American Minorities

A TEXTBOOK OF READINGS IN
INTERGROUP RELATIONS

American Minorities

A TEXTBOOK OF READINGS IN
INTERGROUP RELATIONS
EDITED BY

Milton L. Barron
THE CITY COLLEGE OF NEW YORK

ALFRED A. KNOPF
NEW YORK
1958

L.C. catalog card number: 57–5816

© Milton L. Barron, 1957

PUBLISHED 1957

REPRINTED 1958

FOR MAC

14114

Preface

For more than half a century American sociologists and other social scientists have been making available a vast and rich store of literature on the relations between racial, religious, and nationality (ethnic) groups in the United States. Few, if any, other social problems in America have been subject to so much theoretical analysis and empirical research. Nevertheless it has been virtually impossible to make readily available to courses on intergroup relations an adequate sampling of this literature.

This volume represents an attempt to remedy the situation. The editor has selected, in many cases excerpted, and integrated what he considers to be the more pertinent and readable articles, essays, and chapters in social science literature on the problems of American minorities. The organization and development of the book are adapted to the general scheme that has become standard in most sociology courses on "race" relations, intergroup relations, and American minority groups. Section I, the Introduction, is concerned primarily with providing a broad perspective on the problems of dominant and minority group relations throughout the world. It concludes with a summary picture of the composition of American society racially and ethnically. Section II is a coverage of the characteristics of race, religion, and nationality, the three primary types of dominant and minority group alignment.

Prejudice and discrimination, the key components in all problems of intergroup relations, are defined and analyzed in Section III. The major theories that have been formulated to explain these problems, and illustrations of prejudice and discrimination in our media of communication and in college admissions are also included here. Section IV deals with the numerically small but sociologically important aboriginal element in American society, the Indians. In Section V the subject is another racial minority generally acknowledged to be the most significant at the present time, American Negroes. Section VI provides the setting for problems involving immigrant minorities. Patterns of immigration and the development of American legislative policy with regard to immigration are examined and critically evaluated. This is followed in Section VII by a discussion of ethnic stratification and the problems of selected ethnic minorities as represented by the South Irish, Poles, South Italians, Japanese, Mexicans, and the most recent of all, the Puerto Ricans.

Section VIII considers religious stratification in American society with special attention to Roman Catholic and Protestant tension, and in Section IX problems in the relations of Jews and Gentiles are reviewed and sociologically interpreted. In Section X typical minority group reactions and adjustments to prejudice and discrimination are examined. Finally, in Section XI, the principal techniques devised to reduce and eliminate the various problems in intergroup relations are covered in detail.

The book is designed primarily for use as a text in courses on American minorities. However, some may find it helpful as a supplementary reading in an introductory sociology course and in the study of social problems as well.

New York, New York   M.L.B.

Acknowledgments

For the kind permission they granted to reprint the copyrighted materials on which this volume depends, the editor wishes to thank the following publications, organizations, and book publishers:

The American Journal of Sociology; The American Political Science Review; American Sociological Review; The Annals of the American Academy of Political and Social Science; Appleton-Century-Crofts, Inc.; The Beechhurst Press, Inc.; Bookman Associates, Inc.; Columbia University Press; *Commentary;* Common Council for American Unity, Inc.; Harper & Brothers; *Harper's Magazine;* Harvard University Press; Jewish Reconstructionist Foundation, Inc.; *The Journal of Social Issues;* Alfred A. Knopf, Inc.; The Macmillan Company; The National Council for the Social Studies; *The New York Times;* Public Affairs Committee, Inc.; *The Public Opinion Quarterly; Social Forces;* Social Science Research Council; *Sociology and Social Research;* Survey Associates, Inc.; and Yale University Press.

To the authors who have contributed to this volume and to the estates of deceased authors for their cooperation, I wish to express my sincere gratitude. Professors Robert Bierstedt of City College and Maurice R. Davie of Yale University read the manuscript and contributed many valuable criticisms and suggestions. My wife has been a constant source of help and encouragement throughout the entire project. Whatever merit is found in the book is due largely to these individuals. The editor assumes full responsibility for any deficiencies.

In many cases footnotes have been omitted where they appeared to be extraneous to the purpose of a textbook. If an excerpt rather than an entire essay, article, or chapter is used, every effort has been made to maintain the continuity of the thought being expounded.

Contributors

ELIN L. ANDERSON is a New England social worker who was awarded the John Anisfield Prize in 1937 for *We Americans,* a study of ethnic cleavage in Burlington, Vermont.

MILTON L. BARRON is the author of *People Who Intermarry* (1946) and *The Juvenile in Delinquent Society* (1954). He is associate professor of sociology at The City College of New York.

BERNARD BERELSON, coauthor of *The People's Choice* (1944), has also written *Content Analysis* (1952) and *Voting* (1954). He was dean of the Graduate Library School, University of Chicago, 1947–1951, and at present he is director of the Behavioral Sciences Program of the Ford Foundation.

PAUL J. CAMPISI, author of many articles published in professional journals, was a pre-doctoral fellow of the Social Science Research Council in 1943–44 and a Fulbright Scholar in Italy in 1952–1953. He is associate professor of sociology at Washington University, St. Louis.

YAROSLAV J. CHYZ has written articles on Ukrainian and Russian Americans, the foreign language press, and nationality organizations for English and American periodicals. Since 1942 he has been in charge of the Foreign Language Press Division of the Common Council for American Unity.

MAURICE R. DAVIE is author of *Evolution of War* (1929), *Problems of City Life* (1932), *World Immigration* (1936), *Refugees in America* (1947), and *Negroes in American Society* (1949). He is professor and chairman of the department of sociology at Yale University.

ALLISON DAVIS is the author of several books, including *Children of Bondage* (1940) with John Dollard, and *Deep South* (1941) with Burleigh B. and Mary R. Gardner. He is professor of education and a member of the Committee on Human Development at the University of Chicago.

IRA EISENSTEIN, the author of *Creative Judaism* (1936, rev. ed. 1953), has also written *What We Mean By Religion* (1940) and *Ethics of Tolerance* (1941). The former president of the Rabbinical Assembly of America, Dr. Eisenstein is now senior rabbi of Anshe Emet Synagogue in Chicago, Illinois.

GALEN M. FISHER who died in 1955 was the author of several works and executive secretary of the Rockefeller Institute of Social and Religious Research.

G. James Fleming is the compiler of *Who's Who in Colored America* (1955). He is associate professor of political science at Morgan State College.

E. Franklin Frazier includes among his publications *The Negro Family in the United States* (1939) and *The Negro in the United States* (1949). Past president of the American Sociological Society and the International Society for the Scientific Study of Race Relations, he is professor and head of the department of sociology at Howard University.

Else Frenkel-Brunswik, the coauthor of *The Authoritarian Personality* (1950), has also written *Motivation and Behavior* (1942) and *Psychoanalysis and the Unity of Science* (1954). She is lecturer and research associate at the University of California, Berkeley.

Winfred E. Garrison has written *Religion Follows the Frontier* (1931), *Intolerance* (1934), *A Protestant Manifesto* (1952), and *Christian Unity and Disciples of Christ* (1955). A past president of New Mexico College of Agriculture and Mechanic Arts and of the American Society of Church History, he is at present chairman of the department of philosophy and religion at the University of Houston.

Rose Kohn Goldsen, coauthor of *The Puerto Rican Journey* (1950), is a research associate in sociology and anthropology at Cornell University.

Milton M. Gordon, the author of numerous articles in sociology journals, was winner of an award by the Institute for Religious and Social Studies in 1948 for the outstanding study of intergroup relations. He is assistant professor of sociology at Haverford College.

Francis J. Haas at the time of his death was Bishop of the Roman Catholic Diocese of Grand Rapids, Michigan. The author of *Man and Society* (1930) and several other books and pamphlets, he was the first chairman of the President's Committee on Fair Employment Practice.

Marcus Lee Hansen, professor of American history at Harvard University at the time of his death in 1938, was author of *The Immigrant in American History* (1940) and *The Atlantic Migration,* the 1940 Pulitzer Prize winner in history.

Douglas G. Haring has written *The Land of Gods and Earthquakes* (1929) and was coauthor of *Order and Possibility in Social Life* (1940). He was editor of *Personal Character and Cultural Milieu* (1948, rev. ed. 1949). At present he is professor of anthropology at Syracuse University.

Hubert H. Humphrey, Jr. is the author of numerous articles on politics, labor law, taxes, unions, atomic power, the legal voting age, and defense as well as on fair employment practices and immigration legislation. At one time mayor of Minneapolis, Mr. Humphrey is now United States Senator from Minnesota.

Andrew C. Ivy is author of *Peptic Ulcer* (1953) and past president of the American Physiological Society. His present position is distinguished professor of physiology and head of the department of clinical science, University of Illinois.

Robert B. Johnson, a sociologist, is director of research for the

National Conference of Christians and Jews. He was formerly associated with the Russell Sage Foundation.

BERNARD JOSEPH is a social scientist educated at McGill University and the University of London. He is a resident of Israel.

JOHN J. KANE is author of *Marriage and the Family* (1952) and *Catholic-Protestant Conflicts in America* (1955). Past president of the American Catholic Sociological Society, he is head of the department of sociology at the University of Notre Dame.

CLYDE V. KISER has written *Sea Island to City* (1932), *Group Differences in Urban Fertility* (1942) and was coeditor of *Social and Psychological Factors Affecting Fertility* (1946). A past president of the Population Association of America, he is adjunct professor of sociology at New York University and research associate of the Office of Population Research, Princeton University.

OTTO KLINEBERG'S works include *Race Differences* (1935), *Social Psychology* (1940, rev. ed. 1954), and *Tensions Affecting International Understanding* (1950). Past president of the Society for the Psychological Study of Social Issues, Dr. Klineberg is professor of psychology at Columbia University.

OLIVER LAFARGE is author of *Laughing Boy* (1929), *Raw Material* (1945), and *Santa Eulalia, the Religion of a Cuuchumatan Indian Town* (1947). Fellow of the American Anthropological Association, Mr. LaFarge won the Pulitzer Prize for fiction in 1929. He is now president of the Association on American Indian Affairs.

READ LEWIS has been executive director of the Common Council for American Unity since 1922.

RONALD LIPPITT'S major publications include *Training in Community Relations* (1949) and *Learning Across Cultures* (1955). Past president of the Society for the Psychological Study of Social Issues and past editor of the *Journal of Social Issues,* his present position is professor of sociology and psychology at the University of Michigan.

EDWARD C. MCDONAGH is coeditor of *Analyzing Social Problems* (1950, rev. ed. 1956) and coauthor of *Ethnic Relations in the United States* (1953). He is professor of sociology at the University of Southern California.

DAVIS MCENTIRE is author of *The Population of California* (1946) and *The Labor Force of California* (1952). Formerly research director of the Commission on Race and Housing, Fund for the Republic, he is now professor of social welfare, the University of California, Berkeley.

CLYDE R. MILLER includes among his publications *Publicity and the Public School* (1924) and *Process of Persuasion* (1946). He suggested the Springfield Plan and served as consultant during its development. Today he is a consultant in the fields of education and public opinion.

C. WRIGHT MILLS has written *New Men of Power* (1948), *White Collar* (1951), and *The Power Elite* (1956). He is professor of sociology at Columbia University.

HARRY A. OVERSTREET is author of *Influencing Human Behavior* (1925) and *The Mature Mind* (1949) as well as other works. He is professor emeritus of philosophy at The City College of New York.

LISTON POPE, the author of *Millhands and Preachers* (1942), is a trustee of the Phelps Stokes Fund and Vassar College. He is dean of the Yale Divinity School and Gilbert L. Stark professor of social ethics.

MARIAN RADKE is coauthor of *They Learn What They Live* (1952) and her present position is social psychologist at the National Institute of Mental Health.

MIRIAM REIMANN has written a discussion guide on the general question of prejudice and children for the American Jewish Committee.

JOHN P. ROCHE's major publications are *Early Development of United States Citizenship* (1949) and *Dynamics of Democratic Government* (1954). He is associate professor of political science at Haverford College.

ARNOLD M. ROSE has written *Studies in the Reduction of Prejudice* (1947), *The Negro in America* (1948), *The Negro's Morale* (1949), *Race Prejudice and Discrimination* (1951), and *Theory and Method in the Social Sciences* (1954). He is professor of sociology at the University of Minnesota.

IRWIN ROSS is a newspaper writer in New York City.

PATRICIA SALTER, the coauthor of *They Went to College* (1951), is at present a housewife.

CLARENCE SENIOR is the author of *Puerto Rican Emigration* (1947), *The Puerto Rican in New York City* (1948), and *Strangers and Neighbors* (1952). A former lecturer in sociology at Columbia University, he is now chief of the migration division, Department of Labor, Commonwealth of Puerto Rico.

CLARIS EDWIN SILCOX, coauthor of *Catholics, Jews and Protestants* (1934), has also written *The Fairfield Experiment* (1927) and *Church Union in Canada* (1933). He represents Church Peace Union in Canada and works for L'Alliance Canadienne, designed to foster improved relations between French- and English-speaking Canadians.

JOHAN J. SMERTENKO, the author of *Alexander Hamilton* (1932) and *Palestine in Revolt: a Factual Report* (1947), has taught journalism and English literature at several colleges. A former vice president of the American League for Free Palestine, he is an associate in English at Barnard College.

WILLIAM CARLSON SMITH's major publications are *The Ao Naga Tribe of Nassam* (1925), *Americans in Process* (1937), *Americans in the Making* (1939), and *The Stepchild* (1952). A former president of the Pacific Sociological Society, Dr. Smith is professor emeritus of sociology at Linfield College.

LEO SROLE has been a frequent contributor to social science journals as well as coauthor of *The Social Systems of American Ethnic Groups* (1945). At one time director of research for the Anti-Defamation League, he is now visiting professor of sociology at the Cornell University Medical College.

ALDEN STEVENS' publications include *Dove Creek Rodeo* (1936), *Arms and the People* (1942), and *Victory Without Peace* (1944). He is secretary of the Association on American Indian Affairs.

MAXWELL S. STEWART is author of *Social Security* (1937), *Building for Peace at Home and Abroad* (1944), and *The Growing Family* (1955). He is secretary of the Public Affairs Committee.

SAMUEL TENENBAUM has written *Why Men Hate* (1947) and *William Heard Kilpatrick: Trail Blazer in Education* (1951). Formerly a professor of education at Brooklyn College, he is now a free-lance writer.

WILLIAM LLOYD WARNER has been author and coauthor of several books, including *A Black Civilization* (1937), *Color and Human Nature* (1941), *The Social Life of a Modern Community* (1941), *The Status System of a Modern Community* (1942), *The Social Systems of American Ethnic Groups* (1945), *Democracy in Jonesville* (1949), and *American Life: Dream and Reality* (1953). He is professor of anthropology at the University of Chicago.

JOSEPH E. WECKLER, a coauthor of *The Police and Minority Groups* and formerly a field representative for the American Council on Race Relations, is chairman of the department of anthropology at the University of Southern California.

GENE WELTFISH's major publications have been *Caddoan Texts* (1936), *Races of Mankind* (1943) and *The Origins of Art* (1953). She is now engaged in research at the Laboratory of Anthropology, the University of Nebraska.

ROBIN M. WILLIAMS, JR. is the author of *The Reduction of Intergroup Tensions* (1947), and *American Society* (1951), as well as coauthor of *The American Soldier* (1949) and coeditor of *Schools in Transition* (1954). He is professor of sociology at Cornell University.

LOUIS WIRTH's publications include *The Ghetto* (1928), *The City* (1925), and *Race and Public Policy* (1944). Past president of the American Sociological Society, at the time of his death in 1952 he was professor of sociology at the University of Chicago.

KURT M. WOLFF is the author of *The Sociology of Georg Simmel* (1950). His present position is associate professor of sociology at the Ohio State University.

ARTHUR EVANS WOOD is author of *Community Problems* (1928), *Crime and its Treatment* (1941), and *Hamtramck—Then and Now* (1955). He is professor emeritus of sociology at the University of Michigan.

TOSHIO YATSUSHIRO's articles on culture dynamics and the relocation of Japanese Americans have appeared in several professional journals. Formerly a fellow of the John Hay Whitney Foundation and the Ford Foundation, he is now assistant professor of anthropology at the University of Kansas.

Contents

xvi   Contents

Page

17. Negro Reactions to Minority Group Status BY ROBERT JOHNSON 192
18. Integration in the Schools BY THE SUPREME COURT OF THE
    UNITED STATES   212
19. Report on the South: The Integration Issue BY THE STAFF OF
    The New York Times   220

VI. AMERICAN IMMIGRATION

20. American Immigration and its European Sources and Patterns
    BY MAURICE R. DAVIE   230

21. The Stranger at Our Gate: A Brief History of American Im-
    migration; A Field for Research BY MAURICE R. DAVIE   240

VII. ETHNIC GROUPS

23. Ethnic Stratification in the Community in 1775 BY SIDNEY   277
    Irish Status in America
25. Italian Marriage and Assimilation in the United States
26. The Italian Family in the United States BY PAUL J. CAMPI
    The Japanese Americans
    The Puerto Ricans in New York

VIII. RELIGIOUS MINORITIES: THE ROMAN
    CATHOLICS

    Characteristics of American Catholicism
31. The Protestant and Catholic Cultures in America
    Professional Status and the Catholic

IX. JEWISH-GENTILE RELATIONS

33. An Elementary Syllabus in the Sociology of the Jews BY GUSTA
    WOLFF
    Social Classes
36. Have Jews a Divided Loyalty? BY JULIUS J. SMERTENKO   401
    WITH Hate Does to the Victims BY SAMUEL TENENBAUM   481
    BY JAN

Page

American Minorities

A TEXTBOOK OF READINGS IN INTERGROUP RELATIONS

I. Introduction

INTERGROUP relations involving races, religious groups, and nationalities have developed into some of the most severe social problems of modern times. This has been true not only in the United States, but, with few exceptions, wherever groups of these types have converged and interacted. The people that have undergone subordination in intergroup relations are generally referred to as minorities; their superordinates in status may be called either "majorities" or dominant groups. According to traditional usage, the concepts minority and dominant or majority do not apply to every conceivable type of social group, but only to racial, religious, or ethnic (nationality) groups. In each case members of the group regard themselves and are regarded by others as distinctive in biological, cultural, psychological, and historical respects.

Besides being subject to subordination, minorities are underprivileged in one or more ways and they are the targets of prejudice and discrimination. Usually they are on the defensive, acutely sensitive to group alignments and their status therein. The characteristics of their counterparts, the dominant groups, have been given considerably less thought. Students of intergroup relations have been inclined, with few exceptions, to overlook them as social entities worthy of systematic observation. This is not likely to continue indefinitely, for it is becoming increasingly fashionable to speak of majority or dominant group problems rather than exclusively of minority group problems.

Justification for this is found in the growing conviction that the former play a more strategic role than the latter in responsibility for either intergroup conflict or harmony. In any case, a working knowledge of the traits of those groups in power is essential.

Like minorities, dominant or majority groups do not necessarily depend on their numerical position in relation to other groups to account for their social status. They are not statistical categories, despite the literal meanings of the terms minority and majority. A majority group need not be larger in numbers than a minority group. Sociologically speaking, majorities are those races, religious groups, and nationalities that have social power, the ability to exploit the service or regulate the subservience of other groups. This they can do by utilizing any source of power—weapons, property, financial resources, special knowledge, managerial and executive function, and eminence derived from myths, legend, and history.

The social power enjoyed by majorities or dominant groups becomes embedded in the mores. Furthermore, their domination of minorities is supported by systems of enacted law and status ascription. It is rationalized by ethnocentrism, stereotypes, and elaborate theories of biological determinism. In the power relations between dominant and minority groups there is persistent conflict varying in degrees of intensity and explicitness. Whereas dominant groups tend to seek to suppress minority assertion and to retain the *status quo* in the distribution of power, minorities attempt either to gain autonomy or to achieve equality of status and opportunity.

Reciprocally perceptible differences are helpful in perpetuating dominant and minority group relations. These may be alleged as well as real, and they may be somatic, cultural, or both. In the course of time, the relations between dominant and minority groups are institutionalized by a "vicious circle" of stimuli and responses. The social inferiority of the minority group tends to provide justification for the dominant group's discrimination against them. This, in turn, works to make minority group individuals respond in ways that further strengthen the stereotypes held about them.

Memberships in minority and dominant groups are not mutually exclusive. It is possible for a person to have dominant and minority roles simultaneously. This possibility stems from the fact that the minority-dominant group typology has a threefold foundation in race, religion, and nationality. In addition there are secondary status-providing traits such as nativity. For example, while most people think of American Negroes as a minority group, one must remember that American Negroes are for the most part native-born, Gentiles, and Protestants. As such they cannot avoid much of the dominant-group psychology and inevitably many of them share the hostility against the foreign-born, Jews, and Roman Catholics. Similarly, most Roman Catholics in the United States, members of a prominent religious minority, are simultaneously not only Gentiles but preponderantly whites. These identifications give them two significant dominant-group roles. American Jews, too, as whites, are also in a position to couple a dominant group status with the minority status of being Jewish. These are but a few of the many varieties of jointly held and conflicting roles played by a given race, religious group, or nationality.

What are the implications and ramifications of hostility and tension between dominant and minority groups? They are extensive, ranging far beyond the immediate participants and their problems. Aside from the self-evident social repercussions that weaken and divide the society, intergroup problems—especially in the United States where democratic ideals and creeds abound—raise political and economic issues and stimulate ethical and moral controversy. All Americans are equal, but it appears that some are "more equal" than others.

Thus Gunnar Myrdal, the eminent Swedish social scientist, studied America's paramount intergroup problem, the so-called Negro problem, and came to the conclusion that it was more appropriate to refer to it as "an American dilemma." True, there is an American creed, a system of general ideals and norms governing human relations. All Americans, regardless of group affiliation, find that the Declaration of Independence, the preamble to the Constitution, the Bill of Rights and their Judaeo-Christian heritage offer them formulas such as the essential dignity of the individual, the fundamental equality of all, and inalienable rights to freedom, justice, and fair opportunity. But in addition to this official creed there is an unofficial creed implicit in secondary legislation and explicit in the remarks of the philosophers of racism and ancestor worship. According to the latter creed, America belongs to "real" Americans, not to Negroes, Catholics, Jews, and "foreigners."

As a leading world power, the United States has found that a dilemma of this kind generates serious international as well as internal effects. Rivals of this country in the struggle for political and economic leadership have been quick to seize upon minority group problems here and to exploit them to their own advantage in the struggle for world power.

With these fundamental traits of minorities and dominant groups, and the implications of their relations brought to our attention, it is now appropriate to turn to the late Louis Wirth's analysis of the problem of minority groups. Especially valuable is Professor Wirth's classification of minorities throughout the globe: (1) the pluralistic, (2) the assimilationist, (3) the secessionist, and (4) the militant.

1. THE PROBLEM OF MINORITY GROUPS
BY *Louis Wirth* *

THE MINORITIES question in all parts of the world is coming to be more and more indivisible as internal disturbances in any one country become a threat to the peace of all and as the ideals and ideologies originating in one group are soon shared by others in remote corners of the earth. In this shrunken and interdependent world, social movements of all sorts assume a progressively universal character and recruit their supporters and adversaries among peoples near and far, irrespective of national boundaries. The implications of this trend are of special significance to the United States since, aside from its traditional championship of movements of liberation of oppressed peoples, virtually every minority group in the world has its representatives among our population. Our domestic and our foreign policies are thus closely bound up one with the other.

We may define a minority as a group of people who, because of their physical or cultural characteristics, are singled out from the others in the society in which they live for differential and unequal treatment, and who therefore regard themselves as objects of collective discrimination. The existence of a minority in a society implies the existence of a corresponding dominant group enjoying higher social status and greater privileges. Minority status carries with it the exclusion from full participation in the life of the society. Though not necessarily an alien group the minority is treated and regards itself as a people apart.

To understand the nature and significance of minorities it is necessary to take account of their objective as well as their subjective position. A minority must be distinguishable from the dominant group by physical or cul-

* From Ralph Linton (ed.), *The Science of Man in the World Crisis* (New York: Columbia University Press, 1945), pp. 347–72. Reprinted by permission.

tural marks. In the absence of such identifying characteristics, it blends into the rest of the population in the course of time. Minorities objectively occupy a disadvantageous position in society. As contrasted with the dominant group they are debarred from certain opportunities—economic, social and political. These deprivations circumscribe the individual's freedom of choice and self-development. The members of minority groups are held in lower esteem and may even be objects of contempt, hatred, ridicule, and violence. They are generally socially isolated and frequently spatially segregated. Their subordinate position becomes manifest in their unequal access to educational opportunities and in their restricted scope of occupational and professional advancement. They are not as free as other members of society to join the voluntary associations that express their interests. They suffer from more than the ordinary amount of social and economic insecurity. Even as concerns public policy they are frequently singled out for special treatment; their property rights may be restricted; they may not enjoy the equal protection of the laws; they may be deprived of the right of suffrage and may be excluded from public office.

Aside from these objective characteristics by which they are distinguished from the dominant group and in large measure as a result of them, minorities tend to develop a set of attitudes, forms of behavior, and other subjective characteristics which tend further to set them apart. One cannot long discriminate against people without generating in them a sense of isolation and of persecution and without giving them a conception of themselves as more different from others than in fact they are. Whether, as a result of this differential treatment, the minority comes to suffer from a sense of its own inferiority or develops a feeling that it is unjustly treated—which may lead to a rebellious attitude—depends in part upon the length of time that its status has existed and in part upon the total social setting in which the differential treatment operates. Where a caste system has existed over many generations and is sanctioned by religious and other sentiments, the attitude of resignation is likely to be dominant over the spirit of rebellion. But in a secular society where class rather than caste pervades the stratification of people, and where the tradition of minority status is of recent origin, minorities, driven by a sense of frustration and unjustified subordination, are likely to refuse to accept their status and their deprivation without some effort to improve their lot.

When the sentiments and attitude of such a disadvantaged group become articulate, and when the members become conscious of their deprivations and conceive of themselves as persons having rights, and when they clamor for emancipation and equality, a minority becomes a political force to be reckoned with. To the individual members of such a group the most onerous circumstance under which they have to labor is that they are treated as members of a category, irrespective of their individual merits. Hence it is important to recognize that membership in a minority is involuntary; our own behavior is irrelevant. Many of us are identified with political, social, and intellectual groups which do not enjoy the favor of the dominant group in society, but as long as we are free to join and to leave such groups at will we do not by virtue of our membership in them belong to a minority. Since the racial stock from which we are descended is something over which we have perhaps least control and since racial marks are the most visible and permanent marks with which we are afflicted, racial minorities tend to be the most enduring minorities of all.

It should be noted further that a minority is not necessarily an alien group. Indeed, in many parts of the world it is the native peoples who constitute the minority, whereas the invaders, the conquerors, or the newcomers, occupy the status of dominant groups. In the United States the indigenous Indians occupy the position of a minority. In Canada the earlier French settlers are a minority in relation to the more recent English migrants. In almost all colonial countries it is the "foreigners" who are dominant and the indigenous populations who are subordinate.

Nor should it be assumed that the concept is a statistical one. Although the size of the group may have some effect upon its status and upon its relationship to the dominant group, minorities are not to be judged in terms of numbers. The people whom we regard as a minority may actually, from a numerical standpoint, be a majority. Thus, there are many parts of the South in the United States where the Negroes are the overwhelming majority of the inhabitants, but, nevertheless, are an unmistakable minority in the sense that they are socially, politically, and economically subordinate.

It may even be true that a people may attain the status of a minority even though it does not become the object of disesteem, discrimination, and persecution. If it considers itself the object of such inferior treatment, an oppression psychosis may develop. If a group sets itself apart from others by a distinctive culture and perpetuates itself in this isolated condition long enough, the social distances between itself and others may grow so great as to lead to the accumulation of suspicion and non-intercourse which will make it virtually impossible for members of these groups to carry on a truly collective life. Lack of intimate knowledge of and contact with others may in the course of time generate an incapacity for mutual understanding and appreciation which allows mental stereotypes to arise which the individual cannot escape. What matters, then, about minorities is not merely their objective position but the corresponding patterns of behavior they develop and the pictures they carry around in their heads of themselves and of others. While minorities more often than not stand in a relationship of conflict with the dominant group, it is their nonparticipation in the life of the larger society, or in certain aspects thereof, that more particularly marks them as a minority people and perpetuates their status as such.

It is easy enough to catalog the minority peoples in various parts of the world in accordance with a set of criteria such as race, national origin, language, religion, or other distinctive cultural traits. Thus it is possible to define the areas of the world where one or another racial, ethnic, linguistic, or religious group occupies a subordinate status with reference to some other group. In different parts of the world different groups are consigned to minority status. A given racial, ethnic, linguistic, or religious group may be dominant in one area and be the minority in another. Similar variations are found throughout history. Groups which in one epoch were dominant may in another be reduced to subordinate status. Because of the colonizing enterprises of some of the nation-states of Western Europe a large part of the rest of the world has been subordinated to their political rule, their economic control, and the technology and culture which the European settlers managed to superimpose upon the peoples and areas which they brought under their domain. On a world scale, therefore, there is an extraordinarily close association between the white Western Europeans as colonizers and conquerors and their status as dominant groups. Correspondingly, there is a close association between the nonwhite peoples of the world as the conquered and enslaved peoples and their status as minority groups. There are notable exceptions, however, both in time and in space. In an earlier period of European history the yellow peoples of the East overran vast stretches of the European continent and for a time at least reduced the natives to inferior status. There had been similar, though temporary, invasions of Europe from Africa in the course of which Negroid groups became dominant over the white Europeans. Similarly, the enterprise and military prowess of the Japanese has led to the subjugation of vast stretches of the Orient beyond their island empire which contain many areas and great populations of non-Japanese stock, including European whites. On the whole, however, the expansion of European civilization to the ends of the earth has been so irresistible that from a racial standpoint, virtually the world over, the whites constitute the dominant group and the colored peoples the minorities.

We are less concerned, however, in this analysis, with racial minorities than with ethnic minorities, and hence it will be well to examine in some detail the linguistic, religious, and national minorities within the white group in Europe and in America. The existence of such groups in virtually every European and American country calls attention to the fact that the modern nation-states into which we are accustomed to divide the world and to which we are wont to ascribe a high degree of ethnic homogeneity are far from being as closely knit by intermarriage, in-breeding, social intercourse, and freedom of opportunity for everyone as the stereotypes of national cultures appear to indicate.

In Europe and in America there are today vast differences between the status of different ethnic groups from country to country and from region to region. . . . During the brief period of Nazi domination the Sudeten Germans of Czechoslovakia reveled in their position of dominance over the Czechs among whom they had only recently been a minority. The European immigrants to the United States from such dominantly Catholic countries as Italy and Poland, for instance, find themselves reduced from a dominant to a minority group in the course of their immigration. It is not the specific characteristics, therefore, whether racial or ethnic, that mark a people as a minority but the relationship of their group to some other group in the society in which they live. The same characteristics may at one time and under one set of circumstances serve as marks of dominant status and at another time and under another set of circumstances symbolize identification with a minority.

It is much more important, therefore, to understand the nature and the genesis of the relationship between dominant group and minority group than it is to know the marks by the possession of which people are identified as members of either. Once we know that almost any distinctive characteristics, whether it be the physical marks of race, or language, religion, and culture, can serve as criteria of membership in a minority we will not be inclined to construct a typology of minorities upon the marks by which they are identified. A fruitful typology must rather be useful in delineating the kinds of relationships between minorities and dominant groups and on the kinds of behavior characteristically associated with these types of relationships.

An adequate typology of minorities must, therefore, take account of the general types of situations in which minorities find themselves and must seek to comprehend the *modus vivendi* that has grown up between the segments of those societies in which minority problems exist. There are a number of axes alongside which the problems of minorities range themselves. Among these are: (1) the number and size of distinct minorities in the society in question; (2) the degree to which minority status involves friction with the dominant group or exclusion from participation in the common life of the society; (3) the nature of the social arrangement governing the relationship between minority and dominant group; and, (4) the goals toward which the minority and dominant groups are striving in quest of a new and more satisfactory equilibrium. A survey of historical and contemporary minority problems along these lines will probably not cover the whole range of minority problems and to that extent the typology will be partial. At the same time it should be understood that as long as the relations between minority and dominant groups are fluid—and wherever they do not rest upon long-accepted and settled premises—any rigid typology will prove unsatisfactory. Conversely where the minority's relationship to the dominant group is definitely structuralized and embedded in the mores, laws, and institutions a typological approach may be highly rewarding.

The number of minorities that a country has appears to have a significant effect upon minority-dominant group relations. Where there is just one minority the attitudes of the dominant group are molded by the unique characteristics of that particular minority. This tends to bisect the country into two contending groups. This happens to be the case in Belgium where the Flemings and Walloons stand in relationship of dominant and minority group, respectively, to each other. The situation is quite different in the United States, where aside from the Negro, the Indian, and the Oriental, who constitute our leading racial minorities, we have many ethnic minorities consisting of our European immigrant groups and their descendants and such religious minorities as Catholics, Jews, and Mormons in a predominantly Protestant country. A singular and unique minority must absorb all of the anxieties, frustrations, fears, and antipathies of the dominant group. But if dominant group attitudes are directed toward a number of minorities, some of these may escape relatively easily and often at the expense of the others. There is little doubt but that the Negro in the United States has become the principal shock absorber of the antiminority sentiment of the dominant whites. The Negro in this country has been so clearly our leading minority that in comparison with his status the ethnic minorities have occupied a relatively dominant position. Indeed the attitude of the ethnic minorities toward the Negro differs little from the attitude of the long-established white Protestant settlers. Where there are several distinct minorities in a country the dominant group can allow itself the luxury of treating some of them generously and can at the same time entrench itself and secure its own dominance by playing one minority against another.

Similarly, the extent to which a minority differs from the dominant group conditions the relations between the two. Where the groups differ widely in race and culture and are thus easily distinguishable in appearance and behavior, the lines separating them tend to persist without much overt effort. Where the dominant group is the bearer of an advanced civilization and the subordinate group is without modern technology and is characterized by a folk culture, as is the case in colonial situations, the dominant group can maintain its superior position simply by manipulating the military and administrative machinery. Where, however, the respective groups are of the same racial stock but differ only as regards language, religion, or culture, the tension between them becomes more marked, and the attempts at domination of the minority become more evident. The segregation of minority groups may be relatively complete or only partial, and their debarment from rights and privileges may be negligible or severe. Much depends upon their relative numerical strength and the extent to which they are believed to constitute a threat to the existing order.

The nature of the social relationships existing between the dominants and the minorities comes closer than either of these factors to illuminating the problems that arise. When the relationship between the two groups is that of master and slave, of rulers and ruled, of exploiters and exploited, the conflicts that arise are those characteristic of situations of super- and subordination. They become essentially power relationships involving on the part of the dominant group resort to the sanctions of custom, law, and force, whenever persuasion, prestige, and the manipulation of economic controls do not suffice. Where the minority occupies the position of a caste the sanctions of religion and custom may be quite adequate, but in secular societies the perpetuation of a group in minority status requires the manipulation of public opinion and of economic and political power, and, if these fail, the resort to violence.

Thoroughgoing differences and incompatibilities between dominant and minority groups on *all* fronts—economic, political, social, and religious—or consistent and complete separation and exclusion of the minority from participation in the life of the larger society have tended toward more stable relationships between dominant and minority groups than similarity and compatibility on merely *some* points, and the mere segmental sharing of life on a few frontiers of contact. The granting of some political and civil rights to hitherto submerged groups has inevitably led to the claim for the full rights of citizenship and of equality of opportunity in other respects. Slavery as an institution in the Western World was moribund as soon as the religions of the white man invested the Negro with a soul.

While the above criteria might give us a basis for the classification of minorities, they do not come as close to the actual minority problems that plague the modern world as we can come by analyzing the major goals toward which the ideas, the sentiments, and the actions of minority groups are directed. Viewed in this way minorities may conveniently be typed into: (1) pluralistic; (2) assimilationist; (3) secessionist; and (4) militant.

A pluralistic minority is one which seeks toleration for its differences on the part of the dominant group. Implicit in the quest for toleration of one's group differences is the conception that variant cultures can flourish peacefully side by side in the same society. Indeed, cultural pluralism has been held out as one of the necessary preconditions of a rich and dynamic civilization under conditions of freedom. It has been said in jest that "tolerance is the suspicion that the other fellow might be right."

Toleration requires that the dominant group shall feel sufficiently secure in its position to allow dissenters a certain leeway. Those in control must be convinced either that the issues at stake are not too vital, or else they must be so thoroughly imbued with the ideal of freedom that they do not wish to deny to others some of the liberties which they themselves enjoy. If there is a great gulf between their own status and that of the minority group, if there is a wide difference between the two groups in race or origin, the toleration of minorities may go as far as virtually to perpetuate several subsocieties within the larger society.

Even in the "sacred" society of medieval Europe dominated by the Church, there were long periods when heretics were tolerated, although at other times they faced the alternatives of conformity or extermination. The history of the Jews in medieval Europe offers ample evidence of the ability of a minority to survive even under minimum conditions of toleration. It should be noted, however, that at times the margin of safety was very narrow and that their ultimate survival was facilitated by the fact that they formed an alien cultural island within the larger Christian world and performed useful functions such as trade and commerce in which the creed of the dominant group would not allow its own members to engage. The coexistence of the Jews and Christians in the same countries often did not transcend the degree of mutuality characteristic of the symbiotic relations existing between different species of plants and animals occupying the same habitat but which are forced by their differential structure to live off one another. It involved a minimum of consensus.

The range of toleration which a pluralistic minority seeks may at first be quite narrow. As in the case of the Jews in medieval Europe, or the Protestants in dominantly Catholic countries, it may be confined to freedom to practice a dissenting religion. Or, as in the case of the ethnic minorities of Czarist Russia and the Austro-Hungarian empire of the Hapsburgs, it may take the form of the demand for the recognition of a language as the official medium of expression for the minority and the right to have it taught in their schools. While on the one hand the pluralistic minority craves the toleration of one or more of its cultural idiosyncrasies, on the other hand it resents and seeks protection against coerced absorption by the dominant group. Above all it wishes to maintain its cultural identity.

The nationalities of Europe, which in the nineteenth and early twentieth centuries embarked upon a course of achieving national independence, began their careers as pluralistic minorities bent merely upon attaining cultural autonomy. Some of these minorities had enjoyed national independence at an earlier period and merely wished to recover and preserve their cultural heritage. This was the case in Poland, for instance, which sought to recover from Czarist Russia a measure of religious and linguistic autonomy. Czech and Irish nationalism was initiated under similar historic circumstances.

It would be an error, however, to infer that the claims for cultural autonomy are generally pursued independently of other interests. Coupled with the demand, and often precedent to it there proceeds the struggle for economic and political equality or at least equalization of opportunity. Although the pluralistic minority does not wish to merge its total life with the larger society, it does demand for its members a greater measure of economic and political freedom if not outright civic equality. Ever since the revolutionary epoch of the late eighteenth century the economic and political enfranchisement of minorities has been regarded not merely as inherent in the "rights of man" but as the necessary instrument in the struggle for cultural emancipation. Freedom of choice in occupations, rights of landownership, entry into the civil service, access to the universities and the professions, freedom of speech, assembly, and publication, access to the ballot with a view to representation of minority voices in parliament and government—these and other full privileges of citizenship are the foundation upon which cultural freedom rests and the instruments through which it must be achieved and secured.

Throughout the period of awakening of dominant ethnic minorities in Europe in the nineteenth century and subsequently in all parts of the world the first stages of minority movements have been characterized by cultural renaissances. The primary emphasis in this stage of development has been upon accentuating the religious, linguistic, and cultural heritage of the group and driving to obtain recognition and toleration for these differences. This movement goes hand in hand with the clamor for economic and political equality. In the course of such movements what at first are marks of inferiority—a homely folk tongue, an alien religion, an obscure lore, and eccentric costume—are transformed into objects of pride and positive group values in which the intellectuals among the minority take an especially avid interest and the promotion of which becomes the road to their leadership and power. The aim of the pluralistic minority is achieved when it has succeeded in wresting from the dominant group the fullest measure of equality in all things economic and political and the right to be left alone in all things cultural. The atmosphere of liberalism in which pluralistic minorities developed has emerged since the Renaissance and has found expression in the movements for religious toleration at the end of the sixteenth century; it was further elaborated by the constitutional bills of rights wrested from absolute rulers in the course of the English, American and French revolutions, and found formal acceptance on a world scale in the minorities clauses of the treaties at the conclusion of the first World War. If the legal provisions of the minorities clauses have not been fully observed in practice, they have at least furnished a standard by which the relations between minorities and dominant groups may be more universally appraised by enlightened world opinion. If formal resolutions on such matters are valid as signs of the trend of opinion, the Catholic, Jewish and Protestant Declaration on World Peace, of October 7, 1943, may be adduced. On the Rights of Minorities this declaration says:

> National governments and international organizations must respect and guarantee the rights of ethnic, religious and cultural minorities to economic livelihood, to equal opportunity for educational and cultural development, and to political equality.

It should be recognized however that pluralistic minorities, like all structures expressive of dynamic social movements, are merely way-stations on the road to further developments. They move on inexorably to other stages where correspondingly new types of social structures emerge. Unlike the pluralistic minority, which is content with toleration and the upper limit of whose aspiration is cultural autonomy, the assimilationist minority craves the fullest opportunity for participation in the life of the larger society with a view to uncoerced incorporation in that society. It seeks to

lose itself in the larger whole by opening up to its members the greatest possibilities for their individual self-development. Rather than toleration and
autonomy, which is the goal of the pluralistic minority, the assimilationist
minority works toward complete acceptance by the dominant group and a
merger with the larger society.

Whereas a pluralistic minority, in order to maintain its group integrity,
will generally discourage intermarriage and intimate social intercourse with
the dominant group, the assimilationist minority puts no such obstacles in
the path of its members but looks upon the crossing of stocks as well as
the blending of cultures as wholesome end products. Since assimilation is a
two-way process, however, in which there is give and take, the mergence of
an assimilationist minority rests upon a willingness of the dominant group
to absorb and of the minority group to be absorbed. The ethnic differences
that exist between the minority and the dominant group are not necessarily
an obstacle to assimilation so long as the cultural traits of each group are
not regarded as incompatible with those of the other and so long as their
blending is desired by both. The "melting pot" philosophy in the United
States which applied to the ethnic minorities but excluded the racial minorities, notably the Negro, in so far as it was actually followed, tended to develop both among immigrants and natives an atmosphere conducive to the
emergence of a crescive American culture to which both the dominant and
minority groups contributed their share. This new culture, which is still in
the process of formation, comprises cultural elements derived from all the
ethnic groups constituting the American people, but integrates them into a
new blend.

The success with which such an experiment proceeds depends in part
upon the relative numbers involved and the period of time over which the
process extends. Although since the beginning of the nineteenth century the
United States absorbed some 38 million immigrants from abroad, the influx
was relatively gradual and the vast spaces and resources of the continent
facilitated the settlement and absorption of the newcomers. America was a
relatively young country, dominated by the spirit of the frontier and by a
set of laws and social ideals strongly influenced by the humanistic, liberal-
istic doctrines of religious toleration and the rights of man. This, together
with the great need for labor to exploit the vast resources of the continent,
contributed to keeping American culture fluid and its people hospitable to
the newcomers and the heritages they brought with them. No one group in
the United States had so much power and pride of ancestry as to be able
to assert itself as superior to all others.

Nevertheless as the immigrants came in great waves, and as the wide
margin of economic opportunity shrank periodically, outbursts of intolerant
and sometimes violent nativism and antialien feeling became manifest here
too. As newer immigrant groups followed older waves the latest comers increasingly became the objects of prejudice and discrimination on the part

of natives and older immigrants alike. Moreover, as the various ethnic groups concentrated in specific areas and in large urban colonies and thus conspicuously unfolded their old world cultural heritages, their life became virtually autonomous and hence, by isolating themselves, their contact with the broad stream of American culture was retarded. In addition, their very success in competing with native and older settlers in occupations, professions, and business provoked antipathies which found expression in intolerance movements and in the imposition of official and unofficial restrictions and handicaps.

Although the ethnic minorities in the United States suffer mainly from private prejudices rather than restrictive public policies, their path of assimilation is not without its serious obstacles. The distinctive cultures of the various ethnic groups are not merely assemblages of separable traits but also historically welded wholes. Each immigrant group not only has its own language or dialect which serves as a barrier to intergroup communication and to the sharing of common ideas and ideals, but also its own religious, social, and even political institutions which tend to perpetuate group solidarity and to inhibit social intercourse with members of the "out" group. Moreover, each ethnic group in the United States, especially in the early period after its arrival, tends to occupy a characteristic niche in the economy which generates certain definite similarities among its members in occupation, standard of living, place of residence, and mode of life. On the basis of such likenesses within the group and differences without, stereotypes are built up and fixed attitudes arise which inhibit contact and develop social distances and prejudices. Overanxiety about being accepted sometimes results in a pattern of conduct among minorities that provokes a defense reaction on the part of the dominant group; these defense reactions may take the form of rebuffs which are likely to accentuate minority consciousness and thus retard assimilation.

No ethnic group is ever unanimous in all of its attitudes and actions, and minority groups are no exception. They, too, have their internal differentiations, their factions and ideological currents and movements. It should be understood, therefore, that the difference between a pluralistic and an assimilationist minority must be sought in the characteristic orientation and directing social movement of these groups. The Jews furnish an excellent illustration of a minority which especially in modern times has vacillated between these two types. When the "out" group was favorably disposed toward the Jews, assimilation proceeded apace, even in the face of occasional rebuffs and persistent discrimination. When the dominant group made entry of the Jews difficult, when intolerance movements became powerful and widespread, and when persecution came to be the order of the day, the Jews as a minority group generally withdrew into themselves and by virtue of being excluded became clannish. The most conspicuous example of this transformation is to be found in the shift in the attitude of the German Jews who—before the anti-Semitic wave climaxed by the Hitler epic—could have been correctly characterized as an assimilationist minority and whose optimum longing upon the advent of Hitler was for even a modicum of toleration. Among Jews in this country a similar differentiation is contemporaneously found. The older settlers and those who have climbed the economic and social scale seek on the whole full incorporation into the larger society and may truly be regarded as an assimilationist minority; but the later comers and those whose hopes have been frustrated by prejudice, those who through generations of persecution in the Old World retain a more orthodox ritual and a more isolated and self-sufficient community life, generally do not seek full cultural identification with American society at large. To be sure they aspire to full social and economic equality with the rest of the population but they seek to retain a degree of cultural autonomy. . . .

The secessionist minority represents a third distinct type. It repudiates assimilation on the one hand, and is not content with mere toleration or cultural autonomy on the other. The principal and ultimate objective of such a minority is to achieve political as well as cultural independence from the dominant group. If such a group has had statehood at an earlier period in its career, the demand for recognition of its national sovereignty may be based upon the cultivation among its members of the romantic sentiments associated—even if only in the imagination—with its former freedom, power, and glory. In such a case the minority's cultural monuments and survivals, its language, lore, literature, and ceremonial institutions, no matter how archaic or reminiscent of the epoch of the group's independence, are revivified and built up into moving symbols of national grandeur.

In this task the intellectuals among the minority group play a crucial role. They can find expression for their talents by recovering, disseminating, and inspiring pride in the group's history and civilization and by pleading its case before world public opinion. Having been rejected by the dominant group for higher positions of leadership, and often having been denied equal opportunity and full participation in the intellectual, social, economic and political life of the larger society, the intellectuals of such minorities tend to be particularly susceptible to a psychic malady bordering on an oppression psychosis. They find their compensation by plunging into the life of the smaller but more hospitable world of their minority.

The Irish, Czech, Polish, Lithuanian, Esthonian, Latvian and Finnish nationalistic movements culminating in the achievement of independent statehood at the end of the first World War were examples of secessionist minority groups. The case of the Jews may also be used to illustrate this type of minority. Zionism in its political, as distinguished from its cultural, variety has acquired considerable support as a result of the resurgence of organized anti-Semitic movements. The forced wholesale migration out of the countries practicing violent persecution and extermination has changed the conception of Palestine from a haven of refuge in which Jews are tolerated to a homeland to which Jews lay official claim.

The protest against the dominant group, however, does not always take the form of separatism and secessionism. It may, under certain circumstances express itself in movements to get out from under the yoke of a dominant group in order to join a group with whom there exists a closer historical and cultural affinity. This is particularly true of minorities located near national frontiers. Wars, and the accompanying repeated redefinitions of international boundaries rarely fail to do violence to the traditions and wishes of some of the populations of border territories. It is generally true that these marginal ethnic groups exhibit more fervid nationalistic feelings than those who have not been buffeted about by treaty-makers.

The solidarity of modern states is always subject to the danger of the undermining influence of secessionist minorities, but it becomes particularly vulnerable if the minorities are allied with neighboring states which claim them as their own. Out of such situations have arisen many of the tensions which have provoked numerous wars in recent times.

There is a fourth type of minority which may be designated as militant. Its goal reaches far beyond toleration, assimilation, and even cultural and political autonomy. The militant minority has set domination over others as its goal. Far from suffering from feelings of inferiority, it is convinced of its own superiority and inspired by the lust for conquest. While the initial claims of minority movements are generally modest, like all accessions of power, they feed upon their own success and often culminate in delusions of grandeur.

Thus, for instance, the Sudeten Germans, aided and abetted by the Nazi propaganda, diplomatic and military machine, made claims on the Czecho-Slovak republic which, if granted, would have reduced the Czechs to a minority in their own country. . . . The none too generous treatment accorded by the newly emancipated Poles between the two World Wars to the Ukrainian, White Russian, Lithuanian, Jewish, and other minorities allotted to the Polish state offers another case of the lack of moderation characteristic of militant minorities once they arrive at a position of power. . . .

The justification for singling out the four types of minorities described above for special delineation lies in the fact that each of them exhibits a characteristic set of collective goals among historical and contemporary minority groups and a corresponding set of motives activating the conduct of its members. These four types point to significant differences between actual minority movements. They may also be regarded as marking crucial successive stages in the life cycle of minorities generally.

The initial goal of an emerging minority group, as it becomes aware of its ethnic identity, is to seek toleration for its cultural differences. By virtue of this striving it constitutes a pluralistic minority. If sufficient toleration

and autonomy are attained the pluralistic minority advances to the assimilationist stage, characterized by the desire for acceptance by and incorporation into the dominant group. Frustration of this desire for full participation
is likely to produce: (1) secessionist tendencies which may take the form
either of the complete separation from the dominant group and the establishment of sovereign nationhood, or (2) the drive to become incorporated
into another state with which there exists close cultural or historical identification. Progress in either of these directions may in turn lead to the goal
of domination over others and the resort to militant methods of achieving
that objective. If this goal is actually reached the group sheds the distinctive characteristics of a minority.

It should be emphasized, of course, that this typology of minorities is
a theoretical construct, rather than a description of actually existing groups.
We should not expect to find any one of these types to occur in pure form
either in history or in the present. All minorities contain within themselves
tendencies and movements in which we can discern the characteristic features of one or more of these types. Using such a typology as a tool we are
in a better position to analyze the empirical problems of minority situations
and to evaluate the proposed programs for their solution.

The basic fact accounting for the emergence of minorities is the lack
of congruence between political and ethnic groups. Political boundaries are
definite and almost always arbitrary. Cultural and ethnic areas are more
difficult to delineate. Political areas can be gerrymandered, whereas cultural
areas are the product of growth. Virtually every contest of power between
nations, whether around the diplomatic conference table or on the battle-
field, is followed by some redrawing of boundaries, leaving cultural pockets
enveloped islandlike by an alien sea. Even in the absence of territorial re-
visions, the indeterminate fringes along the frontiers, where marginal groups
are interspersed, tend to be chronic danger spots of ethnic friction.

A second factor causing minority groups to arise lies in the fact that
culture and people are seldom coterminous. Every living culture must be
carried by some people. But culture consists of many elements which may
be carried in varying combinations by diverse groups of people. Thus, for
instance, a group of people who speak the same language, have the same
religion and have an ancient common cultural heritage, is capable of more
effective collective action than a similar group with the same religion but
different language, or the same language but an otherwise different cultural
heritage. It is sufficient for the formation of minorities if merely a few of
the ethnic characteristics that give them distinctiveness coincide, especially
if these include such elements as language or religion. But if a group should
by accident of history and geography find itself united on a great range of
cultural characteristics and fairly densely concentrated in a compact area
so that the contrast between its status and that of its neighbors stands out
sharply, the emergence of that group as a minority is almost inevitable.

The genesis of minorities must therefore be sought in the fact that territory, political authority, people, and culture only rarely coincide. Since the disintegration of tribal society the human stocks occupying virtually every area of the world have become progressively diversified. Through the rise of the modern state the parochial principalities of earlier ages have disintegrated and heterogeneous groupings of people and diverse areas have been consolidated into vast political domains. Through conquest and migration formerly compact groups have become dispersed and split up among different political entities. Through modern transportation, communication, commerce and technology, the surviving folk cultures are being increasingly drawn into the vortex of world civilization. There still remain, in various parts of the world, some relatively limited islands of homogeneity and stability in a sea of conglomerate and swiftly moving heterogeneity, but on the whole the civilizing process is leveling them. Minority problems are symptomatic of this profound world-wide transition. . . .

In modern times, besides the technological and social changes that have profoundly affected the nature and significance of minority problems, there have been set afoot certain ideological forces which bear even more directly upon them. Of these, nationalism, the democratic ideology as applied to persons and groups, and secularism and science seem the most relevant.

The nineteenth century, which has often been called "the age of nationalism," saw the birth of a series of movements of national awakening, liberation, and consolidation resulting in the formation of modern Italy and Germany. It also saw the rapid development of modern empires and the crystallization of such movements as Pan-Slavism and Pan-Germanism, which became formidable threats to a state system based upon the balance of power. The lesser ethnic groups which were involuntarily enveloped by the nascent nations were frustrated and retarded in realizing their national aspirations. There were thus kindled seething movements of unrest which threatened the stability of the newly established states and the peace of the world. Minorities, especially those of the secessionist and militant variety, are in large part by-products of the ideology of nationalism, whose fundamental tenet it was that every people ought to have its own state but which failed to take full recognizance of the fact that political and ethnic lines do not always neatly coincide.

The forces of democracy and of nationalism were closely allied throughout most of the nineteenth century. The coalescence of these two ideologies became the principal weapon of the nationalities which were aspiring to independence at the peace discussions following the first World War. At Versailles the principle of national self-determination was invoked. It was construed to mean the right of every nation to form an independent state. But the conception of "nation" was far from clear and failed to take account of the many lesser ethnic and cultural groups which were not far enough advanced in the life-cycle of minorities to be considered eligible for nationhood and hence statehood. Versailles heard the articulate voices of the secessionist and militant minorities of the time, but failed to hear the softer whispering and petulant pleading of the pluralistic and assimilationist minorities who were put at the mercy of the former without more protection than the pious enunciation of high principles of toleration and non-discrimination. . . .

The problems and the very existence of minorities rest upon the recognition of the rights of peoples, notably the right of self-determination. Ever since the revolutionary era of the late eighteenth century the liberation of oppressed peoples has been a cause which has enlisted the support of liberal thinkers. Though some of its advocates thought of this principle —which was implicit in the democratic ideology—as a step toward cosmopolitanism, its immediate effect was to intensify nationalism. The general principle of the Versailles treaty in effect proclaimed that any group belonging to a minority, whether ethnic, cultural, or religious, was entitled to equal protection and opportunity with others. This principle was easier to proclaim than to put into practice, especially among some of the newly created states comprising former minorities. Having gained their freedom, these militant minorities not infrequently reduced their fellow nationals with different ethnic characteristics to a state of barely tolerated minorities, and sometimes even made them objects of violent persecution. . . .

The strategy for equalizing the opportunities of minorities has in the past been based upon the doctrine of the rights of man, which presumably applied to majority and minority alike. Only recently, however, has it been recognized that the subordination of minority ethnic groups and racial groups results in great cost to the whole society. From a military point of view it is undesirable because it weakens national loyalties and solidarity. The stunting of minority development reacts unfavorably upon the entire economy. As long as minorities suffer from discrimination and the denial of civil liberties the dominant group also is not free.

Another ideological factor that has appeared upon the modern scene and has left its impact upon the minorities problem is secularism. The secular trend in the modern world, which manifests itself in the spread of rationalism, science, and the general skepticism toward ideas and beliefs inherited from the past, has already made substantial inroads on parochial cults, on the divine right of some to rule, and on superstitions concerning the innate inferiority of racial and ethnic groups. It promises even greater progress in the future. Rigid caste systems, supported by sacred sanctions, are fast disintegrating. The separation of church and state has advanced to a point where a state religion is already regarded in most countries as intolerable. Even a "holy war" is almost inconceivable in modern times. With the spread of the ideal of equality of opportunity for all men there has come in most countries of the West a greater access for the masses of men, irrespective of race, ethnic affiliation, religion, or even economic status, to educational and cultural possibilities. The findings and methods of science may consequently find greater acceptance. The symbol of "the common man," despite the ridicule to which it has been subjected in some quarters seems to be on the way to making its influence felt the world over.

From anthropological studies of the last half century we should have gained a recognition of the inapplicability of the concept "race" as applied to the hybrid stocks comprising the European and American peoples. It is not race but culture—that is, linguistic, religious, economic, and social habits and attitudes, institutions, and values—that mark these people off from one another. And if science has demonstrated anything, it has shown conclusively that these traits are subject to human intervention, that they can be changed. The possibility of the ultimate assimilability of ethnic groups is thus beyond doubt.

It is coming to be recognized, moreover, that varying religious beliefs and cultural traits need not be a threat to national solidarity and are not necessarily disruptive of national loyalty. The private life of the individual is considered to an ever greater degree inviolable. What is required of the individual and of minority groups is that there be an adjustment to the social order and not necessarily that there be complete assimilation. Isolation of the minority from the body politic and social, on whatever ground it may be based and by whatever means enforced is increasingly regarded as the road to the perpetuation and accentuation of previously existing differences and as contrary to civilized public policy. . . .

EDITORIAL COMMENT

American society has long been racially, religiously, and ethnically heterogeneous. Today its population ranks among the most complex of all. First there was the heterogeneity represented by the invading and conquering Europeans and the native Indians. Almost from the outset there were Negroes and whites. Then came variation as a consequence of diversity among European immigrants and nativity differences, differences represented by the English and Germans in Pennsylvania, Latins and British on the Gulf Coast, Scandinavians and westward-moving Yankees west of the Mississippi—to mention only a few.

One type of grouping has often coincided with another. Religious affiliation in the United States, for example, rests to a considerable extent on a nationality or ethnic basis. The British-derived groups have tended to be associated with the Congregationalist, Baptist, Episcopalian, Presbyterian, and Unitarian churches; the Scandinavians and Germans with the Lutheran church; the South

Irish, Lithuanians, Poles, Italians, and others from central, southern and eastern Europe largely with the Roman Catholic and Eastern Orthodox churches. Even in its claims of universality, the Roman Catholic church has clearly recognized differences in nationality among its adherents with regard to language, liturgy, and saints.

In the following article, Kiser explores racial and nationality diversity among the American people from colonial to modern times. Because of the negative attitude in the United States since early days regarding the enumeration of population along religious lines, census materials are not available on religious groups and a discussion of this aspect of American diversity is not included in Kiser's analysis. However, estimates of the composition of the major religious groups are available in Sections VIII and IX, which deal with Roman Catholic–Protestant and Jewish–Gentile relations respectively.

2. THE DIVERSITY OF AMERICAN SOCIETY
BY *Clyde V. Kiser* *

COLONIAL ORIGINS OF . . . DIVERSITY

The origins of our . . . diversity are to be found in the conditions under which the area now constituting the United States was settled. In the first place, the Indian-white dichotomy began when the first white settlers arrived. The persistence of that dichotomy is a matter of history. It is a history first of attempted extermination, of the whites pushing the Indians westward, and later of establishing the surviving Indians on reservations as wards of the Federal Government.

The importation of Negro slaves brought another white-colored demarcation early in our population history. First imported as slaves about the time the Pilgrims were settling at Plymouth, the Negroes increased rapidly during the colonial period and were destined to become our largest minority group.

The origins of our intra-white . . . diversity are to be found in the multiple-power attempts at colonization. Although the English became the dominant colonists in early areas of settlement, the Dutch left their stamp on New York, the French on Louisiana, and the Spanish on California and the southwest.

* From Clyde V. Kiser, "Cultural Pluralism," *The Annals of the American Academy of Political and Social Science,* 262 (March 1949), 117–30. Reprinted by permission. Most footnotes omitted.

Furthermore, although the settlers of the British colonies were predominantly from the mother country, sizeable groups also came from other areas—particularly from northwestern Europe and notably from Germany. In numerous instances small groups of non-English peoples were allowed or even encouraged to come because of political and religious persecution. Some of these afford the best examples we have of the role of noneconomic factors in our early immigration.

It is not possible to determine exactly the net effect of these policies relating to Indians, importation of slaves, and origins of white settlers on the size and ethnic composition of this country's population by the close of the colonial period. Records of colonial censuses carried out about 1770–75 in most of the provinces are available, but these did not enumerate Indians in most instances and simply differentiated the Negroes from the whites with no indication of the ethnic origin of the latter. On the basis of these and other materials, however, Sutherland has concluded:

> In the period of 167 years elapsing between the settlement of Jamestown in 1608 and the outbreak of the Revolution, the population of the American colonies grew to 2,507,180, exclusive of Indians. . . . About 533,500 were Negroes, and perhaps 200,000 more were of German or other alien stock; the remainder were British.[1]

According to Sutherland's figures, Negroes constituted about 21 per cent of the total population (exclusive of Indians), and about 90 per cent of the white persons were of British origin. The latter figure corresponds closely to, and is probably based upon, the United States Census Bureau's estimated distribution by ethnic origin of the whites enumerated in the 1790 Census of the United States.

COMPOSITION OF OUR POPULATION IN 1790

In 1790, according to our first census, Negroes comprised 19.3 per cent of the total population enumerated within the United States boundaries of that date. That census did not enumerate Indians and gave no direct information on ethnic stock of the white population. In a special volume published in 1909, however, the Bureau of the Census provided an estimated distribution of the whites in the 1790 Census, according to country of origin, based largely on family names. According to these estimates, 82.1 per cent of the whites enumerated in the United States in 1790 were of English lineage, an additional 7 per cent were of Scottish descent, and 1.9 per cent were Irish. In other words, about 91 per cent of the whites were from, or

---

[1] Stella H. Sutherland, *Population Distribution in Colonial America* (New York: Columbia University Press, 1936), p. 271.

descendants of people from, the British Isles. Most of the remainder were German or Dutch. . . .[2]

The above figures, however, have not been universally accepted. Many students have stressed the possibilities of serious pitfalls in the use of family names in this country as a basis for determining national origin. In 1927 the American Council of Learned Societies appointed a committee of experts in historical and genealogical research to study the problem. The report of this committee, which was released in 1932, not only presented a reclassification of the enumerated white population of 1790, but also provided estimates of whites in unenumerated areas.[3] According to this reclassification, persons of English origin formed only about 60 per cent of the whites in continental United States in 1790. Those of English, Scotch, and Irish descent combined accounted for about 78 per cent. In general, however, although this later analysis of the family names in the 1790 Census suggests a wider variety of origins of the original white population, it does not alter the general conclusion that the British constituted the dominant element and that there were few people from southern and eastern Europe at the time of the first census of the United States. Rare also were the Orientals.

SUBSEQUENT INCREASES IN DIVERSITY

The subsequent increase in diversity of the population was due to the great influx of immigrants from varied sources during the nineteenth century and early part of the twentieth.

To summarize very broadly, three distinct periods stand out in our immigration history both with respect to origins and policy. Prior to 1882 the immigrants were mainly from northern and western Europe. Attracted by the opportunities for free land, they and their descendants helped to push our frontiers westward and their dispersal facilitated rapid mergence into our culture. It was a period of virtual absence of Federal restrictions against immigration, and during the last thirty years of it many Chinese took advantage of this situation.

The second period, 1882–1923, was characterized by declining immigration from northern and western Europe, and by the ascendancy of migrants from southern and eastern Europe. Just as the British, Irish, and Germans predominated in the earlier movement, the Italians, Russians, and Poles were especially conspicuous in the second period. Besides these peoples, however, hundreds of thousands of immigrants from other southern

[2] U.S. Bureau of the Census, *A Century of Population Growth* (Washington: Government Printing Office, 1909), p. 121.

[3] American Council of Learned Societies: "Report of the Committee on Linguistic and National Stocks in the Population of the United States," *Annual Report of the American Historical Association, 1931,* Vol. I (Washington: Government Printing Office, 1932), p. 124.

and eastern European countries helped to swell six annual totals above the million mark during 1905–14. The whole period was one of declining opportunities for free land but of increasing opportunities for industrial employment. Hence, it was the period of urban concentration of immigrants and of the formation of ghettos—Little Italys, Little Hungaries, and Little Russias in New York, Pittsburgh, and other large cities. . . .

The third and last period, that since 1924, is characterized by small numbers of immigrants from any source, by quotas favoring northwestern Europe, by the higher relative importance of immigration from countries of the Western Hemisphere, and by the admission of a fairly sizeable body of refugees in recent years.

Owing to our past history of immigration, our population is considerably more heterogeneous than it was in 1790. This is true to some extent for the colored population; it is conspicuously the case for the whites.

Proportionate Declines

Negroes easily form our most numerous minority group, white or colored, and Indians, though numbering only about 334,000 in 1940, are the most numerous of our non-Negro colored elements. Negroes have declined in proportionate importance in the total population from about 19 per cent in 1790 to 10 per cent in 1940. This is attributed mainly to the fact that since 1808 (when further importation of slaves was banned) the growth of the Negro population has been limited to natural increase. Accretions through voluntary immigration have been very small.

Likewise, although no figures can be given regarding size of the Indian population in 1790, there is no doubt that until recently Indians have formed a constantly decreasing percentage of our population, despite the accession of new groups with the westward extension of United States boundaries. As late as two decades ago these peoples could be aptly described as our "vanishing Americans." Furthermore, the heterogeneity of the colored population is increased by the presence of the Japanese, Chinese, and other Asiatics. Although these groups are small in proportion to the total or even to the total colored population, they were scarcely represented at all in 1790.

Several types of census materials are available for studying changes in the ethnic composition of the white population, but each has definite limitations. The central difficulty is the lack of data, or even the virtual impossibility of securing accurate data, on ethnic origin of all native whites of native parentage.[4] Since 1850, however, the census has provided data on country of origin of the foreign-born population, and since 1890 such data have been available for the total "foreign-white stock" (foreign-born

[4] Probably the two chief reasons for the census omission of this question for native whites of native parentage are (1) the presumption of minor influence of national origin on these people, and (2) the existence of multiple origins due to intermarriages.

whites, plus native whites of foreign or mixed parentage). In addition the Census Bureau has collected data on mother tongue of certain elements of the population since 1910.

ACLS and Other Estimates

Changes in the ethnic composition of the total white population since 1790 can best be shown by comparing the ACLS estimates for 1790 with those that were made for 1920 as a basis for our present immigration quotas, as is shown by Table 1. The latter work was done by a committee set up by Departments of State, Commerce, and Labor. It should be emphasized that the limitations of the data and the nature of the problem itself preclude precise comparisons. Each of the classifications listed in Table 1 was originally submitted with accompanying statements regarding the difficulty of classifying peoples of mixed strains and emphasizing that the distributions should be interpreted simply in terms of the relative importance of the various national origins in the total white population considered.[5]

Whatever the limitations of the data may be, there is no doubt about the decrease in the proportionate importance of English stock in our white population. On the basis of the two estimates mentioned above, 74.1 per cent of our white population was of British and North Irish origin in 1790; the proportion was 41.4 per cent in 1920. On the other hand, "Irish Free State" origins accounted for 3.6 per cent in 1790 and 11.2 per cent in 1920. German origins formed 8.6 per cent in 1790 and 16.3 per cent in 1920. Southern and eastern European origins, scarcely represented in 1790, collectively formed over one-tenth of the white population of the United States in 1920. The two chief origins in this category were Poland (4.1 per cent) and Italy (3.6 per cent).

Country-of-birth Data

Next to immigration statistics themselves, the census data on country of birth of our foreign-born population are most sensitive to changing origins of our immigrants. Thus . . . in 1850 about 43 per cent of our foreign-born population were from Ireland, 26 per cent from Germany, and 17 per cent from England, Scotland, and Wales. Southern and eastern European countries collectively were represented by only one-half of 1 per cent of the foreign-born population. In 1940, on the other hand, natives of Italy outnumbered those of any other country in our foreign-born population and constituted 14 per cent of the total. Those of Germany stood in second place with 11 per cent. Close behind, each group constituting 8–9

---

[5] The chief fault that the ACLS committee found with the Census Bureau's estimate of the 1790 composition was that it was based simply on a tabulation of reported family names and that no account was taken of changes in names. The persons responsible for the 1920 estimates had the benefit of help from the ACLS; they also had the benefit of census data on country of origin and mother tongue of the foreign-white stock.

TABLE 1.

PERCENTAGE APPORTIONMENT OF THE WHITE POPULATION OF THE UNITED STATES IN 1790 AND 1920, BY COUNTRY OF ORIGIN

Country of origin	1790		1920
	U.S. Bureau of Census estimates of 1909	*ACLS Comm. estimates of 1932*	*Prepared as bases for immigration quotas*
Total	100.00%	100.00%	100.00%
Quota countries (for 1920 data)			94.5
Northwestern and central Europe (approx.)	99.7	92.4	83.0
England	82.1	60.1	
Wales	(Included with English, 1790)		41.4
Scotland	7.0	8.1	
North Ireland	⎰	5.9	
Irish Free State	⎱ 1.9	3.6	11.2
Austria	b	b	0.9
Belgium	b	b	0.8
Czechoslovakia	b	b	1.8
Denmark	b	b	0.7
Estonia	b	b	0.1
Finland	b	b	0.4
France	0.6	2.3	1.9
Germany	5.6	8.6	16.3
Hungary	b	b	0.6
Latvia	b	b	0.2
Netherlands	2.5	3.1	2.0
Norway	b	b	1.5
Sweden	b	0.7	2.1
Switzerland	b	b	1.1
Southern and Eastern Europe (approx.)	b	0.8	11.2
Greece	b	b	0.2
Italy	b	b	3.6
Lithuania	b	b	0.2
Poland	b	b	4.1
Portugal	b	b	0.3
Rumania	b	b	0.2
Spain	b	0.8	0.2
Turkey	b	b	0.1
U.S.S.R. (Europe and Asia)	b	b	1.8
Yugoslavia	b	b	0.5
All other quota countries (1920)	b	b	0.3
Nonquota countries (1920)	b	b	5.6
Canada & Newfoundland	b	b	4.3
Latin America	b	b	1.3
Other or unknown (1790)	0.3	6.8	

b. Included with "other or unknown" if represented at all in 1790 per cent of our foreign-born population, were immigrants from Canada, Russia, Poland, Great Britain (England, Scotland, and Wales), and the Scandinavian countries combined. Ireland contributed only about 6 per cent. Collectively, 38 per cent of our foreign-born population of 1940 came from countries of southern and eastern Europe, 46 per cent from north-western and central Europe, 14 per cent from countries of the Western Hemisphere, and the remainder from other places.

Although the foreign-born whites in 1940 numbered only 11.4 million and constituted only about 9 per cent of our total population, there were about 23.2 million native whites of foreign or mixed parentage. Hence, about 34.6 million, or about 26 per cent of our total population, were classified in the 1940 Census as members of "foreign-white stock." Among the persons of foreign-white stock those of German origin stood in top position numerically with about 15 per cent of the total. In descending order of magnitude these were followed by Italians with 13 per cent, British (including North Irish) with 9 per cent, Russians, Canadians, Poles, each with about 8 per cent, and Free State Irish with 7 per cent. . . .

MOTHER TONGUE

In the 1940 Census "mother tongue" was defined as "the principal language spoken in the home of the person in his earliest childhood; English was reported as the mother tongue only if no foreign language was spoken." On the basis of returns from a 5 per-cent sample of the total population, tabulations have been published regarding mother tongue of the total white population, and these are also given separately for the foreign-born whites, native whites of foreign or mixed parentage, and native whites of native parentage.

Among the total whites English was reported as the mother tongue by 78.6 per cent, German by 4.2 per cent, Italian by 3.2 per cent, Polish by 2.0 per cent, Spanish by 1.6 per cent, Yiddish by 1.5 per cent, and French by 1.2 per cent. No other single foreign mother tongue was re-ported by as much as 1 per cent of the total white population. The fore-going percentages represent the following total numbers of whites: English mother tongue, 93 million; German, 4.9 million; Italian, 3.8 million; Polish, 2.4 million; Spanish, 1.9 million; Yiddish, 1.75 million; and French, 1.4 million.

As one might expect, the proportion reporting English mother tongue was lowest (22.6 per cent) for foreign-born whites, intermediate (52.6 per cent) for native whites of foreign or mixed parentage, and highest (93.1 per cent) for native whites of native parentage. Within each of these three groups, German was the most frequent foreign mother tongue re-ported and Italian stood second within the two foreign stock groups. Thus, among the foreign born, German was reported by 14.3 per cent, Italian by 14.1 per cent, Yiddish by 8.3 per cent, Polish by 7.2 per cent, Spanish by 3.9 per cent, Swedish by 3.8 per cent, and French and Russian each by 3.2 per cent.

No census prior to that of 1940 collected data on mother tongue of native whites of native parentage. In the 1930 Census, the collection of such data was restricted to persons of foreign birth and the published tabulations to foreign-born whites. In the 1910 and 1920 censuses the published data related to persons of foreign-white stock but . . . only those for the foreign-born whites are comparable with the 1940 materials for whites of corresponding nativity. In general, the 1910–40 comparisons for the foreign born point up the shift of linguistic origins from northwestern and central Europe to southern and eastern Europe. For instance, in 1910 German was reported as the mother tongue by 20.7 per cent of the foreign-born whites and Italian by 10.2 per cent. In 1940, as already noted, these two languages were about equally represented; the percentages were 14.3 and 14.1, respectively. . . .

II. Race, Religion, and Nationality

THE principal types of minority and dominant groups, as we have noted, are races, religious groups, and nationalities. Important variables in qualifying and refining the situation of any given group are state or country of origin, nativity or generation, and language.

Many people claim their racial distinction from others on the basis of several allegations. First of all, it is alleged that there are hereditary factors that determine not only allegedly significant physical differentials but also alleged differentials in aptitudes and capacities, personality traits, and performance. Physical anthropologists have had little success in discerning distinguishable races along hereditary-biological lines. Nor have they revealed any conclusive proof of a causal relationship between skin color, head shape, and other "racial" traits on the one hand, and capacity, personality, and culture on the other. But races are social and psychological realities as long as people themselves feel, think, and behave racialistically. In the words of W. I. Thomas, "If men define situations as real, they are real in their consequences." The so-called Negroid, Mongoloid, and Caucasoid races and their subdivisions exist in racial thinking and behavior, even though efforts to delineate them physically are largely inconclusive.

Religious groups differentiate themselves from each other on the basis of cultural rather than hereditary factors, and then on the basis of only one aspect of culture. Religion has been defined sociologically as the social institution revolving about the idea of a supernatural being or beings, and the relation of humans to them. This idea becomes formalized into a social pattern, and the pattern comes to be known as "the religion" of a particular group. Every group's religion has three essential aspects: (1) a conception of the supernatural; (2) a set of doctrines concerning the reciprocal obligations and duties between the supernatural and human beings; and (3) a set of behavior patterns designed to conform to the will of God and to assure to the individual believer the approval of his conscience and whatever rewards or freedom from penalties in this world or the next are included in the doctrines of faith. Subdivisions among religious groups occur not only in terms of denominations and sects, but there may be stratification on the basis of race, nationality, country of origin, nativity, and language. A given religious group is seldom homogeneous racially even according to its own thinking. In fact members of two or more religious groups are often racially identified with each other to an extent far greater than they are with their co-religionists.

Nationality (or ethnic group) is frequently confused in people's minds with nation or state, that is, a political grouping organized on a territorial basis. A nationality is a tribalistic group whose members conform to—or at least are expected to be sympathetic with—a number of cultural traits and institutions such as language, dress, food, and family patterns. Nationalities generally antecede the establishment of nations or states. Very few nationalities are situated in a state exclusive of other nationalities. Not only are two or more nationalities usually found within a given nation or state, but a given nationality typically is located in two or more different states. Most nations or states of the Western world include in their populations a dominant nationality—often using its name as the state label—and one or more minority nationalities. Frequently a nationality dominant in one state or nation is a minority in other nations. Like races and religious groups, a given nationality is, more often than not, marked by internal differences as well as resemblances. It may, for instance, have clearly outlined religious and even racial demarcations within its membership. Regional forces may produce still other cultural differences within the group.

In summary, specific groups can and do have ambivalent social relations with each other. They can be psychologically allied racially but stratified from each other in religion and nationality, as in the case of English Protestants and Irish Catholics. Or there may be similarity in religious identification but differentiation in race and nationality, as is illustrated by American Negro Protestants and Welsh Protestants. Again, people may be of the same nationality but of contrasting races and religious groups, a case being German Protestants, some of whom consider themselves Nordic in race, as opposed to those Germans who are Roman Catholics and who may consider themselves Alpine in racial type.

In the readings that follow, race, religion, and nationality are considered in the order given. The first selection by Professor Haring is an account of race from the physical anthropological point of view. It presents all the essential data concerning the history of the race concept and the alleged hereditary and somatic foundation of this intriguing form of human alignment.

3. RACIAL DIFFERENCES AND HUMAN RESEMBLANCES BY *Douglas G. Haring* *

SCARCELY a day passes without news of 'racial' conflict somewhere in the world. Social relations, economic organization and politics are bedevilled constantly by 'racial' alignments and discriminations. . . . What are the underlying facts of race?

Ancient peoples paid little attention to differences in skin color and bodily form. Legend asserts that King Solomon's distinguished friend, the Queen of Sheba, was black-skinned. Mummies indicate that Egypt's Pharaohs ranged in color from chocolate brown to white with red hair. In the Roman Empire generals and officials ran the gamut of human colors and rarely was it noted which were white and which black. . . .

The very word *race* is a late addition to European languages. Sixteenth century France witnessed the gradual acceptance of such a word though its origin is disputed. By the seventeenth century "espèces ou races d' homme" was used to refer to family or breed. About 1700 Leibnitz introduced the word *Rasse* to the German language, but he used it to mean

* Douglas G. Haring, "Racial Differences and Human Resemblances" (2d ed.; Syracuse: published privately, 1947) 24 pp. Reprinted by permission. Footnotes omitted.

something like the English 'generations.' Kant, in 1775, first spoke of the 'races of mankind' and thenceforth the Germans accepted that meaning. The idea of superior and inferior races is still more modern. Probably it arose in demand for labor in the American colonies. Columbus and his men enslaved Indians in the Caribbean; subsequent colonists, pressed to obtain cheap plantation labor, eagerly bought slaves. American Indian slaves had proved too independent and intractable, and demand arose for more docile workers. In Africa the aggressive Negro kingdoms of the Slave Coast and the Gold Coast found it highly profitable to raid the inland tribes and sell their captives to European traders. At first the slavers had trouble because their cargoes could talk among themselves without being understood; consequently mutiny wrecked the profits and hopes of many a shipowner. So the traders hit upon the device of sorting together Negroes from different tribes to make sure they could not talk and conspire among themselves. At the slave markets in America this process was carried further, and the Negroes on any one plantation were rendered helpless against their masters. Not knowing English they often misunderstood orders—a situation which fostered the dogma that all Negroes are stupid.

Since in American experience slaves usually were Negroes and Negroes were slaves, it was easy to conclude that the color of the Negro foreordained him to bondage. In Europe, Asia, and Africa, slaves had been of all colors—every military victory flooded the slave markets with prisoners of war, and slaves were of whatever color happened to have been defeated. Thus events conspired to preclude emphasis upon racial differences in the Old World, while residents of the New World were led to stress the color line.

Abolition of human slavery in the New World—and later, in South Africa—did not change the beliefs about race. Gradually all sorts of phenomena were ascribed to racial differences, and the topic of race is marked by confusion in the modern world. That confusion can be clarified only by discriminating analysis of the facts of human bodily differences.

The ideas most frequently confused involve race, language, and learned social behavior such as customs, religions, forms of government, and knowledge. The word race often is used mistakenly when languages or customs are indicated. Thus Jews are called a 'race'; actually Judaism is a social tradition which each individual Jew learns in home and synagogue. Jews . . . are tall and blond, others short and dark; some resemble the general population of South Russia, some who live in India look like Hindus, and one Chinese city includes descendants of Jews who look and act like Chinese. Similarly, people speak carelessly of a 'German race,' a 'French race,' or a 'British race' when in actuality many different types of physique and bodily characteristics occur in all three nations. Language and physical type also are confused in common belief; thus it is assumed that all who speak English are of one race, while those whose mother tongue is French constitute another. The United States, however, includes millions of Negroes who know no language other than English; French North Africa is home to many thousands of individuals . . . who all speak French. There are Americans of Chinese and of Japanese ancestry whose 'mother tongue' is English, while in China a few children of white parents have grown up speaking only Chinese. In this discussion, the term *race* refers only to *bodily characteristics;* language and other learned habits are discussed specifically as such.

The bodily features of mankind are investigated systematically in the science of physical anthropology, which is the study of man as a species of living organism. Precise definition of a species is difficult, but in general, a species is a plural number of organisms biologically alike who interbreed to produce offspring like the parents. In this sense human beings are a distinct species; no other animal ever is mistaken for a human being, nor can a human being be mistaken for any other kind of organism. All human beings interbreed and the offspring resemble the parents. Although it has been argued by some writers that the races of mankind are distinct species, no attempt to define races as separate species has gained scientific recognition. . . .

CONTEMPORARY HUMAN TYPES

Schoolbooks often repeat the ancient legend that there are five human races: white, yellow, red, brown, and black. Actually few 'whites' are very white, 'yellows' and 'reds' are neither yellow nor red, and 'blacks' range from creamy tan to deep chocolate brown. Of course, this naïve classification ignores all features other than skin color, which depends on two factors: the amounts of brown and yellow pigment, and the 'thickness' of the skin. Thin skin looks pink where the red color of the blood shows through. Moderately pigmented thin skins appear bronzed; thicker skin with similar pigmentation has a yellowish cast. In all 'races' the pigments are identical chemically, but the amounts vary. Certain diseases that disturb bodily chemistry and allow pigment to accumulate may turn white skins brown. And a few individuals in every race—including the Negroes—manifest a hereditary absence of pigment known as albinism; these persons have white skin, pinkish eyes, and colorless hair. . . .

Human hair varies in color, texture, shape, and distribution on the body. Round hair is straight; the more highly elliptical the cross-section of the hair, the more it curls. Straight, wavy, curly, and 'frizzly' hair occur in all colors from straw-blonde through red and brown to black. Nearly all colors and forms of hair may accompany any of a variety of skin colors. . . .

The kind and amount of hair of the beard and on the body vary greatly. Some males grow abundant beards, others almost none; beards may differ in color from the scalp hair. The 'white races' are the hairiest and many white persons have thick growths of hair on chest, legs, and arms. In Negroes and Eastern Asiatics this kind of hairy covering is almost unknown. . . .

The iris of the human eye is predominantly brown. Small numbers in the populations of Europe, North Africa, and Central Asia exhibit eyes that range from pale blue through grey and greenish tints to light brown. The two eyes of the same person—even parts of a single iris—may differ in color. Light colored irises occur more frequently though not uniformly in individuals whose skin and hair also lack pigment.

Variations in the bony skeleton appear conspicuously in the differences between tall, thin, long-faced, long-limbed individuals, and short, wide-faced, plump, short-limbed persons—as well as the whole gamut of intermediate types. So universal and so common are these differences that most talk about race has ignored them. Nevertheless, these inherited bodily characteristics are just as important as skin color.

Stature varies from an average of four feet six inches among Pygmies to six feet two inches among some tribes of the Upper Nile. Shoulder breadth, pelvic measurements, relative massiveness of bones, and proportions of limbs and trunk vary widely in every part of the world. In all 'races,' however, homologous bones are arranged in the same distinctively human pattern. The number of bones is uniform, save for an extra bone in wrist or ankle. Teeth vary in minute details, but the basic pattern of human dentition is uniform.

Skulls range from long-narrow to short-broad, combined variously with different heights and differing degrees of slope of the forehead. Bony eyebrow ridges are frequent in Europeans and Australian blacks, but are absent in a large majority of Chinese. Proportions of the skull seem to vary with diet and methods of infant care; thus infants who are tied tightly to a wooden cradleboard may develop skulls flat in the back and rising to a high point—a fact which has led to erroneous racial classifications. Sometimes the teeth of the two jaws meet vertically, again they protrude somewhat. Chins slope at many different angles from the vertical. Noses vary from high and narrow with pronounced bridge and small nostrils to broad and flat with almost no bridge; some are convex in profile, others concave. A wag has remarked that in most Chinese a fly can walk on the level from one eye to the other, but must be a mountain climber to accomplish a like journey on many European faces. . . .

Eyelids manifest numerous minor variations. At the inner epicanthus (the junction of upper and lower eyelids nearest the nose) the two eyelids usually meet evenly; in some individuals, however, a fold of the upper lid covers the inner end of the lower one. About 2% of Europeans show this feature, while in China it characterizes from 20% to 50% of the population, depending on the locality. Hence it has been called the "Mongoloid fold" and people often refer to the Chinese as "slant eyed" or "almond eyed" even though a majority of Chinese lack this feature. In many Chinese the almond effect is enhanced by absence of the bridge of the nose. A Mongoloid fold may escape notice in a European because it may be combined with a high nasal bridge, beetling eyebrows, and blue eyes. These latter features prompted the Chinese to call Europeans "dog-eyed"—a characteristic naïvely verified when a European fondly boasts that his pet dog's eyes are 'almost human.' In turn, many Europeans exhibit another kind of fold of the eyelid that is rare in Chinese; this is the so-called Nordic fold, which is an extra fold of the upper lid that conceals the outer epicanthus (the junction of the two eyelids furthest from the nose). . . .

To what extent do visceral and other internal organs vary? In general, internal organs vary much as do external features. In no human 'race,' however, are these variations so great that a surgeon about to operate on a specific organ would be in doubt as to the proper place for incision. The same organ turns up in the appropriate place and performs the same physiological function, whatever the 'race.' Perhaps such external variations as those in stature, bodily contour, skin, and hair are related to the relative activity of many endocrine or ductless glands; thus far, however, attempts to define 'race' in terms of glandular functioning are unsatisfactory. . . .

Conspicuous is the fact that, excepting pathological cases, all these human bodily variations 'work' for practical purposes. For example, tropical sunlight injures light-skinned persons and does not injure the dark-skinned. The white-skinned individual, however, can either stay indoors during the peak of the day or may wear a pith helmet. A tall man picks cherries from a tree more easily than a short man; but the short person can get a ladder and pick just as many cherries. Long slender fingers may be an asset to a pianist—or to a pickpocket—but stubby fingers have made good in both professions. All shapes of noses manage to breathe; all shapes of jaws chew and talk; mathematics, golf, or Sanskrit are learned equally well by the thin or the fat, the blonde or the brunette, the kinky-haired or the straight-haired. Even badly mutilated bodies function effectively when the owner has courage and resourcefulness, as many a war casualty has demonstrated. Abraham Lincoln struck at the heart of the problem; asked what should be the length of a man's legs, he replied soberly, "I think they ought to be at least long enough to reach from his body to the ground."

Observations throughout the world show that all these variable features are combined in diverse patterns. All normal human beings are fertile with mates of any physical type, and the offspring combine parental features in unpredictable ways. Negro-White matings have produced offspring who are tall, lanky, with red kinky hair, narrow noses, blue eyes, freckles, and dark brown skin; as well as other offspring with light skin, dark eyes, stocky build, straight black hair, broad nostrils, and protruding jaws. The children of Chinese-White matings combine the parental features in ways that seem just as strange. Tall Mongolians with round heads, heavy build, almost hairless bodies and straight black scalp hair have mated with small, slender, wiry, wavy-haired, long-headed Malays to produce offspring with hair and head form like the Mongol parent and the small wiry build of the Malay—as well as big-boned children with Malayan features and hair. Matings of Japanese with African blacks have resulted in bewildering combinations of the distinctive features of the two parents. Such mixed matings have occurred in all times and places. Consequently the majority of mankind exhibit features in combinations that can only be called scrambled. No known human hybrid is infertile like the mule.

Wars and migrations have provided the warp of history. Always they are accompanied by matings of contrasted physical types. . . . So freely and frequently have both Negroes and Asiatics mingled with Europeans for centuries past that the family trees of most of the readers of these words probably include both Negroid and Mongoloid twigs in a not-too-remote past. Most of the variations appearing in mankind occur sporadically in any local population. In any one region, the accidents of history and of local isolation have produced specific combinations of features that differ from combinations observed elsewhere, so that to some extent all of the inhabitants in a long-settled population look somewhat alike. These more or less definite local patterns of bodily characteristics underlie the belief in clear-cut racial differences.

Attempts to classify mankind in a specific number of well-defined 'races' invariably fail. The great mixed populations defy attempts to fit all their members into any definite 'race.' No one can draw boundaries within which all 'whites,' all 'negroids,' or all 'mongoloids' fall. Classifications based on color are vitiated by the predominance of intermediate colors. If hair be used as a standard, the color groups are broken up. For example, skin color puts the aboriginal Australians with the Congo Negroes; but hair form puts them with the European 'whites.' Which is correct? Both—and neither.

Prior to the invention of the steamship, railway, motor-car, and airplane, small local populations often experienced long isolation from the outer world. Of necessity, these groups inbred. Contrary to popular superstition, inbreeding does not necessarily result in inferior offspring. In domesticated animals, for example, inbreeding fixes a type and may improve it. This happened among isolated human groups. Thus there developed tribes of common descent whose members all, or nearly all, manifested similar bodily characteristics. . . .

In rich, accessible regions, however, no group remains pure. Travel, immigration, and invasion effect intermixture. The larger the population and the more different physical types it includes, the more hazily defined are the racial types. . . . Historically, civilization and race mixture have

gone together; achievements in civilization are the work of mixed peoples
—not because mixed peoples are superior but because racial purity depends on isolation.

Despite scientific inaccuracy, convenience has led to a rough division
of mankind into three major stocks and several minor groups. The *Cauca-*
soids include the light-skinned, highly variable Europeans and their descendants in the New World, South Africa, and Australia, and also the
dark-skinned Hindus. The term *Mongoloid* denotes the Chinese, Mongols,
Japanese, and aboriginal Americans, plus several variable minor stocks.
Negroids include the many dark-skinned peoples of Africa and Oceania.

The inclusion of so many and varied physical types in these three
general categories obviously involves fallacious classification. For example,
many and diverse 'racial types' inhabit Europe, North Africa, Western Asia,
and Northern India. Their resemblances are so vague and general that it
is misleading to lump them together as 'Caucasoids.' Among these peoples
the blue-eyed, fair-skinned, light-haired individuals, though numerous in
the Baltic area, constitute a decided numerical minority. The brown-skinned
Hindus are included because of historic affiliations and physical resemblances other than skin color. Similarly, 'Negroid' is an omnibus term for
dark-skinned peoples as diverse as the Pygmies, the tall Melanesians with
their Roman noses and mops of frizzly hair, and the long-limbed woolly-
haired tribes of the African Congo. Under 'Mongoloid' are classified the
tall northern Chinese and their Mongol neighbors, the short southern Chinese and the Japanese, the Burmese and various Malayan tribes—most of
whom are broad-headed, with bridgeless noses, scant beards, and sallow of
complexion—and also the varied physical types of the American Indians.

Bodily types that cannot be fitted into this somewhat Procrustean classification are observed among the following: the light-skinned, hairy Ainu of
north Japan; the black Australians, who resemble white Europeans save
for black skin and broad nostrils; the Polynesians of the Pacific islands;
the South African Hottentots and Bushmen with their tufted hair and their
steatopygous females; the Veddah aborigines of Ceylon; and others. . . .

EDITORIAL COMMENT

A corollary of the efforts recounted by Haring to describe and classify the races of mankind in the physical sense of the term has
been the oft-repeated attempt to demonstrate innate psychological
differences between races. Just as those high in status have strenu-
ously argued that their physiques are superior, so racially minded
people have maintained that mentally they are superior, regardless
of the criteria of mentality one chooses.

Here, too, racists find their contentions subject to serious doubt and question. Clear differences and superiority and inferiority that presumably stratify races in regard to such traits as intelligence and temperament are more easily claimed than verified. Unless the methodology and tools used in demonstrating one's position are scientific, not much support can be given to the substantive conclusions. Secondly, even when the findings are derived by scientific method, they must be carefully interpreted. Mental performances, for example, may be just as much a function or expression of opportunity as an indicator of aptitude. Furthermore, if psychological tests ostensibly reveal significant differences between racial groups, it must be stressed that the differences are found on statistical averages rather than on qualitative factors distinguishing each and every member of one group from all members outside the group.

Closely related to the concept that races are physically and psychologically differentiated in meaningful patterns of superiority and inferiority is the philosophy of racial determinism. According to the racial determinists, man's cultural variation can be explained by his racial variation. Different races produce different cultures, and a given race is capable of producing only a given culture. It also follows that if some races are physically and mentally superior to others, their cultures fall into a correspondingly stratified pattern. The racially backward peoples, says the racial determinist, are also culturally backward; their behavior and appearance are more closely akin to those of the anthropoid apes than to those of the determinist's own race.

Racial determinism, which emerged in the nineteenth century and reached its highpoint as an operational philosophy in Nazi Germany in the twentieth century, is scientifically obsolete. It is a special form of biological determinism, and social science has come to minimize the importance of biological factors in shaping culture. But like the unfounded dogma extracted from the physical anthropology of race and from racial psychology, racial determinism continues to be especially useful to conquerors and exploiters in rationalizing their superior status.

It is erroneous to assume that only the ignorant accept race as a significant determining factor in physical and mental performance and in the formation of cultural patterns. Race thinking manifests itself to a surprising extent among many scholars, intellectuals, and artists as well. Even scientists often ignore the scientific method and consciously subscribe to race thinking.

Anyone who identifies, categorizes, and characterizes large groups of people as races without sufficient evidence is, of course, engaging in unjustified behavior from the scientific point of view. References to pure or mixed blood, to the Negro's "thick" skull, the Jewish nose, the Nordic soul, and others too numerous to mention are obviously derived from race thinking. Somewhat less obvious indications of race thinking are found in such sayings as, "That is very white (i.e., decent) of you."

These are some of the important issues that must be considered in the study of racial psychology and sociology. Several of them are discussed in further detail in the following essay by Klineberg.

4. RACIAL PSYCHOLOGY
BY *Otto Klineberg* *

AMONG the problems which concern anthropology and related sciences probably none has aroused more popular interest or has had more far-reaching practical implications than that of psychological differences between races. The uncritical belief in the innate superiority of one's own group over others has helped to explain, or at least to rationalize, a substantial proportion of the world's organized aggression. It was a fundamental aspect of the ideology of the Nazis and of the Japanese militarists, and plays its part in our own attitudes toward, and treatment of, American minority groups. It may not be the primary cause of such aggression, but it has certainly contributed a portion of the psychological ammunition with which the aggression has been implemented.

The belief in inherited psychological differences between groups is widespread. In September, 1939, a *Fortune* survey (conducted at the request of the Carnegie Corporation Study of the Negro in America) asked the question: "Do you think Negroes now generally have higher intelligence than white people, lower, or about the same?" In all sections of the country the majority of those interviewed regarded the Negroes as inferior, the figures for different regions varying from 60.0 to 76.9 per cent. Those who believed Negroes to be inferior were then asked the further question: "Do you think this is because: (1) they have lacked opportunities, or (2) they are born less intelligent, or (3) both?" The percentages attributing the inferiority to innate factors alone ranged from 28.7 to 54.8 per cent. The percentages of those, however, who regarded the difference as due at least in part to heredity (that is, those checking the second or third answers) ranged from 55.5 to 79.2 per cent.[1] These last figures should not be

* From Ralph Linton (ed.), *The Science of Man in the World Crisis* (New York: Columbia University Press, 1945), pp. 63–77. Reprinted by permission.

[1] From E. L. Horowitz, "Race Attitudes," in *Characteristics of the American Negro,* ed. Otto Klineberg (New York, 1944).

misunderstood; they are percentages not of the total population but of those who regard the Negro as inferior. They do at the same time give some indication of the extent of popular belief in the biological inequality of racial groups.

The present position of American scientists, on the other hand, appears to be overwhelmingly on the side of those who believe that the differences in the behavior of various racial or national groups have not been demonstrated to be of biological origin. With few exceptions, such differences as exist can be and have been explained on the basis of historical and cultural conditions, variations in opportunity, in education and experience. It is perhaps worth noting that, as Gunnar Myrdal puts it: "Hardly anywhere else or on any other issue is there—in spite of intensive and laudable efforts to popularize the new results of research—such a wide gap between scientific thought and popular belief." [2] In the following pages the attempt will be made to provide some of the evidence on which the present anthropological viewpoint is based.

The emphasis on the word "present" in this context should not be interpreted as meaning that the position here adopted is a temporary one, or that it is likely to be superseded in the near future; it is meant rather to indicate the contrast with the past. In a significant summary of the "errors of sociology," Odum includes "the assumption that races are inherently different rather than group products of differentials due to the cumulative power of folk-regional and cultural environment." [3] This error, it may be added, was not confined to sociologists but was shared by many psychologists and some anthropologists as well. In several instances writers who, in their earlier works, had more or less accepted the popular opinion concerning racial differences in psychology later renounced that opinion completely; this fact is perhaps the best evidence of the change which has occurred in this whole area of investigation. . . .

The problem of racial psychology has been approached from a number of different directions, and with the application of several distinct criteria or principles of evaluation. A study of the physical characteristics of racial groups, for example, led some of the earlier investigators to the conclusion that such groups differed in their degree of evolutionary development; some were more "primitive," others more advanced. The inference was that as a consequence the psychological level of these groups would differ correspondingly. It has been repeatedly demonstrated, however . . . , that the alleged hierarchy in the morphological structure of living races rests upon a one-sided and incomplete reading of the evidence and that, when all the available data are considered, no such hierarchy emerges. . . . In the present context it may be sufficient to point out that

[2] Myrdal, *An American Dilemma* (New York, 1944), p. 93.
[3] H. W. Odum, "The Errors of Sociology," *Social Forces*, XV (1936–37), 327–42.

most of the observed physiological differences appear to be secondary to other factors. To take only one example, variations in basal metabolism apparently occur under the influence of variations in climate, occupation, tempo of activity, emotional experiences, and the like, and cannot be used convincingly as explanations of differences in behavior.

Another approach to the problem is represented by the attempt to deduce differences in racial psychology from the contributions made by different racial groups to the sum-total of the world's culture or civilization. Perhaps the outstanding historical example of such an attempt is represented by de Gobineau in his *Essay on the Inequality of Human Races,* which appeared in the middle of the last century and which helped to develop a vogue in racial theorizing, the effects of which have by no means disappeared. Apart from the fact that the "race" glorified by Gobineau consisted of the "Aryans," that is to say, no race at all, this whole type of approach is unconvincing for many reasons. For one thing, there is no satisfactory criterion as to what constitutes a superior culture, and the decision as to which contributions point to biological superiority will vary according to the prejudices and preferences of the individual writer. For another, the same group may vary so much throughout its history that the judgment concerning its abilities will depend not only upon bias but also upon the particular moment at which the judgment is made; the unflattering description of North European peoples by Aristotle provides a striking contrast to the assumption of Houston Stewart Chamberlain, in his *Foundations of the Nineteenth Century,* that North Europeans, and specifically Teutons, are superior to all others. In addition, the fact that two different samples of the same racial groups may represent such divergent cultures adds to the difficulty of relating culture to race. Some of the simplest tribes of the Burmese jungle are similar in physical type to the Chinese, who built one of the most complex of the world's civilizations; and the warlike Apache of our own Southwest are of the same "race" as the much more peaceful Pueblos.

From still another direction, the belief has been expressed (and rather widely accepted by laymen and even by some scientists) that the very fact that groups differ physically makes it exceedingly probable that they should differ psychologically as well. Even Franz Boas wrote, in the first edition of *The Mind of Primitive Man:*

"It does not seem probable that the minds of races which show variations in their anatomical structure should act in exactly the same way. Differences of structure must be accompanied by differences of function, physiological as well as psychological; and, as we found clear evidence of difference in structure between the races, so we must anticipate that differences in mental characteristics will be found." [4]

It is significant that this passage does not appear in the 1938 edition

[4] New York, 1911, pp. 114–15.

of the book, and it seems highly probable that Boas changed his opinion on this point. In any case, the inference from physical to psychological differences is a highly dubious one. In the first place, there has been no acceptable demonstration of any relationship between physique and personality within the normal range of individual variations. The correlations between traits of intelligence or temperament, on the one hand, and anatomical characteristics (stature, skin color, shape of head, size of head, height of forehead, and so on), on the other, have almost invariably yielded results of no predictive value. Even the approach in terms of constitutional type, as represented by the work of Kretschmer [5] has failed to fulfill its earlier promise and in its application to normal personalities has proved quite unconvincing. A still more recent attempt to link constitution with psychology has been made by Sheldon and his collaborators.[6] This investigation marks a definite advance as far as the description of human constitutional types is concerned, but the alleged relationship between such types and the varieties of temperament remains a matter of controversy and cannot as yet be regarded as established. In other words the statement that "differences of structure must be accompanied by differences of function" remains an unproved assumption with regard to the normal range of human physical characteristics. . . .

One final consideration in this connection. If the anatomical variations that constitute the basis of racial classification have taken place in relation to conditions in the geographic environment, there is no reason to assume that such variations must have psychological significance. To take a specific example, it has been suggested that variations in skin color may be due to certain processes of differential selection related to the effects of the actinic rays of the sun. In northern Europe a relatively unpigmented skin would be an advantage for survival, since such a skin would aid in the absorption of the comparatively weak actinic rays. Conversely, in the tropics a dark skin would have survival value, since the pigment would act as a preventive against too large an amount of such absorption. Given enough time, we would expect those with fairer skins to survive in the north and those with darker skins in the tropics. Under these conditions (or similar selective influences) there would be no reason to assume that psychological factors played any significant part in the development of these anatomical variations. There would be no reason to anticipate any relationship between traits of personality and the amount of melanin or other pigment in the skin.

This description of various approaches to racial psychology is far from exhaustive, but it may perhaps give some idea of the complexities of the

[5] Ernst Kretschmer, *Physique and Character,* trans. W. J. H. Sprott (New York, 1925).

[6] W. H. Sheldon, S. S. Stevens, and W. B. Tucker, *The Varieties of Human Physique* (New York, 1940).

problem and some justification for the unwillingness of so many social and biological scientists to accept the popular view that races differ in their inherited mentality. There is one further method of investigation in this area which has attracted a great deal of attention in recent years, and which requires somewhat more extensive consideration.

The use of mental tests in this controversial field appears to have certain advantages over most, if not all, of the other methods suggested. A test does have a certain objectivity. It yields results which can be checked by another investigator who can repeat the study, using similar tests on more or less similar groups. It furnishes a quantitative score permitting statistical analysis, so that differences between any two samples of races or nations can be judged in relation to whether they satisfy the statistical criteria of significance. It gives some indication not only of average performance, but also of the range and variability of the scores of the individuals who comprise the group. It has, however, one serious if not insurmountable drawback; namely, it furnishes individual and group variations which can safely be attributed to heredity only if the individuals and groups concerned have had, in the broadest sense, similar environmental opportunities. In the case of a relatively homogeneous group, the wide range of scores obtained by the application of mental tests almost certainly points to a wide range of inherited mental abilities. In the case of the comparison of two distinct racial or national populations, such a degree of homogeneity is almost impossible to find, and the differences in test scores will therefore always be subject to the widest differences in interpretation.

Differences occur in the average test scores reported for various ethnic groups studied in the United States. In comparison with the results obtained on American control groups, the results show that subjects of English, Scotch, German, Jewish, Chinese, and Japanese origin test at or near the American norm. Other groups fall, on the average, definitely below. In twenty-seven different studies of American Negroes, for example, the median result was an intelligence quotient of 86 (the norm, of course, being 100); it should be noted, however, that the range of the average scores reported in these studies was from an I. Q. of 58 (in Tennessee) to 105 (for Negro children tested in Los Angeles). Other groups which also rank, on the average, below the American norms are Americans of Italian origin, among whom sixteen different studies yielded a median I. Q. of 85, the results of the individual studies ranging from 79 to 96; Portuguese, with six studies, a median I. Q. of 84 and a range from 83 to 96; Mexicans, with nine studies, a median I. Q. of 83.4 and a range from 78 to 101; and American Indians, with eleven studies, a median I. Q. of 80.5 and a range from 65 to 100.

The wide range in the averages reported for various American Negro groups—from an I. Q. of 58 to one of 105—raises the problem of variations within the same "racial" group living under different conditions. It has, of course, long been recognized that Northern Negroes obtain, on the average, better test scores than do Negroes from the South. The examination of army recruits in the first world war, for example, demonstrated this superiority unequivocally.[7] At the same there was evidence to indicate that Negroes from some of the Northern states obtained average scores superior to those of the white recruits from some of the Southern states. This was true at least for those who took the Army Alpha examination. Frequent mention has been made of the fact that Negro recruits from Ohio, Illinois, and New York obtained higher scores on this test than did the whites, for example, from Mississippi, Kentucky, and Arkansas. In previous discussions of this comparison (including those by the present writer) it was not made sufficiently clear that these comparisons referred only to the Army Alpha. Since this is a "language" test which was not taken by all the recruits, a fairer statement would run somewhat as follows: that the literate Negroes from certain Northern states who took the Army Alpha obtained higher average scores than the literate whites from certain Southern states who were examined by the same test. . . .

The most probable interpretation of this finding is that when American Negroes live under relatively favorable environmental conditions their test scores are correspondingly high, and when whites live under relatively poor conditions their test scores are correspondingly low. It is apparently not "race" but environment which is the crucial variable. As for the factors in the environment which are mainly responsible for these and similar results, it is likely that the nature of the available schooling plays a major role. A glance at the figures for per capita expenditures for Negro and white children in the segregated school system of the South brings into sharp focus the handicaps of the Negro children; the figures also reveal that Southern white children suffer similar, though not such extreme, handicaps. . . . In the light of the known relationship between good schooling and performance on tests of intelligence, it is hardly surprising that Southern whites obtain lower scores than those from the north or that Southern Negroes usually make such a poor showing.

There remains the possibility that the superiority of Northern over Southern Negroes is due not so much to differences in schooling as to "selective migration"—a movement of the most intelligent Negroes away from the South. This explanation has been offered, for example, by Peterson and Lanier [8] to account for the fact that in their investigation, whereas Nashville whites were markedly superior to Nashville Negroes, Chicago whites were only slightly superior to Chicago Negroes, and in New York

[7] See R. M. Yerkes, ed., "Psychological Examining in the U. S. Army," *Memoirs of the National Academy of Science,* XV (1921).

[8] J. Peterson and L. H. Lanier, "Studies in the Comparative Abilities of Whites and Negroes," *Mental Measurement Monographs,* V (1929), 1–156.

City there were no significant differences between the two racial groups. They write: "There is apparently developing in New York, under the more severe struggle for existence, a highly selected Negro population which represents the best genes in the race." This remains an hypothesis, however, for which there is little concrete evidence. People migrate for many different reasons, and it has never been demonstrated that it is always the brightest ones who leave and the least intelligent who stay behind. A series of studies directed at this problem [9] failed to discover any evidence that the migration of Southern Negroes was "selective" with regard to intelligence. It was, on the other hand, possible to demonstrate that among Negro children now living in New York but born in the South there was, on the average, a close correspondence between their test scores and the length of time they had lived in the superior Northern environment. To put it in other words, those Negro children who migrated from the South to the North gave no evidence of being superior in "intelligence" (as measured by the tests) when they first came North; rather, they became superior under the influence of the better schooling and wider opportunities for learning provided them in the new environment. . . .

Since these environmental effects can be demonstrated even in the case of white children of native white American parentage, it is perhaps unnecessary to labor the point that interracial comparisons by means of intelligence tests will always be suspect as long as discrepancies exist in the environmental opportunities of the various groups tested. Reference has already been made to the discrepancy in schooling, most marked in the case of the Southern Negro. This is only one of a number of factors which have some effect on the test scores. For example, many studies have demonstrated a hierarchy in the intelligence quotients of children living under different economic conditions; children of farmers and of day laborers do not do so well on the tests as children of doctors or bankers. There is of course the possibility (not as yet established) that genetic factors contribute to these differences. For present purposes, it is sufficient to point out that whether or not heredity enters here, environment certainly plays a part. This comes out clearly in the studies of foster children, whose test scores rise when they are adopted by well-to-do families. That being the case, the inferior economic position of the Negroes, Italians, Poles, Portuguese, and other groups who fail on the average to meet the test norms, cannot be disregarded in any interpretation of the results.

The fact that many of these groups are bilingual also has the effect of handicapping them in test comparisons.[10] To cite one representative study, it was found that a group of Ontario Indians, all of whom spoke

[9] Otto Klineberg, *Negro Intelligence and Selective Migration* (New York, 1935).
[10] A review of studies in this field is found in S. Arsenian, *Bilingualism and Mental Development*, "Teachers College Contributions to Education," No. 712 (New York, 1937).

English but usually with some difficulty, obtained much lower I. Q.'s on the linguistic than on the performance (non-language) tests. In addition, the monoglot Indian children, who spoke only English, were superior to the bilingual children on all tests except the Pintner-Paterson performance scale.[11] This result has been repeated with many other groups. Children who are bilingual are at a definite disadvantage, in most cases, when the usual type of intelligence test is used. On performance tests their inferiority is much less noticeable and often disappears entirely.

This raises the question as to whether it might be possible to devise tests of intelligence which would be entirely free of cultural or environmental influences. There have been many attempts to devise such "culture-free" tests, but it appears unlikely that they will ever be successful. Even if the specific content is equally familiar (or unfamiliar) to the groups concerned, it would still be impossible to equate the groups for other, more indirect factors. One group may be more strongly motivated, more anxious to succeed; one group may have a friendlier attitude to the tester; one group may be more at home in the testing situation; one group may be more accustomed to tasks involving competition between individuals; one group may have a stronger pattern of getting things done quickly. Differences of this kind are familiar to all ethnologists, but it is doubtful whether their influence could be adequately measured—or even estimated—so as to allow the proper weight for their contribution to the final test score. Until that is done for these and other factors, present and potential, the prospect of constructing a truly "culture-free" test seems almost to be a contradiction in terms.

There is another problem which runs through all of these test comparisons, namely, that of obtaining a representative sample. Suppose tests are given to a group of Italian children in one of the schools in New York City. The question arises as to whether this group is representative of all Italian children; or of all Italian children living in the United States; or of all Italian children in New York; or even of all Italian children in that particular school. There is evidence to show that one Italian group in the United States may differ markedly from another; that Italian girls tested in Rome, Italy, obtain superior scores to those tested in New York City, and so on. It has already been pointed out that groups of Negro children varied in average I. Q. from 58 in Tennessee to 105 in Los Angeles. Some of the methods used in obtaining samples for Public Opinion polls might profitably be applied here. The mere increase in the number of cases would not be sufficient—as was demonstrated by the failure of the *Literary Digest* political poll of 1936 when two million ballots were received. It should be pointed out, however, that even the use of a truly representative sample would not eliminate the other difficulties discussed here.

If the samples can be demonstrated to be adequate and representative, the test scores may be very useful as a measure of present achievement in

[11] E. Jamieson and P. Sandiford, "The Mental Capacity of Southern Ontario Indians," *Journal of Educational Psychology,* XIX (1928), 536–51.

the particular abilities involved (though not as a measure of inherited capacity). As such, they may serve as indications of the extent to which individuals and groups fall below the standards set by one particular culture. They may uncover weak points and indicate the directions in which remedial measures may profitably and effectively be applied. In the case of the Southern Negro, for example, the low test scores may legitimately be used to demonstrate a present inferiority based in large measure upon inadequate schooling—and such schooling may then be regarded as the first line of attack directed to the more complete incorporation of the Negro in the American community as a whole. Only when the Negro has been given the same opportunities for learning will the test scores serve as an indication of possible limitations in learning capacity.

In any interpretation of group differences in test scores it must not be forgotten that the difference is one of averages, and that the overlapping is great. There are always some Negroes who do better than some whites, no matter how unfavorable to the Negro the environmental factors may be. As a matter of fact, there are some Negroes who do better than almost all whites. The upper and lower limits of achievement, even under present testing conditions, are the same for the two groups. There are some Negroes and some whites who are so feeble-minded that they cannot do anything with the problems presented by the tests. At the other extreme, there are Negro children who obtain an I. Q. equal to that of the most successful white children. There is one report [12] of a Negro girl who at the age of nine years and four months obtained a Stanford-Binet I.Q. of 200. This child was apparently of unmixed Negro origin; there is no record of any white admixture on either side of the family. Her background was superior; her father was a former college teacher who later became a practicing electrical engineer, and her mother formerly taught school in a large city. This case is of course exceptional, and would be so in any group, but it at least indicates that the upper limit of abilities as measured by the tests is just as high for Negroes as for whites.

The criticisms that have been leveled against the use of intelligence tests in the field of racial psychology apply even more strongly in the case of most tests of personality. Such tests are so deeply impregnated with the culture in which they have originated that their direct application to other groups and other cultures yields results that may be very misleading. To mention one specific example, the Pressey X-O test, which is designed to measure emotional responses, was administered to Indians of varying tribal origin, now living in Nebraska, Montana, California, New Mexico, and Oklahoma.[13] The investigators report that the Indians were less mature

[12] P. A. Witty and M. A. Jenkins, "The Case of 'B'—A Gifted Negro Girl," *Journal of Social Psychology,* VI (1935), 117–24.
[13] S. L. Pressey and L. C. Pressey, "A Comparative Study of the Emotional Attitudes and Interests of Indian and White Children." *Journal of Applied Psychology,* XVII (1933), 227–38.

emotionally than the whites with whom they were compared. "The Indian tends to remain immature; either he is incapable of a more mature adjustment or else his environment has been so simplified that adjustment on a childish level is good enough." In view of the cultural relativity of the concept of emotional maturity, this statement does not seem especially meaningful. Even if we grant that this particular test has validity in a more or less homogeneous American community, its use "cross-culturally" will always be suspect. The investigators themselves realize this at least in part, for in a subsequent study [14] they point out that the tribes with the greatest degree of white contacts (like the Crow) are "less retarded emotionally" than those which have remained relatively isolated (like the Hopi). This conclusion closely parallels the finding in the case of intelligence tests: that the more similar the environments of the groups compared, the smaller the difference in their average test scores.

One more example of the effect of cultural background on personality test scores may be mentioned. When a Chinese translation of the Thurstone Neurotic Inventory was administered in various Chinese universities, the the results showed much more "neuroticism" among those students than among the American students with whom they were compared.[15] The investigators apparently accept this result at its face value, since they express some concern over the "lack of adjustment" among Chinese students, and advocate a mental hygiene program in their universities as a corrective. Such an interpretation is warranted only if the items in the Inventory have the same significance and fit into a similar "frame of reference" in China as in the United States. That this is not the case is recognized by other investigators [16] who obtained results similar to those of Chou and Mi, but who point out that the answers are in many cases affected not by "neuroticism" but by specific viewpoints resulting from Chinese (Confucian) precepts and principles.

These and similar considerations apply so widely in the field of personality tests, that, as measures of "racial psychology," the results must be dismissed. As indications of group differences in culturally determined attitudes, however, they may have considerable interest. Findings such as those of Pressey and of Chou and Mi, when combined with an adequate ethnological picture of the groups concerned, may be valuable in bringing out such differences in greater detail as well as in demonstrating the amount of variation among individuals within any one culture.

There is some evidence to the effect that the Rorschach test may be

[14] "A Comparison of the Emotional Development of Indians Belonging to Different Tribes," *Journal of Applied Psychology*, XVII (1933), 535–41.

[15] S. K. Chou and C. Y. Mi, "Relative Neurotic Tendency of Chinese and American Students," *Journal of Social Psychology*, VIII (1937), 155–84.

[16] T. Pai, S. M. Sung, and E. H. Hsü, "The Application of Thurstone's Personality Schedule to Chinese Students," *Journal of Social Psychology*, VIII (1937), 47–72.

somewhat more "culture-free" in its application to personality than the other tests so far considered. Even if this should turn out to be true, however, it would probably mean that the Rorschach could be used to discover the personality organization of an individual apart from the impact of his culture upon him; it would not mean that cultural differences would be irrelevant to the group comparisons. Nor would it mean that "racial"—that is, hereditary—group differences could be discovered by this method, since even within our own culture Rorschach specialists do not claim that their method is capable of differentiating between genetic and environmental influences upon personality organization.

The conclusion is therefore justified that mental tests, whether of personality or of intelligence, cannot be used as a foundation for a racial psychology. This method, like the others previously discussed, is open to so much criticism that in this case also the conclusion must be that racial differences in psychology have not been—and perhaps cannot be—demonstrated.

At the same time, it can hardly be denied that there are significant psychological differences between ethnic groups. The rich and varied material collected by ethnologists, the life histories of individuals of minority status (for example, Negroes) in this country, the descriptions of variations in "national character," all point in that direction, though these approaches raise methodological problems of a controversial nature. They do not, however, constitute a "racial" psychology. They indicate differences, but these are differences which are almost certainly the product of historical and environmental factors rather than genetic or racial. . . . "Race" and psychology appear, in the present stage of our knowledge, to be unrelated.

This conclusion has certain important practical implications. If there is no racial psychology, discrimination against minority groups on the basis of their alleged hereditary inferiority is completely unjustified. If there is no racial psychology, the behavior of large national communities is to be ascribed to environmental factors (in the largest sense) and not to the germ plasm, which means that it may change with time and with new conditions. And if there is no racial psychology, any hope that we may have of making our own democracy broader and more efficient rests not so much on an improvement in our "stock" as on making available to the whole community the educational and economic opportunities which pave the way for fuller and richer living.

EDITORIAL COMMENT

There is considerably less difficulty in delineating religious groups and their subdivisions than in the case of race. The population of American society and of the societies from which it is derived by colonization and immigration is composed, for the most part, of Protestants, Roman Catholics, and Jews, and to a much lesser extent of such groups as the Eastern Orthodox, Uniats, and Moslems. In almost all cases the religious group is subdivided either by denominational, sectarian, geographic, or nationality differences.

Religious differences and their ramifications in dominant and minority group relations were usually part of the tradition of each group long before their departure to the New World. In the old country it had been a typical pattern for the dominant religious group to entrench itself in "established" or state churches. As a result, one of the major sources of European immigration to America has always been the dissenting or minority religious group. This gave early American religious life a foundation of dissenting Protestantism, and undoubtedly it accounts not only for the continuing, prolific sectarianism in this country today, but also for the traditional American insistence on the "separation of church and state."

The historical background and social significance of religious stratification in American society are traced in detail by Silcox and Fisher in the reading that follows.

5. THE SOCIAL SIGNIFICANCE OF RELIGIOUS DIFFERENCES
BY *Claris Edwin Silcox* AND *Galen M. Fisher* *

FEW problems in the field of socio-religious relations can be more fascinating, more intricate and more far-reaching than those surrounding the actual relations of Protestants, Catholics and Jews living in the various communities of the United States and Canada. Some sociologists avoid the consideration of such problems, possibly because they are too full of dynamite, perhaps more because the fundamental data requisite to objective treatment are too often lacking.

Nevertheless, the religious differences which separate the various groups in a community tend to color their whole existence. They determine the attitude toward the newly-born-child—shall it be baptized or circumcised? In a large measure they define the type of education which is provided for the pre-adolescent and the adolescent. They influence, if they do not definitely restrict, the sexual selection of mates, provide the cere-

* From Claris Edwin Silcox and Galen M. Fisher, *Catholics, Jews and Protestants* (New York: Harper & Brothers, 1934), pp. 1–31. Used by permission of Harper & Brothers. Footnotes omitted.

monies with which marriages are solemnized, and except in a . . . hybrid
civilization afford the orientation of entire groups toward the home. They
select the pictures on our walls and the books on our shelves. They create
a variety of institutions which minister to the orphaned, the delinquent, the
unmarried mothers, the impoverished, the aged; and when we are caught
in the bitter throes of financial depression, they determine most frequently
the agency from which we seek the saving dole. They inspire the building
of almost countless academies, colleges, universities and hospitals. To a very
large extent they choose the circles in which we find our intimate friends and
sometimes determine the way in which we exercise our franchise. They
may prevent one group from eating pork or rabbits or oysters, while
another group "religiously" refrains from beefsteak on Fridays. The law of
Israel forbade the wearing of garments of divers sorts, such as woolen and
linen together. This law may, at an early date, have contributed to Jewish
involvement in the clothing industry, and if such was the case, the fact
provides an interesting example of the interpenetration of economic life by
religious motivations. Thus religious affiliation may affect all of life, and it
even seems to cast its shadow over us in death, for when we are buried, the
grave is dug in a plot which may have been consecrated by our co-religionists. Religious differences divide us in various ways from the cradle to the
grave. Why not, therefore, frankly face the issues created by such distinctions, and ask ourselves that solemn sociological question: What about it?

. . . Most of us inherit our religion as we inherit our nationality or
our mother tongue, and far from encouraging people to select their religion
on the basis of personal conviction, religious groups seek to immunize youth
against any possible defection in later years, and they erect every conceivable type of barrier which may keep the over-adventurous sheep within
the fold.

If religion were purely a personal matter, as some maintain that it is,
society would rejoice at every manifestation of spiritual emancipation. When
the Jewish boy reached thirteen years of age we should not observe Bar
Mitzvah for him; we should ask him to make his own choice from the
menu-card of available religious delicacies. We should ask the Christian
boy of the same age if he would not care to join the Brahma-Samaj, or a
Roman Catholic Christian if he would not consider possible affiliation with
the Quakers or the Mennonites. But of course we do nothing of the kind.
. . . No, religion is not primarily an individual matter; it is rather a method
of social control and social discipline, and since it is so, any defection is
interpreted as a form of high treason except among those who have already
become déraciné, lost their essential loyalty to the group and grown careless and indifferent in the observance of its discipline. . . .

What is more, the religious group may be, and often is, highly supra-
national. Nations, in their ardent chauvinism, have ever sought to control
and dominate their churches. . . . Here is a dichotomy of more than pass-

ing interest; here emerges the clear significance for all narrowly nationalistic ideals of a supra-national body of believers, a universal "household of faith". . . . We must therefore always bear in mind, in our consideration of the significance of religious differences, the fundamental distinction between such groups as seek quite definitely an international discipline and those that express primarily the will and aspirations of a particular people. We must also remember that over against both the international and the national groupings are the "sects," whose idiosyncrasies are neither national nor international but more purely local and individualistic. . . .

The sociologist, attempting to delineate the various problems created in the field of interfaith relations in either the United States or Canada, may begin with some case studies of Middletown or Cobunk's Corners, but before he has penetrated very far, he will inevitably be searching for the roots of the phenomena in the pages of history, and if, by some strange deficiency in early training, he has been led to believe that history is bunk, he had better abandon his study before he becomes too deeply involved. Indeed, in no other phase of sociological inquiry, is some knowledge of history more imperative. However difficult it may be to discover in annals of the past "the truth, the whole truth and nothing but the truth," the effort must be made if our social judgment on the functioning of religious differences is to be at all adequate. If the psychologist does not exaggerate unduly when he affirms the significance of childhood memories for later experiences, so the sociologist cannot fail to underscore the significance of the whole story of the struggle for so-called religious freedom if he is to appraise aright the social distance between religious groupings in his own day and in his own nation.

HISTORICAL BACKGROUNDS

. . . Some, indeed, aver that if we seek peace and understanding, we should try to forget the past and let the dead bury their dead. The Jews, they say, should forget their persecutions; the Catholics, their martyrs; the Protestants, the Inquisition. A well-known Catholic layman prominent in every work for interfaith good will writes on this point:

I never could see much advantage in going into the details of the unpleasant things of the past which includes the Civil War, but rather prefer to paint a picture of what our relations should be and the progress being made. I know that Jews, Catholics and Negroes like to have told the many injustices to which they have been subjected, but it is not helpful with the people whose cooperation for better relations is desired.

He might have included in his category the Protestants who also feel their backs stiffen at the tales of the Waldensians in Italy, the Huguenots in France, the Covenanters in Scotland and that struggle for freedom which led to the landing of the Pilgrims on Plymouth Rock.

The immemorial observance of Purim on the part of the Jews, with the annual re-reading of the story of Esther and the wicked Haman, may create in the Jewish people an expectancy of persecution and induce in them attitudes that make for persecution, while every man who believes that he is right, or that his church is right, finds a strong rhetorical appeal in the picture of the Christians being thrown to the lions—"the blood of the martyrs is the seed of the church."

The historically-minded, however, seek in history not fresh appeals to fanaticism, but explanations, and not until all three groups adopt a more objective attitude towards their respective pasts can present peace be assured. Objectivity need not involve indifference; it does demand the effort to understand.

Although this delineation of the past does not fall within the exact scope of this study, it may not be amiss . . . to indicate certain aspects of history which the student of interfaith relations has a duty to examine, and which shed light on present attitudes.

Antiquity of Anti-Semitism

In the first place, the phenomenon of anti-Semitism is certainly not new in civilization. Frequently it has been interpreted by Jewish writers largely in terms of the relations of Jews and Christians. But the book of Esther is sufficient evidence that it antedated the Christian era. Whatever the causes, the historic fact seems to be that, wherever the Jews have existed in considerable numbers, anti-Semitism has arisen, sooner or later. The "Jewish problem" existed for the Pharaohs in Egypt, for Ahasuerus in Persia, for Nebuchadnezzar in Babylon, for Antiochus Epiphanes and his Seleucid successors in Asia Minor, for successive Roman emperors before Christianity became the state religion of Rome, for Mohammed and his followers, as well as in Nazi Germany. Even in ancient Palestine, the Jews had no dealings with the Samaritans. Anti-Semitism can never be reduced to a mere struggle between the Star of David and the Cross. Religion, folkways, race, economics, politics—all are involved, and possibly at no time in history was one of these elements the only factor in the situation. . . .

Lack of Objectivity in Studying Church History

In the second place, there has been far too little objective study of the history of the Christian church except among the experts. History has been used to stimulate faith rather than to understand how we got this way. The problem of the relation of Church and State has often been confused with that of Roman Catholicism and Nationalism, while fundamental differences in the partial reading of history keep apart and probably will continue to keep apart the Protestants and the Catholics, however loyal either or both groups may be to certain fundamental emphases in Christianity. Even among the experts few Protestants or Catholics approach the study of history dispassionately or without preconceived ideas, while for the rank and file the infinite possibilities of the story of the church as a means of spiritual culture have been neglected by both groups alike. The less men know about the past, the more they argue, and even when they know enough to know better, they select such facts as will give support to their own point of view and try to forget those facts that will upset their theories. To limit the whole question to only one phase, when may we expect the history of Ireland to be subjected by all concerned to objective analysis? The Catholic Irish who came to the United States and the Protestant Irish who came to Canada were nursed on tales of cruelty and persecution—which were probably true in both cases—and such tales made these groups quick to look for trouble wherever they went and to find it.

Protestant and Catholic in the New World

There is, however, for the student of interfaith relations in the United States and Canada, one great aspect of the Protestant-Catholic impasse which deserves far more extended treatment than such a study as this can give to it. The whole discovery of the New World must be read against the picture of the clash of two cultures—one dominantly Latin and Catholic, the other dominantly Anglo-Saxon (whatever that means) and Protestant. The capture of Constantinople by the Turks, in 1453, brought to an end all hope of a European advance into Asia, and turned the hopes of Europe to a possible road to Asia via the Atlantic. It also rendered the Eastern Church more impotent in the larger affairs of Europe. Then came the discovery of America, in 1492, a date which, for the student of interfaith relations, is also significant because of the expulsion in that year of the Jews from Spain. While the Renaissance of learning and the revival of nationalism were paving the way for the Reformation, this latter movement was to affect Northern Europe rather than Southern Europe. Spain was at the height of her power when the Reformation broke upon her, and in a glow of religious ecstasy she had expelled both Moor and Jew and effected her new unity. She, therefore, remained peculiarly impervious to the shock of the Reformation and, enjoying with Portugal the division of the New World decreed by the Pope in 1493 and modified in the Treaty of Tordesillas (1494), was free to undertake the further discovery and subjugation of the western hemisphere. . . .

France and England were too badly shaken by the religious disputes of the time to participate actively in the conquest of the New World for nearly a century. The English Kings might establish certain rights to Newfoundland, and four hundred years ago (1534) Jacques Cartier made his "discovery of Canada," but no considerable efforts at settlement were attempted by either country. Neither France nor England was strong enough on the sea to venture much against the naval strength of Spain, while within their boundaries there was a constant struggle between Puritan or Huguenot on the one hand, and the Catholic, on the other. . . .

The Wars of religion in France (1562–1598) made any attempts at settlement without that country hopeless until the Edict of Nantes, in 1598, established a temporary inward peace. Almost immediately certain French Huguenots received authority to establish posts in Canada, while in that very year a French settlement was effected at Sable Island. These first settlements seem to have been due largely to Huguenot initiative, although in these early enterprises and until the rise of Richelieu, both Catholics and Huguenots engaged. Then, in 1627, it was decreed that French Canada should be closed to all Huguenots and only Catholics were permitted to go to New France. This was enforced until the Treaty of Utrecht, in 1713, gave Acadia to England, but continued in Canada proper until the fall of Quebec in 1759. It may be that Richelieu's policy of excluding Protestants, while temporarily successful, in the end led to the troubles at home which culminated in St. Bartholomew's Massacre (1572) and definitely cost France her hegemony in the New World. Had French Huguenots participated in the building up of New France, they might have carried the arts of France with them and made of Canada a great power paralleling New England; their removal might have solved the internal conflict in France; while the struggle between New England and New France might have been a purely political struggle and not, as it became, a struggle between two religions as well as between two peoples. At all events, it is futile to attempt to understand the religious backgrounds of America without making proper allowance for the constant threat of New England to New France, and of New France to New England. Out of this struggle came more than the story of Evangeline.

While England had sent expeditions into the northern seas and, along with the French, the Spanish and the Portuguese, fostered fishing, she made little attempt at permanent settlement until her first colonists touched the Virginia capes in 1607. From that time on, the struggle for the continent was waged between Protestant England on the Atlantic seaboard, Catholic Spain to her south, and Catholic France to her north. As the Protestant English pushed southward they made, despite the tolerant arrangements in Maryland in 1633, a rule against Catholic settlements. Thus, the first charter of Georgia, in 1732, excluded from the new colony liquor, slaves and "papists." The exclusion of "papists" was probably due to the fear of the Spaniards around the Gulf of Mexico, and perhaps accentuated by the bitter experiences of the English governors in persuading the Acadians to take the oath of allegiance. Certainly the struggle for the New World involved religious factors and gave to later generations a tradition of antipathies which died hard, if indeed, they ever died. . . .

After 1783, the American colonies, now having achieved their independence, ventured on their new experiment. Their population was almost exclusively Protestant, and the inner problem of interfaith relations was at first largely intra-Protestant. As the Catholics came in by immigration —some from France escaping the ravages of the French Revolution, others from Ireland escaping the endless internecine conflicts of that island, and still others with the increments of territory purchased from France —new problems arose which not even the constitutional provision for freedom in religious worship could solve. Canada, on the other hand, began with an almost compact French-Canadian Catholic population under the rule of the British Crown, which was pledged to Protestantism. The Protestant population of Canada was recruited from the Loyalists in the revolutionary war and later, after the Napoleonic wars, by immigration from England, Scotland and Ireland. . . . In time the French Canadians poured into New England, until today in many sections of those states one wonders whether New England has not become New France. . . .

An evidence of the attitude of colonial New England Protestantism towards Roman Catholicism may perhaps be gathered from the terms of the Dudleian lecture which was annually delivered at the Chapel in Cambridge, Mass., on the first Wednesday in September on one of four topics to be considered in rotation. The third of these topics was:

For the detecting, convicting and exposing the idolatry of the Romish Church, their tyranny, usurpations, damnable heresies, fatal errors, abominable superstitions, and other crying wickednesses in their high places; and finally, that the Church of Rome is that mystical Babylon, that man of sin, that apostate church, spoken of in the New Testament.

Catholicism grew, however, by immigration and by annexation, but the Catholics who migrated to the United States did not for the most part move forward into the West as the territory west of the Ohio River was opened up. . . . Although the Irish immigrants had been for the most part peasants in Ireland, they settled mostly in cities, and when some laymen urged Catholic bloc settlement on the land, their efforts were apparently opposed by the Archbishop Hughes of New York. They settled not only in the cities, but in northern cities, for it was hopeless for the Irish immigrant to compete with slave labor in the south. Thus, during the nineteenth century, American Catholicism was largely concentrated in the great northern and eastern cities. This was a factor in the large degree of municipal power exercised by the Irish Catholics in many cities and as in New York State, in the political opposition which arose between the city of New York and upstate. . . . At the same time it accentuated the clash with Protestants; in city after city Protestant churches were left enisled by the wave of Catholic immigration and their membership hopelessly disrupted. Large capital investments in such churches were of necessity wasted. The contact of the cultures also led to the political clash; while the Protestants continued to be an overwhelmingly dominant force in the country as a whole, in the strategic cities of the North, political control was largely held by the Catholics, of which Tammany in New York is perhaps the most conspicuous instance. Finally, in the competition for jobs, an economic struggle was precipitated in which, for many years, employers were supposed to discriminate against both the Irish and the Catholics.

The control of the wealth of the East was largely left in the hands of the older Protestant families, and thus were accumulated the gigantic fortunes which have made "rich Americans" almost notorious. But the fact is clear that a large number of Protestants who might have stayed in the East and kept the eastern cities Protestant went West in search of new lands, leaving the vacuum created by their departure to be filled by Catholic immigrants from other countries.

Had the Catholic immigrants been scattered over the rural areas as thoroughly as were the Protestants, much of the tension which later developed might have been avoided, and the common struggle with the soil might have done much to blend the two groups. The Protestants in the cities, however, felt a menace in the waves of Catholic migration, and this stirred their old (culturally) inherited animosities. Behind it all, too, was the inevitable clash between city and country—a clash which is far from resolved as yet. . . .

Another factor that played a great role in Protestant development was the Negro. It was only natural that the African slaves should be instructed in the religion of their owners, whether the latter were Protestants or, as in Maryland, often Catholics. It was also natural that the more "aristocratic" types of Protestantism, whether Anglican or Calvinist, should yield to the more "sectarian" types in missionary activity among the submerged Africans. Hence, nearly all Negroes became either Baptists or Methodists. Indeed, had the great migrations from Europe to the United States in the 'forties never taken place, the complexion of the country today would be much darker, for in 1840, out of a total population of 17,-062,566, there were no fewer than 2,878,458 colored persons, of whom only 386,245 were free. At that time 15.5 per cent of the entire population was colored.

The effect on Protestant mentality of the combined influence of early African slavery and later immigration from Europe needs to be studied. Protestant whites, except perhaps the German and Scandinavian, tended to withdraw from all forms of menial service and to be decidedly "bourgeois" in their occupations and habits. With their wealth and their more "refined" occupations, their viewpoint became increasingly aristocratic. As the immigrant classes rose in the social scale and challenged not alone the political power but the social prestige of the Protestant, resentment was practically inevitable, and with the resentment was the fear that the institutions which reposed in part on Protestantism might be overturned. Thus, the religious issue permeated economic, racial, political and social problems.

Protestant Solidarity Shaken by Sectarianism

Throughout the formative period of American life, Protestantism was handicapped by its sectarianism. The constituent elements of the population, while dominantly of English extraction, were quite mixed, and even the Protestant immigrants brought the form of faith peculiar to the country of their origin with them. Indeed, it has been estimated that approximately one-third of the more than two hundred Protestant sects which exist in the United States today have a European origin. Certain of these sects, such as the Mennonites, exercised a rigid discipline over their membership, forbade intermarriage with non-Mennonites and practised the ban. The denominationalists were, and are, tenacious of their peculiar loyalties, and cooperative effort within Protestant circles, while making headway steadily, has been a slow and difficult process. In general, within American Protestantism, two diametrically opposite tendencies prevail—in "bloc" settlements there is often found a certain narrowness and intensity of religious outlook and discipline with internal difficulties frequently leading to further schism, notably in the case of the Mennonites and the Quakers; in other and more sophisticated areas are found a certain latitudinarianism and religious indifference. Both these tendencies may be observed in almost any part of the country today.

The Jews in the United States and Canada

A word, too, needs to be said in regard to the general history of the Jew in the United States and Canada. The Jew was shut out of Canada as effectively as the Protestant by the government of France after 1627 and until 1759. During the last years of the French regime, however, practically the entire provisioning of Canada was entrusted by the French King to a Jewish family of Bordeaux, named Gradis. When Quebec fell in 1759, the commissar of Wolfe's army was a Jew, and a few Jewish families resided in Canada from the date of British occupation down to the present. The great bulk of the Jewish population of Canada arrived, however, only in the eighteen nineties and after the turn of the century when the persecutions in Russia drove them to seek sanctuary in the New World.

When the British first colonized America, Jews were not allowed to reside in England. They had been banished from the kingdom in 1290. Cromwell, however, watching Holland closely, perceived that part of the success which the Dutch were winning in the commercial world was due to its Jewish merchants, and he sought ways and means to induce some of these merchants to come to England. In December, 1654, he called a committee of lawyers, theologians and merchants and put to them two questions: "Whether it be lawful to receive the Jews. If it be lawful, then upon what terms is it meet to receive them?" The lawyers answered the first question in a manner favorable to the return of the Jews. On the question of expediency and conditions, however, there was hopeless differ-

ence of opinion. In disgust, Cromwell put an end to the discussion and decided to let in whomever he chose. In this year, 1654, Portugal expelled
the Jews from Brazil. Some of these came to New Amsterdam (later New
York) where they were reinforced by other Jews from Holland. At first
Peter Stuyvesant, the governor, hesitated to receive them, but finally
yielded when he was assured that "the poor among them shall not become
a burden to the community, but be supported by their own nation." In
1658 fifteen Jewish families arrived in Newport, Rhode Island, bringing
with them, according to tradition, the first three degrees of Masonry.
Rhode Island was probably selected because Roger Williams had said of
his colony that "all these consciences, yea, the very consciences of the
Papists, the Jews, etc. . . . ought freely and impartially be permitted
their several respective worships." We find also some Jewish names among
the earliest colonists in Maryland, one of them, Jacob Lumbrozo, "late of
Lisbone, Portugal," is usually referred to as "the Jew doctor." He was in
Maryland as early as 1656.

Growth of Jewish Population
     . . . There were, however, few Jews in the United States before
1800. In 1818, Major Noah, who later served the United States as consul
to Tunis, 1813–16, and whose spectacular effort to establish a Zionist state
on Grand Island in the Niagara River is one of the delightful episodes
in the history of Buffalo, estimated the Jewish population of the United
States in 1818 at about 3,000. Of these it is safe to say that over 80 per
cent were Sephardic, i.e., Spanish or Portuguese Jews who had come to
the United States either via Holland, England, Brazil or the West Indies.
About 1840, however, following the revolutionary periods in Germany,
many German Jews began to arrive, and in 1848 the Jewish population
was estimated at about 50,000. Considerable numbers went to Cincinnati,
Pittsburgh and other rising industrial cities. A few, however, went into the
frontier areas, not as farmers but as peddlers, with packs on their backs.
In states like Kentucky, they intermarried and the first Jewish settlers were
absorbed by the Gentile population. Not all the Jews of this period came
from Germany, for when the government in Poland sought to force them
to serve their terms in the army, an exodus of Polish Jews began.
     By 1859 the Jewish population had only increased to about 200,000,
and of these more than 50,000 were found in New York. For the next
twenty years few Jews arrived, for the Jewish population in 1880 was estimated at only 230,257. Then, between 1881 and 1886, 114,000 Jews arrived, mostly from Russia. The persecutions within the Pale were forcing
them out, and there began a steady migration that ceased only with the
Great War. . . .
     There are therefore, three major types of Jewish migration to the
United States:

1655–1840, nearly entirely Sephardic Jews
1840–1880, largely German Jews
1880–1933, mostly Russian and Polish Jews

Early Tolerance and Intolerance

There is little evidence of severe anti-Semitism in colonial or post-colonial days. To be sure, even in the liberal states, the law protected from molestation only persons "professing belief in Jesus Christ" and an act was passed in Maryland in 1723 to the effect that "if any person shall hereafter within this province deny our Savior, Jesus Christ, to be the Son of God or shall deny the Holy Trinity, he should, for the first offence, be fined and his tongue bored; for the second, be fined and have his head burned; for the third, be put to death." Under such circumstances, it might be needful to guard one's utterances, although even in England the Acts of Toleration supposedly extended only to those who believed in the Trinity; but there, as in the colonies, the Jews were unmolested. . . .

There was, on the whole, friendliness, respect and collaboration between Jew and Gentile. What troubles the Jews experienced were largely due to the clash between Reformed and Orthodox Judaism, and thus were intra-Jewish rather than Jewish-Christian. Many of the early Jews married Gentiles, and their descendants today are in Christian churches. This was particularly true of the Middle West and the South.

Effect of Coming of Eastern European Jews

The consciousness of tension arose only when the Russian persecutions drove great numbers of Jews to asylum in America. Their coming at first disturbed the Jews already in the United States, but they organized to help them and thus to facilitate their absorption into American life. . . .

There must have been evidences of anti-Semitism as early as 1890, for in that year the *American Hebrew* published a symposium by foremost Christians under the caption "Prejudice Against the Jew". . . . This early anti-Semitism was in part social and manifested itself in the occasional rejection of Jews as guests in certain hotels (e.g. in Saratoga about 1875). . . .

While the Jews in the United States addressed themselves heroically to the task of absorbing their persecuted brethren from Russia it must be admitted that there was not a little feeling against the eastern European Jew on the part of many of them. As a matter of fact, the epithet "kike" applied to the eastern European Jew, is of Jewish, not Gentile, coinage. Whatever its origin, it was used to express the attitude of German Jews to their brethren from Russia and Poland. The peculiar situation in the United States and Canada has been largely created by the character of Jewish immigration into these two countries since 1880.

This general outline of the prevailing course of interfaith relations in the United States and Canada is given with a full appreciation of its inadequacy, but it contains certain fundamental facts which must be taken into consideration in any proper study of the problems to be later presented. . . .

SOCIOLOGICAL PROBLEMS

But apart from these historical . . . difficulties, the sociologist will encounter still others which are, possibly, more germane to his normal processes of thinking. After all, who and what are Protestants, Catholics and Jews? In any strict categorical classification, are these the names of *genera* or of *species?*

A Race or a Religion?

To begin with the Jew, does the Jew cease to be a Jew when be becomes a Christian Scientist or a Two-Seed-in-the-Spirit Baptist? In all his criticism of the discrimination to which he is often subjected, the Jew usually speaks of religious discrimination, but the Gentile almost universally repudiates the allegation and claims that religion has little, if anything, to do with it. . . . Scholars sometimes say that the roots of anti-Semitism are to be found in the religious struggles of the first eight centuries, but most anti-Semites of our own time assert with great emphasis that their controversy with the Jews is due not to their faith (of which they know little or nothing, and care less), but to their social manners and habits; that they have no objection at all to "nice" Jews whose way of living approximates their own, but that they have no use for "kikes." This stereotype is familiar to all students of the problem, and suggests that the major difficulty here may not be religious at all, but purely economic or social. Further, the bitterest comments against the Jews come, not from the people who are the most intimately associated with the churches, but from those on the periphery, if not entirely outside church life altogether. In their expressed antipathies, they distinguish between Jews and Jews, and their principle of differentiation is hardly ever religious. Indeed, while the difficulty of converting Jews to Christianity is well known, it is perhaps not as well known that an almost greater difficulty confronts the missionaries to the Jews when they seek to persuade Christian Churches to receive their converts.

We face, then, the persistent question; *What are the Jews?* Do they constitute a racial group, a religious group, a national group, or just *a* group? There is little unanimity in the answers to this point to be found among Jewish writers themselves. Attention is frequently called to the fact that because of the Diaspora, Jewish "blood" has been greatly attenuated in the group which now calls itself Jewish. Some insist that the ancient Hebrews have practically disappeared from the face of the earth.

Thus, in his . . . book on *The Jews Across the Centuries* Dean Willett, of the University of Chicago, writes: "It would be as appropriate to speak of the English people of the times of Henry VIII as Americans, as to describe the Hebrews of Isaiah's day as Jews."

. . . The modern Jew is the child of many peoples. There is at least one notable case in history where an entire people, the Khazars, living between the Caucasus, the Don and the Volga, accepted Judaism about the year 740 A.D., and continued as a powerful Jewish state until about 1016 A.D., when it was extinguished by a joint expedition of Russians and Byzantines. What happened to these Jews? It may be that some of them migrated in a north-westerly direction and became the nucleus of the so-called Eastern Jews of today, while their children mingled their blood with that of the Jews of Western Europe who migrated eastward in the time of the Crusades and the Black Death and sought refuge in Poland. If this be true, then it may be claimed that the Eastern Jew has little connection with the ancient Hebrews. . . . At the beginning of the Christian era, these Khazars were already a mixed people—Scythians, Finns and Sclavonians—and they are hence no more the . . . descendants of Abraham, Isaac and Jacob than are the Falasha Jews of Abyssinia. . . .

At all events, there is possibly no such thing today as the purity of "Jewish blood," and as a result so many Jews do not "look Jewish" . . . while so often Gentiles do look Jewish! To revert to our former classification, it may be that the "nice" Jews are those who do not look Jewish, while the Jews that are not "nice" are those with pronounced Jewish features. Even so, in the early struggles between Judaism and Christianity in the first eight centuries, we learn that the Christians appropriated the Jewish scriptures and then went through the Old Testament, designating all the noble Jews of history as pre-Christian Christians, while all the "dirty" Jews in those sacred pages were definitely classified as Jews.

Are we then to accept the contention of many of the Jews that they must be considered primarily as a religious group? Rabbi Philipson, in his book on *Reformed Judaism* insists that "the national existence of the Jews ceased when the Romans set the Temple aflame and destroyed Jerusalem. . . . The Jews are a religious community, not a nation." The Canadian census secures from each resident both his religious affiliation and his "racial" origin (by father). In its classification of religious affiliations, it includes "Jews," while in its classification of racial origins, it indicates "Hebrews.". . . Nor does it diminish our difficulty when we frankly recognize a large number of "unsynagogued" Jews. We all know that there are many . . . Jews who disown all religion and a small number who call themselves "Hebrew Christians"; there are, in addition, a considerable number who for economic or other reasons do not identify themselves with a synagogue, just as there are many Protestants whose loyalty to any particular church is, to say the least, most spasmodic, although, on occasion, they may easily develop a very boisterous type of Protestantism. On the great Jewish festivals, however, the synagogues will be crowded, even as on Easter lukewarm Christians throng the churches, and on Rosh Hashana and Yom Kippur these semi-Jews testify to their solidarity with the Jewish community. But if the community be essentially religious, then one may aver that it is far from a unity. Judaism reveals almost all the colors of the theological spectrum, from unadulterated humanism to unadulterated fundamentalism and orthodoxy. . . . Where such diversities of religious outlook exist as within Judaism, it seems somewhat difficult to consider it as essentially a religious unit.

The answer of the Zionists is that the essential unity of Jewry is neither racial nor religious; it is national. The Jews are a people. . . . To this, the Jewish group responds with its inner division between Zionists and non-Zionists. . . .

Moreover, while the Gentile world might be very glad if the Jews had a national home, it is subject to constant irritation by its uncertainty whether to treat the Jews as a race, or religious group, or nationality, and the net result of it all is that in the Gentile mind, the Jew emerges essentially as an international irritant, resisting assimilation and finding ever-shifting grounds on which to found his right to a separate existence. . . . In short, the whole situation is a frightful mess, and by his strange dexterity in playing the triple role of a racial, religious and national group, the modern Jew brings down upon his head a triple type of antipathy.

What Is a Protestant?

If we have found it difficult to answer the question, "What is a Jew?" we find it also difficult to answer the question, "What is a Protestant?" The Jew divides the human race into Jews and non-Jews; the Catholic into Catholics and non-Catholics. Where does the Protestant come in? . . .

We all know the wide variety of Protestants, but only those who study religious statistics realize the complications of classification. Shall we include Mormons and Christian Scientists, Theosophists and Spiritualists as Protestants? Where in the doctrinal spectrum of Protestantism shall we find a place, if any, for Unitarianism and Universalism? Or may there not be more important lines of differentiation *within* any of the recognized Protestant denominations than *between* them . . . ? Then again, is the Protestant Episcopal Church Protestant or Catholic? No student of Protestant cooperation fails to appreciate the almost endless complications that inhibit Protestant action. Some Protestant ministers consistently refuse to attend the meetings of local ministers; some denominations will give only a restrained cooperation to certain movements, and some will give not even that; too frequently, the only successful bit of cooperation involves something that nobody cares about anyway. The differences here are largely temperamental, sometimes "racial" and historical, occasionally doctrinal, and not infrequently almost purely social—the social set go to the church where their social standing is reinforced, while the bourgeois middle class seek out their own little conventicles where they can indulge their sense of self-importance, and the proletariat can go to a mission, join the Pentecostals or the Salvation Army, or go nowhere. Then there is that large number of American or Canadian people who, when asked their religious affiliation, reply simply "Protestant," meaning for the most part that at all events they are not Roman Catholics. Sometimes, indeed, it seems that the most inclusive definition of a Protestant is one that stresses his repudiation of the authority of the See of Rome.

Varieties of Catholics

Then, we have the Roman Catholics, and in the interest of simplicity, we put aside for the time being the much-discussed problem involving the Catholicism of Anglo-Catholics and Old Catholics. We limit ourselves to Roman Catholics, although of course we recognize the importance of the Greek Catholics, and of the Uniat Church, which is of growing importance in the United States and Canada. We also pass over the Catholic group which calls itself the Polish National Church, although in some cities this is a very important communion. Limiting ourselves strictly to *bona fide* Roman Catholics, we discover here a much greater unity and less ragged edges than in either the Jewish or Protestant community. There is more centralization in administration and general policy; there is a more fundamental recognition of territorial responsibility through definite parishes with the enhanced emphasis on community life which such parochial responsibility inevitably means; there is far less overlapping and wasteful duplication of institutions and effort than in Protestantism.

With all such apparent unity, however, there are still within Roman Catholicism manifold differences and perhaps the superlative genius of the organization is its extraordinary capacity to deal with human idiosyncrasies. We must recognize, however, that . . . lines are not obliterated entirely. Thus, we have national churches almost side by side with parish churches. The Irish Catholics, the French Catholics, the German Catholics, the Italian Catholics and the Polish Catholics—just to mention a few of them—seem to require special handling, while the Uniats have their own administration for the entire country. . . .

Catholicism not only provides inner variety by reason of its multiplicity of . . . national groupings, but also because of its various orders and communities. The Directory of Catholic Colleges and Schools . . . gives the names of no less than 139 different orders or communities in the United States engaged in teaching alone, and in addition to these there are communities devoted to hospital work, the redemption of fallen women, the care of the poor, etc., to say nothing of the better known communities such as the Jesuits, the Dominicans, the Vincentians, the Sulpicians, the Basilians, the Marists, the Paulists, etc., each with its own distinctive personality and its own distinctive privileges and responsibilities. . . .

Because of their greater centralization, however, many Protestants or non-Catholics come to believe that in their relations to the larger community, all Catholics tend to feel and act alike. It must, however, be urged that while unity is a note of Catholicism, diversity is also present, and cooperation between Catholics and non-Catholics is dependent in a large measure upon the personal attitudes of given parish priests, and especially of the various bishops. . . . There are areas in the United States where the Catholic bishop is most popular in non-Catholic circles; and he is often the best apologetic for Catholicism in non-Catholic circles; there are other areas where the bishop is aggressively disliked and, by his ecclesiastical seclusion or his uncompromising manner, does more to intensify anti-Catholic feeling than any other factor in the situation. . . . It is impossible to exaggerate the importance of the personal factor in considering the future cooperative adjustments between Catholics and the larger community. . . .

While we have thus indicated chiefly the points of difficulty that confront the scientific student of interfaith relations, we have also sought to emphasize the fundamental importance of the more accurate and unimpassioned study of the differences and similarities between religious groups. Tensions develop which, not properly studied and relieved, create various types of social conflagrations. Intransigence breeds intransigence, and unless the roots of these difficulties are adequately traced and provided against, complications of the first magnitude develop for all social relations. . . . The main point to remember is that while these various groups are all seeking passionately to develop their inner solidarity, they find it necessary at the same time to make terms with one another and with that larger group—the community or the nation—to which all belong. This larger integration between the household of faith and the household of economic and political interest is far from easy, and hence much of the criticism directed today against the international Jew and the international Catholic. But this integration must be made—not on any basis of complete indifference, not by hoping that in time all the structures of faith will crumble away into nothingness and their place be taken by the purely secular state, but by a greater insight into the social function of religion. The sociologist who leaves such problems severely alone, trusting entirely to the erosions of time to settle the conflicts of religious groups and standing cynically, like Werther, "above it all—alone with the stars," will need to guess again. Temples may mix with the dust of the desert, but new temples arise, and ancient gods have strangely resurrective powers.

EDITORIAL COMMENT

Nationalities, as we have seen, are tribal or extended kinship groups that can boast of historical precedence not only over the modern nation or state, but even over most religious groups. For example, long before the founding of Protestantism and of the United Kingdom, there were the English (Angles and Saxons); when Roman Catholicism, Eire, and Poland were established as distinctive religious and state entities, there had already been for centuries the Irish and the Poles.

Religious differences have served as a rallying point for nationality separatism, adequately illustrated in the history of the aforementioned Irish and Poles. In the Irish struggle against the Protestant English and in the Polish struggle against the Orthodox Russians, Roman Catholicism functioned to reenforce the nationality striving for identification and independence. At the same time, a common religion has brought together two or more nationalities in marriage, politics and hostility against other religious groups.

The dominant and minority group relations of nationalities in the old world have not had the same formal structure as in American society. In Europe, our main source of immigration, a nationality dominant in one state oftentimes has existed simultaneously as a minority elsewhere on the continent. This has led to invasions aimed at "rescue" of the "persecuted" members of the group across the border, or, at the very least, to the annexation of its territory. The technical term for this European phenomenon of redeeming coethnics located elsewhere is irredentism.

Much of European history, too, has been colored by the efforts of the dominant nationality in a country to suppress the culture of minorities and absorb them, or to expel them. This frequently has stimulated, instead, the minority reaction of belligerent reaffirmation of ethnic identification. Minority nationalities living under these conditions have either sought political independence, or have attempted to rejoin their "brothers" in their more privileged position across the border. Failing to achieve these solutions, a popular alternative has been to emigrate from the intolerable conditions to an immigrant-receiving society like the United States.

Immigration and census statistics gathered in the United States on the Old-World background of the American people refer to the nation or state of derivation, ignoring their nationality. Consequently, these statistics conceal the facts that two individuals arriving in this country from the same European state may not necessarily have been of the same nationality. On the other hand, if they have come from two different countries or states they may well be of the same nationality. Indeed, because of territorial exchanges after wars in Europe, two brothers immigrating to the United States ten years apart from the same village, while obviously of the same nationality, may be identified in terms of different nation-state labels. One, for example, may be referred to as Polish, the other as Russian; or one will be labeled German, the other French.

Distinctions between nationality on the one hand, and nation and citizenship on the other are clarified in the next selection by Bernard Joseph.

6. NATIONALITY: DEFINITION OF TERMS
BY *Bernard Joseph* *

IT will hardly be disputed . . . that before any attempt can be made to discuss intelligently the problems of nationality, pains must be taken to clarify the meanings of the various terms used in relation to nationality and to minimize their misuse. Doubtless much could be done to facilitate a common understanding, at least as regards fundamentals, if some use of specific terms to express particular meanings could be universally attained.

The term "nation" is derived from the Latin word *Natio* which was commonly used to mean "birth" or "race." It also signified a tribe or social group bound together by actual or imaginary unity of blood. In the seventeenth century, the word began to be applied to describe the population of a state regardless of any racial unity, and this meaning has in large measure persisted up to the present day.

It was after the partition of Poland and during the French Revolution that the term was first popularly employed. It was then synonymous with "country" in the same way as "nationalism" was synonymous with "patriotism." Nationality was at this period a collective sentiment.

As early as the beginning of the nineteenth century there arose a distinction between a nation and a nationality. The former term was applied to those groups which governed themselves, that is to say, which formed independent states; whilst the latter was applied to groups such as the Poles or Italians who lived under foreign domination and did not con-

* From Bernard Joseph, *Nationality: Its Nature and Problems* (New Haven: Yale University Press, 1929), pp. 17–30. Reprinted by permission. Footnotes omitted.

stitute independent states. . . . Soon after it [nationality] also acquired another sense, indicative of citizenship. . . .

The term "nationality" has been diversely defined in the light of varying interpretations of its essentials. . . . It will suffice for the present to set out several of the best known. According to Bluntschli the term "nationality" designates "a union of masses of men of different occupations and social strata . . . , of common spirit, feeling . . . bound together especially by language and customs in a common civilization which gives them a sense of unity and distinction from all foreigners quite apart from the bond of state."

Professor Von Engeln defines it as "a group of people bound together by some condition that makes for likemindedness in each particular group and that develops, incidentally, in each group certain characteristics, readily discernible by members of the other groups, that serve as criteria for distinguishing between nationalities."

The term is also employed abstractly to describe "a corporate sentiment, a kind of fellow-feeling or mutual sympathy relating to a definite home country and binding together the members of the human group irrespective of differences of general economic interests or social position more intimately than any other similar sentiment.". . .

It is clear from this use of the term that it must perforce serve to convey two senses: (i) when it is used concretely and refers to a group of persons bound together by certain common attributes, and the other (ii) when it is used abstractly in relation (a) to a certain group consciousness and (b) to the idea of the grouping of persons in national groups. In the latter sense it has been characterized by some writers as the quality of uniting men and women of the same nation.

A simple provisional definition of the term which conveys an immediate and clear understanding of its meaning is that nationality is the distinguishing mark attaching to those of the various groupings of the inhabitants of the civilized world whose members consciously have certain attributes in common in the nature of a common . . . origin, historic tradition[s], religion or language, each group being differentiated from the others by the special peculiarity to it of certain of such attributes.

The true meaning of nationality, used concretely, as distinct from nation, can best be appreciated by realization of the fact that a nation in the proper sense of that term is a group of persons who constitute the population of a single state, and that a nation consequently may embrace several nationalities. Viscount Bryce has pointed out that a nationality may or may not be also a nation. The people of Great Britain are a nation including three nationalities: English, Scotch and Welsh, which are parts of a larger British Nation.

The correct meaning of the term "nation" was recognized by Mazzini, the great prophet of the Principle of Nationality, who said, "By nation we understand the totality of Italians bound together by a common past and governed by the same laws." To him the word represented unity of aims and rights, which alone, according to his understanding, could transform a multitude of men into a . . . whole—a nation. He held that a multitude of men could with propriety be considered a nation only when the rights purporting to constitute them such were founded upon bases that were permanent, that is to say, when they were organized and formed the population of an independent state. . . .

A further correlated word in common use is the term "people." The distinction between the words "people" and "nation" is at once apparent in the German language which translates the English "people" by "nation" and the English "nation" by "volk." In English, unfortunately, the words are ordinarily used indiscriminately as if they were synonymous.

The distinction in meaning between the two terms is similar to that between the terms "nationality" and "nation," the word "people" implying the notion of a civilization and the word "nation" expressing a political concept. The fundamental difference is the greater organic unity of a nation, for a nation is conscious of a developed sense of political connection and unity which causes it to organize into a political body. In a nation, community of rights is developed more extensively than among a people. This is also true of its desire to regulate the communal life of its members, and to give expression to their common will to create and maintain for themselves a state of their own.

"People" is the broader and more comprehensive term. In the same way as in the instance quoted of the British Nation, it was indicated that a nation can consist of more than one nationality, so a people may be divided up into more than one nation. There is, for example, a German people greater in numbers than the German Nation, of which individual sections form parts of non-German nations and states. In the same way the inhabitants of Sweden and Norway may be deemed to belong to the Scandinavian People, though they form two distinct nations. . . .

We must next consider the term "citizenship" and distinguish it from "nationality," with which . . . it is frequently confused. Etymologically the term citizen means the inhabitant of a city in the original use of that word as equivalent to a state. Citizenship properly used describes the status of a person as a constituent member of a state who possesses full national rights of that state and owes it his allegiance.

It is, however, the common practice to refer to a person's citizenship as his nationality, because in most countries the term nationality is used improperly when citizenship is intended, by the very official bodies who might be expected to practice exactitude. The fundamental difference between nationality and citizenship is that nationality is subjective whilst citizenship is objective. Nationality relates to a condition of the mind or feelings or mode of life; whilst citizenship is a political status.

The two terms which are most often interchanged in apparent ignorance that they stand for entirely separate and different things are "nationality" and "nationalism." Like the word nationality, nationalism, apart from being confounded with nationality, is also given several meanings by different writers. An analysis of the principal literature on nationalism discloses that it is used in four different senses. It signifies an actual historical process, that of developing nationalities into political entities, of evolving out of national groups the modern institution of the national state. Secondly, it refers to the activities of a particular political party, combining an historical process and a political theory; this meaning is clearer when the adjective "nationalist" is employed. In this sense it relates to the deliberate effort of a nationality to dominate the state in which it lives or to establish an independent state of its own. Thirdly, it represents the principle or ideal implied in the actual historical process. In this sense a political philosophy of the state is described as nationalism. Finally, "nationalism" is used to denote a frame of mind among members of a nationality in which loyalty to one's national state is exalted as the primary loyalty and of which pride in one's nationality and belief in its intrinsic excellence are indispensable elements. It is this nationalism which plays an important role both in national and interstate politics. . . .

Amongst the improper uses to which the word is put may be mentioned that which gives it the meaning of the right of a people to decide for itself how and by whom it shall be governed, that is to say, the right of self-determination. It has also been employed to indicate the self-consciousness of a nation.

The most common application of the term is to describe the sentiment which forms the basis of nationality when this sentiment is exaggerated and perverse. . . . Nationalism in this meaning usually takes the form of expecting and requiring of the members of a nation not only blind obedience and unquestioning loyalty to their nation, but in addition, absolute faith in its superiority over all other nations. This exaggeration of the sentiment of nationality which enjoins upon the members of a nation to refrain from any criticism of their own nation and to see only good in it and its deeds is of recent growth.

The improper use of this term is fraught with considerable significance. A moment's reflection will show that the severest critics of the idea of nationality really intend to aim their strictures not at the system of social organization by virtue of which nationalities exist, nor even against the sentiment of nationality which is in a degree necessary and desirable. Their objection is to the exaggeration and perversion of the sentiment. It would clarify matters considerably if the term were confined to the description of (a) the historical process of establishing nationalities as political units, or (b) a movement to manifest the sentiment of nationality.

The sentiment which forms the basis of nationality should be designated as the sentiment of nationality and not as nationalism.

A consideration of the foregoing statement as to the diverse meanings given to relevant terms and their true import will, it is hoped, make it clear that such interchange and confusion of terms as exists is etymologically and historically unwarranted; and that with the exercise of reasonable clarity of thinking, the misapplication of the terms in question may be entirely avoided.

III. Prejudice and Discrimination

THE principal forms of intergroup conflict, whether it concerns races, religious groups, or nationalities, are prejudice and discrimination. By general consensus, prejudice is the term used with reference to the *subjective* aspects of conflict, covering both emotional and cognitive components. Discrimination, on the other hand, is the overt or *objective* manifestation of intergroup conflict and it refers to any observable behavior in intergroup relations that deliberately differentiates between the two or more groups in the direction of inequality.

Many people believe that the greater the diversity of a society, the more intense is its intergroup conflict. Yet intergroup relations on the whole are better at the present time in a more heterogeneous Hawaii than in a less heterogeneous Union of South Africa.

Actually, hasty characterizations of intergroup relations in a heterogeneous society are not feasible. Any such society may experience at one given time the whole spectrum of interaction ranging from one extreme of virtual acceptance of outgroups to the other extreme of explicit, violent and persistent conflict. This is especially true in the United States because of the variables in geography, history, and social, cultural, political, and economic conditions. There are also variations in the spectrum of intergroup relations through time in any given society. The dynamics of urbanization and industrialization are bound to stimulate changes from one period to the next.

Basic to much of this variation in the intensity of American prejudice and discrimination is the presence of two sets of traditions, pulling and guiding the American people in diametrically opposed directions. We have already seen that "the American Creed" insists upon the essential dignity of the individual, the fundamental equality of all, regardless of group identification and derivation. The other American tradition, though less formal and explicit than the first, encourages ethnocentrism, stereotypical attitudes, and discriminatory behavior.

Theories of the genesis, development and processes of intergroup conflict began to be seriously formulated in the nineteenth century. One of the first theories posited an instinctive basis for prejudice and discrimination. It had its philosophical origin in Darwinism which viewed man as a biological creature. Later it was proposed that cultural, not biological, differences inevitably lead to intergroup hostility. Then came a host of other theories pointing to frustration and aggression, the dynamics of economic gain and competition, striving for status ascendance, scapegoating, and personality deviation as well as other factors and processes for the ultimate etiological answer.

In the first reading of this section, Arnold M. Rose presents a review of these traditional and new theories of causation. He also carefully explores their respective strengths and weaknesses, and concludes with his own effort to arrive at an integrated theory of prejudice and discrimination.

7. THE CAUSES OF PREJUDICE
BY *Arnold M. Rose* *

THE NATURE OF PREJUDICE

Speculation and study regarding the causes of prejudice have been carried on for a long time, yet a satisfactory answer has not been achieved. The theories advanced are based on a wide range of causal phenomena,

* Reprinted from *Social Problems,* edited by Francis E. Merrill, by permission of Alfred A. Knopf, Inc., pp. 402–24. Copyright 1950 by Alfred A. Knopf, Inc.

and the findings of the studies do not fit into an integrated pattern. Included among those who propound explanations of the causes of prejudice with great certainty are: (1) propagandists for a certain type of policy toward minorities; (2) advocates of certain monistic explanations of social phenomena of the type that includes prejudice; or (3) those who are ignorant of the range of manifestations of prejudice and of the diverse theories and empirical generalizations in the literature. At the present time, it would thus appear wise not to set our minds too exclusively on one explanation, and instead to remain open to explanations that seem at first impression to be bizarre. Accordingly, this essay will offer the theories and facts relevant to the causes of prejudice, will criticize this information, and will point out some possibilities for integration.

Most of the theories and related studies deal with prejudice against Jews and Negroes, probably because those groups are the objects of the most continuing and widespread prejudice. Many of the writers on anti-Semitism, and some of the writers on anti-Negro prejudice, consider prejudices against Negroes and Jews to be entirely different in origin and psychological make-up. Other writers deny the distinctions and treat prejudice as a unitary psychological phenomenon. Evidence for the former point of view is offered by those sociologists, like Frazier,[1] who point to the unique historical development of antagonism against one minority group, and by psychologists, like Frenkel-Brunswik and Sanford,[2] who find unique personality characteristics among those strongly prejudiced against another minority group. Evidence for the latter point of view is offered by various studies showing the high degree of relationship between anti-Semitism and anti-Negro prejudice. A notable example of the latter kind of studies is that of Hartley,[3] who showed that anti-Semites said they were also against Danireans—a nonexistent group—as well as against Negroes.

OLDER THEORIES OF PREJUDICE

1. *Prejudice and Difference*

One of the oldest explanations of prejudice against all minorities is made in terms of fear or dislike of differences. A person who is physically different or culturally different (a Jew or a Negro, for example), is said to cause an instinctive antipathy. This instinctive fear of the unknown or the unusual is supposed to have developed among animals for self-protec-

[1] E. Franklin Frazier, *The Negro in the United States* (New York: Macmillan Co., 1949).

[2] E. Frenkel-Brunswik and R. N. Sanford, "Some Personality Correlates of Anti-Semitism," *Journal of Psychology*, 20 (1945), 271–291.

[3] Eugene Hartley, *Problems in Prejudice* (New York: King's Crown Press, 1946).

tion and to have continued in modern man as a vestige. The weakness in the theory is that within most species (dogs, for example), different breeds excite no such antipathy in each other. Studies of children show that younger ones do not manifest any inherent antipathy towards members of other races, but are trained to do so, sometimes with great effort. History shows that group differences do not inevitably and naturally lead to dislike and hostility, and it also shows that there is as much dislike of imagined or stereotyped differences as of real differences. In our own day, the syndrome of red hair, ruddy skin, and freckles has no social significance, whereas the combination of dark skin, broad nose, and thick lips provokes some people to intense hatred. While the theory in its pure form is thus disproved, it nevertheless conforms with observations that men tend to form in-groups in opposition to out-groups, and to avoid sympathetic contacts with members of out-groups that would tend to break down the barriers which are artificially set up.

Two implications for social action could be derived if the theory were correct. One is that prejudice is inevitable as long as group differences exist. The other is that—to the extent that group differences are removable—the minority group is responsible for the prejudice by not looking and acting like the majority. History has given us several examples in which prejudice has declined or changed its character without the minority group changing its characteristics or its behavior (e.g., the Scotch in England in the seventeenth century; the Japanese in the United States after World War II). Studying the incidence of prejudice against Negroes, for example, reveals that there may be no less prejudice against those whose physical features and manners are like those of white people. In fact, in the American South, the Negro who acquires education or wealth or who acts too much like a white man is likely to attract the most extreme antagonism of whites.

Many Jews report quite the opposite experience. Long-Americanized Jews of the upper-income class frequently are told by those who manifest anti-Semitism that this behavior is directed not at them but at the "kike" Jews whose manners are so bad. We do not know whether this observation of the prejudiced can be trusted or whether it is simply a manifestation of the well-known phenomenon that those who are known as individuals are never fitted into stereotypes. The most extreme manifestation of prejudice in modern times occurred in Germany, where Jews were more like non-Jews than in any other country in the world. Other evidence points to the fact that, under many circumstances, the strange or the bizarre may be the most attractive. Certainly the evidence is so complicated that not much validity can be attached to the "dislike of differences" theory. It should be thought of as a rationalization of prejudice rather than as an explanation of it.

2. *Prejudice and Competition*

Another early explanation of ethnic prejudice is in terms of *economic competition*. When two groups of people are competing for the same economic values—the same jobs or the same markets—they are likely to become antagonistic to each other. Rationalizations for the prejudice may appear, such as charges by one group that the other is unfair, but the essential element is competition. In its original form this theory included a postulate of some biological instinct, such as the instinct of self-preservation, to "explain" why competition took a strong and personal form. In its modern form, it is held by economic determinists, especially by Marxists, who find the economic struggle the central fact in all social phenomena. For them the motivating force behind competition that turns it into group antagonism is not an instinct but the capitalistic system. The capitalistic system thus creates a scarcity in the midst of plenty and one worker is encouraged to pit himself against another. The division can be of one ethnic group against another if historical circumstances have naturally placed workers into such groups. But the motive forces behind antagonism are still competition and the capitalistic system which profits from it.

An example frequently offered is that of Negro and white workers in the South. The white workers are encouraged by the capitalists to express all their dissatisfaction—arising out of working at unpleasant tasks and out of discomforts caused by low pay—against Negroes. Prejudice thus provides an outlet for unrest which might otherwise turn to revolution, and allows the capitalists to exploit both white and Negro workers.[4] Prejudice takes place not only at the worker level but at all occupational levels, since competition occurs throughout the capitalistic system. Businessmen in the United States, for example, became antagonistic to Jews when the latter began to rise out of the working classes toward the end of the nineteenth century and to compete against the established businessman.[5]

The competition theory seems to explain a good number of historic facts. Slavery in the United States was on its way to gradual and unopposed extinction in the 1790's, when techniques were discovered to make the production of cotton and sugar cane enormously profitable if slave labor were available. Slavery was then rapidly extended and cemented into the social structure by the growth of racist attitudes of prejudice. Whereas slavery had formerly existed as a weak institution, an economic incentive made it strong and apparently provided the stimulus for the introduction of race prejudice. Another historical evidence for the

---

[4] This point of view is expressed by, among others: (1) Herbert Aptheker, "A Liberal Dilemma," *New Masses* 59 (May 14, 1946), pp. 3–6; (2) Oliver C. Cox, *Caste, Class and Race* (New York: Doubleday & Co., 1948).

[5] This point of view is expressed, for example, by: Carey McWilliams, *A Mask for Privilege* (Boston: Little, Brown & Co., 1948).

competition theory is provided in the history of the Chinese in America. When the Chinese were first brought to this country to do the undesirable work of building the Western railroads, there was no prejudice against them. When they first shifted into mine work, there was still no prejudice against them and no competition for their jobs, since whites were engaged in more lucrative pursuits or were prospecting for precious metals. But when it became apparent, in the later 1870's, that few further discoveries of precious metals were likely, and furthermore that the miners' work was steady, whites began to move in and compete with the Chinese. Soon great hostility grew up against the Chinese, and the whole pattern of discrimination was put into operation against them.

Yet the theory has a number of grave weaknesses. Social patterns may continue for reasons other than those which caused them in the first place. In fact, a force which causes a social pattern may later unsuccessfully operate against it. That has occurred in the case of anti-Negro prejudice. There is no longer much economic gain in the South from the exploitation of Negroes that could not be more successfully had from other activities. If the same amount of time, capital, and other resources now spent in cotton growing with hand labor were diverted to other economic pursuits (including industry and some cotton growing with machines), more profit could be made. But many Southerners are tied to the past and to the exploitation of Negroes so strongly that they cannot see better economic opportunities in other directions. The economic situation is obviously not the most important factor in determining attitudes toward any minority group in the United States today (with the exception of Mexicans), although it might become so again in the future. Another criticism of the economic-competition theory is that this factor is never sufficient by itself to explain prejudice. Competition may exist at an even keel, and yet prejudice will have its ups and downs. Clearly the explanation is too simple, even if it has an element of truth.

3. *Prejudice and Social Control*

A third "classical" theory is based on the sociological concept of *social control*. Like most other social patterns, prejudice against certain groups can become a tradition. Studies of prejudice among children [6] show how parents, older playmates, and the formal institutions of society not only transmit race prejudice to young children, but force them into the social groove which requires that their actions show discrimination. The theory helps to account for the continuation of prejudice when its original cause has disappeared. It also helps to explain why antagonism begun against a particular group continues against that particular group, when

[6] See, for example, Bruno Lasker, *Race Attitudes in Children* (New York: Henry Holt & Co., 1929).

other theories simply give a cause of prejudice and do not indicate why one or another group is more hated.

The theory obviously fails to account for the original cause of prejudice. It also fails to account for its motive force. Manifestations of prejudice have an element of violence in them; anyone who examines them closely will see an element of aggression in even the most traditional and mildest prejudice. The sociologists' explanation of violence in social control is best expounded in Sumner's theory of the mores. Notions of social welfare thus sometimes become attached to traditional ways of doing things and then their violations come to be regarded as an attack on society which must be speedily and rigorously punished. Those who consider prejudice a tradition in the mores frequently take their illustration from the treatment of Negroes in the Southern states. They say that violence occurs when the Negro seeks to get out of his place, and not when he maintains his subordinate role. This, however, is much more a Southern myth than a reality. Violence is associated much more with conditions affecting the white man than it is with changes in the behavior of Negroes.[7] The concept "mores" does not fit the Southern pattern of prejudice in other respects. The mores are universally accepted and not discussed, whereas the Negro problem is constantly being discussed in the South. Furthermore, those who are most aggressive against Negroes in the South are not the leaders of white society but those who are least integrated into the society in general. Clearly, the theory of traditional social control fails to do justice to the facts about prejudice.

4. *Prejudice and Experience*

A minor theory of prejudice explains it in terms of some unpleasant early experience with a member of a minority group. Quite a number of admittedly prejudiced people will seek to explain their behavior and attitudes in terms of some traumatic experience, usually occurring in childhood.[8] The weaknesses of the theory are apparent. Children and adults are constantly having major and minor traumatic experiences involving all sorts of people of their own race as well as of other races, but they do not acquire prejudice against all persons with the physical or social characteristics of the hated individuals. There must clearly be some sensitization to the concept of race as a category before a trau-

[7] C. I. Hovland and R. R. Sears, for example, have demonstrated a correlation between high lynching rate and low cotton prices. Cf. John Dollard et al., *Frustration and Aggression* (New Haven: Yale University Press, 1939).

[8] A study by Gordon W. Allport and Bernard M. Kramer shows that persons with strong prejudice say they have had unpleasant childhood memories of members of groups against which they are prejudiced, to a much greater extent than do less prejudiced persons. "Some Roots of Prejudice," *The Journal of Psychology,* 22: (1946), 9–39.

matic experience with one individual can cause hatred of that individual's ethnic group. Psychiatrists have also revealed many individual cases in which the "traumatic experience" proved to be imaginary. From these considerations, it would appear to be as accurate to say that prejudice causes traumatic experiences as to say that traumatic experiences cause prejudice.

PSYCHOLOGICAL THEORIES OF PREJUDICE

1. *The Frustration-Aggression Theory*

The frustration-aggression theory was developed at the Yale Institute of Human Relations as a general concept to explain several kinds of human behavior, of which prejudice is only one. Prejudice is considered to be a type of aggression, which is a universal response to frustration. When people's needs are unsatisfied or their acts are interrupted, they respond with aggression. Aggression takes many forms, but these have psychological equivalence. Therefore it is just as satisfactory to be aggressive against a minority group as to be aggressive against the source of the frustration. In this simplified form, the theory is equivalent to the even more generalized Freudian concept of "displacement," in which an attitude toward one object can be shifted to another object and still maintain psychological equivalence.

In his study of race relations in the South,[9] Dollard observed an unusual amount of dissatisfaction with social conditions. Whites of the lower and middle classes could get substitute satisfactions ("gains") of an economic, sexual, or prestige nature at the expense of the helpless Negro. In other words, hatred for an exploitative economic system and a drab life was displaced onto a convenient, easily identifiable object— the Negro—which could provide substitute satisfactions. Later studies of frustration and aggression included an experiment on prejudice.[10] In a boys' camp, the boys were obliged, unexpectedly and arbitrarily, to take a long and difficult examination which prevented them from attending the movies. Half the boys were given a scale to rate Mexicans before the examination, and Japanese afterwards. The other half rated the Japanese before, and the Mexicans after, the examination. The attitudes toward the set of foreigners rated after the frustration (that is, the examination which prevented them going to the movies) were in each case the more unfavorable.

The displacement theory has been used for scientific support by the economic determinists and is subject to some of the same defects of their theory. Specifically: (1) it basically holds that one frustration, or one

[9] John Dollard, *Caste and Class in a Southern Town* (New Haven: Yale University Press, 1937).
[10] John Dollard et al., *op. cit.*, p. 31.

type of frustration, is the determining factor in a group's whole relation with another group; (2) it assumes that frustration must always have an outlet in aggression; (3) it does not satisfactorily explain why one group, rather than another group or another object, is chosen as the object of aggression.

2. *The Projection Theory*

Closely related to the concept of displacement is the Freudian concept of *"projection."* Here people attribute to others motives which they sense in themselves but which they would not wish to acknowledge openly. Fascists whose aim is world dominance thus accuse the Jews of plotting to seize control of all countries. White Southerners who hunger for an unbounded sex life accuse the Negroes of being naturally immoral. People who are fearful because of the many uncertainties of modern existence are likely to persecute all the people they can, especially the minorities, because the latter are weak. The fearful "persecute so that they may project upon others the fear that is gnawing at their own hearts. By creating in others terrors greater than they themselves experience men seek to build up for themselves an illusion of security and safety." [11]

Projection is a valuable concept since it describes a frequently acting psychological mechanism. It has a counterpart in everyday speech in the notion of "using a scapegoat." However, it cannot be regarded as a theory of prejudice unless it is combined with a conception of motive that tells why people sometimes project. Assuming that there is a need to create in others fears, lusts, and designs which we unhappily cherish within ourselves, the theory still does not explain why *certain* undesirable attitudes are projected on *certain* other groups. Neither the choice of attitude nor the choice of group is explained.

3. *Symbolic Theories of Prejudice*

Various symbolic theories have been advanced that attempt to explain choice and motive force. Most of them make use of the concept of projection and all of them can be regarded as supplementary rather than opposed to the frustration-aggression theory. A symbolic theory assumes an ambivalent attitude toward an important object, for which social pressures and one's own values demand an ostensibly favorable attitude. The individual still has an unfavorable attitude (usually unconscious) toward this object, an attitude driven to expression every time its favorable twin gets openly expressed. To get expression, the unfavorable attitude attaches itself to an object which has psychological equivalence to the desired or revered object. This object—the symbol—is thus cordially hated or despised.

[11] David W. Petegorsky, "The Strategy of Hatred," *Antioch Review,* I (September, 1941), 377.

Freud's theory of anti-Semitism [12] is one of the most complicated of the symbolic theories. It finds the object of the ambivalent attitude to be "God the father." God must be revered and obeyed, but he is also hated as he is the source of repression and authority. Freud developed a pseudo-history to aid his explanation: Moses introduced monotheism, with its repressive morality, among the Jews. After years of driving leadership, he was assassinated by his followers, who thereupon felt guilty for their crime. They repressed the memory of the murder and identified the stern leader they had killed with the strict God they worshipped. St. Paul discerned this guilty ambivalence and hit upon an idea for getting rid of the sense of guilt. Guilt can be expiated; execution of the murderer removes the guilt. Since the Jews considered God as a father, the Son of God could ceremonially allow himself to be killed and this punishment would expiate the crime. St. Paul fastened this role on Jesus, a minor religious leader who had recently been crucified, and so invented Christianity. The Jews who followed St. Paul—that is, the Christians—now felt cleansed of the murder of God, but hated the other Jews who still would not admit the ancient murder and would not accept the cleansing baptism. In this manner anti-Semitism was born and for this reason it was continued. Freud recognizes other contributory motives for anti-Semitism, such as fear of cultural differences, the alleged conceit of the Jews, the numerical weakness of the Jews, fear of circumcision as a symbol of castration, and hatred of Christ as a Jew. But his central notion is that anti-Semitism is symbolically a rejection of the guilt for killing God the father.

Maurice Samuel [13] has developed a variation of Freud's symbolic theory. For Samuel, anti-Semitism is psychologically Christophobia, that is, a real hatred of Christ has been displaced onto the Jews because they gave Christ to the world. Anti-Semites hate Christ pathologically because he is a symbol of peace, equalitarianism, brotherhood, and the other elements of Jewish morality which Christ taught the world. The Nazis, who wanted force to dominate the world, recognized the symbolic connection between Jesus and the Jews, and so were out to kill all Jews with the ultimate aim of destroying the nonforce philosophy. Samuel holds that it does no good simply to disprove rationally the charges against the Jews, or to ask the anti-Semites to excuse the Jews as Christ-killers because they are also the Christ-givers. The real propaganda which will force the anti-Semites to retreat, and make the neutral Christians realize the true significance of anti-Semitism is to reveal to the world the morality of the Jewish religion and to prove that Christ's teachings were fundamentally Jewish teachings. Several other writers have expressed belief in the partial validity of Samuel's theory—for example, Herman Rauschning (the ex-

[12] Sigmund Freud, *Moses and Monotheism* (New York: Alfred A. Knopf, 1939).
[13] *The Great Hatred* (New York: Alfred A. Knopf, 1940).

Nazi), Carl Friedrich (the American historian), and Jacques Maritain (the Neo-Thomist Catholic). They all hold to a modified theory that the anti-Semites are out to kill the spirit of progressivism and other principles of the French Revolution, and are using the Jews as a symbol of these principles as one line of attack.

Still another symbolic theory of anti-Semitism is one suggested by Lewis Browne,[14] and developed by Arnold Rose.[15] This is that the Jews are a symbol of urbanism, with its emphasis on individualism, intellectualism, ambition, impersonality, money as a common measure, the possibility of revolution, and so on. Most Gentiles have a rural background not so many generations old, and they still fear and hate these urban values. At the same time, they realize that the city is economically essential, and they also enjoy the many cultural and entertainment opportunities that the city has to offer. In order to resolve this mental conflict, which requires that people both hate and like the city, a symbol of the city is sought that can be freely hated, while the city itself can be the object of more rational-appearing attitudes. The Jews have been historically associated with city life, and so they are a convenient symbol of what is hated. Miriam Beard [16] contributes to this theory by pointing out that Christian capitalists of past centuries often sought to absolve themselves of the stain of being "tradesmen" (in order to gain status with the aristocrats) by seeking to transfer the blame for being capitalists to the Jews. She points to historical evidence to disprove the Sombart thesis that Jews were the fathers of modern capitalism, but admits that this false thesis is widely believed.

Another evidence for the theory that Jews are the symbol of hated urbanism and capitalism is the attention given by German anti-Semites to the distinction between *schaffendes* and *raffendes* (productive and destructive) capital. The former refers to heavy industry and commercial agriculture; the latter refers to banking, the entertainment field, and other industries that do not produce material "good." The latter is believed to be exploitative, and the real or supposed concentration of Jews in these industries makes them an object of hatred.

We may now turn to a symbolic theory of anti-Negro prejudice, which has been variously expressed in both popular and scientific form by Halsey, McLean, Rose, and Smith.[17] The heart of this theory is that

[14] *How Odd of Jews* (New York: Macmillan Co., 1934), esp. pp. 225–238.
[15] "Anti-Semitism's Roots in City-Hatred," *Commentary* VI (October 1948), 374–378.
[16] In I. Graeber and S. Britt, *Jews in a Gentile World* (New York: Macmillan Co., 1942), esp. p. 367.
[17] Margaret Halsey, *Color Blind* (New York: Simon & Schuster, 1946); Helen V. McLean, "Psychodynamic Factors in Racial Relations," *The Annals of the American Academy of Political and Social Science* 244 (March 1946), 159–166; Arnold M. Rose, *op. cit.;* Lillian Smith, *Killers of the Dream* (New York: W. W. Norton & Co., 1949).

Negroes are the objects of the whites' desires for, and yet fear of, uninhibited sex. White Americans have a traditional attitude that sex is sinful, and that relations between man and wife are for the purpose of procreation and not pleasure. Yet they desire sex pleasure, and insofar as that desire is denied in marital relationships, it seeks outlet in other forms. Especially in the South, Negroes are thought to be less sexually inhibited (which they are) and more capable of passion (which they are not). The whites who have sex relations with Negroes feel guilty; those who do not do so feel that temptation must be vigorously repressed. The prejudice against Negroes is thus not simply a matter of personal antipathy but rather of *righteous hatred*.

The psychoanalyst McLean extends this general notion by saying that Southern whites lack the capacity for expressing all the warm sentiments, including those of sex, but realize that the Negro has what they lack: "They anxiously search for something which will give meaning to their lives through their contacts with the Negro. These contacts, however, are fraught with the terror of the forbidden. Their inflexible consciences, in seeking a victim to punish for all manner of forbidden impulses, must keep in subservience those who represent the temptation. Occasionally a lynching relieves the corporate guilt of the white community." [18] In other words, the Southern white's emotional dependence on, and jealousy of, the Negro and his need to repress these feelings cause his constant manifestations of prejudice.

Lillian Smith adds another twist in her statement of the theory. The Negro woman is not only a desired sex object to the Southern white man, but she is so because she represents the Negro mammy. The mammy is the symbol of the gentle and permissive mother, whereas the biological mother plays a repressive role. There is displacement from both mother symbols for the young white male, and he grows up with a dual sex interest. In a monogamous society this creates conflict for him, and he reduces the conflict by expressing callousness and antagonism toward the Negro attraction.

The major weakness of all symbolic theories is that they have never been subjected to a rigorous test. They are based on inferences from observable facts rather than on the facts themselves—that is, the evidence is purely circumstantial. One theory is substitutable for the other, and there could possibly be an indefinite number of theories to explain the same phenomenon. They have the advantage of offering a possible explanation of why certain groups are selected out for prejudice and of the peculiar forms prejudice takes. They also indicate the complex and fantastic nature of the attitudes we call prejudice. These symbolic theories are supplementary, rather than opposed, to such other theories as that of

[18] Helen V. McLean, *op. cit.*

frustration and aggression. But a systematic test needs to be devised to prove or disprove them before they will be of real use either as theory or in practice.

PREJUDICE AND PROPAGANDA

In two of the theories we have already examined, prejudice was seen to have advantages which a certain group could capitalize on. In the Marxist economic competition theory, the capitalists could use prejudice to "divide and conquer" the workers, and so might well devote their conscious efforts to spreading prejudice. In one of the projective theories, the Nazis are explained as accusing the Jews of plotting to seize control of the world so that they might themselves do this very thing under the guise of saving the world from the Jews. Evidence does exist, therefore, that prejudice can be spread by deliberate propaganda to serve selfish purposes.

Donald S. Strong [19] made a study of organized anti-Semitism in America during the 1930's and showed how it was a bid for political power. Anti-Semitism involves an appeal to nationalism and an underlying contempt for democracy, liberty, and equality and the other values associated with the French and American Revolutions. Strong's chronological distribution of 119 anti-Semitic organizations in the United States is suggestive of the tie-in with the Nazi bid for world domination. Between 1915, when the first organization was started, and 1932, the year before Hitler came to power, there were only five organizations started. In 1933, nine more were started, and the succeeding years saw the birth of, respectively, 19, 13, 18, 22, 24 and 9 new anti-Semitic organizations.

McWilliams' [20] study of prejudice against Japanese-Americans in California shows that this prejudice has been largely the result of agitation by vested interests. For example, he points out that the peak years of anti-Japanese agitation were election years: "Dozens of California Congressmen were repeatedly elected to Congress by their sponsorship of this agitation." McWilliams also points out that agitation mounted after the Japanese had been evacuated from the West Coast in 1942. This agitation was economically motivated; many persons had benefited from the removal of the Japanese during the war and did not want them back. There is little present feeling against the Chinese in California because there has been no organized agitation against them for about twenty years.

This and other evidence clearly suggests that propaganda can spread

[19] *Organized Anti-Semitism in America* (Washington: American Council on Public Affairs, 1941).
[20] Carey McWilliams, *Prejudice. Japanese Americans: Symbol of Racial Intolerance* (Boston: Little, Brown & Co., 1944), esp. pp. 3, 25, 44, 235.

or intensify prejudice. But there is also evidence that propaganda is often unsuccessful,[21] and it is known from history that prejudice has often been strong without being stimulated by its beneficiaries. Propaganda must then play only a supplementary role, under some circumstances, in the spread of prejudice. These conditions need to be studied, but a whole theory of prejudice can never be built on the analysis of propaganda and its effects.

PREJUDICE AND PERSONALITY

A number of students have sought to explain prejudice as a sort of mental disease. Functional mental disorders can usually be traced to inadequacies in personality development, and prejudice is regarded under this theory as resulting from a particular kind of misdevelopment. Most of the studies in support of this theory take the form of comparing groups of prejudiced and unprejudiced persons on a number of questions about personality characteristics and personality development. The items where significant differences appear are then integrated into a clinical picture of "the prejudiced personality." One study, by Frenkel-Brunswik, Sanford, and others at the University of California,[22] is based on a detailed comparison between the personality traits of known anti-Semites and the personality traits of known non-anti-Semites. The typical anti-Semite was found to be a compulsive conformist, exhibiting anxiety at the appearance of any social deviation. He appears to be a person with little insight into himself, who projects his own undesired traits onto other people. He has a tendency toward stereotyped thinking, is unimaginative, and tends to have unconscious inferiority feelings. He consciously expresses strong parental and religious devotion, but unconsciously manifests hatred of parents and little concern with values. He exhibits aversion against emotionality but unconsciously has a feeling of inferiority toward it. He is prone to aggressive fantasies.

Another study was conducted in New York City by Jahoda and Ackerman. They obtained detailed reports on fifty patients who had expressed anti-Semitism while undergoing psychoanalytic treatment, and tried to determine what role, if any, anti-Semitism played in their unstable mental make-up. It seemed clear that anti-Semitism was derived from some distortion in personality structure, and fulfilled certain needs in this respect. Anxiety and lack of security in group membership are

---

[21] The history of the Dreyfus affair in France is a classic on the role of propaganda and counterpropaganda in prejudice in which the deliberate propaganda for prejudice had an initial success but an ultimate failure.

[22] Reported in: Ernst Simmel (ed.), *Anti-Semitism: A Social Disease* (New York: International Universities Press, 1946), pp. 96–124. Also see: E. Frenkel-Brunswik and R. N. Sanford, "Some Personality Correlates of Anti-Semitism," *Journal of Psychology*, 20 (1945), pp. 271–291.

the major and uniform traits of this type. Fearing attacks on their integrity as individuals, these personalities counterattack against Jews, the handiest object. The anti-Semitic personality type in this study also has an overwhelming desire to conform, to appear "respectable," to attach itself to dominant organizations, and is characterized by outward submissiveness and inward aggressiveness.

Hartley [23] also made a study of the personality traits of the prejudiced person. Since he found that intolerance toward one minority group is usually accompanied by intolerance toward other minority groups, his description applies to all prejudiced people and not only to anti-Semites. He also obtained expressions of attitudes toward nonexistent groups, and found that prejudiced people expressed prejudice even against them. Hartley's subjects were college students at several colleges. His summary of the characteristics of the intolerant personality follows: "unwillingness to accept responsibility; acceptance of conventional mores; a rejection of serious groups; rejection of political interests, and desire for groups formed for purely social purposes and absorption with pleasure activities; a conscious conflict between play and work; emotionality rather than rationality; extreme egocentrism; interest in physical activity, the body, health. He was likely to dislike agitators, radicals, pessimists. He was relatively uncreative, apparently unable to deal with anxieties except by fleeing from them. Often his physical activity had in it a compulsive component. (It may be that this compulsion to be on the move, that is, constantly occupied with sport, motoring, traveling, etc., served for him the same function as did study and activities with social significance for the individual with high tolerance.")

Personality disorder can also involve the concepts of projection and symbolism, as we see in a clinical interpretation of a notorious anti-Semite by the psychoanalyst Gertrude M. Kurth.[24] Her subject is Adolph Hitler, and since he was in a position to propagandize most of Europe into anti-Semitism, the theory has broader implications than the explanation of prejudice in one man. The explanation is in terms of Freudian theory and assumes that desires for incest can be displaced and that guilt feelings can be projected. Hitler's complex was that Jews were constantly seeking to rape non-Jewish girls. Hitler himself had an unusually affectionate relationship with one of his sisters, who later became his housekeeper, and he took her daughter as his mistress. He had apparently entertained incestuous feelings toward his sister since childhood, and probably transferred them from his mother. Hitler hated his father, who died while he was young, but it seems that a Jewish doctor took the father's place in

[23] Eugene Hartley, *Problems in Prejudice* (New York: King's Crown Press, 1946).

[24] "The Complex Behind Hitler's Anti-Semitism," *Commentary* V (January 1948), 77–82.

the Hitler household. According to the theory, Hitler abhorred his own incest feelings and hated and feared the person (the Jewish doctor) who was suppressing them. Hitler later thought of the Jew, who was (allegedly) always trying to rape girls, as black-haired, which he himself was. The theory holds that Hitler feared his own incestuous desires and felt a need to exterminate them. The "black-haired Jew boy waiting in ambush to rape an unsuspecting girl" was thus a symbol to Hitler of his own hatred of self. By exterminating the Jews, Hitler was trying to kill the evil in himself. He could then live with his sister, have sex relations with her daughter, and still be at peace with himself.

Aside from any technical defects in these various studies of prejudice as the expression of a warped personality, there are certain conceptual inadequacies. They assume a particular background of personality development, but as yet beg the question of the nature of the development. They say nothing about the situational influences affecting prejudice. They give the impression that prejudice is never a matter of degree, but rather of kind of personality. Nevertheless, the facts that are turned up regarding the personality characteristics of the strongly prejudiced suggest many important problems for further study.

An Integrated Theory of Prejudice

In addition to the studies in support of theories we have mentioned, there are many other studies that attempt to throw light on the causes of prejudice. There is thus a great deal of information, but no real integration, of this information. The studies and theories cannot simply be added together, as many of them are obviously opposed to each other. What is needed is an effort to find similarities in the theories despite differing terminologies and a determination of what parts of a theory are essential for explaining certain facts and what parts are not essential. A first approximation of such an integration will be attempted here.

The older theories can be fitted in large part into the modern theories. The economic competition theory fits in well with the frustration-aggression theory, if we recognize that the frustrations involved in earning a livelihood are major ones. The question of whether the capitalist system contributes more to the workers' frustration than do alternative economic systems can be left to empirical determination, and economic frustrations must take their place along with noneconomic ones. The distinctive implication for action characteristic of the economic competition theory then loses its force. Changes in prejudice can occur by means other than revolution, and revolution is not a sure cure for prejudice.

The notion that vested interests can benefit from prejudice by using it to divide workers and keep them hostile to each other agrees with the modern conception that prejudice may be deliberately propagated. The inconsistency in the economic competition theory can then be eliminated. If prejudice can be spread and intensified through propaganda, it should also be susceptible to reduction by the same means. The economic competition theory identifies the objects of prejudice as groups with which the prejudiced are in competition. That fails to explain such a widespread prejudice as that against the Chinese, who are in competition with practically no one. This theory would also give the patently false advice to a small minority group that, if it wishes to avoid prejudice, it should withdraw from competition to presumably inferior positions. Actually there is evidence that Negroes have been experiencing less prejudice recently because they are achieving more equal economic status and are in greater contact (and competition) with white workers. It would seem that the part of the economic competition theory which identifies the object of prejudice had best be dropped.

The "dislike of differences" theory is obviously false, as we have noted, when applied to all differences. But when applied to differences of unconscious symbolic value, and thus fitted in with symbolic theory, it seems to have some truth. If there is something in "Negro-ness" that arouses the ire of the anti-Negro white, then the Negro with fewer of these traits (that is, with more education, more Puritanism, lighter skin perhaps) will arouse this antagonism less. Of course, even if this be true, it helps very little in either understanding or reducing prejudice. Only when it promotes other values, such as getting a better education, will Negroes wish to direct their efforts to minimizing the differences that disturb the prejudiced white man. Otherwise there will be inquiry into what makes the differences disturbing rather than into locating and abolishing the disturbing differences. In dealing with group differences, we should examine the fact that most strongly prejudiced persons live in a world of exaggerated and imaginary differences. Such persons will go quite beyond the evidence of their senses in finding differences and will even ignore most of their everyday experiences. Under these circumstances, expressions of differences provide clues to symbolic meanings.

The social control theory makes the valuable point that culture tends to perpetuate itself, but beyond that it does nothing to explain the rise and fall of group prejudices or the violence or hatred which attend expressions of prejudice. Traditions are calm behavior patterns and could not exist with the excitement that attends prejudice. Violations of the mores are attended by excitement, but excitement regarding minority groups is more or less continuous for the strongly prejudiced, even when the minority persons are meek. The final proof that the social control theory is inadequate reveals itself when prejudiced people appeal to it to oppose social change affecting minorities. This observation might give rise to a concept of "pseudo-mores," or a system of rules to which some people adhere allegedly out of deference to tradition but actually out of inner psychological compulsion. It would be of great interest to conduct a study of the "prejudiced personality" type in a region (like the South) where apparently most people are strongly prejudiced. Such a study might reveal that certain people are enforcers of the anti-Negro customs and other people simply passively go along with the "rules." Such a study would help us integrate the social control theory with the newer theories and findings about prejudice.

The essential weakness of the traumatic experience theory has already been demonstrated. An unpleasant experience with a member of a minority group might accentuate prejudice for some people. It might also transform a latent prejudice into an active one. But the improbability of finding that most white Southerners had strongly unpleasant experiences with Negroes when they were children, and no such unpleasant experiences with whites, shows that the traumatic-experience approach cannot be a significant one. The statement of many prejudiced persons that they had traumatic experiences with minority persons suggests that some symbolic theory is necessary to explain the incidence and role of the traumatic experiences.

The "prejudiced personality" and "deliberate propaganda" theories of the causation of prejudice provide valuable supplementary insights but obviously cannot be sufficient in themselves. Those who have made studies of the personality characteristics of strongly prejudiced persons recognize that they must next delve into the developmental histories of these persons. Their findings will then be more amenable to integration with other theories. In the case of the deliberate propaganda theory, the next phase of investigation would bring one to ask the question, "What propaganda is effective, and why?" Answers to this question will also allow the fact that propaganda has been effective in increasing prejudice—especially in the case of attitudes toward the Japanese and Jews in the United States— to be integrated with other theories.

The central theories today which seriously attempt to explain prejudice are based on the concepts of frustration-aggression, projection, and symbolic substitution. These theories have a good deal in common despite the differing kinds of evidence which lead to their formulation. All of them postulate (1) a need to express antagonism (2) toward something which is not the real object of antagonism. The motive force behind the need might be an external frustration, or a major dissatisfaction with some aspect of oneself, or a social pressure to express only favorable attitudes toward something for which one really feels ambivalent attitudes. Which of these three sources of the motive strength is most important needs to be settled by research, but it is possible that all three operate. Not only is there an essential similarity among the three theories, but they complement each other at their weakest points. The symbolic theory does most to explain which group is selected for prejudice and why.

The frustration-aggression theory does most to explain the strength behind prejudice. The projection theory offers a plausible explanation of the psychological function of prejudice—as a cleansing agent to dissolve inner guilt or hurt.

The problem of reconciling the apparently divergent symbolic theories with each other will have to await the development of keener research tools. In the meantime we can point to the likelihood that the outstanding symbolic theories are not so divergent as they appear. If we consider civilization to be the object of ambivalence, we remember that Freud always equated a repressive father—God—with a repressive civilization, we recognize that urban values represent the highest values of civilization (the Latin word "civitas" is the root of both "city" and "civilization," as Simmel pointed out), and we observe that Christian values of peace and cosmopolitanism arise out of an urban civilization. This type of integration may put too much of a strain on the original theories, but we present it as an interesting possibility.

In our excursion through the various theories of prejudice we have observed something of the complexity of the human mind. The layman—especially the prejudiced layman—usually thinks of prejudice as the simplest thing in the world. This attitude helps him to ignore what the facts of complexity reveal—that prejudice lies very close to the core of our culture and its characteristic personalities. In dramatic terms, it is indeed a problem of the national conscience.

EDITORIAL COMMENT

Although some questions are still unresolved, research has shed considerable light on the significance of such factors as age, culture, and personality in the etiology of prejudice and discrimination. In recent years solutions of some of the problems have been sought more and more in the study of children. Where, if not early in life, can the origins and processes of dislikes of racial, religious, and ethnic outgroups best be unravelled? The age at which this antipathy appears, its functions in the child's personality development and socialization, and the roles of different social institutions in transmitting or hindering it are issues with implications for all age groups. It is also felt that if intergroup prejudice and discrimination can be controlled and prevented early in life, then the solution of the problem is within easy reach.

In the article that follows, Miriam Reimann traces a cross-section of social psychological studies that have considered the question of prejudice and discrimination in children. What is its genesis among them? What are the etiological factors? In what ways do children express their antagonism against members of other groups? Special attention is given to the theories and researches of Lasker, Minard, Zeligs, Frenkel-Brunswik, Rokeach, Axline, Horowitz, Radke, Trager and Davis, and Allport. In conclusion, Reimann outlines further tasks in research on the intergroup behavior of children.

8. HOW CHILDREN BECOME PREJUDICED
BY *Miriam Reimann* *

A GROUP of seven-year-olds at a progressive school were reporting what they had done over their Thanksgiving vacation. A dark-skinned Negro boy, one of the most popular children in the class, said he had gone to watch television at the home of his uncle, Jackie Robinson.

"That's impossible! His uncle can't be Jackie Robinson," a white boy shouts out.

"Why is it impossible?" the teacher asks.

"Because Jackie Robinson is colored!"

The seven-year-old already knew that "colored" meant something to the world, but it meant nothing concrete to him; and his bizarre confusion is typical of children's awareness of race. But his ability to use such general terms as "colored" will grow as he grows; in a year or so he will know that Jackie Robinson is colored, and that his schoolmate is colored, too. Whether he will also be "prejudiced" toward Jackie Robinson and his schoolmate, and just what his "prejudice" will consist of— these are more difficult questions.

In the last fifteen years, psychologists and sociologists have been exploring the origins and development of children's attitudes to "minority" groups. In the long run, sound intercultural education programs, designed to reduce prejudice and increase the rational acceptance of differences, will have to be built on such knowledge. But the results of research are now fragmentized into a great many articles published in scientific journals, much of it unknown to the thousands of teachers and community leaders concerned with developing intercultural education. Moreover, for all the effort so far expanded, our knowledge is still very incomplete, and researchers' conclusions are, or appear to be, contradictory.

Four groups of questions are asked by those studying prejudice in children:

* Miriam Reimann, "How Children Become Prejudiced," *Commentary,* XI (January 1951), 88–94. Reprinted by permission.

(1) At what age do signs of prejudice appear among children? Does prejudice increase or abate with age? And what are the usual manifestations of prejudice at various age levels?

(2) Is prejudice in children a social habit acquired from the culture, or is it largely a compensation for personal insecurity springing from the needs and defects of the individual personality?

(3) What social experiences most affect children's group attitudes? The conscious lessons in tolerance of a teacher? The unconscious lessons of prejudiced parents and other adults? The unthinking remarks of other children? How does the child handle the contradictions between the viewpoints of teachers, parents, and other children?

(4) What can be done about children's prejudices? Does organized contact—in school or clubs—with members of minority groups prevent the acceptance of prejudiced stereotypes? What techniques might schools adopt for the prevention or elimination of childhood prejudices?

Some answers to the first set of questions can be found in Bruno Lasker's *Race Attitudes in Children* (Holt, 1929), an impressive collection of anecdotal material and speculations about children, assembled from adults in all parts of the country. This book was not an attempt to "measure" childhood prejudice, nor even a proof of anything—except that children are prejudiced and in many confused ways. From all parts of the country, from school teachers, parents, social workers, and group leaders, come reports and examples of prejudiced behavior.

Lasker's informants found evidence that children were aware of other groups, and prejudiced against them, as early as in the kindergarten years. (Many educators . . . still maintain that few children under eight or ten even recognize group or color differences. Lasker's conclusions, however, have been supported by the work of later investigators in the field, notably that of Radke, Davis, and Trager, discussed below. And what many adults take to be innocence on the part of young children may be rather a sophisticated reluctance to exhibit what is officially forbidden.) Lasker observed that what we might consider prejudice is variously signified in various age groups: "The small child is more apt to exhibit signs of fear, the child of early school age teasing and combativeness, either associated with or soon followed by a sense of ridicule— more amused than malicious—for strangers in appearance, language or manners. . . ."

Prejudiced attitudes, Lasker generalized, are not deliberately taught but are transmitted without conscious intention to the growing child by parents and other adults, and children. (Later, Eugene L. and Ruth E. Horowitz showed that the parents of prejudiced children in Tennessee specifically disclaimed teaching their children prejudice, and that older children denied their parents had had any role in forming their attitudes —"Development of Social Attitudes in Children," *Sociometry,* 1938.)

Indeed, it appeared to Lasker that prejudice flourished *despite* the formal ideology of racial equality fostered in many public schools. A Midwestern high school teacher, who is quoted often in the book, claimed that "it is quite practicable to eliminate race prejudice as an active force in school matters," but that even the complete absence of racial discrimination within the school had nothing to do with what the children did outside the school. Colored and white boys formed distinct groups on the street during noon hours. "It is a question with me," this teacher concluded, "whether mixed education is likely to touch the social separation of the races." Another Midwestern teacher reported the same phenomenon in the primary grades. In their school games the children chose foreigners as partners as often as any others, but their choice of partners when they were unsupervised—while leaving the building or on the playground—was not so "democratic." Thus, even at the ages of five to eight, these children had learned the niceties characteristic of prejudiced but well-mannered adults.

Among adolescents, Lasker found that the split between "official" and actual behavior widened. On the one hand, adolescents have a deeper understanding of history and of the ideals of the American creed. On the other, their more conscious competitiveness in scholarship and in sports, and their awareness of the sexual implications of intergroup mixing, predispose them to greater prejudice.

Lasker observed, on the basis of this and other evidence, that it is questionable whether individual contacts with members of other groups effectively offset other, prejudice-forming influences. . . . The public school system is commonly supposed to be America's great democratizing influence. But clearly the unsegregated school is not the only or major influence shaping the child's attitudes on race. If Lasker's premise of the unconscious learning of prejudice is correct, one might have to borrow a concept from psychoanalysis and consider whether the best way to combat children's prejudices is not by revelation of the sources of their prejudices rather than simply by ideological counter-propaganda. Or perhaps we should look toward a change in the social situation that creates these attitudes.

Dr. Lasker's book was frankly exploratory. A later attack on the problem concentrated on the question: How does the child reconcile conflicting influences? This study was R. D. Minard's *Race Attitudes of Iowa Children* (University of Iowa, 1931). Minard gave a verbal questionnaire to 1,641 Iowa children from grades seven to twelve. The questions asked were of two types: those requiring a judgment of the behavior of fictional persons, and those requiring the subject to indicate how he would act in hypothetical situations.

A typical question of the first category ran: "A young lady belonged to a sorority at a state university. There was a faint trace of Negro blood in her ancestry, although no one would ever have suspected the fact from her appearance, and the young lady was herself unaware of the fact. The truth was revealed by accident. After the discovery, it was suggested that she resign from the sorority, and she did so. *Question:* Ought this young lady to have been asked to resign from the sorority?"

Questions of the second type inquired if the subject would just as soon have a trace of Negro blood that didn't show, or if the subject would just as soon marry a person who did have such a trace.

The interesting fact revealed in this study is that, as the children got older, their objective *judgments* of situations involving members of minority groups (that is, their answers to questions of the first type) became more tolerant, but their *personal responses* (that is, their answers to questions of the second type) indicated greater prejudice. Apparently their personal emotional responses were somehow immune to their intellectualized attitudes. . . .

We can observe how the growing child's attitudes toward minority groups become immunized to official ideology by looking at another study, which tested the attitudes of some twelve-year-old children in Cincinnati in 1931, and retested them in succeeding years (Rose Zeligs, "Children's Intergroup Attitudes," *Journal of Genetic Psychology,* 1948). Dr. Zeligs concluded that race and nationality prejudices seem to be supported and perpetuated by patterns and stereotypes "deeply ingrained in our children's social environment and . . . molding their attitude." It is especially interesting to observe in the following series of responses how one girl's prejudiced feelings were rationalized and reconciled with other conflicting feelings and opinions:

"*1931.* The Negro isn't of my race of people. Most of the time white people don't associate with Negroes. They are not clean. Some of the girls are rough and not careful when they play.

1933. I don't like the Negro race. I know the ones in our school are awful wild. They are unclean, unpleasant race to have around.

1937. In some respects I dislike the Negro intensely because of their unclean ways of living, and yet, at times I pity them because people are so prejudiced against them."

At the age of twelve, this girl gave as her first reason a strong ingroup feeling ("the Negro isn't of my race"); as her second, social requirements ("white people don't associate with Negroes"); as her third, a popular stereotype ("they are not clean"); and finally, almost as an afterthought, her personal experience ("some of the girls are rough . . ."). At the age of fourteen, she raised her personal experience to first place. At the age of eighteen her childhood stereotypes remained in force, but she had developed some conflict about allowing them completely to dominate her, and we hear the echo of the conflict when her answer implies that unprejudiced views are supposed to be part of the "American way." This very awareness, however, permits her to remain prejudiced because she now feels she has taken the demands of tolerance into account. Her prejudice is legitimized by lip service to tolerance.

In recent years the personalities of prejudiced and unprejudiced persons have been studied, and significant correlations between personality and prejudice have been found. The most intensive study on this subject was done by a research group at the University of California at Berkeley, whose work on adults is reported in *The Authoritarian Personality* (Harper, 1950). One of the authors of this work, Else Frenkel-Brunswik, also studied a group of children aged eleven to sixteen ("A Study of Prejudice in Children," *Human Relations,* 1948). And for this group, too, she found that prejudice is not an isolated sentiment but part of a complex of attitudes toward men and society; and that this general complex is in turn related to the whole emotional orientation of the individual.

Fifteen hundred children were presented with a series of about fifty slogans relating to race attitudes as well as to more general social attitudes, and on the basis of their scores were divided into an upper 25 per cent of children considered "unprejudiced" or "liberal," and a lower 25 per cent considered "prejudiced" or, in the researcher's term, "ethnocentric."

The prejudiced children tended to have what might be called a conservative and self-oriented attitude toward society. For example, answering the questions, "What is wrong with America today, and how would you change America?" ethnocentric children gave such answers as:

"Taxes on everything, and the cost of living."

"Clean up the streets—all that garbage lying around! See that everything is in order."

The unprejudiced children, on the other hand, mentioned the "atomic bomb, the condition of the Negroes in the South, the need for world peace," and so on.

Ethnocentric children tended also to be conservative in their attitudes toward the roles of the sexes in society. Prejudiced girls and boys both tended to agree that "girls should only learn things that are useful around the house." An ethnocentric girl said that when girls are around boys, they should "act like a lady, not like a bunch of hoodlums. Girls should not ask boys to date. It's not ladylike." Ethnocentric children placed a high premium on good manners, order, social approval, cleanliness. The stress on social approval and on power converge to produce an attitude of awe toward money, which is considered as having an exaggerated power for good or evil. A typical comment of a prejudiced child was: "No dollar, no friend; have a dollar, got a friend"; and the reverse of the coin: "It [money] helps make enemies. Money is the root of all evil, they say."

The prejudiced children's aversion to weakness extended to those who have power over them, their parents and their teachers, from whom they demand harsh discipline and punishment for misdemeanors and failures. "For what should the hardest punishment be administered?" elicited the following replies from some of them:

"Naturally for murder, the next is for not paying attention to her mother and father. She should be sent to a juvenile home for not paying attention to her parents."

"Talking back, not minding; for example, if you are supposed to saw a certain amount of wood in one hour and don't do it, you should be punished for it."

The ethnocentric children looked toward their parents as a source of power rather than of love. Liberal children stressed a comradely relationship to their parents.

In short, Dr. Frenkel-Brunswik concludes that the attitudes of ethnocentric children are outgrowths of their central personality, and indeed of the type of personality depicted (in adults) in *The Authoritarian Personality*—though in general it is less firmly established. Their prejudice stems from their effort toward rigid conformity to what they conceive to be the values of awe-inspiring and authoritarian figures. Their rigid conformism obstructs a flexible social attitude, and facilitates the acceptance of black-or-white group stereotypes, particularly those they see dominant in society.

This analysis applies only to the extremely prejudiced children on the one hand, and those most free of prejudice on the other. We should realize there has been no such exhaustive inquiry into the personalities and attitudes of the large group that falls into neither the upper nor the lower quarters, but is in the middle ground comprising 50 per cent of the children (although a study by Milton Rokeach, "Generalized Mental Rigidity as a Factor in Ethnocentrism," *Journal of Abnormal Psychology,* 1948, found a positive correlation among the entire population studied between prejudice and general mental rigidity). Conceivably, the study of milder prejudices might not reveal this psychological pattern linked with prejudice.

The conclusions to be drawn from the University of California study might indicate that the ethnocentric person requires psychotherapy for his prejudices. Other studies, however, suggest that the milder prejudices of children, as seen in verbal expressions and behavior, can be modified by a less intensive attack.

Virginia M. Axline ("Play Therapy and Race Conflict in Young Children," *Journal of Abnormal and Social Psychology,* 1948) has presented an extremely interesting report on a play therapy course conducted with four seven-year-old public school children, one of whom was colored. The children were what was formerly called "bad," now "disturbed," and were taken for a one-hour session once a week to a room for non-directed therapy under a trained therapist. The atmosphere was completely "permissive"—no behavior was prohibited except direct physical violence against persons.

The race problem came up five times, and did not arise at all during the last five meetings. Miss Axline reports the children's statements and actions in stenographic detail, and we see how the immediate hurt reaction of a Negro girl to verbal attacks by one of the boys eventually leads him to try to make amends. Miss Axline's conclusion was: "When one provides a stiuation wherein the children are given an opportunity to be themselves—and an opportunity to react in a very permissive situation, then it seems that they can more readily come to terms with their own attitudes and emotions; and in a face-to-face situation . . . they *can* and *do* assume responsibility for their attitudes. . . ."

But most children rarely if ever have the "opportunity to react" provided by the completely permissive situation of play therapy. It is a delicate task to elicit frank and uninhibited responses from children on a subject that is as embarrassing and taboo to them as sex used to be. To meet this problem, many psychologists have employed rather subtle and indirect approaches to the study of race attitudes.

Eugene Horowitz ("The Development of Attitude toward the Negro," *Archives of Psychology,* 1936) showed pictures of white and colored faces to comparable groups of New York City and Southern schoolboys and asked the subjects which they preferred: "Show me which you like best; show me which you would like to live next door to you," and so on. He found a continuous development of prejudice from year to year, but no significant differences in prejudice scores between the Northern and Southern groups, and no evident correlation of prejudice with the amount of contact by white subjects with Negro schoolmates. Among the groups tested was a class which had a very popular Negro boy in it, and several other classes in mixed public schools, but these did not diverge from the general results obtained. . . . Two years later, E. L. and R. E. Horowitz ("Development of Social Attitudes in Children," *Sociometry,* 1938) conducted another "show-me" study among Tennessee boys and girls, but this time pictures of both sexes as well as both races were shown. To these children, race was a more important factor than sex in their choices; that is, a white boy, presented with a picture of a white girl and a colored boy, would be more likely to prefer the white girl, although in tests (written tests requiring the subject to state whom he would prefer to sit next to) given in Northern communities, sex had been found more important than race in comparable age groups. In other words, among Northern children one's own sex is preferred to one's own race; among Southern children, one's own race is preferred to one's own sex.

The Horowitzes suggested ("Race Attitudes," in *Characteristics of the American Negro,* ed. Otto Klineberg, Harper, 1948) that while his earlier study indicates there is no apparent difference between Northern and Southern children in the prevalence of anti-Negro prejudice in the population, his later one suggests that there is a difference in the relative *weight* of prejudice in relation to other factors.

Summarizing the results of the studies reported to this point, it would appear that the questions asked at the beginning of the article might be answered in the following way:

(1) Prejudice appears during early childhood, perhaps in the preschool years, and increases with advancing age (Lasker, Minard).

(2) Prejudice seems to be instilled by the unconscious example or teaching of the social environment formed by parents, adults, and other children (Lasker and E. L. and R. E. Horowitz, 1938).

(3) Prejudice is closely tied to the basic personality of the individual (Frenkel-Brunswik).

(4) Prejudice is on the whole stronger than the counter-propaganda of democratic teachers and the influence of democratic ideology, and becomes more organized and more rigid as the child grows older (Minard, Zeligs, Horowitz). Further, prejudice does not seem to be closely dependent on personal contact with members of minority groups, for whether we study children in the North or South, or children in segregated or unsegregated classes, the pattern of prejudice is more or less the same (Horowitz).

What is implied for the educator by these theories of the source of childhood prejudices? The implications of Frenkel-Brunswik's personality-and-prejudice correlation might be that the educator is powerless to alter the consequences of unsound parent-child relationships. Another study, which adheres more closely to the social-influences line of Lasker, Horowitz and Zeligs, however, has a more hopeful view, and offers positive suggestions for possible educational techniques to deal with children's prejudices. This is the study of Marian Radke, Helen Trager, and Hadassah Davis, conducted under the auspices of the Bureau for Intercultural Education ("Social Perceptions and Attitudes of Children," *Genetic Psychology Monograph Series,* 1949). The conclusions in regard to personality and prejudice made by these authors are directly opposed to those of Frenkel-Brunswik: " . . . conformity to environmental standards and expectations rather than individual securities or insecurities would appear to be the root of the child's earliest content and valences for social groups. . . ."

Radke, Trager, and Davis presented two hundred fifty Philadelphia school children, aged five to eight, with a series of eight pictures about which they were asked to make up stories and express attitudes. In one picture, for example, a colored child is seen standing aside from a group of white children playing together. In another, two boys are seen emerging from a synagogue, while four boys stand down the street watching them.

The premise of the test is that the subjects project their own feelings and attitudes in discussing the pictures.

Many subjects at the beginning of the interview were uneasy and seemed to wish to avoid the questions of race and religion, but became actively interested when confidence in the interviewer was established. Reserve and conflict were particularly apparent among the Negro children tested; at one moment, they rejected the white group and at the next rejected their own. Jewish children valued their own group much higher than did Negro children, and expressed their valuations more emphatically than did Christian whites; they also referred to their group more frequently than did children of other groups, and almost half of the Jewish children projected "Jewish" into pictures where there was no such identification by the tester.

The study found an increase, with age, in the percentage of children expressing prejudice and showing an awareness of group tensions. The presence or absence of minority groups in the subjects' neighborhood or school had little effect on their attitudes. The authors concluded that it was not contact with minorities, but *contact with prevailing social attitudes* toward minorities, that was the foundation for prejudice.

Radke, Davis and Trager found in the children's early inhibitions and later eagerness in regard to race discussions a clue to the kind of pedagogy required. Their fears, fantasies, curiosities, and misconceptions must not be suppressed but openly discussed. "A rule of silence about differences," they wrote, "not only fails the child in not helping him to achieve a better understanding . . . but the silence may also be perceived by the child as tacit agreement with societal prejudices." The authors also argued that the specific problems of prejudice which the child meets in his school, his neighborhood, and his home must be discussed frankly. The successes of the play therapy course by Axline reported above would seem to support such a program.

The author's own inquiries into New York City educators' attitudes toward intercultural education indicate that these suggestions are not widely followed. Whether because of fear of antagonizing some members of the adult community or because of the theory that such discussions only aggravate children's prejudices, many educators carefully refrain from mentioning to the children that there are significant differences among various groups, that there is some degree of prejudice in almost every community and institution in the nation, and that the children themselves are frequently the objects or the subjects (or both) of prejudice. In many schools there seems to prevail a kind of liberal over-optimism that may be as ineffectual in intercultural education as a reactionary fatalism. The ignoring of differences is expected to lead to the early disappearance of all the problems they create. In effect, the children are told there is no real problem, at least not where they are concerned—whereas, as a matter of fact, there is.

The Philadelphia experimenters concluded that prejudice is largely a matter of social imposition upon the individual; the California group, as we saw, held that it is a response of the individual personality to inadequate social and emotional satisfactions. Both studies were carefully conducted and in neither does it appear that there were unwarranted generalizations of the empirical conclusions.

However, there is one way of reconciling the apparent contradictions of the California and Philadelphia studies while accepting their results. There is within our society a very wide range offered to the individual between tolerance and prejudice. He may choose any one of a number of positions, or several positions simultaneously or successively, without departing from what is regarded as the cultural norm. The "normally" prejudiced person accepts and perpetuates on the one hand a formal ideology of tolerance ("live and let live, equal opportunities for all, the American creed") and, on the other, a fluctuating set of invidious stereotypes. Which social attitudes he will accept as his own depends on personal as well as social factors. And within the "normal" range of prejudice and tolerance, it is probably not easy to distinguish the personality elements from the complicated interplay of social influences.

Thus for any random population—and such a random population was studied in the Philadelphia research—it is not easy to find a correlation between personality factors and prejudice. Most people will indeed pick it up "out of the air," from the "social atmosphere." And for these people, their prejudices will be virulent or mild, as the situation demands. But those persons who have really developed the kind of personality that *requires* prejudice to balance it—that is, the authoritarian personality—will develop more consistent and perhaps more violent attitudes, and will show up in studies as extremely prejudiced. Consequently, when we approach the limits of the scale of prejudice, we will find personality and prejudice linked together. From this point of view, the "liberal" child and the "ethnocentric" child, as they appear in Dr. Frenkel-Brunswik's study, are deviants from a norm of mild prejudice, since the completely secure and loving family held responsible for the former, the completely unprejudiced child, is probably as rare in our society as the completely hostile and rejecting family that is believed to produce the latter.

Whether "normally prejudiced" children can be taught finally to resolve the conflicts between a formal creed of tolerance and stereotyped prejudicial attitudes in favor of the former, is a question that educators like to answer in the affirmative, but that psychologists have not answered at all—unless we take their more general comments on attitudes. Thus, Gordon Allport writes ("Attitudes," in *A Handbook of Social Psychology,* ed. Carl Murchison, Clark University Press, 1935): "An attitude seldom changes as rapidly as a faithful following of experience would require. . . . Because they save both time and effort, stereotyped attitudes offer great resistance to change. They resist the inroads of new contradictory experience and are retained as long as they satisfy and protect the individual."

In such a situation, what is the value of intercultural education, and what type of formal education is most valuable? To my knowledge, no follow-up tests have been made on children subjected to the various programs of intercultural education. The employment of such projective techniques as those used by Radke, Davis, and Trager, on a before-and-after basis, would seem to be an excellent means of testing the effectiveness of different pedagogical procedures—including the one suggested by these authors.

The subject of children's prejudices is also deficient in another type of study—one that would consider it in a non-laboratory atmosphere, in the ordinary relations of social life, in terms of *social behavior* (physical and verbal) rather than *verbalization;* i.e., the individual's report on his behavior. The laboratory emphasis may be responsible for the fact that more general social and economic causes of prejudices have only rarely been considered.

While a few studies have failed to discover any simple correlation between economic status and prejudice, no studies—that is, in the sphere of children's prejudices—have been made on the relation of change in economic status, and particularly loss of economic security, to prejudice. Indeed, the whole larger social background of prejudice—in the school, on the street, at home—is often filled in rather shallowly, if at all, in these studies. Yet many students believe that it is only in a time of economic crisis and general insecurity, that prejudice becomes dangerous. A long-term study of the relation between economic factors and prejudice might give us some insight into the dynamics of the frightening shifts we have witnessed in our time from a relatively tolerant to a violently discriminatory social atmosphere. The fragmentary research we have summarized . . . will go on, we may hope, to fill in this social and economic setting.

EDITORIAL COMMENT

One of the questions posed in the previous selection—the socio-cultural versus the personality origins of intergroup hostility—signals the latest important development in the pursuit of answers to the etiology of our problem. As Reimann's review of research on children has made abundantly clear, the most popular version of the theory of prejudiced and unprejudiced personalities grew out of the Berkeley studies conducted by Adorno, Frenkel-Brunswik,

Levinson, and Sanford. It is best known as the theory of the "authoritarian personality."

While few would argue today that personality structure offers the sole basis for prejudice, intolerance, and discrimination, most scholars concede that it is, at the very least, an important component in the still-unknown total answer. An essay by Frenkel-Brunswik is presented below because her research testing the theory of prejudiced personalities has included both child and adult subjects, and because she has emerged as the theory's most vociferous and articulate spokesman.

It should be emphasized at the very beginning that the so-called authoritarian or prejudiced personality described by the author and her colleagues is a composite portrait, and so is its counterpart, the unprejudiced personality. Both represent extremes on a scale that measured the subjects who were studied.

9. THE AUTHORITARIAN PERSONALITY
BY *Else Frenkel-Brunswik* *

THE DISTINCT personality pattern which emerged from two Berkeley studies . . . we have chosen to call "the authoritarian personality." . . . The material evidence of the two Berkeley projects . . . takes its start from questionnaire scales designed to elicit responses to a variety of slogans or statements involving social and political attitudes, with special emphasis on "ethnocentrism"—commonly known as racial or national prejudice—including attitudes toward parents, authority, conventional values, criminality, superstition, fellow men, fate, etc. Individuals found to be either extremely high or extremely low on ethnic prejudice were subjected to further study by intensive interviews and by the so-called projective techniques, such as the Thematic Apperception Test. The interviews delved, among other matters, into the subjects' images of various social "outgroups," their spontaneous ideas and conceptions of major political and social events, of religion, of parents and childhood, of friends and of people in general, and of their experiences with, and expectations of, the other sex.

Intercombination and synopsis of results from the various methods employed show that intolerance toward one minority group correlates with

* From Else Frenkel-Brunswik, "Interaction of Psychological and Sociological Factors in Political Behavior," *The American Political Science Review*, XLVI (March 1952), 44–65. Reprinted by permission. Footnotes omitted.

intolerance toward other minority groups. This rejection of everything that is "different" goes hand in hand with an undue glorification of one's own group; it is for this reason that the term "ethnocentrism" was introduced. This attitude in turn is related to a broader socio-political outlook which can be described as a kind of pseudo-conservatism, since it combines rigid adherence to the *status quo* with readiness to use force for the restoration of what is extolled as, say, "the true American way of life." Because these various attitudes are closely interrelated, such terms as "authoritarianism," "ethnocentrism," "prejudice," and "antidemocratic" attitude will be used interchangeably throughout this presentation. . . .

1. CLINICAL DESCRIPTION

The distinct personality syndromes of the two extreme groups, those "high" and those "low" on ethnocentrism, evolve in the main from the analysis of the interviews for which the present writer was mainly responsible. The method of evaluation represents a compromise between individual case studies and quantification. As much as possible of the richness and intricacy of the material was encompassed by a number of specially instructed raters. A number of broadly conceived categories, such as submission to family and degree of aggression and repression, were set up on the basis of a preliminary survey of the interviews. Each subject was then rated on these categories by clinically trained persons who did not know whether the person in question had an authoritarian-ethnocentric or a democratic orientation; the diagnosis of attitudes toward family, sex, etc., thus was always a "blind" one.

The description which follows is a statistically substantiated composite picture; few, if any, single individuals exhibit at the same time and to a marked degree all of the traits listed under either of the two syndromes. From a psychological point of view, an overall summary of the authoritarian personality must first stress the great number of discrepancies and discontinuities—seldom conscious, to be sure—which can be found in this type of individual. The ethnocentric individual is less likely than the ethnically unprejudiced to face within himself such emotional tendencies as ambivalence, passivity, fear, aggressive feelings against parents and authorities, and . . . impulses which are considered "bad" or immoral. Because he usually fails to integrate these tendencies with the conscious image he has of himself, he rather tends to ascribe them to the outside world and to fight them there. Closely related to this tendency is his moralistic condemnation of other people. For him the world itself comes to appear as a dangerous and hostile place, to be viewed with distrust, suspicion, and cynicism. An undercurrent of panic is evident in his fear that food and other supplies may run short and that he may be left helpless in the face of danger, which he is all too ready to anticipate. Asked to retell a story in which aggressive as well as friendly characters were described, the prejudiced children as a group recalled a greater number of aggressive characters, whereas the unprejudiced children recalled a greater number of friendly characters than had been mentioned in the story originally read to them. Moreover, the total distortion of reality—here the original story —was greater among the ethnocentric children.

It is easy to understand that persons so fear-ridden will tend to be unusually manipulative and exploitative in their relations with others. Fellow men become, to borrow a term from Otto Fenichel, mainly "deliverers of goods." Thus, along with the self-centered overpersonalization of the social scene, human relationships become depersonalized. The kind of material-magic dependency just described extends not only to people and authority but also to inanimate forces; ethnocentric subjects subscribe more often to superstitious beliefs. It seems to be important for them to use devices by which they can get evil and dangerous forces to join them on their side. Such support should be considered a substitute for an underdeveloped self-reliance; and it is apparently this same feeling of helplessness, together with underlying destructive impulses, which leads the ethnocentric subject to agree more often than others with questionnaire statements which describe or predict doom and catastrophe, the spread of contagious diseases, and so forth.

The prejudiced person's attitude toward work shows an externalization similar to that just noted in his attitude toward people and animistic forces. He is indifferent toward the content of work and lays emphasis upon work mainly as a means to success and power.

Prejudiced individuals also tend to create and adopt extreme and mutually exclusive pairs of values such as dominance-submission, cleanliness-dirtiness, badness-goodness, virtue-vice, masculinity-femininity, and so forth. They consider the absoluteness of such dichotomies to be natural and eternal and so exclude the possibility of any intermediate or overlapping position. Their adherence to these delineated norms is likely to be rigid, even though it may imply restrictions and disadvantages for their own group. Thus it is that not only the prejudiced men but also the prejudiced women favor restricting women to narrowly defined fields of activity which are considered to be "feminine."

In an attempt to understand these rigidities and dependencies, we may turn to the childhood situation of our authoritarian-minded subjects. Here we find a tendency toward rigid discipline on the part of the parents. They demand that their children learn quickly the external, rigid, and superficial values which they themselves have adopted but which are beyond the comprehension of children. This insistence may be explained by the fact that faithful execution of prescribed roles and the exchange of duties and obligations is, in the families of the prejudiced, often given preference over the exchange of free-flowing affection. In telling of their parents, ethnocentric children tend to think in the category of strictness and harshness, whereas the unprejudiced tend to think primarily in terms of companionship. We are led to assume that an authoritarian home regime, which induces a relative lack of mutuality in the area of emotion and shifts emphasis on the exchange of "goods" and of material benefits without adequate development of underlying self-reliance, forms the basis for the opportunistic type of dependence of children on their parents which is described here, and that the inherent general stereotypy is an outcome of this orientation.

However, it is of great importance that, although he tends to submit to the authority of his parents on the surface level, the authoritarian child harbors an underlying resentment against them. Along with conventional, stereotypical idealization of the parents, we find indications that the child feels, without being fully aware of it, that he has been victimized by them. Frequently ethnocentric children tend to begin, when speaking of their parents, somewhat vaguely and on a note of general admiration; but the praise will likely be followed by descriptions of specific episodes of neglect, unjust discipline and the like. Fear and dependency seem not only to discourage the child from conscious criticism of his parents but further to lead to an acceptance of punishment and to an identification with the punishing authority.

It is especially the male authoritarian who seems intimidated by a threatening father figure; and we may note here that our material shows the family of the ethnocentric individual to be more often father-dominated, whereas that of the unprejudiced is more frequently mother-centered. However, since in the prejudiced home the closeness of the parent-child relationship is based more on fear than on love, and since the punishments and rewards meted out must seem inconsistent to the child, no genuine identification with parents nor real internalization of values can be achieved. . . .

In addition to the dichotomizing of the sex roles *per se* by the prejudiced, we also find among them dichotomous sex attitudes in a broader sense of the term, such as the sharp opposition of "sex" versus "marriage," of "pure" versus "low" women, and so forth. This explains why the prejudiced woman clings to a self-image of "femininity" defined by subservience to, and adulation of, men at the same time that she shows evidence of an exploitative and hostile attitude toward men. . . . .

2. PERCEPTION AND THINKING

In the foregoing we have seen that the authoritarian personality tends to resort to black-white judgments and to unqualified and unambiguous overall acceptance or rejection of other people. In his descriptions, whether of ingroup or outgroup, of parents, or of a political leader, this individual displays both stereotypy and lack of differentiation—in short, an all-or-nothing approach. His opinions are "closed" and cannot be modified; new experiences are immediately viewed from the standpoint of the old set and are classified in the same way as the earlier ones.

The rigidity of the ethnocentric person which is implied in this presentation seems to a certain extent to be a generalized personality trait. Experiments on perception and thinking carried out with the children in our study show that stimuli which are unfamiliar, ambiguous, or subject to change are experienced by the prejudiced as strange, bewildering, and disturbing. . . . Children in the group tend either to jump to premature conclusions or to hold rigidly to a familiar stimulus and to ignore the changes that may prevail. In the retelling of the story mentioned above, the ethnocentric children reproduce literally some of the phrases but misrepresent the essence of the story more often than do the unprejudiced children. Clinging to a concrete, isolated detail of reality and overgeneralizing are two alternative ways of avoiding complexity and of making things definite at the expense of the existing facts. Indeed, with the ethnocentric child, the intolerance of ambiguity seems to pervade the solving of problems ranging from those of parent-child relationship and sex roles to simple perceptual and intellectual tasks. In the course of these attempted solutions a subtle but profound distortion of reality must necessarily take place, since stereotypical categorizations can never do justice to all of the aspects of reality. . . .

Our observations have led us to believe that the adjustment of the authoritarian person is confined to narrowly circumscribed conditions. It is precisely his extreme conformity, rigidity, and need to ascribe all his own weaknesses and shortcomings to a scapegoat which account for the restricted conditions of his functioning. . . .

Concerning the democratic-minded person, it may suffice here to emphasize that he is generally better able to face uncertainties and conflicts, as indeed he must in order to master the physical and social realities. Readiness to recognize, to accept, and to master diversities, conflicts, and differences in oneself and in others, as contrasted with the need to set off clear demarcation lines, was found to be one of the most basic distinguishing criteria of the two opposite patterns in our studies.

3. SOCIAL-PSYCHOLOGICAL DESCRIPTION

We may now turn back and interpret much of what we have said about the authoritarian personality pattern in the light of a further fact, that is, his rigid conformity to cultural clichés. It must be stressed that this conformity does not consist in a genuine identification with traditional values. Our evidence points to the fact that the authoritarian person has frequently lost his roots in tradition and has made an attempt to compensate for this loss by a rather nonfunctional, forced, and rigid conformity. This surface-conformity to externalized values can be observed in a variety of spheres of life. One of the earliest expressions is to be found in his attitude toward parents. His conception of sex roles is likewise highly conventionalized, with emphasis on activity, determination, toughness, and success in the masculine ideal, and on passivity and subservience in the feminine ideal; and in all personal relationships preference is given to restricted roles rather than to vaguely defined ones. Thinking in hierarchical terms—such as dominance versus submission, orientation toward power and success, dichotomizing of sex roles, and the like—would have to be considered part of this conformity. In fact, most of the dichotomies which imply valuation, such as good and evil, strength and weakness, dirtiness and cleanliness, masculinity and femininity, can be seen as mirroring a conventional inventory of social clichés. The ethnocentric group, which desperately wants to "belong" and to be successful, acts as custodian of these distinctions, keeping them always in mind as the approved vehicles by which its most obsessively cherished goals may be reached. . . .

Because of their real or imagined marginality, some individuals feel persistently threatened with being degraded in one way or another. It is in defense against the possibility of being grouped with the underdog that identification with the privileged groups is so insistently asserted. Apparently the great number of conflicts and confusions concerning personal, sexual, and social roles are responsible for determined efforts to eliminate uncertainties in all contexts of life; yet our interview material furnishes ample evidence that chaos and violent destructiveness lurk behind the rigid surface, posing dangers to the very society to which there seems to be conformity. . . .

As mentioned above, external criteria, especially social status, are the yardsticks by which the ethnocentric individual tends to appraise people in general; these criteria furnish the grounds on which he either admires and accepts or rejects his fellow men. The ethnocentric person tends to take cognizance primarily of whether the behavior of individuals is appropriate to alleged social roles, and tends to ignore the intrinsic values of the individuals themselves. He takes social institutions so literally that his personal orientation and behavior reflect in many ways the basic structure of certain gross features of our culture. The relative uniformity in the personality structure of individuals in the ethnocentric group is derived from this adoption of status and role values. However, this does not mean that the behavior and feelings of these individuals represent our social institutions in *all* of their essential aspects. We have evidence that, in their reactions to perception, thinking, and memory tasks, ethnocentric individuals show great fidelity with respect to concrete details but tend to miss the overall problems. A similar quality can be discerned in their interpretations of social institutions. Among other distortions, they tend to simplify the meaning of these institutions and interpret the predominant values too homogeneously and too absolutely in the direction of status values, ignoring other trends in the culture. In the final analysis, rigid adherence to conventional values turns out to be no more than a superstructure beneath which operate many tendencies which are self-destructive of the society to which superficial conformity has been achieved.

It was . . . psychoanalysis which introduced the differentiation between manifest and latent content, a distinction which is seen to be especially important for an understanding of the authoritarian personality. In the tradition of a pre-Freudian social psychology, we would have to take exaggerated conformity at its face value and would thus overlook the fact that it stems from feelings of social insecurity and resentment and that it can switch dramatically into its opposite. Both conformity and its reverse, chaotic upheaval, are considered by the authoritarian person to be useful means for gaining power, and he will give preference to whichever appears more likely to succeed.

4. SOCIOLOGICAL CONSIDERATIONS

In the preceding few pages we have begun to discuss some psychological findings in more nearly sociological languages. It is now appropriate to inquire whether or not the feeling of social marginality, which is so characteristic of the ethnocentric individual, is related to distinct socioeconomic factors. In an attempt to determine the sociological factors in the background of the authoritarian personality, we used a variety of approaches. A questionnaire was used to ascertain the political preferences, group memberships and incomes of our subjects. An analysis of the responses to questions on political party preference indicates that no relationship exists between ethnocentrism and preference for either the Democratic or Republican Party as such, but that New Deal Democrats and Willkie Republicans obtain significantly lower scores on ethnocentrism than do members of the traditional wings of the Democratic and Republican Parties. . . . Further analysis reveals that in the middle-class groups the relation between ethnocentrism and political preference is much closer than in working-class groups. Different individuals seem to support a given political group for different reasons, and inquiry into the basis of selection is as important as establishing group membership. There is, furthermore, a significant difference in degree of ethnocentrism between those individuals who agree with the politics of their parents and those who disagree. As we might expect from the psychological data, the subjects who disagree with their parents on politics are significantly lower on ethnocentrism than those who agree.

Economic and social stratification may to a certain degree determine party preference, but they seem to have little to do with such social and political attitudes as ethnic prejudice. We find that members of a CIO union had a slightly higher mean score on ethnocentrism than a Parent Teachers Association group composed largely of middle-class members of a relatively high educational level. Members of a women's club were substantially higher on ethnocentrism than were a group of members of the League of Women Voters. In the latter instance, neither actual class nor educational level differentiated the two groups; but such factors as upward economic mobility, pseudo-conservative values, and the like, did.

There is a slight tendency for the lowest and highest income groups to score higher than the middle-income group on ethnocentrism, while within the latter ethnocentrism seems to decrease as income increases. These relationships, however, are so tenuous as to support the hypothesis that economic factors as such are not closely related to ethnocentrism so far as individuals are concerned. These findings are in line with those of other observers to the effect that economic factors alone are insufficient to account for the occurrence of fascist movements. We must view the economic and sociological factors in the light of their meaning to the individual and to society as a whole if we are to increase their predictive values.

Over a period of time the present writer was able to collect extended data on the socio-economic history of the families of extremely ethnocentric and of non-ethnocentric children. One of the chief purposes of obtaining this material was to see whether or not the feeling of marginality which is so important to ethnocentrism is determined by sudden changes in the socio-economic status of the families. The assumption in collecting such data was that loss of status might undermine an individual's social security and that gain in status might lead to all kinds of attempts to maintain the gain. This hypothesis has been only partially confirmed in the sense that families with a long history of privileged socio-economic status seem to be on the whole less ethnocentric than families with unstable histories; but instability of status, *per se,* goes almost as often with tolerance as it does with ethnocentrism.

For the most part the families studied had been recruited from lower-middle-class and middle-class sectors of the population. As a group, the ethnocentric families do not differ to any marked degree from the more democratic-minded families in purely economic terms, i.e., difference in income, housing conditions, number of cars, radios, etc. However, within the group studied, the few individuals whose living conditions fell decidedly below middle-class standards were mostly ethnocentric and those whose conditions were definitely above them were mostly liberal. Since the neighborhood of the schools from which our subjects were drawn would indicate middle-class identification on the part of all the families studied, the differences in ethnocentrism which we observed may thus hinge upon the relation of level of status-aspiration to actual status rather than upon status *per se.*

Ethnocentrism also seems more closely related to the occupational affiliation of families than to purely economic factors. The parents and grandparents of unprejudiced children are significantly more often from professional fields, such as medicine, law, teaching, the ministry, etc., than are those of ethnocentric children. . . . In the relatively rare cases where the father or grandfather of our ethnocentric subjects comes from one of the professions, it is likely to be the engineering profession.

These results point to a certain relationship between education and freedom from prejudice. Information, and especially information along the lines of social science, is by no means directly related to economic factors, however. The crucial factor seems to be a certain psychological receptiveness accompanied by accessibility to facts. This is why experiments have shown that extensive information about minority groups does not markedly alter the beliefs of ethnocentric persons.

We find, furthermore, a higher percentage of non-ethnocentric families among the small merchants in our sample and a higher percentage of ethnocentric families among the workers. This circumstance may be an indication that the small merchant in America, in spite of the big monopolies, does not yet feel basically threatened. (In Germany, as we know, the small independent lower middle-class groups contributed the greatest number of Nazi followers.) Among employees as a whole, we find an even distribution of ethnocentric and unprejudiced families. In particular, however, the salesman, policeman, fireman, etc., are more frequently among the prejudiced, while bus drivers, accountants, and government workers are more frequently among the unprejudiced. Some of these relationships can perhaps be explained psychologically. Thus, choosing the occupation of salesman may indicate self-promoting tendencies and choosing that of policeman may reveal identification with authority and aggression. . . .

In general, the ethnocentric individual tends toward a more unstable history of work than the non-ethnocentric. He seems to be less rooted in his daily task, and there is a greater discrepancy between aspiration level and performance. . . .

While these socio-economic considerations throw some light on our problem, the fact remains that certain families or individuals accept their objective social marginality cheerfully while others develop rigid defenses against it; the latter apparently have to reject the "outgroups" in order to demonstrate that they themselves are not weak or different. Economic deprivation may be one differential factor, but there undoubtedly are others. . . .

EDITORIAL COMMENT

Prejudice toward minority groups, regardless of its reasons, form, or intensity ordinarily entails the process of stereotyping—the tendency to evaluate a person not as an individual, but in terms of his or her group membership. When one stereotypes, the essential likeness of all members of the outgroup is uncritically assumed and stressed. The belief, whether expressed or not, is in the superiority of one's own group and in the inferiority of the outgroup.

Stereotyping is often described succinctly as the process of tabloid thinking. Its function, among other things, is to simplify by reducing people and their behavior to a few clearcut traits. Walter Lippman, who originally coined the concept "stereotype" in his classic work *Public Opinion,* said at that time: "For the most part we do not first see and then define. We define first and then see." Today this process is frequently referred to in social science as "selective perception." By and large, stereotypes of the outgroup in intergroup relations are uncomplimentary; those of the ingroup are favorable.

There is probably no more convincing method to demonstrate the function of the stereotype than by a content analysis of the mass media of communication. One of the best analyses of this kind was done on magazine fiction by Berelson and Salter. The primary value of their findings, presented in the article that follows, is to reveal how much stereotyping exists even on the relatively innocuous level of communication and in what are generally reputed to be "respectable" publications.

10. MAJORITY AND MINORITY AMERICANS: AN ANALYSIS OF MAGAZINE FICTION
BY *Bernard Berelson* AND *Patricia J. Salter* *

. . . THE FIGHT against prejudice and discrimination is most likely to take place in areas where they are the most overt and intentional. But it is not only these overt and intentional areas of attack upon minority groups and support of "Americans" which serve as sources of such discrimination. Prejudice also finds its way into innocuous areas where people are exposed to them without consciousness that an ethnic problem is being raised at all.

This is a study of the latter kind of exposure to anti-minority and pro-majority discrimination: the treatment of majority and minority

* From Bernard Berelson and Patricia J. Salter, "Majority and Minority Americans: An Analysis of Magazine Fiction," *The Public Opinion Quarterly,* X (1946), 168–90. Reprinted by permission.

groups in the popular fiction appearing in mass magazines. How do people meet the various ethnic and religious groups of this country in this channel of communication, which reaches a large number of people in their relaxed, leisure hours? Are some groups presented as more important or more personable or wealthier than others? Do some groups in these stories get more of society's rewards, such as love or high position? What picture is presented of the relationships between different ethnic groups? In short, what kinds of people appear in typical magazine short stories in terms of their racial, religious, and national backgrounds, and how are they treated?

THE SAMPLE AND THE STORIES

The Sample

The object of analysis was a sample of 198 short stories published in eight of the country's most widely read magazines in 1937 and 1943. The magazines included in the study are the following: [1]

GENERAL WEEKLIES:	*Saturday Evening Post*
	Collier's
GENERAL MONTHLIES:	*American*
	Cosmopolitan
WOMEN'S:	*Woman's Home Companion*
	Ladies' Home Journal
CONFESSIONALS:	*True Story*
	True Confessions

The years 1937 and 1943 were selected in order to investigate the effect of World War II upon the fictional treatment of various groups. The standard analysis was done for a total of 185 stories—those with a United States locale or a "transferred" U.S. locale (i.e., the fifteen or so stories laid outside the United States but containing a predominantly American cast of characters). A special analysis was done for the thirteen stories in the sample which were laid in foreign countries and peopled with predominantly foreign characters. For each magazine for each year, four issues were selected at regular intervals (in order to avoid the possible bias of seasons or events), and the first, third, and fifth short stories were analyzed in each of the selected issues (in order to avoid the possible bias of placement in the magazine).[2] Serial and "short short stories" were omitted altogether.

[1] The results reported . . . are substantially the same for each magazine, so they are presented for the group as a whole.

[2] This procedure calls for a total of 192 stories, but it could not be fulfilled in seven instances, leaving a total of 185 stories actually analyzed.

The Stories

The majority of the analyzed stories were of the romantic love, boy-meets-girl type. Others dealt with family or domestic or marital problems. and there were some adventure and mystery stories. In the 1943 sample, several war-related stories appeared, but their plots were usually the standard romantic models with military personnel or settings appended, rather than treatments of wartime or military problems. On the whole, the stories were light-hearted in tone and were designed primarily if not solely for purposes of entertainment. They were chosen exclusively as a representative sample of the short stories appearing in such popular magazines and *not* with reference to their treatment of ethnic problems. . . . Almost all the stories (about 90 per cent) were laid in the contemporary world. Their locale strongly favors the East Coast, especially New York City, and discriminates against the South.

THE METHOD

The Analysis Procedure

The central problem of the study was to investigate the existence and nature of differential treatment accorded various ethnic groups in magazine fiction. The procedures and techniques of the analysis can be described in the following stages, listed here in roughly chronological order.

1. On the basis of general knowledge of such stories, supplemented by the focussed reading of a few of them, a set of hypotheses dealing with the problem at hand was formulated. For the sake of simplicity, the hypotheses were formulated in terms of two major groups—the "Anglo-Saxons" and the "foreigners"—with the understanding that the actual analysis would establish empirically the ethnic composition of these two groups in the stories. The hypotheses dealt with the frequency of appearance of various groups, their characteristics, cultural contributions, relative status positions, and social interaction. In addition, hypotheses on time and locale differences were also formulated. From time to time during the study, some of the hypotheses were modified and a few were added.

2. The conversion of the hypotheses into analytic operations took two forms, based upon two different units of analysis. The first unit was a character in the story and the second was the story as a whole. The first called for the coding of eight characteristics for each of the speaking characters (or groups) in the story.[3] The eight characteristics for which data were secured whenever possible were the following: *Role* in the story (major, submajor, minor; hero, heroine, villain); *Sex; Status position* (occupation, economic status, educational level, "class"); *Social origin*

---

[3] In the 185 stories, a total of 889 characters and groups were identifiable by racial, religious, or national origins. Of these, only 25, or less than 3 per cent were groups.

(nationality, race, religion); *Personality traits; Goals or values* (the ends the characters were trying to realize, such as economic advancement, romantic love, settled marriage state, social position, etc.); *Plus-minus position* (the approval or disapproval of the character: sympathy-hostility, liking-disliking, desirability-undesirability, pleasantness-unpleasantness, etc.); *Summary identification* by ethnic groups (using both explicit and implicit indicators).

The analysts not only checked each of these categories for each speaking character, whenever applicable, but also documented their entry with a brief summary of or quotation from the appropriate story content, which were used to standardize the indices used by the analysts for certain categories.

The second form of analysis dealt with the story as a whole. The hypotheses not covered directly by the character analysis—e.g., the hypothesis that the stories do not *explicitly* deal with problems of ethnic relationships in American life—were listed, with five possible entries for each: confirmed; refuted; both confirmed and refuted in the same story; indeterminate as between confirmation and refutation; not applicable. An entry for each hypothesis for each story was required, together with full documentation of the basis for decision.

3. After a period of instruction in the procedures of the study, the eight analysts (all graduate students in sociology) coded the same story. Differences in interpretation were discovered and minimized through redefinition of the disputed categories. In addition, the supervisor of the analysts checked a random sample of each analyst's work during the early stages of the study and standardized analytic procedures among the workers.

4. After the analysis of the story had been completed, codes were inductively constructed for the "open" categories in the character analysis, such as goals and traits. The codes were based upon a total of about a third of the analysis sheets; at about that point, additional analyses failed to yield additional categories for the code. The character analysis was coded for transfer to punch cards. The story analysis was hand-tallied because of the progressive re-definition of hypotheses in the course of the study and the necessity for standardization.

So much for the procedures. Now let us turn to the findings of the study. Did magazine short stories "prefer" some kinds of people to other kinds? If so, how did such preferential treatment operate? We shall present the results of our analysis in five main sections:

The distribution of the characters
Their role
Their appearance
Their status
Their goals.

DISTRIBUTION OF CHARACTERS

What was the composition of the fictional population? What groups of people appeared more and less frequently in the stories? The brief answer is that characters identifiable only as "Americans" more than filled the center of the stage.

The Americans and the Field

Of all the identifiable speaking characters, fully 84% were presented just as Americans (Table 1). The others were about equally divided between the various American minorities on the one hand and various foreign groups on the other. The nearly 200 stories, containing nearly 900 identifiable characters, included only sixteen Negroes and only ten Jews. On the whole, this small number of minority and foreign characters is spread very thin throughout the stories. Very seldom did more than one of them appear in a single story. They typically filled isolated roles in order to provide background or "tone" or some other specialized function within the stories.

But what about the ethnic composition of the characters as compared to the ethnic composition of the people of the United States? Perhaps the distribution of the fictional characters simply reflected census statistics. Actually, however, census data only accentuate the differential treatment accorded "natives" and "minorities" in the stories. Although the "minorities" (as here defined) make up 40% of the population of the United States, they make up only 10% of the population of the short stories. Every "minority" group appears less frequently in the stories than in the country. Only the "Americans" appear more frequently.

Thus we start with a fundamental conclusion: in popular magazine short stories laid in the United States, minority and foreign groups were seldom represented. The American minorities appeared much less frequently in magazine fiction than in the population. Overwhelming attention was given to the "Americans." The stage and the spotlight belonged to them.

The Three Basic Groups of Characters

Three ethnic groups of characters in these stories were accorded differential treatment. The first group is composed of *The Americans*—white Protestants with no distinguishable ancestry of foreign origin. They are called "The Americans" here because that is the stereotypic designation for this type of "unadulterated" person.

Not all the non-Americans were treated alike, and the other two groups are composed of sub-groups within the minorities, and foreigners. The basic distinction is *not* that between all American minorities on the one hand and all foreigners on the other; these two groups were approved and disapproved to the same extent. Rather, the important distinction appeared between those American hyphenates and foreigners with Anglo-Saxon and Nordic backgrounds, on the one hand, and the Jews, the Negroes, and the hyphenates and foreigners with other European, Latin-

TABLE 1

MINORITY AND FOREIGN GROUPS IN MAGAZINE SHORT STORIES ARE DWARFED
BY *The American* GIANT [4]

"Americans"		84%
American Minorities		8.5
Anglo-Saxon and Nordic Hyphenates	3.0%	
Other Hyphenates	2.5	
Negroes	2.0	
Jews	1.0	
Foreigners		7.5
Anglo-Saxon and Nordic Groups	4.0	
Other Foreign Groups	3.5	
Total Number of Identifiable Characters (equalling 100%)	889	

American, and Oriental backgrounds, on the other. On all the important considerations, the former group showed up to better advantage than the latter.

Accordingly, the findings shall be presented as comparisons of these three groups:

1. *The Americans*—84% of the total group of characters
2. Anglo-Saxon and Nordic minorities and foreigners (abbreviated *The AS & Ns*)—7% of the total
3. Other minorities and foreigners—Jews, Negroes, Italians, Germans, Poles, Orientals, etc. (abbreviated *The Others*)—9% of the total.

Since World War II did not serve to increase or otherwise modify

[4] Since relatively few of the characters were explicitly identified by national origin, it was necessary to classify them by other indicators. The following sources of identification were used (the total is more than 100% because some characters were identified in more than one way):

Explicit Identification	21%
Identified by: Name	58
Language	21
Appearance	17
Position	8
Other indicators	2

In both the American minority and the foreign groups the following classification is used:

Anglo-Saxon and Nordic: English, Irish, Scotch, Canadian, Scandinavian (Norwegian, Swedish, Finnish, Danish); *Other:* German, Polish, Italian, Russian, Austrian, Czech, Portuguese, Spanish, Latin-American, Oriental.

the treatment of minority and foreign characters in these stories, the data reported in this study include both the 1937 and the 1943 samples.[5]

THE ROLES OF THE CHARACTERS

The characters in these stories play all sorts of parts, ranging from the central and highly approved figure appearing throughout the action to the marginal and unsympathetic figure appearing only for a few lines. What about the importance to the story of our three basic groups of characters?

The Majors and the Minors

The characters in these stories can be conveniently classified into three groups—major, sub-major, minor—in terms of their importance to the story (as measured by the amount of attention given to them). Those playing the most important roles, i.e., given the most space, are the major characters. The characters given a medium amount of space in the stories are the sub-major and those who appear in incidental roles are the minor characters.

TABLE 2

The Americans APPEARED MORE OFTEN IN THE MAJOR ROLES

	The Americans	The AS & Ns	The Others
Major characters	52%	38%	30%
Sub-major characters	16	18	14
Minor characters	32	44	56
Total No. of Identifiable Characters (equalling 100%)	745	61	77

The Americans appeared as major characters just over half the time and as minor characters only about a third of the time (Table 2). But *The AS & Ns* appeared slightly more frequently in minor roles than major, and *The Others* much more frequently. Not only did *The Americans* appear more often than the rest, but they also got more than their share of the important roles. When *The AS & Ns* and *The Others* did get into the stories, they were placed in smaller roles.

The heroes and heroines occupy the best roles of all. Again *The Americans* furnished more than their share, and so did *The AS & Ns*. About 35% of all *The Americans* and 31% of *The AS & Ns* were heroes or heroines, as against only 10% of *The Others*. In other words, the

[5] Only about 5% of the stories in these magazines were laid in foreign countries. In such stories, too, the Americans and the Anglo-Saxons received preferential treatment. If anything, the descriptions of the foreigners were even more stereotyped in these stories than in those laid in the United States.

heroes or heroines in these stories were almost exclusively either of "pure" American or else of Anglo-Saxon or Nordic stock. *The Others*—Italian-Americans, Jews, Negroes, *et al.,*—rarely reached such lofty positions.

The Approved and the Disapproved

Similarly, the characters can be differentiated on the basis of the approval or disapproval attached to their roles in the stories. The approved characters were likeable, personable, wise, desirable, respectable, honest, upright; the disapproved characters were the opposite. In such "light" fiction as these magazine stories—which are entertaining and pleasant rather than "realistic" or "serious"—the large majority of the characters are approved. This was true, in this sample, for all three groups—but not equally true (Table 3). Here *The Americans* and *The AS & Ns* were approved more often than *The Others*. Incidentally, the heavy appearance of neutral characters among the minority and foreign groups reflects the colorless roles to which they were assigned.

TABLE 3

THE CHARACTERS WERE DIFFERENTIATED BY THEIR APPROVAL IN THE STORIES, WITH *The Others* THE LEAST APPROVED OF ALL

	The Americans	The As & Ns	The Others
Approved characters	80%	78%	62%
Neutral characters	4	14	14
Disapproved characters	16	8	24
Total No. of Identifiable Characters (equalling 100%)[6]	726	60	77

This tendency of the minority and foreign groups to draw minor, less approved roles and seldom to reach the positions of hero or heroine obviously places serious limitations on the extent to which their personalities can be developed. Space limitations, together with the general lack of sophistication of these stories, impose a low level of complexity for all characters, and have a particularly strong impact upon the minority and foreign groups. Since they were more often hand-maidens to the plot, they must more often be one-dimensional in personality. They were usually developed only in that aspect of their personalities necessary to their dramatic function, namely, the most obvious or sterotypic aspect which made the author's point facilely and quickly.

Indeed, some of the minor non-Americans, falling even lower on a scale of personalities-in-their-own-right, came to serve the function of *things* in the stories. That is, they merely provided atmosphere and mood

[6] These figures are not exactly alike from table to table because of varying numbers of indeterminate characters for the different categories.

or dramatized the broadminded or cosmopolitan nature of *The Americans*. A typical case, for example, was the American heroine who was seen "talking charmingly to the quaint Italian flower vendor," who in that sentence fulfilled his role in the story.

THE APPEARANCE OF THE CHARACTERS

By its nature, this sort of magazine fiction capitalizes on quick stereotypic delineations of characters. Such delineations apply to most of the characters in the stories—whether major or minor, approved or disapproved, American or not. The easy description of personality *types* which are considered desirable or acceptable, rather than the difficult and complicated elaboration of an individual *personality,* is the custom. As a result, some facets of the characters—those which are thought to be representative or at least familiar to a wide audience—are often made to serve as the complete personality.

For example, the American heroes in the stories were typically tall, blonde, and handsome in the best Hollywood tradition, and the American heroines were stereotyped in similar fashion. Other American characters were similarly drawn from standard patterns—the "darling" Southern girl, the "stalwart" college athlete, the "efficient" career girl, the "modern" housewife and mother. However, such stereotypes are seldom invidious or even implicitly disparaging and, more important, they are not attached to socially distinctive groups in the sense in which that term applies to Negroes or Jews or Italian-Americans.

But this function of the stereotype to compress the members of a group into a common mold operates in these stories not only artistically as the enemy of individuality in fictional characters. When the stereotype applies to ethnic groups like Negroes or Jews or Italian-Americans, it also operates socially as a stimulus of xenophobia. Studies of popular attitudes have repeatedly shown that people hold certain settled opinions about the traits and behavior of members of "outgroups"—mental pictures of what other "different" kinds of people believe and do. Such stereotypes, to which they think the others actually correspond, may arise from personal contact with some individuals in the other group, or from general hearsay, or from reading and listening, or from some other source. But whatever their source, their function is to label the "outsider" as an outsider, so that he may be easily identified, appropriately reacted to, and conveniently rejected.

Minority and Foreign Characters Described Stereotypically

The representatives of minority and foreign groups were usually tailored to the stereotypic dimensions of their respective groups. Of all the stories including one or more minority or foreign characters, familiar and usually disparaging stereotypic descriptions were employed in fully three-fourths.[7]

Stereotypes were found for virtually every minority and foreign group in the fictional population. The Negro, the Irishman, and the Italian appeared most frequently in this connection, but many others were given the same sort of treatment: Jews, Poles, Filipinos, French, Chinese, Scandinavians, and even South Sea island natives. (Of the very few non-stereotypic descriptions, half involved Canadians, the out-group closest to *The Americans*.) The following are only a few examples of the stereotypic treatment found in the sample of stories:

The amusingly ignorant Negro: Rosemary is a "generously upholstered" maid who "cackles" and "rocks back and forth from her rounded hips." Her "golden eye-teeth" reveal themselves "in an affectionate smile, her flat feet toed out at a forty-five degree angle, her bulgy body solid enough but looking perilously safety-pinned together." She leaves a note for her mistress: " 'I taken the gray evening dress like you said. Will leave it at the diars on my way home tonite. I allso taken some of your lonjourey and your lecktrick ion because I got time to do some wash on my oather job. Will bring the ion in the mourning. If you needed it tonite you find me att my oather place till 8 clock.' "

The Italian gangster: Louie di Paolo, an amiable racketeer with a debt of loyalty to an heiress, furnishes her with money and a kidnapping so that she can get her own way with a young man. Louie is "a sinister-looking individual with a white scar over one eye . . . known as Blackie, Two Rod, and Smart 'Em Up in various police precincts, and among the underworld citizenry. . . ." Says he: "'Beer was my racket. I made my pile and been layin' low ever since. If you want twenty-five G's, all I got to do is stick up my own safe-deposit box.' " He drives "a coupe with bulletproof glass and a specially built steel body, ready for anything."

The sly and shrewd Jew: Jew Jake, manager of a troop of barnstorming stunt flyers, shows greater concern for money than for the safety of his employees. He has an "ungainly and corpulent figure" and he rubs his hands "in a familiar and excited gesture." In answer to his question, " 'Maybe you'd like to make five bucks easy?' " the hero says: " 'Jake, you would not put out five bucks for anything less than a suicide.' " Another character says: " 'You ought to know the way Jake is. He'd like it better if I did not pull it (the parachute cord) at all. It would give the customers a thrill.' "

The emotional Irish: Ellen, an Irish cook, is overwhelmed by her

[7] A character delineation was accepted as a stereotype when a sizeable proportion of the American public would have identified it as such, according to our assumption based upon knowledge of the experimental studies. The examples cited in the text are typical illustrations.

first sight of the new baby: "Ellen—who, being a Celt, was easily moved—flew out of the kitchen, saw a fraction of David's face, and burst into a flood of tears."

The primitive and "backward" Pole: A Polish-American girl thinks of escape from her national community. "I began to despise our way of life. . . . The American men did not value a wife who could work all day on her knees at his side, taking only a day or two off to bear a child. They love the weakness, not the strength in their women; love the job of looking after and supporting them. . . ."

In addition to these, there are the humorous Chinese servant, the correct Filipino houseboy, the volatile Latins, the extravagantly romantic Frenchman, the hard-working and thrifty Scandinavian. And in most of the cases, there is also a patronizing tone in these stereotypic descriptions of minority and foreign characters.

THE STATUS OF THE CHARACTERS

Now let us turn to the characters' position in the socio-economic hierarchy. Did differences appear between *The Americans* and the rest in the possession of man's worldly goods? What kinds of jobs were held by what kinds of people? What sort of social interaction, if any, occurred between different groups of characters?

Status-Possessed and Deserved

The general economic level of characters in these stories was assessed as an interviewer for an opinion survey would assess the economic level of a respondent—by the person's appearance, clothes, home, possessions, etc. The characters were classified on four levels, designated A, B, C, and D. The A people have the most money, influence and prestige and the D people have the least.

Again, *The Americans* showed to better advantage than *The AS & Ns* or *The Others* (Table 4). Almost three-fourths of the former fell on the upper two levels of this status index as against less than half of the latter. This simple index reflects substantial differences in characters' standards of living. *The Americans* lived better in various ways: they ate better food, wore better clothes, resided in better homes, and generally enjoyed more material conveniences and luxury possessions.

Not only that, they also seemed to *deserve* their higher status; it was usually taken for granted. People can achieve wealth, power and prestige in a variety of ways—through fortunate birth or fortunate marriage or hard work or crooked dealing or luck. In these stories, only infrequently were the sources of *The Americans'* high status positions explicitly mentioned. However, when the representatives of minority and foreign groups appeared in high status positions, *their* paths to power—whatever they

TABLE 4

The Americans ENJOYED HIGHER SOCIO-ECONOMIC STATUS
THAN THE REST [8]

Socio-Economic Status	The Americans	The AS & Ns	The Others
A	39%	24%	16%
B	33	18	28
C	23	49	37
D	5	9	19
Total No. of Identifiable characters (equalling 100%)	722	55	76

were—were more often explicitly mentioned (Table 5). In other words, the claim of *The Americans* on society's rewards was presented much less as a matter for explanation or justification. Their acceptance at the top, without elaboration, subtly suggested that they belonged there. But when the rest appeared at the top, their rise had to be explained more often, because they did not belong there.

TABLE 5

FEWER EXPLANATIONS WERE FORTHCOMING OF *The Americans'* HIGH
STATUS POSITIONS

	The Americans	The AS & Ns and The Others
Source of high status not explained in the story	78%	43%
Source of high status explained in the story	22	57
Total number of stories with characters in high status positions (equalling 100%)	93	14

Occupational Level—"Positions" and "Jobs"

The Americans also engaged in pleasanter and more desirable work than the members of minority and foreign groups. For the sake of convenience, the occupations have been grouped in a few major categories. Once more *The Americans* came off best, *The AS & Ns* next, and *The Others* worst (Table 6). Not only did *The Others* contain many more

[8] These status differences are not simply a reflection of the differences in role among our three basic groups of characters. The status differences remain even when role is held constant. The data:

	Percentage with A & B Status:	
Role	The Americans	The AS & Ns and The Others
Major	71% (387)	58% (46)
Sub-major and Minor	68% (353)	32% (94)

There was thus a stronger association between *The Americans* and high status than between major role and high status. Similarly, it can be shown that *The AS & Ns and The Others* were approved less than *The Americans* when status is held roughly constant; thus, the fact that they were approved less is not simply the result of their lower status. (Although similar control tables do not appear in the text in connection with other tables, the differences have all been tested in this way.)

TABLE 6

The Americans HAD MORE DESIRABLE OCCUPATIONS THAN
THE OTHER GROUPS [9]

	The Americans	The AS & Ns	The Others
High occupations	59%	29%	20%
Middle occupations	19	23	20
Low occupations	11	27	36
Illegal and "suspect" occupations	1	2	15
Members of the armed forces	10	19	9
Total No. of Identifiable characters (equalling 100%)	602	52	66

characters in illegal and "suspect" occupations; in addition, they were more likely to be enlisted men rather than officers in the armed forces (two-thirds of *The Others,* one-half of *The AS & Ns,* and one-fourth of *The Americans*). Thus the distinctions among the groups extend even into the military hierarchy.

Social Interaction—The Upper and the Lower

These stories contain whole networks of personal interactions, some conducted on a basis of equality but others serving to place one character in a lesser position relative to another. Such social interaction varies from the intimate to the incidental; that is, two characters can marry each other or they can have a chance meeting in a restaurant when one serves the other. How did such social interaction take place among our groups of characters?

The distribution of occupations suggests the answer. Whenever social interaction in these stories occurred *on the job,* it was the members of minority and foreign groups who were found in the subordinate roles. They were the servants, the dressmakers, the liverymen, the restaurateurs, the peddlers. The "quaint flower vendor" was Italian; Mr. Beilstein was a butcher; Mr. Casparri ran a restaurant; Silva was a Filipino houseman; Ella was an Irish cook and Hong a Chinese cook; Rosemary and Bessie and Sidonia, and many others, were Negro servants. They worked for, and served, *The Americans.*

In some cases, the minority and foreign representatives appeared subordinate to *The Americans* in non-occupational roles. For example,

[9] *The high occupations:* Business executives; the "idle rich"; parent-supported college students; lawyers, doctors, professors, ministers, architects, artists, musicians, and other professions; entertainers; major government officials; "luxury" housewives.

The middle occupations: White-collar workers, minor government officials, small businessmen, farmers, housewives who do their own housework.

The low occupations: Fishermen, skilled laborers, servants, building maintenance workers, unskilled laborers.

The "illegal" and "suspect" occupations: Racketeers, thieves, gamblers, nightclub proprietors (suspect in these stories).

an Irish mother pleaded with a wealthy American for her criminal son; an Italian gangster was slavishly devoted to an American heroine who once helped him; Tanya Verriki was an inmate of a home for delinquent girls where all the staff members were Americans. And when social interaction between *The Americans* and the rest did occur on a basis of equality, it was usually *The AS & Ns* who participated. The English girl entertained American soldiers; British army officers (aristocrats) were invited to dinner; the Irish-American flyer became his ship's hero; the Scotch-American photographer won the motion picture actress; the Irish sea captain was fully accepted and admired by his American fellows. Only occasionally did *The Americans* associate with *The Others* on an equal basis and even in such cases it was usually the former who monopolized the spotlight.

But the acid test for personal relations is courtship and marriage. Who married whom in these stories? What boys won what girls? The distribution of marriages and successful courtships in these stories, closely paralleling the distribution of characters, reveals the slight extent to which *The Americans* courted or married members of minority and foreign groups (Table 7). It also shows the still smaller extent to which either *The Americans* or *The AS & Ns* courted or married *The Others*. Interlove and inter-marriage were not sanctioned in magazine fiction.

TABLE 7

ON THE WHOLE, COURTSHIP AND MARRIAGE WERE INTRA-GROUP

Love or Marriage Partners	Frequency
The Americans—The Americans	85%
The Americans—The AS & Ns	5
The Americans—The Others	4
The AS & Ns—The AS & Ns	3
The AS & Ns—The Others	2
The Others—The Others	1
Total identifiable courtships and marriages (equalling 100%)	153

In sum, then, not only did *The Americans* play the leading roles in the stories. In addition, they were also represented as getting more of the world's material values and they occupied the superordinate roles in most of the human relationships. They made more money, lived more comfortably, had better occupations, gave more orders. In these stories, the world belonged to them, and they ran it.

THE GOALS OF THE CHARACTERS

Finally, what were the different groups of characters striving for in these stories? What did they want from life? People in magazine fiction pursue a variety of goals—romantic love, settled marriages, money, power, prestige, idealism, and a few more. These goals were classified into two broad categories—"heart" goals, which are emotional and effective, and "head" goals, which are rational and calculating. These specific goals subsumed under each category, and the frequency with which they appeared, are these:

"Heart" Goals	"Head" Goals
ROMANTIC LOVE (231)	SOLUTION OF AN IMMEDIATE CONCRETE PROBLEM (94)
SETTLED MARRIAGE STATE (190)	
IDEALISM (74)	SELF-ADVANCEMENT (92)
AFFECTION AND EMOTIONAL SECURITY (62)	MONEY AND MATERIAL GOODS (58)
	ECONOMIC AND SOCIAL SECURITY (51)
PATRIOTISM (57)	
ADVENTURE (20)	POWER AND DOMINANCE (22)
JUSTICE (9)	
INDEPENDENCE (8)	

The "heart" goals are "in the clouds" and the "head" goals are "down-to-earth." In these stories, *The Americans* were less encumbered with such down-to-earth goals (Table 8). Their goals were more frequently pleasant and idealistic and "pure." Particularly *The Others* were bound to mundane and calculating aims.

TABLE 8

The Americans PURSUE "HEART" GOALS MORE THAN THE OTHER TWO GROUPS

	The Americans	The AS & Ns	The Others
"Heart" goals	69%	61%	49%
"Head" goals	31	39	51
Total Number of Identifiable Goals (equalling 100%)			

SUMMING UP

This concludes the analysis of the differential treatment of characters in magazine fiction. On the whole, life in the United States as reflected in these stories was lived differently by our three basic groups. On almost every index—frequency, role, delineation, status, goals—*The Americans* received better treatment, both qualitatively and quantitatively, than the minority and foreign groups. And within the latter, a preference operated in behalf of *The AS & Ns*. The rules seem to be that the character receives better treatment the closer he is to the norm of *The American,* i.e., white, Protestant, English-speaking, Anglo-Saxon. Common ancestry and common characteristics are decisive.

And even within *The Others* some kinds of people came off better than others. The minority and foreign groups from the other European and Oriental countries, deprived as they were, received preferential treatment in these stories over two critical American minorities—the Negroes and the Jews. On several characteristics this distinction held up. The Negroes and Jews never appeared as heroes and heroines. No Negroes or Jews were depicted as members of the armed forces. They had the lowest occupational rating. They constituted the only group with more disapproved than approved traits. In short, of all the distinguishable groups of characters in magazine fiction, the Negroes and the Jews were depicted least favorably.

INTENT AND EFFECT

Such a description of magazine fiction (or of any other communication content) supports two sets of interpretations. One set deals with the *intent* behind the communication; how did it get that way? The second set deals with the *effects* of the communication; what difference does it make in the readers' attitudes? The communication itself—in this case short stories in popular magazines—occupies a midway position between the writers and the readers.

Presumable Intents

How do these stories happen to be written in this way? We can undoubtedly discount at once any malice on the part of the writers and editors responsible for these stories.

First, it is a convenient method of writing. Such short stories call for brief, compact plots in which the action begins immediately and moves rapidly, and any techniques which facilitate "getting the character across" easily and immediately are at a premium. Thus, many stock roles must be filled by stock characters, and they are often conveniently found in minority groups. For example, whenever the plot requires a gangster, it is the simple and "natural" thing to cast an Italian in the role and put it up to the reader to fill in the overtones for himself on the basis of the familiar stereotypes. Although this practice makes for shallow and cliché-filled writing, it does save time and space in the development of the story.

Secondly, the standard pattern for such short stories demands, and gets, conformity. Inertia on the one hand and fear of changing a "successful" formula on the other, combine to keep the stories within designated bounds. Just as certain language is proscribed, so are certain ("controversial") topics and certain uses of fictional characters. An editor or publisher who would eagerly accept another variant of the typical boy-meets-girl story starring Julie Britton and Bill Davis would not consider printing the same story if the leading figures in it were called Sadie

Horowitz and Abe Goldstein, or Lorenzina Sereno and Sebastian de Grazia.

Further, the heterogeneity of the audience to whom such stories are directed may necessitate the use of the broadest symbols of identification. As the types of readers in an audience increase in diversity, both the variety and the complexity of communicable ideas decrease. Heterogeneity breeds generality, and thus the leading characters become members of the dominant and presumably the best-recognized group.

Finally, insofar as the leading roles are taken by members of probably the most respected and certainly the most envied group in the community, these stories correspond to the historical bias of literature in centering upon the economic-, prestige-, and power-elites of every age. On the one hand they have traditionally been considered the people most worth writing about, and on the other hand, as the people most deferred to, they present a convenient focus of attention for large groups of readers who seek to identify themselves with the rich and the powerful.

Presumable Effects

These stories are probably offered and accepted purely as entertainment. Their typical effect upon readers is a respite effect; that is, they normally provide a satisfying and enjoyable vacation from daily routines and daily cares. That may be the typical effect, but it is certainly not the only one. Many communications have other than their intended effects upon readers or listeners and this is probably such a case. In all likelihood, the consistent deprivation of *The AS & Ns* and especially *The Others* in these stories, over a long period of time, serves to activate the predispositions of a hostile or even an indifferent audience. Readers with latent tendencies to assign the usual stereotypic descriptions to groups whom they do not know, or toward whom they are unsympathetic, or with whom they do not come in personal contact, can find support for their convenient tags, labels, and aggressions in such magazine fiction. And this is all the more striking as a result of the implicit comparison with *The Americans*. Thus the condition and behavior of fictional characters can readily be used to "prove" that the Negroes are lazy or ignorant, the Jews sly, the Irish superstitious, the Italians criminal, and so on.

THE IMPLICIT YES AND THE EXPLICIT NO

The nature of these stories, then, tends to perpetuate the myth of the "100% American" by differentiating, subtly and consistently, between *The Americans* and the representatives of other groups. Such differentiation in itself constitutes an implicit recognition of a "minority problem" in this country. What about the *explicit* handling of the problem in these stories? Was the direct relationship between various ethnic groups overtly discussed in these stories, and if so, how?

One of this country's favorite ideologies claims equality for the diverse national, racial, and religious strains which make up the United States. In one sense, it is "immoral" to suggest that inequality actually exists or, if that is acknowledged, that it cannot be attributed to biological factors or individual inadequacies. This ideology is not challenged in these stories. Minority differences are regularly recognized but the minorities are not *overtly* depreciated.

Of our sample of 185 stories, only four contained a direct reference of any kind to this problem area in American life. Only four brought the issue into the open:

> An Indian girl is subject to conflict between loyalty to and marriage into her own people and assimilation into the American culture. Her ambivalence is resolved by acceptance of Indian social life (marriage to an Indian) and by acceptance of material conditions characteristic of American life (clothes, household appliances, etc.). Caste lines are maintained.
>
> A Polish girl rebels against the traditional life of the American-Polish community, notably by dating an outsider. She is shamed by her people, almost loses her fiancé, acknowledges her mistake, and ends by accepting the traditional life of her community.
>
> An upper-class American girl tries to evade jury duty and is chastised: " 'This country would get into a pretty mess if a girl of the more intelligent class, why, she just checked aside and let the foreign element administrate justice in our courts.' "
>
> An "American-born" man protests against being identified with French-Canadians living in New England: " 'But I'm an American.' " A character refers to such French-Canadians as " 'kind of American—but ain't.' "

The latter two references were only incidental comments on the problem. Only the first two—involving the adjustment problems of the Indian and Polish girls—contained "serious" and extended considerations of the problem itself. And in each case, the "out-group" heroine solved her problem by remaining within her own group. In each case social assimilation was unsuccessful—although in each case the material trappings of American civilization, such as washing machines and radios, were secured. The moral for these stories was sounded by an Indian character: " 'We want to win a place among the white people by our efforts and our determination, but we can never hope to be accepted socially.' "

Thus the consistent deprivation of the minority groups is indirect;

it is present in the stories but only seldom is it directly acknowledged or its implications discussed. The readers of short stories in popular magazines are constantly exposed, implicitly, to the prejudices and stereotypes attached to minority problems in the United States. But they are almost never exposed to serious and direct presentation of the problems themselves. Minority representatives are consistently deprived within an atmosphere which acknowledges no basis for such deprivation.

Minority problems in the United States are serious and deep-rooted. They will not be solved by symbols alone, but symbols will help. So will recognition of the pervasiveness of the problems. Even here, in ephemeral fiction fashioned of sweetness and light and designed purely for entertainment and divertissement, a subtle discrimination against minorities and foreigners has found its way. Even here, there are different classes of citizenship for different classes of people.

EDITORIAL COMMENT

We have observed how readily prejudiced attitudes directed against racial, religious and ethnic groups can be detected in fiction. In this manner discrimination comes into existence, for it is the translation of prejudiced attitudes into overt behavior.

The practice of discrimination, however, is ordinarily looked upon as something more intense and overt than that found in oral and written communication. As we shall see in the subsequent section, minorities face discrimination in their work, housing, institutional life, and efforts to exercise civil rights.

One of the most painful expressions of such discrimination from the point of view of the student is found in the admission policies of many colleges and universities. The problem is usually not the complete closing of doors to particular minority groups. Instead, it is a question of how far the doors are open—whether all applicants receive equal consideration, or whether there is a restricted allotment (*numerus clausus*) for minorities.

The opportunity to discriminate occurs in at least five distinct stages in the process of an applicant seeking admission either to college or to graduate school. Each of the stages affords both direct and indirect means for identifying the applicant and discriminating against him or other members of his group. It is true that some institutions have removed direct questions about race, religion, or nationality and have done so in good faith for the purpose of eliminating such criteria in the selection of their students. But the removal of specific questions concerning group identification from application forms is no guarantee of equal treatment for all. Identification can still be made in any one or combination of the following stages: (1) letter of request for an application form, in which the name of the applicant and his or her place of residence are used for discriminatory purposes; (2) preliminary application; (3) the application form, which may require the parents' birthplace, the mother's maiden name, and a photograph of the applicant; (4) letter of recommendation from the clergyman of the candidate; and (5) personal interviews conducted by an alumni representative or by a college administrative officer.

The following selection on discrimination in college admissions is based on several research projects.

11. DISCRIMINATION IN COLLEGE ADMISSIONS BY *A. C. Ivy* AND *Irwin Ross* *

CONCRETE evidence of discriminatory practices has been provided by several recent studies of the acceptance of college applicants. The most exhaustive survey of this sort—made possible by a grant from the Anti-Defamation League of B'nai B'rith and the Vocational Service Bureau —was recently conducted for the American Council on Education by the Elmo Roper organization.

The goal of the survey was to discover "what characteristics, or combination of characteristics make a high-school graduate admissible under present-day conditions; what characteristics make him inadmissible. The special contribution of the study is its objective approach in securing answers to these questions. Instead of asking for the opinions of college admissions officers, high-school principals, or high-school students on what *would* happen to the applications of different kinds of high-school seniors, it was proposed to find out what actually *did* happen to a representative sample of applicants. . . ."

The survey was based on two large, carefully selected samples. The first was a group of 10,000 high-school students in the class of 1947, selected in proportions representative of all parts of the country and of all types of high schools—public, private, and parochial. The second group was a sampling of 5,000 students from large cities only. The survey was limited to white students, largely because so few Negroes apply to college that a huge number of interviews would have been required to produce scientifically accurate results.

Each of the students in both samples was interviewed and questioned in detail on every aspect of his college application, and *subse-*

* From A. C. Ivy and Irwin Ross, "Religion and Race: Barriers to College?" (New York: Public Affairs Committee, 1949), Pamphlet No. 153. Reprinted by permission.

quently revisited to determine the outcome of his efforts. By the time the survey was complete, a wealth of information had been collected on who wants to go to college—and who gets in.

Who Wants to Go to College?

From the national sample of 10,000 seniors, Roper discovered that approximately one-third sought a college education. Thirty-two per cent applied and expected to enroll if admitted; another three per cent had also applied but were uncertain as to whether they would actually attend.

Who were these students? As might be expected, there was a disproportionate number from the higher economic bracket, more from professional families than from farm and middle-class families. More boys than girls wanted to go to college; more Jews than Protestants; and more Protestants than Catholics. This was true of both bright and dull students, of students from well-to-do families as well as from those of moderate incomes. Sixty-eight per cent of all Jewish students applied, as compared with 35 per cent of all Protestants and 25 per cent of Catholics.

There was a good deal of pessimism among the students interviewed about their chances of getting into college. Eighteen per cent of the students who applied regarded their prospects as "only fair" and 2 per cent as "poor." Rather significant variations showed up according to religious affiliations. Only 69 per cent of the Jewish applicants thought their chances "good," as compared with 73 per cent of the Catholics and 82 per cent of the Protestants. Nevertheless, half of the Jewish students who were doubtful about their chances applied, as against 14 per cent of the Protestants and only 11 per cent of the Catholics.

Another indication of student pessimism was the fact that three out of every ten students did not apply to the college of their first choice. Equally significant was the great number of students who applied to more than one college. "By this index," the Council's study declared, "boys are slightly more insecure than girls, Jews very much more uncertain than either Protestants or Catholics, and residents of New England and Middle Atlantic states more uncertain than students in other parts of the country." This uncertainty led the Jewish students, particularly the brighter ones, to apply to several colleges in the hope of getting into one.

Who Gets into College?

A total of 87 per cent of all applicants in the Council study was accepted by a college. But the chances of being accepted were affected by a number of factors beside scholarship, including sex, geography, and religion. Specifically, it was found that:

1. Boys had more difficulty getting into colleges than girls: 90 per cent of all female applicants and only 84 per cent of the males were accepted.

2. Students who lived in the northeastern part of the country were at a great disadvantage in gaining admittance: the percentages of acceptance were 80 per cent for the Northeast, 88 per cent for the South, 90 per cent for the Far West, and 91 per cent for the Midwest.

3. Catholics had less success than either Protestants or Jews—88 per cent of all Protestant, 87 per cent of all Jewish, but only 81 per cent of all Catholic applicants were accepted.

What Happens to the Application?

The fate of individual applicants may be all-important, but it tells only a part of the story about college admission policies. More significant than the *applicant,* from the standpoint of analysis of policy, is the fate of each *application.* For each college deals only with the applications submitted to it; it makes its decisions without reference to the fortunes of the applicant elsewhere. Hence the percentage of applications that are accepted gives the best indication of whether discrimination occurs.

Now the figures become much more significant, and the discrepancies greater. To start with, we find that 72 per cent of all applications are accepted. The Northeast is at an even greater disadvantage than previously. Only 58 per cent of northeastern applications are accepted. The rate for the South is 81 per cent, for the Midwest 80 per cent, for the Far West 84 per cent.

Next to area, the most important factor in application success is academic standing: the brighter students consistently do better. Sex is also relevant: only 68 per cent of the applications from boys were accepted, as against 76 per cent from girls. This may be due, at least in part, to the fact that girl applicants tend to have a better scholastic standing. The findings also show that it is easier to get into a school close to home.

A number of other factors, generally thought to be important, have little appreciable influence on the success or failure of an application: participation in extra-curricular activities, definite plans for a career, or the level of education of the applicant's father.

Religion, however, is of crucial significance.

The Religious Factor

The national figures show the Jewish application at a startling disadvantage—and the Catholic at a somewhat lesser disadvantage. Only 56 per cent of Jewish applications are accepted, as compared with 67 per cent of the Catholic and 77 per cent of the Protestant applications. These figures, however, are somewhat misleading in the case of the Jews —for most Jewish applicants (80 per cent) come from the Northeast and that section, it will be recalled, has a much lower acceptance rate than the country as a whole.

Let us, then, look at the Northeast sample separately. It will be seen that the discrimination is not quite so severe as it seemed. Viewed regionally, the Jewish application appears to be at less disadvantage, although still in a prejudiced position. The chances of an application's being accepted are: 54 per cent for Jewish, 59 per cent for Catholic, and 61 per cent for Protestant. In the rest of the country, the Jewish application was more readily accepted. The rates are 76 per cent for Jewish, 78 per cent for Catholic, and 82 per cent for Protestant. However, Jews and Catholics still do worse than Protestants.

Several more comparisons must be made before we can conclude that the bulk of the Jewish students in the Northeast are discriminated against. For if that generalization is to hold up, we must be certain that all other factors are equal; that we are comparing groups of students of about the same academic standing, nativity, family background, and so on.

When these comparisons are made, it develops that whatever way you adjust and reassemble the data, applications made by Jews to northeastern colleges are less often accepted than those of the Protestant and Catholic. For instance, if you take applications from male students in the Northeast who are in the upper fifth of their class, you find that a Jewish application has a 53 per cent chance of acceptance, a Catholic 71 per cent, and a Protestant 74 per cent. For girls with the same academic standing, the figures are 65 per cent for Jews, 80 per cent for Catholics, and 72 per cent for Protestants.

Similarly, if we compare the acceptance of applications from native-born students in the Northeast who are in the upper fifth of their class, we find the acceptance rate for Jews is 57 per cent, for Catholics 78 per cent, and for Protestants 76 per cent.

These comparisons show that "the lowest success rate almost always belongs to Jewish high-school seniors rather than to the Catholics or Protestants. Out of thirty-one instances where the classification shows significant differences between one religious group and others, twenty-nine show the Jews in the less favorable position, one shows Jews and Protestants both with a lower rate than Catholics, and one shows the Catholic group in the worst position. *If we use the term 'discrimination' solely as an objective label for a difference in application success rates, leaving out any overtones concerning the social attitudes of the responsible college admissions officers, we can certainly say on the basis of these data that discrimination against Jewish high-school students appears evident."*

Bright Students Handicapped

As the figures are examined further, several oddities become apparent. For one thing, a Jewish youngster in the top two-fifths of his class encounters special difficulty in getting into a college of his first choice. The superior Jewish student did relatively worse, compared with non-Jews of similar grade, than the dullard. The explanation may be that the poorer student, pessimistic over his chances both because of his religion and his grades, may apply only if he has some special asset, such as a parent who previously attended the college in question.

But it is not only the bright Jewish student who is handicapped. Jewish students who seemed to have many assets—parents of the professional and executive class, parents who were well-to-do, or who themselves went to college—were frequently turned away by the college of their choice. Thus a northeastern Jewish applicant, in the upper fifth of his class, whose father attended college, has a 60 per cent chance of gaining admittance with any one application, as compared with a 74 per cent chance for a Protestant.

Geography also determines the extent of discrimination against Jews. A Jewish student has as good a chance as a Christian of comparable academic standing in gaining admittance to a college in his home city. But again the bright Jew is at a decided disadvantage, as compared with a Protestant or Catholic, when applying to colleges outside the home city or state. Larger colleges did not discriminate against superior Jewish students as did the smaller colleges. . . .

Discrimination in Graduate Schools

The position of a Jewish or Italian [Catholic] college applicant is bad enough. But he confronts a much greater degree of discrimination after he completes his undergraduate course and seeks admission to a graduate school. In innumerable cases, despite high academic qualifications, he never gets admitted anywhere. This holds for medical, engineering, law, and many other graduate schools. Frank Kingdon [1] presents a typical case history:

> "Leo, a bright and personable American lad, dreamed of becoming a great physician. . . . After graduating from Thomas Jefferson High School in New York City, he took his pre-medical course at the University of Ohio, and made an excellent scholastic record. In college, he became a member of the Student Council and the debating team, and also distinguished himself as a star track man. Upon graduation, he filed his first application for admission to a medical school and, in view of his record, he was confident of being accepted.
>
> "But his application was mysteriously turned down. He filed another, and another—at eighty-seven schools—always with the same heartbreaking result. Though the rebuffs piled up, Leo kept trying. That fall he took his M.A. degree at Yale, receiving top honors. One of the professors, impressed by his mind and personality, made a personal effort to enroll him

[1] "Discrimination in Medical Colleges," *American Mercury,* October, 1945.

in a medical school, but without success. Not one of the schools had the courage to inform Leo frankly that he was being excluded because he was a Jew.

"Frustrated everywhere, Leo gave up his dream of becoming a doctor. . . ."

Leo's experience has been shared by thousands of young people. . . . Over the years, the proportion of Jews enrolled in the nation's medical schools has fallen drastically. In a recent survey conducted by the B'nai B'rith, Jewish enrollment in fifty-seven medical colleges was compared for the years 1935 and 1946. During that period, enrollment increased by 557, but the number of Jewish students dropped by 408. In 1935, Jewish students constituted 16.1 per cent of the total roster; by 1946 the figure had fallen to 13.3 per cent.

Kingdon reported that, on the average, three out of every four non-Jewish applicants are accepted for admission—but *only one out of every thirteen Jews can enter*. Sometimes applicants with Jewish names are not even sent application blanks when they request them.

The discriminatory practices of the medical colleges are equally prevalent in other types of professional schools. In the same B'nai B'rith survey, it was found that in the case of law schools (77 out of 166 reporting) Jewish enrollment fell from 25.8 per cent in 1935 to 11.1 per cent in 1946.

In privately controlled engineering schools, Jewish enrollment dropped from 6.5 per cent to 5.6 per cent; in architecture, from 8.5 per cent to 4.4 per cent; in dentistry, from 28.5 per cent to 19.7 per cent; in social work, from 13.6 per cent to 11.1 per cent; in commerce, from 16.7 per cent to 10.7 per cent; in fine arts, from 15.5 per cent to 8.4 per cent. Jewish enrollment in journalism remained at 10.4 per cent. In nursing, it increased from 0.8 per cent to 2.6 per cent and in education from 3.1 per cent to 4.7 per cent. The only sizable increase over the eleven-year period was in osteopathy—from 9.1 to 20.3 per cent.[2]

BARS AGAINST NEGROES

The discrimination suffered by Negro students differs considerably from that of the other groups. In the first place, few Negroes, in comparison with whites, go to college. Primarily, it is poverty that keeps them out; but poor elementary preparation is also a factor. The 1940 census figures showed that only 1.3 per cent of Negroes had a four-year college education, as contrasted with 5.4 per cent of native-born whites and 2.4 per cent of foreign-born whites. Moreover, of the Negroes who do go to

[2] A more recent survey reveals that the tide of discrimination against Jewish students may be on the decline. Between 1945 and 1955, Jewish enrollment at eight Ivy League colleges rose by fifty per cent, i.e., from 15 to 22.9 per cent of the total enrollment.–ed.

college, only a small proportion go to northern colleges. Of the estimated 75,000 Negroes in college in 1947, 85 per cent were attending 105 segregated schools.

There are two reasons for this preference: Most Negroes cannot afford the fees at privately supported colleges in the North, and a good many Negro students believe they will have a fuller college life at a Negro institution. There is, of course, less of a financial obstacle to attendance at publicly supported colleges in the North, but the second factor still acts as a deterrent. The end result is that the quota system in undergraduate colleges is of much less importance to the Negro than to the Jew or Italian. (It is another matter entirely with professional schools.)

In spite of recent progress, Negro education in the South is still Jim Crow. Segregation inevitably takes a toll in psychic distress, if nothing else. But in most instances the handicap is material. Although segregation legally involves the obligation to provide "separate but equal" facilities, the equality is usually a fiction. The Negro college nearly always has less money, poorer teachers, poorer laboratories and libraries than the white college. According to the President's Commission on Higher Education, "for all types of institutions, whether publicly or privately controlled, the ratio of expenditures of institutions for whites to those of institutions for Negroes ranged from 3 to 1 in the District of Columbia to 42 to 1 in Kentucky." There are relatively few Negro institutions that offer reasonably good undergraduate, graduate, and professional training.

It so happens that the seventeen southern states which maintain segregated colleges are among the states which can afford the smallest appropriations for education, whether it be primary, secondary, or collegiate. Financing dual school systems is a substantial drain on their slender resources—the result being that the white student, like the Negro, receives a poorer education than would otherwise be the case.

The Negro is much worse off in regard to the professional and graduate school than the college—and here the quota system, as well as poor preliminary education, takes its toll. Negroes get many fewer advanced degrees than do white students. In 1940, Negro institutions granted 5,201 degrees, of which 97 per cent were bachelors, and 3 per cent masters. There were no doctorates. Of the degrees granted by white institutions, 86 per cent were bachelors, 12 per cent masters, and 2 per cent doctorates. In 1947, Negroes received only eight of the more than 3,880 Doctor of Philosophy degrees granted in the United States.

Medical schools discriminate against Negroes to a much greater extent than against Jews. There are seventy-seven medical colleges in the country. The twenty southern ones do not accept Negroes; the others admit to no exclusion policy, but actually only one-third will take Negroes. In 1946, there were 592 Negro medical students. Only 85 were enrolled in twenty non-segregated schools; the others all studied at Meharry Medical College and Howard University, both Negro institutions. These two schools annually receive a volume of applications far beyond their capacity. Howard, for instance, can accommodate 75 students in its freshman class; in 1946 and 1947 it received 1,350 applications. The Negro student faces an equally tough problem getting professional training as a dentist, pharmacist, lawyer, social worker, or engineer. A highly restrictive quota system operates in all these fields.

Bad as the situation is, it represents a vast improvement in higher education for Negroes over the past decade. An increasing number of institutions, formerly limited to white students, have admitted Negroes. . . .

THE APPLICATION BLANK

The President's Commission on Higher Education holds that a case of discrimination can be made against virtually any educational institution which includes questions about religion, race, nativity of parents, and similar data on its application forms. Obviously, a considerable amount of information is necessary if a college is to maintain an intelligent, democratic admissions policy. But some of the information requested by some colleges seems pointless unless the college intends to establish racial or religious bars.

Sometimes the college inquires forthrightly about the candidate's religion, color, or nationality. In other cases, the approach is more indirect. There is an inexplicable request for the mother's maiden name, or for the birthplaces of both parents. On the other hand, some application forms are scrupulously nondiscriminatory, but the inquisitive admissions committees pick up the required information on various supplementary forms—health blanks, the regular report from the high-school principal, and so on.

A spot check of typical practices was recently undertaken by the New York State Commission on the Need for a State University. Application forms of 125 New York State institutions were examined. A total of 67 per cent asked for a photograph; 32 per cent inquired about the applicant's religion, 63 per cent about the mother's maiden name, 53 per cent about parental birthplace, 16 per cent about race or color. Many colleges which did not ask one type of question asked another.

It is possible, of course, for a college to collect racial and religious data without making discriminatory use of them. But the practice of asking such questions inevitably arouses distrust, particularly when the means of eliciting information are indirect. It is also possible that a college may have legitimate use for such information quite apart from the admissions process. The solution here is simple: Let the statisticians collect the data after the student has been admitted rather than before.

The Connecticut Inter-Racial Commission points out that the application blank is by no means the only way by which some colleges gain information which might be used for racial or religious discrimination. The discovery can be made at five convenient stages of the application process:

1. *Letter of request for the application blank.* The name of the ap-

plicant is often sufficiently revealing; so is the place of residence, in some cases. Right at this point, the college can deny the student the chance to submit an application.

2. *Preliminary application form.* The same telltale evidence of minority affiliation. And it's a little more discreet to halt the application process here rather than at the first stage.

3. *The application form.* Various kinds of indirect questions are possible.

4. *Letters of recommendation.* An approving line from a clergyman is sometimes requested—if everything else has failed to reveal the identity of the candidate.

5. *Personal interviews.* Conducted either by college representatives or local alumni. In a half hour, an astute interviewer can discover what he wants from even the most guarded subject.

The Commission concludes: "This sequence in the processing of applications is presented as an indication that *no* institution of higher learning is operating in a vacuum with respect to racial, religious, or national origin criteria merely because it has removed a specific question on race, religion, or national origin from its application forms."

THE DEFENSES OF DISCRIMINATION

Jim Crow education is usually defended on the same grounds as is all segregation. . . . On the most sophisticated level, the defense is based on the notion that no matter how irrational the fear and distrust of the white for the Negro, prejudice must be respected; it is impossible to erase the patterns of prejudice through law; it may be catastrophic to try. In short, segregation is deplorable, but it is too deep-rooted to be eliminated by law; the process involves the changing of basic attitudes through education.

Often the crudest folk prejudices are used in defense of the Jim Crow colleges. It is said that the Negro is not capable, or worthy, of a decent education; that his presence is likely to contaminate the white college community; and that non-segregated education will also lead to the erasure of Jim Crow barriers in other fields, a prediction which takes on the qualities of a nightmare.

The arguments justifying discrimination through the quota system, however, are often more rational and are worth considering in detail.

Six main arguments are advanced in favor of minority quotas:

1. *The colleges must cater to the prejudices of the student body. Otherwise the morale of the college community will suffer irreparable damage.*

This argument assumes a degree of student prejudice that probably does not exist. Actually, students have usually proved to be more democratic than their elders. The current revolt in dozens of college fraternities over the traditional policy of excluding Negroes and Jews was sparked by the students themselves, not by the old grads or the college administrations. On the other hand, suppose we grant the assumption that the mass of white Protestant students are prejudiced. Is it the job of the colleges to endorse the ignorance of their charges—or to enlighten them? The colleges pride themselves on their role as leaders in a democratic society. Passively reflecting the prejudices of the majority is not a principle of leadership.

2. *Colleges and universities must accommodate themselves to the prejudices of the community, lest they lose status and (particularly in the case of professional schools) their students have difficulty getting jobs after graduation.*

The same observations about the colleges' leadership role are relevant here: Do the colleges want to lead the community or trail behind it? Moreover, the maintenance of a quota system does not merely reflect outside prejudice; it reinforces it. Even if the colleges wanted to abdicate their leadership, they would be unable to do so. Their practices and their values are endowed by the community with a degree of propriety such as is the portion of few other institutions in American life. The colleges inevitably *lead*. The question is, *where* do they lead?

The argument about vanishing job opportunities is based on the third point:

3. *Colleges which did not maintain quota systems would be inundated by minority group members.*

Obviously, if just a few colleges abolished the quota system, they would probably find themselves enrolling a volume of minority group members disproportionate to the population-split in the nation. But if *all* colleges—or most of them—let down the bars, there is no reason to believe that any school, or group of schools, would be flooded. As Dan W. Dodson has observed, this particular defense "is a better argument against quota systems than for them, because the quota systems of some schools create a special hardship and handicap for those schools which strive to conform to the American tradition of equal educational opportunity for all."

4. *There is simple logic, as well as rough justice, in having quotas involving the same percentages as the racial and religious divisions in the general population.*

This argument has no place in any democratic philosophy. It certainly has no basis in American tradition. We have all been brought up to believe that an individual stands on his own merits, regardless of his race or religion or the nativity of his parents. He may not be endowed with the same talent as his fellows, but he is supposedly accorded an equal opportunity to acquire the good things of life. Equality of opportunity does not square with the notion that an individual's range of choice is limited by a quota imposed by his minority status.

In America, there are supposed to be no minorities in the race for preferment. There are no laws, for instance, restricting the number of Jewish or Italian politicians, judges, or civil servants; there are no legal limitations on entry into any field of business or profession. How can it be said, then, that if Jews—for example—constitute some 4 per cent of the population, their enrollment in any institution of higher learning can properly be held to this figure? . . .

5. *Quotas are good for the minority groups—they tend to keep down the incidence of anti-Semitism, for example.*

This argument assumes that minority groups can depend on a tolerant reception only so long as their numbers are small and their conduct unobtrusive. Not only should they be seen and not heard, but they should not be seen too much. Any other line of action will wound the frail sensibilities of the majority-group members.

Merely spelling out this argument indicates its absurdity. Moreover, no noticeable anti-semitism has occurred in those privately controlled colleges where Jews make up a substantial minority of the student population. The argument presumes a lack of tolerance which does not actually exist among most students. It is also based on the fallacy that the abolition of quotas will lead to an overwhelming influx of minority-group members. This would not be the case if all—or a majority of—institutions eliminated quotas. But the major objection to this whole line of reasoning is the notion that appeasement will buy tolerance. Succumbing to bigotry has never been a way to combat it.

6. *Although geographic quotas often cause hardships to minority groups, they may be necessary if a college is to become a truly national institution.*

The American Council's survey established the fact that proportionately more students from the Northeast than from other parts of the country want to attend college. And most private colleges set up some limitations on the number of Northeasterners accepted. This action would appear unobjectionable, so long as minority and majority groups receive equal treatment.

It may be sound educational policy for a college to seek a student body representative of the country as a whole. But too often this objective serves as a subterfuge to discriminate against minority groups. Under the circumstances, the burden is on the college to demonstrate that geographic quotas are discriminatory solely in a *geographic sense.*

What Can Be Done to Abolish Discrimination?

To achieve the elimination of discrimination in education, the President's Commission on Higher Education has set forth a program of vigorous public action.

First, in regard to Negro segregation: the only long-run solution compatible with our democratic beliefs is the complete abolition of Jim Crow practices. . . . The task, however, will not be an easy one. "Deep-seated, long-standing forces of opinion and sentiment are obviously involved. Segregation laws cannot be wished away or eradicated by executive order. But influences looking to their repeal are at work; time and more vigorous effort will change public sentiment."

. . . The Negro colleges in the South must be greatly strengthened to bring them up to the standards of the white institutions. When federal funds are made available to support higher education, there should be no discrimination in their apportionment. Also recommended is the establishment of regional educational centers "attached to strong colleges and open to both white and Negro students, with broad curricular offerings and high standards of scholarship and research."

The Commission proposes another series of steps to eliminate the restrictive quota system:

1. Discriminatory questions on application blanks should be outlawed by statute.

2. State laws should be passed removing the accreditation and tax exemption of colleges and universities which are proved to discriminate on grounds of race, religion, or national origin. This is a persuasive force well within the power of every state.

3. Passage of Fair Educational Practices Acts similar to the New York State law is recommended. Under the New York legislation, in operation since September 15, 1948, discrimination on grounds of race, creed, color, or national origin is declared illegal. (Denominational institutions, however, may maintain religious qualifications for admission.) The State Commissioner of Education is empowered to receive the complaints of individuals who allegedly have suffered discrimination. The Commissioner can also initiate such complaints. An elaborate procedure for fact-finding and informal adjustment of grievances then goes into operation. If quiet persuasion is unavailing, legal compulsion can be resorted to. Public hearings, resulting in cease and desist orders, are authorized. Such orders would be enforceable through regular court proceedings; they would also be subject to judicial review. . . .

The President's Commission is well aware that reform by compulsion is regarded with distaste by many enlightened persons who abhor all forms of discrimination. They believe that voluntary change will bring more lasting results. The Commission argues cogently, however, that "the urgency of this issue in our national life, in education, and in the growing sense of grievance in the minds of all minority group members does not promise to let a satisfactory democratic outcome wait upon statements of pious intention or upon tardy voluntary action. . . . Where assurance of good conduct in other fields of public concern has not been forthcoming from citizen groups, the passage of laws to enforce good conduct has been the corrective method of a democratic society. Extension of this method into the educational field . . . is, therefore, not only a defensible measure; it is also . . . the logical next step. . . ."

iv. American Indians

ONE of the most conspicuous racial minorities in the United States is the Indians. They comprise our earliest minority group, having been forced into their subordinate status by conquest. The situation of the American Indians is one of the most serious and at the same time probably the least understood aspect of all minority problems in American society. Even among people living near the Indian reservations the extent of misconceptions about the Indian and his status as a citizen is astonishing. Indians are often arbitrarily defined as any native American who has one-half or more Indian ancestry. Actually this definition does not go far enough sociologically, for there are many Americans who are called and who consider themselves Indians with no more than a thirty-second part of Indian descent. The government shelters on its reservations for Indians large numbers of these near-whites and near-Negroes.

Estimated to number more than 400,000 at the present time, the Indians of the United States are no longer "the vanishing American." The low point in decimation of the Indian population was reached at the beginning of the twentieth century. The trend toward their extinction as a result of violent contact with conquering and disease-carrying whites has been virtually brought to a halt. The population trend among the Indians has been recently one of increase. Not only have many diseases been curtailed among them, but their birth rate is still almost twice that of the white population in the United States as a whole.

There is no typical American Indian either in physical makeup, culture, social organization, or economy. The Sioux have, on the whole, high cheekbones, straight noses, and thin lips like the Indian who appears on the nickel coin. But the faces of Shoshone Indians are round, with full lips and broad noses. Housing ranges from the picturesque reed-woven lodges of the Kickapoos to the sturdy adobe dwellings of the Pueblos. The semi-nomadic Navajo people have eight different kinds of conical hogan. Among the various ways in which Indians earn their living, farming, stock-raising, and work for wages prevail.

Most Indians in the United States are poor, for the major problem is, as it has always been since the European invasion and conquest, that of land. By 1933 Indian land holdings had dwindled to about 48,000,000 acres. Almost two thirds of the Indians at that time were landless or had land too poor in quality to provide them with a decent living. Within the next few years, through a drastic change in governmental policy toward them, 2,780,000 acres were restored. But most of the land still owned by Indians is insufficiently productive or not productive at all.

Governmental policy toward the Indians has changed from time to time. At the beginning the goal was to destroy them. Everything possible was done to turn Indian children away from all things Indian and to draw them into a European-derived culture alien to their own traditional ways. This policy succeeded only in driving them back to their own reservations confused, discontented, and bitter. More recently the policy has been to revive Indian culture and to train the Indian child for the life he or she will follow as an Indian. There has been heated controversy about this plan. Among other things, critics claim that assimilation is being delayed needlessly and that the underlying assumption appears to be that someone else must forever do the planning for the Indian.

Even though Indians have been wards of the government for more than 130 years, they are citizens and they have had the right to vote for more than a generation. Many whites persist in the belief that every Indian is a pensioner of the government. In reality, Indians are dependent upon such income as they can derive from their tribal lands plus whatever work they can obtain outside the reservation.

In the first reading of this section, Alden Stevens reviews the plight of the American Indians up through the New Deal in the third decade of this century, and describes a dynamic Indian Bureau policy in effect between 1933 and about 1950.

12. WHITHER THE AMERICAN INDIAN?
BY *Alden Stevens* *

A CENTURY AND A HALF OF DISHONOR

. . . Since the beginning of white occupation of the North American continent the Indian has been trampled upon and exploited. Treaties have been made and violated; tribes deprived of their land, their living, their customs and religion. In 1838 the Cherokees were mercilessly driven westward from their homes in North Carolina and Georgia clear across the Mississippi. A few hid out in the mountains, but only a few. It was winter, and the soldiers who drove them cared little whether they lived or died. The best thing was to get rid of them anyway. One-third of the tribe was buried or left to rot along the way.

At about the same time, on the Western plain, the fur trading posts systematically debauched the Indians with cheap liquor, cheated them of their furs and sometimes of their land. Did a tribe rebel? Soldiers came quickly and taught them their place. Usually their place was underground.

Every effort was made, over a long period of time, to get rid of the Indian; to kill him off, starve him and discourage him . . . in an effort to solve the Indian problem by eliminating the Indian. It did not work, and today the Indian is actually gaining in numbers at a rate faster than that of the white population of the United States.

When Helen Hunt Jackson wrote "A Century of Dishonor" in 1881, the fashion of making treaties with tribes, and then conveniently breaking them by writing new ones, had just been abandoned. The book tells a long story of broken promises, systematic destruction and demoralization, exploitation by traders, railroad companies and politicians. How much the book had to do with it is hard to say, but shortly after it was published a new Indian policy came into effect, based on the land needs of the tribes. This was urged by Carl Schurz and approved by Helen Hunt Jackson and other good friends of the Indian. It was recognized that ruthless destruc-

* Alden Stevens, "Whither the American Indian?" *Survey Graphic*, XXIX (March 1940), 168–74. Reprinted by permission.

tion must stop. Instead, the Indian should be assimilated, gradually losing his identity until he became indistinguishable from a white man. This done successfully, the Indian problem would disappear, for certainly the Indian was dying out at that time—or being killed off; and Indian culture would not possibly last more than a few years, anyway. As a matter of fact little was said about Indian culture, the general feeling being that there wasn't any.

The General Allotment Act was passed in 1887, and many people regarded it as the final solution of the Indian problem. Each Indian was to be given 40 to 160 acres of land, with the stipulation that it must not be sold for twenty-five years except with the consent of the government. Agents were supposed to give instruction in farming methods and help along a little during the first few years.

It is doubtful whether anyone suspected that this act would work out even one-tenth as badly as it did. In the first place the Indians were expected to adapt themselves almost immediately to a completely new way of life. The very concept of land ownership by individuals was foreign. Few of the tribes had done any farming or were interested in doing any. The facilities for educating them to the new ways were pitifully inadequate.

When all the Indians on a reservation had received their allotments, the remainder of the land was thrown open for white settlement. Nobody thought this mattered very much, since the Indians were a dying race, anyway, and would never need the land, especially now that each had a nice farm of his own. The tribes lost 20 per cent of all their land within two years. By 1933 they had lost 90 million of the 138 million acres they had when the act was passed—nearly two-thirds. "Checkerboarding" of reservations, leaving blocks of Indian land completely surrounded by white holdings, led to the gradual break-up of tribal life without the substitution of any other kind of community life. Whites more often than not regarded the Indians as inferior, and almost never would the two cultures mix.

But probably the worst feature of the allotment act was its inheritance provision. On the death of the original allottee, the land was to be divided among his heirs. Why no one thought of the way this would work out is hard to say; maybe some legislators did think of it, but they didn't do anything. Indians sometimes live a long time, and when old Charley Yellowtail dies at the age of ninety-nine, the number of heirs may be something little less than astronomical. Forty acres of land divided among, say 120 heirs, gives each just about enough room to pitch a tepee.

The Indian Bureau attempted to solve this difficulty by renting and in some cases selling the entire parcel, and dividing the proceeds among the heirs. More often than not a white man was on the other end of the deal. The Indians were left landless, and the rental checks sometimes amounted to as little as two or three cents a year. Some Indians might have these microscopic shares in a dozen or more estates. The bookkeeping was about all the Indian Bureau had time to handle.

It was an impossible situation, of course, and quite insoluble under the allotment act. Fortunately for them, the act was never applied to some groups, such as the Pueblos in New Mexico, who retained their land as tribes and lost nothing through allotment.

A DECADE OF PROGRESS

The groundwork for a change was laid in 1928, when Lewis Meriam and his associates published their Institute of Government Research report, "The Problems of Indian Administration." In this comprehensive and fundamental study, the failure of the assimilation policy was boldly drawn, and practical, specific recommendations were made. Under President Hoover, Charles Rhoads and Henry Scattergood administered the Indian Office and began making the government a helpful friend instead of a despotic manager. A good spirit of cooperation between the government and the Indians came about. New emphasis on day schools marked the beginning of a better educational policy. Tribal skepticism and the novelty of the approach slowed the work, but a new day had definitely begun.

John Collier became Commissioner of Indian Affairs in 1933. For a number of years he had headed the militant Indian Defense Association, had saved the Pueblo lands from seizure by associates of Albert B. Fall by forcing the defeat of the anti-Indian Bursum bill, and had demonstrated his devotion to the Indian cause in many other ways.

Collier's plan was to make a clean sweep of the old ways and make it possible for Indians to live as Indians until a more natural and less destructive assimilation could come about, no matter how long this might take. His first step was to get through a none-too-willing Congress the Wheeler-Howard bill, largely his own work, assisted by Nathan Margold and Felix Cohen, two Interior Department attorneys. In the end this emerged almost intact as the Indian Reorganization Act, and was the legal basis for Collier's program.

The act did not apply to any tribe which rejected it in an election, and though it did not appear that a tribe had anything to lose by accepting it, a considerable number voted it down, including the Navajo. The administration frankly urged its adoption, sometimes with a fairly high pressure campaign, but there is no evidence of discrimination against those who rejected it and nothing to cast suspicion on any of the elections. No tribe in the country has had a more comprehensive program of conservation work and general economic rehabilitation than the Navajo—but space is lacking for adequate discussion of this unique and particularly difficult situation.

REORGANIZATION

The allotment policy is ended, and while present holdings of individuals are not affected, no more allotments will be made. Indian owners of reservation land may now sell it, but only to the tribe, a provision which prevents further alienation of Indian land. Ceded lands which have neither been allotted nor settled by whites are returned to the tribe, and provision is made for small additions to Indian holdings where necessary. Management is by an elected tribal council, which (except where there is a shortage) assigns each member as much land as he can actually use. Thus, one of the worst administrative headaches is on the way to a cure, and the shrinkage of Indian holdings is halted except for some of those tribes which have rejected the Reorganization Act. It is true that the problems of the checkerboarded reservations are not solved, and most of the old difficulties of rental and division of proceeds among heirs of allottees remain. But the new policy does turn land management back to the Indian; it goes far toward stabilization of the situation. . . .

No less important than the land provisions are the sections of the Reorganization Act enabling Indians to organize, adopt a constitution, and to incorporate. These give a measure of self-government greater than ever enjoyed before, though approval of the Secretary of the Interior is still required on many important matters. The constitutions are supposed to originate with the tribes, but government lawyers have usually helped frame them, and each must be approved by the Secretary before the tribe votes acceptance or rejection.

It is the Secretary of the Interior, too, who issues a charter of incorporation when petitioned to do so. This also is subject to a vote on the reservation. Indians have never before had an opportunity to do much voting on what they wanted or didn't want, and not all tribes have taken kindly or intelligently to the democratic process thrust suddenly upon them. . . . On some reservations, such as the Hopi, the idea of an all-tribal elected council is so foreign that many Indians simply do not recognize its authority and pay little attention to its activities. Poorly educated people commonly miss the full implications of an election and ignore it. After it is over, they may resent the powers acquired by the council members and regard them simply as government stooges.

Congress is authorized to appropriate $10 million as a revolving fund from which loans may be made to these chartered corporations for the purpose of promoting the economic development of the tribes. Repayments are credited to the revolving fund and are available for new loans. It was this fund which made possible the fresh start of the Mescalero Apache tribe. The record of collections on these loans has been very good.

More than seventy-five of the tribal corporations are now functioning, with varying degrees of success, and the number continues to grow.

The Jicarillas have bought their trading post and are running it; the Chippewas run a tourist camp; the Northern Cheyennes have a very successful livestock cooperative; the Swinomish of Washington have a tribal fishing business. There are plenty of others to prove these corporations can be made to work.

So far, however, it has shown up best where a small, close-knit group is involved, but less satisfactorily on such large reservations as those of the Sioux, where distances are great and there is a certain amount of mutual distrust and jealousy between communities. . . .

In the case of the Blackfeet, the tribal council, when elected, proved to be predominantly Indians of "mixed blood," and the "full bloods" of the reservation, amounting to about 22 per cent of the population, complained that their interests were being subordinated and neglected wherever they conflicted with those of the "mixed bloods." The election system was adjusted later to insure fair representation of the minority group. The difficulty about the system is that so many Indians on large reservations— and some on small—do not have a sense of common interest. The nine Hopi villages in Arizona have a long tradition of independent action as city states, with very little cooperation or friendly feeling between them. In other cases, the desperately poor circumstances prevailing and the lack of resources to start with have caught tribes simply too run down and discouraged to put their shoulders to the wheel.

But all this new machinery gives Indians for the first time an opportunity to run their own affairs, to a limited extent it is true, but previously everything was handled by the government, and the Indians had to take it or leave it. Now a tribe, as a corporation, may purchase, operate and dispose of property, may hire counsel, engage in business enterprises of nearly any sort, and generally enjoy the legal privileges of a corporation. Management by the elected council is not always good, but at least it is management by Indians through democratic processes, and a period of adjustment to the new way must be expected to produce mistakes and failures as well as successes. . . .

INDIANS AT WORK

About 40 per cent of all Indians over ten years old are engaged for at least a part of the year in pursuits which bring in cash. Half of these are unskilled laborers, the other half do various types of semi-skilled and skilled work. Fishing brings in sizeable amounts to some tribes in the Pacific Northwest. Lumbering is carried on in Oregon, Montana, Arizona, Wisconsin and other states. The sustained yield management of timber reserves now almost universally applied should insure an income indefinitely for the relatively small number of Indians with commercial forests. Nearly all Indians are farmers or stockbreeders, and as such raise at least a part of their own food supply. The cooperatives which are springing up all over the Indian country help with marketing and do much to improve farming methods and increase production of saleable crops.

A growing source of income has been the sale of arts and crafts. This has long brought in sizeable sums to the Southwest tribes, and everyone is familiar with Navajo blankets and jewelry and with Pueblo pottery. In fact, the popularity of these products has brought out a flood of inferior factory-made imitations which has hurt the sale of authentic items. . . . Arts and crafts will never be one of the most important incomes sources except locally, but an increasing number of Indians are finding that there is money in it.

HOMES AND HEALTH

Housing has been for years as serious a problem on the Indian reservations as in city slums. Best housed are the Pueblos of New Mexico and Arizona, who escaped the destructive effects of the allotment act and early white penetration of their traditional homeland. Since they live in a mild climate, and have plenty of building materials—stone and adobe —they have managed well, and still do. On the plains it has been a different story. Nearly landless, penniless, with no way to make a living, and no satisfactory natural building materials at hand, such tribes as the Sioux, Winnebago, Cheyenne and Arapaho have lived through the cold winters in dirt hovels, tar-paper shacks, ancient tents and other makeshift dwellings for many years. . . .

Health, so closely related to housing, is also still far from satisfactory, though probably better today than it has ever been before. Somewhat better food and shelter have made a difference, particularly in the greatest Indian scourge, tuberculosis. There is some indication that Indian resistance to disease is increasing, and certainly Indian resistance to white medicine is decreasing. When the new Navajo-Hopi health center was opened . . . at Fort Defiance some of the prominent Navajo medicine men participated in the ceremonies with chants, speeches and offers of cooperation—evidence of an entirely new attitude toward the Indian Service, and one which has been brought about by the new attitude of the service itself toward the Indian. . . .

EDUCATIONAL ABOUT-FACE

The original colonies showed little concern for Indian education, although several colleges, including Dartmouth and Harvard, made provision for tuition-free admission of Indians, and the Continental Congress in 1775 employed a schoolmaster for the Delawares and made motions toward doing something for other tribes. The Revolution interrupted, and until 1819 Indian education was left entirely to a few missionary societies.

From that year to 1873, $10,000 was appropriated annually for the work, and most of this was turned over to the missions. From 1873 on, the appropriations increased fairly regularly. . . . Until 1929, Indian education was pretty much a hodgepodge. More Indians attended public schools than any other kind—this is still true. Large numbers were in mission schools. Many attended boarding schools both on and off the reservations. These were established late in the last century when the accepted theory of Indian education called for removal of the children from their parents and home life as much as possible so that they might be "civilized." Often the children were taken by force from their homes and subjected in the schools to a rigid discipline and a standardized, outmoded course of study. Half their time was devoted to school work, the other half to doing routine institutional tasks such as laundering, cleaning, wood-chopping and food preparation. Often this work was too hard and too many hours per day were devoted to it, so that it had a serious effect on health. Insufficient operating funds made the school and living standards dangerously low.

Forbidden to speak their own language in school, out of touch with family and tribal life, denied the normal experience and education needed to prepare them for life as Indians, the children would return home from school dissatisfied misfits, unable to readapt themselves to reservation life and equally unable to find a place in a white community. They had learned to read and write, but they were unfamiliar with the customs and language of their own people, and found their schooling of little use in making a living. . . .

The "about-face" in Indian education is designed to mesh with the "about-face" in general policy. Recognizing attempts to drag children from their families and "civilize" them as a total failure, the aim now is to give a basic education in the three R's without detaching them from their families, to teach hygiene and such mechanical skills as will be useful to each group. This is accomplished to an increasing extent in day schools, which are being established on as many reservations as possible. The children live at home and walk or ride to school. Native tongues are not forbidden, and an increasing number of Indians are on the teaching staffs. . . .

The truth is that the . . . Indian administration is neither as successful as its publicity says it is, nor as black and vicious a failure as the severest critics would have us believe. Many Indian problems remain unsolved, but every one has been attacked. If eddies have been stirred up, there is still a powerful current in Indian affairs, and it seems to be in a direction which gives the group an opportunity to shape its own destiny.

EDITORIAL COMMENT

The ultimate goal of governmental policy toward the American Indians at present is that they should attain economic self-sufficiency and develop skills in retaining their lands and natural resources. Presumably this will make them no more vulnerable than other Americans and enable them to compete with all. The goal also is to have the Indians assume full responsibilities of citizenship, including payment of taxes on land now held in trust for them by the government. However, in the opinion of many specialists, this is not likely to be reached any earlier than the year 2000.

In fact some critics claim there still is no firm, definitive program to reach the goal summarized above, and no rigorous timetable for achieving it. Nor, they say, is there even a real trend of policy or a vigorous drive among officials to head for it. The Bureau of Indian Affairs has been accused of arbitrary methods that inadvertently reverse the advance of the Indians toward complete self-reliance and delay the end of their paternalistic supervision by the government.

In the selection that follows, Oliver La Farge, long a student of Indian culture and problems, pleads for a "square deal" for the Indians.

13. A PLEA FOR A SQUARE DEAL FOR THE INDIANS
BY *Oliver La Farge* *

THE LATEST official figures show that there are more than 420,000 Indians (including a few Eskimos and Aleuts) in the United States and Alaska now under Federal supervision. The figure is surprising. In the early Nineteen Twenties when no one thought Indians important enough to be counted carefully, the official estimates ran around 250,000, and certainly for a long time we have assumed that they were rapidly dying out. Now we learn that they are not; on the contrary, "full-bloods" as well as "mixed-bloods" are increasing slightly more rapidly than our general population.

Of the 420,000 Indians in the United States and Alaska, now under the jurisdiction of the United States Bureau of Indian Affairs, 395,000 live in continental United States. About two-thirds (252,000) are concentrated in Oklahoma (110,000), Arizona and New Mexico (98,000) and the Dakotas (44,000). The Navajo people of the Southwest, who number about 61,000, are by far the largest single tribal group. There are 220 In-

* From Oliver La Farge, "A Plea for a Square Deal for the Indians," *The New York Times Magazine*, June 27, 1948, pp. 14, 37. Reprinted by permission.

dian reservations in twenty-six states. An unexpected contrast is that there are about 9,000 reservation Indians in New York State and only 368 in Texas.

The Indians are going to be with us for quite a while, then. They are a factor in our total citizenry. Some 25,000 of them served in the armed forces in World War II—women as well as men. . . . Many thousands served in war industries. The Marines had a special corps of Navajos who were used to communicate by radio from ship to shore in landings—as simply by talking in their own language they used an unbreakable code. . . . We should be glad to have them around.

Yet in one area their situation has become so extreme as to catch public attention. Our greatest tribe, the 60,000 Navajos, is locked by illiteracy and endemic disease into a desert reservation which can hardly support half that number. Their condition has become so shocking that we now have under consideration in Congress a program which typifies what we need throughout. This program contemplates large-scale medical assistance, the building and staffing of schools for some 17,000 children now receiving no schooling, development of resources, encouragement of industries, and general economic rehabilitation which, if carried through, will change the Navajos, perhaps in a generation, from very primitive, half-starved herdsmen into a modern people, engaging in as wide a variety of gainful pursuits as the rest of us, and moving freely in the American world. . . .

This is an extreme example, and the remedy required is equally extreme, but in lesser degree this situation is repeated among many of the once famous Plains Indian tribes of the North, and in many other sections.

We took the whole country from the Indians, leaving them tracts of land, often the poorest there was, sometimes purely worthless, on which to try to get by. We shattered the simple and satisfactory life which they had been living, and in return we inflicted upon them a vast variety of diseases, above all tuberculosis, against which they had no immunities. Conquest, despoliation, disease and mistreatment they have repaid with loyalty and patriotism. . . .

The predicament of the majority of them is a combination of ignorance and poverty, with ill-health thrown in for good measure. The areas of land, whether reservations or individual holdings, which they have been able to hang on to are too small and too poor to support them as farmers and herders, even if they were taught the most modern agricultural methods. In practice, most of them follow relatively primitive methods, partly because they receive only a fraction of the agricultural extension service extended to every white man living off the land.

In all the years that they have been under our control, the majority of them has still not been brought far enough along in literacy, command of English, and understanding of our complex and often cut-throat civilization, to be able to contemplate leaving their reservations except in desperation, to sink to the lowest slum levels of white communities.

The Indian Bureau, often mistaken, often fumbling, hampered by a magnificent inheritance of red tape, is striving with entirely inadequate funds and far too few employees to bring these hundreds of thousands up across centuries of cultural evolution to a merger with ourselves. So far the result tends to be poverty and a long frustration which ends in hopelessness and the loss of the will to struggle.

One of the reasons why Indians do not get a square deal today is that the American public not only knows almost nothing about them, but is loaded with misinformation. There is the stereotype of the Indian himself, a befeathered, half-human creature of unnatural dignity with a habit of saying "ugh!"

Indians today run from very able lawyers, doctors, businessmen, trained nurses, to people who speak no English and still retain much of their ancient way of life, although very few now wear Indian costumes except for special occasions. They are notable for their keen sense of humor, ready laughter and fondness for singing. On the whole their greatest desire is to become completely equal to white men in general education and knowledge of the world, and to compete with them on even terms.

All sorts of wild ideas exist as to the status of an Indian and the meaning of the "reservations" on which many of the Indians live. By the exploiting of these misconceptions, millions of acres of Indian land and millions of dollars of Indian money have been stolen from them, and the drive to get the rest still goes on. It is well worth taking a little space to tell what the Indian's status really is.

The average Indian lives on a reservation. This is *not* a sort of large concentration camp. No one is compelled to live on a reservation. The Indians go and come as they please. A reservation is an area of tax-exempt land, owned by the tribe, or originally so owned, and held in trust for the Indians by the United States. It cannot be taxed, levied upon, or alienated. The Indians have received these tracts of land, inadequate though they are, in recognition of their inherent right as the original settlers of this country. Obviously, tax-exempt, inalienable land, even poor land, is a valuable asset.

The Indian is a ward of the United States. Originally when we were dealing with recently conquered, resentful, warlike tribes, wardship included various restrictions upon personal freedom. . . .

As a person, the Indian is completely free. Wardship consists in the trusteeship over the reservation, and a similar trusteeship over funds which essentially derive from the reservation or from the Indians' status as Indians—that is, such funds as royalties on oil from trust lands, or damages paid to tribes for claims against the government. It also consists in the right of Indians to receive education, medical care and other such services from the Federal Government. Like reservations, then, wardship is not a restraint, but an asset. In fact, Indians as advanced as the late Vice-President Curtis retained wardship status because of the advantages involved.

It is essential to grasp these two points, because the cry of "set the Indians free" by abolishing wardship and reservations is the standard device by which the plunderers lead well-intentioned citizens to acquiesce in new raids upon the Indian estate.

"Setting the Indians free" resulted, between 1880 and 1930, when the process was halted, in the acquisition by various devices—really legalized theft—of more than 100 million acres of Indian land. . . .

Indians are citizens as well as wards. They enjoy every right of any citizen. . . . It would look, then, as if our Indians enjoyed special advantages. In theory they do. In certain areas, as in parts of Oklahoma, you will find Indians who by means of these aids and their own efforts have advanced themselves to complete equality with the rest of the population. In all too many parts of the United States and Alaska, however, sheer ignorance, wide-spread disease and wretched economic conditions hold them in a sort of slavery. That is the plight the Navajos enjoy, already described.

In Oklahoma you will find Cherokees in the cities and on good ranches, businessmen, politicians, professional men—and you will find several thousand Cherokees in the backwoods able to speak very little English and not long ago trying to survive on a per capita income of $34 a year.

We have had these people in our charge for anywhere from seventy-five years to a couple of centuries, and this is what we have to show for it. The usual way of dodging the blame . . . of such a record is to talk vaguely about the wicked Indian Bureau, as though the citizens were in no way responsible for the failure of a branch of their Government. As a matter of fact, the Indian Bureau of the past twenty years has earnestly tried to help the Indians, although it has made many mistakes. It can do its work only as the people, through Congress, will enable it to do so.

There is a clear goal in our handling of our Indians. That is to give them all the education, medical care and economic assistance which will put them on their feet as healthy, well-informed, self-supporting citizens of the United States. When that is done, there will be no more need for an Indian Bureau. In fact, the Indian Bureau's own brief summary of its policy is that it is trying to work itself out of a job.

When the last Indian is ready to sink or swim in even competition with the rest of us, when we can say that our conquest of what is now the United States has brought full opportunity for a better life than the old one to all the descendants of the conquered, within the limits of their individual abilities, then we can relax. Then it will no longer be necessary to give Indians special status or special advantages.

If we destroy those advantages before the Indians are ready, we simply project them into the relief rolls, as has been demonstrated over and over again. If we merely help them in status quo and neglect them, we build up miserable populations who will continue indefinitely to be a drain upon the Federal purse and will increasingly become a liability instead of the very real asset which our Indians potentially are.

The greatest long-range economy we can make in connection with them is to spend enough on them now to give them the opportunity which they themselves so greatly desire. It is worth noting that each white citizen receives an average of $300 per year in services from the Federal, state and local Governments, exclusive of what is spent on the armed forces, while Indians receive an average of $166 per year from the Federal Government and nothing else. This is second-class citizenship. . . .

Wherever the Indians have had a chance they have proved their capacity for advancement. If we will insure them all that chance, we shall get out of it in the end half a million or more (at the rate at which they are increasing now) extremely desirable fellow-citizens whose loyalty to this land goes back even farther, is even deeper, than that of any of us.

If we keep on passing by on the other side, a few of them will pull themselves up by desperate efforts. The spoilers and plunderers who never forget them for a moment will go on "emancipating" them from what few assets they have. The Indians will not solve our problem for us by dying out. They will live on, ever poorer, ever sicker, an infection in our body politic and a disgrace to our nation before the world.

v. Negro-White Relations

THERE were approximately 15.5 million Negroes in the United States at mid-century. Of these, 99.4 per cent are American-born and 97 per cent are of native parentage. Of the total population of the United States, nearly 10 per cent are foreign-born and only 70 per cent are of native parentage.

To define an American Negro is not as easy as it may seem at first thought. Dictionaries often crudely describe Negroes as belonging to the "black" race and having traits that apply correctly only to a caricature—wooly hair, large teeth, everted lips, etc. Somewhat more sophisticated definitions are to be found in a few encyclopedias where the point is made, for example, that the term American Negro refers not so much to a race as it does to a social entity. An American Negro is any person who is known to have a Negro ancestor; he or she may, accordingly, be a person who has no so-called Negroid traits at all.

Obviously American Negroes are not a race in the physical anthropological meaning of the term. They are enormously varied in pigmentation, hair, features, and other physical traits. In thousands of cases Negroes in American society are physically indistinguishable from whites. Although they show a preference for Protestantism, as do other Americans, they are affiliated with all major religious denominations and many of the minor religious sects and cults. Like the Indians, no label of nationality other than American describes them, for they are not an immigrant group.

One of the most useful approaches to defining Negro-white relations in the United States began in 1936 with John Dollard's application of the concept of caste to the two groups in a southern community. Castes, like social classes, are groups in which the privileges, duties, obligations, and opportunities are unequally distributed among the superordinate and the subordinate. In a caste system, however, there exist taboos against marriage between the two groups and severe prohibitions and sanctions of vertical intergroup mobility.

The relations of American Negroes and whites meet eight criteria of caste: [1]

(1) A degrading historical experience—slavery—stratified Negroes from whites.

(2) As is typical in a caste system, the statuses of Negroes and whites are ascribed, not achieved; an individual automatically inherits the group affiliation of his parents, and, should the parents belong to the two different groups, he or she inherits the lower status of the two. To "pass" as a white is the only way to escape identification with the lower caste.

(3) There exists a taboo against intermarriage of the two alleged castes, often enforced by enacted law, but also informally and effectively sanctioned by the mores. In this country a majority of the states have legislated against Negro-white intermarriages, and in the southern as well as many of the western states this legislation is still in effect. Where such legislation does not exist today, the rate of intermarriage is, nevertheless, negligible.

(4) A caste system is marked by separate and parallel social organizations, the lower caste establishing its own equivalents of the upper-caste social structure. Thus, American Negroes have established their own clubs, professional associations, fraternities, and sororities when they have been excluded from similar white organizations.

[1] However, in discussing the applicability of the concept of caste to Negroes in the United States, it is necessary to point out a major distinction between the situation here and that of caste systems elsewhere. The members of a lower caste generally accept their status and do not struggle against it. This has not been true of American Negroes.

(5) In a caste system the lower caste is restricted in the use of public accommodations (such as hotels, restaurants, waiting rooms, and water fountains), education, and places of residence. There are countless examples of such restrictions of the American Negro.

(6) Some of the qualities considered virtues in the upper caste are looked upon by members of that caste as vices when manifested by the lower caste. Upward social mobility in American society, for example, is glorified in the "log cabin to White House" and the "rags to riches" traditions, but whites tend to interpret the Negro's social and economic progress as more desirable if it proceeds at a slow pace.

(7) Stereotypes are strongly etched in a caste system, each caste having tabloid beliefs about the other. American Negroes are stereotyped by whites as lazy, childlike, uninhibited, promiscuous, untidy, stupid, etc. Whites are said by Negroes to be overbearing, rude, lazy, arrogant, cruel, cheating, etc.

(8) In a caste system, occupational stratification is sharply drawn—the upper caste is eligible for skilled, administrative, professional, and lucrative positions, and the lower caste is concentrated mainly in unskilled, poorly paid, and marginal types of work. The gains made by American Negroes since World War II do not offset the fact that a disproportionate number of Negroes are indigenous farmers, ditchdiggers, porters, hotel and restaurant workers, cooks, and laundresses.

Two schools of thought exist regarding the significance of the African background to the present cultural patterns and the problems of American Negroes. One school, represented by Melville J. Herskovits of Northwestern University, maximizes the extent to which the American Negro's African culture has been perpetuated. Besides some evidence in vocabulary, culture parallelism between the Old World and the new is claimed for Negro secret societies, funeral rites, agricultural cooperatives, religion, family structure, gambling, and music.

The second school of thought, represented by E. Franklin Frazier, minimizes the importance of the African background, asserting that many characteristics of American Negroes can be explained by disruption and disorganization of their earlier culture rather than its transplantation from Africa to America.

The first Negro slaves were brought to this country in 1619 when a Dutch ship from Guiana reached Jamestown, Virginia, and sold 20 slaves to the plantations. By 1750 slavery was recognized by law in every American colony. It was attempted everywhere, but it became profitable only in the South.

The first action to abolish slavery was taken by Vermont in 1777, followed shortly thereafter by Pennsylvania, Massachusetts, New Hampshire, Rhode Island, and Connecticut. By 1790 all states north of Maryland except New York and New Jersey (which waited until 1827 and 1829, respectively, to take action) had emancipated the slaves.

Although few in numbers in the North, in the South Negroes soon became so numerous that in some areas they outnumbered the whites. The 1790 Census revealed that on the one hand only 1.2 per cent of northeastern families and 7.5 per cent of those in the middle states owned Negro slaves; on the other hand a third of the southern families had them. There were almost one million Negro slaves in the United States at that time, and nine tenths of them were in the South.

In the article that follows Frazier develops the thesis that problems in race relations were of lesser importance during slavery itself because the statuses of Negroes and whites were stabilized. With emancipation and the struggle of the Negro for higher status the "race problem" accelerated and intensified.

14. ROLE OF THE NEGRO IN RACE RELATIONS IN THE SOUTH
BY *E. Franklin Frazier* *

IN OUR interpretation of the role of the Negro in race relations in the South, it may be well to state the two assumptions upon which this brief discussion is based. First, race relations, according to our understanding, refers, on the one hand, to those attitudes and sentiments of the whites which have established social distances between the races and, on the other, to the customary and institutionalized practices which define the

* E. Franklin Frazier, "Role of the Negro in Race Relations in the South," *Social Forces*, XIX (December 1940), 252–8. Reprinted by permission.

status of the Negro. Second, by the role of the Negro in race relations we refer to the manner in which the Negro's behavior or more specifically his struggle for status within the social organization, has affected the social distance between the races as well as the customary and institutional practices involving race relations. Within the compass of this paper we can only indicate, what seems to us, some of the more significant ways in which the Negro may be regarded as thus playing a role in the problem of race relations.

DURING THE PERIOD OF SLAVERY

From the beginning, it appears, the presence of the Negro in America gave rise to some race consciousness on the part of the whites. Unfortunately, we do not have much information on the nature of race relations during the seventeenth and eighteenth centuries when Negro labor became indispensable to the cultivation of tobacco and rice. But from the time of the establishment of the Cotton Kingdom in the nineteenth century, we have fairly definite knowledge on the course of the race relations in the antebellum South when the majority of the Negroes were subject to the regime of the cotton plantation.

Under the plantation regime, which was a social as well as an industrial institution, race relations became stabilized and institutionalized or tended to disappear in the sense in which we have defined the term. . . . Naturally, relations between masters and slaves varied, but from the general standpoint of race relations, an important fact stands out. The status relation of the two races was not affected even though the maximum intimacy might develop as the result of close association within the same household. This presents a strange paradox if social distance is thought of only in terms of personal intimacies and not as what Durkheim regarded as the objective "social facts." But, as we know, the intimacies which the slave system permitted did not destroy the social distance between the two races so far as their status in the social structure was concerned. . . . Moreover, when the plantation regime was disrupted, the sympathies and understandings which had been created during slavery lessened the possibilities of a racial struggle on a purely physical or biological level.

But slavery did not provide a perfect adjustment for the two races and there were Negroes and whites more or less outside its influence. Attention should be called first to the fact that the mixture of the races tended to dissolve the formal and objective social relations and thereby created a problem of race relations. The "mixed-bloods," no matter how they were treated by their white parents, were conscious of their relationship to the master race and were not inclined to accept the traditional status of the black slaves. Then, since the Negro was not completely isolated from the outside world, there was always some unrest which was shown in the number of fugitives. Moreover, we are becoming conscious of the fact that crimes were more frequent among slaves than we had once thought. It was, however, the slave revolts, both in the United States and in the West Indies, that did more than anything else to make the whites conscious of a race problem, or that there were Negroes who wanted to change their status. For the whites there was no place for the Negro race in the social order except as slaves.

Of course, there were free Negroes in the South; but they were always suspected, especially during periods of insurrections and disorders. In fact, free Negroes, who were an anomaly within the slave system, were not found in large numbers where the plantation system flourished. They were found in large numbers only in Maryland and Virginia where the plantation system was breaking down among the heterogeneous elements in cities. In Charleston, South Carolina, and New Orleans, where they had found a niche in the economic organization, they formed a distinct caste. One should not overlook the fact, however, that the majority of these free Negroes were of "mixed-blood" and were, therefore, an intermediate race as well as an intermediate caste. In considering the role of the free Negro in the development of race relations in the antebellum South, one should also note the participation of free Negroes living in the border and Northern states in the abolition movement. The constant agitation and conventions of the free people of color in behalf of the enslaved members of their race tended to keep before the minds of Southern whites the presence of an alien race among them. Having to defend slavery because of such agitation as well as the emancipation of the Negroes in the West Indies, the South built up rationalizations of slavery. The most extensive and important rationalizations of the system are to be found in the theories of society in George Fitzhugh's *Sociology for the South* and Henry Hughes' *A Treatise on Sociology*.

The Negro's relation to the so-called "poor whites" was also a factor in the development of race relations in the antebellum South. Between the slave-trader and the Negro slave, who regarded the former as his worst enemy, there was scarcely any sympathy and understanding. This was natural in a relationship where the rational economic interest of the speculators in the human commodities precluded almost entirely a social relationship. The mere assertion of normal human impulses might be regarded as "mulishness" or resistance on the part of a subhuman species. Then there were the relations of the slaves to the overseers and patrollers who were recruited from the "poor whites." Although these "poor whites" had to make some concessions to the humanity of the slaves, they regarded them as a subhuman group or at best a barbarous and exotic species of mankind. The slave's response to such an attitude was one of hatred and contempt. On the other hand, the bitter racial antipathies of the "poor whites" were aroused especially when free Negro and slave artisans were placed in open competition with them.

EMANCIPATION AND RECONSTRUCTION

From the foregoing analysis one will understand why it may be asserted that race relations or what has come to be known as the race problem was created in the South by the emancipation of the Negro. The social consequences of Emancipation so far as it involved changes in the relationship of the two races were more important than the economic consequences. In fact, the revolutionary changes in land ownership implicit in the contest between the industrial North and the agrarian South were never realized. Some of the Radical Republicans might have envisaged a system of peasant proprietorship for the emancipated blacks; but it is apparent that Northern leaders were not disposed to carry out a revolutionary assault upon private property in land. Although the freedman has been ridiculed because he expected to receive "forty acres and a mule," the newly emancipated Negro was fundamentally right in regarding land-ownership as the substance of a free status. Even if the abandoned lands entrusted to the Freedman's Bureau had been given to the freedmen it would have made little difference in their economic status. But as it turned out, most of the land was returned to the former owners and the freedmen found themselves dependent upon their former masters. The institution of the "black codes," which were designed in part to secure a regular labor supply, represented an attempt to secure through formal controls the type of subordination which had been based on habit and tradition.

The racial conflict which ensued as the result of the breakdown of the traditional relationships between the two races was intensified by the political struggle. Although in the political struggle the freedman was on the whole the pawn of the Republican Party which was intent upon consolidating the triumph of the industrial North, the Negro played an active role in the struggle and thereby affected race relations. The political activities of the Negro were related to some extent to his economic interests. But it appears that his chief efforts were directed toward securing civil and political equality, or social equality in the broader sense, with the whites. One cannot assume that if the freedman had sought landownership instead of civil and political rights, he would have prevented racial antagonism. In fact, the impoverished freedman could not buy land. Like other submerged groups, he hoped through political means to secure the symbols if not the substance of freedom. The "mixed-blood" Negroes who had been free before Emancipation naturally played an important role in the political struggle. They became the leaders of the struggle for status which is the central fact in race relations. In the end, many of the "mixed-blood" leaders lost their lives; others either migrated voluntarily or were forced to leave the South.

A consolidated white South was the final result of the Negro's struggle, with the aid of political allies, to achieve equality. When freedmen attempted to assert their right to equal accommodations in public places, they were either violently ejected or the whites offered passive resistance by withdrawing from such places. But violent methods of suppressing the Negro were the rule where he insisted upon asserting his newly acquired rights. Negroes were not only denied civil rights but were also driven from the fertile lands, their school houses were burned, and their leaders murdered. Nor is it to be forgotten that the monopoly which the Negro slave labor had enjoyed in the economic organization was broken and competition with "poor whites" often resulted in open conflict. The newly formed trade unions refused Negroes membership and denied them an opportunity for apprenticeship. The solidarity of the whites was only slightly broken during the agrarian movement when "poor whites" were arrayed against the large planters and the financial interests. But even in this conflict the "poor whites" often turned their hatred against the Negro as the supporter of the Bourbons.

The demoralized elements in the Negro population, who swarmed into cities and constantly came into conflict with the law, helped to create the stereotypes concerning the post-bellum Negro. But despite the racial conflict which characterized the period of reconstruction, the traditions which had regulated relations between the two races during slavery made possible some cooperation between the races. In fact, the great masses of the Negro population not only accepted their economic dependence under a modified form of the plantation system but resigned themselves to a subordinate social status. The struggle for equal status was carried on by a minority, who in the end were killed off, forced to migrate, or accommodated themselves to an inferior status.

It appears that by the time Booker T. Washington announced his formula for the accommodation of the two races, the Negro had been forced to accept an inferior status and the period of conflict was drawing to a close. At the very time that Washington was announcing his formula, the South was giving content and meaning to his phrase, "In all things that are purely social we can be as separate as the fingers." With Mississippi setting the example in 1890, between 1895 and 1910 seven other Southern states disfranchised the Negro through changes in their constitutions without violating the Federal Constitution. By 1891 nine states had passed legislation requiring separate accommodations on railroads; and between 1898 and 1907 five other states followed suit. While the conservative whites were inclined to give "poor whites" and Negroes the same educational facilities, when the "poor whites" came into power around the nineties, they paid little heed to the educational needs of the voteless blacks.

SINCE THE OPENING OF THE PRESENT CENTURY

By the opening of the present century the new status of the Negro in the South had become relatively fixed and the conflict between the races had subsided. A rough index to the subsidence of racial conflict is provided in the number of lynchings which have gradually declined since 1900, with the exception of flare-ups in 1908 and 1919. There are, of course, other indications that new forms of accommodations had become established and that bitter racial antagonisms were tending to disappear. Although in the new accommodation of the two races the Negro was forced to accept an inferior status, he could no longer be treated as a slave.

The pattern which race relations have assumed in the South is similar in many respects to a caste system. One might say that from the standpoint of racial orthodoxy all Negroes have a social status lower than the lowest white in the social scale. But a realistic analysis of the manifold and changing relations between the two races must go beyond the static concept of caste. In a highly mobile and dynamic society like ours, it is impossible for race relations to become fixed and sacred as in a stable society. It is because of the mobile and dynamic character of our society that a race problem or race relations exist in the South. In other words, it is inevitable that the Negro continues to "get out of his place."

An outstanding feature of the racial situation in the South has been the emergence of a bi-racial organization. In fact, during the period when a new type of accommodation between the two races was being established, some of the Negro leaders in the conflict area of politics withdrew to become leaders of the separate Negro institutions. These leaders have accepted and urged the masses to accept the various forms of accommodation which have become established. In such institutions as the schools which depend upon the larger community for support, their vested interests have played some role in their conciliatory attitudes toward the whites. Moreover, such institutions have tended to select a Negro leadership which has the "right" attitude toward the interracial situation. Institutions and organizations, developed through the cooperation of the Negroes, have provided a field in which natural leaders among Negroes could find a place and the more aggressive among them could avoid contacts with the whites.

The bi-racial organization in the South has permitted some occupational differentiation and social stratification of the Negro population, a fact which is of importance in considering the role of the Negro in race relations. Upper-class Negroes, whose economic security has depended upon the white community, have accepted discrimination, though utilizing in many cases their position to avoid the cruder forms of racial discrimination. They as well as those who draw their support from the Negro community and enjoy a similar advantage do not fail to escape periodically from Southern discrimination. Moreover, many upper-class Negroes in urban areas, where there is less danger of mob violence, do not fail to use their buying power to enforce respect on the part of whites. But this does not mean that they as well as the lower class Negroes have not developed deferential attitudes toward whites and that the prestige of the whites, especially those of the upper-class and the relics of the aristocracy, is not sufficient to cause some at least to acquiesce in their inferior social status. Nothing betrays this more than their desire to appear respectable in the eyes of the whites. It is this class that urges the Negro, who agitates for equality, not to disturb the "good" race relations and, if he is not satisfied, to leave the South. Finally, in appraising the role of the upper-class Negro in race relations, the fact should not be overlooked that his status among Negroes in the bi-racial organization provides some satisfactions which compensate for being excluded from the advantages that might be enjoyed by participating in the larger society.

If we turn our attention from this more or less sheltered group to the masses of Negroes, we shall see how the role of the Negro in race relations is influenced on a broader scale by the dynamic factors in the Southern situation. The first factor of importance is the urbanization of the Negro population. From the standpoint of race relations the movement of over a million Negroes from rural areas to hundreds of towns and cities of the South has tended to secularize the relations between the two races. The personal loyalties and sentimental ties between the races are destroyed. It means also that the Negro is brought into contact with a larger world which influences his conception of himself. Where urbanization has been accompanied by the employment of the Negro in industry with whites, it has had even greater consequences for race relations. For example, even such impersonal factors as technology have in some cases tended to have important effects upon the association of white and Negro workers. In a competitive industrial system, traditions concerning the relations of the races however sacred are bound to give way where they are opposed to economy and efficiency. Then, where, as in the case of the C. I. O., the contest between capital and labor depends upon the organization of the masses of laborers, new forms of cooperation between the two races become necessary. The race issue may be raised not by the participants but by those who wish to defeat such a movement. For example, . . . in a small town in Virginia, the industrialists and businessmen attempted to make a race issue of the efforts of the C. I. O. to organize Negro and white workers. But in this instance the race issue failed to deter the cooperation of white and Negro workers.

What has been called the collapse of cotton tenancy or the crisis in

Southern agriculture is another indication of the manner in which dynamic factors have affected the role of the Negro in race relations. . . . The stirrings of Southern white tenants and the sharecroppers have brought the rural Negro into a new relationship with the whites. . . . For example, in some cases the Negro, who has had some training in his own organizations, has been able to assume certain duties of leadership, because the "poor white" lacked this experience. . . .

In summing up our brief discussion, it might be stated that since the break-up of the slave regime no type of social organization has emerged in which the two races have found a comparable form of accommodation. Although bitter racial antagonisms have subsided since the period of internal race conflict during Reconstruction, the struggle of the Negro for status which is the heart of the race problem continues. The bi-racial organization represents a form of accommodation in which the leaders in the struggle for status have found a way of life which offers some compensations for the status denied them in the larger world. But the Negro world is not isolated from the larger white world and the relations of the masses of Negro workers to the economic organization are constantly creating or re-creating the problems of race relations. Then, too, the secularization of race relations as the result of urbanization precludes an accommodation on the basis of personal loyalties and sentimental attachments. Thus, because of the dynamic character of our culture and the social and economic forces inherent in Southern society, the Negro continues to be the central figure in race relations.

EDITORIAL COMMENT

Notwithstanding the economic, social, and cultural dynamics described by Frazier as affecting the status and role of American Negroes since the nineteenth century, the present era still finds a great disparity between the official American creed of equality and the actual subordinate position of America's largest minority group.

Negroes have contributed considerably to the development of American land and resources. Yet they still have far from proportionate representation in the higher, remunerative skills and positions. Consequently, their purchasing power, while increasing, is still limited. In all respects, no one but the bigot will deny that the Negro is American. He is overwhelmingly native-born, and his cultural and artistic contributions are preponderantly indigenous. But because of the persistent obstacles of caste, Negroes still cannot freely partake of all the opportunities that American life has to offer.

In the selection which follows, Maxwell Stewart summarizes

the most pertinent survey findings of Gunnar Myrdal, author of the thesis that contemporary Negro-white relations in the United States are best understood in terms of values in conflict and a moral dilemma.

15. THE NEGRO IN CONTEMPORARY AMERICA BY *Maxwell S. Stewart* *

. . . RECOGNIZING the importance of the Negro problem in American life, the Carnegie Corporation several years ago determined to bring the resources of the social sciences to bear on the problem. In order to avoid all danger of bias or partisanship in this study, it decided to bring a scholar from abroad "who could approach his task with a fresh mind." It was felt that it was important that such a scholar should be chosen from a country with no background or traditions of imperialism which might lessen confidence in the impartiality of the study. These considerations led to the selection of Dr. Gunnar Myrdal, a distinguished social economist from the University of Stockholm and economic advisor to the Swedish government, to undertake the task. The following pages represent a brief summary of his four years of intensive study as contained in his two-volume report entitled *An American Dilemma,* and four other volumes prepared by noted scholars associated with him.

NATURE OF THE PROBLEM

Dr. Myrdal discovered a striking difference between what many Americans *say* about the Negroes and what they really *think.* As he traveled over the country he found that many Americans indignantly deny that there is a "Negro problem" in America. They insist that if there ever was one, it has been solved to the satisfaction of both parties. This view is heard most frequently in the Deep South. It is usually accompanied by a statement that the Negroes are all right in their place, but they must be kept there or they will cause trouble.

Denial of Problem Symptom of Tension

But Dr. Myrdal is doubtful whether those who most fervently insist that the problem has been solved actually believe it. For the white South seems to be "obsessed by the Negro problem." The very vigor with which people deny that it exists reflects the intensity of the race tension. This

* From Maxwell S. Stewart, "The Negro in America" (New York: Public Affairs Committee, 1944), Pamphlet No. 95. Reprinted by permission.

may easily be seen if one suggests the possibility of a Negro uprising. Many Southerners immediately show alarm. And the persons who are most cocksure in insisting that there is no Negro problem and that the Negroes are content with present conditions often display the greatest fear. Without seemingly being aware of a contradiction, the same person may in one sentence defend the suppression of the Negroes on the ground that they are satisfied with things as they are and in the next explain that the Negroes must be kept down because they are always wanting to be like white people.

Statements that no problem exists are not limited to the South or even to white people. Negroes often declare that there is no difficulty between the races in their part of the country. Such statements are made by some Negro college presidents, principals, and teachers of Negro schools whose jobs are dependent on white boards of directors. They seem to be expected of Negro leaders at all public interracial affairs. They are, however, usually different from the similar statements made by white persons. They are nearly always limited to the local community and are qualified by mention of some particular situation which might be improved. And they are rarely, if ever, made by Negroes when talking "off the record" or among friends. As with similar statements by white persons, the assertion that there is "no Negro problem" is an indication of the unhealthiness of the situation. Actually, the problem not only exists but is of great importance in many parts of the United States.

In the South the Negro is almost never discussed formally. He is almost never referred to in schools or in the church. Southern newspapers, with remarkable exceptions, ignore Negroes except for their crimes. For a long time there was an unwritten rule that a picture of a Negro should never appear in print; and even now it is rare. Yet the extent to which the Negro dominates people's thinking may be seen in a story reported by Ray Stannard Baker a generation ago, and which still crops up in the South.

A Negro boy went as a sort of butler's assistant in the home of a prominent family in Atlanta. His people were naturally curious about what went on in the white man's house. One day they asked him:

"What do they talk about when they are eating?"

The boy thought a moment, then he said: "Mostly they discusses us cullud folks."

Mr. Baker adds that Negroes display the same consuming interest in white people and the race question.

Ignorance about the Negro Is Widespread

In his travels throughout the country, Dr. Myrdal was astonished at the lack of correct information about Negroes which he found in all walks of life. He found physicians who held absurd ideas about the amount of disease among Negroes; educators who knew nothing of the results of modern intelligence research; lawyers who believed that lynchings are practically all caused by rape; and ministers who knew practically nothing about Negro churches in their own town.

"The ignorance about the Negro is the more striking," Dr. Myrdal writes, "as the Southerner himself is convinced that he 'knows the Negro,' while the Yankee is supposedly ignorant on the subject." In insisting that they have reliable and intimate knowledge about the Negro problem, the Southern whites are only fooling themselves. "The average Southerner 'knows' the Negro and the interracial problem as the patient 'knows' the toothache—in the sense that he feels a concern—not as a diagnosing dentist knows his own or his patient's trouble. He further 'knows' the Negro in the sense that he is brought up to use a social technique in dealing with Negroes" by which he is able to lord it over them. "The technique is simple: I have often observed that merely speaking the Southern dialect works the trick."

In the North the Negro problem is not nearly as important as in the South. Northern whites believe that they treat Negroes, on the whole, much better than Southerners do. Do they not allow the Negro to vote, and to attend the same schools as white children? Having thus consoled himself, the average Northerner wants to forget about the whole matter. The result is an astonishing ignorance about the Negro. Many educated Northerners are far better informed about foreign problems than about Negro conditions in their own city.

Conflict with the American Creed

. . . Ignorance about conditions under which Negroes live probably explains in part the gap between America's professed belief in equality and democracy and its manifestly unequal treatment of Negroes. . . . Every American believes in the principles set down in the Declaration of Independence and the Bill of Rights. Americans believe that "all men are created equal," in freedom of speech, freedom of religion, and racial tolerance; they believe that America is the "cradle of freedom," the "land of opportunity," and the "home of democracy." In principle, most Americans in the North at least, concede that the Negro has the same right to freedom and justice as other citizens. But, in practice, Negroes have not shared many of these rights. This gap between our profession and our actions constitutes, according to Dr. Myrdal, "the Negro problem. . . ."

DISADVANTAGES OF BEING A NEGRO

Most Negroes Are Poor

Most Negroes are poor. This is true in the North as well as the South. Most Negroes own little property; what furniture and household goods they have are badly dilapidated. They not only are poorly paid when they work but they are much more freqently unemployed than whites. They are forced to live from day to day with little chance to plan for the future.

In the South the Negro's poverty is connected with the decline of King Cotton and the overcrowding of Southern farm lands. More than half of America's 30,000,000 farm population is in the South. But the South has only a little more than one-third of the country's farm land. In value, the proportion is even less—28 per cent of the total.

The Decline of King Cotton

The backwardness of the South agriculturally is largely the result of too much dependence on cotton. . . . Cotton growing in the Southeastern states became less and less profitable in the period between World War I and World War II. Prices were driven down by competition with cheap labor in Brazil, India, China, and other countries. Cotton was more seriously affected by the depression than other crops and recovered less afterwards. The AAA helped the South in many ways, but the Negroes did not get their share of these gains. More Negro tenants than whites were driven from the land by its crop-reduction program. Most of these were reduced to wage laborers.

Erosion

Furthermore, cotton growing is extremely wasteful of the soil. It robs the soil of its fertility and causes widespread erosion. The Southeast pays more than half of the nation's bill for commercial fertilizers. One of the effects of erosion in the Southeast has been to encourage the development of cotton growing in Texas and other parts of the Southwest. This has resulted in still lower prices for cotton.

Although both whites and Negroes suffer from the traditional dependence on King Cotton, the Negroes have been more dependent than the white farmers.

Negroes produce one-third of the total cotton crop. As long ago as 1929 it was estimated that three Negro farmers out of every four received at least 40 per cent of their incomes from cotton. There are 4,500,000 Negroes who live on the land.

Tenancy

A large part of these . . . are tenants or sharecroppers. The South has long been cursed by tenancy. Almost three-fourths of the cotton farms are operated by tenants or croppers. The economic position of this group, white and Negro, has been peculiarly difficult because of its association with a credit system carrying extremely high interest rates. This credit system, in turn, has increased the pressure for a cash crop which in the South usually means cotton.

This completes the circle. The South grows cotton because it needs cash. Cotton growing is traditionally carried on by tenants and sharecroppers. This system not only robs the soil and interferes with the education of the next generation, thus preventing agricultural progress, but it requires the assistance of money lenders. And the Negro, being poorer and more dependent on cotton than the white farmer, is the chief victim of this circle.

Negro Landowners

Some Negro farmers do, it is true, own their land. But the number is not greater than one out of every seven and has declined in the past twenty years. Only in Florida and Virginia do a majority of Negro farmers own land, and in Virginia the number has declined drastically since 1910.

Moreover, the Negro's farm is usually small. . . . The farms owned by Negroes average less than half the size of farms owned by whites. In crop value the Negro-owned farms show up even less favorably. This may be explained both by the fact that the land owned by Negroes tends, on the average, to be less valuable and by the fact that the Negroes have less farm equipment at their disposal.

There are several reasons why so few Negroes own their farms. Starting as slaves, they were never encouraged to do much for themselves. Instead, they were taught to look to the white man for everything. And of course they had no capital with which to buy land. In many parts of the South the whites have banded together to prevent Negroes from obtaining land in white neighborhoods. Most Negro-owned farms are on back roads or in areas which the whites do not think good enough for farming.

Plantation Tenants and Wage Laborers

Although the plantation system is breaking up in many parts of the South, some hundreds of thousands of Negroes still work as plantation tenants. These are really ordinary laborers. Their work is usually supervised by the landlord or foremen. They often work by the clock in gangs. But unlike laborers, they are not paid regular wages. Like sharecroppers, they receive a certain proportion of the crop. They share the risk of bad weather, the boll weevil, and low cotton prices. In fact, they often assume more than their share of the risk. For in nine cotton states the landlord has the legal right to sell any and all property the tenant may have to recover rent or any money that may have been advanced by the landlord.

At one time the wage laborers on Southern farms were mostly Negro. But at present somewhat more than half of them are white. Yet two out of five Negroes who work the land are wage laborers. Since they work only part of the year, these wage laborers are even worse off than tenants or sharecroppers.

Other Opportunities for Negroes

Outside of farming, the Southern Negro has also had to compete more and more with whites for what used to be regarded as purely Negro jobs. . . . In many of the cities of the old South there are still a number of Negro carpenters, masons, and painters, but not nearly as many as there were formerly. In other cities there are only Negro helpers. And in some places they are not even permitted to be helpers. In a few cities along the Atlantic Coast, the old Negro barber may still be found. Negro waiters are still common everywhere, but white waitresses are rapidly taking their place. The entry of white women into industry has caused even more headaches, since white women and Negroes are not allowed to work together in the South on an equal plane.

White pressure is particularly strong in Southern industry. From 1890 to 1910 the number of male white workers more than doubled. The number of male Negro workers rose by only two-thirds during the same period. Such increase as did occur was due mainly to the growth of certain industries which are traditionally reserved for Negroes, such as coal mining, work in lumber mills, and railway maintenance-of-way work. From 1910 to 1940 there was a much slower increase in the number of Negro jobs. In the last ten years of that period the Negro population of the cities increased by 20 per cent as Negroes were forced out of agriculture. But the number of male Negro workers increased only 12 per cent. Comparatively few Negroes obtained factory jobs before the war. Although the textile industry has grown tremendously in recent years, only 26,000 out of its 635,000 Southern workers in 1940 were Negroes. Only in domestic service has the Negro retained a practical monopoly in the South.

In the North

Contrary to the views held by most Southern whites, the Negro has had a much better chance for a good job in the North. For one thing, Negroes hold many more different kinds of jobs. Even before the war, many more were employed in skilled factory work. Tremendous gains were made during World War I and in the 1920's. Between 1910 and 1930, the number of male Negro workers in the North outside of farming rose by 480,000. This was a much better showing than the South made, despite the fact that the South had many more Negroes.

But even in the North the Negro has been kept out of many of the more desirable kinds of work. He has had little chance of getting a skilled job, for instance, in textile factories, sawmills, shoe factories, bakeries, or furniture factories. Few Negroes were employed by the railroads or utilities except as porters and similar work. And during the depression of the 1930's, the Negroes were first to lose their jobs. As Negroes continued to move from the South to the North during the depression, the unemployment situation among Negroes in Northern cities became extremely serious—much more serious than in the South. Strangely enough, young Negroes usually were able to find jobs about as easily as white youths, but middle-aged Negroes, particularly those listed as skilled workers, suffered much more from unemployment than whites of similar experience. This seeming good luck on the part of the young Negroes is probably due to their willingness to accept almost any kind of unskilled work. White young people are more likely to hold out for better jobs.

White Collar Opportunities

With all of these handicaps, a Negro wage-earner has a much easier time finding a place for himself than a Negro white collar employee or professional man. . . . Most Negro workers work for white people. But the Negro professional or business man is usually limited to the Negro community. Since the Negro community is extremely poor, this means that the Negro professional is badly paid as compared with white persons in the same field. It means also that while there are many Negro ministers, teachers, and storekeepers, there are very few openings for Negro engineers, architects, or industrial managers. And few Negroes are engaged in clerical work.

In 1930 only 254,000 Negroes were listed in the census as white collar employees, business or professional men. Only one out of every fifteen Negro workers, not including farmers, had entered the white collar field. Among whites the ratio was two out of five. Nor does the situation seem to be improving. The Negro's share in white collar and professional jobs declined in the twenty years between 1910 and 1930.

Teaching

School teaching is the chief Negro profession. It is confined chiefly to Negro schools, or schools in which most of the students are Negro. Actually, Negroes are not more than half as well represented in the teaching profession as they are in the population. And although the teaching load of Negro teachers is much heavier than that of white teachers, their salaries, particularly in the South, are much lower than those of white teachers with similar qualifications.

Ministry

The profession with a large proportion of Negroes is the ministry. This may be because Negroes are more regular church-goers than are the whites and because they tend to divide up into more small sects. Most Negro ministers are poorly paid. Although a few Negro ministers in the cities receive reasonably high salaries, most of them have to be content with a few hundred dollars. A large number of Negro clergymen have other jobs on the side. Or, more frequently, the ministry is a side line for men who follow other occupations during the week.

Medicine

In contrast to teaching and the ministry, the medical profession has been almost closed to Negroes. In 1940 there were only 4,000 Negro physicians and surgeons in all of the United States. Negroes find great difficulty in gaining entrance to white medical schools. Only a few hospitals admit Negro and white doctors on a basis of complete equality. Negroes are likewise barred from specialized work. This accounts for the widespread but unfounded belief that Negro physicians are ill trained. Since most Negro physicians draw their patients entirely from the Negro community, their incomes are far below those of white physicians of similar training and ability. The same applies to dentists and nurses.

Law

Negro lawyers have even harder sledding. While there would seem to be a great need for Negro lawyers to fight for the rights of their race in the courts, most Negroes have found that a "respectable" white lawyer could help them more before a white court than the best of Negro lawyers. As a result there were only 1,200 Negro lawyers in the entire country in 1930. About two-thirds of these lived outside the South. Out of 600 lawyers in Alabama, for example, only six were Negroes. Negro artists, musicians, and actors fare somewhat better. But competition is severe and their opportunities are much narrower than those of whites. . . .

Educational Handicaps

Although Negroes have shown themselves capable of skilled work of all kinds, they have much greater difficulty than whites in getting the education and training necessary for better jobs.

Their difficulties start in the grade school. . . . In most instances the Negro schools are inferior to white ones. The buildings are old; the equipment out-of-date; and the teachers are poorly trained and poorly paid. In parts of the South, the Negro schools are not open during the planting and harvest seasons.

Although many more Negroes are in school today than were twenty or thirty years ago, today's Negroes reflect the lack of educational opportunities of a generation ago. . . . When it comes to higher education, the Negro is still worse off. Only a few have money enough to attend college, and they have difficulty getting good training. Negroes are [generally] not admitted to the state universities or private white colleges in any of the Southern states. Several of these states support small Negro colleges; but none of them has as high standards as the average Southern state university. No Northern state university excludes Negroes, but they are often treated rather badly once they are enrolled. . . . Most of the smaller [private] colleges . . . either bar Negroes or restrict their number. Only a limited number of Negroes are admitted each year to the better white medical or law schools.

The Negro has also had a tough time getting vocational training for skilled work even in wartime. Although they were in greater need of training than any other group, Negroes constituted less than 5 per cent of the persons accepted in the preemployment or "refresher" courses offered by the U.S. Office of Education and Employment Service up to May, 1942. In some of the Southern states, where most of the Negroes live, Negroes were kept out of the war training program altogether.

Citizenship Rights

Parallel to the economic [and educational] limitations imposed on the Negro are severe political restrictions, particularly in the South. Although the Constitution declares specifically that "the right of citizens of the United States to vote shall not be denied or abridged . . . on account of race, color, or previous condition of servitude," Southern tradition is strongly opposed to permitting Negroes to vote, except when their voting serves the white man's purpose. Various means are used to restrict or prohibit Negro voting in the Southern states. One of the most effective has been the rule that Negroes could not participate in the Democratic primary. This action has been enforced on the theory that the Democratic party is a voluntary organization entitled to determine its own membership. Since the Democratic party [usually] is the only party that counts in the South, its primary really determines who is to be elected. In view of this, the Supreme Court . . . held that it was illegal to deprive the Negro his right to vote in the primary. . . .

Another device commonly used to prevent Negroes from voting is the poll tax . . . a small fee before voters can register to vote. Although whites as well as Negroes may be compelled to pay the fee, election officials enforce the ruling much more strictly with Negroes. Moreover, since Negroes are poorer as a group, fewer of them are willing or able to pay the tax. Similar to the poll tax in that they restrict Negroes because they are poor, are property, educational, and "character" requirements for voting. These are seldom applied to whites but almost always to Negroes. And they may be applied most unfairly, as in the instance of an intelligent Negro woman in North Carolina who was not permitted to register because she mispronounced the words "contingency" and "constitutionality" in reading the state constitution.

Despite these restrictions, . . . Negroes do vote in the South, especially in the border states. Just how many vote is not known since election statistics are not divided according to race. . . . In the North Negroes vote in large numbers. In fact, in some cities more Negroes vote in proportion to their numbers than whites. But despite the large number of Negroes who vote, they get much less proportionately for their vote in the country as a whole, than the whites. For example, Negroes cast about the same number of votes throughout the United States as the whites cast in the seven states of the Deep South. Yet Southern whites get incomparably more benefits from politics than do Negroes. . . . In recent years, however, Negroes have increased their political influence by abandoning their traditional Republican allegiance and becoming "fluid," ready to support the party that offers them the greatest benefits. And in some cities, Negroes are coming to exercise important political influence in local affairs.

THE NEGRO AND COMMUNITY LIFE

In addition to being poor and being denied a fair chance at an education or in political life, Negroes suffer from many other handicaps. Although they have lived in this country since the founding, they have been kept outside the main currents of American life. They are Americans by birth, by citizenship, and in the social habits—more American than millions of white people of recent European origin. Yet most of them live apart from other Americans; they attend their own churches; patronize their own stores; have their own social and cultural organizations; and, in many places, work at "Negro jobs."

Segregation

Negroes and whites are kept apart from each other by a series of restrictions and taboos, some formal and legal but mostly informal and traditional. For example, the two rarely mingle in the same part of town. This is true in the North as well as in the South. Since the Negroes have few social contacts with whites, it seems almost "natural" for the Negroes to have their own churches, hospitals, stores, and playgrounds. And since the Negroes are poorer, on the average, than white people, it seems almost "natural" that they should live in a more dilapidated part of town, with fewer paved streets and fewer hospitals, schools, and playgrounds.

On top of this, the Negro sections of town are always overcrowded. In the North, particularly, the Negro population has grown much more rapidly than the areas in which they are encouraged to live. Because so few houses are available for them, Negroes nearly always are compelled to pay much more than white families for a decent place to live, or else put up with much worse conditions. Many find that even after paying rents which most whites would consider out of reason they still cannot get decent housing.

This segregation has not been achieved by housing laws. Several attempts have been made to enforce segregation by means of zoning ordinances, but the Supreme Court has ruled that all such ordinances are unconstitutional. Segregation has usually been maintained by informal social pressure or property agreements. . . . Few white property owners in white neighborhoods will even consider selling or renting to Negroes. Neighborhood associations often devote their energies to keeping the Negroes out of white communities. Threats and violence are sometimes used if the more peaceful methods fail. . . . Although the United States Housing Authority has provided a considerable amount of low-cost housing to Negroes, it has usually built separate projects for whites and Negroes. Even where mixed projects were undertaken, they were forced by public opinion, except in one or two instances, to keep the Negroes at one end of the project and the whites at the other. This practice was later modified.

Jim Crow and Other Practices

Outside of housing, there is considerable difference between the South and the North in the extent to which Negroes are kept from mixing with whites. In the South, the race line is sharply marked. . . . Some Southern cities have special facilities for Negroes but they are never quite so good as those provided for whites. . . . Negroes are ordinarily barred from white hotels, restaurants, places of amusement, and cemeteries. Some hospitals admit Negro patients, but they are kept in separate wards. And although there are Negro Baptists and Methodists, there is [virtually] no mixing of the races in the Southern churches.

Although there are no Jim Crow laws in the North, Negroes are often barred from schools, parks, playgrounds, and other places of amusement by social pressure. Many stores, hotels, and restaurants refuse to serve Negroes unless someone threatens to call in the police. In some cities the more expensive stores are more likely to turn Negroes away than the inexpensive ones. Churches in the North do not prohibit Negroes or even keep them separate, but Negroes rarely feel welcome enough to wish to attend. The Y. M. C. A.'s ordinarily segregate Negroes even in the North, the reason usually given being that they are equipped with swimming pools. The Y. W. C. A. is somewhat more tolerant.

Differences Bewildering to Negroes

Curious differences in the rules of segregation exist not only between the North and the South, but between cities both in the North and South. Many of these differences [seem to] make no sense whatsoever and are bewildering to visiting Negroes. In some office buildings in Atlanta, for example, all Negroes must ride up in special Negro elevators, but they may come down in any of the cars. A federal office building in Nashville has separate rest rooms for white and Negro employees, but the public rest rooms are open to both races. The border states have harsher rules on some things than the South, while on others they are more lenient. . . . In the North, Negroes are never quite sure how they will be treated in a restaurant until they have tried it out.

Social Taboos

The strongest forces keeping Negroes and whites apart, however, are social. In the South the most powerful of all are those separating white women from Negro men. The desire to "protect" white women from Negro men amounts to an obsession in the South. A discussion of the justice of "keeping the Negro in his place" often ends by a Southerner asking heatedly: "Would you want your daughter to marry a nigger?"

Actually, of course, the question is an idle one. Marriages between Negro men and white women occur but rarely in the United States. Mixed marriages are prohibited by law in the Southern states and some of the Western states. And there are few such marriages even where they are allowed. It is true that many American "Negroes" are actually largely of white descent. But the mixing of the races has been due almost entirely to white men taking advantage of Negro women. Such relations have rarely involved marriage, and appear to be decreasing. Illicit sex relations between Negro men and white women are uncommon.

Nevertheless, the Southerner's fear of intermarriage is a very real thing. It accounts for many of the social restrictions placed against Negroes. Negroes and whites practically never dance together, for example, in the South. Even in the North, Negro students are usually expected to stay away from high school or college dances, or, if they attend, they dance with each other. In many parts of the country Negroes are prohibited from using public swimming pools or beaches when whites are present. Even the shaking of hands is ruled out in the South, except for a servant's greeting his master. Eating together is also frowned on in many places. In the South it seems to be regarded as almost as bad as intermarriage. Like the other barriers, this has broken down only to a slight extent. A Southern writer explains that "the table, simple though its fare may be, possesses the sanctity of an intimate social institution. To break bread together involves, or may involve, everything."

Even conversation between the races is, in the South, heavily restricted by custom. Serious discussion is ruled out except as it concerns business affairs. The only Negro men whom the ordinary Southern white woman is likely to have occasion to talk to are her servants—although she may interest herself in a certain amount of polite welfare work among the Negroes. The form of the conversation is of great importance. A Negro is expected to address a white person by the title of "Mr.," "Mrs.," or "Miss." White men may be called "Boss," "Cap," or "Cap'n." But a white person is expected to address a Negro by his first name, or by

such terms as "boy," "uncle," or "aunty." "Mr." and "Mrs." are practically
never used by a white person in referring to a Negro unless it be by a salesman anxious to gain customers. A Negro is expected to beat about the
bush and never to contradict a white man or mention a delicate subject
directly.

These restrictions on conversation are important because they impose a very real barrier between the races. They keep each from knowing
what the other is really thinking about. This obviously has a bearing on the
Southerners' idea that they "know" their Negroes. The North has no
restriction on conversation, but since the two races ordinarily live apart,
they rarely have a chance to get to know one another.

ARE NEGROES DIFFERENT?

The result of all this is that many white people think of the Negro
as "different." He is thought to be good only for unskilled work and wholly
unfitted for leadership. Also many whites say that Negroes are not to be
trusted, citing their high crime rates as evidence of supposed criminal
tendencies. Careful examination shows both of these ideas to be wholly
false.

Negro Achievements.

Despite the many restrictions placed upon them, Negroes have
achieved outstanding success in many fields. These achievements are
naturally the greatest in the fields where Negroes have suffered the fewest
handicaps, and the least in fields where they have found little or no opportunity. For example, few Negroes have achieved fame in national, state,
or local politics. Few have been outstanding in business. In both fields
they suffer from tremendous handicaps. In the field of entertainment, on
the other hand, many Negroes have made outstanding contributions. . . .
In athletics, too, Negroes have won their full share of fame. . . .

Although we may search in vain for Negro Senators, Cabinet members, or state governors this does not mean that the Negroes are lacking
in statesmanlike qualities. It merely means that professional politics is
largely a white domain. For outstanding Negro statesmen we shall have
to turn to the field of race leadership. If we include this field with politics,
we may say that some of the most capable statesmen in the United
States have been Negroes. This is certainly true of such men as Frederick
Douglass, Booker T. Washington, W. E. B. DuBois, and James Weldon
Johnson. Many of the younger Negro leaders of today are displaying
similar qualities of statesmanship.

Crime and Negroes

At the other end of the social scale, much emphasis has been placed
on the large number of Negro criminals. Many Americans firmly believe

that the Negro is a born criminal. They read in their newspapers almost every day of crimes that were committed by Negroes. In fact, a large part, perhaps most, of the news about Negroes in the papers, in both North and South, is about crime. This is partly due to the way that the papers handle news. When a Catholic, a German, or a Swede commits a crime, his religion or nationality is rarely mentioned. But when a Negro commits a crime, his race is usually stated in the headlines.

Statistics can be quoted to "prove" that Negroes are much more likely to commit crime than whites. For example, there are more than three times as many Negroes in prisons and reformatories, in proportion to the population, as there are native whites. But what do these figures mean? Scientists have been trying to find out for years, and as yet no one really knows. Obviously, there are no statistics which reveal the amount of crime committed by the two races; what we have are figures on arrests, convictions, and imprisonment—which are much smaller than the number of crimes committed. It would seem that Negroes are more likely to be arrested for crimes than whites. This is particularly true in the South, where a crime committed by a Negro against a white person seldom goes unpunished, while crimes by whites against Negroes are likely to be overlooked. Some of the Negro "crimes" in the South are merely violations of segregation laws or "disorderly conduct," a term used to cover such things as failing to treat white persons with proper respect. In the North, white criminals are more likely than Negroes to have political "pull" protecting them from arrest and conviction. And, finally, Negro criminals are arrested more frequently and sent to jail for longer terms, thus warping the crime statistics.

Although no one can say so positively, it is quite possible that Negroes do commit more crimes, proportionately, than whites. This would be expected from a sociological point of view. Slavery brought about a low regard for human life. . . . Because of poverty and weak family bonds, prostitution seems to be more common among Negro women than among white women. Poverty and slum conditions, under which most city Negroes live, encourage the formation of criminal gangs. In fact, white criminals often operate in the Negro areas because slum areas are rarely well policed. Negro children brought up under such conditions have two strikes against them before they come of age. Negroes are no more likely to be born criminals than whites, but their social handicaps are so great that it is a wonder that their crime record is as low as it appears to be.

The Negro Protest

For years most Negroes accepted the severe handicaps forced upon them because there seemed nothing else to do. In the South, particularly, Negro leaders were largely men who "knew how to get along with whites."

For years "Uncle Tom" was regarded as the symbol of a good Negro who knew his place. Most Negroes, desiring to avoid serious trouble, have been humble and subservient in the presence of whites—regardless of how they may have felt.

Gradually, however, a change has taken place. Although all Negro leaders must work with whites, the Negro leaders of today have been more aggressive in fighting for full equality. Their protest has been gaining in strength since the early 1900's and reached a climax in World War II.

Organizations

The Negro's struggle has been led in recent years by three interracial organizations. Oldest of these is the National Association for the Advancement of Colored People, founded in 1909. It operates primarily in the field of civil liberties. . . . In this struggle it has won many notable victories. . . . Although often attacked by militant Negroes, particularly in recent years, as being too cautious and conservative in its tactics, its achievements are undeniable.

The Urban League was founded in 1910 as a result of a merger of three older organizations. Its main aim has been to get equal job opportunities, with equal pay for equal work, and an equal chance for advancement. In this struggle the League has concerned itself with such things as the problems of education, home and neighborhood, problems of youth, recreation, vocational guidance, housing, and welfare work. Local branches of the League maintain employment agencies, day nurseries, child placement agencies, clubs for boys and girls, neighborhood groups, parent-teacher associations, and study groups in trade unions. In many cities the League has worked closely with the trade unions in efforts to improve conditions for Negro workers. Although it too has been criticized by the extremists for being too timid, the League has rendered real service within its field.

Operating solely within the South, the Commission on Interracial Cooperation has been concerned with breaking down the barriers between the races and solving race problems so far as possible from within. Its emphasis has been largely on research, education, and publicity. But it has undertaken legal activities in its fight against lynching and on behalf of the Negro's civil rights. And it made interracial work socially respectable in the South. This organization has been replaced by the Southern Regional Council, which has a somewhat broader scope of activities. . . .

Grounds for Hope

. . . There are solid grounds for believing that solution of the Negro-white problem can be reached. Much of the difficulty is due to misunderstanding arising out of the fact that the two groups rarely have an opportunity of talking matters out around the table. When asked to rank,

in order of importance, the types of discrimination they consider important, white Southerners usually list them in the following order:
1. The ban on intermarriage and sex relations involving white women and colored men;
2. The established etiquette governing personal relations between individuals of the two races;
3. Segregation in the schools and churches;
4. Segregation in hotels, restaurants, and theaters;
5. Segregation in trains, street cars, and busses;
6. Discrimination in public service;
7. Inequality in political rights;
8. Inequality before the law;
9. Inequality in jobs and relief.

Thus, while white Southerners are completely opposed to intermarriage, and strongly opposed to calling Negroes "Mr." and "Mrs." or mixing with them socially, they say they do not object as strongly to seeing them obtain job equality, or even their rights as citizens of the United States.

This is hopeful because Negroes would rank their demands in almost exactly the reverse order. They are interested, first of all, in equality of jobs and pay, and second, in their rights as American citizens. Contrary to the white belief, few, if any, Negroes are concerned about intermarriage, and the question of civil courtesies is of much less importance than such things as decent schools, playgrounds, and housing. Segregation is not as burning an issue as equality.

In view of the fact that the Negro places the greatest store on those rights which the Southern white says he considers least important, it would seem that some basis of understanding could be achieved once the white man recognizes the need for it. . . .

EDITORIAL COMMENT

More convincing to many people than the Myrdal thesis that prejudice and discrimination against American Negroes have created a moral dilemma is the pragmatic argument that a caste system is too expensive in actual dollars and cents to maintain. Concomitantly, it is argued that the end of the Jim Crow system would ultimately be to the economic and financial advantage of minority and dominant groups alike.

Segregation and inequality require, among other things, duplication of facilities in the region of this country least able to afford the cost. Lower educational standards, poorer health, and smaller incomes for Negroes have meant throughout American history that Negroes cannot purchase and consume goods and services to the extent that others can. The result is that the entire economy suffers incalculable losses. Frustration of ambition, talent, and personality development have negative consequences in other institutional aspects of life as well. Illiteracy and poor health, for example, have reduced by thousands the Negroes who could serve in the armed forces of the country.

The late Louis Wirth, sociologist at the University of Chicago, was a proponent of this point of view, and in the following article he discusses in detail the "price" of prejudice all people in American society must pay.

16. THE PRICE OF PREJUDICE AGAINST NEGROES BY *Louis Wirth* *

| FOR WHITE | FOR COLORED |

To the visitor from the North such signs in Southern railroad stations come as something of a shock. No one has ever calculated the cost of these signs, much less of the practices which they symbolize.

The determination of the cost of segregation is not a simple problem in accounting. It is much like calculating the costs of disease, of ignorance, of crime, or of war. It involves not merely those costs of material things which can be translated into dollars, but also of more intangible, but none the less real, values of a human, a social and psychic nature which have an indeterminable order of magnitude.

Some of the costs of segregation are direct—such as what it costs the South to maintain a dual school system as over against what it would cost to maintain an integrated system of the same quality in which whites and Negroes shared equally. Other costs are more indirect—for instance the loss in productive capacity or in per capita wealth or income due to the lowered educational standards affecting both whites and Negroes under a system of segregated schools. Such loss, insofar as it expresses itself in public and private income and expenditure, is easily enough calculable. But who shall put a dollar value upon a human life wiped out by preventable disease, by a lynching or a race riot? Upon fear and suspicion which divide a community? Upon a frustrated ambition, a stunted personality, or an embittered soul?

* Louis Wirth, "The Price of Prejudice," *Survey Graphic*, XXXVI (January 1947), 19–21. Reprinted by permission.

The struggle against racial segregation and discrimination has been based in the main upon the claim that these practices are un-Christian and undemocratic. It might with equal validity be based upon the fact that they are uneconomical. The price of race prejudice has apparently not been too high to discourage even so relatively impoverished a region as the South from continuing to pay it. Yet if its sum total could be made clearly and widely known, it would conceivably add force to the moral, religious, and legal sanctions against racial discrimination.

There is, of course, no assurance that so rational a procedure as the weighing of gains against losses will commend itself to people who are under the spell of profound emotional urges, however thoroughly their prejudices may be rationalized by pseudo-scientific arguments that the existing practices are necessary and justified.

Indeed, segregation has even been justified on economic grounds. Thus, for example, it has been claimed that as long as the Negro can be served by segregated schools, the total cost of education for the entire community will be less than would be the case under an integrated educational system meeting the minimum expectations of the whites.

To the extent, however, that minimum standards of living and of public services are established for the nation at large, it is no longer possible to invoke this type of reasoning even in areas where the segregated services to the Negroes of the community, because of their number, constitute a large proportion of the total cost.

The Negro thus gains in some measure as the community as a whole advances. This has been notably true of federal programs in education, health, housing, and welfare during the period of the New Deal. On the other hand, the experience of philanthropic agencies interested in, among other things, the education of the Negro, indicates that financial support to segregated schools for Negroes can serve as an incentive to the whites in the community to improve their own schools.

METHODS—DIRECT AND DEVIOUS

The perpetuation of minorities rests upon the maintenance of segregation. As the physical and social barriers that keep racial and cultural groups apart diminish, the differences between dominant group and minority are minimized, and ultimately their separate identity is lost. In the largest sense, therefore, the very existence of minorities and the personal and social consequences that flow therefrom are part of the cost of segregation.

Whenever racial and cultural minorities exist in a society, some degree of segregation is practiced. Segregation is both public and private, formal and informal, direct and indirect. Its consequences affect not merely the minority, but also the dominant group and the society as a whole. The segregation of the Negro in the U.S.A. illustrates all these forms and effects.

In the North, segregation is for the most part private, informal, and indirect, whereas in the South it is public, formal, and direct. Although the North generally avoids frank measures designed to prevent or discourage free association between whites and Negroes, the physical and social distances between the races are nevertheless obvious. In contrast, it might be said of the South that, despite ceremonial and legal segregation, there is actually a greater degree of intimacy between Negroes and whites than there is in the North. This is indicated by the clearly demarcated and compact Negro residential ghettos or Black Belts in the Northern cities in contrast to the sprawling and more or less random location of Negro dwellings in the South.

DUAL ESTABLISHMENTS

It would take much more space than is at our disposal here to trace the effects of segregation as currently practiced in the United States against even a few of our leading minorities. The case of the Negro, as the outstanding minority, must suffice, and even in his case, only a few aspects can here be mentioned.

Since the Negro furnishes the most glaring instance of segregation covering the whole range of the forms and consequences of the phenomenon, his experience illustrates what is true to a greater or less extent in the case of all minorities. It happens that in the case of the Negro the segregation that is operative is perhaps more overt and deliberate than of other minorities, and the record is therefore more easily accessible.

There is scarcely an aspect of American life in which segregation of the Negro is not in evidence. In the South, until recently, segregation was rigidly and invariably enforced in respect to: transportation facilities, drinking fountains, toilets, waiting rooms, schools, clinics and hospitals, welfare institutions, jails, penal institutions, churches, cemeteries, theaters, parks, playgrounds, and housing.

If "separate but equal" facilities and services, as the legal phrase puts it, had actually been furnished to Negroes, the cost of duplicate institutions would have been enormous. Although the economies are usually practiced in the case of facilities for Negroes, the total cost of the dual establishments is obviously excessive and the quality of the services must necessarily suffer. Even if the South had not been under the pressure to maintain duplicate facilities, it would have had to strain its limited resources to keep pace with the more prosperous North. As it is, the economic plight of the South is substantially aggravated by its thoroughgoing racial segregation.

Hand in hand with a racially segregated system of institutions and physical facilities goes also dual administration and personnel. The South, which is economically a handicapped region, thus puts further brakes upon its progress by insisting upon dividing its limited supply of trained people into two staffs—one to serve whites, the other to serve Negroes.

Furthermore, as any intimate student of the segregated Negro community well knows, there is another complicating factor. This arises out of the fact that the Negro leader or professional person, confronted as he is by limited opportunities, is inclined to accept segregation either because of the increased power to bargain with whites for a greater share of the available resources, or else because the minority leaders have developed a vested interest in freezing the *status quo*. . . .

School Costs

The costs of segregation to the Negro, to the South, and to the nation have been most thoroughly documented in the field of education. The enormous differential in educational opportunities between Negro and white youth is shown in virtually every index of educational excellence. Grossly inferior as are the provisions for Negro children compared with those for white children on the elementary level, they are even greater on the high school level. When we come to the colleges and universities the situation is even worse, because the segregated higher institutions of learning, unlike the elementary and most of the secondary schools, are largely excluded from the benefit of public funds and must depend upon philanthropy. . . .

Considering the need of the Negroes under a system of segregation which, especially in the South, makes them largely dependent upon the services and leadership of their own educated and professionally trained personnel, it is obvious that the discriminatory practice of segregated education has a crippling effect upon Negroes. Segregation hinders them in developing the talents required for self-maintenance and social ascent. It also blocks their full participation in the responsibilities of democratic citizenship.

Since in our modern social order education is rightly considered the high road to personal and social progress, segregated education—which means inferior education—is a major road block which affects Negroes as well as whites, North as well as South. . . .

If the most glaring instances of segregated education are to be found in the South, it should by no means be inferred that segregated education is not practiced in the North. . . . Although education is not formally segregated—indeed, that is prohibited by law in many Northern states—it is nevertheless a fact, brought about by residential segregation, economic and cultural stratification, and the persistence of race prejudice. The truth is that openly acknowledged segregation probably has less embittering personal effects, and can be more readily adjusted to, than the subtly concealed but none the less effective discrimination against which there is little opportunity for concerted defense.

The personal and social losses incident to segregated education are similar to and have their repercussions upon health, welfare, economic opportunities, and the whole complex of living. As in education, so in health there is ample evidence to show that racial segregation in institutions and services is tied up with discrimination—and results in stupendous losses. . . .

A convincing documentation of the over-all cost of segregation and discrimination was developed . . . as part of the Carnegie Corporation's study of the Negro in America under the leadership of Gunnar Myrdal. Richard Sterner, in "The Negro's Share," analyzed the income, the employment trends, the occupational opportunities, the family expenditures, the food consumption and other items in the family budget, the housing conditions, the public relief assistance, and public emergency employment of the Negro. His findings show that although through federal welfare programs commendable progress has been made in the equalization of opportunities, the Negro gets far less, in relation to his needs, than the general population.

Similar evidence, though less carefully and systematically assembled, is available elsewhere concerning the practice and the cost of segregation in private employment, in labor, in the professions, in business, in the military field, politics, religion, in the press, the arts, and in science.

NEEDED: A BALANCE SHEET

It took the crisis of war to bring the American government and the American people to fuller awareness and the frank recognition of the enormous waste of manpower, of talent, and of the human, material, and spiritual resources that derives from our practice of racial segregation.

We took some resolute steps toward integrating the Negro and other minorities into the armed forces and into our industries. We began to realize the corroding effect of segregation upon our national unity and upon the effectiveness of our public and private institutions and organizations. We became conscious of the disintegrating effect of racial tensions upon every form of collective effort to strengthen ourselves against the enemy from without.

What was done during the war to reduce the practice and mitigate the destructive influences of segregation gave us a conception of what is possible in a society which seeks to achieve the promises of democracy. . . .

Even if we could afford to indulge our prejudices from a material standpoint, we would find it more difficult to do so in the future than we did in the past because of the nature of the war we fought, and the new position of leadership we have achieved in the modern world. . . . Moreover, the expectations we have aroused among our own minorities will lead them to resist any backsliding with greater militancy and with greater force—derived in part from our own admission of the incompatibility of segregation with our national principles and ideals. A searching calculation of the stupendous cost of our own folly might not help much, but to us in America, who are a practical as well as an idealistic people, it would give pause.

When humanitarian appeals prove impotent by themselves, they may find reinforcement in the red figures appearing on the nation's balance sheet.

EDITORIAL COMMENT

The caste system in American society includes a class system for whites and a similar one for Negroes. Since slave times, small but powerful middle and upper classes have evolved among the Negroes. They comprise such personnel as ministers, educators, doctors, lawyers, social workers, and businessmen. According to the sociologists who have studied caste and class, the emergence of middle and upper classes among Negroes has swung the caste line on its axis in the sense that some members of the lower caste are actually higher in class status than some members of the upper caste.

Some Negroes who have an economic advantage find their positions so profitable only because of the segregated *status quo*. They fear and resist changes leading toward desegregation, for to them the breakdown of the walls of segregation would mean initially competition with whites and loss of the social class status and the economic superiority which they now enjoy.

But obviously only a small proportion of American Negroes react to their minority group status by exploiting other Negroes and thereby developing a vested interest in segregation. No one reaction to their minority status prevails among American Negroes. Like other minorities, they react in various ways. Robert Johnson's findings, based upon intensive community research, substantiate this point. He shows that complete unanimity in Negro response may be said to exist only in their realization of minority status, their expectation of prejudice and discrimination by whites in the community, and their reaction to racial epithets. Otherwise, differentials can be observed in terms of five principal continuums. These are hostility and friendliness, insulation and integration, lassitude and militancy, avoidance and "whiteward" mobility, and self-hatred and race pride.

17. NEGRO REACTIONS TO MINORITY GROUP STATUS [1] BY *Robert Johnson* *

I. INTRODUCTION

In the current international crisis of conflicting group attitudes, sentiments and loyalties, men are fortunate in having available to them a vast amount of academic and empirical literature on the subject of minority group relations in world society. Most of these studies of minority group problems have dealt with (a) the position of minorities in the stratification of social structures; (b) the clarification of thinking on the subject of race, and on the relation of race and culture; (c) the psychological, sociological and economic analyses of the nature of race prejudice and discrimination; and (d) the discussion of techniques for the reduction of intergroup tension and the improvement of minority group status.

The present article is an attempt to contribute to a fifth area of interest: the differential reaction of minority group members to their minority group status. This subject has received intensive study by Myrdal, Frazier, Johnson, Strong, Rose, Cox, and numerous other social scientists. However, this study is the outgrowth of an intensive two-year investigation in a single community, using as a setting the general community as well as the rest of the American Negro world. In this study, the research techniques of participant-observation and of the cross-sectional survey method have been combined to determine how the American Negro in this community feels and reacts toward his minority status.

We are generally familiar with the current credo of the American Negro as expressed by Negro leaders, organizations and publications on the national level. This credo implies the desirability of concerted movement toward two goals: (a) the promotion of a general American drive toward the 'More Perfect Union,' and (b) the improvement of the Negro's status within the framework of the democratic creed. Militancy is urged,

[1] This study was conducted as part of the Cornell Intergroup Relations Study, sponsored by Rockefeller Foundation and directed by Dr. John P. Dean, Dr. Edward A. Suchman, and Dr. Robin M. Williams, Jr. The author, as research associate, has included this study in a final report, "The Nature of the Minority Community; Internal Structure, Reactions, Leadership and Action" (Doctoral thesis, Cornell University, 1955).

* Robert Johnson, "Negro Reactions to Minority Group Status" (Unpublished manuscript). Reprinted by permission.

self-hatred is decried, interest in international events is encouraged, friendliness and goodwill toward whites are advocated (with notable exceptions). In addition, a seemingly contradictory but actually realistic dual value is implied: (a) the desirability of strengthening Negro group identification and race pride, and (b) the desirability of struggling for full integration into American society.

On a local community level, it is evident that adherence to this National Negro Credo will be strongly affected by the socio-economic position of the individual Negro, by the background of racial experience that colors his current attitudes, by the nature and frequency of his interracial contacts, and by the attitudes of his reference groups and 'significant others.' This intensive community-wide examination of intergroup contacts, attitudes and social relations has selected, as part of its scope, the relevance of the national Negro credo to Negro attitudes in a specific locus.

II. THE GENERAL COMMUNITY SETTING

The study was made in a middle-sized, upstate New York community of 60,000 persons which we shall call 'Hometown.' It is a predominantly industrial community boasting twelve locally-owned and twelve absentee-owned relatively small industries, and one large industrial plant with 7000 employees. The city was selected on the basis of these criteria: (a) its economic and industrial organization was relatively representative of most middle-sized American cities, (b) it was not a 'boom town' nor was it 'dominated' by large nearby cities, large industries or educational institutions, (c) it had a fair distribution of ethnic groups. The Negro and Jewish communities were of approximately equal size, each comprising close to three per cent of the city's population. Roughly, 6% of the community members were of Italian-American descent. In addition, the community contained several Irish, Russian-Ukranian and Polish families.

After compiling relevant data on the history, demography and ecology, economic organization and social structure of the community, and after making 'quickie' surveys in six similar cities, the research group devised a questionnaire which was administered to 529 adult 'NaM's' (native American white gentiles), 150 Jews, 150 Negroes and 150 persons of Italian ancestry. The questionnaire contained an exhaustive inventory of contacts between majority and minority group members, an inventory of personality traits (authoritarianism, 'Jungle' outlook, frustration, and indices of psychoneurosis) and an intensive inventory of the elements of prejudice—hostility, antipathy, scapegoating, social distance, and stereotyped thinking.

When the majority group was asked about the Negro community, it soon became evident that most majority group members had (a) very little contact with Negroes, and (b) a great deal of prejudice against them. Half of the majority group members in the community had *no* contact with *any* minority group member (Negro, Jew or Italian) in any of the four areas investigated—job, neighborhood, organization or informal social group.

Respondents were asked about actual and hypothetical contacts with Negroes in these four areas. Fourteen per cent stated that there were Negroes living within a block or two of their home, 13% reported contact with a Negro fellow-worker or employee on their job, 10% belonged to organizations with Negro members (half of these were unions or veteran's organizations) and none of the respondents interviewed reported any Negroes in their informal social group. Attitudes toward Negroes in these four areas took this form:

Those who had Negroes	*Respondent 'feels different'*	*Others 'feel different'*
In their club (52)	10%	23%
On their job (67)	17%	33%
In their neighborhood (74)	27%	46%
In their social group (0)	—	—

Those who contacted no Negroes in these areas were asked:

Suppose a Negro wanted to come into:	*Respondent would object:*	*Others would object:*
Your club (205)	43%	68%
Your work group (226)	33%	47%
Your neighborhood (448)	60%	86%
Your social group (293)	77%	93%

It may be consistently shown that respondents reacted more favorably to the presence of Negroes in these four areas than they responded to the *hypothetical* possibility of Negroes in these areas, and also that in every single case, the respondent was more likely to say that *others* would object than to admit that he himself would object.

The researcher began the study with the assumption that most prejudices arise not from contact with minorities but from contact with other prejudiced people. This was confirmed by the fact that despite the lack of contact with Negroes, most whites expressed some type of prejudice against them. When presented with a social-distance scale (known as the 'distastefuls') Hometown whites answered as follows:

I would find it distasteful:
1. To eat with a Negro	49%
2. To dance with a Negro	82%
3. To go to a party and find that most of the people there are Negro	80%
4. To have a Negro marry somebody in my family	99%

When asked a modified version of the 'Chicago Tension Barometer,' 20% of Hometown residents said that they disliked Negroes, 22% thought that Negroes are demanding more than they have a right to (and 26% of these said that this made them feel 'pretty angry'); 41% felt that Negroes were pushing in where they were not wanted (of these, 23% averred that it bothered them a good deal). In addition, 42% agreed with the stereotyped statement that "generally speaking, Negroes are lazy and ignorant."

Allied to this statistical picture of anti-Negro prejudice in Hometown (though not always directly related to it) is the pattern of racial discrimination in the community and the configuration of operating policies and procedures by which Negroes are admitted to or barred from various institutional and organizational structures, depending on the will of 'gate-keepers' in power roles. In a state that has reasonably strong civil rights laws for the protection of minorities, outright discrimination against Negroes in jobs and housing, public facilities, or social groups is difficult to enact in a direct manner, and is, in some cases, impossible. However, more subtle ways of practicing racial discrimination often take their place. For example, although a direct refusal to serve a Negro in a restaurant might bring about a legal suit, the Negro may be otherwise discouraged by such devices as slow or careless service, overcharging, caustic glances and remarks, or the breaking of the Negro's dishes after the meal. In the face of this partial discrimination and fuzzy uncertainty about the possibility of 'runarounds,' the Negro frequently finds it easier to completely avoid the situation.

III. BARRIERS TO COMMUNICATION: ON THE WHITE MAN'S SIDE

In addition to the factors of prejudice and discrimination against the Negro, a third factor contributes to his isolation from the general life of the community. Woven into the speech of many Americans are elements of 'the *language of prejudice,*' derogatory remarks, slurs, and epithets that are insulting to the Negro. The content of interracial contacts is frequently (and negatively) loaded and charged with affect by the white person's careless or non-insightful employment of these elements.

The following are some of the elements of the language of prejudice, ranging from little minded careless expressions to the words that make any Negro "spit fire."

1. Phrases pertaining to color; equating whiteness with desirability and blackness with evil: 'that's darn white of you,' 'free, white, and twenty-one,' 'your face may be black but your heart is as white as mine,' 'he treated me white.'

2. Racial 'testimonials'—Statements from whites explaining that 'you're as good as I am,' 'I like you people,' 'I've loved the colored ever since I was rocked to sleep in the arms of my black

mammy' (a popular southern eulogy and indirect status attribute).

3. Jokes about other minorities, or disparagement of other minorities: 'You people are all right with me, but it's those Jews. . . .'

4. Imitating Negro dialect, staging minstrel shows or parodying the stereotype of the Negro, referring to Negroes as 'boy' or as 'Sambo,' 'Nicodemus,' 'Rastus,' etc.

5. Prejudgements and stereotypes—expecting the Negro to be able to dance, sing and clown merely because he is Negro, assuming that every Negro knows all there is to know about Negro history, traditions, attitudes on every subject, assuming that each Negro in America knows the other fifteen million.

6. 'Darky jokes,' comic stories about Negroes using dialect, or songs with racially derogatory content such as "you can hear those darkies singing."

7. 'Slips'—accidental use of racial epithets as: 'I worked like a nigger,' 'I Jewed him down,' 'there's a nigger in the woodpile.'

8. Intentional use of racial epithets such as "coons," "shines," "jigaboo," "smoke."

The varied interrelationships of these three factors: the patterns of prejudice, the patterns of discrimination, and the elements of the 'language of prejudice' constitute the 'Gestalt' that confronts the Hometown Negro. The expectation of prejudice in most whites, the fear of a rebuff or ambiguously embarrassing discrimination, the tense wait for the almost inevitable 'language of prejudice' (including what one Negro called the possibility of being *stabbed* with the word nigger') produces in the Hometown Negro a pattern of avoidance and defensive insulation, prompting the frequent white statement that 'the Negroes prefer to be by themselves.'

IV. Barriers to Communication: on the Negro's Side

While observing a variety of superficial, uncomfortable and sometimes frictional interracial contacts, the participant-observer developed a series of hunches on Negro reaction to these contacts. By interviewing a cross-section of 150 Negro adults, the researchers were able to verify some of these hunches in three areas: the interracial situations that make Negroes uncomfortable, the barriers to interracial contact, and the Negro's reaction to the language of prejudice. The results were these:

A. Situations That Make the Negro Feel Uncomfortable

When a group of Negroes gets noisy and boisterous around white people	88%
When a white person tells you "you're as good as I am"	44%
When you are with Negroes that are trying hard to impress the white people	37%
When a white person starts talking to you about Paul Robeson	31%
When a white person asks you how it feels to be a Negro	29%
When you are discussing race relations with white people	23%
When you are the only Negro in a group of people	21%
When you see white people in the Negro business establishments	9%
When a white person talks to you about Jackie Robinson, Ralph Bunche and other 'credits to your race'	0

(Only 8 Negroes [5%] stated that none of these situations made them feel uncomfortable.)

B. Factors That Deter Contact

Since avoidance patterns are developed in the American Negro as part of the socialization process, at an extremely early age, it is often difficult for him to articulate his reasons for avoiding contacts with whites as an adult. Many respondents were not sufficiently in touch with their own feelings to give a definite answer on the question of self-limiting contact. Thirty-two percent of the Negroes were unable to select any answer to this card question although the pattern of their group memberships and informal associations showed that they clearly *did* avoid interracial contacts. However, the 102 respondents who gave an answer other than 'nothing' replied, in answer to the question:

"Which of these things keeps you from contacting more white people than you do now?"

"I expect the white person to make a 'slip' and say something wrong about Negroes"	50%
"I have to keep up appearances so I won't reflect badly on the Negro Race"	30%
"I expect most white people to be prejudiced"	27%
"I have to avoid touchy subjects like intermarriage"	21%
"I don't understand white people"	21%
"I'm afraid my family and friends wouldn't like it"	11%
"I suspect that most white people are 'after something'"	9%
"I don't like white people"	3%
Other answers	13%

C. Reactions to the 'Language of Prejudice'

The four paramount elements of the 'language of prejudice' were considered to be the 'testimonial,' the faulty rapport device, the 'slip' and the epithet. The 150 Negro respondents were asked: "Which of these things make you angry, which just annoy you, and which don't bother you at all." The response was as follows:

	Makes Me Angry	Annoys Me	Doesn't Bother Me
When a white person tells you how much he likes Negroes ('testimonial')	9%	32%	59%
When a white person tells you how much he dislikes some other minority such as Jews or Catholics (faulty rapport device)	26%	36%	38%
When a white person forgets or "slips" and uses the word 'darky' (the 'slip')	57%	26%	17%
When a white person uses the word 'nigger' (the epithet)	74%	15%	11%

Violent negative reaction to the epithet was further documented by the Negro youths. At the end of a battery of questions about their white best friend, they were asked: "If your white *best* friend 'slipped' and called you a nigger, what would you do?" The response was explosive. Only six youths said they would assume the white friend didn't mean it, 13% said they would ignore it, or do nothing, 2% said they would sympathize, 23% said they would make a vigorous verbal protest ('wise him up,' 'tell him to watch his tongue,' 'I'd resent it and tell him so in strong words.'). Twenty-four per cent mentioned physical violence ('Slap her face, but good,' 'I think I would find myself fighting,' 'I would dip my fist into his mouth,' 'give him a black eye,' 'Sock him in the teeth.'). Only one charitable-hearted thirteen year old girl said:

"I would forgive."

V. The Negro Community

The Negro's expectation of white prejudice, discrimination, and careless 'language of prejudice,' coupled with the linkages caused by family and kinship ties, membership in the segregated Negro lodges and churches, physical proximity and mutual use of the community's contact centers produces a heterogeneous but isolated ghetto of individuals, who are generally lumped together in the minds of whites under the heading 'Negro community.' The researchers went into the field employing this unreflective term, and regarding all community members as one. Soon, an obvious division emerged: that between old settlers and newcomers, or floaters, transients, 'beanpickers' and 'gandies' (transient railroad workers). This evolved into a fourfold division based on length of residence; it became apparent that the lifetime residents were almost as inactive in their social participation as were the newcomers (5 years or less), while the people who had lived in the Negro community over twenty years (but not life) were by far the most active participants. Later, the community was divided into five discrete strata on the basis of socio-economic status: (a) the isolated 'elites,' (b) the 'stable pillars,' (c) the 'steady industrious' migrants, (d) the working 'floaters,' and (e) the indigents, seniles and 'winoes.'

Still later, using criteria of sex, age, status and social participation, it was possible impressionistically to place sub-groupings at various points until approximately *fifty* clearly discernible sub-worlds were plotted, each with its own style of behavior, physical locus, pattern of belief, and reference group. When these divisions are viewed, one after another, it becomes evident that it is difficult to generalize about a 'Negro community.' It becomes a unit only because the general community (with a few exceptions based on social status or personal intimacy) defines nearly all Negroes in a similar, and usually negative, manner.

The 'Negro community' is an isolated one and there are several evidences of it. Questionnaire evidence shows not only that contacts with whites are quite limited in quantity and in depth, but also that Negroes viewed many issues more as part of a psychological community of 1200 members than as part of a Hometown community of 60,000. For example, when asked the question: "If you were asked to put yourself and your family into one of these classes, which would you say you are in: the upper class, the middle class, the working class or the lower class?" 20% of the 150 Negro adults said *upper* class, because their reference group was the working-class Negro community rather than the predominantly middle-class general community.

Casual statements of community members also reflected the isolated social world. The statement 'It's all over town' generally meant 'all over the Negro community' and even this takes in only the solid core of the Negro community, and not its indefinite periphery. 'The prettiest girl in town,' or 'the meanest man in town' referred not to Hometown but to its Negro community. The term 'we' usually turned out, under probe, to refer to Hometown Negroes or to Negroes throughout the country, rather than to Hometown in general. At one time, the observer was reassured by a lifetime resident that he could feel free to discuss confidential subjects over the telephone, since the only people who would possibly be listening on the party line were white people who were so removed from the Negro's life that it didn't matter what *they* heard.

VI. THE NEGRO'S RACE ATTITUDE COMPONENTS

A general survey of the Negro's reaction to his minority status indicates these facts: The historical position and past southern experience of the Hometown Negro strongly affect his present relations with whites; the Hometown Negro community is socially almost completely isolated from the general community; the Hometown Negro feels strongly identified with the national Negro community and much less identified with the Hometown community; the Hometown Negro maintains a high level of consciousness on intergroup relations; a good deal of confusion, status dilemma and bitterness is produced by the Hometown Negro's uncertainty of his position in interracial situations; a number of the face-gaining and face-losing attributes in the Negro community are connected with ingroup-outgroup relations; the undefined nature of many interracial contacts, and the fear of insult or rebuff from outsiders erect strong barriers to interracial communication; the attitude of the Hometown Negro toward other minorities and toward himself are strongly conditioned by the majority definition of minority groups; the integration of the Negro into general community life is most likely when a new in-group definition is created, transcending racial lines.

Yet, complete unanimity in the Negro community seems to hang only around realization of minority status, expectation of white prejudice, and reactions to racial epithets. Even within the realm of racial attitudes, there is a vast difference of opinion within the community depending on (a) personality factors, (b) regional origin and length of residence, (c) current contacts and experiences with whites, (d) exposure to the media of Negro life and Negro protest, (e) exposure to "significant others" who mold opinion on race as well as other issues, (f) social position and social mobility, (g) conforming to the role that the community has created for the individual, and (h) success or failure in the enactment of that role. The Negro's reaction to his minority status may be described (in addition to differential reactions to the "language of prejudice") in terms of five main continuums:

1. Hostility	Friendliness
2. Insulation	Integration
3. Lassitude	Militance
4. Avoidance	Whiteward mobility
5. Self-hatred	Race pride

These five continuums cannot be separated within the individual personality, but rather, hang together in a configuration of "creeds" as we shall show. However, they may be discussed separately.

1. *Hostility and Friendliness*

It is certain that every Hometown Negro has encountered at one time or another, evidences of white prejudice or differential treatment from whites. In addition to his own experiences, he may feel *vicariously* the experiences of other Negroes, transmitted through the endless racial conversations, and through the militant Negro press which seldom hesitates to present in graphic detail the inequities, discriminations and atrocities perpetrated on Negroes throughout the country. Consequently, every Negro has experienced the emotion of hostility toward whites at one time or another. This hostility is usually only sporadic and occasional, rising under stress, and receding under pressure of a favorable interracial contact or under the necessity of turning attention to other things. However, in several cases, this hostility is generally resting near the surface, and is tapped in our questionnaire through reactions to the following questions, based on the responses of 150 adult Negroes:

"I would like to get even with the white man for some of the things he has done to Negroes." (25% agree.)

"No matter how nicely he treats a Negro, a white man doesn't really mean it." (26% agree.)

"Sometimes I hate white people." (33% agree.)

In general, Negro hostility is more prevalent among the less educated, among the southern-born, the youths and adults under 45, the female, the isolated, and the Negroes whose interracial contact was minimal. Often, this hostility is deflected at specific groups, particularly the foreign born, who are resented as having greater privilege on their first day in America than the Negro.

Hostility in the Hometown Negro community was most closely related to place of birth. Lifetime residents were least hostile, and the southern born were most hostile. As C. S. Johnson states:

> There is a considerable amount of racial discrimination in the north but it is a common observation that the Negroes who discuss these discriminatory practices most frankly are those who originally came from the south. The Negro pattern of behavior outside the Negro residence areas is carefully molded to permit maximum freedom within the vague margins of acceptability. Within the Negro areas, there is more realization and sense of both security and possession. Buried racial antagonisms can easily be called to the surface, however, in a variety of overt expressions with or without strong provocation. Migrants from the South in particular who have stored away memories of deep-cutting offenses discreetly tolerated in the South, may reveal undue aggressiveness in the areas of open competition.[1]

[1] Johnson, Charles S., *Patterns of Negro Segregation,* Harper & Brothers, 1943, p. 310.

The greater hostility of southern Negroes is shown by this table:

	Born in Hometown	Born in other Northern city	Born in South, came here from other North	Came from South
Per cent who agree that:				
I would like to get even with the white man for some of the things he has done to Negroes.	18%	13%	32%	37%
No matter how nicely he treats a Negro, a white man doesn't really mean it.	4%	24%	27%	42%
Sometimes I hate white people	12%	41%	33%	42%

2. *Insulation and Integration*

Minority group reactions have often been described in terms of a cycle; first, an absorption of majority group attitudes toward the subject's minority group and a consequent development of self-hate feelings toward his group; second, an attempt to integrate into the majority group; third, a rebuff from the majority group and a subsequent development of feelings of hostility, avoidance, and defensive insulation. According to Everett Stonequist's description of the "Marginal Man," a fourth process is possible: the development of in-group identification, pride and militancy.

There is evidence that Hometown's Negro youths may follow a cycle similar to this description. At any rate, the life history of almost every Negro's reaction to minority status will include a variety of rebuffs ending in a general withdrawal and isolation from the stresses of interracial contacts. This withdrawal results in a syndrome of attitudes that characterize what we call the "insulated personality." The insulate is characterized by his endorsement of the following statements:

"Negroes should live around their own people." (27% agree.)

"If I had a choice between an all-Negro club and a mixed club, I would join the all-Negro club." (50% agree.)

"I would find it a little distasteful to:

Eat with a white person 9%

Dance with a white person 17%

Go to a party and find that most of the people there were white 21%

Have a white person marry somebody in my family." 42%

Like the hostile personality, the "insulate" is likely to be southern-born, less educated, relatively non-participant, and predominantly female.

The insulate is also likely to be older than the non-insulate. In addition, the insulation responses tend to cluster together, or "scale;" that is, any person who would find it distasteful to go to a party and find that most of the people are white will also agree that Negroes should live around their own people, and prefer an all-Negro to a mixed club.

In reference to background characteristics, the most significant variables that will condition the Negro's attitude toward insulation are his education and his regional origin. Educational level was divided between those who had some high school education or better (only two of the 150 had college training) and those who had a grammar school education or less. Regional origin was defined by whether the respondent was northern-born or southern-born. Results are as follows:

	Better educated northern born (33%)	*Better educated southern born (19%)*	*Less educated northern born (15%)*	*Less educated southern born (33%)*
Per cent who agree that:				
Negroes should live around their own people	12%	21%	23%	47%
I would prefer an all-Negro club to a mixed club	31%	43%	59%	69%
I do not think it is all right for a Negro to marry a white person	29%	21%	50%	49%
I would find it distasteful to: Go to a party and find that most of the people are white.	12%	11%	14%	37%

3. *Lassitude and Militancy*

The Negro community is also divided on the necessity and possibility of militant action to improve the status of Negroes. The existence of militant feeling on the part of some Negroes is an argument against the allegation that the northern Negro is a caste member, since one of the characteristics of caste is the member's complete acceptance of his caste position. Myrdal has stated:

> [The Protest] attitude is not so uncommon as one would think, even among Negroes of humble status. But with the individual Negro there is always a tendency for the protest to become bent into defeatism. Negroes on all class levels give vent to this feeling of defeatism in expressions such as "niggers ain't got a thing," "We're the underdogs," "Negroes can't win," "there is just no hope for Negroes," "why bother?"
> This cannot be said publicly though. The protest motive

does not allow it. No Negro leader could preach it. No Negro newspaper could print it. It must be denied eagerly and persistently. But privately it can be said and it is said.[2]

This ambivalence about lassitude and militancy is frequently present in the Hometown Negro. On the one hand, it is status-losing for him to articulate publicly statements of defeatism about the Negro's position, except in an intimate circle of friends. On the other hand, disparagement of the Negro and joking references to the Negro's incapacity is sometimes acceptable and is often the subject of much banter and levity. Even the Race Leader sometimes pauses from his denouncement of prejudiced whites and directs amused or angry criticism at the Negro community, provided no whites are present. At an NAACP meeting, the chairman of its membership campaign shouted:

> I get sick of working for people with no thanks and no help.
> I asked one man to join the NAACP and he told me: "You
> know what—that thing ain't legal."

Thirty-five per cent of Hometown Negroes, and 51% of the even less potent Negro youths agreed with the statement: "I don't worry about the race problem since I can't do anything about it." When asked what they would do if refused service in a Hometown restaurant, 60% of the adults said they would leave without saying anything, 12% said they would protest to the manager, 13% said they would try to sue, 8% would report it to the NAACP, and 7% gave other answers. Like the hostiles and insulates, the lassitudinous Negroes tended to be older, less educated, southern-born, less participant, and female.

4. *Avoidance and 'Whiteward Mobility'*

Most Negroes tend to avoid the ambiguous interracial contacts that abound in northern cities. Sixty-four per cent of Negro adults agreed that "Negroes shouldn't go into business establishments where they think they are not wanted." The 100 Negro youths were also asked a battery of avoidance questions, and showed a similar tendency. Ten per cent of the youths agreed that "I keep away from white people as much as I can," 29% agreed that "it is best to stay away from white people; then you will avoid all embarrassing situations," 57% agreed that Negroes shouldn't go into business establishments where they think they're not wanted," and 77% agreed that "If a business place refuses to serve me, I think I should leave without causing any trouble."

On the other hand, 38% of Negro adults and 39% of youths agreed that "I would prefer to live in a neighborhood where there are not many Negroes"; 46% of adults and 62% of youths said they would prefer a

[2] Myrdal, Gunnar, *An American Dilemma,* Harper & Brothers, 1944, p. 758.

mixed social club to an all-Negro club. Statements like "I would like to know more white people than I know now," "Colored and white people should try to mix together more often," and "I wouldn't mind having white people in my social group" were dropped from the youth question-naire after the first 25 interviews because everybody agreed with them.

5. Self-Hate and Race Pride

The nature of self-hatred has been clearly expressed by the late social psychologist, Kurt Lewin:

> "There . . . seems to exist in every underprivileged group a tendency to accept the values of the more privileged group in a given society. The member of the underprivileged group there-fore becomes excessively sensitive to everything within his own group that does not conform to these values, because it makes him feel that he belongs to a group whose standards are lower. Such feelings against one's own group conflict with the natural tendency of the individual in favor of it. The result is a typically ambivalent attitude on the part of members of an underprivileged group toward their own group." [3]

The Negroes of Hometown are caught in this cross-pressure be-tween the high value placed on race pride and group identification of the National Negro creed, and the disparaging view of the Negro which they have absorbed from the general community. The tendency to disparage the in-group was strongly shown by Negro youths in response to these questions:

	Per cent who agree
If Negroes would prepare themselves, the white man would give them good jobs	59%
Negroes blame whites for their position, but it is really their own fault	50%
Negroes in this country need a lot more education before the white man gives them equal rights	47%
Negroes will never get ahead, because when one is succeeding, the others pull him down	41%
The white man is always trying to help the Negro but the Negroes won't try to help themselves	31%
Negroes are always shouting about their rights, and have nothing to offer	28%
Negroes would be better off if they acted more like white people	20%

On the other hand, it is status-losing to admit to others or even to one's self that one has no race pride or strong group identification. Most

[3] Lewin, Kurt, *Resolving Social Conflicts*, Harper & Brothers, 1948.

respondents said they were proud to be Negro and hopefully pointed to the Negro's past, his progress, and to current Negro heroes like Ralph Bunche, Jackie Robinson and Marian Anderson, as the basis of their pride. Only 28% of Negro youths said they would rather work for a white person than a Negro; 23% agreed that "Sometimes I wish I were anything but a Negro," 9% agreed that they would rather play with white kids than with Negro kids, and only 5% agreed that "If I could be born again, I would like to be born white." Eight per cent indicated 'white American' as the group they would like most to be born into, while 46% mentioned it as the group they would like *least* to be born into. Eighty-two per cent maintained that they would like most to be born Negro, 26% mentioned 'Spanish,' 17% mentioned 'Mexican,' and 17% said 'French.'

Efforts to work up a spirit of pride often conflicted with the obvious disadvantages of minority group status, as shown in these ambivalent statements:

> "I'm proud to be a Negro, but it's an ordeal and a struggle. You have a hard time to get anywhere. In view of the treatment, I wouldn't 'pick to scuffle.' "

> "Lots of people are worse off than we are. Negroes are advancing faster than any other race."

> "I'm proud of being a Negro—no use wishing—I've got to bear with it and make the best of what comes."

> One 78-year-old Negro woman summed it up by saying: "Being a Negro is no disgrace, but it sure is an inconvenience."

VII. A Social Typology

In a study of Negroes in Chicago, Samuel Strong adopted the method of empirical typology to reflect the nature of race relations in a large metropolis. Strong says:

> The assumption is that socially isolated minority groups, resenting their exclusion from the larger society, develop their own universe of discourse which is likely to express many reactions usually withheld in conventional communication with the outgroup. Under such conditions indigenous social types arise and are referred to in the everyday language of the group in a distinctive way that reveals their connotation. By isolating empirically the significant social types recognized by a minority group and studying the various characterizations attributed to them, it is possible to ascertain the meaning they have in the life of the community.[4]

[4] Strong, Samuel, "Negro-White Relations as Reflected in Social Types," *American Journal of Sociology,* July 1946, p. 23.

Since the main focus of the Hometown research was intergroup relations, certain individuals in the Negro community attained special significance because of the role they played in Negro-white relations. It soon became apparent that as far as race relations were concerned, there were discrete 'types' in the Negro community who were expected by the community to play certain roles in interracial elements of community life. Some of the more articulate community members were asked to formulate the racial types in Hometown and other communities. One picturesquely expressive respondent explained:

> (a) The type that accepts first-hand impressions—they don't think. (b) The "overbearing" type—he craves white people. (c) Always looking for "Uncle Charlie" to give them something—the freebe (gift-hunting) type. Can change conditions, but won't. (d) The type that thinks white folks owe us something. (e) The cautious type Negro—so scared he's gonna hurt the white man's feelings. (f) Untrained Negroes—don't know how to act around white people. (g) Uncle Tom type—the "white man's nigger"— always hanging on to some white peck.

Combining this community articulation with the observer's impressions, it was possible to designate five social types in the Negro community which we have designated as (a) the "Race Men," (b) the "Interracial Duty Squad," (c) the "Whitewardly Mobiles," (d) the "Uncle Toms" and (e) the "Hostiles."

1. *The Race Man* is generally the spearhead of militant race leadership in these smaller communities. He has achieved a measure of personality adjustment on racial matters, but sees the world through race-colored glasses and interprets most events in their racial context—how they will affect the Negro. He strongly distrusts whites, has a life history of frictional interracial experiences about which he is very bitter, and is uncompromisingly militant and hostile toward whites in general. However, he is able to completely waive this hostility when he encounters whites of whatever motivation, who are interested in helping the Negro through militant action. The Race Man is bitter not only at whites but also at more accommodating Negro leadership, at the indifferent Negro masses who won't support him, at the more disorganized areas of Negro life, and at all persons who are able or qualified to help in the struggle for Negro rights, but refuse to do so.

On the other hand, Race Men are favorably disposed toward all liberal elements in the community who are willing to help them—unions, the Democratic party, Jews, and many organizations that the general community regards as left wing. The credo of the Race Man may be summed up thusly:

The white man has been depriving us for years; profiting off our labor and taking our women. He can't be trusted; he will smile in your face and then stab you in the back. I will fight him at every opportunity and make him accord our people their rights. If I encounter discrimination through the courts, through picketing, through boycott, I will fight back by any legal means available. "Our people" take too much of this discrimination lying down. We should stick together, give each other a boost, and fight the white man until he gives us our rights.

2. *The Interracial Duty Squad* (researcher's term) are middle-class Negroes, generally in the highest socio-economic strata of the Negro community. They are actively participant in community life, particularly in interracial activities. They feel it their duty to represent the Negro at interracial gatherings, at banquets where a brown face is wanted at the "Democracy in Action" table, in organizations that encourage a *few* Negro members or in programs where the four "faiths" (Catholic, Protestant, Jew and Negro) are represented. They generally feel that Negroes should take advantage of these invitations to interracial activities; however they feel that they should delegate *themselves* rather than some other less middle-class Negro who might reflect badly on the race as a whole. One prominent middle-class Negro woman explained:

> The colored people don't like it because my husband and I are active in the Little Theater. They say "Humph, she thinks she's white folks." But the white people have invited Negroes to participate and *somebody* ought to go. And my husband and I get along with whites better than most people do.

This group is frequently placed in a "representative leadership" role by the Negro community. However, they are less militant than the Race Men, more inclined to disparage the working-class Negro, and more likely to participate in conciliatory negotiation with whites than in contention.

3. *The "Whitewardly Mobiles"* (researcher's term) are also usually of higher socio-economic status, but have an almost minimal identification with the Negro community and a low degree of group identification. They idealize all things white and disparage all things Negro. They have somewhat concealed but strong self-hate feelings and resent being classified with the Negro community in general. They are upwardly mobile but must strain toward integration into white middle-class life since they are already near the top of the Negro status hierarchy. Because of their obsequious and ingratiating behavior toward whites, they are often despised and disparaged by Negroes with stronger in-group ties and loyalties. On the surface, their hostilities are turned back toward the Negro group,

and whatever hostility they bear toward whites is deeply buried, except under stress. They are in the extremely small proportion of the Negro community (5% to 10%) who admit that they would rather be white than Negro and would rather associate with whites than with other Negroes. Such admissions are so face-losing that they must be uttered in secret, if at all.

4. *The "Uncle Toms"* are such a familiar part of Negro community life in America that the term is now being employed in the general community to describe an ingratiator and a "sellout." This is the term most frequently recognized and used by Negroes, and is probably the worst epithet that one Negro can hurl at another. Myrdal has stated:

> Especially since the time of the Washington-Dubois controversy, Negroes have been somewhat divided in their ideas as to what they should do about different aspects of the Negro problem. The major division today is between those who would be aggressive in the Negro protest and those who would compromise. The former call the latter "Uncle Toms" and "handkerchief-heads," while the latter call the former "radicals" and "hotheads." It is a serious charge in the Negro community today to call a person an "Uncle Tom." [5]

On the local community level, whether it be deep south or extreme north, the "Uncle Tom" is characterized as a person who "sells out" the Negro race, grins, clowns and ingratiates in the presence of whites (while other Negroes grit their teeth), tells the gossip and secrets of the Negro community to whites, and places self-advancement and white favors ahead of allegiance and loyalty to the Negro community.

The person designated by the community as an "Uncle Tom" usually tries to rationalize his behavior by explaining that the whites are fine and generous and that the Negroes themselves are responsible for the prejudice and discrimination that exists. However, the social pressures in the Negro community are so strong in the current era of growing group identification that it is now difficult for any person to practice "Uncle Tom" behavior and still be accorded respect from the Negro community.

5. *The "Hostiles"* are not frequently found in these smaller northern communities although they abound and are well recognized in the south. Recall Richard Wright's statement in "Black Boy":

> Having grown older and taller, I now associated with older boys, and I had to pay for my admittance into their company by subscribing to certain racial sentiments. The touchstone of fraternity

[5] Rose, Arnold, *The Negro's Morale,* University of Minnesota Press, 1949, p. 79.

was my feeling toward white people, how much hostility I had toward them, what degree of value and honor I assigned to race. None of this was premeditated but sprang spontaneously out of the talk of black boys who met at the crossroads.[6]

In the Hometown community, a Negro who was articulately and violently hostile would not be supported by the community in quite the same manner; he would more likely be thought "queer" or "soreheaded." However, a few are known. One 25-year old Negro male referred the researcher to one of his friends, saying:

> He hates a white man's guts. If he hears a man was killed some-where, he'll ask, "White or colored." If twenty white men get killed somewhere, he'll say, "Good. Should have been two hun-dred." He loves to read in the papers about some white man getting killed. He is the only guy in this town who *really* don't like a "paddy" (white man). My father don't like 'em either. But what you gonna do? You got to like 'em. They got all the money—they control the wealth. We'd look mighty funny not liking "paddies." We'd starve to death.

Interviews with "hostile" Negroes show that they usually have a basis for their hostility, rooted in a bitter past experience. However the fact that many less hostile Negroes (even "Uncle Toms" and "White-wardly Mobiles") have had equally bitter experiences suggests that the violent hostility toward whites may be the outgrowth of a larger person-ality problem.

In terms of approval or disapproval on these five social types, the Negro community was asked: "How do people in this town feel about this kind of person: would you say they strongly approve, mildly approve, mildly disapprove, or strongly disapprove?" They answered as follows:

	Race Man	Interracial Duty Squad	Whitewardly Mobile	Uncle Tom	Hostile
Strongly approve	45%	50%	12%	9%	7%
Mildly approve	39%	30%	23%	5%	7%
Don't care either way	2%	5%	12%	12%	23%
Mildly disapprove	3%	2%	17%	15%	25%
Strongly disapprove	2%	2%	22%	45%	24%
I don't know	9%	11%	17%	14%	14%

The results of this cross-sectional inventory of social types clearly indicate that the Negro community is aware of these types, is willing to identify them, and has a clear-cut perception of Negro community ap-proval or disapproval, depending on the service that each social type performs for the Negro race.

[6] Wright, Richard, *Black Boy,* Harper & Brothers, 1937, p. 23.

VIII. SUMMARY

From observation of hostile "Race Men" and ingratiating "white-wardly mobiles" in action, it was assumed that hostility in the Negro community would correlate with militance and that friendliness would correlate with lassitude. Analysis of the questionnaire results did not bear out this assumption, mainly because the social types are deviant cases, and are noticeable and outstanding in the community because of their atypicality. Actually, the community is divided into two opposed con-figurations of attitude which we may call the "Old Negro Creed" and the "New Negro Creed," with the social types falling somewhere between them. Omitting the Interracial Duty Squad (which represents more of a high-status pressure for participation than a configuration of attitudes), we could diagram the social types and the "creeds" in a six cell table, as follows:

Lassitude-Hostility-Insulation	Lassitude-Friendliness-Insulation	Non-lassitude-Hostility-Insulation	
"Old Negro Creed"	The "Uncle Toms"	The "Hostiles"	
	Lassitude-Friendliness-Integration	Militancy-Hostility-Integration	Non-Lassitude-Friendliness-Integration
	The "Whitewardly Mobiles"	The "Race Men"	The "New Negro Creed"

The characteristic racial attitude of the "Race Man" is directly opposed to that of the "Uncle Tom," the "Hostile" is the opposite of the "Whitewardly Mobile," and the old and new Negro creeds are diametri-cally opposed to each other. Since the vast majority of community mem-bers in the cross-sectional survey fall into either the old or the new Negro creed, we may summarize by describing the two creeds as follows:

1. *The Old Negro Creed*

The people who endorse this creed are generally likely to be older, less educated, of lower socio-economic status, southern-born, less partici-pant in either all-Negro or interracial activities. They are likely to endorse all the items of lassitude, hostility, insulation, self-hatred, avoidance, and "angry" reactions to the "language of prejudice." They are likely to have fewer interracial contacts than the rest of the community, likely to avoid or withdraw from interracial contacts, likely to feel "uncomfortable" in most interracial situations, and likely to have a high number of "distastefuls." They are strongly opposed to racial intermarriage. Their hostility is also directed towards the foreign-born, though not toward Jews. They are likely to admire any Negro who fights vigorously for the rights of Negroes in preference to the Negro leader who concentrates on general community improvements, but express inability, disinterest, or lack of qualification to fight the Race's battle themselves.

2. *The New Negro Creed*

Community members who endorse this creed are the younger, better educated, of higher socio-economic status and likely to be northern-born. (Exception—the educated southern-born). They have almost no "distasteful" reactions, express a belief in militancy, and maintain an attitude of friendliness toward whites in general. They have a large number of favorable interracial contacts and are interested in joining interracial clubs and promoting more tranquil contacts between the races. They have few discomforts in interracial situations and have a more temperate reaction to the language of prejudice, i.e., they are more likely to be annoyed than angry.

They are likely to deplore the incendiary aspects of the Negro press or the all-out, violent crusades of the "Race Man," but on the other hand, they have a high degree of racial optimism and are committed to an unwavering race pride and support of militant endeavor. They strongly believe in the possibility and desirability of an integrated society in which the Negro is accorded equal rights which are reinforced by law. They hold complete integration as their goal, have a somewhat more permissive attitude toward intermarriage, and regard the struggles of the Negro as part of a general drive toward "The More Perfect Union."

Thus, the National Negro Creed which is continually reiterated by Negro leaders, organizations and publications, finds its almost exact counterpart in the Hometown community, and, to varying degrees in all Negro communities throughout the American land.

EDITORIAL COMMENT

While advances made by Negroes in the United States were notoriously slow in the decades immediately following their emancipation from slavery, improvement in status has been very pronounced in recent times. Improvement can be measured in numerous ways. Some measurements are economic—beginning with the drastic manpower shortages in World War II and the role played by Negroes in meeting the demands for unskilled and skilled positions. Others are the achievement of social, legislative, judicial, and political successes. Economic advances undoubtedly opened the door to many of the other improvements in status.

A study made by the Census Bureau in the summer of 1955 revealed that Negroes were holding better jobs than they did at the end of World War II. It described the steady improvement in the economic status of American Negroes as one of the most important developments in this country in several decades. On the whole, the report emphasized, Negroes still lag behind whites in education, income, and type and adequacy of employment. But the historical differentials between the two have been narrowing. Twelve per cent of the employed nonwhites (mostly Negroes) in the United States in 1955 held white collar, managerial or professional jobs. This compared with 9 per cent at the end of World War II. On the other hand, 42 per cent of the employed whites held such positions in 1955, and about the same percentage had held these positions ten years earlier.

What about the Negro's advances in human relations? Ambivalence in the American creed guiding relations between Negroes and whites has long been expressed in the principle of "separate but equal." This came to be the official rationalization for the legally enforced segregation of Negroes without violating the theme of equality that is crucial to the "American Creed." The principle has been based since 1896 on the Supreme Court decision in the case of *Plessy v. Ferguson*. The specific issue in that case was whether a Louisiana provision for separate railroad accommodations for Negroes and whites denied the equal protection guaranteed by the Constitution. Asserting that "separate but equal" facilities in transportation were not unconstitutional, the Supreme Court's decision was confirmed in subsequent decisions on issues such as education.

There have been reasons for believing that the Supreme Court might one day reverse itself. One is the fact that the decision of 1896 was itself a reversal of an earlier Supreme Court decision in 1873 which had ruled that separate accommodations were not equal under the Constitution. The second has been a new trend in Supreme Court decisions. For example, in 1945, one of its decisions opened the political party primary to Negroes. Also there was a series of decisions against segregated interstate travel. In 1948, too, the Supreme Court ruled that covenants which would prevent the sale of real estate to Negroes were not legally enforceable in the lower courts. The third indication of possible reversal has been the growing conviction that the principle of "separate but equal" is a fundamental contradiction; segregation implies inferiority and inequality for one of the parties in question.

At mid-century, the Supreme Court of the United States had still left untouched its ruling of 1896 that segregation in itself was not necessarily unconstitutional. True, it had a few years before decided against segregation on interstate buses and trains, but it limited itself to saying Negroes were not getting equal treatment on segregated vehicles. In 1950 the Court decided that Texas and Oklahoma must admit Negroes into their graduate schools, but again it did so only on the grounds that Negro graduate schools in those states were not equal to those for whites.

The National Association for the Advancement of Colored People, together with other Negro and white lawyers, concluded that a more drastic step should be taken. It asked the Supreme Court to rule that segregation of Negro children in public schools, whether or not the schools were as good as those for white children, is inherently unconstitutional.

Seventeen southern states and the District of Columbia were requiring school segregation by law. This covered 40 per cent of the nation's public school enrollment. A total of 8,200,000 white children and 2,530,000 Negro children were attending elementary and secondary schools in these segregated areas. Four other states —Arizona, Kansas, Wyoming, and New Mexico—had local option, permitting the local communities to decide whether Negro and white children were to go to the same or segregated schools.

The issues were argued first during the 1952–53 terms of the Supreme Court and reargued in the subsequent terms. A wide range of arguments was presented by lawyers for the Negroes and those for the states. Only two arguments were central, however. The plaintiffs contended that segregation in any form is unconstitutional. The Fourteenth Amendment, they maintained, was intended to proscribe all forms of state-imposed racial distinctions and to give complete equality to Negroes. On the other hand, the basic argument of the states, led by South Carolina, was that laws providing for separate schools were constitutional under the police powers of the states. School segregation was not expressly proscribed by the Fourteenth Amendment, they asserted, and hence it came within the powers reserved by the states. If equal facilities were provided for Negro and white children, constitutional requirements were met.

On May 17, 1954, the Supreme Court's unanimous decision against segregation in the schools was read by Chief Justice Earl Warren, sustaining the argument that even with equal school buildings, segregated Negro children receive a substantially inferior education. The decision itself follows.

18. INTEGRATION IN THE SCHOOLS
BY *the Supreme Court of the United States* *

THESE cases come to us from the states of Kansas, South Carolina, Virginia, and Delaware. They are premised on different facts and different local conditions, but a common legal question justifies their consideration together in this consolidated opinion.

In each of the cases, minors of the Negro race, through their legal representatives, seek the aid of the courts in obtaining admission to the public schools of their community on a non-segregated basis. In each instance, they had been denied admission to schools attended by white children under laws requiring or permitting segregation according to race. This segregation was alleged to deprive the plaintiffs of the equal protection of the laws under the Fourteenth Amendment. In each of the cases other than the Delaware case, a three-judge Federal district court denied relief to the plaintiffs on the so-called "separate but equal" doctrine announced by this court in Plessy v. Ferguson, 163 U.S. 537. Under that doctrine, equality of treatment is accorded when the races are provided substantially equal facilities, even though these facilities be separate. In the Delaware case, the Supreme Court of Delaware adhered to that doctrine, but ordered that the plaintiffs be admitted to the white schools because of their superiority to the Negro schools.

The plaintiffs contend that segregated public schools are not "equal" and cannot be made "equal," and that, hence, they are deprived of the equal protection of the laws. Because of the obvious importance of the question presented, the court took jurisdiction. Argument was heard in the 1952 term, and reargument was heard this term on certain questions propounded by the court.

Reargument was largely devoted to the circumstances surrounding the adoption of the Fourteenth Amendment in 1868. It covered, exhaustively, consideration of the Amendment in Congress, ratification by the states, then existing practices in racial segregation, and the views of proponents and opponents of the Amendment. This discussion and our own investigation convince us that, although these sources cast some light, it is not enough to resolve the problem with which we are faced. At best, they are inconclusive. The most avid proponents of the postwar Amendments undoubtedly intended them to remove all legal distinctions among

* Text of the Supreme Court of the United States decision in the racial segregation cases (*Brown et al.*, v. *Board of Education of Topeka, Briggs* v. *Elliott, Davis* v. *County School Board, Gebhart* v. *Belton*, 347 U.S. 483) as reprinted in *The New York Times*, May 18, 1954. Footnotes omitted.

"all persons born or naturalized in the United States." Their opponents, just as certainly, were antagonistic to both the letter and the spirit of the amendments and wished them to have the most limited effect. What others in Congress and the State Legislatures had in mind cannot be determined with any degree of certainty.

An additional reason for the inconclusive nature of the amendment's history, with respect to segregated schools, is the status of public education at that time. In the South, the movement toward free common schools, supported by general taxation, had not yet taken hold. Education of white children was largely in the hands of private groups. Education of Negroes was almost nonexistent, and practically all of the race was illiterate. In fact, any education of Negroes was forbidden by law in some states. Today, in contrast, many Negroes have achieved outstanding success in the arts and sciences as well as in the business and professional world. It is true that public education had already advanced further in the North, but the effect of the Amendment on northern states was generally ignored in the congressional debates. Even in the North, the conditions of public education did not approximate those existing today. The curriculum was usually rudimentary; ungraded schools were common in rural areas; the school term was but three months a year in many states; and compulsory school attendance was virtually unknown. As a consequence, it is not surprising that there should be so little in the history of the Fourteenth Amendment relating to its intended effect on public education.

In the first cases in this court construing the Fourteenth Amendment, decided shortly after its adoption, the court interpreted it as proscribing all state-imposed discriminations against the Negro race. The doctrine of "separate but equal" did not make its appearance in this court until 1896 in the case of Plessy v. Ferguson, supra, involving not education but transportation. American courts have since labored with the doctrine for over half a century. In this court, there have been six cases involving the "separate but equal" doctrine in the field of public education. In Cumming v. County Board of Education, 175 U.S. 528, and Gong Lum v. Rice, 275 U.S. 78, the validity of the doctrine itself was not challenged. In more recent cases, all on the graduate school level, inequality was found in that specific benefits enjoyed by white students were denied to Negro students of the same educational qualifications. Missouri ex rel. Gaines v. Canada, 305 U.S. 337; Sipuel v. Oklahoma, 332 U.S. 631; Sweatt v. Painter, 339 U.S. 629; McLaurin v. Oklahoma State Regents, 339 U.S. 637. In none of these cases was it necessary to reexamine the doctrine to grant relief to the Negro plaintiff. And in Sweatt v. Painter, supra, the court expressly reserved decision on the question whether Plessy v. Ferguson should be held inapplicable to public education.

In the instant cases, that question is directly presented. Here, unlike

Sweatt v. Painter, there are findings below that the Negro and white schools involved have been equalized, or are being equalized, with respect to buildings, curricula, qualifications, and salaries of teachers, and other "tangible" factors. Our decision, therefore, cannot turn on merely a comparison of these tangible factors in the Negro and white schools involved in each of the cases. We must look instead to the effect of segregation itself on public education.

In approaching this problem, we cannot turn the clock back to 1868 when the amendment was adopted, or even to 1896 when Plessy v. Ferguson was written. We must consider public education in the light of its full development and its place in American life throughout the nation. Only in this way can it be determined if segregation in public schools deprives these plaintiffs of the equal protection of the laws.

Today, education is perhaps the most important function of state and local governments. Compulsory school attendance laws and the great expenditures for education both demonstrate our recognition of the importance of education to our democratic society. It is required in the performance of our most basic responsibilities, even service in the armed forces. It is the very foundation of good citizenship. Today, it is a principal instrument in awakening the child to cultural values, in preparing him for later professional training, and in helping him to adjust normally to his environment. In these days, it is doubtful that any child may reasonably be expected to succeed in life if he is denied the opportunity of an education. Such an opportunity, where the state has undertaken to provide it, is a right which must be made available to all on equal terms.

We come then to the question presented: Does segregation of children in public schools solely on the basis of race, even though the physical facilities and other "tangible" factors may be equal, deprive the children of the minority group of equal educational opportunities? We believe that it does.

In Sweatt v. Painter, supra, in finding that a segregated law school for Negroes could not provide them equal educational opportunities, this court relied in large part on "those qualities which are incapable of objective measurement but which make for greatness in a law school." In McLaurin v. Oklahoma State Regents, supra, the court, in requiring that a Negro admitted to a white graduate school be treated like all other students, again resorted to intangible considerations: ". . . his ability to study, engage in discussions and exchange views with other students, and, in general, to learn his profession." Such considerations apply with added force to children in grade and high schools. To separate them from others of similar age and qualifications solely because of their race generates a feeling of inferiority as to their status in the community that may affect their hearts and minds in a way unlikely ever to be undone. The effect of this separation on their educational opportunities was well stated by a finding in the Kansas case by a court which nevertheless felt compelled to rule against the Negro plaintiffs: "Segregation of white and colored children in public schools has a detrimental effect upon the colored children. The impact is greater when it has the sanction of the law; for the policy of separating the races is usually interpreted as denoting the inferiority of the Negro group. A sense of inferiority affects the motivation of a child to learn. Segregation with the sanction of law, therefore, has a tendency to retard the educational and mental development of Negro children and to deprive them of some of the benefits they would receive in a racially integrated school system."

Whatever may have been the extent of psychological knowledge at the time of Plessy v. Ferguson, this finding is amply supported by modern authority. Any language in Plessy v. Ferguson contrary to this finding is rejected.

We conclude that in the field of public education the doctrine of "separate but equal" has no place. Separate educational facilities are inherently unequal. Therefore, we hold that the plaintiffs and others similarly situated for whom the actions have been brought are, by reason of the segregation complained of, deprived of the equal protection of the laws guaranteed by the Fourteenth Amendment. This disposition makes unnecessary any discussion whether such segregation also violates the due process clause of the Fourteenth Amendment.

Because these are class actions, because of the wide applicability of this decision, and because of the great variety of local conditions, the formulation of decrees in these cases presents problems of considerable complexity. On reargument, the consideration of appropriate relief was necessarily subordinated to the primary question—the constitutionality of segregation in public education. We have now announced that such segregation is a denial of the equal protection of the laws. In order that we may have the full assistance of the parties in formulating decrees, the cases will be restored to the docket, and the parties are requested to present further argument on questions 4 and 5 previously propounded by the court for the reargument this term. The attorney general of the United States is again invited to participate. The attorney general of the state requiring or permitting segregation in public education will also be permitted to appear as amici curiae upon request to do so by Sept. 15, 1954, and submission of briefs by Oct. 1, 1954. It is so ordered.

EDITORIAL COMMENT

Increasingly instrumental in efforts to achieve the goals of equality and integration, especially in Negro-white relations, is litigation such as that behind the Supreme Court decision of May, 1954.

In results obtained, court decrees have been a weapon similar to the executive order and enacted legislation. Supreme Court decisions in recent years have been but part of a judicial revolution in which the federal courts have spelled out the fundamental civil rights of minorities.

While the Supreme Court in May, 1954 ruled that segregation in public schools was unconstitutional, it did not at that time implement its decision with a directive as to how any school system should desegregate. There were many practical questions to be settled. Therefore the Court postponed formulating specific decrees until plans could be made throughout the South and the border states and further arguments before the Court could be heard.

Ultimately, on May 31, 1955, the Supreme Court ruled that desegregation should proceed with "deliberate speed." But its opinion on implementation of desegregation also cautioned: "Full implementation of these constitutional principles may require solution of varied, local school problems. School authorities have the primary responsibility for elucidating, assessing, and solving these problems; courts will have to consider whether the action of school authorities constitutes good-faith implementation of the governing constitutional principles. Because of their proximity to local conditions and the possible need for further hearings, the courts which originally heard these cases can best perform this judicial appraisal. Accordingly, we believe it appropriate to remand the cases to those courts."

In 1956 the Supreme Court affirmed a lower court decision against racial segregation in tax-supported colleges and universities. The effect of this decision was to extend to higher institutions of learning the decision of May 17, 1954, banning segregation in the elementary and high schools.

Although private schools were not subject to any of these Supreme Court decisions, many parochial schools, especially those of the Roman Catholic church, complied nevertheless. In fact some of them had been desegregated even before the decision.

In March, 1956, *The New York Times* reported at length on a special survey made by ten of its reporters on what had been happening in the South with regard to the Supreme Court decision of May 17, 1954. The reporters were assigned to various states in the South and spent five weeks investigating the situation. The following selection is a summary of their detailed findings dealing with six major questions.

19. REPORT ON THE SOUTH: THE INTEGRATION ISSUE

BY *The New York Times**

1. How Much Integration Has There Been?

The degree of compliance with the Court's ruling ranges from complete defiance to complete implementation. Following are the states that have (1) made no progress at all, (2) made a token beginning, (3) made very substantial progress, and (4) completed the task.

No Progress. In eight states, not one Negro has been integrated. These states are Alabama, Florida, Georgia, Louisiana, Mississippi, North Carolina, South Carolina, Virginia. Furthermore, the Legislatures of five of these—Alabama, Georgia, Mississippi, South Carolina, and Virginia —have passed laws to thwart and contest the Supreme Court ruling with the obvious purpose (since the general expectation is that the laws will not survive court tests) of postponing integration by legal delays.

Token Progress. Arkansas, Kentucky and Tennessee have a few —very few—Negroes attending schools with whites. Texas has 10,500— but still only 5 per cent of its Negro students.

Substantial Progress. Five border states—Delaware, Maryland, Missouri, Oklahoma and West Virginia—have made considerable progress. In Maryland and Missouri, 80 per cent of the Negro students have been integrated; in Oklahoma, slightly over half; in West Virginia, two-thirds; in Delaware, 11 per cent.

Completely Integrated. The school system of the District of Columbia is now completely integrated. Of the District's 169 schools, there are, however, twenty-seven that are still entirely white or Negro, or have no more than one white or one Negro. This is due to neighborhood racial patterns.

The over-all figures above do not always convey an accurate picture of the situation within a state—or the prospective situation. For example, although only 313 of Kentucky's 38,760 Negro students were integrated last fall, next September Louisville plans to integrate, and most of the Negro population of the state is concentrated in that city. Again, while not a single Negro has been integrated in North Carolina, four cities— Greensboro, Charlotte, Winston-Salem, and Asheville—have indicated a willingness to begin integration.

A contrary prospect is offered by Maryland and Delaware. Baltimore's schools are integrated; Wilmington's will be next year. But on Maryland's Eastern Shore and in southern Delaware, integration is bitterly opposed.

* "Report on the South: the Integration Issue," *The New York Times,* March 13, 1956. A summary of this article appeared in *The New York Times,* March 18, 1956. Reprinted by permission.

II. WHAT HAVE BEEN THE PATTERNS OF COMPLIANCE WITH, AND RESIST-
ANCE TO, THE COURT'S ORDER?

From the outset it has been assumed that the percentage of the
Negro population would be the prime determinant in compliance with,
or resistance to, the Supreme Court ruling. Generally this has been true,
not only as between states, but within each state. Thus Missouri, where
Negroes comprise 8 per cent of the population, and West Virginia, where
they comprise 6 per cent, have been moving rapidly toward compliance,
and have experienced almost no difficulty.

In Fayetteville, seat of the University of Arkansas, in the northwest
corner of the state, Negroes are only 2 per cent of the population. There
was no opposition when school officials decided to integrate Negro high
school students who had been formerly sent to a Negro high school sixty
miles away at an annual cost of $500 to $600 per pupil. The school
superintendent said: "Segregation was a luxury we no longer could afford."
But in the Hughes school district in east Arkansas, a cotton-economy
area near the Mississippi, the school superintendent said: "Forced 100
per cent integration would destroy the public school system . . . I would
never let my two daughters attend an integrated school with two Negroes to
one white."

But there are very important exceptions to this general rule. These
exceptions indicate that—in some areas at least—there are other factors
in compliance more important than the number of Negroes in the population.

The outstanding examples of progress to date are Washington,
Baltimore and St. Louis. Yet Negroes form 64 per cent of Washington's
public school attendance, 41 per cent of Baltimore's, 35 per cent of St.
Louis! All three are border cities; they have ties with the North as well
as the South; they are cosmopolitan; they are centers of industry (if the
Federal Government is classed as an industry). During the war thousands
of Negroes got Government jobs in Washington of varying degrees of
responsibility; they streamed north to work in Baltimore's shipyards and
steel plants and in the manifold industries in St. Louis.

Some of The Times reporters believed that the improvement of the
Negro's job and economic status had lessened white opposition to school
integration. Thus, one reporter said in a memo to an editor: "Job-equality
tends naturally to facilitate race acceptance in other fields, through human
contact and understanding." This process will certainly be slower in the
South, for there—with some exceptions—Negroes are still given menial
jobs in factories.

Nevertheless, The Times reporters felt that generally the resistance
to integration would crumble sooner in the cities than in small towns and
rural areas. In part, they believed, this would be due to a larger, more
metropolitan outlook, and a better educated citizenry. But only in part.

Many urban Southerners, they believed, would be finally reconciled to integration in law because they knew that, owing to residential patterns, most Negro children would continue to be concentrated in the same schools. This would be probably true of Atlanta, for example.

For the reverse reason, the opposition to integration in the rural back country is likely to be hard and long. Negro field hands and share-croppers live close by white farmers. Under integration, their children would all attend the same county or district school. Similarly the housing pattern of many cities and towns—Charleston, S.C., is a notable example —where whites and Negroes live on alternate streets (a pattern dating back to antebellum days when slave quarters were in the rear of the big house) may make opposition to "legal" integration more durable than in cities where the Negroes are grouped largely in their own neighborhoods.

III. WHAT IS THE WHITE POINT OF VIEW?

There is some pro-integration sentiment—not merely resigned but positive—in the South. But not much. It is found chiefly among the Catholic clergy (the Catholic Church has taken a firm position that seg-regation is morally wrong), among some Protestant ministers, social work-ers and those working in the various state Councils on Human Relations, which have been created by the Southern Regional Council. These voices undoubtedly have had a moderating and leavening influence in the past, and that influence will be increasingly felt if (and this is a large if) the present tension is relaxed and outbreaks of violence can be avoided. But at the moment, most Southern advocates of integration speak softly when they speak at all.

At the other end are the voices of racial hate. These voices do not all belong to the "red necks" and "wool hats" in the back country reaches. Some of them belong to men of means and position in town and city. These are the men who have repaired together in some of the White Citizens' Councils (though not all the White Councils are characterized by "yahooism"), and in such various organizations as "White America, Inc.," in Arkansas and the "Christian American Segregation Association" in Delaware, which has trappings of Ku Kluxism. Most Southerners condemn this extreme element and its venomous racism. But the general feeling among the reporters was that its influence could unquestionably grow if tension in some areas degenerates into violence.

But on the assumption—an assumption which men of good will on both sides of the Mason-Dixon line pray will be borne out—that reason will prevail, then the fate of the Supreme Court order will rest with that vast middle group of Southerners who do not want integration, will use every legal resort to evade and delay it, but who deplore racism and rabble rousing, and fear violence. In this vast middle group are to be found many members of the more temperate Citizens' Councils and such groups as the Federation for Constitutional Government and Patriots of North Carolina. The doubts, hesitations, fears and opposition of this group were expressed this way by Russell Porter, who reported on Georgia: "The viewpoint of these Georgians is intellectually intersectional and international but emotionally Georgian. They recognize in their mind the need for social change, but in their heart and soul they cannot endure the actuality of breaking with ancient customs."

Repeatedly—in Mississippi's Black Belt and in the border states— The Times' correspondents heard the phrase, "We know integration is inevitable, but—." The key to the temper of the South lies in that word "but." The South—for several good historical reasons—is deeply conservative. Conservatism is a way of life dedicated to the belief that "the old ways are the best ways." Segregation is the old way. Many moderate Southerners, who quite willingly concede that segregation may violate religious and political ideals of equality, still feel that, in this imperfect world, it is—as one Dallas lawyer said—"a sort of natural thing." And they resent a dictated change in "the Southern way of life."

But one Times reporter at least felt that there was a deeper, more profound reason for the refusal to move more quickly toward the "inevitable." This was a desire—perhaps unconscious—to "save face." This is how Gladwin Hill, who reported on Louisiana and Mississippi, summed it up:

> These people are not so averse to changes in the segregation pattern as they are, subconsciously, to an embarrassing acknowledgement of a change in policy, to a tacit admission that to some extent the prevailing system has been wrong or at least obsolete. . . . But where this embarrassment can be avoided, these people tend to go along. . . .

> In this unconscious desire to save face, in this very conscious determination not to be held up to judgment and rebuke by other sections whose treatment of the Negro they regard as "hypocritical or fraudulent," are to be found the reasons for the reiterated pleas of many Southerners, "Don't push us too hard."

IV. WHAT IS THE NEGRO POINT OF VIEW?

Again and again, in talking with white Southerners, The Times reporters met with variations of "the Negroes don't want integration—my cook told me." While this cliché was delivered with all sincerity, the reporters agreed it was—as one of them said—a sentiment "confined largely to cooks, if it exists at all."

If one thing was made clear in The Times survey it was that the generality of Negroes want an end to legal discriminations. The executive director of the Negro Chamber of Commerce in Dallas, Texas said: "There is not a Negro alive who does not want first-class citizenship." The emphasis is placed on the words "legal" and "citizenship." Most Negroes fully realize that the abolition of Jim Crow practices would not bring social acceptance by whites. They know equally well that because of housing segregation in most cities, school segregation will remain practically in effect. But it is the legal branding that burns most deeply. One Negro in Little Rock put it this way:

> Negroes are still interested in their own institutions, their churches, their communities, their theatres. But . . . when I go downtown and want a cup of coffee I like to feel free to go into a restaurant and get it.

Another—an official of the National Association for the Advancement of Colored People—gave his opinion that: "Once the stigma, the barrier is removed, there will be no rush into white schools. Housing and choice will keep most people right where they are."

But beyond this legal recognition, the Negro hungers to be part of a larger community, to assume his responsibilities as a citizen, to participate in civic affairs and have some voice in them. Reporting from Mississippi, Gladwin Hill quotes a kindly white business man: "Why, every Negro here knows some white person he can discuss his problems with." But, Mr. Hill points out, this paternalistic kindliness, however well meant, is blind to the Negro's need and desire. What the Negro wants is to be able in a representative group to "discuss things as simple as a leaky school roof."

But the Negroes of the South know very well that they will not be accepted as part of the civic community until the Negro educational level is raised. Despite the fact that many states are trying to equalize the physical school facilities, generally the money spent per Negro child is below that spent per white student. Therefore, the Negro sees in legal integration the means to a very practical end—better education. A Florida Negro Ph.D., the executive secretary of the State Teachers Association, comprising 6,000 Negro teachers, said: "We realize social change can't come overnight. However we don't want to wait until the year 2000. For the present, lower classroom standards might result from integration. It wouldn't take very long to catch up. Integration would stop Negroes from having inferior books, facilities and teachers."

The N.A.A.C.P. does not underestimate the strength of the opposition. But it is not dismayed. One N.A.A.C.P. official said: "We've had a long way to go. We've had to overcome a lot of apathy built among the colored over the years." The N.A.A.C.P. does not intend to let this apathy take hold again. Its officials impress on Negroes that integration is "their due and their duty."

The Times reporters everywhere found N.A.A.C.P. officials convinced, on the basis of experience, that the only way to meet the opposition was by direct attack. Over the past several years the N.A.A.C.P. has used court action to level, one after another, the legal barriers to equality. Its strategy now is adapted to the situation in each state.

Generally where a state has made a tentative beginning on integration, or set a time-table for doing so, the N.A.A.C.P. has been holding legal action in abeyance, giving the state every opportunity to show "good faith." But in those states bent on defiance or indefinite delay, the N.A.A.C.P. intends to press to court tests.

V. What Problems, Social and Educational, Has Integration Brought?

Even the stoutest advocates of integration conceded that it might—at least in the early stages—create headaches for school administrators. There was, first, the possibility that racial intermingling would bring major disciplinary and moral problems. Second, there was the question whether, and how much, educational standards would be affected, since Negroes as a group are on a lower educational level than the majority of whites. Third, there was the problem of Negro teachers. Some of them would continue to teach in schools largely Negro; but others, if they were to be retained, would have to teach mixed classes. Could Negro teachers also be integrated?

On the basis of those states where there has been considerable integration, these are the answers—so far tentative—that The Times reporters found:

Social effects. Generally integration has been effected without trouble between Negro and white students. At the outset, there was a four-day strike of white students in half a dozen Washington schools and a flare-up in several sections of Baltimore. But the protests and demonstrations collapsed against the firmness of civic authority. In the Washington schools, Times reporter Luther Huston reported there has been little mixing so far in social situations. In cafeterias, for example, the two races have tended to sit apart. Although segregationists had expressed fears that there might be trouble at dances, these fears have not been borne out.

Educational standards. Whatever the reasons—lack of opportunity, poorer teaching, home environment, economic status—the fact is that Negroes are, as a group, on a lower educational plane than whites. This has been established by repeated tests. For example, a survey of about 6,000 students in the seventh grade in Washington, D.C., showed 65 per cent retarded two or more years in reading and arithmetic. Three-fourths of the 65 per cent were said to be Negroes.

Mr. Huston reported the feeling of Washington teachers that integration has slowed the pace of classroom teaching, with a consequent resentment of white parents. Many white parents, who can afford it, are sending their children to private schools. However, Washington school officials believe that, by the very fact of integration this lag will be largely eliminated in a few years, and that this progress can be speeded by reducing the size of classes.

Negro teachers. In Washington, Baltimore and St. Louis, Negro teachers have not been displaced by integration. Many are teaching mixed classes. In other places, however, there has been considerable opposition to Negroes teaching mixed classes. For example, in Oklahoma, 150 Negro teachers have lost their jobs as the result of integration. In Missouri many Negro teachers have been dismissed. Negro educators recognize the problem, but many of them are prepared to make the immediate sacrifice. The president of Kentucky State College, which has trained most of that state's Negro teachers, said: "I believe the same people who resisted integrating children and came to it will come to integrating teachers eventually."

VI. WHEN WILL INTEGRATION BE GENERALLY ACCEPTED?

What is the end date on "inevitable?" Obviously there can be no sure answer to this. Much depends on chance—incidents of violence could delay integration for years. Much depends on the politicians—their words can inflame passions or moderate them. Much depends on the influence of a younger generation in the South.

Depending on the states they visited, the degree of opposition they found, the people they talked to, The Times correspondents put various dates on "inevitable"—ten years, fifteen years, fifty years.

Despite the apparent intransigence in many states, some of the reporters felt the segregation walls might tumble sooner than expected or predicted. Following are two of those feelings as set forth in memos to the editor from reporters who covered areas where opposition was most determined:

The first reporter writes: "Segregation is bound to go because (1) its illogic is becoming increasingly apparent, with separation on street cars, but none in elevators, bank window lines or stores; (2) its inequity is increasingly pronounced, with payment of substantial taxes by Negroes and then the expenditure of tax money on a one-horse-one-rabbit basis; (3) a multitude of economic squeezes make it too costly."

The second memo reads: "I feel that in spite of the allegiance to the old ways, there is that vague something that tells you that integration is coming. I personally do not see it in terms of fifteen or twenty years. If something like the Lucy case breaks out, resistance will harden. But if the tide of integration keeps moving, then resistance may go with a quick, total collapse once the outer wall is cracked."

VI. American Immigration

U NLIKE the Indians and Negroes, the bulk of the American population, whether dominant or minority groups, came here from Europe and Asia by the process of immigration. Immigration is merely the most recent phase of the overall process of migration, earlier phases having been dispersion, invasion, conquest, and colonization. The continuation of migration during the modern era has led to convergences in immigrant-receiving countries like the United States, Canada, Australia, New Zealand, the Union of South Africa, and the South American states.

Europe's position as a major source of emigrants is indicated by the fact that at least one eleventh of the earth's population presently comprises European emigrants and their descendants. The reasons for emigration from European countries and immigration chiefly to the several countries listed above, including the United States, are to be found in the general differences between the two sets of countries. Immigration-receiving countries are usually newer, less densely populated, and offer greater economic opportunities, lighter military burdens, and broader opportunities for social relations and religious expression than the emigrant-sending countries.

After the period of colonization, American immigration took on a meaningful sequence of patterns. The first pattern, "old" immigration, lasted until the eighth decade of the nineteenth century. Like colonization, it drew people mostly from northern and western Europe. The decade of 1880 to 1890 saw the transition from "old" to "new" immigration, and from 1890 until approximately 1930, the new immigrants came predominantly from central, southern, and eastern Europe. In the meantime, during the nineteenth century, there was Asiatic immigration, and immigration from other American countries proceeded into the twentieth century. Since the middle of the 1930's, refugees and displaced persons have come primarily from central and eastern Europe. Lastly, we have received Puerto Rican migrants who, technically not immigrants because of their American citizenship, nevertheless have had problems of adjustment similar to those of immigrants in previous movements, especially "new" immigration.

As the most popular destination of so many earth-hungry and freedom-seeking emigrants, the United States in the nineteenth century found it necessary to develop immigration policies regarding the numbers and characteristics of the people it would receive. The evolving policies came to represent still another part of the struggle between the two conflicting American traditions and creeds discussed in earlier sections of this book. On the one hand, there were the democratic ideas and sentiments expressed in Emma Lazarus' famous words: "Give me your tired, your poor, your huddled masses yearning to breathe free." In conflict with these were the discriminatory, selective beliefs that only certain types of immigrants had the potential of becoming desirable Americans. Thus, American immigration policies have at one time or another been based on free immigration, exclusion, selective (qualitative) regulation, and restrictive (quantitative) regulation. People entering the United States have become quota immigrants, nonquota immigrants, and nonimmigrants. Immigrant laws themselves have frequently been combinations of two or more of the various policies. Earlier laws have not necessarily been made obsolete by subsequent laws.

One of the most influential factors in stratifying the American population in intergroup relations was the time-sequence of arrival of the various immigrant groups. If American immigration had drawn people indiscriminately and simultaneously from all parts of the world, especially Europe, it is most unlikely that our problems of dominant and minority group relations would have been as intense as they came to be.

Because immigration, unlike invasion and conquest, is a peaceful process and those who enter the country do so in deference to the wishes and rules of the natives and those who immigrated earlier, the time of arrival becomes crucial in determining group status. Accordingly, the earliest immigrants who came mostly from northern and western Europe were at an advantage in later years; those who arrived in recent times from central, southern, and eastern Europe were subordinate. This pecking-order or step-ladder character of American immigration, as Davie implies in the following selection, accounts substantially for the unofficial dominance and prestige associated with Protestantism and derivation from the British nationalities. The minority group status logically ensued from non-Protestant affiliation and from nationalities derived from central, southern, and eastern Europe.

20. AMERICAN IMMIGRATION AND ITS EUROPEAN SOURCES AND PATTERNS
BY *Maurice R. Davie* *

WHAT is immigration? How does it differ from other forms of population movement? What is its historical setting? Throughout the whole history of mankind migration has been an ever-recurring phenomenon. Immigration, as a distinctive movement, is simply the most modern phase of the age-long tendency of men to migrate in order to improve their conditions of life. In prehistoric times these movements of population probably took the form of more or less blind dispersions or wanderings, a type of migration characterized by a slow movement of groups, with no strict destination, into uninhabited territory and therefore unopposed and peaceful. In some such way, over a long period of time, mankind spread from its cradle or cradles to occupy practically the entire earth before the dawn of history. Among historic peoples four types of movement have been distinguished,

* From Maurice R. Davie, *World Immigration* (New York: The Macmillan Co., 1936), pp. 1–11, 96–8, 179–83. Used with the publisher's permission.

to which the terms invasion, conquest, colonization, and immigration have been applied. These represent not so much a chronological order as a given type of cultural development. . . .

Types of Migration

The most important types of migration which history has recorded have generally been distinguished as follows. We are interested in these definitions only as a means of bringing into sharper relief the particular phase of migration we are concerned with.

Invasion is characterized by a movement *en masse* of a people whose culture is less advanced overrunning the territory of a more highly developed group. It is a concerted, hostile movement of whole peoples acting as military or political units. The end sought is the benefit of the tribe as a whole. The migrations of the semi-barbaric tribes into the countries of southern and western Europe are classic examples: the invasion of the Goths from the middle of the third century to the end of the fifth, that of the Huns in the fourth, that of the Vandals in the fourth and fifth, and that of the Magyars at the close of the ninth. Another example is the spread of the Arabs and Turks over Europe and northern Africa.

Conquest is the reverse of invasion, in that a people of higher culture takes the offensive, conquers a less advanced people, imposes its political system on them, and lays them under tribute. This is an enterprise of the state, seeking its own glory and aggrandizement. It involves but a slight movement of population. The great historical example of conquest is of course that of Rome. Another striking illustration is provided by the empire of Alexander the Great. . . .

A new era in population movements was inaugurated by the voyages of discovery in the fifteenth and sixteenth centuries. Earlier migrations had been mainly overland or across land-locked seas. Oceans had been barriers; gradually they became highways. The oceanic period or modern migratory epoch has been characterized, unlike its predecessors, by changes of residence occurring increasingly and at last predominantly over the water. Other new features were the enormous extent of the new lands and the small power of resistance of the inhabitants. Man's new power to traverse the oceans almost at will disturbed the equilibrium previously existing between different human groups and started currents of migration which grew in volume and spread from area to area until the present time. Associated with these migrations was a great and accelerating growth of the population of the earth, which has probably quadrupled since the middle of the seventeenth century. "The greatest source of these migratory currents was Europe, and today one-eleventh of the earth's population consists of Europeans . . . who are living outside of that continent. There are between one and a half and two times as many such European folk living elsewhere as there were living in Europe in the seventeenth century. From these currents of migration within the oceanic period swarming into and multiplying in a sparsely settled region of surpassing natural resources the United States has arisen as the one full-grown child of Europe. Of all the Europeans now living elsewhere three-fifths are in the United States." [1]

The new form of movement following the Discoveries Period has had two phases: colonization and immigration. The fundamental ideas of colonization are a movement of population and an extension of political power. It is a state enterprise, the state sending out its citizens to settle in new countries. The motive is the commercial advancement of the state, on a non-military plane if possible, as contrasted with the military or political aggrandizement of conquest. The great colonial expansion took place in the seventeenth and eighteenth centuries. It may be said to have come to an end with the Treaty of Paris (1763) which settled the colonial possessions of the European powers, although there were subsequent discoveries and subsequent changes in the ownership of colonies. In the case of the United States a more appropriate date for the ending of the colonial period is 1783, when the treaty of peace was signed with England.

Distinctive Features of Immigration

Immigration differs from colonization in being a mass movement composed of individuals or families not forming a coherent association. Though governments may encourage or regulate immigration, it is not a state enterprise, but results from the spontaneous decision of individuals on the ground of personal motives. Even when the current appears to be a collective whole, it is seen on closer examination to be only a loose association of interested individuals. It is essentially a peaceful movement, in which citizens of a foreign country have been allowed free access to a modern state, provided they come as individuals and on their own initiative. This feature sets immigration off as something entirely different from any previous population movement.

A further characteristic of immigration is that . . . there has never been any appreciable amount between the Temperate Zones and the tropics, in either direction, nor have the Polar Regions ever been concerned. In fact, "practically all immigration, historically speaking, has been between different countries in the Temperate Zones." [2] That is, immigrants have not moved out of their natural environment, as was true in some instances of colonists.

The reasons for immigration will be found in the differences between

[1] Walter F. Willcox, "Introduction," *International Migrations*, New York, National Bureau of Economic Research, 1931, Vol. II, p. 30.

[2] Henry P. Fairchild, *Immigration*, New York, The Macmillan Co., rev. ed., 1925, p. 25.

the countries concerned with the movement. The country which receives the stream of immigration is newer, much less thickly settled, than the other, and living conditions are more favorable. The ratio between population and land is low. As a consequence, the immigrant-receiving country is more democratic, its people enjoy greater social and political equality, there is more individual freedom of conduct, traditional and legal restraints are fewer, military burdens are lighter, and there is greater latitude for religious belief and practice. Here are the chief motives for immigration. The new country is attractive economically, politically, religiously, and socially; the old country is repellent in these respects. . . .

Immigration has generally been directed toward the less fully occupied regions because there the competition of life is less severe. Population density, considered concomitantly with the level of civilization, is an index to the direction of the movement. . . . As matters now stand, Europe and Asia, with two-fifths of the world's area, support nearly four-fifths of the world's population. As long as differences exist in birth rates, in density of population, in economic pressure, and in social, political, and religious conditions, the drive to migrate to new and better lands will continue. Struggles will continue to arise from inequalities in population density, for example over the question whether nations with vast unexploited areas are justified in excluding less fortunate peoples.

Historically, immigration is the most recent type of population movement. As a world phenomenon it was made possible by the Discoveries Period which opened up the outlying continents, the great immigrant-receiving regions. As a mass movement it was conditioned by the Commercial Revolution which introduced rapid, easy, and inexpensive means of transportation. It may be laid down as a rule that the volume of immigration is determined in part by the cost and the degree of hardship involved in transit. Immigration is also ultra-modern in that it is conditioned by individual freedom to migrate. It could not exist so long as the old idea prevailed of the feudal bond between the person and the land. It presupposes the right of expatriation. Strictly defined, it does not include the cases of forced migration, such as the expulsion of the Jews from various European countries during the Middle Ages, of the Moors from Spain and the Huguenots from France, or the exportation of slaves from Africa or the transportation of criminals to penal colonies. It is essentially, though not solely, a voluntary movement on the initiative of the individual. . . .

The broadest possible definition would include migrants whose destination was a colonial possession of the country to which they belonged; but more strictly speaking, the country of destination is not a dependency or colony but a sovereign nation. The typical immigrant is an alien, and because of this fact the problem of naturalization has arisen.

The term migration includes all changes of abode, even the shifting of animals on land, in water, or in air. But emigration and immigration by their prefixes imply the existence of an organized state in which the migrant has resided or intends to reside. The words are different names for one and the same change of place, regarded from the point of view now of the state which is left and now of the state which is entered. They exclude the many cases of human migration, a large majority of the entire number, in which the change of residence does not take the individual out of one country or into another. . . . Only the foreign-born are immigrants; the others are simply migrants.

True emigration and immigration involve a permanent change of residence. Yet much of the movement in recent years is not of this type. In the eighteenth and early nineteenth centuries, when the voyage was prolonged, trying and dangerous, and when many of the emigrants died en route, emigration was almost unchangeable and final. Today, when the voyage takes only a few days in safe and comfortable ships without hardship or danger and at low rates, a removal overseas has ceased to be an irrevocable step. Indeed, here and there seasonal emigration has developed, that is, workers who transfer their domicile to an overseas country to profit by its economic opportunities, temporarily or for a favorable season. Therefore the term "emigrant" must be defined more loosely than before, as one who departs from the mother country to gain his living abroad. . . . According to the United States Bureau of Immigration, an immigrant is an alien officially admitted into the United States whose last permanent residence was in some foreign country and who comes with the declared intention of residing here permanently. Residence of twelve months or more is considered permanent. This definition includes the essential characteristics of immigration. . . .

Historical Perspective

In the first half of the nineteenth century the largest emigration was from Great Britain and Germany, while that from other European countries, notably France, Scandinavia, and Switzerland, was a small part of the whole, although large perhaps in comparison with their own populations. The movement from Asia had scarcely begun. During that period emigration was directed principally towards territories where the emigrant found racial connections, language, religion, and institutions similar to those of his mother country. The citizens of the United Kingdom thus went in large numbers to the United States or to British possessions. Until about 1850 the movement was determined mainly by conditions in European countries. Emigration was practically confined to persons who were driven to it by economic, political, or religious circumstances in the mother country. The new lands beyond the seas were not well known or attractive, and no one knew what fate awaited him there. Moreover, the high cost of the journey and grievous conditions in the emigration ports and on board ship were added deterrents, while transportation by land was extremely troublesome, so that many persons never reached the port of embarkation. Nevertheless, at the beginning of the nineteenth century there was a fairly large movement, but not until the 1840's did it become a mass movement of European populations and that principally because the legal obstacles to emigration had been gradually removed.

Everywhere serfdom was coming to an end. One of the results of the French Revolution was the freedom of the individual to migrate within and from his country. The increase in population, made possible by technological advance, provided labor for overseas territories. The recurring depressions of the economic cycle involved periodic unemployment. One relief measure was emigration, sometimes spontaneous but frequently assisted by the authorities. The number of emigrants was also increased by the impoverishment of agriculture. Countries where large estates and a tenant system prevailed, notably Ireland and Germany, suffered severely from periodic depressions. In countries where small holdings existed, as in southern Germany and Switzerland, the progressive subdivision of the land frequently led to considerable emigration. Certain political disturbances, such as the despotism in Germany after the Napoleonic period and the democratic revolution in 1848, induced large sections of the middle classes to seek a livelihood in the New World.

Emigration from these countries of northern and western Europe reached a peak in the 1880's. As soon as it began to decline, the great steamship companies became interested in drawing the high wages in the Americas to the attention of the agricultural proletariat of southern and eastern European countries (especially Italy, Austria-Hungary, and Russia) in which the system of large estates had brought about unfavorable living conditions. Satisfactory terms of transportation offered them the prospect of greatly improving their economic and social position in the New World, and the movement from these quarters soon amounted to hundreds of thousands annually. Meanwhile emigration from certain Asiatic countries had begun as a means of escaping from hard conditions of life.

Emigration did not become a mass movement until the 1840's, due primarily to the fact that until that time legal obstacles to emigration had not been removed. Laws restricting emigration were common in the seventeenth and eighteenth centuries in most European and Asiatic countries. But during the first half of the nineteenth century under the influence of economic liberalism many of these restrictive laws were repealed, and by the end of the century practically all of them were removed. The right to emigrate, however, is still not complete. In no country is the principle recognized without exception. The interests of justice, national defense, and sometimes even of the intending emigrants themselves, frequently bring about limitations. . . . Thus an individual may emigrate only if the country of which he is a citizen grants him permission to do so, and his admission to the country of destination depends upon the willingness of that country to accept him. . . .

SHIFTING OF THE SOURCES OF IMMIGRATION

As was mentioned above, in the decade of the 1880's the main sources of immigration shifted from northern and western to southern and eastern Europe. By the following decade the "new" immigration had surpassed the "old.". . . The date 1882 may be taken as marking the transition. It is the most prominent landmark in the history of immigration to the United States. In that year the first inclusive federal immigration law was passed; also the first Chinese Exclusion Act. The total immigration in 1882 (788,992) was the highest point yet reached, and it was not surpassed until 1903. With one or two exceptions, the year 1882 marked the climax of the movement from northern and western Europe, and it coincided with the appearance of streams of immigration from southern and eastern Europe of sufficient volume to command attention.

A line drawn across the continent of Europe from northeast to southwest, separating the Scandinavian Peninsula, the British Isles, Germany, and France from Russia, former Austria-Hungary, Italy, and Turkey, divides the old source of immigration from the new. . . . This line also separates the countries of representative institutions and popular government from absolute social systems; lands where education is universal from lands where illiteracy predominates; countries of low birth and death rates from countries of high birth and death rates; manufacturing countries, progressive agriculture, and skilled labor from primitive land industries, backward agriculture, and unskilled labor; and educated, thrifty peasantry from a peasantry scarcely a generation or two removed from serfdom. . . .

REASONS FOR THE CHANGED CHARACTER OF IMMIGRATION

Various reasons may be ascribed for this change. Special causes which earlier operated in the case of northern and western Europeans were removed, such as the famine in Ireland in 1847, political and religious intolerance in Germany and other countries. On the other hand new special causes in the later period operated in the case of the southern and eastern Europeans, such as the anti-Semitic riots in Russia in 1881–83, the failure of the currant market in Greece, and the reversal of Russian policies regarding the Finns in 1901. Moreover, the difficulties of travel in the earlier days were so great and the knowledge of the New World so vague that very few persons in the more backward and less maritime countries had the courage to attempt the long and arduous journey. In addition, during the period of old immigration many of the southern and eastern Europeans were serfs bound to the soil, and not permitted to emigrate.

Another reason for the changed character of immigration is that it was deliberately induced by American employers, padroni and other middlemen, and steamship agents. While immigration has always been to a certain extent stimulated, this became very noticeable after 1880. When the forces retarding the older movement became operative, immigration agents swarmed into the virgin fields of Italy, former Austria-Hungary, Russia and the Balkan States, where they told the peasants and poorly paid agricultural laborers glowing stories of opportunities in America. Letters written back home by immigrants who met with economic success here were also an important factor. Nearly all the immigrants admitted were according to their own statements, coming to join friends or relatives. Steamship companies also early entered the picture, and their ticket agents conducted extensive propaganda abroad in "the great drive for emigrants." The profits in the immigrant-carrying trade were very great; the immigrant was the cheapest kind of cargo to carry, for he loads and unloads himself and his baggage.

A more fundamental reason for the changed character of immigration from the European standpoint is the fact that by 1880 northern and western Europe, especially Great Britain and Germany, had become industrialized and thus furnished work opportunities at home for those surplus laborers from the rural districts who had constituted most of the emigrants. Due to industrial development migration within the country from rural districts to the cities replaced emigration out of the country. It is a significant fact that by and large immigrants have come primarily from the agricultural classes and from the agricultural countries. With the industrial expansion the governments, notably in the case of Germany, began to look unfavorably upon emigration; they enacted laws prohibiting the solicitation of labor by outsiders and aimed in other ways to prevent the exodus of their laboring element. These nations were also taking great strides in labor organization, advance of wages, improvement of working conditions, and in supplying accident, invalidity, and other types of social insurance. These improvements, so noticeable in northern and western Europe at the time (modern social insurance began in the 1880's in Germany), largely removed the inducement to emigrate, by making general conditions at home nearly equivalent to those prevailing in America.

Another fundamental reason is that beginning with the 1870's and 1880's the birth rate in countries of northern and western Europe began markedly to decline. By 1900 the birth rate was declining faster than the death rate in most of these countries, so that altogether there was much less cause to emigrate than had earlier been the case. While northern and western European countries have balanced their population, the opposite situation prevails in the South and East. These countries, with their high birth rates, have lagged behind. In many respects it would seem that southern and eastern Europe has experienced a development parallel to that of the northern and western sections, except a generation or two later. Generally speaking, the effects of the industrial, agricultural, social and political revolutions were not so noticeable in the earlier years of the century in the countries of southern and eastern Europe as they were in the countries of the "old" immigration. Religious and political persecution which was common in northern and western Europe in the earlier days subsided after the middle of the nineteenth century; it persisted until later in the South and East. Northern and western Europe were agricultural and rural until the 1870's and 1880's; the southern and eastern section is still largely so. This lag in the case of the southern and eastern Europeans is also evident in the characteristics of immigrants to the United States: the "old" immigrants started out like the "new"; the "new" immigrants occupy the same relative status that the "old" immigrants held a generation or two earlier.

The main reasons for the changed character of emigration to the United States will be found not so much in a changing European situation as in changing economic and social conditions in America. During the period of the old immigration we were primarily an agricultural nation. The density of population was low, cities were few, and an extensive frontier with an abundance of free land existed. The main attractions offered to immigrants were in agriculture, and the government land policy was such as to make these attractions all the greater. The United States government has held in its own name nearly three million square miles of land. Its policy has been to encourage the rapid settlement of this territory by disposing of the land to individuals at a merely nominal price. . . .

By 1890 the public lands were practically all gone and the frontier had disappeared. Our chief known deposits of gold, silver, copper, and other metals had passed into private control. The lavishness of the various federal measures led to the conservation movement, which was inaugurated by the Act of 1891. The passing of the frontier marked the closing of an epoch and the removal of the main drawing card to northwestern Europeans.

The decade of the 1880's was marked by an immense industrial development and expansion which has continued until the United States is now the leading manufacturing nation in the world. The period of the 1880's was the great turning point in the economic and industrial history of the United States. The expansion of communication and transportation, the removal of manufacture from the home to the factory, the development and perfection of machinery, the increase in size of the units of business, together with the introduction of the corporation, all these established a new era in American history. From being primarily an agricultural nation we have become an industrial and urban nation. The great growth of cities has occurred since the 1880's and now over half of our population is urban. These economic changes are also reflected in the development of the wage-earning class which has been especially marked since that time. It is significant that the American Federation of Labor was organized in 1881 and also that American socialism began in that period. Henry George's *Progress and Poverty* appeared in 1879 and Edward Bellamy's *Looking Backward* in 1888. Now this development and concentration of industry, the disappearance of free land, the change from agriculture to manufacturing as the predominant occupation, the development of the laboring class, and the growth of cities go far to explain the changed character of immigration. It is no longer of marked advantage for northwestern Europeans to come. Our chief drawing card now is our industries. Our need is no longer for agriculturists, but rather for miners, steel mill hands, and unskilled industrial laborers, a distinctly laboring element. This has been the main type of immigrant we have received since 1880. Southeastern Europe has been the main source of supply because there the standard of living is lower and more cheap labor is available. The differential between the opportunities now offered by America and those available in the home country is appreciably greater in southeastern than in northwestern Europe. . . .

EDITORIAL COMMENT

American immigration policy took a long time to unfold. Until 1882 there was only one federal policy regarding immigration: free immigration. Individual states, to be sure, attempted to restrict certain ethnic and religious groups from settling among them, but they could not deter those who wanted to come to American shores from finding a haven somewhere.

In 1820, immigration statistics began to be collected, a sign of growing national concern for the numbers and quality of immigrants. But nothing concrete was accomplished in the form of federal legislation until 1882 when a law was passed with exclusion features aimed at the Chinese, and selective regulation directed against "undesirables" (convicts other than political offenders, lunatics, idiots, and persons "likely to become public charges") coming from any country.

Next there was the Gentlemen's Agreement of 1908. While this was not enacted legislation but an executive agreement, it functioned as a part of American immigration policy, excluding Japanese laborers except those returning to their former domicile in this country, those coming to join parent, husband, or child, and those assuming active control of an already possessed interest.

With the passage of the Immigration Act of 1917, restrictive or quantitative regulation, a fourth type of immigration policy, was added to the previous policies of free immigration, exclusion, and selective regulation. The new policy was implicit in the literacy test, a device designed to reduce the numbers of immigrants, especially those from central, southern, and eastern Europe. Two of the earlier policies—selective regulation and exclusion—were expanded in other parts of the Act of 1917.

The end of World War I gave rise to renewed anxiety that the United States was receiving too many of the "wrong" kinds of people as immigrants. The temporary act of 1921 and the permanent law of 1924 (which actually went into effect in 1929) both featured a new form of restrictive regulation in the adoption of the quota system. The quotas established by law favored northern and western Europeans, the people most closely resembling old-stock immigrants, and they discrimininated against central, southern, and eastern Europeans. Asiatics were barred by (a) the Asiatic Barred Zone, and (b) the ineligibility to citizenship clause. Token quotas of 100 per Asiatic country each year were established. But the quotas for these countries were only for persons born there of non-Asiatic parentage and therefore eligible to have United States citizenship.

World War II and the postwar period indicated how severely this type of discrimination could harm the foreign policies of the United States. An amendment to the law of 1924 gave a "real" annual quota of 105 to our wartime allies—the Chinese—and other Asiatic peoples were given similar consideration in the years following the war.

In 1948 a special Displaced Persons Act, above and beyond the provisions of the law of 1924, was passed to take care of a temporary but acute problem created by wartime conditions and the aftermath in eastern Europe. The act, nevertheless, was alleged to discriminate indirectly against Jews and Roman Catholics.

For several years after World War II, dissatisfaction with the permanent features of immigration law enacted from 1882 until 1924 was expressed vehemently in and out of Congress. The feeling of the critics was that all permanent immigration provisions should be revised and coordinated into one system. Controversy between the restrictive and liberal points of view concerning the direction the coordinated policy should take finally resulted in the victory in 1952, over President Truman's veto, of the forces favoring immigration restriction. The McCarran-Walter Bill became Public Law 414, an act revising the laws relating to immigration, naturalization, and nationality.

Among other things, this revision and coordination of all permanent immigration law in the United States perpetuated the quota system. It allowed a potential annual quota of immigrants at 154,658, or only 308 more than what had been previously allowed. The year 1920 continued as the base year for computing quotas, thereby continuing to ignore the contemporary composition of the American population, and discriminating against those ethnic groups whose representation in the population was lower in 1920 than it is at the present time. Selective grounds were increased, and priority in quotas was given to those having superior education and skills needed in this country.

Instead of resolving the complaints against previous immigration law, the McCarran-Walter Act has intensified the objections of those who feel strongly that legislation consistent with the official American Creed is needed. They have argued that the new permanent legislation is merely the continuation of most of the worst aspects of discrimination that characterized the laws from 1882 thereafter. They have urged that a coordinated system of immigration fair to all ethnic groups should be passed in replacement of the act of 1952.

One of the most ardent voices in opposition to the McCarran-Walter Act and in favor of more "humane and generous" legislation has been Senator Hubert H. Humphrey, Jr. of Minnesota. A former professor of political science and a student of the problems inherent in establishing immigration policies, Senator Humphrey, in the following selection, unravels five myths about immigration and proposes several fundamental changes in our present legislation.

21. THE STRANGER AT OUR GATE
BY *Hubert H. Humphrey, Jr.**

IMMIGRATION LAWS crystallize and express a society's basic human values, for they deal with our relationship to people other than our immediate neighbors. In a sense, they may be said to codify our prejudices or our freedom from prejudice. They reveal how our actual practices correspond with our professed ideals. A nation's immigration policy is thus an index of its strength, wisdom, and morality. Our immigration laws recall the biblical admonition to "Love ye therefore the stranger: for ye were strangers in

* From Hubert H. Humphrey, Jr., *The Stranger At Our Gate* (New York: Public Affairs Committee, 1954), Pamphlet No. 202. Reprinted by permission.

the land of Egypt." (Deuteronomy 11:19.) It is well to remember that at one time we or our ancestors were all immigrants to this country.

From the beginning of our history those who founded the United States recognized a national need not merely to tolerate immigration but to encourage it; not alone to admit those who were wealthy or skilled, but in the words of George Washington, to give haven to "the oppressed and persecuted of all Nations and Religions."

Indeed, one of the reasons announced in the Declaration of Independence for the American Revolution against England was the British effort to impede free immigration into the colonies. In the first years of our Republic we deliberately sought to stimulate immigration. We needed help to build our industries and to assist in the development and expansion of our frontiers. The wisdom of this policy is now manifest everywhere in our land. Refreshed by a constant stream of new settlers with new ideas and new imagination, and with fresh yearning for freedom, we have erected a vast industrial network and created a democratic community. James Madison's predictions at the Constitutional Convention of 1787 have been confirmed: "that part of America which has encouraged them [the foreigners] has advanced more rapidly in population, agriculture, and the 'arts.' "

Abandoning Our Traditional Welcome

Not until 1882 did we depart from our original policy of unimpeded immigration. Then, under the influence of ideas similar to those expressed earlier by the Nativist and Know-Nothing movement, we permitted for the first time bars against the entry of an immigrant class because of its race. Between 1882 and 1924 we did a complete about-face in our immigration policies.

At first Chinese alone were excluded. But the categories of excludables were swiftly expanded. In 1917, after three different Presidents had vetoed a similar measure, Congress enacted a literacy test for admission aimed at shutting off entry of the so-called "new" immigrants from southern and eastern Europe. The 1917 law also established the notorious "Barred Zone" provision, sealing off immigration from most of the Orient. When, in turn, these devices were found insufficiently restrictive, they were supplemented by the rigid quota plans of 1921 and 1924 which represented the final hardening of a national anti-immigration mood into a national policy. The basic principles of the 1924 law without the Oriental exclusion provisions were re-enacted in the McCarran-Walter Immigration Act of 1952.

Since the 1880's, arguments for a more humane and generous immigration law have largely gone unheard. Despite the contributions to our national economy and our national culture made by our immigrant populations, despite their energy, their creativeness, and their industry, despite the crying need for charity and generosity in the face of the growth of oppressive European totalitarianisms, it has nevertheless become increasingly difficult to persuade Congress of the need for an immigration law premised on reasoned hospitality.

The Price We Paid

Our immigration laws represent the face we turn to the rest of the world. Other nations may be impressed by our strength but they will not be impressed with our humanity as long as our immigration policy enacts or reflects hostility toward strangers.

It is a profound error to regard immigration as a one-way street— as an area in which the benefits all flow one way. All competent observers agree that the very diversity of the peoples who have made up our immigrant population has been crucially responsible for enriching our culture. American democracy has no simple genealogy. Its family tree is not easily traced. It reaches back into the most varied of backgrounds. Our history is in a real sense a history of many peoples.

Immigration Contributed to America's Greatness

Our economic progress has been advanced and secured by the efforts of large numbers of immigrants who came to this country in the latter part of the 19th and the early part of the 20th century in time to construct the mines, the railroads, the farms, the canals, and the highway systems which now abound in our land. The immigrants came to this country to lend their muscles and their energies to the creation of a new, better, and more prosperous community, one in which they would earn and deserve their rightful place. It is a matter of history that in the long period of unrestricted immigration the number of new immigrants rose during periods of prosperity but automatically and of itself dwindled in depression.

The liberal immigration policy of our early years was of critical importance in the development of our industrial and technological strength. The rich diversity of traditions and cultures it introduced into the United States contributed to an acceptance and understanding of ethnic differences. Our early immigration laws were a source of hope and a model for the world; they were a symbol of the sympathy and goodwill that free men can extend to each other.

All this being so, why then has it been so difficult to get a similarly liberal immigration law enacted in recent years?

FIVE MYTHS OF IMMIGRATION

In the first place, immigration laws are not easy to understand. Few citizens or Congressmen have time to digest the mass of scientific and historical material required for an appreciation of the problems in this field. The McCarran-Walter Act runs to 302 pages, and is virtually un-readable by anyone except an expert.

In addition, certain persistent myths have become widely accepted as facts. They almost always turn up in discussions in this area and they account for some of our undemocratic immigration policies. These myths are:

1. Rigid laws are needed to prevent the country from being flooded with immigrants.

2. Immigration threatens American living standards.

3. Certain races or nationalities are undesirable.

4. Immigrants do not make good citizens.

5. There isn't room for many more people here.

Not one of the five assumptions can be supported by statistics, science, or history. Let's look at them:

Myth No. 1: Rigid laws are needed to prevent the
country from being flooded with immigrants.

If that is so, why haven't millions, eligible under immigration laws, migrated from Canada and South America which are exempt from quota limitations? The fact is that most people cling to familiar soil or well-known pavements. They will suffer poverty or endure dictatorship rather than turn from friends and relatives to start afresh in a strange country where a strange language is spoken. We do not know how many people from southeastern Europe would come to our shores if allowed to do so. But it is interesting to remember that even when immigration from Europe was unlimited—which no one proposes today—the highest average annual immigration, in ratio to the total United States population, was only 1.28 per cent of our population for the decade 1840–1850. This peak figure certainly does not represent a tidal wave.

Myth No. 2: Immigration threatens American
living standards.

Organized labor, which is sensitive to any attack on living standards, has tossed this myth into the ashcan. Leaders of both the American Federation of Labor and the Congress of Industrial Organizations opposed the McCarran-Walter Act and argued for a liberalized immigration policy. Labor has learned that immigration normally creates more jobs and in-creases the national wealth. Millions of native Americans earn good livings from industries founded or developed by immigrants. The type for this pamphlet (and for practically every newspaper, magazine, and book pub-lished in the United States) was set at low cost on the linotype machine in-vented by Otto Mergenthaler, an immigrant from Germany. Other immi-grants gave us the typewriter, the telephone, the electric elevator, the blast furnace, the oil refining process, and many other sources of wealth.

Recent immigrants have brought old world skills and technical processes with them. Judah Lifszyc, a Polish scientist, had a secret process for producing clear dextrose syrup. He opened a factory in Wenatchee, Washington, cooperatively owned by some 700 farmers, which is producing 30 tons of syrup daily from surplus wheat and potatoes that used to be dumped. Refugees from Amsterdam created high-paid jobs for Americans when they moved the center of the world's diamond industry to New York City.

Immigrants are consumers as well as workers and producers. The more consumers, the more capital investment and the more employment. During the great period of immigration, from 1870 to 1930, the population increased about three times, but the number of jobs—despite widespread adoption of labor-saving machinery and techniques—increased about four times.

Myth No. 3: Certain races or nationalities are undesirable.

Like the old belief that the world is flat, this myth has been hard to dispel. As recently as a generation ago a few scientists still clung to the idea that certain people were inherently or biologically inferior, but today not a single competent authority accepts the theory of superior and inferior peoples. Dr. Margaret Mead, the distinguished anthropologist, says "all human beings from all groups of people have the same potentialities." The concept of inferior peoples, she adds, "is artificial, and cuts off good ancestors for our great-great-grandchildren." Dr. Ralph L. Beals, former president of the American Anthropological Association, comments: "All scientific evidence indicates that all peoples are inherently capable of acquiring or adapting to our civilization. Upon this point of view the American Anthropological Association has unanimously endorsed an official statement by its executive board."

There will be marked individual differences, of course, in any national group. There will be idiots and geniuses, scoundrels and statesmen, weaklings and Samsons. But the average person, whether he be an Eskimo or an Ecuadorean or a resident of Easton, Pennsylvania, is the same fellow the whole world over. He has the same innate ability to compose a great symphony, invent a better mousetrap, or develop a spineless artichoke. And there's the same risk that he may abuse his dog, yell at telephone operators, or pilfer the poorbox.

Myth No. 4: Immigrants do not make good citizens.

The Scots were once rated as poor timber for citizenship and for decades it was widely believed that the Irish could never become good Americans. History has shown otherwise. The slurs against recent immigrants have no more validity.

Again and again it has been demonstrated that the foreign-born commit proportionately fewer crimes than the native Americans. E. H. Sutherland, an authority on criminology, found in 1933 that 536 native whites per 100,000 were committed to prisons of all types as against only 402 foreign-born whites. The sons and daughters of immigrants contribute more to delinquency than the foreign-born.

Home ownership is a good index of adjustment to a new environment. The 1940 census showed that proportionately more foreign-born people own homes than native whites.

Recent immigrants have made rich contributions not only to industry and science but also to music, literature, drama, and art. Over the years the foreign-born have changed our eating habits. What would our diet be without occasional opportunities to sample ravioli, chile con carne, blintzes, shish kebab, sukiyaki, and crepes suzettes?

Myth No. 5: There isn't room for many more people here.

There is plenty of room and plenty of need for them. Representative Harrison Gray Otis of Massachusetts was wide of the mark when he declared: "When this country was new it might have been good policy to admit all. But it is so no longer."

Mr. Otis was speaking in 1797.

In 1950 the United States had 51 persons per square mile. Compare this with 480 in Great Britain and 807 in Belgium. How large a population could be comfortably supported cannot be forecast exactly, but the experience of the past fifty years shows that the limit is not yet in sight.

Some experts predict that at the present small rate of immigration the population will reach a peak of about 190,000,000 in 1975.

OUR PERMANENT IMMIGRATION LAWS

Our permanent immigration laws were codified in June, 1952, when the Congress enacted, over President Truman's veto, the McCarran-Walter Immigration and Nationality Act (Public Law 414). This new act is the first comprehensive revision of our immigration statutes ever attempted.

The law has some good features. It was sensible to make an orderly codification of the many haphazard and piecemeal laws on immigration and naturalization. It was wise to remove the long-standing prohibition against citizenship for Japanese and other Asian aliens. It was encouraging to permit the entry, for the first time since 1917, of Asians who were formerly ineligible for permanent residence, although only a handful were allowed to come.

While the new law takes these steps forward, in the opinion of many authorities it takes other steps backward. It has been argued that it reaffirms and even strengthens the racist provisions of the old laws, that it rates northern and western Europeans as superior people, and that it classifies southern and eastern Europeans, Asians, and Africans as inferior.

Few of our federal laws are based on racial prejudice. Critics of the new law assert that none results in more serious racial discrimination than our new 1952 immigration act. They point to the fact that the peoples whom they claim have been classified as inferior have been outspoken in their resentment.

Northern and western European countries have been scarcely less bitter. Visitors and seamen from England, France, Norway, Denmark, Sweden, and other western European states complained that the new law requires that they undergo complicated loyalty checks as if they were potential criminals. The world's leading scientists have, in some cases, been reluctant to arrange international conventions in the United States lest their delegates suffer needless insult.

Reports from abroad indicate that the McCarran-Walter Act is intensifying the ill-will toward the United States that stemmed from previous immigration laws. The hundreds of millions of dollars we are spending to cultivate allies will be at least partly offset if our immigration law implies that most of the world's people are not good enough to live in the United States. You can't call a man inferior and then expect him to be on your side.

Why should the United States care whether other nations like or dislike us? That was the attitude of some of our Congressmen when the 1924 immigration law was drafted. A clause excluding Japanese was debated. The Japanese embassy warned that the proposed law would weaken the democratic forces in Japan and give the militarists the anti-American ammunition they were looking for. Secretary of State Hughes agreed and urged Congress not to "affront a friendly nation." But the insult was voted. The Japanese militarists strengthened their grip. Seventeen years later they considered themselves strong enough to attack Pearl Harbor.

This doesn't mean that the 1924 immigration law was the direct cause of the Pearl Harbor raid. But our international rudeness may have been one factor contributing to the build-up of the Japanese war parties. To a far greater extent than most Americans think, other nations judge us by our immigration laws.

THE NATIONAL ORIGINS QUOTA SYSTEM

The major target of our restrictive immigration policy was southern and eastern European immigration. Bias against immigration from this area grew rapidly as the influx of northern and western Europeans slackened. For some years Americans who regarded Italians, Greeks, Poles, Hungarians, Russians, and their neighboring peoples as inferior looked for a way to make discrimination against this group effective. They found it in the National Origins Quota System, first written into the 1924 immigration act.

The National Origins Quota System lies at the heart of the McCarran-Walter Act. The quota for any given nationality is determined by finding out what proportion that nationality contributed, by birth or descent, to the total American population of 1920—a most difficult statistical problem —and then applying this percentage to the total quota of 154,000. The result of this system is that about five-sixths of the over-all quota goes to northern and western countries of Europe, while one-sixth goes to the southern and eastern European countries. For example, Great Britain is entitled to send 65,361 persons a year; Germany, 25,814; and Greece only 308.

The quota system is in some measure supplemented by the issuance of immigration visas outside the quota system, but these are granted mainly to immigrants who are the children or spouses of citizens or to persons born in Canada or Latin America.

Most of the quotas of the favored countries are wasted because their citizens don't wish to emigrate. From 1930 to 1944 the northern and western nations used on the average only 17 per cent of their quotas. The total authorized quota ceiling for the 28-year period from 1925 to 1952 is 4,362,354. Of this, a total of only 1,923,509 was used. In other words, 56 per cent of the quota has been wasted.

In the southern and eastern countries qualified applicants for visas must wait years—and sometimes more than a lifetime—to be considered. Displaced persons admitted to the United States in the postwar years were charged against one-half of their countries' quotas for future years. By this plan, the quota for Greece has been reduced 50 per cent until the year 2013; for Yugoslavia until 2114; for Estonia until 2146, and for Latvia until 2274.

The National Origins Quota System would appear to be a futile attempt to turn the clock back a hundred years and restore the immigration pattern of the mid-19th century. The purpose—to discriminate against southern and eastern Europeans—was publicly acknowledged when the system was devised in 1924, and many feel that it was reaffirmed in 1952 by the Senate Judiciary Committee, which wrote the McCarran-Walter Act. A slight relaxation of the National Origins Quota System had been proposed in order that unused quota numbers might be redistributed to countries that wanted them. The change was rejected because—"To distribute the unused quotas on the basis of the registered demand would shift more quota numbers to the countries of southern and eastern Europe."

Individual Congressmen were even more candid in the debate. One member said that although he was not a follower of Hitler's theory of racial origins, "there is something to it."

"I believe," he continued, "that possibly statistics would show that the western European races have made the best citizens in America and are more easily made into Americans."

The Congress of 1924 at least used the most recent census figures on the national origins of the population. Knowing that the percentage of southern and eastern Europeans had increased since 1920, the framers of the McCarran-Walter Act refused to accept 1950 census figures for the national quotas. The 1920 census is still used as the base, and only the white population is included in the calculations. By the 1952 act, the annual quota of any country is fixed at one-sixth of 1 per cent of the number of inhabitants in continental United States in 1920 of that national origin.

Quotas based on one-sixth of 1 per cent of the 1920 white population are much smaller than they would be if they were based on the same percentage of the 1950 population. A nation that has increased its population 43 per cent in thirty years is thus restricting its immigration out of all proportion to its capacity to absorb new people. Instead of being a law to regulate immigration in the wisest and most humane manner, the McCarran-Walter Act thus becomes primarily a stop sign.

Discrimination Against Asiatics

Sponsors of the new law have argued that the law does not discriminate. They point out that small quotas have been assigned to Asian countries for the first time and that Japanese may now become United States citizens. But what offends Asian peoples and those Americans who find prejudice repugnant is the broad use of a relatively new device for discrimination. The McCarran-Walter Act endorses the fiction that there is a huge geographical area inhabited by inferior peoples. This area, called the Asia-Pacific triangle, is defined as including every country that is wholly situated north of the 25th parallel of south latitude and between 60 degrees east and 165 degrees west longitude. Immigration of persons born in countries wholly situated in this area is sharply restricted. Except for slightly higher quotas for China and Japan, not more than 100 persons a year may ever enter from any of the countries in this zone. The 25th parallel bisects Australia; the 60th meridian is on the eastern edge of Iran and 165 degrees west longitude is just west of the Aleutian Islands.

The McCarran-Walter Act not only discriminates against every person born within this vast triangle, which includes the populations of Afghanistan, Burma, China, Indonesia, Japan, Korea, India, and the Pacific Islands, but also discriminates against those born elsewhere if half of their ancestry can be traced to the triangle. The law says that any prospective immigrant "born outside the Asia-Pacific triangle who is attributable by as much as one-half of his ancestry" to peoples within the triangle shall be chargeable to the annual quota of 100 for the Asia-Pacific triangle or, in certain cases, to the token quotas of 100 for Asian countries.

Thus the English-born son of an English father and an Indian mother cannot use the liberal English quota. He would have to wait at least a decade or so under India's quota of 100.

The code of racial prejudice twists like a cowpath. To keep out Italians, Greeks, Turks, and Slavs, the McCarran-Walter Act relies on place of birth, not the ancestry of the applicant. To keep out Asians, the law ignores place of birth and relies on ancestry. For both groups, however, the law consistently ignores individual worth.

The Immigration and Naturalization Act of 1952 brings racial prejudice to our front door by penalizing, for the first time in the history of our immigration laws, the predominantly Negro population of the British West Indies. Immigrants from these colonies formerly were permitted to enter without restriction under the liberal quota of the mother country, and at the most about 2,500 did so each year. The new law sets a limit of 100 for each colony or dependent area that may be charged to the quota of the governing country. This limitation has been denounced by the colonial legislatures, by newspapers, and by West Indian leaders. They have pointed out that there are no quotas for the neighboring states of Cuba, Haiti, and the Dominican Republic.

There would appear to be no explanation that squares with American traditions. During debates on this measure in the House, one of the authors of the bill announced that the reason for this provision is that the St. Thomas Labor Conference in the Virgin Islands and the Virgin Islands Civic Association had written the House Immigration Sub-Committee urging the new limitation as a means of "protecting" those islands from large migrations from Jamaica. This hardly appears to be a sufficient justification for so grievous a discrimination against colored immigrants. In the minds of most people this provision looks like an expression of anti-Negro prejudice.

BARRING THE GATE

In practical effect our immigration code keeps many deserving people out of the United States even when the quotas for their countries are still unused. One way in which this has long been done is by giving authority to consular officials abroad to bar visa applicants if for one reason or another those applicants are believed to lack the qualifications established in the immigration laws. The discretion of subordinate officials on these matters is virtually absolute since there is now no way to prosecute an administrative appeal or to secure judicial review of an adverse decision regardless of its accuracy.

Thus, persons of adequate means may be excluded if they "in the opinion of the consular officer or the attorney general are likely at any time to become a public charge." An unfavorable determination of a consular official may be right or wrong, but under this provision a wrong opinion would bar the immigrant just as surely and just as completely as a correct one. An American citizen can challenge the decision of a customs official who tries to prevent him from importing a sack of beans but he cannot appeal the ruling of a consul who prevents him from bringing in his mother or any other person whose admission he wishes to facilitate.

Also barred is any applicant who the consular officer or Attorney General "has reason to believe" might "incidentally" engage in activities "prejudicial" to the United States. This loose language could conceivably be used to keep out almost anybody. A member of the British parliament, resolutely anti-Communist but also critical of United States actions in the United Nations, could be denied a visa because a consular official feared that he might express his differences with American policy on the lecture platform.

Our present immigration law excludes persons convicted of two or more nonpolitical crimes with sentences totaling five years. This provision gives foreign courts the power to screen our immigrants. It even means accepting the verdicts of totalitarian courts that operate under laws alien to our concepts. Thus, the Belgian war bride of an American airman has not been allowed to enter the United States because, as a slave laborer for the Nazis, she was convicted of falsifying documents to get food ration tickets.

While the victims of Fascist courts are excluded, the ex-Fascists themselves get two advantages under the new act and, although once barred along with Communists, they now are eligible for admission. First, the present law provides that former members of totalitarian parties may qualify if they terminated their membership five years earlier and have since opposed the party's ideology. This test is relatively easy to meet since the Nazi-Fascist parties which we fought in World War II technically went out of existence more than five years ago, and since the State Department has ruled that a former member need not prove affirmatively that he opposed such a totalitarian program for the last five years but merely prove that he did not advocate it. Secondly, the present law includes a definition of "totalitarian" which restricts the term to those who have advocated a dictatorial rule "in the United States," a phrase which has been interpreted by the State and Justice Departments as inapplicable to the Nazi and Fascist parties.

The 1952 Immigration Act further removed foreign professors from the non-quota status which traditionally they had enjoyed. It subjected their entry to the red tape and delay of obtaining a regular quota visa or of securing a preference quota visa as one whose presence is "needed urgently" in the United States. This change reflects a fear of ideas and a lack of confidence in the ability of our universities to select only well-qualified persons for their teaching staffs.

A Medieval Punishment

A case can be made for deporting a person who used fraud to enter the United States. But many competent critics feel that the McCarran-Walter Act unnecessarily goes to the extreme length of deporting immigrants for minor reasons, even when no law of the United States has been violated.

The new law makes it easier to deport an alien who is suspected of having become a public charge within five years of entry. Under the old law, the government had to prove the alien was in fact a public charge. But the McCarran-Walter Act permits deportation if in the "opinion" of Attorney General (and, realistically, an immigration inspector) the alien is such a charge.

Similarly immigration officers are given authority to decide whether an alien committed to a mental hospital is suffering from a condition that developed in the United States or in the country from which he came. Experienced psychiatrists often find it hard to tell when mental diseases began. But the alien is nonetheless required to prove conclusively that his mental sickness began after a certain date.

Deportation is also made an extra penalty for violation of the alien registration law, which carries stiff penalties of its own. An alien can be deported if he neglects to notify the Attorney General of a change of address within ten days and if the Attorney General does not think the oversight excusable.

Membership—at any time after entry—in an organization required to register under the McCarran Internal Security Act is made a ground for deportation. The publication of lists of subversive groups is a relatively new device. Many good Americans and many good immigrants innocently joined, ten, fifteen, or twenty years ago, "front" organizations that have since been declared subversive. There is no penalty whatever for comparable membership by native citizens but aliens may be deported even though they may have long since rejected the organization and the principles it represents. The failure of this section of the law to recognize repudiation of totalitarian beliefs denies us the association and support of many persons who are today more firmly welded to democratic beliefs.

This feature of the new law introduces for the first time in American history a system of retroactive punishment for aliens.

The United States Constitution prohibits *ex post facto* laws. But this has been held applicable only to criminal cases and the Supreme Court has ruled that deportation is not technically criminal punishment, although in many respects it is admittedly harsher and severer. Deportation punishes not only the alien but also his wife and children who in fact may be citizens. This situation has long been recognized in our immigration code which has always included some provision for relief in hardship cases. The possibility that injury may be worked on innocent parties, however, is intensified under the 1952 Act which sharply restricts the grounds for suspension of deportation and establishes almost impossible conditions for the adjustment of the status of an alien no matter how worthy his claim.

Moreover, the McCarran-Walter Act does much to deprive resident aliens from ever attaining a feeling of security. The new law prescribes deportation *at any time* if it is discovered that the immigrant should have been excluded originally because of his race, nationality, politics, or anything else. There is no statute of limitations as long as he is unnaturalized. An alien who has been a model resident for twenty-five or thirty years is no safer than the person who arrived last month. Indeed, the long-time resident's position is worse. There may have been nothing fraudulent in his case, but how can he find witnesses so many years later to help establish his innocence? And if witnesses are found, how can they be positive in their recollection? That is why every crime save murder has a statute of limitations.

Much is rightly said about the immigrant's responsibility to his new country. More should be said about America's responsibility as a host to newcomers. Pulling up roots from foreign soil and moving a family to the United States is an enterprise that demands courage, vision, and money. The average immigrant family plans, sacrifices, and saves for months and years to fulfill its dream. When the family reaches American soil, there is no overnight indoctrination in United States laws and customs. Our language, our cities, our people, and our concepts cannot be assimilated in a couple of years.

What the immigrant needs is time to get settled and to learn about the United States. He should have friendly help during this period.

SECOND-CLASS CITIZENSHIP

Chief Justice Marshall wrote that a naturalized citizen becomes "a member of the society, possessing all the rights of a native citizen and standing, in the view of the Constitution, on the footing of a native. The Constitution does not authorize Congress to enlarge or abridge those rights."

An immigrant who obtained his citizenship through fraud should, of course, be deprived of it. But if citizenship was fairly won, there should be no strings attached.

Although native Americans may live abroad until they die without losing their citizenship, the new law terminates the citizenship of any naturalized American who is absent anywhere abroad for five years or more. This provision was aimed particularly at Jews who left the United States to help develop Palestine. The drafters of the bill which ultimately became the Nationality Act of 1940 had not thought of including this provision until after receiving testimony from an official of the State Department. The enactment of this section of the law seems largely attributable to his observation that "it will be desirable to put in a provision to cover each person who goes to a third country. The principal cases we have, I may say, are these scientists that are principally Russian and German Jews who have been naturalized in this country and later went to Palestine. We have other cases but I mean that there are more of that particular body than in any other category." Thus, Ezra Pound, who broadcast for Mussolini during the war, is still an American citizen—but a naturalized citizen who spent more than five years in Israel or Germany would lose his citizenship.

Second-class citizenship is humiliating to the naturalized immigrant, unbecoming to our democratic tradition, and hurtful to the nation. The person who knows he is getting an unfair deal cannot serve his country as well as the citizen who is treated fairly.

Any American citizen who helped the Russians in their campaign to alienate our friends would be denounced in Congress for subversion and hustled off to jail. Yet there are many who feel that the McCarran-Walter Act has gratuitously placed a powerful propaganda weapon in the hands of the Russians, and the Russians are making the most of it. Philip M. Hauser, professor of sociology at the University of Chicago and former acting director of the Census Bureau, reported after a long stay in the Orient:

> Public Law 414 (the McCarran-Walter Act) is well known to the peoples of the world and it is not favorably known. It does untold damage to the United States in creating attitudes of distrust and hostility. . . . It is absurd to think that we can retain our position as the world leader in the fight for freedom and democracy with the peoples whom we explicitly and openly brand in our legislation as undesirable and inferior. . . . We have unwittingly placed into the hands of the ruthless, adroit and unscrupulous propagandists of the U.S.S.R. a major weapon with which to attack us. . . . The U.S.S.R. is skillfully and continuously making the most of our ethnic and racist doctrines as promulgated in Public Law 414.

Professor Hauser's opinion is supported by the first-hand observations of many other experts. Our new immigration law has created resentment and hatred not only in Asia but also in Africa, in the Caribbean, in Latin America and, of course, in Italy and Greece.

The mistrust of non-Americans that is manifested in the new law is one reason why international scientific congresses are keeping clear of our shores. The International Congress of Psychology [was] held in Canada, not the United States, in 1954, to avoid any embarrassment to delegates who might be refused visas. The International Congress of Genetics decided that Italy and Canada would be more hospitable than the United States for its next two meetings. The International Astronomical Union and other important scientific groups have likewise turned down invitations to America. Leading American scientists are gravely concerned about their foreign colleagues' boycott.

Congress has been alert to catch even the slightest flaws in the Voice of America program. Many citizens of other nations do not hear the Voice of America broadcasts because the McCarran-Walter Act speaks so loudly.

How about the Reds?

Some good Americans, admitting that the McCarran-Walter Act is marked with racial bias and other defects, say that a tough law is essential to keep out Communist agents.

No American could object if the provisions of the Act had a reasonable relationship to our national security. But the McCarran-Walter Act gives no more protection against Communist immigration than a more equitable and less discriminatory law would give.

The National Origins Quota System certainly is no safeguard against Communists. Neither is the Asia-Pacific triangle. And France, the western nation with the heaviest proportion of Communists, enjoys a fairly liberal immigration quota under the McCarran-Walter Act.

Moreover, those who pushed hardest for the adoption of the present act seemingly show little concern with the influx of illegal migrants from Mexico and Canada. Communists could easily, if they so wished, bypass our consular officers by sneaking across the line from Canada and Mexico, as hundreds of thousands of persons do every year. No real effort has been made to stop them.

Gladwin Hill, the New York *Times* correspondent, reported in January, 1953, that an estimated 1,500,000 Mexican "wetbacks" entered the United States in 1952 without the formality of tipping their hats to an immigration officer. This illegal immigration was about ten times greater than the 154,000 persons allowed from Europe and Asia by the McCarran-Walter Act.

Why hasn't Congress cracked down on the vast, illegal migration from Mexico? Because, Mr. Hill says, farm owners want cheap Mexican labor.

No good American opposes statutes designed to protect us from invasion by agents of a foreign power or by those bent upon espionage or subversion. The McCarran-Walter Act, however, cannot be justified or explained in these terms. Its most restrictive and unfair provisions bear no relation whatever to considerations of internal security. Many devoted Americans believe that attempts by the sponsors and authors of the McCarran-Walter Act to masquerade the discriminatory provisions of the laws as a protection against Communist infiltration into the country represents an effort to exploit anti-Communist feelings for purposes totally unrelated to our security.

A NEW LAW?

The United States has an unparalleled opportunity to write a good immigration law—a law based on common sense and decency, with no taint of racial prejudice.

Four circumstances make this an ideal time to erase the prejudice we have been writing into our immigration laws since 1882:

First, the general condemnation of the unfortunate provisions of the McCarran-Walter Act by national organizations of all kinds, by leading newspapers, by foreign experts and government officials. Among the organizations that have advocated basic changes are the National Council of the Churches of Christ in the U.S.A., the National Catholic Welfare Conference, the National Council of Catholic Men, the National Council of Catholic Women, the National Lutheran Council, the Protestant Episcopal Church, the Baptist World Alliance, the Synagogue Council of America, the National Community Relations Advisory Council, the American Jewish Congress, the Congress of Industrial Organizations, the American Association for the Advancement of Science, the American Friends Service Committee, the Young Women's Christian Association, the American Hellenic Educational Progressive Association, the Federation of American Scientists, the American Academy of Arts and Sciences, the American Jewish Committee, and the National Federation of Settlements.

Second, the report of the President's Commission on Immigration and Naturalization, appointed by President Truman, which investigated the McCarran-Walter Act and recommended a substitute that would square with American tradition and American requirements.

Third, President Eisenhower's criticism of the 1952 Act.

Fourth, the introduction in the first session of the 83rd Congress of an omnibus immigration and naturalization bill to supplant and replace the McCarran-Walter Immigration Act.

The President's Commission

The President's Commission, headed by former Solicitor General Philip B. Perlman, was appointed September 4, 1952, at the request of every major religious faith in the country. The members included Earl G. Harrison, former commissioner of immigration; Monsignor John O'Grady, secretary, National Conference of Catholic Charities; the Reverend Thaddeus F. Gullixson, president, Lutheran Theological Seminary of St. Paul, Minnesota; Clarence E. Pickett, honorary secretary, American Friends Service Committee; Adrian S. Fisher, legal advisor to the State Department, and Thomas G. Finucane, chairman, Board of Immigration Appeals, Department of Justice.

The commission held hearings in eleven cities from coast to coast. About 400 persons testified and 234 others submitted written statements. "It is fair to say that approval of the new law was voiced by comparatively few, and that in practically all such instances the favorable opinions were not supported by factual information," the commission said in its report, *Whom We Shall Welcome*. Some of the conclusions were:

> The commission believes that although immigrants need the United States, it is also true that the United States needs immigrants, not only for its domestic or foreign benefit, but also to retain, reinvigorate, and strengthen the American spirit.
>
> The commission believes that we cannot be true to the democratic faith of our own Declaration of Independence in the equality of all men, and at the same time pass immigration laws which discriminate among people because of national origin, race, color, or creed. We cannot continue to bask in the glory of an ancient and honorable tradition of providing haven to the oppressed, and belie that tradition by ignoble and ungenerous immigration laws. We cannot develop an effective foreign policy if our immigration laws negate our role of world leadership. We cannot defend civil rights in principle, and deny them in our immigration laws and practice. We cannot boast of our magnificent system of law, and enact immigration legislation which violates decent principles of legal protection. . . .
>
> The commission believes that laws which fail to reflect the American spirit must sooner or later disappear from the statute books.
>
> The commission believes that our present immigration law should be completely rewritten.

Presidential Criticisms of the McCarran-Walter Act

The need for extensive revision of the McCarran-Walter Act is in no way a partisan political issue. This is evident from the statements

made by both Democratic and Republican presidents. In a speech during
his campaign in Newark, New Jersey on October 17, 1952, General
Eisenhower said:

> A new immigration law was certainly needed. . . . We should
> have had, and we must get, a better law than this McCarran
> Act. . . . Obviously, there must be limits to the number of im-
> migrants this country can or should absorb. We must develop a
> system of limitation in line with our concept of America as
> the great melting pot of free spirits, drawn here from all the
> nations. . . . Ladies and gentlemen, the McCarran Immigration
> Law must be rewritten.
> A better law must be written that will strike an intelligent
> balance between the immigration welfare of America and the
> prayerful hopes of the unhappy and the oppressed.

After becoming President, Mr. Eisenhower emphasized this position
in his State of the Union Message on February 2, 1953:

> It is a manifest right of our Government to limit the number
> of immigrants our nation can absorb. It is also a manifest right
> of our Government to set reasonable requirements on the
> character and the number of people who come to share our land
> and our freedom.
> It is well for us, however, to remind ourselves occasionally of
> an equally manifest fact; we are—one and all—immigrants or
> the sons and daughters of immigrants. Existing legislation con-
> tains injustices. It does, in fact, discriminate. I am informed by
> members of Congress that it was realized, at the time of enact-
> ment, that future study of the proper basis of determining quotas
> would be necessary.
> I am therefore requesting the Congress to review this legislation
> and to enact a statute which will at one and the same time
> guard our legitimate national interest and be faithful to our
> basic ideas of . . . fairness to all.

Similarly President Truman in vetoing the McCarran-Walter Act
on June 25, 1952, declared:

> A general revision and modernization of these laws unques-
> tionably is needed and long overdue, particularly with respect
> to immigration. But this bill would not provide us with an im-
> migration policy adequate for the present world situation. Indeed,
> the bill, taking all its provisions together, would be a step back-
> ward and not a step forward. . . . (this legislation) would per-
> petuate injustices of long standing against many other nations

of the world, hamper the efforts we are making to rally the men of the east and west alike to the cause of freedom, and intensify the repressive and inhumane aspects of our immigration procedures. The price is too high and, in good conscience, I cannot agree to pay it.

The imperative need for thoroughgoing amendment of the McCarran-Walter Act has been acknowledged by thinking Americans of every political background, by both Republican and Democratic national administrations. It represents a challenge to be met by the common action of all the American people, no matter what their party affiliation.

PROPOSALS

Many proposals have been made. The recommendations of the President's Commission and the suggestions made by major civic and religious organizations in testimonies before legislative committees in large part have been embodied in an omnibus immigration and naturalization bill which was introduced during the last days of the first session of the 83rd Congress by a group of eight Senators and twenty-four members of the House of Representatives. Intended as a more equitable substitute for the present permanent immigration law, the new bill proposes the following fundamental changes:

1. *Creation of a single independent government agency with full responsibility and jurisdiction over immigration and naturalization.* This new agency, to be called the Immigration and Naturalization Commission, would be charged with the application, administration, and enforcement of national immigration and naturalization policies.

2. *Issuance of visas to all qualified applicants throughout the world without regard to national origin.* This means replacing the National Origins Quota System. The new plan for the first time would place all immigration for permanent residents, including that from the Western Hemisphere, within the framework of a liberal quota system which would be completely nondiscriminatory.

3. *Establishment of an annual immigration quota of 1/6 of 1 per cent of our national population as reported by the most recent decennial census.* This formula applied to the 1950 census would permit annual immigration of approximately 251,000. A definite quota ceiling would thus be firmly fixed. Immigrants would then be admitted on the basis of need and our own national welfare.

This would be achieved by creating a system of priorities within the "first-come, first-served" plan.

These priorities would be created to encourage (a) reunification of families; (b) asylum for the persecuted; (c) haven for refugees and displaced persons; (d) preference for persons with specially needed skills.

In addition, a basic percentage of the total annual immigration would be allocated for a fifth group, persons who represent new and self-initiated immigration, with arrangements to insure that their group would represent peoples of varied cultural and ethnic background. Thus our native culture would be constantly refreshed by the introduction of peoples with new points of view and new insights.

4. *Curtailed use of deportation as a punishment.* It is proposed to establish statutes of limitations requiring that deportation proceedings must be commenced within ten years of the act which constitutes the ground for deportation. Moreover, if an alien has lived in the United States for twenty years or more he is to be protected against deportation just as a citizen is.

5. *Elimination of present insupportable distinctions between native-born and naturalized citizens.* Citizenship acquired by naturalization could be revoked only on the grounds of fraud perpetrated in acquiring it. In the proposed bill no act which a native-born citizen can perform with impunity can serve as a ground for revocation of citizenship of a naturalized American. Residence abroad is eliminated as a ground for revoking citizenship acquired by naturalization.

6. *Creation of machinery for appeal from the decisions of visa officers abroad.* At present neither the applicant nor his friends or relatives in the United States can appeal if a consular officer abroad refuses a visa on the basis of unfounded suspicions.

7. *Modification of unduly harsh restrictions.* The proposed measure would recognize the possibilities of reform and change of heart both for political error and for single acts of minor crime, such as stealing a loaf of bread. Aliens would be judged for purposes of admission and of deportation on the basis of their character and record rather than on the basis of long-past and isolated incidents.

There is also before Congress at this time a less comprehensive bill (S. 2545) designed to eliminate some of the most glaring defects in the present immigration code. These proposed amendments include:

1. Restoration of professors to non-quota status;

2. The pooling of unused quotas;

3. Repeal of the "mortgage" on quotas as required by the Displaced Persons Act;

4. Abolition of the "Asia-Pacific Triangle"; and

5. Creation of a Visa Review Board.

CONCLUSION

No doubt other immigration proposals will be introduced during the next few years to achieve many of these same reforms. Bills have been introduced to minimize the discriminatory features of the national origins system by pooling immigration quotas and assigning them on the basis of need and national interest. No matter which of these measures ultimately becomes law, one thing appears certain: a basic rethinking of our present inflexible and restrictive immigration policies is necessary to bring our immigration practices into accord with our democratic aspirations. Ill-conceived and bigoted immigration laws have been a blemish on our record of democratic achievement. The immigration laws of any society both reflect and shape its fundamental character. Freedom of movement, both in emigration and immigration, have long been acknowledged as among the most fundamental of human freedoms; it is the hallmark of totalitarianism that it seeks rigidly to limit the free movement of people. It seeks to deny to its own subjects the freedom to live elsewhere. It seeks to deny to others access to its soil or contact with its peoples. Conversely, the very essence of democracy is that people remain free to choose where and in which country they wish to live and build their future. It is essential that so fundamental and significant an area of American life and law as immigration be revised so that bigotry may give way to knowledge, and expediency to the justice of humanitarianism.

EDITORIAL COMMENT

Notwithstanding the arguments and pressures brought to bear on the problem by Senator Humphrey and others, the only immigration legislation passed in the United States subsequent to the McCarran-Walter Act of 1952, was the special Refugee Relief Act of 1953. Like the Displaced Persons Act of 1948, it was a temporary law to supplement permanent legislation. It was designed to admit 214,-000 refugees, displaced persons, and orphans over the three-year period ending in 1956, and it was carefully constructed to aid anti-Communists and to block the entry of Communists. Almost one fourth of the number was allotted to people of German ethnic origin who had been natives behind the "Iron Curtain" but who in 1953 were residents of western Germany and western Austria. Smaller allotments were made for people of other origins who had also fled from Communism; Italian, Greek, and Dutch refugees with American relatives; refugees from any part of Asia; non-Asiatic refugees from the Far East; Chinese refugees from the island of Formosa; Arab refugees; escapees living in any of the NATO countries except Britain; refugees who had been members of the armed forces of Poland in World War II, residing in Britain and not having acquired British citizenship; refugees now in this country on temporary visas; and orphans from anywhere in the world.

The net effect of all immigration provisions, however, has been to curtail immigration considerably below that of the early decades of the century. Since the end of World War II, immigrant aliens entering the United States have averaged fewer than 200,-000 a year. From 1903 through 1914, on the other hand, the annual average exceeded 750,000. First and second generation Americans have been decreasing in number. At the time of the 1950 Census, the white foreign-born and the native-born children of foreign or mixed parentage totaled 33.8 million, a decline of 15.2 per cent from the peak of nearly 40 million in 1930. During these two decades, the population of native parentage rose by 43.6 per cent.

Not being replenished by immigration, the foreign-born population in the United States has been aging rapidly. By 1950 three fourths were 45 years of age or older, with somewhat more than one fourth of the total at ages 65 and over. Of the second generation, the native population of foreign or mixed parentage had one third of its number at ages 45 and over, compared with less than one fourth at this age for the population of native parentage.

Since the foreign born tend to settle near their place of entry into the United States, they are heavily concentrated in the northeastern part of the country. In fact, in 1950 more than two fifths of the country's foreign born lived within the area of four states—New York, Pennsylvania, Massachusetts, and New Jersey. Second generation Americans were dispersed only slightly more throughout the United States, 45 per cent of them residing in the Northeast, whereas the proportion was only 21 per cent for persons of native parentage. Only a small proportion of first and second generation Americans—less than 8 per cent—live in the South.

Foreign-born Americans and their second-generation children are predominantly urban dwellers. More than four fifths of them live in urban areas, compared with less than three fifths of the population of native parentage. The educational attainment of the foreign born is somewhat below that of the native born, judging by the proportion with high school, or more advanced, educations. However, the United States Census does show that the children of immigrants have had more formal schooling than children of native parentage through 35 for males and age 25 for females. Among both the foreign born and the native born, the proportion with at least a high school education was much higher at age 25 than at age 35—indicating the long-term rise in the level of education.

At the prime of working life—ages 25 through 64—about the same proportion of immigrants and native born participate in the labor force. Differences are observable, however, at the extremes of working life. Under age 18, the foreign born have the larger proportion in the labor force, whereas at the older ages the native born are the more fully represented, especially among the males. In the latter case the difference probably reflects the much higher proportion of farmers among the native born—an occupational group which often continues to work well into old age.

The concluding essay in this section on immigration is by an eminent historian, the late Marcus Lee Hansen. In 1941 the Common Council for American Unity said of this piece that it "indicates hundreds of topics worthy of study and practical lines of approach to a rich and too neglected field in American scholarship. Many of these topics are matters for documentary research, but many are matters still within the personal experience of thousands of students—and their immigrant parents and grandparents—now attending our colleges and universities. Not to enlist their interest, study and collaboration will be to lose an opportunity that will never come again. . . ."

22. IMMIGRATION: A FIELD FOR RESEARCH
BY *Marcus Lee Hansen* *

THE addition to our population between 1815 and 1914 of thirty-five million Europeans marks an era in American history no less significant than the two centuries of colonization that preceded. In time, the change in sovereignty that occurred in 1776 will be regarded as an unnatural dividing line, and settlement will be viewed as a continuous process from its beginning in 1607. . . . By common usage, however, the term "immigration" applies to the period since the Revolution or, more specifically, to the still later period characterized by individual as distinguished from group migration.

A study of the various waves which have marked high points in the immigrant tide reveals a definite geographic origin for each. The adjectives "old" and "new" are commonly used to describe the change from Northern and Western Europe to the south and east late in the 19th cen-

* Reprinted by permission of the publishers from Marcus Lee Hansen, *The Immigrant in American History* (Cambridge, Mass.: Harvard University Press, 1940), pp. 191–217.

tury; but this general shift was no more significant than the deviations within each area. At any given time the phenomenon of emigration characterized not a nation as a whole, but a comparatively restricted part of it; and when it again made its appearance, though the participants were still listed as Germans or Italians, their origin was distinct. In every case, the exodus in that district was accompanied by a social and economic reorganization usually indicating an adjustment to modern life. Such reorganizations sometimes took place without emigration to America; but they were always attended by changes in population—perhaps a drift to the cities, perhaps a movement to hitherto waste lands or to other parts of Europe. On occasion they resulted in a congestion of population which produced great social unrest. To the United States the people went only when American industry was prospering, and each wave of migration coincided with an era of unusual business activity. During the century, therefore, it may be said that America was a huge magnet of varying intensity, drawing the people of Europe from those regions where conditions made them mobile and from which transportation provided a path. American conditions determined the duration and height of the waves; European, the particular source.

Accordingly, both Europe and America comprise the field for research. Because students of 19th century Europe have concentrated upon political developments, the student of American immigration will be forced to do much pioneer work which at first glance would seem to have little bearing on his topic. The fact is that emigration has been connected with as many phases of European life as immigration has of American life. Freedom to move, desire to move, and means to move summarize these phases. Each requires research, and each is a wide field. Freedom to move involves the process by which the remaining feudal bonds were loosened and the systems of land tenure revolutionized—in short, that break-up of the solidarity of the community which, in making the individual mobile, forced him to shift for himself. Desire to move concerns political, economic, social, and psychological motives, and its roots may be found now in one, now in another, of the great movements of the century. How the emigrant obtained the means to leave is part of the history of the transfer of property and of the development of land and sea transportation.

Until a cheap and safe crossing of the Atlantic was provided, mass emigration was impossible. A study of the emigrant trade from the days when the captain journeyed inland to solicit passengers for his spring voyage to the time when no village was without its agency and no day passed without an emigrant ship leaving some European port would be a contribution to the history of both migration and commerce. But much preliminary work must be done, for the subject is bound up with technical progress, sanitary regulations, and the economics of return cargoes.

When upon the high seas, the emigrant was in the hands of some shipping company, and its policies exerted a vital influence on his movements. After the Civil War the rivalries of the lines often proved the dominant factor, as would be shown by a study of the competition of the German and English companies for the control of the Scandinavian trade, or the more general struggle to capture that of the Mediterranean. Rate wars upon the North Atlantic determined the extent and character of American immigration in certain years; and the peace terms which closed these wars had more influence upon the movement in succeeding years than any contemporary American legislation. Moreover, every port of embarkation has its own history, concerned, on the one hand, with the development of its interior net of communications and, on the other, with the nature of its Atlantic commerce. The tobacco trade of Bremen, the cotton trade of Le Havre, and the timber trade of Liverpool dictated the American termini of voyages from those ports and thereby determined the racial complexion of certain sections. Were the archives of shipping companies opened, we could see the agents in operation, and how, when one reservoir of mankind was becoming exhausted, steps were being taken to educate another as to the advantages of emigration.

Though American tariff policy has long been a subject of historical research, the development of the legal conditions under which the most valuable of all our imports has entered has been entirely neglected. The state laws of immigration and settlement are usually characterized as dead letters, but neither the shippers nor the immigrants thought them such. The eventual assumption of regulation by the Federal government marked the culmination of a long agitation which concerned the Supreme Court, the transportation companies, organized labor, and the farmers. A cross section of these influences could be obtained by studying the Immigration Convention which met at Cincinnati in 1870. The progress of the movement for restriction, leading up to the present-day legislation, involves much social and political history. Castle Garden and Ellis Island are each worthy of a volume; and the administration of laws, the state labor bureaus, and the welfare activities at Boston, Philadelphia, Baltimore, Charleston, and New Orleans should not be neglected.

An integral part of the history of immigration is the process of distribution of the newcomers. . . . Why was it that the periods of small immigration were the periods of most active dispersion? The immediate destination of immigrants during each era of prosperity should be studied, and their participation in the landward movements following the crises in 1819, 1837, 1842, 1857, and 1873 determined. The return European migrations after 1893 and 1907, when it was easier for the immigrant to obtain land in Italy than in America, should receive attention. Not until much detailed research has been done can a theory of distribution be formulated. The investigation of many single aspects will be valuable contributions toward such a theory.

Before the days of the railroad, immigrants considered the journey from the seaport to the interior as difficult as crossing the Atlantic. Often it was as expensive and lasted as long. The immigrant trade on the great natural highways—the Hudson River, the Mississippi, the Ohio, and the Great Lakes—should be studied in the same way as that of the Atlantic, in relation to the commerce carried. Pittsburgh and Buffalo, Chicago and St. Louis, should be investigated as immigrant distributing centers. Local ordinances and police restrictions will reveal how the hotels, land offices, and labor exchanges were regulated. We should know the reasons for the popularity of certain states or regions at certain times, as Pennsylvania and Illinois in the 20's, Missouri and Ohio in the 30's, Wisconsin in the 40's, and Iowa and Michigan in the 50's.

With the era of internal improvements a new factor in distribution appears. The census of 1850, the first providing statistics of the foreign-born by countries, reveals all the principal lines of immigrant travel. The zones of settlement represent, in part, accessibility and, in part, the residue left by the construction gangs. An analysis should be made of the labor policy of canals and railroads—the hierarchy of contractors and subcontractors, the recruiting of men, labor conditions, and the methods of preserving order. The history of a shanty town may be as rich in primitive self-government as any mining gulch in California.

These alien fringes sometimes resulted from the absconding of the labor contractor; but more often such communities comprised the staff necessary for the upkeep of the canal or railroad, together with those who judiciously chose uncleared lands or snapped up improved farms, and others attracted by the stimulated industrial activity. A study of biographies, in local histories or obituary notices, will reveal how often the nucleus of a later extended immigrant settlement began with such pioneers. When the railroads and canals themselves possessed lands, their land policy will explain much settlement. That the great Western railroads rank with the Colonial trading companies as American colonizers is becoming recognized, but the influence of the railroads in the older sections should not be overlooked. The opening of the Erie Railroad, for instance, brought thousands of newly arrived immigrants into southern New York and northern Pennsylvania. Access to a market was demanded by the immigrant who settled upon the land, whereas the native American was more self-sufficing.

When the rail net was completed to the Mississippi, the carriage of immigrants became an important feature. This business was sought by the railroads not only for the immediate revenue or the disposal of their lands, but for the more permanent income to be derived from settlement.

Hence tickets were sold in the interior villages of Europe, alliances were formed with steamship lines, competition was bitter in the ports, and fares were reduced to ridiculous figures, as in the railroad war of 1885 when for a time the flat rate from New York to Chicago was only a dollar. The varying policies of individual roads, the relation of rates to settlement, the demands of certain industries for the supply of labor, as well as the history of the immigrant train itself as an institution, are all topics worthy of investigation. Nor should the "home seekers' excursions" be forgotten, which in times of industrial depression drew away persons who had settled in congested urban centers.

Land companies and individual landowners supplemented the activities of the railroads. The rise of great land fortunes, the creation of these estates of hundreds of thousands and even millions of acres, is a phase of American settlement as yet obscure. The dissolution of these estates was intimately connected with the immigration of foreigners, as advertisements in the German and English agricultural journals of the 70's and 80's reveal. Agents of such estates were active in European villages, sticking up their posters in public houses, lecturing to improvement clubs and, allied with the railroad and state representatives, smoothing all the difficulties of migrations. Though this mode of settlement is most noticeable in the last quarter of the 19th century, the same influence operated from the very beginning and often decided the permanent character of a given region. Thus, it was probably the opening of the Astor lands at an opportune moment that turned the tide of Germans to Wisconsin.

But there were also other factors influencing the process of distribution. Religious ties, which must be interpreted as including language and social customs as well as spiritual needs, played an important part. The early history of many rural parishes will show how the minister or priest turned solicitor and, working quietly year after year, changed his feeble missionary charge into a vigorous church. Ecclesiastical administrators undertook comprehensive plans, the Catholic Church producing a group of colonizing bishops in Fenwick of Boston, Ireland of St. Paul, and Byrne of Little Rock. The activities of each will repay study. The Irish Colonization Convention, which met at Buffalo in February, 1856, at the suggestion of D'Arcy McGee, proved a failure; but an analysis of the plans there promulgated will prove an interesting indication of ethnic consciousness, and their final wreck, due to the opposition of Bishop Hughes of New York, will provide an enlightening picture of rival group ambitions. Many congregations, especially of Germans and Scandinavians, migrated as a unit; but although almost any county history of the Middle West mentions the arrival of some such body, the economic history of no one of them has ever been written.

Through the operation of these factors of distribution the immigrant entered some line of economic activity in country, village, or city. His energies usually raised him to a different social plane and, at the same time, influenced the material welfare of his American neighbors. The economic history of "foreign" farming communities has varied with the local conditions existing upon the arrival of the immigrants and their financial resources. Many were left stranded in the small towns and villages. Here they served as carpenters, masons, blacksmiths, and casual laborers. Some obtained a footing in commercial life and their children became merchants and bankers. Professional men of immigrant parentage were recruited almost exclusively from this class, so their influence as leaders of the second generation was far greater than their numerical proportion would warrant. Others of this group, however, were the ne'er-do-wells that have contributed so much to the flavor of Main Street literature.

Industry played a part in the initial stages of dispersion by providing jobs, from the savings of which the immigrant might acquire a farm. Some "foreign" groups, however, preferred the opportunities and sociability of the cities. The ethnic evolution of a purely manufacturing city, such as Lowell, Massachusetts, will provide illustrations—with the Irish displacing, or at least taking the place of, the Yankees; the French Canadians succeeding the Irish; and they in turn followed by the Greeks and Slavs.

When the process of distribution had been completed and a definite economic status achieved, social life took on clearer form. If the immigrant's lot was cast in a purely American environment, he soon lost his characteristics or became a social hermit. More often, he was surrounded by hundreds who had the same life history and, in company with them, he built up a society neither European nor American. At present there exist probably a score of types of these societies. Research should begin with the effects of the American scene upon the individual. How did it influence his health? When did he discard his old clothing, and when and why did he become ashamed of being "different"? What changes occurred in his principles and morals, and why did he become more ambitious? What new interests did he most easily adopt and which of the old most quickly disappeared? The determination of how immigrant reaction has varied with time, place, and nationality may seem to present insuperable difficulties. But it is not impossible. Biographies, reminiscences, and letters exist by the thousand; acute observations were made by travelers; and the missionary reports teem with comments.

The social history of the alien family provides a clue to much community development. What variations in internal administration and authority resulted from the migration? The persistence of family traditions, customs and even names, the training of children in the years before going to school, the family pastimes and mutual obligations are pertinent topics. In time the second generation became a disturbing element. Unnumbered household revolutions occurred, the rebels demanding modernization of furniture, food, and dress, and often a change of religion. When they succeeded in securing control of the family, the strongest bulwark of hyphenism was carried. The success or failure of such movements should be related to nationality, location, religion, and community type.

Finally, community activities demand research. Everyday life in Boston and Milwaukee and a score of other immigrant "capitals" should be described. The sociology of the 160-acre farm is as worthy of investigation as that of the ante-bellum plantation. What amusements, festivals, commercial and social habits prevailed? How was an immigrant aristocracy created, and was it an expression of European or American standards? What was the opinion as to intermarriage with other groups, and what was the social effect of such alliances? Did each nationality manifest a characteristic attitude toward social problems, such as temperance and Sunday observance? At what stage and why did native prejudice express itself, and did it cause an intensification of peculiarities? What traits persisted after the first generation had passed, and was a constant influx necessary to maintain group individuality?

As long as any community retained its own language, amalgamation with American social life was impossible. From the first, immigrant leaders complained of the eagerness with which the people discarded their mother tongue. Its retention became the cornerstone of all efforts to maintain solidarity. Historically, therefore, the problem has two aspects: first, the varying circumstances that led to the adoption of English; and, secondly, the positive language-policy of the leaders. The matter being so personal, the materials for the study of the first are scant. But the second generation, now so widely represented in the colleges, might be subjected to a questionnaire, for it was in the inner life of the bilingual families that the transition took place. For the second point the materials are abundant. Sooner or later in every denomination the language question arose, and the proceedings of church conventions and the columns of the official organs are filled with debates and resolutions. Even more abundant are the materials for a history of the teaching of foreign languages in the public schools. Every state board of education was subjected to tremendous pressure, and in many states every ward and school district witnessed similar propaganda. The language legislation during World War I, interesting as a manifestation of war psychology, can be more clearly understood in the light of these concessions.

But the language question is but one phase of the much broader subject of the immigration of institutions. How these institutions were set up, how they throve in the American atmosphere, and how they competed with the native institutions form part of the history of immigration. The process of their transplantation is obscure, though a few years after settlement we can see them in full bloom—churches, parochial schools, academies, fraternal organizations. There are Portugese bands, Welsh eisteddfods, German turnvereins, Bohemian sokols and Polish falcons. Each nationality at every period demands special study. What applies to the Irish differs from what applies to the Hungarians; and conditions among the Germans in 1840 are different from those in 1880. The situation varies with the intensity of national feeling in the European countries, with the amount of support given by organizations at home, with the internal politics of the immigrant group in America, and with the amount of opposition which native institutions exhibited.

It was the American churches and their missionary activities that offered the strongest resistance. They met the invaders on their own ground and fought them with their own language. Maintaining seminaries on American soil, they had an advantage which the European training schools could not duplicate, and their success was the despair of the early missionaries from the churches of Europe. Psychologically, the years of migration provided a fertile field for the propagation of new faiths, and the result was the division of the nationalities, especially the old immigrants, among sects, and the breakup of migrating denominations into many branches. Much as three divisions were to be deplored from the point of view of effective religious service, they did act as agents of Americanization by dissolving the ties with European hierarchies and placing administration in the hands of those who were directed by American organizations.

This mingling of social systems raises the natural question: What has immigration as a whole, or any national stock, contributed to American culture? Many intellectuals among the newcomers thought of themselves as the bearers of a higher civilization, and their descendants have been assiduous in pressing these claims, so that today the national origin of every man who achieved distinction has been duly acclaimed. We have lists of statesmen, soldiers, poets, novelists, engineers, and educators, presenting a formidable array. But this method does not reach the heart of the problem. It is in the township, the village, or the city ward that the leaven in the lump can be detected. There the investigator will find the German singing society, which gradually took into its ranks non-Germans, stimulated the formation of other organizations and provided a winter's concert course. There he will find the immigrant music teacher, who passed on the training of his Old World masters to the offspring of a dozen nations. He will see a reading circle develop into a library reflecting the particular bent of its originators, thereby helping to determine the literary character of the community. He will see the immigrant schoolmaster transmitting his own training and producing among his pupils an unusually large proportion of scientists, philosophers, or farmers. When a few hundred such studies have been made and compared, we can more confidently say what each group has contributed to the cultural possessions of American society.

In certain centers the mingling of immigrant contributions may be analyzed. There are the universities, many of whose professors have been drawn from European institutions, and whose training is reflected in the organization and scope of the curriculum. Hundreds of each nationality have sat in Congress and in the State Legislatures. Have they been conspicuous in producing legislation to foster the arts and sciences? In the cities theaters have been promoted by almost every alien group. When they disappeared, did they leave any trace of their influence upon the American stage? At what times and for what reasons have European classics become popular, either in the original or in translation? What scientific, literary, artistic, or musical causes have been championed by the immigrant groups? What literature did the immigrants beget, and what characteristic traits of American literature derive from such origins?

These questions can be answered only by access to sources that depict the inner life of a group. Such a source is the widespread foreign-language press. To peruse its pages gives a vivid cross section of community activities. But it is as a political exponent or political instructor that the immigrant press merits the greatest attention. With the increasing percentage of naturalized voters, its relation to the succeeding political crises becomes of greater significance. In another and increasingly important field it became the guide—foreign affairs. Whatever may be said of the course of the American press generally in respect to European news before World War I, the foreign-language newspapers were not ignorant, and did not slight such topics. Each of the diplomatic crises that mark the advance to August, 1914, forms the basis of news and editorial comment that reflected prevailing opinion in the country of origin. Consequently, these people in America were almost as prepared for war, psychologically, as any in Europe; and when the conflict did come, the whole battery of the press was turned upon the American policy of neutrality, thus creating many of the internal problems of the troubled years from 1914 to 1917. The historian who attempts to unravel the political skein of that period must first trace the development of the international state of mind of these groups.

In the formation of this state of mind the press was by 1914 receiving the assistance of powerful allies. The new-immigrant elements were becoming more conscious of their origin. Immigrants of forty years' residence were becoming reflective. An unusually large number of reminiscences appeared; histories were being written; and alliances, foundations, and leagues were being organized. Though largely cultural in their ambitions, these societies could not exclude politics in times of crisis, and in 1914 they played the role in national politics which for practically a century as local societies they had enacted in their own neighborhoods.

It is in these local circles that the student of the political influence of immigrant groups will make his start. There are perhaps a hundred such clubs that demand a historian. He will investigate the circumstances attending the organization of each, trace the political allegiance of the moving spirits in the venture, analyze its program, ferret out the speakers, and interpret the toasts at the annual banquets. Soon he will find its leaders becoming aldermen and its more prosperous members being favored with city and state contracts. The advantages of naturalization are urged, and committees appointed to welcome the immigrants and train them in the political way in which they should go. These features, be it emphasized, are not necessarily the most important activities of the society; but this approach to the problem is the direct path into the maze of local politics, where new and bewildered voters are captured for this or that party, and in turn the party is influenced in its attitude toward public issues.

The immigrant came with preconceived attitudes which conditioned his reaction to American life. One of them relates that for ten years before his departure he read all the letters which reached the village from those who had already migrated; and when he heard that here or there within the range of a dozen miles someone had returned to visit relatives or friends, he called on foot to catechize him more particularly. From such reminiscences, in newspapers, magazines, and books, an attempt should be made to deduce the prevailing attitude toward American problems at various periods, in order to estimate the background of political reactions. Important among such sources are the addresses and writings of the many successful immigrants who later returned to their native country to serve as ministers and consuls.

The political machines found the alien voters susceptible. The issues that were emphasized, the attentions paid to visiting foreign notables, the injection of religious controversies, were all means to an end. The fire, police, and street departments of every city have an immigrant history. Naturalization clubs flourished in all large communities, some of them bona-fide efforts to train immigrants to become citizens, others the creatures of the machine. As early as the decade of the 30's, efforts to secure the German or Irish vote may be recognized locally. The spread of such tactics from city government to state government and thence into national politics should be traced.

In the rural regions the "foreigners" in a township were either so few that they did not count, or so many that they had entire control. A township of the latter type provides an enlightening laboratory. Here is a community governed by men who perhaps had no training in democracy. Under such circumstances what type of men came forward? Did they merely imitate their neighbors, or were they more progressive or more conservative? To which did they pay the more attention, schools or roads?

Were the German immigrants after 1848 more politically minded than their predecessors, and did any change occur after 1871? It is questions such as these that the student who has before him the records of a North Dakota or a Wisconsin township can answer.

With these matters disposed of, it will be more possible to generalize as to whether the immigrants have contributed anything to American political ideals. . . . On occasion, they have been more interested in fighting the battles of the old country than in participating in the affairs of the new. Irish, German, Hungarian, Polish, and Italian patriotic movements operated from an American base about the middle of the last century; and research will probably reveal that the emergence of the new nations of Eastern and Central Europe in consequence of World War I was possible only because there had existed in America, for a generation or two, active colonies of those nationalities, which had kept alive the ideal of independence and could offer financial support and political pressure at the critical moment. Such activities, which to the natives seemed alien to American life, prepared the way for the anti-"foreigner" movements from the time of the Know Nothings down to the era of the present immigration act.

Countries of origin were dismayed by their loss when they saw their ports thronged with the sturdiest of their peasantry. Efforts to stem the movement were attempted. Special attention should be directed to the Scandinavian societies which agitated against emigration, and the relation of empire settlement to variations in the flow of the British current. The positive policy of Italy in securing economic advantages from the movement will be found an essential factor in the development of the characteristics of the "new" immigration.

European governments, moreover, realized that their political as well as their economic life was involved. Experience with a few returned radicals revealed a new threat to their institutions. Consequently, persons who had been in America were regarded with suspicion and, if necessary, their freedom in action and speech was limited. At times newspapers, periodicals, books, and even personal letters were subjected to censorship. Here is a rich field for those who would trace the development of 19th-century democracy. What influence American political theory had upon the minds of those who were the leaders; how the framework of the American republic was the model for projected European republics; and how the peasant who had neither political theories nor visionary governments in mind began vaguely to feel that things could be better because they were better across the Atlantic—these matters require investigation.

The source material from which the history of immigration can be drawn is infinite. Not until the movement was clearly defined were bureaus for its supervision created by the European governments. Long before their reports appear, however, pertinent official documents are available. There are ponderous investigations of land tenure, feudal services, taxation, marriage laws, poverty, and military affairs. Petitions to legislatures provoked debates in which members gave testimony and suggested remedies. Consuls residing abroad reported on the fate of fellow-countrymen who had settled in their districts. Charitable organizations investigated the feasibility of obtaining relief by systematic emigration and, in doing so, laid bare the social maladjustments that were stimulating departure. Farmers discussed the problem of rural labor at their meetings, and local correspondents of agricultural journals commented on the changes in population that were effecting a revolution in local society.

In the countries of Northwest Europe, emigration produced a literature of its own. Before commerce undertook the task of watching over the voyager from his native village to his new home, emigrants traveled "by the book." A comparative study of these guidebooks reveals the changes that took place from decade to decade in the routes, difficulties, costs, and even motives of emigration. The files of emigrants' periodicals also present a rich opportunity, with their advertisements of land and transportation companies, news items, letters from settlers, notes on labor conditions, and descriptive poetry and fiction.

In time, the business of catering to the needs of emigrants became a major concern of the ports of embarkation. Their newspapers and commercial journals and the official city and port documents report the almost daily variation in the flow as well as the general trade conditions influencing transportation. City information bureaus were established, protective societies formed, and religious organizations were not slow in undertaking missionary work. All these left records. The actual trans-Atlantic journey is depicted in the works of travelers, most of whom inspected the steerage. The less picturesque aspects of the traffic may be discovered in the annual reports of shipping companies, the columns of commercial periodicals, and the findings of official investigations.

In America all sources of pioneer history can make a contribution, but there are two which bear directly on the immigrant elements. One is the immigrant press discussed above, the other the great mass of literature connected with the religious conditions of the immigrants. Bishops and missionaries on their travels could not overlook the material situation of their flocks, and in their reports this interest is reflected. How much lies buried in church archives can only be imagined; the great amount that found its way into print has hardly been touched. In Europe societies were formed to promote the spiritual welfare of the emigrants, and their publications are even more informative.

But such materials can be found in few libraries to which students have ready access. A painstaking search is necessary before the investigator can attack his problems. Accordingly, it is suggested that, as the first step in developing the field, a survey be made to locate the raw materials.

Such a survey would extend beyond the libraries of universities and the great public libraries. It would explore the riches of the theological institutions and the archives of church headquarters. It would reveal unexpected treasures on the shelves of local historical societies and in the libraries of immigrant communities. Such a comprehensive investigation would do more than shorten the labors of the student. It would be the best guarantee that the history of American immigration will be written on the broad and impartial lines that its place in our national development deserves.

VII. Ethnic Stratification and Selected Ethnic Minorities

T HE experience of ethnic minorities in American society has been largely that of stratification, not only
in relation to their dominant group counterparts, but in relation to
each other. In many instances even the experience of sharing the same
period of immigration, and in other instances, of having cultural ties
such as religion, language, and region of old-world origin, did not dispel the separation engendered by nationality differences. Stratification
has been partly self-imposed and partly forced upon the groups from
without by prejudice and discrimination.

The process of stratification of nationalities can still be observed
in virtually all areas of American life. In the community it manifests
itself most clearly in the ecological distribution of the population, in

levels and types of occupational concentration, and in the creation by each group of a number of institutions and organizations that have served to obstruct intimate contact and interaction with members of outgroups. Indeed, some sociologists specializing in the study of the urban community maintain that recurrent patterns of stratification of nationality groups suggest a generalized history, summarized as follows.

Usually the first representatives of the ethnic group to immigrate to the United States settle near the center of the city or close to some industrial section. There they work as unskilled and semiskilled laborers. As their relatives and countrymen join them in this "area of first settlement," a distinctive ethnic neighborhood emerges. Subsequently, the expansion of industrial and commercial land usage or the arrival of a newer immigrant nationality drives them to seek housing elsewhere. In addition, with an improvement in their own occupational, income, and educational levels they are attracted more and more to middle-class areas in the community. The second and third generations, becoming acculturated, tend to drift away individually from the ethnic neighborhood. In this manner it is possible to speak of a cycle comprised of recurrent, successive ethnic groups entering and dispersing through the larger community.

On the eastern seaboard—the leading region of immigrant settlement—the first prominent ethnic minority was the South Irish. Succeeding them were dozens of other groups, mostly from central, southern and eastern Europe. The stratification of the South Irish and of a representative sampling of other ethnic minorities throughout the United States, namely, the Poles, South Italians, Japanese, Mexicans and Spanish Americans, and Puerto Ricans, is discussed in this section.

The first selection is a description of the overall stratification of nationalities in a New England community, Burlington, Vermont. While no two communities have had precisely the same pattern of stratification, the major features of Burlington's pattern have been so frequently repeated elsewhere that it can serve as a general introductory description of community stratification.

23. ETHNIC STRATIFICATION IN THE COMMUNITY BY *Elin L. Anderson* *

WALKING along the streets in Burlington, the visitor sees nothing in the appearance of the citizens to remind him of the not-too-distant past when the shawl or apron of a foreigner was a usual part of an American street scene. The women he sees dress in identical styles of similar materials, wear their lipstick in the same way, and have the same swirl in their new permanent waves; the men, too, dress alike, in casual suits not too carefully pressed. Nor does their activity give any impression of cleavages in the community, of barriers separating group from group. On a Saturday night, for example, with stores open until nine or half-past, the citizens of Burlington, the farmers from the country, and visitors from nearby towns, all mingle together. They are going to a Saturday movie, doing last-minute shopping, or just being downstreet with the crowd. It is the end of the working week and there is a relaxed, carefree buoyancy about the group as they go in and out of the chain stores, department stores, five-and-ten-cent stores, along the main street. They rub shoulders together, give a cheery greeting, stop for a few minutes visit, laugh over the jostlings of the crowd. In this moment of common activity they all bear the stamp of Americans.

But to a Yankee farmer they are not all alike. To him Burlington has a lot of foreigners. . . . Going into a store he may be greeted by a proprietor. . . . While waiting to be served he may listen to an animated conversation between the clerk and a customer only to realize suddenly that he is listening to a foreign language. "French," he probably decides, as he turns to give his order. He goes into another store to be waited on by the Jewish proprietor, and comes out a little fearful lest he may have met his match in bargaining. If he stays in town for lunch, he will have to look hard along the main street to find a restaurant which is not Greek, or Syrian, or Chinese, or run by some other "foreigner." It is only when he goes into the bank that he can breathe easily, knowing that here he is still on Yankee ground.

Burlingtonians themselves are occasionally interested in speculating on the extent to which the city is no longer an Old American community. The Federal Census gives them some picture of the changes: according to the figures . . . 40 per cent of the population of 24,789 are either immigrants or children of immigrants, 12 per cent being foreign-born and 28 per cent of foreign or mixed parentage. This group of immigrants and children of immigrants is composed of several elements. The French-Ca-

* Reprinted by permission of the publishers from Elin L. Anderson, *We Americans* (Cambridge, Mass.: Harvard University Press, 1937), pp. 16–34.

nadian, with 4,895 members, is the largest; it comprises one-half of all the people of foreign stock belonging to the first and second generations, and one-fifth of all the people of the community. The next largest group is that of English-speaking Canadians, who number some 1,208 persons. The Irish come next with 1,102; and the Russians and Poles (most of whom are Jews) come fourth with 741 persons. Other groups of some size are the English, with 457 members; the Italian, 392; and the German, 309. In addition to these, twenty-nine other nationalities are represented in lesser numbers.

The Census, however, does not tell the whole story, for it does not distinguish the nationality or stock of the grandchildren of immigrants. It is therefore only by a count of the three Catholic parishes—two French-Canadian and one Irish—that a more comprehensive picture may be obtained of the size of the ethnic groups of the city which have been here for more than two generations.

Such a count reveals that the French-Canadian element is much larger than it appears to be from the Census enumeration. By the priests' estimate there are in St. Joseph's, the first French-Canadian parish, some 6,000 souls of French-Canadian stock; in St. Anthony's, some 1,500; and in Cathedral, the English-speaking parish, at least 2,000. Hence, according to this count, the people of French-Canadian stock number approximately 9,500 and comprise almost two-fifths of the total population of the city. In Cathedral, the English-speaking parish, there are also some 5,000 persons of Irish stock, and 1,000 Italians, Syrians, and persons of other smaller groups. In this Yankee community, therefore, 15,500 persons, more than three-fifths of the population, are members of ethnic groups identified with the Roman Catholic faith; and when to this total is added the Jewish group, numbering 800 persons, the elements foreign to the Old Yankee stock are found to comprise 66 per cent of the population of the city.

This does not mean that the remaining 34 per cent is a "pure" Yankee group. Rather, it, too, is composed largely of foreign elements, though of kindred ethnic stocks—English, English Canadians, Germans—with the Old Americans themselves, those of the fourth generation or more in this country, making up an extremely small part of the population of the city. Their ranks are reenforced by the peoples of the related ethnic stocks who are of the Protestant faith, and it is chiefly as Protestants in contrast with Roman Catholics that these form a cohesive group.

The city itself is interested in the whole question from the point of view of the comparative size of each religious, rather than of each ethnic, group. Speculation as to the proportion of Protestants to Catholics is a frequent topic of conversation; an old Protestant Yankee does not like to think that he is being crowded out by these newer peoples of a strange faith, and it is with some apprehension that he estimates that the proportion by now may be 50–50, while an Irish Catholic, interested in the growing strength of the peoples of his communion, estimates the ratio at 60–40 in favor of the Catholic group.

The surprise with which the average Yankee in Burlington greets the information that his community is largely of foreign stock attests to the fact that Burlington wasn't always like this and that the change that has come over it came so gradually as to be almost imperceptible. The first settlers, to whom the charter of the town was granted in 1763, were adventurous Yankees who built up a prosperous timber trade with Europe via Lake Champlain and Quebec. Later a few French Canadians came down from across the border, but not until 1812 was there a sufficient number of them, 100, for the Catholic See at Boston to send up a priest to be their pastor. They intruded very little on the community; and it was not until 1849, with the building of the railroads, that some Irishmen came to town and made the Yankees aware that there were "furriners" in the land. The story goes that when two gangs of Irishmen working on the railroads met at Burlington a serious quarrel arose between those from County Cork and those from County Connaught, the upshot of which was that a number quit their jobs rather than work with the Irish from another county, and, finding other work in Burlington, decided to build their homes there.

Between 1860 and 1875 the influx of foreigners increased with the boom in the lumber industry. The demand for laborers brought more French Canadians and Irishmen; by 1880 there was a small colony of Germans; by 1885 there were enough Jews to support a synagogue, and by 1890 a group of Italians had come in to dig sewers, and to build roads at the military post situated five miles from Burlington. In the late nineties Burlington felt the reverberations of the wave of immigration which brought hundreds of new Americans from southeastern Europe: a Greek started a restaurant, a Syrian set up a fruit store. Thus by the turn of the century the character of Burlington had altered markedly from that of its early beginnings. The change since then has been slower. The only continuous movement of recent times has been that of the French Canadians, who still come down across the border to find work in the textile mills which were Burlington's last gesture toward becoming an industrial city before it settled into its present character as a commerical and educational center.

The role played by each of the main ethnic groups in the life of the community is in part dictated by its historical place in the development of the city and in part by the essential motivation of the group—what it selects out of American life to make its own, what essentially it contributes to the larger community. In order to appreciate the life of the community and the place of each group in that life, it is necessary to make some analysis of the role of each.

Every community contains its corps of people who consider themselves its charter members. They have determined its nature, created its organizations, fostered its development. In Burlington this corps consists of Old American Protestants—the Yankees, as they still are called. They have always lived there, they love the place, they own it. No matter what changes may come over the city, no matter how far it has lost its early character, they watch over its development and growth with a certain sense of responsibility born of the feeling of proprietorship. This feeling is justified in a sense by the fact that most of the institutions around which the life of the city centers today were founded by their forefathers. These had, immediately upon their settling in 1763, set up a town government and public schools, and, as early as 1791, the University of Vermont. After these agencies symbolic of the principles of free government had been established, they turned their attention to the organization of a religious society, which was formed in 1805. Today the descendants of these Old Americans have to a large extent retreated from the commerical life of the city, but they still control the banks, most of the city's manufacturing, and the University. Furthermore, they have through their institutions, and aided by the fact that the immigrant "invasion" was never great enough to threaten their position of dominance, set an indelible stamp upon the life of the community. . . .

The small Old American group has been helped to maintain its predominant position by the strength of its traditional feeling of the racial superiority of the Anglo-Saxon. As one woman, concerned about a more successful interrelationship between the various ethnic groups of the community, explained: "Of course you do believe that the English are the finest people yet produced on earth. You do believe that they have the most admirable human qualities and abilities that any people have ever had!" Interestingly enough, the newer peoples on the whole accept the Old Americans at their own valuation, perhaps partly because the premium placed on conformity to standards already set has not permitted them to value their own standards and interpretations of America. At any rate, they always speak highly of the Old Americans as fine people with superior ability, shrewd businessmen, and leaders of the community; though some qualify their appreciation by commenting that the Old Americans tend to be snobbish and ingrown, and that they place undue emphasis upon the forms of their culture, which they expect all newer peoples to emulate. The criticism, however, is always good-humoredly qualified by: "But they can't help themselves, you know. A Yankee just is like that. You have to accept that when dealing with him."

Traditions of family and name, of power and influence in the financial and civic life of the community, of race-consciousness, plus a very deep conviction that the Protestant traditions of their forefathers are basically important to the development of free institutions in America, set the Old Americans apart as a group distinct from other people. Within that group there are the usual divisions of classes and cliques, of rich and poor; but the common elements of culture and tradition give an impression of a common unit in relation to other ethnic groups in the community. The Old Americans are charter members; they give a kindly welcome to newcomers, as behooves people of their position, but they expect in return the respect that is due charter members. One who can claim even remote blood connections with any of the group is cordially welcomed without question; he is "one of us," while one who cannot claim such connection is "accepted" only as he obeys the forms and the codes of the group, because, after all, he is "not one of us."

Freed from the kind of economic pressure that is known to a great proportion of the people in the other groups, the Old Americans are concerned primarily with "nice living." Their interests and activities connect them with persons outside the community more than with those within; thus they have broad views, wide interests in the arts, literature, and even international relations. In the community, however, their interest is in keeping their place and their prerogatives; their influence tends to preserve the *status quo* and puts a check on too rapid an invasion from the lower ranks into their society.

The Irish are the leaders of the opposition. With the same fighting spirit that they showed in Ireland against the English, under the banner of their religion and their political party they aggressively assert their difference from the Old Americans and take it upon themselves to champion the rights of the immigrant, casting their lot not with the dominant element but with the "have nots." This role for a people who speak the English language and identify themselves more or less with the English tradition has made for a conflicting situation even more complex than that known to their forefathers in Ireland.

Wherever they have settled in America the Irish have set up such conflict situations, but nowhere more so than in New England. Their criticism of all things English and their loyalty to the Roman Catholic Church went deeply against the grain of the descendants of the Yankee settlers, who were proud of their English origin and traditions and of the independence of religious thought expressed in Protestantism. As a result, to many Old Americans the Irish have epitomized differences in social philosophy which are deeply opposed to the English and Protestant principles upon which this country's institutions were built. To be an Irishman —a Papist and a Democrat—is as a red flag to a bull to many a Puritan Yankee. The failure of each to appreciate the other or to understand the principles for which the other stands is the basic tragedy which disturbs the equanimity of any community where Irish and Old Americans are found together.

In Burlington also the Irish have assumed the role of champions of political justice for the newer immigrant groups and leaders of the Catholic Church in America, while at the same time they have a strong conviction that as the Old American political leadership diminishes the Irish will be the inevitable leaders in the political and civic life of the community. . . .

The role chosen by the Irish is beset with many difficulties. On the one hand, the newer elements at times find the leadership of the Irish officious and irksome; on the other hand, the older elements sometimes find them pushing, and carry over from their English forebears a distrust of their dependability. As a whole, however, the Irish are spoken of highly by all groups, with qualifications such as those indicated in the comments: "The Irish are loyal and faithful first to their church, second to their kind. When these obligations have been fulfilled, they make excellent citizens, contributing to the best interests of the community."

The difference between the French Canadians and the other groups in Burlington cannot be understood without a recognition of the attitude with which the French Canadians regard the territory itself. They may not proclaim it from the housetops, but to them Burlington is a French city and they are its true citizens. To all of New England they have felt a peculiar claim. After all, they say, was it not French explorers and priests who opened up much of the country? Did not Samuel de Champlain discover this very territory, and were not the French the first white settlers on the shores of Lake Champlain? Certainly a military conquest could not entirely take away the feeling that they have a right to this territory. . . .

With this belief deep within them, their settling in New England has differed from that of other people. Their migration has been a "peaceful penetration" across an imaginary line; indeed, at first their migration was largely seasonal. Some Burlingtonians still recall the trainloads of French Canadians, through with their work on the farms, who would arrive each fall to work in the lumber yards and mills and after staying for a short season to earn, as they said, some of the gold and silver that America had to offer, would return to their poor Canadian farms. On the farms of Quebec, as in Europe, "The States" was pictured as a land with streets of gold. Gradually they began to lengthen their stay here from one season to two, from two seasons to three; then they came for a period of two or three years, until they settled permanently. When they did, it was not so much like settling in a new land as extending the boundaries of the old. The tie with Canada has always remained strong, partly because the short distance to the home land makes close contact possible, partly because the continued migration without restriction of French Canadians has constantly reenforced the Canadian national spirit.

Although they are French, they differ markedly from the Frenchman

of today and are, in habit of thought and behavior, more closely akin
to his forebears. They have been separated from France for over 170
years and have known nothing of the great liberalizing movements, such
as the French Revolution, the great literary revolution, and other up-
heavals which have so greatly influenced modern France. Their way of
life in Canada has therefore remained essentially that of a simple peasant
folk whose most vital cultural element has been their religion; as in any
primitive society, the forms of that religion govern every aspect of their
lives. This circumstance has made far more for docility and obedience
to rules than it has for the quality of individual enterprise and responsibility considered characteristic of America. They have willingly accepted
the leadership of the parish priest as their forebears did two centuries
ago. In the French-Canadian community around the cotton mill in Burlington, today, the priest is spiritual guide, lawyer, doctor, friend, and com-
forter, to his people. Such complete acceptance of a single cultural force
has resulted, in the estimation of many students, in a lack of interest in
other forms of development, a result manifested in the lack of schools
and free libraries in French Canada.

In Burlington those of French Canadian descent form a bloc of
nearly ten thousand people. . . . As a peaceful, unaggressive people,
they have won to some extent the sympathy of the Yankee group, whose
social and economic position is not threatened by their advancement. This
Yankee sympathy is based partly on the belief that they have had to
submit to Irish leadership in religious organization and partly on the belief that they have been held back in Canada as a conquered people.
There is also in it, however, something of the attitude of an adult to a
child, an appreciation of their warm, earthy simplicity and a delight in
the "quaint" aspects of their behavior, as presented in the poems of
Rowland Robinson. But this attitude is accompanied by a rejection of
some of the very qualities which make them charming.

The Jews, destined to be dispersed among all peoples on the face
of the earth, have a quota of 800 in Burlington. With a long history of
persecution and suffering behind them, they have sought to find a place
of freedom for the oppressed. Perhaps the principles on which this country
was based have meant no more to any group than to the Jews. The intensity of feeling may be seen in part by the remark of one Jewish woman
who said: "The first thing I did when I came to America was to kiss
the ground. This was a free land—my country. Here there would be no
more pogroms."

In Burlington they have pursued the dual role the Jews have had
to assume in America as much as in any other country. On the one hand
much of their life is within the group, centered around the synagogue and
the Talmud Torah, for even in America, though they may enjoy equality
before the law, they know discrimination born of prejudices ingrained for

centuries in the Gentile mind. On the other hand, showing their appreciation of the liberty that America offers, they actively participate in all civic and philanthropic enterprises. In Burlington their presence is being more and more felt, and some people worry that their influence is becoming an irritant in the life of the community; but their role essentially is that of the impersonal outsider whose support is sought in times of intra-community conflict between the two main branches of the Christian faith.

The Germans have nearly as much right as the Yankees to the claim of first citizens of Burlington. When Ira Allen came in 1773 he found two Germans settled on the shores of Shelburne Point. According to Allen, they "had the appearance of peaceable men, and on their promise to behave were suffered to remain undisturbed." Whether because of this "peaceableness" or because their numbers have never been large, the Germans have quickly become almost indistinguishable from the rest of the community. Today they number 300 persons, but it was not until 1880 that enough of them found their way from the surrounding towns to form a little German neighborhood in the city. Those who came were largely from one section of the country, Silesia, where they had been farmers, weavers, and artisans; in Burlington they fitted into the lumber mills and trades. The German love of music, of intellectual discussions, and especially of *Gemütlichkeit* led them to organize as early as 1891 a German club, a branch of the National Order of Harugari, which is still the center of German social life in the town. It aims to preserve and transmit to the second and third generation an appreciation of German culture.

Two Italians reached Burlington in 1890. A few years later, while working under their padrones on the Delaware and Hudson Railroad on the New York side of the lake, some came over in search of a suitable location for their families. When they found that in Burlington they could secure work in building some of the streets and sewers, they decided to settle. For some time, while there was work on the roads and in building the nearby army post, there were more Italians in Burlington than there are at present. Now, though few in number, they are not a compact group—the three or four families from northern Italy distinguishing themselves from the majority who have come from the southern part. Unlike the Irish or the French Canadians, they have made no effort to center their life around a church of their own. This is due partly to their small number, but also partly to traditions of a state-supported church which make Italians slow to establish and support a church of their own. They are more or less lost in the English-speaking parish; and only at times of baptisms, funerals, and marriages do they feel the need of seeking the services of a French-Canadian priest who is well versed in Italian. In 1934, for the first time, they organized an Italian club. This has been an important social center for all the Italians in Burlington and Winooski, and an educational force aiming to make them feel at home in America and understand its ways and laws.

Representatives of other peoples have added their peculiar qualities to Burlington, but they are too few to form distinctive groups, or they have already fused into the larger blend. The English and English Canadians, with traditions so similar to those of the Old Americans, have merged with that group. Syrians and Greeks, part of the last great migration from southeastern Europe, are few in number. The Syrians comprise some thirty families, the first of whom came to Burlington in 1895; they have established no church of their own but have become members of the English-speaking Roman Catholic parish; their unity is expressed through the social activities of the Lady of Mount Lebanon Society. The Greeks number some twenty families, or 130 persons; one or two Greeks were in Burlington in 1902 in small fruit stores and restaurants. The Greeks remain individualistic, and come together as a group only on special occasions, as when a Greek Orthodox priest comes to town; ordinarily they attend the Episcopal Church, which has been the most hospitable to them as well as nearest in teaching to their own. The American Hellenic Educational Patriotic Association is an important force in uniting all the Greeks of Vermont, emphasizing pride in the Greek heritage. Other people, such as Norwegians, Swedes, Finns, Armenians, Turks, Negroes, and some representatives of seventeen other nationality groups, are too few in number to do much more than add a touch of color to the pageant of peoples who have found their way to Burlington.

The life of all these people is the story of the process of becoming at home in the ever-changing, increasingly complex, American world. They are all intent on realizing the hopes and dreams which America has symbolized to them or their forebears. Each group, according to its need, clings to its customs and traditions as to things assured in an unsure world; each has had to realize that this country has welcomed not only its own group but also those that have been traditional enemies. Only slowly has each realized that the large economic and social forces affecting all America are drawing them all together in common concerns: all are concerned with earning a living, bringing up their children, keeping up their religious practices; all hope that their children may realize what they did not enjoy; all hope for a little fun; all worry over their old age.

In the process of adjusting to their new American environment, different potentialities within the groups have been brought out—special interests in educational training, in the kinds of jobs they have taken. Thus, slowly, new divisions are arising within the groups; and those with similar interests have begun to reach across barriers of nationality or religion, which once were all-important in American life. New divisions are being formed. The old, however, those of nationality or religion, may often color these new developments, especially as each group has not fully realized the sense of freedom that it hoped to find in America.

In Burlington it is possible to observe the advances and checks experienced by each group in its attempt to share in the common life of the community and to see therein the part that these early differences in America play in the new cleavages which inevitably form in a more settled society. It is possible to see the advantages and the disadvantages of preserving the old lines against the rapid social change in the world about us.

EDITORIAL COMMENT

Of all the ethnic minorities in the United States, few have been as conspicuous as the South Irish, a group not to be confused with the North Irish and Scotch Irish. The immigration of the South Irish began at a comparatively early period in American history. Even in the Colonial period some of them arrived to join the first settlers of several towns and villages in the Northeast.

The bulk of the South Irish immigrated in the nineteenth century when they were driven out of their homeland by overpopulation, land hunger, crop failure, and famine. They were attracted here by the country's demand for laborers. This was long before most other ethnic minorities arrived. This historical precedence and their ability to speak English gave the Irish a position of leadership over the other Roman Catholic nationalities that eventually entered the growing urban communities of the eastern seaboard. Because of their economic, political and religious roles, the South Irish have had extremely high visibility in American intergroup relations.

In the next selection an attempt is made to define the status of the South Irish in terms of the concept of "intermediacy."

24. IRISH STATUS IN AMERICA
BY *Milton L. Barron* *

PERSISTENT and generally accepted efforts among sociologists and anthropologists to identify American Negroes and Jews by status concepts,

* Milton L. Barron, "Intermediacy: Conceptualization of Irish Status in America," *Social Forces,* XXVII (March 1949), 256–263. Reprinted by permission.

especially caste, quasi-caste, and marginal man [1] lead inexorably to these theoretical queries: Are these the only minorities in American society to which characterization by the same or related status concepts can be applied? Can status conceptualization of other groups avoid the pitfalls of over-generalization and group fallacy?

It is the purpose of this paper to establish that the status concept of "intermediacy" applies to American Irish Catholics, a religio-ethnic group seemingly neglected by sociologists in inverse correlation to its "high visibility" in American intergroup relations. We begin with the hypothesis that the various economic, political and religious roles which give this group "high visibility" among European-derived ethnic groups are not exclusively the product of Irish cultural traits acquired and transplanted from Europe. Rather, they constitute to a considerable extent the expression of an intermediate ethnic status which evolved from an historically "mean" and culturally and demographically "median" positions in the American immigration process. It is proposed that this hypothesis is most readily substantiated in urban communities of the New England, Middle Atlantic and East North Central States, the area which has experienced the most heterogeneous range of immigration from Europe and the greater part of Irish Catholic settlement.

THE INADEQUACY OF NUMERICAL STRENGTH

Oft-repeated observations hold that American Irish Catholics have played outstanding roles in trade union leadership, municipal and state politics and the Roman Catholic hierarchy. To account for this situation by a theory of numerical strength is a facile but inadequate pursuit. The American Irish Catholics in contemporary America do not have overwhelming numbers nationally and—except for a minority of communities—locally.

Sociologists who have attempted to unravel the ethnic composition of American society know only too well that "it is difficult . . . to evaluate with any definite degree of exactness the relative importance of different national groups. . . . After two or three generations in the United States intermarriage and intermixture make it impossible accurately to apportion the population into national-origin groups." [2] The United

---

[1] John Dollard, *Caste and Class in a Southern Town* (New Haven: Yale University Press, 1937); Allison Davis, Burleigh B. and Mary R. Gardner, *Deep South* (Chicago: University of Chicago Press, 1941); Raymond Kennedy, "The Position and Future of the Jews in America," in I. Graeber and S. H. Britt (eds.), *Jews in a Gentile World* (New York: The Macmillan Co., 1942); Everett Stonequist, *The Marginal Man* (New York: Scribner, 1937); Edward C. McDonagh, "Status Levels of American Jews," *Sociology and Social Research*, XXXII (1948), 944–53. The latter, the most recent of such studies, is unique in its conclusion that the status levels of American Jews vary with the particular status—ethnic, educational, legal, economic —selected for analysis.

[2] Joseph S. Roucek, "National Minorities in Domestic Politics," in F. Brown and J. Roucek (eds.), *One America* (New York: Prentice-Hall, 1945), p. 400.

States provides reasonably accurate statistics only for the foreign born and their children. Another handicap has been the classification of immigrants according to "the country of last permanent residence" rather than the country of nativity. Irish immigrants have come to America after brief residences in England, Scotland and Canada. One is also confronted with the facts that prior to 1820 the number of immigrants from each country was not recorded, and that the number of those returning to their homes in Europe prior to 1907 is not known.

Nevertheless, there are useful contemporary estimates of the numbers of Irish in the United States; the most generally accepted is that 10 per cent of the American people are Irish. Even if the frame of reference is a single community rather than the entire United States, the Irish are frequently estimated to be as small as 10 per cent of the population and of the groups in a community the Irish group often is mediocre in size. At the same time their economic, political and religious roles are conspicuous in the manner described above.

THE AMERICAN IRISH AS A HISTORICAL MEAN

A more feasible explanation for the roles of the American Irish is their time-position in the immigration process. Despite the nuances in the shifting source of European immigration, the detailed classifications of periods or phases of immigration, and the distinctions between colonists and immigrants, it is not an oversimplification to state that until 1882, the most prominent landmark in the history of immigration to the United States, "old immigration" brought mostly people from northern and western Europe, whereas subsequently the predominance was "new immigration" from southern and eastern Europe. It is a popular but false notion that the American Irish were almost exclusively early nineteenth century —therefore "old"—immigrants; conversely it is frequently misrepresented that they contributed insignificantly to immigration before the "potato famine" as far back as the earliest colonial settlements, and relatively little after the famine—that is, the late nineteenth and early twentieth century. The statistics of the United States Census and the Bureau of Immigration and Naturalization, the reconstructionist labors of Irish researchers and historians leave no doubt that the Irish Catholics were represented well in all phases of American immigration, but preponderantly and characteristically in the concluding decades of "old immigration," especially from 1850 to 1870. This era may justifiably be called the "middle" of American immigration. It is also noteworthy in supporting this point that "the Irish were the only group among the older immigrants to concentrate so heavily in the Northeast. . . . In any event, the Irish in their distribution more nearly resemble the new immigrants to come later than they do the other 'old' immigrants who came in at the same time." [3] *The main point, however, is that the Irish were not only characteristic of and conspicuous in nineteenth century immigration but the group among all major groups whose mean average in its spectrum of American entry most clearly fell in the nineteenth century.*[4]

Even when allowance is made for the probable bias and self-eulogism of several Irish-American historians, the evidence is that Irish immigration before 1820 (when official immigration statistics were recorded in this country for the first time) was greater than disinterested students of the subject have allowed. Some Irish-American historians go so far as to claim that the policy of Anglo-Saxons to give American ideology and polity an English aspect and pro-English direction led in turn to a "history" written by men of Protestant affiliation and Anglophile sentiments. The latter minimized mention of the numbers and roles of the Irish Catholic in early American—that is, colonial and post-Revolutionary —times. The Irish historians fortify their stand by the analysis of names and nativity in early American historical documents and conclude that possibly one third or more of the American population in 1776 was Irish. They also have claimed that their rival Anglophile historians fabricated a "Scotch-Irish" myth to further their plot. Others contend that the Scotch-Irish, quite apart from their remote origin in Scotland and their Presbyterian affiliation, are really Irishmen and are to blame themselves for distorting the true picture of the American Irish numbers and their arrival. As one Irishman resolved 80 years ago on the phenomenon of Irish "passing": "Scotch-Irish are those Irish, or descendents of Irishmen, who are ashamed of their country, and represent themselves to Americans as other than what they really are." [5] A more recent observation is that "so many of us financially—therefore socially—successful Irish in America go Scotch over night because, I suppose, the Scotch route is so easy a way out." [6]

An interpretation generally overlooked in explaining the minimization of the Irish in early America is that by virtue of being predominantly male in sex ratio and frequently "gentlemen of substance" they were more likely to lose their identity as Irishmen by intermarriage than in the case of the mid-nineteenth century Irish immigrants. The latter, starved off the land by the millions, were in number, relatively balanced sex ratio, and economic impoverishment better equipped to persevere as

[3] Maurice R. Davie, *World Immigration* (New York: The Macmillan Co., 1936), p. 254.

[4] An apparent competitor in this respect was the Germans. But German immigration is essentially a fictional and retroactive entity, for the German state and nationality were not conceived until long after "German" immigration had begun in colonial times.

[5] John F. Maguire, *The Irish in America* (London: Longmans, Green, and Co., 1868), p. 309.

[6] Frank W. O'Malley, "American Sons of th' ould Sod," *American Mercury,* XVIII (1929), 32.

a group. In short, there are grounds for assuming that more Irish entered this country in earlier and later periods of immigration compared with their high mark in the mid-nineteenth century—the lack of official statistics in the former period (before 1820) notwithstanding.

THE AMERICAN IRISH AS A CULTURAL AND DEMOGRAPHIC MEDIAN

To place the American Irish in a historically "mean" position in the immigration sense of the term does not suffice by itself in accounting for their roles in American life. The significance of this historical position and the development of our hypothesis is brought in terms of the concept of the American Irish as culturally and demographically "median."

It was Commons' keen observation over forty years ago that "old" and "new" immigration were each marked by distinctive cultural correlates. "A line drawn across the continent of Europe from northeast to southwest, separating the Scandinavian Peninsula, the British Isles, Germany and France from Russia, Austria-Hungary, Italy, and Turkey, separates countries not only of distinct races but also of distinct civilizations. It separates Protestant Europe from Catholic Europe; it separates countries of representative institutions and popular government from absolute monarchies; it separates lands where education is universal from lands where illiteracy predominates; it separates manufacturing countries, progressive agriculture, and skilled labor from primitive hand industries, backward agriculture, and unskilled labor; it separates an educated, thrifty peasantry from a peasantry scarcely a single generation removed from serfdom; it separates Teutonic races from Latin, Slav, Semitic, and Mongolian races." [7]

What Commons failed to clarify was that the Irish, whose "mean" position in the immigration process has been proposed above, were in a peculiar cultural situation as far as his schematic dichotomy of Europe was concerned. Their immigration crest did come within "old" immigration, but they deviated markedly in the cultural common denominator shared by other northern and western Europeans, especially in religion. On the other hand, their Roman Catholicism (or more inclusively, non-Protestantism), illiteracy, lack of popular government, backward agriculture, and poverty which gave them an affinity to most southern and eastern European emigrants could not supersede the basic cultural reality of their English-speaking background and the status advantage of a generally earlier arrival. *In other words, the spectrum of major cultural traits with "old" or northern and western European immigrants represented at one*

---

[7] John R. Commons, *Races and Immigrants in America* (New York: The Macmillan Co., 1907), p. 69. See Davie, *op. cit.*, pp. 96–98. The line to which Commons and Davie refer is, of course, a general division between the sources of "old" and "new" immigration.

extreme, and "new" or southern and eastern Europeans represented at the other, found the Irish in an approximately "median" position. Their Roman Catholicism, perhaps more than anything else, set them apart from Protestant "old" immigrants but identified them with the Roman Catholics and other non-Protestant "new" immigrants; the fact that they spoke English had the same key ambivalent effect but in reverse relationships. The following operational illustration serves to demonstrate concisely the significance of this "culturally median" position: "Social habits did not separate Villagers and Irish to the degree that they did Villagers and Italians. Though the Irish looked askance at the behavior of the Villagers, deploring their lack of family life, and though they raised their eyebrows at girls who smoked on the street, and were very dubious of their new neighbors' morality, they were sufficiently used to American habits not to set every Villager girl down as a 'loose woman.'

"To the Villagers, in their turn, the Irish were not wholly mysterious. Some had had Irish cooks or nursemaids in their youth; others Irish schoolmates. There was no language barrier as there was with the Italians." [8]

Whatever research has been done in the neglected area of comparative demographic traits in American ethnic groups points to a "median" position for the Irish. A study [9] in World War II of 3075 white enlisted men measured by the Chemical Warfare Service, comprising a wide sampling of all sections of the United States, correlated eight head and face measurements with national extraction. Six cephalic types were identified, but "the sixth type is really no type at all; it comprises the Irish, who happen to be very close to the general averages of the total American melange. . . ."

With respect to another demographic trait, nativity, it has been noted that today the American Irish are for the most part two or more generations removed from their original stock. On the other hand the descendants of "old" immigrants have an overall higher generational identity and "new" immigrants are still concentrated in the first two generations. A closely related demographic trait, age structure, reveals similar findings. For example, each ethnic group entering Greenwich Village within a fairly short period and more or less homogeneous in age composition at the time of arrival, presented a distinct age pattern. "The Irish group during these years (1920 and 1930) consisted of three generations —the remnant of really old people, born on the other side, who had come to the district as young people fifty years before; the children of these people raised in the district during the last decade of the nineteenth and the first few years of the twentieth century; and thirdly, the children of

[8] Caroline F. Ware, *Greenwich Village 1920–1930* (Boston: Houghton Mifflin Co., 1935), pp. 113–14.

[9] Alice M. Brues, "Regional Differences in the Physical Characteristics of an American Population," *American Journal of Physical Anthropology,* IV N.S. (1946), 463–81.

the latter, the older of whom were beginning to marry and move away in 1920 while the younger were still in school in 1930. Along with these was a mere scattering of those who had not moved out on marriage and who were starting to raise their families in the neighborhood. The study of the Irish must, therefore, be couched largely in terms of the middle generation, the parents of grown and nearly grown children—with some consideration for the youngsters in their teens and the very old.

"The Italian group, by contrast . . . must be studied in terms of this young, second generation element and of their parents—somewhat younger than the middle group of Irish." [10]

THE AMERICAN IRISH AS ETHNICALLY INTERMEDIATE

Out of these historical, cultural and demographic patterns the Irish Catholics in contemporary America have developed ethnic status and roles of "intermediacy." America's continuous immigration has been approximately correlated with a system of upward social mobility. "So long as each year brought large numbers of new immigrants, a shifting and flexible hierarchy could develop in which each new group entered at the bottom of the "pecking order" only to move up later to a position of dominance over newer groups." [11] The Irish, followed by "new" immigrants and replaced by them ecologically, economically and otherwise in the lower strata occupied by whites, moved upward into more prestigeful positions, but seldom into the "upper-upper" brackets of old stock Protestant Americans.

Occupational Structure

This pattern was apparent especially in the occupational structure. The desire of Yankee contractors for cheap labor in building up the new industrial economy before the Civil War channeled Irish males into the unskilled workers class of northeastern urban America and marked them out as the white "hewers of wood and drawers of water," replacing the daughters of New England farmers in the factories. As for Irish women, over a period of 75 years it came to be commonplace to find old-stock American families employing an Irish housemaid or cook. Nonprofessional descriptions of the correlates of this early occupational status of the Irish—that is, poor housing, high morbidity and mortality rates—can now be applied almost as adequately to the plight of Puerto Ricans who entered roughly the same geographical area after World War II. America's Irish moved up the occupational scale when a later gen-

[10] Ware, *op. cit.,* pp. 40–41.
[11] Robin Williams, *The Reduction of Intergroup Tensions* (New York: Social Science Research Council, 1947), p. 3.

eration's "new" immigration brought Poles, Italians and others to replace them in unskilled economic roles. The occupations of foreman, straw-boss and superintendent over these immigrants on behalf of the old American employer became typically Irish; the impetus and needs for such supervisors resulted from an increasing complexity of industrial organization, and the assignment to the Irish derived from their historical priority and ability to speak English. It was perhaps consistent that further manifestations of this intermediate occupational status and role of the Irish became apparent in their roles as first union organizers and labor leaders, urban policemen and firemen. Pertinent to the subject is Anderson's [12] tabulation of Burlington's professions. Whereas the old Americans understandably out-distance in number all other groups as physicians, surgeons and lawyers, the middle position belongs to the community's Irish, and far behind come the professionals of the other groups.

Political Structure

The absence of a serious language barrier, the appeal made by the new Democratic party in the nineteenth century for the rights of foreigners on the one hand, and the old-line American and anti-Catholic orientation of the Federalist-Whig-Republican party on the other produced a near universal American Irish attachment to the Democrats. By 1880 the Irish, congregated and solidified in urban areas, became the northern mainstay of the Democratic party with their own machines and bosses in several cities. Traditionally, the chairman of the National Democratic Committee is an Irish Catholic. The population's growing cosmopolitanism which accompanied "new" immigration—several of whose groups looked up to the English-speaking political leadership of their fellow Irish Catholics in a manner comparable to the worker-foreman relationship—soon congealed into a political pattern which became commonplace in the northeastern communities. That is, the Irish assumed what may be labelled a politically "intermediate" position, as the "champions of the newer elements" on one side of them, and the Republicans of "old" immigrant Protestant stock on the other—"a fact which tends to increase the force of the demarcations already established along economic, cultural and religious lines . . . in the community." [13] This borderline or "intermediate" position of the Irish as expressed in their Democratic party leadership has reached the point of "spilling over," so to speak, in the direction of "Irish Republicanism," according to some observers. Early symptoms in New York state were the nomination of William F. Bleakley as Republican candidate for governor and Alfred E. Smith's "walk." The rise of some Irish to a higher economic status is held primarily responsible.

[12] Elin L. Anderson, *We Americans* (Cambridge: Harvard University Press, 1938), p. 55.
[13] Anderson, *op. cit.*, pp. 211–212.

Religious Structure

The aforementioned expressions of Irish "intermediate" status and role are functionally enmeshed with still another—the religious role—to which several allusions have already been made. When the Irish, as the first large American contingent of Roman Catholics, poured into the predominantly Protestant United States in the decade of 1840, their leadership in the American branch of the Church awaited the subsequent arrival of other Catholic immigrants. Because the Irish furnished most of the Church's priests and nuns in this country, the Catholic hierarchy has become characteristically Irish. To a considerable degree, Catholic organizations, such as the Knights of Columbus, the Catholic Daughters of America and the National Catholic Welfare Conference, are also staffed by Irish-Americans.

An analysis of the names in the present controversy about ideology between Roman Catholics and Protestants—revolving chiefly around the problems of the relation between government and religion and the system of public versus parochial education—reveals a conspicuous number of Irish Catholic spokesmen. Perhaps the best available functional illustration of the intermediate status and roles of the Irish—whether occupational, political or religious—has been made by Ware with reference to Greenwich Village. "In a very real sense the Irish community, rather than the world which the Villagers represented, was the 'America' to which immigrant Italians came. Their ways, in so far as the Italians could observe them, were 'American' ways. They occupied a higher position on the same plane rather than an altogether different and distant plane." [14]

Ecology

There is some evidence that in many eastern communities an "intermediate" position is characteristic of the Irish in the spatial distribution of ethnic residences. For example, the Burlington Irish [15] were found to be dispersed throughout all the community's wards. However, more than half of them resided along the entire slope of "the hill" south of the main body of French Canadians and Jews, but north of the "old American" section on the upper slope of "the hill." In other small New England communities the majority of the Irish live in the two-family homes adjacent on one side to the more exclusive areas and subject to invasion on the other side by Italians and Poles. Davie's classic study of urban ecology in New Haven [16] showed a pattern of scattered Irish distribution. Yet they were found to prevail in areas where two-family homes

---

[14] Ware, *op. cit.*, p. 129.

[15] Anderson, *op. cit.*, p. 38.

[16] Maurice R. Davie, "The Pattern of Urban Growth," in G. P. Murdock (ed.), *Studies in the Science of Society* (New Haven: Yale University Press, 1937), pp. 136–61.

predominated and where they were characterized as artisans, office workers and public-service employees (mail carriers, policemen and firemen).

Intermarriage

A final proposal for the expression of Irish "intermediacy" is intermarriage. What there is appears to support the hypothesis of this paper. Expectations of verification are in terms of Irish cultural and social propinquity to several groups, for "the largest number of intermarriages are those between persons who are neither on the lower nor the higher culture level (as measured by occupation), but on the middle or mediocre plane." [17] Wessel's findings that Woonsocket people choose husbands and wives of their own ethnic identification, and that a secondary outlet for cultural identity in mate selection is the choice of a closely related group, support the expectation of Irish intermediacy in intermarriage.[18] The writer's study of intermarriage provides tentative verification but requires further studies to check the results. Of those who intermarried, the Irish of Derby selected and were selected by the largest number of different groups in the community, a fact which coincides with their composite intermediate and influential status. They have more points of contact historically, politically, economically, and educationally with all groups than any other one group, despite their mediocre numerical rank.[19]

CONCLUSIONS

Sociologists have long been agreed that there is no inconsistency in the juxtaposition of caste and class, for the concepts of caste and quasi-caste apply to American Negroes and Jews at the same time that status distinctions are recognizable within each of the groups themselves. In the same fashion we may conclude that there is nothing irreconcilable between the attempt in this paper to conceptualize the ethnic status of the American Irish and the fact that the group's inner cohesion is disrupted by its members' own system of class differentiation. The concept of American Irish intermediacy proposed in this paper can be of use in clarifying the dynamic and complex nature of intergroup relations in American society.

EDITORIAL COMMENT

Late in the nineteenth and early in the twentieth century, the Poles, a Slavic-speaking group and one of the Roman Catholic

[17] Davie, *op. cit.,* p. 290.
[18] Bessie B. Wessel, *An Ethnic Survey of Woonsocket, Rhode Island* (Chicago: University of Chicago Press, 1931, 290 pp.).
[19] Milton L. Barron, *People Who Intermarry* (Syracuse: Syracuse University Press, 1946), pp. 201–202.

nationalities to follow the South Irish, began to immigrate in large-scale numbers. The Poles, a great number of them from the peasant class, left their homeland primarily for economic reasons. They emigrated from small villages which at that time were under the rule of Russia, Austria, and Germany. Nationalism and Roman Catholicism provided them with a strong, integrating bond, so that even in the United States they tend to form almost self-sufficient communities in which group life is distinctly Polish. Factory work has become their chief source of income. Yet farming is a more extensive enterprise for the Poles in the United States than for most other recent immigrants.

In the following excerpt from his study of Hamtramck, a well-known Polish community in Michigan, Arthur Wood discusses the old world culture and social structure, survivals in the new world, and the signs of ethnic disorganization that have appeared among second-generation Poles.

25. POLISH HERITAGE AND SURVIVALS
BY *Arthur Evans Wood* *

. . . HEADS of Polish families had come mostly from those provinces in old Poland, which, previous to World War I, had been controlled by Russia. The communities from which they came were for the most part rural villages, indicating a peasant background.[1] Our purpose will then be briefly to sketch some of the characteristic features of life in the peasant village. A valuable source of information on this subject is to be found in the novel, *The Peasants,* by the Polish author Ladislas Reymont, which won for him the Nobel Prize for Literature in 1924.[2] Therein is presented a saga of peasant life through Autumn, Winter, Spring and Summer, portraying an unchanging pattern, conditioned by the relation of the folk to the soil. The scene of the narrative is the village of "Lipka," a fairly common name for hamlets in Austrian and Russian Poland. But Reymont's "Lipka" is obviously in Russian Poland of the old days, as the people are often in conflict with the Russian authorities. It is a vil-

* From Arthur Evans Wood, *Hamtramck—Then and Now* (New York: Bookman Associates, 1955), pp. 29–45. Reprinted by permission.
[1] Of 1247 applicants for citizenship checked by the Superintendent of Schools in Hamtramck, 1085 were born in Polish villages or on farms, while only 162 were born in Polish cities.
[2] The one-volume edition, translated from the Polish by Michael H. Dziewicki, and published by Alfred A. Knopf, New York, 1937.

lage of some sixty families, or of about three hundred persons. In the daily round of life of the people there is shown their immemorial activities in making a living, raising families and managing household affairs, spending their leisure, and participating in religious, educational and communal interests. Moreover, there is vividly described the structure of village society, the leading people, and the conflicts both within the peasant group, and between them and the manorial and Russian authorities.

Of the few leaders in the community conspicuous are the parish priest and his organist, the Voyt and the Soltys, the latter two being the political heads of the community. Above all there is Boryna, the wealthiest farmer of the village. Shrewdness characterizes the efforts of these leading persons to dominate all the affairs of the community; and, in the case of Boryna, shrewdness often gives way to violence of speech and action. The priest imposes the enforcement of church obligations through an appeal to fear; the Voyt and Soltys truckle with the manor folk, receiving bribes for favors rendered. Such behavior is more or less expected by the peasants, who remark, "To be an official always ought to mean both honor and profit." Or, they say, "The Voyt holds with the manor folk." As for Boryna, his wealth gives him supreme status, and he lords it over his family and the villagers, until he is caught in the toils of the village harlot, Yagna.

The main business of the community is farming. The farms are small, averaging about twelve acres. From sunrise to sunset the men and women work in the fields, the younger children tending the cattle and doing the chores. One reason for the small size of the farms is that they have been subdivided for the dowries of children. A man's land may not be in a continuous piece, but divided in small strips outside the village. The possession of land is the chief means of attaining status in the community. Apparently land and cattle are held in more affection than are members of the family. The death of a good cow means more to the peasant than the loss of a child. At the lower end of the social scale are the lodgers or *komorniki,* who own no land, but live as renters on tracts of land owned by the manor. The social hierarchy is represented in the church where the richer peasants have the front pews, the poorer ones being arrayed behind them according to their holdings. The *komorniki* are made to stand in the rear of the church; while beggars and servants on festival occasions when the church is filled are forced to stand or kneel outside.

The general condition of the peasantry is one of poverty. This is not due to any lack of desire or capacity for work. Rather it is that the taxes, paid to the manor or the Russian government, are high. Moreover, the land holdings are too small for the support of large families; the church exacts heavy payments for mass offerings; the one miller in town charges exorbitantly for grinding the grain; and, finally, the peasant may be made to pay dearly for the services rendered by the Jew who maintains the one tavern in the village. Such are the reasons alleged by the peasants for their poor condition. A scientific agriculturist might give other explanations. Nevertheless, the hard task of scraping a bare living from the soil is ruefully accepted, often with pious submission. However, it ill becomes Boryna to explain matters by saying, "Try carrying water in a sieve; how much will ye bring in? 'Tis even so with poverty—and to me it seems a divine ordinance that some should have possessions and others only the air they breathe."

The levels of affluence or need are reflected in the homes of the people. The poorer class live in three-room huts, consisting of a store room, a bed room, and a living room with fire place that also serves as a kitchen. These huts have earthen floors. It is otherwise with Boryna's establishment. His house is large and well-built with wooden floors and glass in the windows. The house and out buildings are whitewashed and everything appears neat and cleanly. His servants sleep in the stable with the cattle, whereas in the poorer huts the cattle and fowl are kept inside in severe weather. In good weather life is lived outdoors, so that acute "problems" of housing in our modern sense are unknown.

Among the peasants large families are the rule. The necessities of farm work provide an integration of interests among members of the family, though otherwise there are conflicting issues. Chief of these is the resentment of the dominating influence exercised by the father. Old Boryna storms around, asserting his authority over the family. In spite of his age he refuses to subdivide his land in accordance with custom. When Antek, his oldest son, demands his share of the land, a furious struggle occurs during which Boryna drives Antek from the house with the words, "The land is my own. Let anyone else dare claim my property!"

Parental authority is also manifest in the marital selection of children. Since all values are subordinated to the ownership of land, parents have a sharp eye to the acres which a proposed marriage will bring and they may interfere with the match. Otherwise, romance is a factor in selection, and a man will send a proposer, as an intermediary, to the girl of his choice. If she accepts from the latter a drink of vodka, the engagement is concluded.

Of romance, however, there is slight evidence as between married persons. The power of the husband may be cruelly exercised, as in the case of Yagustynka, a shrewish sort of woman of the village. Of her someone remarks, "Yagustynka has learned—has she not buried three husbands? The first taught her in the morning with a whip; the second at noon with a strap; and the third at night with a cudgel. As our Lord's dog cannot do without men, so women cannot do without beating. The want of that is what makes Yagustynka so spiteful." At best the attitude toward a wife in the household is one of respect conditioned by her economic services. Says Boryna in lamenting the death of his wife:

> "Yes, she was a housewife, indeed, a rare housewife. It's true she had a sharp tongue, and never a good word for anyone. But she was a good wife and manager for all that. Somehow we throve well then. Calves and goslings and suckling pigs multiplied. There was always cash on hand, and money put by for a rainy day."

. . . Education in the village is of a more or less primitive pattern. That is, the children learn their necessary functions and duties through the imitation of their elders. The Russian government attempted to introduce schools in which the Polish language was prohibited, and to tax the people for them. Such efforts were vigorously opposed by the peasants. The result was that the people were generally illiterate, the exceptions being the priest, the organist and the Voyt. Informally, however, the people learn much from old Roch, who goes about the village telling legends; and during the long winters he sits around the firesides, recounting ancient lore, and teaching children their catechism. He is greatly revered.

The life of the folk is enveloped in religion. Rarely does anyone question the authority of the Roman Catholic Church which gives color to the life of the people through its festivals and holidays. The onerous exactions of the church are met submissively, though not without murmurings, as the people pay to safeguard their fortunes in this and the next world. Their attitude toward the priest was one of respect and even fear for his imputed power over their destinies. Such feelings are slightly tinged with cynicism, as the people note that he is not above concern for his own personal profit. Their sense of his aloofness is not weakened as they kiss his hand or give the customary greetings; and on one occasion, when another priest is brought in to hear the numerous confessions at holiday time, the people resent his fanning himself to offset, as they surmise, the odor of the peasants!

Equally important to religion and the priest for keeping people in line is the role of gossip. The closeness of contact between the families of the village make it a primary group, where everyone knows what everybody else is doing. Thus, there are no secrets, and woe betide anyone guilty of a too flagrant violation of the mores.

As is usual among people on a more primitive level of culture, the leisure and play time of the villagers is closely integrated with their religious and economic functions. The church festivals and those at harvest time afford occasions for a letdown from drudgery when excessive drinking and eating may be indulged in. But though liquor flows freely at such times, there is no problem of "alcoholism" in the village. The center for such gala occasions is the Tavern where the people gather on Sunday evenings after a day of church services. Here the young people dance while their elders discuss matters of political importance. The keeper of the Tavern is a Jew. Though held in some contempt, he is tolerated as his financial services are valued. He extends credit to the peasants, knowing that they will keep their word. They sometimes revile him for shrewd dealings, but are well aware that, in a way, he is indispensable. Moreover, he is loyal to the people in their conflicts with the manor estate over the forest lands.

During the great church festivals at Christmas or Easter religious devotion is suffused with a playful spirit which for a time lifts the ever present burden of toil. An atmosphere of superstition gives further color to such occasions, such as the belief at Christmas, that if one is deserving of God's favor, the dumb beasts will talk to him. On Dyngus Monday, the day after Easter, the young men of the village go to their prospective sweethearts to throw holy water on them. The girls then award their suitors with Easter eggs and choice bits of pastry. All this is impressive evidence of the similarity of the functions of play and religion in human living.

Besides the religious festivals the people make a great deal of the Polish national holiday on May third. This is in commemoration of the Polish constitution of 1791 which had never gone into effect because of the partition of that country. The celebration was marked by an elaborate procession in the village, led by the priest who blest the land.

The bitter cold of the long winter evenings was made more endurable when the women gathered about the fire to sew and spin while listening to tales and gossip. If Roch were present he would hold them in wrapt attention by one of his fascinating stories. An amazing one of these was the legend of Jesus and his dog!

Thus, the unchanging routine of life went on from season to season. The few contacts with the outside world were made through the fairs which brought people in from surrounding areas. Other contacts came from pilgrimages to the shrine at Chenstohova. Roch also brought news from afar which he had picked up during his summer wanderings.

Returning to the Poles in Hamtramck, one finds as might be expected, that in the process of migration a large part of their traditions and folkways is lost or profoundly altered. This would be especially so in an urban industrial community such as Hamtramck; it would be less so when the migration is to a rural area, such as that in the neighborhood of Cheboygan, Michigan. There the occupations and way of life resembles more those of the homeland. But even in an industrial city like Hamtramck fragments of the old Polish life are clung to, though with ever diminishing strength. Often this means conflict, sometimes overt, as when a Polish father tries to dominate his wife and American-born children, as he would have done in the old country. Perhaps the conflict is more often silent and even unconscious, deep within the soul of the immigrant himself as he yearns for the old ways to the point of nostalgia. It will not be remiss, therefore, to recall a few of the ways by which shreds of the old culture persist in the new setting.

A most obvious survival is that of language. In the Hamtramck school census for 1927 an item was included concerning the language used in the home. It disclosed that in Polish families, with fathers born in Poland, 47.7 per cent of them spoke Polish *only* in the home, while 50.9 per cent spoke Polish *and* English in the home. The remaining families, 1.3 per cent, were reported as speaking *only* English. A new appraisal was made on this point in the school census of 1945, including nearly 8,000 Polish families with the result that 49.3 per cent of the Polish families were shown to use *only* Polish in the home, and 50.7 per cent both Polish *and* English. Such data reveal a remarkable tenacity in the use of the native language over a period of years.

As a further indication of the hold which the language has upon the people, we may follow a clue given in Reymont's *The Peasants* wherein much is made of the peasants' habit of coloring their speech with proverbial expressions. It was of interest to discover to what extent this picturesque manner of speech survived among the Polish folk in Hamtramck. Accordingly, one hundred Polish proverbs were taken from Reymont's novel, and from other Polish literary works, and these were then submitted in Polish to a large group of men in an Americanization class in Hamtramck. They were asked to check those proverbs which they had used, or heard used, in this country. One hundred thirty-four replies were returned. Each of the one hundred proverbs was checked by one or more of the group. We here submit the English translation of those that were checked by more than fifty members of the class:

> What we can delay will not run away.
> In an old stove the devil fires. (Referring to an old man)
> Between the hammer and the anvil.
> A word to the wise is sufficient.
> What's too quickly done isn't worth a damn.
> Briefly, but concisely.
> How you make your bed, so you will sleep.
> When among crows, crow as they.
> Only God is to be believed, not dreams and visions.
> Better late than never.
> He who drinks lives long.
> Every country has its customs.
> The scythe hit a stone.
> Hit the table and the scissors will answer.

The farther into the forest the more trees there are.

The devil isn't as black as he is painted.

A guest in the house means God in the home.

You become like those with whom you associate.

You can tell a master by his boots.

I'm for that as for summer. (An expression of approval)

As you act toward others, so they act toward you.

The pitcher carries water until the handle breaks.

I say mine, he keeps on saying his.

Hand washes hand.

The awl has come out of the bag.

He who digs holes under someone else falls into them himself.

A promise is a pretty thing and it brings joy to the fool.

The wise man promises, the fool feels pleased.

One may do as one pleases in one's own home.

Wise after loss.

. . . Many of the above proverbs, or their equivalents, are to be found in other languages, but some of them appear to express the peculiar folk spirit of the Poles themselves.

It is to be noted that the survival among the Poles of their native language is encouraged in a variety of ways by community agencies. Thus, Polish is an optional subject for students in the Hamtramck high school, though the enrollment for such work has not been large among the young people. Moreover, the Catholic parochial schools play an important role. There are four of these in Hamtramck with an enrollment of approximately three thousand children in the grades. It is said that nearly all Polish children attend the parochial schools at some time through the grades. In them Polish history and language are taught, though by state law instruction in the common branches must be given in English. The public schools also encourage the reading of Polish by the inclusion of many books in that language in school libraries. Such books are not widely read by the children, but are taken home for use by their parents. In this way the school system is commended to the parents and the community at large. The city library, as well, cultivates the reading of Polish by the inclusion of over a thousand Polish books which have an extensive circulation. Above all, the Polish language is preserved through the church services, through the Polish newspapers in Hamtramck and Detroit, and through numerous community gatherings and societies where Polish is spoken. The situation may alter in a generation or two; but there is no present indication of much change with respect to language habits. So long as Hamtramck maintains its character as a kind of cultural island, we may expect the language bond to be conserved.

Besides language another means of furthering a lively interest in traditional Polish ways is through activities that pertain to ancient customs. The most deep-seated of these are associated with religious rites that find expression at weddings and funerals, or on other occasions. The great religious festivals were commemorated in the old village life with symbolic or playful activities that assuaged the monotonous routine of life with joyous expectancy. They may seem strangely out of place in a sordid, industrial, American community, yet their persistence bears evidence to the strong hold they have upon the people.

In order to discover the degree of survival of such practices an extensive list of customary activities was drawn up by a Polish student at the University of Michigan, and was then submitted to fifty adult residents of Hamtramck who were asked to check those which they knew to have been observed in America. Those customs which were associated with religious holidays were divided in accordance with the season in which the holidays fell. In addition certain wedding and funeral customs were included. The following is a list of such activities, each of which was known to one or more of the selected group:

I. *Customs Associated with Winter.*

    A. ADVENT.
        1. Attending church at 4 a.m. every Sunday in Advent.
        2. Playing on flute during evenings of Advent.

    B. CHRISTMAS EVE.
        1. Breaking and sharing of Christmas wafer among relatives.
        2. Placing hay underneath the tablecloth or platter.
        3. Serving twelve varieties of dishes for Christmas Eve supper.
        4. Going around from house to house with "Christ's Crib" and caroling.

    C. HOLIDAY OF PURIFICATION OF THE BLESSED VIRGIN MARY.
        1. Blessing of candles brought to church by parishioners.
        2. Placing of consecrated candle in hand of dying person.

    D. CARNIVAL PERIOD BETWEEN CHRISTMAS AND LENT.
        1. Masquerade parties.
        2. "Kulig" sleigh ride parties.
        3. Polish dances, such as Polonez, Krakowiak with songs, Mazurka, Oberek, Kujaviak.

    E. ASH WEDNESDAY.
        1. Beating one another with sacks filled with ashes.
        2. Throwing pots filled with ashes in the way of pedestrians.
        3. Pinning chicken's foot on the backs of sophisticated ladies.

    F. HOLIDAY OF ST. GREGORY.
        1. Parents leading dolled-up children to school.

II. *Customs Associated with Spring.*

    A. HOLY WEEK AND EASTER.
        1. Beating on pots and pans.
        2. "Pucherniki," or boys parading with blackened faces.
        3. "Dyngus," referring to boys sprinkling water on girls on the day after Easter.
        4. Christ's tomb exhibited in church on Good Friday.
        5. Taking Easter foods to church on Saturday for blessing.
        6. Dragging Judas through the streets.

    B. WHIT SUNDAY.
        1. Decorating homes with green branches.
        2. Baking various kinds of pastry for the occasion.

    C. ASCENSION DAY, MAY 10.
        1. Taking wreaths to church.

    D. ST. JOHN'S EVE.
        1. Jumping over bonfires.
        2. Hunting for bewitched flower.
        3. Throwing wreaths into water.

    E. HOLIDAY OF KUPAL.

III. *Customs Associated with Summer.*

    A. THE ASSUMPTION OF MARY INTO HEAVEN.
        1. Taking herbs and flowers to church for blessing.

IV. *Customs Associated with Autumn.*

    A. HARVEST HOLIDAYS CELEBRATED WITH GREAT FESTIVITY.

    B. "ZADUSZKI" OR ALL SOULS DAY.
        1. Giving food to beggars who are supposed to have communion with the spirits of the dead.

    C. VIGIL OF ST. ANDREW AND ST. CATHERINE'S EVE.
        1. Much merry-making among young people.

V. *Wedding Customs.*

    A. WELCOMING COUPLE WITH SALT AND BREAD AS THEY RETURN FROM CHURCH.

    B. "OCZEPINY" CEREMONY OF TAKING OFF VEIL AND PRESENTING CAP TO BRIDE.

C. Farewells to Bride with Songs on Threshold.

D. "Poprawiny" or Second Celebration.

VI. *Funeral Customs.*

A. Closing Eyes of Dead Person.

B. All Cooking Stopped While Corpse Is in the House.

C. "Stypa" or Funeral Feast with Songs and Drinking after Burial.

D. Noisy Weeping over Dead.

E. Carrying Out Casket So That Feet of Corpse Leave First.

The foregoing customs may not all have been witnessed in Hamtramck, but all of them were known to the group to whom the list was submitted as having been practiced at some time and place in the United States. Through them, as well as through the use of the native tongue, the old way of life persists in the minds of the Poles. It goes without saying that their influence will diminish with the passage of time, and with the necessity of adjusting to the stark realities of life in an urban industrial community. The list reveals how deeply the traditional life of the people has been imbedded in the church which endowed their work and leisure with a sense of sacredness. If in the new setting the customary activities become impractical or lose their meaning, the loyalty of the people to the church might be adversely affected. They have given sanctity and stability to the life of the folk, and it could be expected that any weakening of their influence would give rise to a degree of personal and social disorganization in the community. Evidence of such a result is presented. . . . Continuity of tradition is a necessary element of stable community life. When this is broken disorder ensues.

Our study of the Polish heritage would scarcely be complete without reference to another account of the subject to be found in *The Polish Peasant in Europe and America* by W. I. Thomas and Florian Znaniecki.[3] The method of these authors was not that of the novelist, as was the case with Reymont, but rather that of social scientists who give their data a conceptual framework. Their leading concepts were those of value and attitude, the former applying to those objective standards of behavior that are imbedded in institutions and mores; while the latter imply the response of the people to those standards. Where agreement exists between values and attitudes there results a large degree of personal and social stability. On the contrary, where values are confused, and people depart

[3] See two-volume edition, New York, Alfred A. Knopf, 1927.

from traditional ways, individual and social disorganization may be expected, until some new value system is established.[4]

The materials for this study were derived initially from letters of Poles in the homeland to members of their families who migrated to America. In these the same patterns of family life are revealed that we have seen in Reymont's story. Family solidarity prevails over individual desire. Loyalties are attached to the fortunes of the group as a whole, whose prestige is the dominant concern of all. The familial bonds are those of duty and respect rather than affection. To augment the family property in land, and to distribute it fairly in accord with custom upon the death or retirement of the father are the leading motives in family affairs. Considerations for property also determine the selection of mates for children.

This study by Thomas and Znaniecki carries the analysis farther than does Reymont, for the former show the breakdown of the peasant system of values. A variety of circumstances may bring this about, but in all cases they are accompanied by new individualized attitudes that threaten family and community integration. Perhaps the most important of all influences that disrupt the family is the emigration of one of its members to America. The physical separation is often a prelude to a weakening of a sense of obligation on the part of the one who has gone. On the other hand, it is sometimes continued through the sending of money to the home folks, with the idea, perhaps, that, should he return, he would have his share of the family property. Or, there are instances where the husband in this country will gradually desert his wife in the homeland, failing to correspond, and developing an immunity to her appeals. If, however, the wife and children are brought to this country, the family then becomes subject to all the individualizing tendencies in our American culture which dissolve the familial patterns of the homeland.

Other situations besides emigration tend to disrupt the traditional family. Among those mentioned by Thomas and Znaniecki are a son's marriage to someone who does not conform to the ways of the family to which she comes; or any other type of violation of the rules of marital selection by the parents. A Polish student of the present writer related how her mother left her family, eventually coming to America, because of a distasteful marriage about to be imposed on her. Still further influences in the breakdown of the peasant mores come from erosive "hedonistic" desires on the part of individuals, such as wanting to sell the farm so as to divide the proceeds among the remaining children. This represents a radical shift in attitudes, as the peasant economy did not sanction that kind of pecuniary interest. Or, again, there appeared an increase in litigation in the courts over family matters, indicating a new disposition to solve family

[4] For a theoretical critique of this work, see "An Appraisal of Thomas and Znaniecki's *The Polish Peasant in Europe and America*" by Herbert Blumer. New York, Social Science Research Council, 1939.

difficulties outside the councils of the family itself, thus lowering the prestige of that group. Finally, increased contacts with the outside world, through travel or employment, led many youths to seek recognition beyond the family circle, revealing a weakening of loyalties. The whole situation may be summed up in sociological terms if one says that the process shows a tendency for the "I" to become dominant over the "We" attitude. In other words, the traditional Polish family was on the road toward the more individualized type of behavior that characterizes western civilization, especially America.

This individualizing tendency evident in the peasant family was accompanied by a growing disorganization of the community, though we are here dealing with a dual phase of a single process. A fundamental aspect of such community disorganization is to be found in the declining role of public opinion. Departure from the traditional mores is led by youth who migrate to work in factories of neighboring cities. There they assimilate new desires and learn devious ways that often lead to crime. Another influence producing a breakdown of older standards of the community is the settling of strangers within its borders who bring different mores. Among these, as mentioned by Thomas and Znaniecki are non-Polish shopkeepers and city workers. The former may engage in questionable activities, such as selling liquor without a license, lending money at usurious rates, receiving stolen goods, and smuggling. It is youth who are chiefly affected by these influences; and their demoralization appears as a phenomenon of the changing culture, rather than as an aspect of merely individual behavior. The increase of crime is met by punishment or ridicule. But an even more compelling check to the rising tide of social disorganization is to be found in religion, as the church tends to hold sway over both young and old, except for a small intellectual class.

These evidences of disorganization in the homeland, arising from the decay of the traditional system of values, are profusely illustrated by Thomas and Znaniecki through the use of case histories. In them one finds particular instances of a lessening sense of social solidarity and a corresponding increase in what is termed the "individualization" of behavior. . . . In Hamtramck one finds a predominantly Polish community with old-world backgrounds. In the American setting many of the old ways survive through language, religion and customary practices. But the processes of disorganization that had already begun in the homeland become even more devastating.

It would be a mistake to regard such phenomena as occurring only among the Poles who are the subject of the present study. Rather, they would be manifest among any group whose traditions tend to dissolve in the profound social changes of our time. Any reintegration must wait upon the discovery and acceptance of new values which place the common welfare above merely personal gratification. There is little evidence that we have arrived at such a happy stage in the life of any American community.

EDITORIAL COMMENT

After 1880, the Italians provided one of the chief sources of immigration from southeastern Europe. Like the Poles and other immigrant nationalities of that period, the Italians, especially those from southern Italy, came to the United States primarily to improve their depressed economic conditions. Emigration seemed to be the only feasible solution in the face of a very high birth rate, absentee landlordism, high rents and low wages, and a relatively high cost of living.

In several respects, the South Italians have not differed from other immigrant groups in this country. They tended, at first, to congregate in their own ethnic settlements and in patterns according to the region of Italy from which they came. They entered unskilled and semiskilled labor initially, but with time and acculturation they have become prominently represented in many of the trades and professions.

The dynamics of Italian adjustment to American life are best observed with reference to family structure and functions. In the following article, Paul Campisi compares the South Italian peasant family with the first and second generation families in America in order to bring out changes that have taken place.

26. THE ITALIAN FAMILY IN THE UNITED STATES BY *Paul J. Campisi* *

THE changes in the Italian family in America can be visualized in terms of a continuum which ranges from an unacculturated Old World type to a highly acculturated and urbanized American type of family. This transformation can be understood by an analysis of three types of families which have characterized Italian family living in America: the Old World peasant Italian family which existed at the time of the mass migration

* From Paul J. Campisi, "Ethnic Family Patterns: the Italian Family in the United States," *American Journal of Sociology*, LIII (May 1948), pp. 443–9. Reprinted from the *American Journal of Sociology* by permission of The University of Chicago Press. Footnotes omitted.

from Italy (1890–1910) and which can be placed at the unacculturated end of the continuum; the first-generation Italian family in America, which at the beginning of contact with American culture was much like the first but which changed and continues to change increasingly so that it occupies a position somewhere between the two extremes; and, finally, the second-generation Italian family which represents a cross-fertilization of the first-generation Italian family and the American contemporary urban family, with the trend being in the direction of the American type. Consequently, the position this family assumes is near the American-urban end of the continuum.

Since there are significant differences between the northern Italian and southern Italian families and since there are even greater differences between peasant, middle-class, and upper-class families, it seems expedient to single out one type of family for discussion and analysis, namely, the southern Italian peasant family. During the period of mass migration from Italy the bulk of the immigrants were from southern Italy (including Sicily). These immigrants came mostly from small-village backgrounds as peasant farmers, peasant workers, or simple artisans, and as such they brought with them a southern Italian folk-peasant culture. It is this type of background which the majority of Italian families in America have today.

This paper cannot possibly present an adequate analysis of all the important changes observed in the Italian family. Therefore, a simple tabular form (see Table 1) is used to display the most important details.

THE SOUTHERN ITALIAN PEASANT FAMILY IN AMERICA

At the time of the great population movement from Italy to America, beginning at the end of the nineteenth century, the southern Italian peasant family was a folk societal family. One of the chief characteristics of the folk society is that its culture is highly integrated, the separate parts forming a strongly geared and functionally meaningful whole. This intimate interconnection between the various parts of a folk culture indicates that it would be artificial and fruitless to attempt to isolate, even for the sake of study and analysis, any one part, such as the family, and to proceed to discuss that as a discrete and distinct entity. All the characteristics of the Old World Italian peasant family are intimately tied in with such institutions and practices as religion, the planting and gathering of food, the celebrations of feasts and holidays, the education of the children, the treatment of the sick, the protection of the person, and with all other aspects of small-village folk culture. In the final analysis Old World peasant-family life meant small-village life, and the two were inseparable aspects of a coercive folk-peasant culture. This fact sharply distinguishes the Old World peasant family from the first- and second-generation families in America.

TABLE 1

DIFFERENCES BETWEEN THE SOUTHERN ITALIAN PEASANT FAMILY IN ITALY
AND THE FIRST- AND SECOND-GENERATION ITALIAN FAMILY IN AMERICA

Southern Italian Peasant	*First-Generation South-ern Italian Family in America*	*Second-Generation Southern Italian Family in America*
A. *General characteristics*		
1. Patriarchal	Fictitiously patriarchal	Tends to be democratic
2. Folk-peasant	Quasi-urban	Urban and modern
3. Well integrated	Disorganized and in conflict	Variable, depending on the particular family situation
4. Stationary	Mobile	High degree of mobility
5. Active community life	Inactive in the American community but somewhat active in Italian neighborhood	Inactive in Italian neighborhood, but increasingly active in American community
6. Emphasis on the sacred	Emphasis on the sacred is weakened	Emphasis on the secular
7. Home and land owned by family	In small city home may be owned, but in large city home usually a flat or an apartment	Ownership of home is an ideal, but many are satisfied with flat
8. Strong family and community culture	Family culture in conflict	Weakened family culture reflecting vague American situation
9. Sharing of common goals	No sharing of common goals	No sharing of common goals
10. Children live for parents	Children live for themselves	Parents live for children
11. Children are economic asset	Children economic asset for few working years only; may be economic liability	Children economic liability
12. Many family celebrations of special feasts, holidays, etc.	Few family celebrations of feasts & holidays	Christmas only family affair, with Thanksgiving variable
13. Culture is transmitted only by family	Italian culture transmitted only by family, but American culture transmitted by American institutions other than family	American culture transmitted by family & by other American institutions
14. Strong in-group solidarity	Weakened in-group solidarity	Little in-group solidarity
15. Many functions: economic, recreational, religious, social, affectional & protective	Functions include semi-recreational, social, and affectional	Functions reduced to affectional, in the main

TABLE 1 (*continued*)

DIFFERENCES BETWEEN THE SOUTHERN ITALIAN PEASANT FAMILY IN ITALY
AND THE FIRST- AND SECOND-GENERATION ITALIAN FAMILY IN AMERICA

Southern Italian Peasant	First-Generation Southern Italian Family in America	Second-Generation Southern Italian Family in America
B. *Size:*		
1. Large-family system	Believe in large-family system but can't achieve it because of migration	Small-family system
2. Many children (10 not unusual)	Fair number of children (10 unusual)	Few children (10 is **rare)**
3. Extended kinship to godparents	Extended kinship, but godparent relationship weakened	No extended kinship to godparents
C. *Roles and statuses:*		
1. Father, highest status	Father loses high status, or it is fictitiously maintained	Father shares high status with mother & children; slight patriarchal survival
2. Primogeniture: eldest has high status	Rule of primogeniture variable; success more important than position	No primogeniture; all children tend to have equal status
3. Mother center of domestic life only and must not work for wages	Mother center of domestic life but may work for wages and belong to some clubs	Mother acknowledges domestic duties but reserves time for much social life & may work for wages
4. Father can punish children severely	Father has learned that American law forbids this	Father has learned it is poor psychology to do so
5. Family regards itself as having high status & role in community	Family doesn't have high status & role in American community but may have it in Italian colony	Family struggles for high status & role in American community & tends to reject high status & role in Italian community
6. Women educated for marriage only	Women receive some formal education as well as family education for marriage	Emphasis on general education with reference to personality development rather than future marriage
7. Individual subordinate to family	Rights of individual increasingly recognized	Family subordinate to individual
8. Daughter-in-law subservient to husband's family	Daughter-in-law in conflict with husband's family	Daughter-in-law more or less independent of husband's family
9. Son is expected to work hard & contribute to family income	Son is expected to work hard & contribute to family income, but this a seldom-realized goal	Son expected to do well in school & need not contribute to family income

TABLE 1 (*continued*)

DIFFERENCES BETWEEN THE SOUTHERN ITALIAN PEASANT FAMILY IN ITALY
AND THE FIRST- AND SECOND-GENERATION ITALIAN FAMILY IN AMERICA

Southern Italian Peasant	First-Generation Southern Italian Family in America	Second-Generation Southern Italian Family in America
D. *Interpersonal relations:*		
1. Husband & wife must not show affection in family or in public	Husband & wife not demonstrative in public or in family but tolerate it in their married children	Husband & wife may be demonstrative in family & in public
2. Boys superior to girls	Boys regarded superior to girls	Boys tend to be regarded superior to girls, but girls have high status also
3. Father consciously feared, respected, imitated	Father not consciously feared or imitated, but is respected	Father not consciously feared. May be imitated & admired
4. Great love for mother	Great love for mother but much ambivalence from cultural tensions	Love for mother shared with father
5. Baby indulgently treated by all	Baby indulgently treated by all	Baby indulgently treated by all with increasing concern regarding sanitation, discipline & sibling rivalry
E. *Marriage:*		
1. Marriage in early teens	Marriage in late teens or early twenties	Marriage in early or middle twenties
2. Selection of mate by parents	Selection of mate by individual with parental consent	Selection of mate by individual regardless of parental consent
3. Must marry someone from same village	This an ideal, but marriage with someone from same region (i.e., province) tolerated; very reluctant permission granted to marry outside nationality; no permission outside religion	Increasing number of marriages outside nationality & outside religion
4. Dowry rights	No dowry	No dowry
5. Marriage always involves religious ceremony	Marriage almost always involves both religious & secular ceremony	Marriage usually involves both but increasing number of marriages without religious ceremony
F. *Birth & child care:*		
1. Many magical & superstitious beliefs in connection with pregnancy	Many survivals of old beliefs & superstitions	Few magical & superstitious notions in connection with pregnancy

TABLE 1 (*continued*)

DIFFERENCES BETWEEN THE SOUTHERN ITALIAN PEASANT FAMILY IN ITALY
AND THE FIRST- AND SECOND-GENERATION ITALIAN FAMILY IN AMERICA

Southern Italian Peasant	First-Generation Southern Italian Family in America	Second-Generation Southern Italian Family in America
2. Delivery takes place in special confinement room in home; midwife assists	Delivery takes place generally in hospital; may take place in home; family doctor displaces midwife	Delivery takes place almost always in hospital; specialist, obstetrician or general practitioner assists
3. Child illnesses are treated by folk remedies; local physician only in emergencies or crises	Child illnesses are treated partially by folk remedies but mostly by family doctor	Child illnesses are treated by pediatrician; much use of latest developments in medicine
4. Child is breast-fed either by mother or wet nurse; weaning about end of 2d or 3d year by camouflaging breasts	Child is breast-fed if possible; if not, is bottle-fed; same practice with variations regarding weaning	Child bottle-fed as soon as possible; breast-feeding rare; no weaning problems
5. No birth control	Some birth control	Birth control is the rule
G. *Sex attitudes:*		
1. Child allowed to go naked about house to age 5 or 6; after this, there is rigid enforcement of rule of modesty	Variable, depending on individual family's situation	Variable, depending on individual family; development of modesty much earlier than in Old World peasant family
2. Sex matters not discussed in family	Sex matters not discussed in family	Sex matters increasingly discussed in family but not as freely as in "old" American family
3. Adultery severely punished by man's taking matters into own hands	Adultery results in divorce or separation	Adultery may result in divorce or separation
4. Chastity rule rigidly enforced by chaperonage; lack of it grounds for immediate separation on wedding night	Attempts to chaperon fail but chastity expected; lack of it grounds for separation; few cases of this kind in America	No chaperonage; chastity expected; lack of it may be reluctantly tolerated

TABLE 1 (*continued*)

DIFFERENCES BETWEEN THE SOUTHERN ITALIAN PEASANT FAMILY IN ITALY
AND THE FIRST- AND SECOND-GENERATION ITALIAN FAMILY IN AMERICA

Southern Italian Peasant	First-Generation Southern Italian Family in America	Second-Generation Southern Italian Family in America
5. No premarital kissing and petting allowed openly	No premarital kissing and petting allowed openly	Premarital kissing and petting allowed openly
6. Boys & girls attend separate schools	Schools coeducational	Schools coeducational
H. *Divorce & separation:*		
1. No divorce allowed	No divorce allowed, but some do divorce	Religion forbids it, but it is practiced
2. Desertion rare	Desertion rare	Desertion rare
I. *Psychological aspects:*		
1. Fosters security in individual	Fosters conflict in individual	Fosters security with some conflict lags
2. Family provides specific way of life; hence little personal disorganization	Family in conflict, hence can't provide specific way of life; yields marginal American-Italian way of life	Family reflects confused American situation, does not give individual specific way of life, but marginality weakened
3. Recreation is within family.	Recreation both within & outside family.	Recreation mainly outside family; but variable depending on individual family situation

THE FIRST-GENERATION SOUTHERN ITALIAN PEASANT FAMILY IN AMERICA

By the first-generation Italian family is simply meant that organization of parents and offspring wherein both parents are of foreign birth and wherein an attempt is made to perpetuate an Italian way of life in the transplanted household. This is a family in transition, still struggling against great odds to keep alive those customs and traditions which were sacred in the Old World culture. As a result of many internal and external pressures which have cut it off from its Old World foundations, the first-generation family is marked by considerable confusion, conflict, and disorganization. The uncertain and precarious position of the first-generation Italian family today is further aggravated by the loss of that strong family and community culture which had been such an indispensable part of the Old World peasant family. It is this loss in the first-generation family which pushes it away from the unacculturated end of the continuum to a position somewhere in the middle.

THE SECOND-GENERATION SOUTHERN ITALIAN FAMILY IN AMERICA

This refers to that organization of parents and offspring wherein both the parents are native American born but have foreign-born parents who attempted to transmit to them an Italian way of life in the original first-generation family in America.

Among the significant characteristics of this type of family is the orientation which the American-born parents make to the American culture. This adjustment tends to take three forms. One is that of complete abandonment of the Old World way of life. The individual changes his Italian name, moves away from the Italian neighborhood and in some cases from the community, and has little to do with his foreign-born parents and relatives. The ideal is to become acculturated in as short a time as possible. This type of second-generation Italian generally passes for an American family and is rare. A second form of second-generation Italian family is a marginal one. In this type there is a seriously felt need to become Americanized and hence to shape the structure and functions of the family in accordance with the contemporary urban American type of family. The parental way of life is not wholly repudiated, although there is some degree of rejection. This family is likely to move out of the Italian neighborhood and to communicate less and less with first-generation Italians, but the bond with the first-generation family is not broken completely. Intimate communication is maintained with the parental household, and the relationships with the parents as well as with immigrant relatives are affectionate and understanding. A third form which the second-generation family takes is of orientation inward toward an Italian way of life. This type of family generally prefers to remain in the Italian neighborhood, close to the parental home. Its interaction with the non-Italian world is at a minimum, and its interests are tied up with those of the Italian community. Of the three, the second type is the most representative second-generation Italian family in America. This is the family depicted in Table 1.

Table 1 reveals the movement of the first- and second-generation Italian families away from the Old World peasant pattern and toward the contemporary American family type. In this persistent and continuous process of acculturation there are three stages: (1) the initial-contact stage, (2) the conflict stage, and (3) the accommodation stage.

THE INITIAL-CONTACT STAGE

In the first decade of Italian living in America the structure of the Old World family is still fairly well intact, but pressures from within and outside the family are beginning to crack, albeit imperceptibly, the Old World peasant pattern. Producing this incipient distortion are the following: the very act of physical separation from the parental family and village culture; the necessity to work and operate with a somewhat strange and foreign body of household tools, equipment, gadgets, furniture, cooking utensils, and other physical objects, in addition to making an adjustment to a different physical environment, including climate, urban ecological conditions, and tenement living arrangements; the birth of children and the increasing contact with American medical practices regarding child care; the necessity to work for wages at unfamiliar tasks, a new experience for the peasant farmer; the attendance of Italian children in American parochial and public schools; the informal interaction of the children with the settlement house, the church associations, the neighborhood clubs, the neighborhood gang, and other organizations; the continuing residence in America and increasing period of isolation from the Old World; the acceptance of work by the housewife outside the home for wages; the increasing recognition by both parents and children that the Italian way of life in the American community means low status, social and economic discrimination, and prejudice; and the increasing pressure by American legal, educational, political, and economic institutions for the Americanization of the foreigner.

Nevertheless, the first-generation Italian family in this phase is a highly integrated one, as in the Old World. The demands of the American community are not seriously felt in the insulated Italian colony, and the children are too young seriously to articulate their newly acquired needs and wishes. The Italian family is stabilized by the strong drive to return to Italy.

THE CONFLICT STAGE

In this period the first-generation family experiences its most profound changes and is finally wrenched from its Old World foundation. It is now chiefly characterized by the conflict between two ways of life, the one American and the other Italian, and by the incompatibility of parents and children. This phase begins roughly during the second decade of living in America—specifically, when the children unhesitatingly express their acquired American expectations and attempt to transmit them in the family situation and when the parents in turn attempt to reinforce the pattern of the Old World peasant family. Conflicting definitions of various family situations threaten to destroy whatever stability the family had maintained through the first period. This is the period of great frustration and of misunderstanding between parents and children. In this undeclared state of war between two ways of life it is the parents who have the most to lose, for their complete acceptance of the American way of living means the destruction of the Old World ideal.

The first-generation Italian family is also constantly made to feel the force of external pressures coming from outside the Italian colony. It is inevitable that the family structure should crumble under the incessant hammering. Not able to draw upon a complete culture and social system to support its position, the family pattern, already weakened, now begins to change radically: the father loses his importance, the daughters acquire unheard-of independence; in short, the children press down upon the first-generation family an American way of life.

ACCOMMODATION STAGE

This period begins with the realization by parents and children that the continuation of hostility, misunderstanding, and contraventive behavior can result only in complete deterioration of the family. The ambivalent attitude of the children toward the parents, of great affection, on the one hand, and hostility, on the other, now tends to be replaced by a more tolerant disposition. This stage begins when the offspring reach adulthood and marry and establish households of their own, for by this time the control by the parents is greatly lessened.

Among the many factors which operate to bring about a new stability in the family are the realization on the part of the parents that life in America is to be permanent; the adult age of the offspring; the almost complete dependence of the parents on the offspring, including use of the children as informants, interpreters, guides, and translators of the American world; recognition on the part of the parents that social and economic success can come to the offspring only as they become more and more like "old Americans"; the conscious and unconscious acculturation of the parents themselves with a consequent minimizing of many potential conflicts; the long period of isolation from the Old World which makes the small-village culture and peasant family seem less real; the decision by the parents to sacrifice certain aspects of the Old World family for the sake of retaining the affection of the children; the acknowledgment by the children that the first-generation family is a truncated one and that complete repudiation of the parents would leave them completely isolated; the success of the first-generation family in instilling in the offspring respect and affection for the parents; and the gradual understanding by the children that successful interaction with the American world is possible by accepting marginal roles and that complete denial of the Old World family is unnecessary.

The accommodation between parents and offspring permits the second-generation Italians to orientate themselves increasingly toward an American way of life. The second-generation household, therefore, tends to pattern itself after the contemporary urban American family. Considerable intermarriage, the advanced age of the parents, the loosening of ties with the Italian neighborhood, and the development of intimate relationships with non-Italians make the transition of the second-generation family comparatively easy.

EDITORIAL COMMENT

Whereas the South Irish, Poles, and South Italians have been discussed as representatives of immigrant minorities from Europe, the Japanese are included in this section to represent Asiatic immigrant groups. For the most part, the Japanese arrived in the United States relatively late, between 1900 and 1910. Most of the first Japanese immigrants were single males who married later in life. As a result, the second-generation Japanese did not appear in significant numbers until 1920 and thereafter.

Concentrated mostly in the three West Coast states, the Japanese have also been concentrated occupationally in agriculture, and wholesale and retail trade. From the beginning, racial attitudes and cultural differences stratified the Japanese still further from other Americans.

The most traumatic experience the Japanese have experienced in the United States and the one that most seriously reflected on American intergroup relations in general occurred during World War II. In the spring and summer of 1942, 112,000 Japanese Americans were evacuated from their homes on the West Coast and herded into ten relocation centers at various points in Utah, Arizona, California, Idaho, Wyoming, Colorado, and Arkansas. Virtually the entire population of Japanese ancestry was subject to this forced migration—the largest in American history—and it was authorized by executive order. The military commander of the West Coast area tried to justify this action affecting native-born and foreign-born Japanese alike by asserting that "the continued presence of a large, unassimilated, tightly-knit racial group, bound to the enemy by strong ties of race, culture, custom, and religion, constituted a menace which had to be dealt with."

Life in the relocation centers obviously disturbed the traditional Japanese cultural stability. Yet even before the war there were signs of acculturation and friction between the first generation (Issei) and the second generation (Nisei). Toshio Yatsushiro, an anthropologist who experienced relocation himself, discusses below the changing patterns of Japanese culture and social structure which began to appear in this country prior to World War II.

27. THE JAPANESE AMERICANS
BY *Toshio Yatsushiro* *

DISTRIBUTION OF THE UNITED STATES JAPANESE POPULATION

According to the 1940 Census, there were 126,947 persons of Japanese ancestry living in continental United States. Of this total, 112,353 or 88.5 per cent resided in the West Coast states of California (73.8%), Washington (11.5%), and Oregon (3.2%). The remaining 11.5 per cent were dispersed throughout other parts of the country, largely in the states of Colorado, New York, Utah, and Idaho.

What is most significant here is the heavy concentration of Japanese on the West Coast, particularly in the state of California, which contained almost three-fourths of the total for continental United States. This concentration is not surprising when one considers that the West Coast represents the area of first contact for the Japanese immigrants. Furthermore, cheap labor for railway construction and other types of manual work was in great demand in the West at the turn of the century, and the young immigrants were readily absorbed into this type of employment. In addition, the area provided conditions which later permitted the immigrants to turn to economic pursuits with which they were familiar, namely, farming and the operation of small businesses.

Within the West Coast area the Japanese population tended to cluster in certain specific districts and communities. The largest single concentration was in Los Angeles County (California), which contained 36,866 Japanese, or 29 per cent of the total for continental United States. . . . The next largest aggregation was in King County, Washington, which contained 9,863 Japanese, most of whom resided in the city of Seattle. Other clusters containing between 2,500 and 1.500 people were found in Multnomah County in Oregon, Pierce County in Washington, and Santa Barbara, San Diego, Orange, Tulare, Placer, and Imperial Counties in California. . . .

GENERAL CHARACTERISTICS

The two most significant characteristics of the pre-war Japanese community, whether urban or rural, were: (1) group solidarity, and (2) the predominance of elements of Japanese culture. The solidarity of the group was maintained and perpetuated by rigid adherence on the part of

* From Toshio Yatsushiro, "Political and Socio-Cultural Issues at Poston and Manzanar Relocation Centers—a Themal Analysis" (Doctoral thesis, Cornell University, 1953), pp. 181–208. Reprinted by permission. Most footnotes omitted.

the members to certain modes of behavior derived from the traditional culture of Japan.

The behavior of the Japanese immigrants, the dominant elements in the community, was basically oriented toward Japanese culture. The immigrants exerted every effort to develop communities which would be socially self-sufficient, and which would provide them emotional security otherwise unobtainable. Attacks upon the group—for example, anti-Japanese agitation and legislation—resulted in driving the members back into their own community and in strengthening solidarity within the group, thereby fostering the Japanese-based culture.

This does not mean, however, that Japanese culture flourished among the Japanese in the United States in the exact traditional form. Certain aspects of the group's traditional culture had to be and were modified to meet the demands of the new situation. As Embree states:

> Throughout the social organization in Kona we find the effects of this changed emphasis from group cooperation to individual initiative, from Japanese peasant ways to those of the American pioneer and business tradition, from an emphasis on the sacred (family ties, hamlet *do,* seasonal festivals) to an emphasis on the secular (individualism, lack of communal unity, no close relaship between society and nature or society and the seasons).

This change, explains Embree, is "due in part to acculturation through 'continuous firsthand contact' with modern American culture, due in part to pioneer conditions, and settling in a new environment which lacks the associations and traditions of an old Japanese village." [1] In the same vein Miyamoto observes:

> By the necessity of participation in an American social order the Japanese community finds at points here and there that their primary-group conceptions of society are inadequate to meet the demands of a new type of social participation. In other words, try as the Japanese may to keep the invasions of individualism and other secondary-group attitudes from seeping into their community, by the very nature of their contacts with American institutional life they have begun to find certain conflicts, between their mode of life and that of the American, that cannot be reconciled except by completely casting off the one or the other. [2]

Although changes were occurring, and there was even evidence of impending disruption of the established group culture, the fact remains

[1] John F. Embree, *Acculturation among the Japanese of Kona, Hawaii,* American Anthropological Association, Memoir No. 59, 1941, pp. 143–144.

[2] Frank Miyamoto, *Social Solidarity among the Japanese in Seattle,* Seattle, University of Washington Press, 1939, p. 125.

that at the time of the evacuation [from the West Coast to relocation camps during World War II] two dominant characteristics of the group were (a) its internal solidarity and (b) the rigid adherence on the part of the members to many Japanese customs, values, and institutions. Recalcitrant members were kept in line by strong social sanctions. . . . The walled-in Japanese community represented not merely a cultural entity, but to a large extent an economic entity. This was true of the rural, as well as the urban, Japanese community. Members became dependent on each other for a living. In Seattle, Miyamoto reports, about half of the earners of income were operators of small businesses (including independent professionals such as lawyers, doctors, and photographers), which catered largely to a Japanese clientele, without whose trade the business establishments would have collapsed. Because their diet consisted of certain foods, such as pickled vegetables, dried seaweed, fish cake, and various by-products of soybean, which were obtainable only at the Japanese stores, the Japanese consumer became dependent on his local community for much of his food supply. Credit buying increased this dependent relationship. In general the people expressed a strong inclination to deal with local merchants rather than outsiders. The Japanese farmers from nearby farm communities visited "Little Tokyo" regularly—sometimes with their families—to sell their farm products or to purchase a supply of needed merchandise and foodstuff, or simply to indulge in such urban offerings as a Japanese movie and a meal at a Japanese restaurant. The farmers, therefore, constituted an important element in sustaining the economic structure of the urban Japanese community.

Of the remaining half of the income earners, the large majority were employed by Japanese firms, which were owned or controlled by the Issei [first generation Japanese]. While there were some who were able to secure private employment outside the Japanese community structure— for example, as city civil service employees, as domestics, or as gardeners —the number was small.

The tight economic structure on which the members of the community were dependent for a living was an important factor contributing to the group's solidarity. Economic sanctions could easily be applied against anyone who violated any established group code. However, a positive factor, namely, the traditional attitude concerning collective responsibility, contributed more toward sustaining the economic structure of the Japanese community than any other single factor. . . .

THE NISEI AND THEIR RELATION TO THE ISSEI

At the time of the evacuation roughly two-thirds of the entire West Coast Japanese were Nisei, the American-born children of Issei immigrant parents, while only one-third was Issei. Statistically, therefore, the Nisei citizens constituted an important segment of the population.

The term "Nisei" is Japanese and literally means "second generation.". . . The term "Issei" is likewise Japanese and literally means "first generation." Unlike the more established European immigrant groups, the Japanese in the United States at the time of the evacuation comprised largely a first and second generation ethnic minority. Only a handful in the group represented the third generation—Sansei—and these were practically all infants or young children.

The Nisei were born in the United States. They are, therefore, American citizens. At the time of the war's outbreak a small proportion of the Nisei held dual citizenship, that is both American and Japanese citizenship. Most of the Nisei who were in possession of dual citizenship were, however, ignorant of this fact until they had completed high school. The Issei parents neglected to inform their Nisei children of this, for in most instances the occasion requiring that they do so never arose. However, upon reaching maturity and learning of their dual status, many Nisei had their Japanese citizenship formally nullified, a process which was both bothersome and time-consuming. During the middle and late thirties, when the Nisei were just coming of age in noticeable numbers, a vigorous campaign was conducted by Nisei civic associations on the West Coast, and in Hawaii as well, to have the Nisei relinquish their Japanese citizenship. It was the first time many of the older Nisei became aware of the significance attached to their dual citizenship, especially by state officials and anti-oriental organizations on the West Coast. . . .

The Issei had done what they did out of practical considerations. Being aliens ineligible to become American citizens, uncertain of continuous residence in the United States in view of mounting prejudice and discrimination against them, and like many other immigrant groups, nursing a secret ambition to return ultimately to their motherland, the Issei wanted to be sure that in the event they did return to Japan with their families, their Nisei children would be welcome there. . . .

The Nisei attended American schools. Most of them completed high school at the insistence of their Issei parents before seeking full-time employment. Some pursued higher education. Studies . . . prior to World War II all indicate that the school record of the Nisei students was very respectable, in fact along certain lines superior to that of other students. While the Nisei were not by any means all "A" students, they took their school work very seriously and were motivated by a strong desire to excel. This was an attitude that to a great extent was instilled in them by their Issei parents, whose traditional culture attaches extreme importance to formal education. . . .

More than any other single force, the American school molded the character of the Nisei. It was in the American school environment that the Nisei came in direct contact with American culture. They responded eagerly to the relatively free and permissive school atmosphere which was in direct contrast to the rigid family life they led. They were able to interact rather freely with the members of the majority group, and in doing so assimilated . . . traits of the majority culture. Among other things, they were quick to pick up slang and cursing, the practice of which was in part evidence of their desire to be identified with the majority group and its culture.

Outside the school situation, the Nisei participated in various American-type community activities, such as the Boy Scouts, Girl Scouts, YMCA, YWCA, club and church activities, and sports. These activities, however, were largely organized on a segregated basis. . . . The Nisei formed their Boy Scout troops, their own athletic teams and sports league, their own fraternities and sororities, and their own Christian church groups. This was in direct contrast to the intermingling that went on in the school.

While the school situation provided a permissive atmosphere which encouraged intermingling among the students regardless of ethnic affiliation, this was not true of the larger community structure. Pressures from the larger American community forced the Nisei to form their own clubs and social groups. More proximity to, and the consequent frequency of interaction with, other persons of Japanese background in the geographically enclosed Japanese community also aided in promoting segregated social activities among the Nisei. This latter factor, however, was secondary in importance to the outside pressures. All this led to a peculiar sense of emotional security which the Nisei derived from being among their kind, a feeling they found lacking in mixed situations outside the school. The Nisei, in other words, led a dual life, intermingling rather freely when at school with persons of other backgrounds and participating in segregated social activities when away from school. . . .

The Nisei strove hard to become Americanized, in speech and in behavior, and in outlook on life. They wanted to get away from their parental culture, which they thought was "old-fashioned" and out of place in the American scene. They laughed at the Nisei who spoke Japanese incessantly or displayed Japanese mannerisms. The Kibei, those Nisei who, because of their extensive rearing and education in Japan, acted very much like the Issei, were a constant butt of jokes of the Americanized Nisei. . . .

The Nisei, on the other hand, were under the constant pressure of their Issei parents and the community in which they lived. The parents wanted their Nisei children to become good Americans, and also to cultivate an appreciation of Japanese culture. Only in this way, the Issei reasoned, was it possible to maintain a harmonious family life. In the eyes of the Issei, the Nisei were becoming Americanized too rapidly. But as they grew older and better educated, the Nisei drew further and further away from their parents, culturally and emotionally, and appeared more and more strange to their bewildered elders. It was as though a hen had hatched ducklings.

In attempting to impart their culture to their children, the Issei established Japanese language schools. The instruction consisted of an hour every weekday after the regular American school, or a few hours on Saturday. The attitude of the Nisei toward language school was generally one of disdain; they often used it as an opportunity for "horse-play." Attendance was irregular, especially on the part of the boys, who were lured into playing baseball or going swimming on their way to school. In the classroom there was much more of a playful air than that prevailing in the American school. Students would converse with each other in English. Often the pupil would address the teacher in English. . . . If ability to speak Japanese adequately was the measure of the effectiveness of the language school, the Japanese school system failed miserably. Although many Nisei understood their parents' Japanese, very few of them were able to express themselves in the tongue of their parents with any degree of proficiency. In regard to reading and writing Japanese, the Nisei were "illiterates." Thus, for example, during the war, when persons who could speak, read and write Japanese were badly needed, the United States Army made a thorough check of all Nisei and found that only fifteen per cent could speak passable Japanese, while only five per cent could pass a reading and writing test.[3]

It was in the home situation that the problem of communication was most acute. The inevitable culture conflict between parents and children would have been eased considerably had this problem been solved more adequately. As it was, the inability of an individual to express his feelings to a family member of the other generation led to frustrating situations in which major and minor family matters were seldom adequately discussed and resolved. . . . The wide disparity between the culture of the Issei and that of the Nisei did not, however, close the door to compromises. For example, in the matter of marriage, most Nisei selected their own mates and sought the approval of their parents, which is in accordance with the American pattern. In return the Nisei accepted the parents' desire to name a *baishaku-nin,* or "matchmaker." Compromises, however, are difficult to achieve when the means of communication are faulty. Because most Nisei spoke Japanese poorly and the Issei knew little or no English, the various issues which arose between the two generations were seldom aired sufficiently and resolved to the mutual satisfaction of both parties. . . .

Lest the impression is created in the minds of the readers that the Nisei were forever doomed to occupy a marginal position in American society, it must be noted that the Nisei were increasingly becoming ac-

[3] Carey McWilliams, *Prejudice: Japanese Americans.* Boston, Little, Brown and Company, 1944, p. 123.

cepted by and absorbed into the larger American society. This was especially true of the period between 1930 and 1940. Thus Opler writes:

> During the decade 1930 to 1940, the Nisei were enjoying an increasing degree of acceptance. This was especially true in school circles but it was true in many other spheres as well. White American manners and idiom of the young people of Japanese ancestry typically impressed American neighbors more and more. The anti-oriental elements had won their great victory by means of the passage of the stricter anti-alien land laws and the exclusion act in the twenties and were less active and hysterical. In fact proposals to place Japanese immigration on a quota basis and to allow resident Japanese aliens to naturalize were gaining considerable support. . . .[4]

Although the Issei aliens in 1940 were in comparison to the youthful Nisei relatively old, they were in fact still in the prime of life. Thoughts of retiring from active life were scarcely in their minds on the eve of Pearl Harbor. They had exercised control over the political and economic affairs of the community without interruption and without challenge in the past, and they expected to retain their group leadership for a number of years to come. In this expectation they were supported by the dominant Japanese-oriented culture of the group of which they were the leading members, for a premium was placed on the qualities of maleness and old age. . . .

Largely because of their extreme youth, the Nisei had not as yet developed political consciousness and mature leadership qualities to any appreciable degree. Although they were beginning to cultivate these qualities through their newly-founded Japanese American Citizens' League—which, it should be noted, was supported by the Issei—the Nisei's collective influence in the more important spheres of community life remained negligible. In short, the Nisei were hardly in any position to assert their leadership effectively, much less to challenge very seriously the firmly established authority and hegemony of their Issei elders.

True, sooner or later the group would have had to cope with the problem of transfer of authority from the older to the younger generation. But all the evidence indicates that at the time of the war's outbreak an immediate transfer was not only quite premature, but in the eyes of most Nisei and Issei, inconceivable. If the pre-war conditions had been permitted to continue, the shift would probably have come about in ten or fifteen years. Even so it is acknowledged that in view of the wide gap in median ages between that of the Issei males (55 years) and that of the Nisei males (18 years), and of the near-absence of a whole generation

[4] Morris E. Opler, *Studies of Segregants at Manzanar, II. United States Citizens Only with no Foreign Travel,* Oct. 26, 1943, p. 54. (Unpublished report.)

of males in the important 30 to 50 age bracket, such a shift in the group's leadership structure would have been accomplished somewhat abruptly. For with a more normal age-sex distribution, the transfer of authority from older to younger generation is a gradual, continuous, and barely perceptible process.

EDITORIAL COMMENT

The Mexicans are one of the largest and most important groups to immigrate to the United States from elsewhere in the Western Hemisphere. Entering in significant numbers at the turn of this century, the Mexicans are preponderantly of mixed Indian and white ancestry ("mestizos"). Even in the second generation they are used as cheap labor and remain a low-income group. Most Mexican Americans live in the Southwest close to their country of origin, and they are constantly being reenforced by new Mexican immigrants. In the United States they have experienced all the major problems of an oppressed minority—occupational and wage discrimination, segregation in schools and housing, and, occasionally, mob brutality.

Unlike the Negroes, however, who have a wider geographic distribution in this country, familiarity with the American cultural patterns, and growing political organization and strength, the Mexican Americans are not yet in a position to struggle effectively against discrimination. The sympathy of people throughout the United States is not easily aroused on behalf of a group living in a remote arc stretching from the Mexican border north to Santa Barbara, California; Santa Fe, New Mexico; and Corpus Christi, Texas. Few people in the North and East know enough about the Mexicans to become really concerned about their welfare.

There is little variation between the social, legal, educational and economic statuses of Mexicans in the United States. Many of the dominant-group Americans with whom the Mexican Americans initially came into contact had brought with them an ideology from the former slave states that welcomed the Mexicans in place of the Negroes as cheap labor and was reluctant to consider them as equals. Given these prejudices, further developments in inferior status were logical. The native-born dominant group insisted on segregation in housing and schools, and Mexican Americans were refused admission to many places of public accommodation. When efforts were made through Mexican farm workers' and industrial unions to achieve higher living standards, organizers and members were jailed, beaten up and otherwise mistreated as alleged dupes of agitators.

In the article that follows, Edward McDonagh analyzes the various status levels of the Mexican American minority in the United States.

28. STATUS LEVELS OF MEXICANS
BY *Edward C. McDonagh* *

I

. . . THERE are several methods of approximating the social status level of an ethnic group. The studies by E. S. Bogardus on social distance give some indication of the status accorded to Mexicans by various ethnic groups in the United States. It is of special importance to observe that the social distance rankings for the Mexicans remained almost constant in spite of the twenty years between the first and second test. In 1926 he obtained the reactions of 1,725 persons in six regions of the United States to a list of ethnic groups nearly the same as was used twenty years later. These persons were selected on the basis of roughly defined stratified sampling. The Mexican was assigned twenty-seventh place in 1926, and twenty years later he had dropped to twenty-ninth place. The Spanish were rated in twelfth place in 1926 and sixteenth place in 1946. On the other hand, the Indian occupied twenty-first place in 1926 and twenty-fourth place in 1946. Of sociological interest is the finding that the off-spring of miscegenation may occupy a lower status than either of its parent ethnic groups.

A recent study of Eugene S. Richards disclosed that the Mexican was assigned the lowest social status of nine ethnic groups. [The ethnic groups considered: Chinese, Filipinos, Foreign-born Whites, Native-born Whites, Indians, Japanese, Jews, Mexicans, and Negroes.] About 1,700 white university students from the states of Texas, Oklahoma, Arkansas, and Louisiana were asked to check traits, either positive or negative, that described the nine ethnic groups under consideration. Of the forty traits considered the following five traits were most often checked as depicting the Mexicans: (1) possess a low moral standard, (2) will steal, (3) are dirty, (4) help to keep wages low, and (5) are spreaders of disease. The Mexican group received 38.5 per cent of the positive items checked and 61.5 per cent of the negative items checked.

* Edward C. McDonagh, "Status Levels of Mexicans," *Sociology and Social Research*, XXXIII (July-August 1949), 449–59. Reprinted by permission. Footnotes omitted.

The low-to-moderate social status of the Mexican may be appreciated by observing the reluctance of many persons to refer to these people as "Americans." In a number of social situations they are designated as Mexican Americans or Spanish Americans, but rarely as Americans. "We're Americans for the draft, but Mexicans for jobs and the police." It appears that "typical Americans," or the majority group, assume that Americans are Anglo-Americans. Another sidelight on the social standing of the Mexicans may be noted by observing the tendency to refer to the favorable aspects of Mexican culture as Spanish, and thus to relegate to the background many of the Indian patterns as primitive and unimportant. One rarely sees an advertisement for Mexican food, but Spanish dishes are common on the menus of restaurants in the Southwest. Since corn is the matrix of most so-called "Spanish foods," it is rather obvious who should get the credit. A Mexican American university student observes: "I am ashamed of my group. So many of my Mexican friends claim to be Spanish in the university. We are Americans in the sense of ancestry and pioneer background, and as to our Indian ancestors we may be proud of their glorious culture." As Mexican American students are graduated from the high schools, it is generally expected that they should affect the role of an American of Spanish ancestry. The role playing involved has a tendency to make it appear that intellectual superiority and Spanish ancestry are definitely related. It becomes easy for the majority group to observe that "Mexicans never finish high school." Hence, the Mexicans become stereotyped in the minds of the Anglo-Americans as persons of lower abilities and cultural attainments. Every American university student who admits his Mexican ancestry tests the misconception that the predominantly Spanish background spells superiority and success.

Another area offering some understanding of the social status of the Mexican American may be found in the development of the zoot-suit cult and the resulting friction in Los Angeles during the recent war. This peculiar garb seems to have won wide acceptance because of its attention-getting qualities, as a symbol of emancipation, and for some as a fashion. The zoot-suit was accepted by some Negroes, Filipinos, and Anglo-Americans of the jitterbug cult. The Mexican zoot-suiters varied their garb with the use of triple-sole shoes and their appearance by the ducktail haircut. Mexicans who accepted the zoot-suits were known as "drapes" and the Mexicans who dressed in conventional garb were referred to as "squares."

The Mexican gangs in Los Angeles involved only a small percentage of the total Mexican population. Bogardus estimates that about one in thirty-six Mexican youths was a member of a zoot-suit gang. For the most part, these Mexican gangs fought each other; however, the daily press now and then featured a story depicting conflict between zoot-suit gangs composed of Mexicans and Negroes. Reporters failed to state that these gangs of American Mexican youth were the products of low social and economic status. These Americans of Mexican ancestry were logical candidates for zoot-suit associations, especially if they had been denied a war job, failed to meet the physical standards for military service, and had been poor students in school. Inasmuch as the zoot-suit gave an immediate status to the wearer, "consciousness of kind" quickly developed among the Mexican youth. A unique garb gave an esoteric status to the wearer. . . .

No doubt one of the major factors in assigning a low social standing to the Mexican is the tendency of the majority group to think of him as a peon. He is too often depicted on post cards as a person sleeping against a shady wall. In a go-getting culture, such as ours, such a stereotype cannot offer status. The American of Mexican ancestry as an artist, a writer, or a scientist is omitted rather completely from this visualization of role. It must not be forgotten that the successful Mexican is likely to define himself as "Spanish," which adds status to the Spanish and detracts from the natural abilities of the Indian ancestry.

II

To some extent the legal status of the Mexican varies from state to state. Perhaps one of the interesting aspects of the legal status of the Mexican immigrant is his adverse reaction to becoming an American citizen. It is known that most of the citizens of the United States of Mexican ancestry acquired that status through birth in this country, not through the process of naturalization. Some of the reasons for the failure of Mexican immigrants to become naturalized citizens of this country may be worth noting: (1) cost of securing the necessary documents, (2) difficulty of speaking in a foreign language, (3) inability to furnish adequate proof of legal entry into the United States and the possibility of deportation once naturalization proceedings begin, and (4) a deep loyalty to a country only a few hundred miles away. Perhaps a fifth reason of signal importance might be added, namely, the foreign-born Mexican cannot always ascertain how he will benefit from the naturalization status. While still a Mexican citizen, the Mexican can call on a Mexican consul for aid when he experiences difficulty, but when he becomes a citizen of the United States this assistance is lost.

Before the United States Supreme Court decision on restrictive covenants in the spring of 1948, the Mexican had been defined legally as "white." Hence, the usual "Caucasian clauses" could not be interpreted to discriminate against the Mexican. The American of Mexican ancestry has few legal prohibitions opposing his free movement. True, there may be . . . discriminatory treatment, but not as a legal policy of separation as in the case of the Negro in the South. Hence, the Mexican and the

Jew find themselves discriminated against largely by persons of prejudice rather than by laws. . . .

There is a history of differential treatment toward the Mexican in the Southwest and Pacific Coast. It was not long ago that a white man might harm a Mexican and suffer no great penalty, but the reverse was rarely true. . . . In California, to cite a contemporary example, many of the automobile insurance companies refuse or discourage applications from Mexicans. Two devices are used to screen the applicants: a statement concerning race and ability to speak English clearly. Upon questioning as to why Mexicans are not insured, one of the automobile underwriters gave the following reasons: (1) we have no chance in a court case, since the Mexican cannot make himself understood to his advantage, (2) the jury may be prejudiced against him, (3) we feel that he is a poor driver, and (4) he will be driving a very old automobile with its inherent liabilities and perhaps without much pride in its possession.

III

The educational development or status of the Mexican is not high. Since the American culture places a premium on the amount of formal schooling an individual attains, the Mexican finds himself at considerable disadvantage. His culture has been geared to an agricultural tempo, and the conflict between rural and urban values is part of the problem. A number of studies are available that point up the fact that the educational status of the Mexican is low because of poor school attendance, limited average grade completion, and frequent school failures. Some of this low educational status may be explained in terms of high mobility necessitated as transient workers, difficulties centering upon bilingualism, and perhaps a culture that values "living" rather than schooling. . . . To some readers it may seem strange that the Mexican has a lower school attendance than the Negro. The poor school attendance record of the Mexican may be appreciated in another light—by a reference to the high percentage of Mexican immigrants unable to speak English. It must be recognized that a superior command of the English language adds status and an inferior command of the language detracts. No doubt some of the first- and second-generation problems result from a differential command of English. Mutual suspicion is encouraged when there is an inability to comprehend the verbalization of either generation.

What factors account for the Mexican's retardation in school and learning to speak English? Some of the prominent factors underlying the low educational status of the Mexican immigrant, and to a limited degree a similar status of the Mexican American, are the following: (1) frequent shifting back and forth between this country and Mexico decreases the importance of becoming Americanized, (2) the high mobility of Mexican labor interrupts regular school attendance, (3) illness and poor medical care depress school attendance, (4) the low wage scale of the Mexican forces the entire family into various jobs to augment the total income, and (5) there is a somewhat futile attitude toward formal schooling which may be expressed in the statement "Why is José going to school? Isn't he going to pick fruit anyway?"

A few psychologists and educators have claimed that the Mexican does poorly in school because of his "limited" intelligence. It must be remembered that the paper-and-pencil tests of intelligence measure alertness in terms of the American culture, not Mexican. Before the proposition can be accepted that the Mexican does not measure up to other ethnic groups in intelligence, the following qualifications must be kept in mind: (1) American tests of intelligence place a premium on speed, (2) the tests are strongly urban biased, (3) command of English is imperative, and (4) the Mexicans who are best educated may pass for Spanish or "white." Cultural factors and certain selective factors probably account for the differential scores made on tests of intelligence better than does a difference in *native* ability between ethnic groups.

Segregation of the Mexican in predominantly Spanish-speaking neighborhoods tends to retard the Americanization process. The segregated school has been abolished, but the fact that Mexicans are likely to live in neighborhoods composed mainly of Spanish-speaking people insulates the Mexican from contacts with other American children. The few English-speaking children may attend school outside the Mexican community.

IV

The limited economic status of the Mexican American is well known. Economic status has great significance in reference to other statuses. Inasmuch as poverty is highly correlated with other social problems, the economic status of the Mexican is of particular importance.

Accurate data setting forth the economic statuses of ethnic groups are difficult to find. However, a number of studies offer some insight into this phase of human relations. The Los Angeles Co-ordinating Council reported that before the advent of World War II the median Mexican family income did not exceed $800, or about $500 less than the minimum required for decent living. Another study indicated the income of Mexican wage earners participating in the Cleland House Program in Los Angeles. Before the war no wage earner associated with the Cleland House Program received more than $190 a month, but during the war 47 per cent earned from $190 to $320 a month. . . .

In conclusion, these status levels may be interpreted as integral aspects of the Mexican Gestalt which is held by many Americans. Social status tends to be a generalized evaluation based on legal, educational, and economic status levels. However, the status within a given category or level is subject to change; hence, the status levels reported in this paper relate to the present situation. The chances are good that in the United States the combined status levels for the Mexican will improve. At the moment the Mexican's status levels appear as follows: (1) social status is probably in the lower quartile of a representative list of ethnic groups, (2) official legal status seems to be equal to the majority group, inasmuch as the Mexican is defined as "white" in most of these relationships; however, the Mexican finds himself discriminated against by the police, who accord him a low legal status, (3) educational status is very modest in terms of formal schooling completed, and (4) economic status is probably in the lower quartile of ethnic groups in terms of pay rates and percentage of Mexicans in skilled jobs and the professions.

EDITORIAL COMMENT

The newest of our ethnic minorities, the Puerto Ricans, are technically not immigrants because they are American citizens. But their cultural and linguistic background and their problems of adjustment are very similar to those of many European immigrants.

Puerto Rico, with 2,000,000 inhabitants, has a population density of 600 per square mile. The majority of people in Puerto Rico depend on agriculture for a living, and less than half of the land area is cultivable. The excess of births over deaths has been between 40,000 and 50,000 a year. Puerto Rican migration to the United States reached its peak in 1947; it was stimulated not only by these homeland conditions of overpopulation but also by exaggerated reports of success from earlier migrants. The center of concentration of Puerto Ricans in the United States is New York City where they comprise 375,000 or 4.7 per cent of the total population.

Puerto Ricans differ from earlier immigrant nationalities in at least three respects. Their entrance was extensively air-borne; they are the only entering group to include a significant proportion of Negroes from a non-English speaking culture; and they have been preponderantly female in sex ratio. Their poverty and difficulty with the English language have been important obstacles in their adjustment to the new environment.

In the following excerpt from their comprehensive study of the Puerto Rican migrant, Mills, Senior, and Goldsen summarize these problems of adjustment and assimilation in New York City.

29. THE PUERTO RICANS IN NEW YORK
BY *C. Wright Mills, Clarence Senior,* AND
Rose Kohn Goldsen *

As established by law, the Puerto Rican is an American, but the contrast between his rural island with its Spanish heritage and the American metropolis makes him, in psychological and cultural reality, a foreigner in the city. The country to which he comes is the classic country of immigration; since 1820, it has been the destination of 61 per cent of all the immigrants in the world. During the last century and a quarter, over 38 million immigrants have come to America, and in the entire country no place of reception has equaled New York City.

New York is a city built by migrations. Time and again its streets and slums have been flooded by people from foreign lands. Even in 1940, over one quarter of New York's population was foreign-born, and many more were the children of foreign-born parents. The lower east side is the world of the Russian and Polish Jew; east of 3rd Avenue, from Sutton Place uptown to Harlem, of the Italian; in Yorkville, of the German; and off the Bowery, on and around Mott Street, of the Chinese.

Each successive wave of migration has been met by various kinds of rhetoric. Newspapers and welfare workers, immigration authorities and politicians have vied with one another in casting aspersions upon, or extending a glad hand to, each set of newcomers. While each of the migratory influxes has followed certain patterns peculiar to itself, there has been a tone and a predictable sequence of rhetoric in one way or another common to them all; there has also been a classic pattern of "adaptation" or "assimilation." As they enter the city, the Puerto Ricans hear this same rhetoric, but whether they can follow the classic pattern of assimilation in the middle of the twentieth century is an open question.

1

The rhetoric of this latest migration reached its peak in the spring and summer of 1947, when, after war, spokesmen for various interests were duly fearful of a slump. Their rhetoric was a whispering echo of that which has been heard at various times throughout American history, especially during the second decade of the century, when the Americanization crusade was under way. It comes out of the same context of

* From C. Wright Mills, Clarence Senior, and Rose Kohn Goldsen, *The Puerto Rican Journey* (New York: Harper & Brothers, 1950), pp. 79–90. Used by permission of Harper & Brothers. Footnotes omitted.

distrust and fear of strangers as the Nativist activities of the 1830's, the Know-Nothing movement of the 1850's, the APA-ism of the 1890's, and the Ku Klux Klan rides of the 1920's.

The Puerto Ricans were seen by many spokesmen and commentators as a continuation of the "new immigration," from South and East Europe rather than of the "old immigration" from West and North Europe. Many of them are dark, even Negro; there is a rather high illiteracy rate among them; they are Catholic; although citizens, they lack training in full political participation; the island from which they come is economically backward.

Comments picked at random suffice to indicate the content of the press about Puerto Ricans. Two authors claim that they are "mostly crude farmers, subject to congenital tropical diseases . . . almost impossible to assimilate and condition . . . a majority of these people are lured here deliberately, because as American citizens they can vote . . . few can obtain employment . . . they were left far behind in their own unhappy land before they left, that was why they left . . . they turn to guile and wile and the steel blade, the traditional weapon of the sugar cane cutter, mark of their blood and heritage . . ." When the Commissioner of Welfare said there was a 54 per cent rise in the non-resident case load in a year due to Puerto Rican arrivals, one newsman wrote: "New York City's relief costs have jumped 54 per cent in areas where Puerto Ricans congregate." Three days later, the city was "reeling under the impact of this continuing immigration, suffering along with the migrants for all the dislocation caused by such an ill-advised, unsound shifting of the population."

Another comment, which seems to come from recent newspaper clippings on the Puerto Ricans, actually was written about the Irish in 1840: "The conditions under which they had been born and brought up were generally of the most squalid and degrading character. Their wretched hovels, thatched with rotting straw, scantily furnished with light, hardly ventilated at all, frequently with no floor but the clay on which they were built, were crowded beyond the bounds of comfort, health, or, as it would seem to us, of simple social decency; their beds were heaps of straw or rags; their food consisted mainly of buttermilk and potatoes, often of the worst, and commonly inadequate in amount; their clothing was scanty and shabby."

Always with each new wave there has been such a cry. "This time it is different"; perhaps "when the country was new it might have been good policy to admit all. But it is so no longer." That is what Representative Otis of Massachusetts told his colleagues in 1797. Nor has this rhetoric been confined to newspapers or officials. As a whole, American historians of older stock have taken a belligerent attitude, declaring for the superiority of the "Anglo-Saxon," maintaining that the immigrant "somehow constituted a threat to what they held dear, ideologically and materially." On the other hand, "the jingoism of the historians of recent immigrant ancestry far exceeded the chauvinism of historians derived from the older American stock."

Examining the record and the rhetoric, one cannot escape the conclusion that streets "filled with wandering crowds of immigrants . . . clustering in our cities, unacquainted with our climate, without employment, without friends, not speaking our language . . ." as the Mayor of New York City described them in 1837, have been a large and continuous part of the American experience, and each time this rhetoric has accompanied it.

2

As successive waves of immigrants have swept into Manhattan and elsewhere in America, a rather clear-cut pattern of their experience and of the reactions of native Americans has been established. Most of the newcomers are poor, and hence forced into the least desirable sections of the city, from two to ten families often living in accommodations built for one. They are uneducated; the ways of the new city are strange and complex; the ways of yet another culture add to their strangeness and complexity; they are exploited by native landlords and sharks, and by some of their own countrymen who already "know the ropes." Entering the labor market, unlearned, unskilled, they seem at the mercy of economic forces. If the business cycle is on the upturn, they are welcome; if it is on the way down, or in the middle of one of its periodic breakdowns, there is a savage struggle for even the low wage jobs between the new immigrants and the earlier ones who feel they have a prior claim.

The new group huddles together for comfort in mutual misery, and then is accused of "clannishness." Yet the immigrant group itself is almost never cohesive, but is crisscrossed by economic cleavages, inter-village rivalries, rural-urban lines, and sometimes by religious differences, educational rank, and vocation. But if the group as a whole has one visibly distinguishing characteristic, it is that all members are usually lumped together by the "natives"; whatever distinguishing tag is given the group is applied willy-nilly to each and every individual in it.

The press and the politicians usually take the lead in influencing public opinion about the newcomers. Foreigners make news, which by definition has to do with the unusual. The more their manners and morals differ, the more newsworthy they become. No matter how bad the slum conditions in which the children of older immigrant groups live, they are not considered newsworthy, but slum conditions in which the children of newscomers live make the front page. High crime rates of slum dwellers as such are not news, but a few crimes committed by the recent immigrants may constitute a "crime wave." The conspicuous strangers become a convenient foil for attacks which give politicians publicity and the backing of the uneducated, the anxious nationalists, the professional patriots, and special interest groups.

The competition and conflict which mark the early years of former immigrant groups gradually give way to accommodation. Older established immigrant groups find that their economic and social status is not actually threatened by the newcomers; businessmen discover that the newcomers are among their customers; employers find that the strangers can do their work; unions find that language barriers can be overcome and that the immigrant in due course may become a loyal union member.

The new group itself begins to adapt to its new environment. English words and phrases begin to replace the mother tongue; some of the newcomers go to night school and learn the new language, new customs, and new skills. The birth rate, originally high because of ignorance and poverty, begins to decline. Finally the migrants begin a slow climb up the American occupational ladder. They establish businesses and churches, mutual aid associations and newspapers. They become citizens. The politicians then find that they are not a "menace to America" after all, but actually are bringing, just as their predecessors did, elements of new life and strength to "the greatest nation in the world."

Having gained acceptance, the newcomers begin a process of "assimilation." They become active outside their own group and occupation, in various civic, business, religious, and labor organizations. They are welcomed at community affairs; they mix with the "old timers" on a more or less equal basis; they have "arrived."

This pattern is subject to local variation by the stratification of each different community, but in general it has been followed by all major immigrant groups since the first wave 300 years ago. . . .

3

Certainly the Puerto Ricans have heard the old, intolerant rhetoric of the middle forties, but whether they will follow the classic pattern of assimilation is a different question. Will they, as a group and as individuals, move gradually, or rapidly, or at all toward some kind of integration with the accepted patterns of New York life? Will their children begin the American climb away from the asperities their parents face into a white-collar job or a secure business?

The Puerto Ricans must be classed as part of "the new immigration," many of whose members have not followed the classic pattern with the ease some liberal commentators suppose, or, indeed, have not followed it at all. Characteristics of the new setting of their migration must be borne in mind when attempting to forecast the possibilities for Puerto Ricans.

The islanders come at a time when the rate of upward mobility, a key feature of the classic pattern, has been slowing down. It is quite possible that again, as during the thirties, the ladder will become something of a treadmill. Between this migration and the migration before World War I stands the fact of the big slump. Before 1920, immigration into the United States aided, and was part of, the rapid expansion of the economy. Indisputably, what happens to a new immigration depends directly upon what happens to the economy. Immigration aside, will the economy continue to expand? Between 1870 and 1930, jobs increased 300 per cent, population 200 per cent. But can this trend begin again?

Puerto Ricans in New York are twentieth-century migrants who have entered the economic framework of twentieth-century America; in particular, they are handworkers who enter a class structure that has become increasingly rigid since the end of the nineteenth century. They are identifiable in New York not only as the representatives of a "foreign culture," but as belonging to a specific economic position. As long as their sphere of experience is closed off by low status and lack of occupational diversity, the opportunity to become assimilated is likewise restricted.

In the city, Puerto Ricans are concentrated in unskilled and semiskilled jobs, mainly in manufacturing and service industries. They are most likely to remain at the skill level at which they enter the New York labor market. Those who do move upward occupationally meet a ceiling at the handwork level. They may rise from unskilled to semiskilled or even to skilled levels, but white-collar work or small business, to which, in the classic pattern they should aspire, is largely closed to them.

The handwork jobs available to the migrants, and the industries in which they are employed, are just those most subject to business fluctuations. Escape from this sort of lower-level working class lies, as the Puerto Rican sees it, mainly in the small business field. In Harlem, for example, many retail grocery stores and other small businesses are owned by Puerto Ricans. . . . Yet these are the very types of business which have the highest mortality.

The "average Puerto Rican," then, can expect to have a harder time following the classic upward pattern in New York City than the European migrant of a generation past. Of course, "the average Puerto Rican" is a statistical abstraction. In any given group there are always individual variations, and it is true that "the Puerto Ricans," like all others are split into many subclasses. There are many older groups of migrants from earlier, small migrations who have already made good, who own grocery stores, small stands, and other businesses. A few Puerto Rican migrants are famous and successful—José Ferrer, the actor and director, Jesús María Sanromá, the pianist, Graciela Rivera, colatura soprano, Noro Morales, composer and orchestra leader, Luis Juero Chiesa, artist and illustrator of children's books. Such variations, however, do not deny the validity of the general sociological type and its typical problems.

4

Yet one reality of United States culture denies that the Puerto Rican is one single type: the Puerto Ricans differ from previous migrants to this country in that a third of them are Negroes. They are the only substantial influx of colored migrants from a non-English speaking culture which New York has known. The world into which they move when they come to the city is largely a Negro world, with all the restrictions imposed upon it by a white society. They enter this country, as migrants, at a time when opportunities for the entire group are by no means large, and when other tensions about them are by no means low. Movement upward in the American social scene for them is not only circumscribed as it is for all immigrants, but also by the ceilings which United States culture places upon the aspirations of all Negroes in America.

But there is a curious contradiction within American society which gives higher status to the foreign-born Negro, and particularly the non-English-speaking Negro, than to the native American Negro. Of necessity, the colored Puerto Rican is encouraged to maintain his identity as a "foreigner" rather than to blend himself in the world of the American Negro. Especially is this true for those in the intermediate colored group, the grifos, whose Caucasian features entitle them to a somewhat higher status on the island than the outright Negro or mulatto, but who in New York may lose that margin of privilege.

These colored Puerto Ricans have less incentive and less opportunity to follow the pattern of Americanization than any other immigrants America has known. Only so long as they continue to remain conspicuously different from the American Negro can they improve their status in America.

5

There is still another important respect in which the Puerto Rican migration differs from nineteenth- and early twentieth-century migrations: it is in larger part a migration of women.

Up to 1930, most immigrants to the United States were men, who, once they managed to make their way, sent for their wives and families. In the decade, 1901–10, only 30.2 per cent of the migrants to the United States were women; in 1921–30, 44.4 per cent. Since the twenties, however, immigration figures have shown increasing proportions of women entering the country; during the thirties, 56.6 per cent of the immigrants were women; in the last half of the forties, 59.0 per cent.

Yet there is a basic difference between the overseas immigrants and the island migrants in this respect. For the most part, women from Europe have been those who could legally join relatives who had entered this country before the immigration laws. In the late twenties and during the thirties, therefore, immigrant women were those who joined husbands, balancing a sex ratio that had previously been overwhelmingly male. Even though the official entry figures show a higher proportion of women, once they entered their ethnic groups in the United States, the statistical ratio disappeared. This is not the case in the Puerto Rican colonies. Since its beginning in the twenties, the Puerto Rican migration has consistently shown a preponderance of women. In New York they outnumber the men about three to two. Among the non-white migrants, this preponderance of women is even more marked.

Many women who leave the island for New York do come to join their families, but there is also a large number of single girls and women who have been divorced, deserted, or widowed. For them, the city becomes a place of new freedom—a place where they can be free of the restrictions Latin culture would place upon them. But their comparative inexperience with an unsupervised life sometimes brings them into conspicuous public view; and here again newspaper assertions about the "loose morals" and the high prostitution rate of the Puerto Rican colony feed the rhetoric of migration. The courting behavior of any women migrants is always particularly dramatic to observers outside the migrant community if it differs in any way from American custom; it feeds the press and rhetoricians, supports and releases other hostilities from the surrounding communities.

The colored women, particularly the intermediately colored, have an even more acute problem. As New York's colonies contain about twice as many of these women as men, the women are forced to seek male companionship outside the Puerto Rican colony, perhaps even outside their color group. The range of their social circulation is defined by mainland standards as the sphere reserved for the American Negro. Yet in the due course of exposure to American prejudice, the colored Puerto Rican woman, especially if grifo or indio, is likely to consider American Negroes beneath her social status. But if she crosses into the white community she is acting conspicuously, focusing mainland attention upon her noticeably "different" behavior.

That the Puerto Rican migration is preponderantly made up of women also affects the way in which and the degree to which migrant colonists become adjusted to continental life. Adjustment to a culture requires the exposure of new members to older ones; association at work is a direct means of such exposure. Although many of the Puerto Rican women do have jobs, there is still a substantial proportion who are housewives. The circulation of these women, like that of all Latin women, is more restricted than that of men. Moreover, the geographical area of their activities is more circumscribed; they confine themselves mainly to the household, the street, and the neighborhood.

While presumably the women who work have a better opportunity to "learn the ropes" in the New York world, actually they are confined to highly limited occupations and industries. Even more than the men they are restricted to semiskilled jobs in manufacturing industries. Thus, although working women have more of a chance than housewives to be exposed to American culture, their chance is limited to a small sector of it. The virtual absence of job mobility among Puerto Rican women seems to deny the likelihood of future change in these conditions.

There is another respect in which the preponderance of women among the migrants seems to affect their chances of adjustment. One of the strongest incentives to adaptation among immigrants is their wish for job advancement. But, unlike the men, the women are likely to view their jobs mainly as a supplementary source of money in the family. They are much less career-minded than the men; Spanish culture does not encourage women to aspire upward occupationally. To them, "job advancement" is more likely to mean either the opportunity to earn more money for the same work, or to leave the labor market entirely to become housewives.

In summary, movement of the Puerto Ricans according to the classic pattern of assimilation is slowed up or hampered by (1) the facts that the Puerto Ricans—men and women, white and colored—are occupationally restricted, and that they enter a social order with a declining rate of upward mobility, so that they have less chance than previous migrants to be exposed to American culture while on the way up; (2) the fact that two thirds of the migrants are, by mainland standards, colored, and thus cannot rise as easily or as far as people of white stock, and may thus presumably develop less motivation to fit themselves into the lower levels of a world of color and caste; (3) the fact that among the migrants there are more women than men, and that women have less opportunity to become exposed to any culture outside their households, the housewives among them because their range of social circulation is so limited, the working women because they are, and are likely to remain, concentrated occupationally.

VIII. Religion and Roman Catholic–Protestant Relations

No aspect of contemporary intergroup tensions in the United States can be divorced from its historical roots. This is especially true of religious intergroup relations—in which the most widespread problem is that of the Roman Catholics and the Protestants.

The first European discoverer of this continent was undoubtedly a Roman Catholic, regardless of his specific identity. But permanent and successful settlement by groups of Roman Catholics did not take place until late in the seventeenth century. Because the Roman Catholics were few in number and without an adequate supply of clergy, the

Protestants set the basic religious tone in the new society of the western world.

Antipathy, grounded largely on nativism, developed when Irish Catholics began to immigrate in conspicuous numbers in the middle of the nineteenth century. This attitude was intensified when "new" immigration after 1880 brought millions of Roman Catholics to this country. But the acculturation of these recent immigrants, the emergence of their own native-born generations, and their assumption in growing numbers of urban, middle-class status have diminished the strength of nativity and ethnic origin as a basis of conflict. The basic issues between the religious groups have become church competition and the clash of religious and other values.

Church competition in the United States is regulated by the first amendment to the Constitution which holds that "Congress shall make no law respecting an establishment of religion, or prohibiting the free exercise thereof." This is usually referred to as the principle of the separation of church and state. It is an outgrowth of the dissenting, minority Protestantism of so many of the early American settlers who had rebelled in the old world against established, state-supported, and dominant churches.

No religious group can ever establish its church as officially dominant as long as the first amendment remains in effect. Nevertheless, there has been apprehension in many of the Protestant sects and denominations concerning the following alleged developments, all of which intensify Protestant feeling against the Roman Catholic church and its members.

(1) Roman Catholics are, according to their own claims, increasing in numbers at a rate more rapid than Protestants and they are converting more Protestants to Catholicism than Roman Catholics are being converted to Protestantism. (There is, of course, the counterclaim by some Protestant organizations that far more Roman Catholics are becoming Protestants than vice versa.)

(2) There have been signs of increasing strength and aggressiveness in Roman Catholic organization.

(3) As an exclusive and highly evangelistic church, the Roman Catholic church seeks to impress its moral precepts and values upon all Roman Catholics, and in doing it seriously influences the lives of Protestants and other non-Catholics as well. The conflict of values be-

tween Roman Catholics and Protestants has revolved mainly about issues such as public versus parochial education, and policies in sex education, mixed marriage, divorce, contraception, and censorship of the mass media.

In the first selection of this section, Winfred Garrison outlines some of the major characteristics of organized religion in the United States as they evolved historically, and he shows how they are fundamental to the present-day conflicts between Roman Catholics and Protestants.

30. CHARACTERISTICS OF AMERICAN ORGANIZED RELIGION
BY *Winfred E. Garrison* *

WHEN organized religion in America is viewed in one continuous panorama, from the beginning of the Federal period to the present time, its most conspicuous and distinctive features seem to be these: the full flowering of the denominational system; revivalism, or evangelism; the "social gospel"; and the trend toward cooperation and union among denominations.

Back of these characteristics of organized religion lie certain environmental factors which are primarily political, geographic, social, and economic. The chief of these are: the complete equality of all churches and of all citizens before the law, regardless of their religion or lack of it, and the absence of governmental control or support for the churches; the newness of the country at the beginning of the Federal period, with a small population in a vast area; the small proportion of church members in the total population at that time; the volume and variety of immigration; an expanding economy, with rapid increase of population, wealth, occupied area, and social and cultural institutions; urbanization and the shift from an agricultural to an industrial economy. . . .

RELIGIOUS MOTIVES FOR COLONIZATION

The religious motive for colonization in America was genuine, though mingled with other factors. The earliest appeals for settlers by the

* Winfred E. Garrison, "Characteristics of American Organized Religion," *The Annals of the American Academy of Political and Social Science,* 256 (March 1948), 14–24. Reprinted by permission.

great companies which had received royal grants of land took account of patriotic, religious, and economic interests on the part of prospective colonists. The geographer Richard Hakluyt, the most ardent apostle of colonization, was a preacher by profession. In the closing years of Elizabeth and the early years of James I, many of the clergy were on the pay rolls of the companies, and their "colonization sermons" sounded these three notes with equal fervor.

The patriotic purpose was to promote British commerce and to establish a British Empire that would be a match for the Spanish Empire which was already great and was still growing.

The religious appeal was twofold: first, a British Empire would be a Protestant counterpoise to Spain's colonial contribution to Roman Catholic power and prestige; second, there were heathen in America to whom the gospel should be preached. The second of these projects failed and was soon forgotten, but the first succeeded. The Protestant motivation was intensified as the British colonies found themselves hemmed in between a French Catholic Canada and a Spanish Catholic Florida, Caribbean, and South America. As the boundaries became settled, the tension of this struggle diminished and other colonial interests, political and economic, took first place. But the colonists along the Atlantic seaboard were not allowed to forget that they were holding a Protestant "rampart" (the word was often used) against an otherwise solidly Roman Catholic New World.

The economic appeal for the enlistment of colonists dwelt upon the fertility of the soil, the rich variety of its products, and the opportunity for the common laborer to become an independent landlord—such an opportunity as the land-hungry commoners of England had not enjoyed since the heptarchy.

The chief motive of the Puritan migration to New England was the desire to set up a Puritan commonwealth. The founders of Massachusetts and Connecticut did not, of course, come to establish a regime of religious liberty for all men. They followed what was the universal pattern of thought—except in the minds of a few despised radicals—when they planned to set up states in which their own type of religion would be dominant and all others either excluded or subordinated. But many came with them who had no religious motive at all. Captain Miles Standish was one of several in the Mayflower company who were not members of the Pilgrim congregation. Thousands came to New England to escape starvation, to find work, to get land, to gain economic security. But, on the whole, the religious motive in the entire enterprise was strong.

GROWTH OF TOLERANCE

Although there were established churches in nine of the thirteen colonies, there was a rapid, though somewhat uneven, growth of toleration for dissenters. The tight New England system of government exclusively by the "saints" broke down in the second generation. Massachusetts persecuted the Quakers and jailed a Baptist preacher in 1665, but these two denominations were operating without interference twenty years later. A Jew received an honorary degree from Harvard in 1720—and that was 150 years before Oxford would admit a Jew to a degree. New York never put restraint upon any Protestants after the days of Peter Stuyvesant, but was harsh toward Catholics, especially priests. The southern colonies, where Episcopacy was established, were tolerant of Presbyterians, Quakers, and Baptists, though occasionally a Baptist preacher would be called to account for refusal to register with the authorities. Rhode Island and Pennsylvania were completely tolerant on principle.

Maryland under its Catholic proprietor, who held his grant subject to the pleasure of a Protestant king, had to tolerate Protestants in order to have toleration for Catholics; but this happy arrangement was ended by the anti-Catholic acts of 1689—just four years after Louis XIV had crowned his campaign of extermination against the Protestants of France by revoking the Edict of Nantes on the ground that (as he supposed) "Protestants in France no longer exist." With every Roman Catholic country in the world banning Protestants, it was too much to expect that the defenders of the "Protestant rampart" would welcome Catholics with open arms.

FREE CHURCHES IN A FREE SOCIETY

The religious situation in America was radically altered by a series of changes which preceded and accompanied the American Revolution and were clinched by its success. The establishments of religion in the separate colonies faded out. One or two lingered on, vestigially, into the next century, but they were obviously outworn. The Virginia "Declaration of Rights," adopted June 12, 1776, expressed an idea which was widely current in all the colonies and was to become the keystone of the national policy with respect to religion. It declared:

> XVI. That Religion, or the Duty which we owe to our Creator, and the Manner of discharging it, can be directed only by Reason and Conviction, not by Force or Violence; and therefore, all Men are equally entitled to the Free Exercise of Religion, according to the Dictates of Conscience; and that it is the mutual Duty of all to practice Christian Forbearance, Love and Charity, towards each other.

Ten years later, the Virginia "Act for Establishing Religious Freedom," written by Thomas Jefferson and adopted January 16, 1786, went still farther. The 1776 declaration had freed the consciences but not the purses of citizens from compulsion by the state on behalf of the church. The 1786 act laid down these principles: (1) that the state has no right to compel the citizen to support with money the propagation even of those religious opinions which he believes, much less those which he disbelieves; (2) that "civil rights have no dependence on our religious opinions"; (3) that eligibility to public office ought not to be conditioned upon the profession or renunciation of any religious opinion; (4) that all men are free to worship as they will, or not to worship at all, without restraint or penalty; and (5) that all are equally "free to profess, and by argument to maintain, their opinion in matters of religion"—which would even include antireligious opinions.

The effect of this act was not only to disestablish the Episcopal Church but to reject decisively the proposal, strongly urged by some, that Christianity should be declared "the religion of the state" and that ministers of all denominations should be supported by taxation. There was a real battle on this point. The sweeping action which brought about genuine separation of church and state was not taken by inadvertence.

Nor was the Congress of the United States unaware of this issue and the implications of Virginia's decision when, only three years later, it voted to submit for ratification the First Amendment to the Constitution. This declared that "Congress shall make no law respecting an establishment of religion." In the light of the Virginia debates and decision, which were a matter of common knowledge, the First Amendment clearly meant: no Federal establishment of any one church (which would have been patently impossible anyway); no establishment of several or all churches by levying a tax to be divided among them; in short, no law whatsoever looking toward the establishment or support of religion by the Government. The phrase "separation of church and state," coined later, describes the situation produced and guaranteed by this amendment.

A NEW IDEA

The separation of church and state was a thing unheard of in Christendom since the fourth century. It is the one thing to which, more than to anything else, the distinguishing characteristics of organized religion in America are due. The fact that the American churches were in an unprecedented position in relation to the political and social order must be emphasized by contrasting the new arrangement with the one which it supplanted.

For more than fourteen hundred years—that is, from a little after the time of Constantine—it was a universal assumption that the stability of the social order and the safety of the state demanded the religious solidarity of all the people in one church. Every responsible thinker, every ecclesiastic, every ruler and statesman who gave the matter any attention, held this as an axiom. There was no political or social philosophy which did not build upon this assumption. From the time when Christianity became the only legal religion in the declining and falling Roman Empire, the rulers of that empire and of all its fragments, extensions, and successors, and all their clerical and lay advisers, and all the makers and interpreters of their laws—*all,* with no exceptions other than certain disreputable and "subversive" heretics, believed firmly that religious solidarity in the one recognized church was essential to social and political stability.

This, if true, obviously justified and necessitated the closest possible collaboration of church and state for their common defense. Dissent or schism necessarily became a crime against the state as well as a sin against the church. The persecution of heretics was the logical corollary. There were other motives for the Inquisition and other agencies of compulsory conformity, but this one was the simplest and would have been sufficient by itself. A church which had a complete monopoly in the field of religion could reasonably appeal to the "secular arm" to exercise its police power for the protection of that monopoly by the restraint or punishment of heretics and schismatics, when the church's monopoly was deemed as essential to the security of the state as to the safety of the church. The state's part in persecution was merely the punishment of a crime equivalent to treason, and toleration would have been compounding a felony.

This theory of the necessary linkage of church and state did not originate in the lay or secular mind. It originated with the church. The reversal of it, however, was almost entirely due to the rise of popular resistance, the experience of lay statesmen, and the thinking of secular philosophers. On the administrative side, the two most profound revolutions which have occurred in the entire history of the church have been these: first, the change of the church, in the fourth century, from a voluntary society having in its membership only those who were members by their own choice, to a society conceived as necessarily coextensive with the civil community and endowed with the power to enforce the adherence of all members of the civil community; second, the reversal of this change. That reversal was completed in America.

This was not an issue between Catholics and Protestants. The theory of compulsory solidarity was, indeed, of Roman Catholic origin, was practiced consistently by the medieval church, and has continued to be practiced with some necessary modifications in Catholic countries; but it was also taken over by the major divisions of Protestantism insofar as these secured establishment as state churches. England concerns us most. Tudor, Stuart, and Commonwealth Protestantism saw an established church, of whatever complexion, struggling to maintain its monopoly and to convince the government that dissent from its norms would be dangerous to the state. This attitude was carried into Puritan New England and into other colonies.

In mother country and colonies alike, the growing sense of man's natural rights made this theory difficult to maintain, and experience proved it false. The pressure of increasing numbers of dissenters was irresistible, and their complete suppression or assimilation was impracticable. It was found that, in actual fact, dissenters were not necessarily disloyal to the state, and that compulsory religious conformity was not the cement of the social order. England learned this slowly and relaxed the pressure on her nonconformists while keeping her established church. The colonies learned it more rapidly and more completely. The founders of Rhode Island and Pennsylvania had known it from the start. Virginia made splendid and memorable record of its discovery.

THE DENOMINATIONAL SYSTEM

By the time the Federal Government was launched, this second revolution in church history—the one in the interest of religious liberty—had been sufficiently achieved in America to ensure the complete detachment of all the churches from the Central Government and the equal treatment of them all by the Government insofar as it had any relations with them. This was the first great distinguishing fact about organized religion in Federal America.

Visitors from Europe frequently mention the multiplicity of sects as the first feature of the religious scene that strikes their attention. The explanation is simple and not too discreditable. America has more sects than any European country because she has received immigrants from all of them—often as refugees. And America has more sects because nowhere else, in the formative period, did all sects enjoy complete freedom, including freedom from the overshadowing prestige of a long-established state church.

The existence of many free and legally equal churches in a free society is the denominational system in its fullest development. Most American churchmen have come to realize that it is not an ideal condition. Division breeds wasteful and sometimes acrimonious rivalry, diminishes efficiency in the pursuit of the common major objectives of all churches, sets narrow bounds to Christian fellowship, and encourages religious provincialism. But it is a stage, perhaps inevitable, in the process of passing from the old regime of compulsory unity to a future condition of unity with freedom. During the first century of American national life, the churches were so exultant in their new-found freedom that their prevailing mood was one of complacent denominationalism. That stage has passed, and they have begun to realize that, since their freedom to separate is secure, they can now safely seek ways in which they can freely unite.

A New Country and an Advancing Frontier

Frederick J. Turner discovered and publicized the significance of the frontier in American history. Mode, Sweet, and others have explored the influence of the frontier on the American churches. The point is valid. America is still young. A British visitor remarks that, by contrast with his own land, America "has no medieval churches." Except for rare colonial landmarks, America has not even any seventeenth-century and very few eighteenth-century churches. As seen through European eyes, this gives a sense of shallow rootage.

But the churches are no newer than the country. In 1800 the United States was a ribbon of settlements along one coast, with a vast and almost empty and unknown hinterland. Ninety per cent of its 5,300,000 people lived east of the Alleghenies, and more than half of the other 10 per cent were in Kentucky and Tennessee. The whole Northwest Territory, later to become the five states north of the Ohio River, had 51,000 inhabitants. Boston had 24,000 people; Philadelphia, 28,000. The center of population was eighteen miles west of Baltimore. No one was very far from the frontier, and every road and trail was a one-way street by which the population was moving west. For a time, the growth of the east was checked by the excess of westward migration over immigration from abroad. A Baptist church had moved in a body from North Carolina to Kentucky, and later a Disciples of Christ church migrated similarly from Alabama to Texas. Each of these was called "the church on wheels." But in a wider sense a large part of the American church was on wheels.

The notable fact is that here was a great new country to be occupied by settlers and by the churches at the same time. Or, to put it another way, the new communities which were coming into existence had to create simultaneously their social, political, and religious institutions. The separation of church and state meant that the religious effort had to be supported on an entirely voluntary basis. The churches had neither subsidies nor endowments; they were strictly on their own.

Though the institutions of the frontier had to be created on the ground, the basic patterns were imported from the east and from overseas.[1] The churches which grew up in the Middle West were new congregations of old types, their coloration but not their fundamental structure determined by environment.

The great "popular churches" of the pioneer period were Baptist,

[1] See Dixon Ryan Fox, *Sources of Culture in the Middle West* (New York: D. Appleton-Century Co., 1934), and *Ideas in Motion* (New York: D. Appleton-Century Co., 1935), which serve as a needed counterpoise to Turner's emphasis on the frontier.

Methodist, and Presbyterian, with Disciples of Christ added after 1830. Only the last of these bodies originated in America; but the Methodist Episcopal Church, which separated from the Church of England in 1784, owed its denominational independence directly to American political independence. Anglicanism's traditional observance of national boundaries in ecclesiastical organization led naturally to an independent Protestant Episcopal Church in the United States as soon as the United States became a nation. Presbyterians similarly saw themselves nationally and organized their General Assembly in 1787. Congregationalists, hesitant about general organization and more interested in education than in revivalism, fell behind in the race to occupy the frontier, but before the middle of the nineteenth century had excelled all others in founding colleges. Methodists and Baptists outdistanced all others in numbers—they constitute half of the Protestants in America today—partly because of their effective use of lay leadership and their easy standards for admission to the ministry when few educated ministers were available, and still more because they developed effective techniques of evangelism. . . .

IMMIGRATION AND ITS CONSEQUENCES

Immigration augmented the general percentage of church members and, more specifically, brought an enormous increase in both the number and the percentage of Roman Catholics. Until 1830, immigration was light enough to leave relatively unchanged the racial, cultural, and religious characteristics of the later colonial and early Federal days. The racial strain and the cultural tradition were chiefly British, and the background was Protestant even though the backsliders and the unregenerate far outnumbered the communicants. There were also German, Dutch, Swedish, and French elements, the last including colonies of Huguenot refugees in the east and Roman Catholic early settlers in the Mississippi Valley. The Irish were Scotch-Irish, Ulster Presbyterians of Scottish ancestry.

At the time of the first Federal census, in 1790, less than 1 per cent of the population was Roman Catholic—30,000 out of 3,900,000. There had been restrictive legislation against Roman Catholics in some of the colonies, though nothing to compare with the proscription of Protestants at the same period and later in Catholic countries. But from the beginning of the Federal period, Catholics had full liberty of worship and civic equality.

Some of the most notable Protestant theologians, like Timothy Dwight, made unflattering identifications of the Roman Catholic Church and the Pope with the most abominable figures in the prophecies of Daniel and the book of Revelation; but such utterances neither voiced nor aroused any great popular feeling. American Catholics had done their share in the War of Independence—naturally, because America was their country, and also because the fight was against anti-Catholic England— and other Americans felt kindly toward them. Moreover, Catholic France had been our ally. The Congress of the United States and the Pennsylvania Legislature in a body attended a service in the Catholic Church in Philadelphia, listened to a *Te Deum,* and heard a sermon by the Abbé Bandol in celebration of the victory. It was an era of good feeling between Protestants and Catholics. But there were not very many Catholics, and most of these had as good a claim as any to the title of "old Americans."

Immigration increased greatly after 1830, and enormously after 1840. The chief influx was from Ireland, and all the Irish were Roman Catholics. Most of them stayed in the eastern cities. There was also heavy Catholic immigration from Germany. By 1860 the initial 30,000 Catholics had become 3,000,000, and their proportion of the total population had increased from .78 to 9.65 per cent. Roughly, the population of the country had been multiplied by 10, the Catholic population by 100. Immigration was the chief source of this increase, aided by the high birth rate in immigrant families.

NATIVISM

The tensions that arose were the resultant of several causes, of which religion was the least. Anti-alien, specifically anti-Irish, and anti-cheap-labor feeling and the fear of anti-republican influences were more basic than anti-Catholic "prejudice." The belief that Catholicism was hostile to what were deemed fundamental American principles seemed plausible because the Vatican was in active alliance with every reactionary and anti-democratic force in Europe during the forty years after Napoleon, and the Popes were constantly denouncing every form of liberalism and declaring that the demand for religious liberty was nothing else than the essentially irreligious attitude of "indifferentism."

Nativist feeling found expression in a series of "American" political parties, under various names, which demanded a period of twenty-one years' residence in the United States prior to naturalization and opposed any candidate for public office who "owes allegiance to any foreign prince or potentate"—meaning, of course, the Pope. The slogan, "No Irish need apply"—often humorously used but meant to be taken as a true word spoken in jest—signified that the Irish were regarded as a lower order of humanity, ignorant, vicious, and unclean, who, if they no longer "kept the pig in the parlor" as they were reputed to do in the old country, would naturally do so if they were not too miserably poor to have either parlors or pigs. That they were Catholics was significant only because of the presumption that such ignorant and superstitious people would vote as their priests told them, and most of the priests were also recent immigrants. Gone were the days when a "Charles Carroll of Carrollton," signer of the Declaration of Independence, would be considered as the typical American Catholic. In the Massachusetts mill towns, the Irish lived in hovels on the other side of the track. In the cities, they crowded the ranks of unskilled labor and competed with "real Americans" for jobs. Labor was unorganized, its condition was bad, and the heavy immigration made it worse.

The anti-Catholic angle, which became very real, had nothing to do with Catholicism as a form of faith and worship. Aside from the fact that these odious immigrants happened to be Catholics, the feeling against the Roman Catholic Church rested on these alleged grounds: (1) that the Pope is a foreign ruler to whom all Catholics give prior loyalty and from whom they, and especially their priests, receive instructions which govern their political action as citizens; (2) that the Catholic hierarchy, from the Pope down, is hostile to democracy and to the civil rights guaranteed by the Constitution, and plans to gain control of the United States so as to transform it into a typical "Catholic country" in which civil and religious liberty would be suppressed, as in Spain and the Papal State itself; (3) that this control is sought by directing the masses of Catholic voters at the polls, and perhaps by armed insurrection when the time is ripe; (4) that the personal morals of the clergy are low and the internal administration of monasteries and convents amounts to a tyranny and a scandal.

Some of the Protestant clergy lent their support to one or all of these charges, but the main force of the organized attack upon what was commonly called "political Romanism" did not come from Protestants as such. Its impulse, its leadership, and its personnel were akin to those of the anticlerical movements which have occurred, with even more vigor and effectiveness, in some Catholic countries where there were practically no Protestants at all. No important leader of any of the nativist and anti-Catholic parties, from the Native Americans of 1836 to the Know-Nothings of 1855, was a figure of any consequence in any Protestant church. This is true also of such later organizations as the A.P.A. (American Protective Association—not American Protestant Association as sometimes supposed) and the Ku Klux Klan.

Nevertheless, the great growth of the Roman Catholic Church in numbers, wealth, and power in a country which began its national life on a set of principles radically at variance with the political and social philosophy of that church as exhibited everywhere else throughout history, has produced a situation which is not only distinctive of organized religion in America but is unique in the history of Christendom. . . .

EDITORIAL COMMENT

The historical forces causing the social stratification of Roman Catholics and Protestants in American society are obviously helpful in accounting for the conflict between the two religious groups. But to what extent is religion related to the social class structure at the present time? Is it true that social class differentials between Roman Catholics and others are as clearly delineated now as they were in the nineteenth century?

To many Americans the relation of these religious groups to the social class structure is clear. They operate on the assumption that Roman Catholicism is still the religion of preponderantly working-class people of first and second generation nativity, and that Protestantism is the affiliation of higher social classes.

In the article that follows, Liston Pope challenges the extent to which this correlation is valid in the face of vast social and economic changes.

31. RELIGION AND THE CLASS STRUCTURE
BY *Liston Pope* *

ARCHIBALD MACLEISH once said that he divides people into two classes: those who divide people into classes, and those who do not. The doctrine of equalitarianism reflected in his statement has been central not only in the modern democratic ethos, but also in the Judaeo-Christian heritage from which modern democracy derived and secularized most of its basic values. Like democratic nations, however, Western religious communities have affirmed egalitarianism more clearly in theory than in practice, and at times they have modified even their theory—generally in terms of a doctrine of hierarchy or of "station"—in such fashion as to sanction social stratification.

BACKGROUND IN AMERICA

Almost from the beginning, Protestantism has tended to be the religion of the ruling and advantaged groups in the United States. In the early New England theocracies, church membership and the political franchise were closely associated, and both were restricted to a small minority. At the time of the first Federal census in 1790, less than 10 per cent of the population were church members; less than 10 per cent of the church members were Roman Catholics. By this time, most of the formal ties be-

* Liston Pope, "Religion and the Class Structure," *The Annals of the American Academy of Political and Social Science,* 256 (March 1948), 84–91. Reprinted by permission.

tween religious affiliation and political power had been broken, but church membership continued to be confined largely to the more privileged groups.

The great Protestant revivals during the nineteenth century broadened the social base of church affiliation immensely. So did the waves of immigration during the latter half of the century; most of the new immigrants after 1880 were Roman Catholics, and their arrival greatly increased the strength of the Catholic Church in the United States, and also gave that church close connections with the growing mass of urban industrial workers. During the same period, Protestant churches were gaining strength in the rural population, among the American Negroes, and in the middle and upper classes of the rising cities. These broad tendencies in the relation of religion to social classes have gradually developed into the present patterns.

NATIONAL PATTERNS BEFORE THE WAR

The popular myth that America has no social classes is obscurantist but not entirely empty—it is hardly a greater misrepresentation than is the Marxist dogma at the other extreme.[1] Social stratification in the United States has been proceeding rapidly for several decades, but according to most indices American society still has the character of a continuum rather than of several discrete planes; it more nearly resembles a ramp than a staircase. Further, the degree and modes of stratification vary considerably by region, by size of town, by the economic and ethnic bases of the community, and perhaps by other factors.[2]

There is no clearly defined national pattern of social classes, except as one may be arbitrarily constructed in terms of income classes or other general criteria—and such procedure falsifies the picture of the actual stratification in most American communities. The most accurate studies of social classes have therefore been pitched at the community level, and generalizations for the Nation as a whole must be rather tentative and abstract.

The over-all pattern for religion and the class structure can be pieced together from information gathered in public opinion polls.[3] Using data

[1] Gunnar Myrdal, looking at American society as a European social scientist, found an impressive degree of social fluidity and mobility still present. *An American Dilemma* (New York, 1944), p. 670.

[2] All these facts are reflected in a continuing debate among social scientists over the validity of various criteria for the study of class alignments, the number of social classes, and so forth.

[3] It is not certain that these polls are entirely adequate for description of religious or class patterns, even when "social" rather than "voting" samples are used. For one thing, the distribution by religious denominations in their samples seldom coincides with the established proportions of these denominations in relation either to the total population or to the total church membership. Similarly, regional distribution of

gathered from approximately 14,000 persons in 1939–40, Hadley Cantril employs a threefold class scheme: upper, middle, and lower.[4] His material (adapted in Table 1) indicates that there was at that time far less dif-

TABLE 1

CLASS COMPOSITION OF CATHOLICS AND PROTESTANTS, 1939–40 [a]

	Per Cent Distribution		
	Upper Class	*Middle Class*	*Lower Class*
Protestants			
In US	14	52	34
In South [b]	8	48	44
In remainder of US	17	54	29
Catholics			
In US	9	50	41
In South [c]	10	42	48
In remainder of US	9	51	40

[a] Constructed from data given by Hadley Cantril, "Educational and Economic Composition of Religious Groups," *American Journal of Sociology,* Vol. 47, No. 5 (March 1943), p. 576, Table 2. Cantril used "social" samples.

[b] The South is overwhelmingly Protestant, and the ratio of church membership to population is higher there than in any other region (see Howard W. Odum, *Southern Regions of the United States* [Chapel Hill, 1936], p. 141). The South is also notoriously poor in comparison with other regions, and has proportionately smaller middle and upper classes. Gross inclusion of its figures in national studies therefore results in considerable distortion of the picture for other regions of the country.

[c] Cantril's sample of Southern Catholics is too small—only 165 cases—to support confident generalizations.

ference in class affiliation between Protestants and Catholics in the Nation as a whole than had been commonly supposed, though differences become more apparent when data from the South are segregated. For every upper-class Protestant in the South, there were six lower-class Protestants; in the other regions of the country, the percentage classified as upper class ranged from 14 to 18 per cent, and the percentage in the lower class ranged from 25 to 32 per cent, leaving a majority in each region in the middle class.

In comparison, the Roman Catholic Church was composed of a smaller percentage of upper-class members (ranging from 6 to 15 per

various religious groups is not always reflected accurately. Further, classification of interviewees into social classes generally rests on rather superficial and subjective methodology; in most cases, the interviewer makes the classification in terms of general impressions as to the type of neighborhood, occupation, house furnishings, dress, and so on.

[4] Hadley Cantril, "Educational and Economic Composition of Religious Groups," *American Journal of Sociology,* Vol. 47, No. 5 (March 1943), pp. 574–79.

cent in the various regions) and a larger percentage of lower-class adherents (varying from 30 to 51 per cent). But the net results of Cantril's study indicate that Protestantism had a larger representation from the lower class and Catholicism had more middle-class members than popular generalizations have assumed.

Cantril also discovered that the proportion of Protestants to Catholics rises as one moves up the educational scale. Protestants have had more schooling in every section of the country, and outside the South the percentage of college graduates is almost twice as high for Protestants as for Catholics. Further, "those who are not church members (whether Protestant or Catholic) are found in increasing numbers as either income or education decreases"—and vice versa.

PRESENT PATTERNS

Cantril's conclusions must be thoroughly revised in the light of a series of studies of similar data gathered more recently. A breakdown of four polls taken in 1945–46 has been made for the Department of Research and Education of the Federal Council of Churches by the same office from which the data for 1939–40 were obtained—the Office of Pub-

TABLE 2

CLASS COMPOSITION OF RELIGIOUS BODIES, 1945–46 [a]

Body	Per Cent Distribution		
	Upper Class	Middle Class	Lower Class
Entire Sample	13	31	56
Catholic	9	25	66
Jewish	22	32	46
Methodist	13	35	52
Baptist	8	24	68
Presbyterian	22	40	38
Lutheran	11	36	53
Episcopalian	24	34	42
Congregational	24	43	33

[a] Derived from a breakdown of four polls taken by the American Institute of Public Opinion in 1945–46, covering approximately 12,000 cases. Each poll covered a "voting sample" of approximately 3,000 cases. See note 3.

lic Opinion Research at Princeton University, of which Dr. Cantril is director. The contrast between Cantril's earlier data and these more recent studies indicates either that information gathered in these various public opinion polls is not reliable for interpretation of the relation of religion to class structure, or else that a profound class realignment has occurred in religious denominations during the war years or that class lines themselves have shifted significantly.

The class composition of various religious bodies as revealed by these more recent studies is indicated in Table 2. If these figures reflect the actual situation, all the major religious bodies in the United States now draw a far higher percentage of their members from the lower class than they did before World War II. There remains a significant difference between the Catholic constituency and all others except the Baptist, which parallels it almost precisely in stratification. Distribution of the Jewish group is very much like that of the Episcopalians; a majority of the members of both still come from the middle and upper classes, and this is even more largely the case for the Presbyterians and the Congregationalists.

The Federal Council studies also provide information on the relation of religious adherents to certain occupational groups, to membership in trade unions, to educational status, to political preferences in 1944, and to other indices of class affiliation. Space permits only a few generalizations derived from the studies.[5]

Occupational Affiliations

Occupation is considered one of the most reliable indices of class affiliation; Table 3 attempts to correlate major religious bodies with certain categories of occupation. The categories are too gross in character to permit exact comparison with Table 2, and the class rank of many occupations varies by social context. The most surprising revelation in Table 3 is the number of trade union members in the churches, and especially the number in the Protestant churches, which have been considered to be largely divorced from industrial workers.[6] The proportion of union members is considerably higher, however, in the Catholic and Jewish groups.

Educational Levels

The Federal Council studies of poll data concerning religious affiliation and educational achievement confirm—and refine—the general conclusions reached by Cantril, as is indicated in Table 4. But significant differences within Protestantism are depicted by this table, ranging from the least-educated Baptists to the most-educated Congregationalists. Meas-

---

[5] Access to this material has generously been made available by the Department of Research and Education of the Federal Council of Churches, and parts of it are used by permission. . . .

[6] Trade union leaders are also more characteristically Protestant than many Protestants realize. A survey of two hundred top American Federation of Labor (AFL) and Congress of Industrial Organizations (CIO) leaders was made in 1945 by the Bureau of Applied Social Research at Columbia University. Fifty-one per cent of the leaders designated their religious preference as Protestant, 35 per cent Catholic, and 4 per cent Jewish. There were no significant differences between AFL and CIO leaders in this respect. Twelve per cent of the AFL leaders and 6 per cent of the CIO leaders had no religious affiliation.

TABLE 3

OCCUPATIONAL CATEGORIES, AND TRADE UNION MEMBERSHIP,
IN MAJOR RELIGIOUS BODIES, 1945–46 [a]

| Body | Percentages by Occupational Categories | | | | Percentage belonging to trade unions |
	Business and professional	White collar	Urban manual workers [b]	Farmers	
Entire Sample	19	20	44	17	19
Catholic	14	23	55	8	28
Jewish	36	37	27	0.6	23
Methodist	19	19	39	23	14
Baptist	12	14	52	22	16
Presbyterian	31	21	31	17	13
Lutheran	13	18	43	26	20
Episcopalian	32	25	36	7	13
Congregational	33	19	28	20	12

[a] For source of data, see note to Table 2. Figures given above pertain to "the principal breadwinner" in the case of each family interviewed, where the interviewee was not personally employed.

[b] This category includes urban manual workers of all grades of skill, and also incorporates a rather diverse group of "service occupations" that are primarily manual in character (such as domestic servants, policemen, firemen). A great deal of variation is represented within each of the categories in this table, and their relative class status varies from community to community.

ured against the Protestant scale in this respect, the Catholics are above the Baptists and almost on a par with the Lutherans; the Jews are near the top, almost precisely on the same level as the Presbyterians. Other data indicate that denominational differences in educational level prevail in all class groups, though they are somewhat less pronounced in the middle and upper classes than in the lower.

Political Preferences

Several studies have shown that religion and class status are important variables in the study of political behavior, and that they often cut across each other, exposing individuals to "cross pressures." [7] Table 5 summarizes the Federal Council poll data covering political preferences of religious groups in the 1944 election. The Catholics and the Jews voted heavily for the Democratic candidate; the Protestants split more evenly, but in most denominations a majority of the votes went to the Republican candidate, with significant variations between the denominations. From the political standpoint, the raw data reveal that 25 per cent of all Mr.

[7] Paul F. Lazarsfeld, Bernard Berelson, and Hazel Gaudet, *The People's Choice* (New York, 1944); Gerhart H. Saenger, "Social Status and Political Behavior," *American Journal of Sociology*, Vol. 51, No. 2 (Sept. 1945), pp. 103–13.

TABLE 4

EDUCATIONAL LEVELS IN RELIGIOUS BODIES, 1945–46 [a]

Body	*Per Cent Distribution*		
	High school incomplete (or less)	*High school graduates (or more)*	*College graduates*
Entire Sample	52	48	11
Catholic	57	43	7
Jewish	37	63	16
Methodist	49	51	12
Baptist [b]	65	35	6
Presbyterian	37	63	22
Lutheran	56	44	8
Episcopalian	35	65	22
Congregational	29	71	21

[a] For source, see note to Table 2.
[b] As the data for this table were drawn from a *voting* cross section, virtually no Southern Negro Baptists are represented in these figures.

Roosevelt's votes came from the Catholic group, as did 12.5 per cent of Mr. Dewey's.

Summary

All told, information derived from public opinion polls indicates that Protestant and Jewish adherents come more largely from the middle and upper classes than do Catholics, with significant differences between the major Protestant denominations in this respect. At the same time, Protestants are more largely represented in the lower class than has been com-

TABLE 5

POLITICAL PREFERENCES IN RELIGIOUS BODIES, 1944 [a]

	Per Cent Voting for Dewey	*Per Cent Voting for Roosevelt*
Entire Sample	32	42
Catholic	20	54
Jewish	6	75
Methodist	38	37
Baptist	24	42
Presbyterian	48	32
Lutheran	42	35
Episcopalian	44	36
Congregational	56	26

[a] For source of data, see note to Table 2.

monly supposed; a significant change in this respect may have occurred during World War II. Protestants, and Jews even more largely, come typically from business, professional, white collar, and service occupations; Catholics are more typically workers; Catholics, Jews, and Episcopalians have comparatively few farmers. Each major religious body has a sizable percentage of trade unionists in its membership. In the over-all picture, Protestants and Jews have had more education than Catholics. Catholics and Jews gave large majorities of their votes to Mr. Roosevelt in 1944; the Protestants divided, with a majority in most denominations voting for Mr. Dewey.

COMMUNITY STUDIES

There have been a number of close studies of social stratification in particular American communities in the last twenty-five years, and they yield more precise information concerning religion and the class structure than can be deduced from public opinion polls. Their findings are too varied in detail (this is their great merit) to permit summary here, but generalizations based on them would include the following:

Social Stratification

1. Every American community, from the most rural to the most urban, from Plainville through Middletown to Metropolis, has some pronounced pattern of social stratification, and religious institutions and practices are always very closely associated with this pattern. The number of classes, or layers, varies from community to community; Old City in the Deep South differs in important respects from Yankee City in New England; not all social hierarchies call their bottom class, as do the residents of Plainville, "people who live like the animals." However much details may differ, the stratification is found in all American communities, and religion is always one of its salient features.

2. Differentiation within Protestantism corresponds fairly closely to class divisions. Individual Protestant churches tend to be "class churches," with members drawn principally from one class group. Even where membership cuts across class lines, control of the church and its policies is generally in the hands of officials drawn from one class, usually the middle class.

Protestant denominations in their total outreach touch nearly all sections of the population. But each denomination tends also to be associated with a particular social status. Such denominations as the Congregational, Episcopal, and Presbyterian are generally associated in local communities with the middle and upper classes; the Methodist, Baptist, and Disciples of Christ denominations are more typically associated with the middle classes. The Lutheran denominations are harder to classify, because of their closer association with farmers, with particular ethnic backgrounds, and with skilled workers.

Though all of these major denominations have adherents from the lower classes, the religious expression of the latter has increasingly taken place in the last quarter-century through the new Pentecostal and holiness sects, which represent on the one hand a protest (couched in religious form) against social exclusion and on the other a compensatory method (also in religious form) for regaining status and for redefining class lines in religious terms. Some of these sect groups are already beginning to repeat the age-old transition toward establishment as respected churches, moving up the social scale (in terms of the class status of their adherents) as they do so. Christianity itself began among the poor, who accepted it less because they were poor than because they were marginal; most of its branches have long since permeated the higher classes of their societies and have relatively neglected the poor.

Ethnic Division

3. Internal differentiation in the Catholic Church tends to follow ethnic lines more largely than economic lines.[8] Ethnic divisions cut across the organization of Catholic parishes by geographical districts, though the latter have often themselves reflected the residential propinquity of immigrants from a particular country. Thus the local Catholic churches in a community may include a French Catholic Church, a Polish Catholic church, an Irish Catholic church, and the like.

"Nationality churches" are found in Protestantism also, but they tend to be exceptional and to be associated more clearly with social (and often spatial) isolation than is the case in Catholicism. There is a great deal of evidence that nationality churches, whether Protestant or Catholic, are gradually losing their peculiar ethnic connections. As the number of foreign born has declined, sermons in English have been introduced to supplement—or to replace—the mother tongue.

The institution has found it very difficult to bridge effectively the cultural gap between its older and younger members. Of most importance, intermarriage is increasingly modifying ethnic divisions in urban centers, though some groups (especially the Jewish, Italian, and Polish) remain more endogamous than others; such intermarriage, however, "is not general and indiscriminate but is channeled by religious barriers; and groups with the same religions tend to intermarry." [9] Religious divisions may

---

[8] See John W. McConnell, *The Evolution of Social Classes*, Washington, 1942; Elin Anderson, *We Americans: A Study of Cleavage in an American City*, Cambridge, Mass., 1938; W. Lloyd Warner and Leo Srole, *The Social Systems of American Ethnic Groups*, New Haven, 1945.

[9] Ruby Jo Reeves Kennedy, "Single or Triple Melting-Pot? Intermarriage Trends in New Haven, 1870–1940," *American Journal of Sociology*, Vol. 49, No. 4 (Jan. 1944), pp. 331–39.

therefore become even more important indices of stratification in the future. Meanwhile, the nationality church continues to serve as a cohesive force, at least for its older members, and at the same time it helps to insulate them against disruptive and assimilative influences.

4. Differentiation within Judaism corresponds to a combination of ethnic and class pressures, with the latter probably stronger in the large. Higher-class and better-educated Jews tend to leave Orthodox synagogues and to join Conservative or Reform congregations, or to become secularized. Studies of this alignment are inadequate, but the general trend appears clear. This trend has not prevailed, incidentally, among the Jews of Great Britain.

Church of the Middle Class

5. Religious organizations decline in influence at both extreme ends of the social scale, among the most privileged (though there is some contrary evidence) and among the most disadvantaged. In this very general sense, the churches are associated especially with the middle classes.

NEGRO STRATIFICATION

A few statistics will summarize the relation of Negro churchmen to the white religious institutions.[10] Of the more than 14 million Negroes in the United States, about 6.8 million belong to some church. Of these, about 300 thousand are Catholics. . . . Of the 6.5 million Negro Protestants, about half a million belong to the predominantly white denominations. While Negroes are integrated into denominational affairs to varying degree in higher ecclesiastical bodies (synods, presbyteries, general conferences, and so forth), there is almost no mixing of whites and Negroes at the level of the individual congregation. According to unpublished studies by Frank Loescher, Dwight Culver, and others, less than 1 per cent of the white congregations have any Negro members (and each of these generally has only two or three), and less than one-half of 1 per cent of the Negro Protestants who belong to "white denominations" worship regularly with white persons.

The remaining six million Negro churchmen belong to all-Negro denominations. Nearly all of them are Methodists or Baptists. There are social classes within the Negro community, though the criteria differ from those operative in the white community. Religion tends to be associated with Negro class divisions in a particular context, however, much as it does among whites.[11]

[10] For fuller details, see the articles by John LaFarge and by the present writer in *Survey Graphic*, Vol. 36, No. 1 (Jan. 1947), pp. 59 and 61.
[11] V. E. Daniel, "Ritual and Stratification in Chicago Negro Churches," *American Sociological Review*, Vol. 7, No. 3 (June 1942) pp. 352–61.

DYNAMICS OF RELIGION AND CLASS

There has been a long debate over whether religion or class is primary in social structure and change, with the other as a function or a secondary manifestation. Max Weber and Karl Marx represent extreme views; Bergson appears to be more nearly correct in the light of evidence accumulated recently.[12] Religion, despite the close association of its institutions with the class structure, is neither simply a product nor a cause, a sanction nor an enemy, of social stratification. It may be either or both, as it has been in various societies at various times.

There is little evidence that religion will operate in the near future to change American class structure appreciably. Several opinion polls have shown ministers to be discontented with many aspects of social organization in this country, and church-leaders—of all faiths—are more concerned about racial patterns in America than ever before. (There is less concern about class lines than about race barriers.) But unless a drastic transformation comes about in the churches, they will probably continue for the most part to adapt to class divisions—and even to intensify them—as they have done in the past.

EDITORIAL COMMENT

No one knows the exact absolute and relative numerical strengths of the chief protagonists in American religious intergroup relations. There are definite discrepancies in the statistics reported by the different groups, a situation that is likely to prevail as long as the Census Bureau, implementing the principle of separation of church and state, does not ask questions about religious affiliation. Nevertheless the statistics collected and published privately by each group are significant. They reveal the claims of each competitor, and they also serve as stimulants to the competitive process, to the fears and the hostilities of each side.

Notably successful in arousing Protestant anxiety are the Roman Catholic statistics. Periodically they describe increases in the numbers of Roman Catholic laity, converts, clergy, educational institutions, hospitals, seminarians, and students in Roman Catholic elementary and secondary schools. In 1954, for example, the Official Catholic Directory reported that the Roman Catholic population in the United States, Alaska, and Hawaii then numbered 31,648,424 as compared to 21,406,507 in 1939; converts to Roman Catholicism in 1954 were 116,696, almost twice as many as in 1939; there were one more Cardinal, fourteen more Archbish-

[12] Henri Bergson, *The Two Sources of Morality and Religion* (New York, 1935).

ops, and 53 more Bishops than fifteen years earlier; the clergy increased to 45,451 as compared to 33,540 in 1939; Roman Catholic churches in 1954 were 30,268, an increase of 11,511 over the number in 1939; and parochial school enrollment went up to 3,367,417, more than 800,000 above the 1939 figure.

On the other hand, the Yearbook of American Churches, published in 1955 by the National Council of the Churches of Christ, a federation of thirty Protestant and Eastern Orthodox denominations, claimed Protestant church membership had increased by nearly 20,000,000 since 1940 to a new total of 57,124,-142. The Yearbook stated that whereas the Roman Catholic population in the United States had increased from 16.1 per cent of the population as a whole in 1940 to 20 per cent in 1954, Protestants had increased from 28.7 per cent to 35.3 per cent during the same period.

In the next article, John J. Kane, a sociologist at the University of Notre Dame, explores the contention that tensions between Roman Catholics and Protestants in American society have increased, and reveals the results of some research on the new areas and issues of tension.

32. PROTESTANT-CATHOLIC TENSIONS
BY *John J. Kane* *

THERE is a current impression that Protestant-Catholic relationships in the United States are shifting in the direction of conflict. Bases for such impression are a best-seller book portraying the Catholic hierarchy as a threat to American freedom; organization of a society known as "Protestants and Other Americans United for Separation of Church and State"; legislation to prevent Catholic sisters from teaching in public schools entirely; and controversies over the use of public school buses by parochial school children. . . .

This paper attempts to discover: (1) what empirical evidence exists to warrant such impression; (2) if tensions do exist, in what areas are they strongest; and (3) what factors appear to underlie such tensions. The term Protestant in this paper refers to persons who are members of those religious bodies such as Episcopalian, Methodist, Baptist, Lutheran, Presbyterian and others stemming from the movement known historically as

* John J. Kane, "Protestant-Catholic Tensions," *American Sociological Review*, XVI (October 1951), 663–72. Reprinted by permission. Most footnotes omitted.

the Protestant Reformation. Catholics include members of the body known officially as the Roman Catholic Church. The term tension is of psychological origin, and as such refers to some degree of disharmony, discrepancy, imbalance or the like in an organism resulting in restlessness, anxiety, desire, need and demands. . . . As the term is employed in this paper it refers to unresolved conflicts which persist below the level of overt conflict.

Throughout the history of the United States relationships between Protestants and Catholics have rarely been static, but on the contrary have shifted from accommodation to conflict to a limited cooperation and back again as situational factors and the definition of these factors have varied. Basically there are fundamental cleavages in the ideologies of the two groups. Despite this, limited cooperation has occurred when both have united in the face of a common enemy, as in war. The hypothesis proposed here is that situational factors and their definition by leaders and members of the respective groups cause shifts in their relationships. Situational factors refer to "a number of stimuli external to the organism but acting upon it, organized as a unit and with a special relatedness to one another as stimuli of the specific organism involved." [1]

For instance, after the colonial period of American history anti-Catholic prejudice on any large scale remained dormant until the advent of Irish Catholic immigrants to the United States in the fifth decade of the nineteenth century. As the French hierarchy gave way to an Irish hierarchy and as the militant brand of Irish Catholicism replaced the less militant French and English varieties, agitation against foreigners and Catholics grew. The Native American Movement of the 1840's became an organized effort to delay naturalization of all foreigners and thus remove the supposed threat of Irish Catholic supremacy. Protestant America of this period was alarmed by such tales as "The Awful Disclosures of Maria Monk at the Hotel Dieu" and statements that the Pope would seize the Mississippi Valley. Discriminations against Catholics, especially Irish Catholics, grew. Schools, hospitals, orphan asylums, prisons and similar institutions were either Protestant-owned, or if state-owned, apt to be Protestant-dominated. Priests were forbidden to enter many of these establishments to administer the last sacraments to the dying or to instruct the young in their religion. Public schools used anti-Catholic textbooks which ridiculed Roman Catholicism, the Pope and the Irish. . . . Catholic churches and property were destroyed and Catholics and Protestants were killed. In this case a constellation of situational factors—the first stream of Irish Catholic immigrants, increased visibility of Catholicism and Catholic power, competition for jobs, the Native American Movement and other factors—were stimuli external to the organism but or-

---

[1] James H. S. Bossard, *The Sociology of Child Development,* New York: Harper & Brothers., 1948, p. 38.

ganized with a special relatedness to Protestant-Catholic relationships. Both sides defined the situation as one threatening their group welfare, and accommodation disappeared in favor of conflict.

From a sociological viewpoint Protestants and Catholics represent an in-group, out-group situation with regard to religion. At times, however, social, political and economic factors broaden the base of this in-group, out-group relationship resulting in an intensification of such sentiments, and in the creation of stereotypes. Thus throughout the history of the United States certain terms have tended to become synonymous with Catholics, such as foreigner, Irish, Democrat, Fascist and authoritarian. On the other hand, Protestants have been stereotyped as Know Nothings, A.P.A.'s, Republicans, and K.K.K.'s. Such stereotypes make the definition of a situation in terms of conflict much easier.

. . . During most of the nineteenth century the attitude of [Irish Catholic] separatism developed, and would have reached its height in the projected goals of the Irish Catholic Benevolent Society. These goals were the establishment of banks, steamship companies, hotels, labor unions and in fact almost a complete Irish Catholic economic system. Obviously this was impractical if not impossible, and if successful would have broken the main link that bound Irish Catholics to the majority economic system. Here Irish Catholics had to meet and mingle with non-Irish Catholics and accommodations proceeded most rapidly in this area.

It cannot be denied that the attitudes of certain Irish Catholic leaders played a part in this separatism. Some of the hierarchy, notably Archbishop John Hughes of New York, appeared to believe that too close contact with American culture would result in apostasy. . . . Only later as the number of American-born bishops increased did these attitudes diminish, but even today vestiges of them remain to plague Protestant-Catholic relationships. In *Time* magazine, December 18, 1950, Father Jean Danielou, S.J., is quoted, "They (the Catholics) tend to constitute a self-sufficing community, and as a result, to live apart within the nation. . . ." Thus the pattern of Irish Catholic adjustment in Eastern United States a century ago tends to persist although conditions necessitating this type of adjustment have considerably changed.

Such separatism tends to result in a parallel set of institutions. Since Catholics represent a minority group in terms of numbers, resources and wealth, it means they are hard put to compete successfully with Protestants in certain areas. Second, the in-group feeling is strengthened and whatever inferiorities or abuses may exist in certain Catholic institutions are rationalized, glossed over or defended while successes are magnified out of all due proportion. Third, Catholic institutions tend to parallel Protestant and other non-Catholic institutions in more ways than one, and in some cases become pale imitations of Protestant or secular institutions, only nominally Catholic. A certain amount of inferiority accruing from this situation is built up into an aggressive defense so that even an objective criticism is labeled anti-Catholic. On the other hand attempts to secure assistance, for instance from the federal government for indirect aid to schools, meets resistance from groups most critical of Catholic institutions.

Protestant objections to Catholicism are not entirely on religious grounds, and none of the powerful anti-Catholic movements has ever been predicated solely on this basis. On the contrary, current attackers attempt very specifically to indicate that they subscribe to freedom of religion, and would in no way impair Catholic rights in this respect.[2] Religion, however, is a culture, a way of life and of necessity spills over into social, economic and political life. . . . Protestantism too is a culture and a way of life, although because of denominations it is not so homogeneous as Catholicism. The really great difference, however, exists in the fact that the United States is traditionally a Protestant country. But what is American and what is Protestant have been frequently confused—a typical value judgment of this type is the title of the organization, "Protestants and Other Americans United for Separation of Church and State"—and such confusion is reflected in the ultimate repeal of the blue laws so long upheld by Protestant support and perhaps also in repeal of the Volstead Act. The fact that Protestant opinion and public opinion of most Americans differed on these issues intimates that the two are no longer synonymous if ever they were. The defeat of Protestant opinion on these issues, however, probably reflects even more the diminished militancy of Protestantism in recent years. Certain signs at present appear to indicate that Protestantism is again prepared to take the field. . . . The militant require a foe, real or imagined, and Catholicism may fit the need.

Protestantism's lack of vigor in the last two decades has probably been the result of urbanism, the attack on fundamentalism by physical science and the inherent weakness or strength of Protestantism—its right to protest, and to make effective its protest by splitting off from the parent organization into numerous sects. Catholicism in America, on the other hand, is predominantly an urban religion, and in the first decade of the twentieth century was considerably strengthened by a heavy influx of Central and Southern European Catholics. These immigrants found a well integrated religious organization with schools and churches ready to receive them and to guard their faith during the period of cultural transition. Furthermore, the Roman Catholic Church's stand on artificial contraception has been a factor in maintaining a higher birth rate for urban Catholics than for most urban non-Catholics. In a word, Roman Catholicism has been growing in power and influence in the United States while Protestantism has shown some decline, or at least not the expected growth.

[2] Paul Blanshard, *American Freedom and Catholic Power,* Boston: The Beacon Press, 1949, p. 303.

To some extent the problem is similar to that which existed in this country in the 1840's and 1850's, when heavy Irish Catholic immigration, occasioned by the famine, sent millions of Catholic Irish to these shores. There are, however, some notable differences, but Protestant strategy tends to overlook them. Protests against Catholicism in the mid-nineteenth century charged that Catholics were largely foreigners, poverty stricken, provided unfair competition with American workmen and were tools of their priests and hierarchy. Then, as now, one of the resounding issues was government aid to parochial schools, then on the municipal or state level, now on the national level. The international problem was also a source of dispute, then regarding relationships of Irish Catholics to Ireland and the Vatican, today to Spain, . . . Russia and the Vatican. Although one hundred years have elapsed, Protestants still protest against Catholics on almost the same issues they used in the mid-nineteenth century. The sole exception appears to be the charge that Catholics were poverty stricken, swelled the tax rolls as dependents and provided unfair competition with American workmen. . . .

Certain significant changes have occurred in the Catholic group during the last century. First, Catholicism can no longer be considered a foreign religion at least in terms of the nativity of its adherents. Many have achieved vertical mobility, and resent deeply any effort to treat them as second-class citizens. This makes contemporary tensions between these religious groups especially dangerous. Today the conflict is still a verbal one, waged mainly between the leaders and spokesmen of the two groups. It has yet to seep down into the rank and file where violence may be the result. So far no new terroristic organizations have been established and none of the old ones seriously revived. The threat of world Communism is certainly one factor that may hold such potentialities in check.

In order to get some empirical check on the impression that Protestant-Catholic relations in the United States are currently becoming more tense, a content analysis was made of the *Christian Century* and *America* for the first six months of 1939, 1944 and 1949. According to Professors Berelson and Lazarsfeld, "Content Analysis is a research technique for the objective, systematic and quantitative description of the manifest content of communication." [3] The basic assumption of content analysis is that inferences concerning the relationship between intent and content, or content and effect can validly be made, or such relationships established. It is also assumed that the meanings ascribed by the researcher to the content as he assigns it to certain categories, corresponds to the meaning intended by the communication or understood by the audience. There is scarcely perfect agreement on this, and some hold that manifest con-

[3] Bernard Berelson and Paul F. Lazarsfeld, *The Analysis of Communication Content*, mimeographed copy, Columbia University, 1948, pp. 5, 6.

tent is limited to the form of black forms on white. Lazarsfeld and Berelson admit certain limitations, but state that there is a continuum of meanings. Some communications are obvious in their intent and audience understanding, such as a factual news story; others, such as an obscure modern poem, may be at the opposite end of the scale and subject to as many interpretations as author or audience wish to place upon them. The last assumption is that quantitative description of communication is meaningful. To some extent this is a matter of choosing important categories for the analysis, and "content analysis should be undertaken only when relative frequencies of content categories are relevant to the problem at hand."

With these considerations in mind, the following standards were observed in the selection of items. First, only three types of communication material in these periodicals were examined: editorials, articles and letters. The section known as Commentary in *America* was considered editorial material since it is, what its name implies, a running commentary on current events. Straight news items out of the *Christian Century* were omitted. Such omissions did not prejudice findings, since they were factual news items, not expressions of opinion by editors or authors as editorials. The length of the item was ignored, short or long it counted as one item, but some clue is given to the length in its classification as editorial, article or letter. Second, for an item to be listed it had to be definitely critical of Protestantism, its policies, practices, or leadership in *America,* or of Catholicism, its policies, practices or leadership in the *Christian Century.* The name of the religious group or one of its leaders or clergymen had to be specifically mentioned, unless the implication was very obvious. All items conforming to these standards and appearing in the sections cited were included. Furthermore a significant part of each item had to be critical of Protestantism or Catholicism, a mere sentence or passing phrase did not justify inclusion of the material. In other words, every item included is one which is definitely an attack on Catholicism or Protestantism and which represents a major theme in the editorial, article or letter, at least in the opinion of this writer.

The *Christian Century* and *America* were selected for analysis because both are national religious weeklies. The *Christian Century* is an undenominational Protestant magazine. *America* is a Roman Catholic publication of the Society of Jesus. Both have a wide circulation and appear influential within their respective spheres. Neither can be considered a Protestant- or Catholic-baiting publication. Since they are national religious periodicals, it was expected that they would be more delicate instruments for measuring religious tensions throughout the country than a sectional daily newspaper or secular magazine catering to a larger and more diversified audience, and interested in many more aspects of life than are these publications.

The answer to the first question, Is there an increase in Protestant-Catholic tensions on the basis of items in these periodicals, is given in Table 1.

These figures show an increase of items critical of the respective groups in each case over the period of five or ten years prior to 1949. While items in the *Christian Century* remained unchanged with respect

TABLE 1

THE NUMBER OF ITEMS IN THE *Christian Century*
AND *America* DURING THE FIRST SIX MONTHS OF
1939, 1944 AND 1949 CRITICAL OF CATHOLICISM
OR PROTESTANTISM RESPECTIVELY

	1939	1944	1949
Christian Century	15	15	42
America	8	3	14

to number in 1944, they had almost tripled in 1949. *America* showed a decrease in items critical of Protestantism in 1944 but in 1949 the number of items almost doubled those of 1939, and were almost five times as great in 1949 as in 1944.

On the basis of these figures, there has been an increase in both the crude number of editorials and articles and the ratio of such items to the total items respectively between 1944 and 1949. If these items are adequate indices of tension between Protestants and Catholics, it appears that such tensions are either more numerous than in 1944, or at least are being made more articulate. Whether such items alone are adequate indices of Protestant-Catholic tensions may be questioned, but they do indicate that two national religious weeklies consider such material significant enough to include in their publications. As such, these items appear to reflect the judgment of journalists editing these periodicals. Furthermore, while it is beyond the scope of this paper, it is probable that such items direct readers' attention to this situation, thus making them aware of it, perhaps enlisting their sympathies on either side and ultimately tending to create such tensions if they had not previously existed. Since this is the case, it is unlikely that editors of reputable magazines, such as these, would publish items of this nature unless seriously convinced that it was in the interest of public service. Other indications of Protestant-Catholic tensions have already been cited and in light of this combination, these items do appear significant.

The second question raised was, In what areas do these tensions appear to be strongest. Table 2 presents a breakdown in terms of areas of the highest frequency.

These categories are the most common in which disagreement or criticism exists in either magazine. There are, however, many others which

TABLE 2

AREAS SHOWING THE HIGHEST FREQUENCY OF CRITICISMS OF CATHOLICISM
OR PROTESTANTISM IN THE *Christian Century* AND *America* DURING THE
FIRST SIX MONTHS OF 1939, 1944 AND 1949

	1939	*1944*	*1949*
International	14—Christ. Cent. 0—America	8—Christ. Cent. 1—America	16—Christ. Cent. 5—America
Federal Aid to Education	0—Christ. Cent. 2—America	0—Christ. Cent. 2—America	11—Christ. Cent. 3—America
Religious Beliefs	0—Christ. Cent. 1—America	0—Christ. Cent. 0—America	9—Christ. Cent. 4—America
Censorship	0—Christ. Cent. 0—America	2—Christ. Cent. 0—America	4—Christ. Cent. 0—America

occur but not with the same amount of frequency. The power and certain religious practices of Catholicism come in for criticism in the *Christian Century*. *America* likewise criticizes certain practices of Protestantism and cites conversions of notable persons from Protestantism to Catholicism, mentioning specifically the son of the Archbishop of Canterbury and the grandson of Charles Dickens.

On the basis of this analysis it appears the *Christian Century* is most critical of Catholicism on the international level. The Cardinal Mindszenty case was the subject of four items in 1949. Criticism of a Vatican envoy from the United States made up three items in the same period, and the persecution of Protestants and Jews in Spain accounted for the same number of items in the same period. Federal aid to education and related material made up eleven items and was second in frequency of complaint. In the field of religious beliefs Catholics were criticized for their marriage legislation in five items. The Boston College controversy over no salvation outside the Church accounted for two items. In this instance the *Christian Century* admitted that the Roman Catholic Church did not teach this doctrine, but claimed it did imply it. Four items deal with censorship exercised by Catholics over the media of communication; one of these cited was the difficulty experienced in advertising Blanshard's book.

America had two items on Cardinal Mindszenty in which attitudes of Protestant leaders on this matter were criticized and a sharp refutation of Bishop Oxnam's statement that Catholics follow foreign directives. A projected prayer room at the United Nations was criticized because "Catholics, for example, cannot very well share a room with 'Christians' who, in the light of Catholic beliefs, mutilate a great part of Christ's teaching."

These constitute rather general examples of the types of criticisms found in the two publications. At times stands are taken in highly controversial language. For instance the *Christian Century* charged that Cardinal Spellman engaged in black marketing, and accused Cardinal Mindszenty of treason and spying at least in the sense that the Hungarian government used these terms. The *Christian Century* predicted in 1949 that if the U.S. House of Representatives passed S-246, aid to education bill, the Roman Catholic Church would have what it has wanted for years, and only the Supreme Court could save American public education from disruption and American religious life from sectarian strife. In an article by Paul Blanshard the Roman Catholic Church was accused of anti-Semitism. In a sarcastic tone the *Christian Century* discussed the marriage of Tyrone Power and Linda Christian referring to "The airy grace with which the Roman Catholic Church waived aside the fact that Mr. Power had been released from his previous marriage." This item concluded by stating, "All this you understand is to protect the 'sanctity of marriage.'" In an article the *Christian Century* warned, "All Protestants and non-Roman Churches must be made conscious of the peril to their liberties and survival."

America too mixes some acid in its comments on Protestantism. In replying to charges of anti-Protestantism in Spain, it cited Sweden where the established Lutheran Church seems unaware of the "great Protestant principle of separation of Church and State." In an article, "The Meaning of Mindszenty," Edward Duff says that the non-Catholic group bowed to the pressure of the Communists and were urged by Karl Barth to get rid of leaders Communists found objectionable. In an editorial on euthanasia headed, "Let's Kill the Poor Beasts," *America* said that this is the reasoning, if it can be called that, behind the petition signed by 379 Protestant and Jewish clergymen calling on the New York state legislature for mercy killings. It also called upon Protestant leaders who disagreed to disown their fellows who preach a doctrine that brutalizes man, violates God's sovereignty and prostitutes the words of Christ.

In summary, the following points appear to be true and to merit further investigation. First, it seems there is some evidence of growing Protestant-Catholic tensions. Second, these tensions find verbal expression in criticisms of Catholicism in foreign lands and the implication appears to be that were Catholics a majority in terms of power, American policy toward Protestantism would parallel Spanish policy. Third, Catholics are attacked for using their power and influence in economic, social and political areas as a means toward achieving control of the country. These criticisms specifically involve federal aid to education, censorship of the media of communication, and appeals to state legislatures to prevent passage of laws contrary to Catholic dogma.

From the viewpoint of sociology at least two observations should be made. First, to the extent that cultural borrowing does occur, it never occurs without some modification. If Catholics did become a majority in the United States, and if they did vote as a bloc, a highly unlikely possibility, there is no conclusive proof that Protestantism would suffer discrimination. The climate of opinion in the United States at least tends toward democracy, and American Catholics have been reared in this tradition. . . . Second, Protestant objections to censorship, appeals to state legislatures and requests for aid to parochial schools on the part of Catholics would have more merit if Protestants had not employed the same tactics. The most famous controversy over aid to Catholic education in the United States was set off in New York in 1840 when Archbishop John Hughes attempted to secure public funds for parochial schools. Actually he had an excellent precedent, for in 1831 the Common Council of New York had granted a share of the common school fund to the Protestant Orphan Society. Catholics are merely trying to do today what Protestants have done so successfully during most of American history. This type of acculturation to Protestant methods, however, arouses ire when employed by Catholics.

The problem, nevertheless, is not one-sided. Catholics, like most minorities, suffer from undue sensitivity. At times they scream when unhurt. Statements of fanatics and bigots sometimes receive undue publicity in Catholic publications, and their refutation may occasion bitterness when it involves the well disposed in a needless dispute. At times Catholics are maneuvered into a position of being entirely opposed to measures which they could support with modifications. At times Catholics fail to participate in certain public enterprises through a sense of suspicion, perhaps not always unfounded, but frequently not yet justified. Furthermore Catholics have failed to develop lay leadership to the extent necessary in a modern, complex world. Because clergymen once represented the bulk of educated persons in Catholic society, cultural lag has tended to throw an increasing burden on them to provide Catholic leadership in almost every field. This not unnaturally directs Protestant suspicion at a church in which laymen appear to comprise only the rank and file. Part of this is the result of the lower class status of many Catholics in the past. Their first efforts were directed toward achieving vertical mobility, most easily gained in American society through those avenues likely to provide wealth. As a result the field of social science has suffered from a lack of Catholic scholarship, and Catholic contributions to literature, the arts and to some extent even physical science have not been so great as might have been expected from a population of twenty to thirty million persons. Exceptions to the above merely serve to highlight the lack of numbers.

An hypothesis has been offered that Protestant-Catholic tensions are contingent upon situational factors and the definition of such factors by the groups involved. Social change has altered traditional stratification between Protestants and Catholics. Federal government has expanded its field of interest to include many things, among which are education and aid to education. The contemporary climate of opinion opposes discrimination toward minority groups. Under such circumstances it was almost inevitable that Catholic leaders should press demands for what they consider justice long denied them. In other words, contemporary Catholics have begun to think of themselves as a minority group only in terms of numbers. Some deny even a numerical minority status, since Roman Catholics outnumber any other single denomination in the United States. Here Catholics make the mistake of believing that differences in dogma which separate them from Protestants are equally effective in dividing Protestant denominations from each other. This is not true and perhaps one of the most obvious indications is that three religious groups are spoken of in the United States, Protestants, Catholics and Jews, recognizing at least colloquially the underlying unity among many Protestant denominations.

Protestantism, on the other hand, has not yet recognized changes in the traditional stratification between Protestants and Catholics. Some Protestant leaders who do recognize it have just noticed it, and are so startled they view with alarm and lead the outcry against Catholicism. In some sections of this country Catholicism does not now occupy, nor has it for some time occupied, a minority status. Yet in these areas Protestantism has not suffered discrimination to any measurable degree. Furthermore, what Catholic leaders frequently attack is not traditional Protestantism at all but rather secularism masquerading as traditional Protestantism. Radical changes have occurred in the "old time religion" as George Betts discovered in his study, "The Beliefs of Seven Hundred Ministers." Sixty-two per cent of the ministers queried but only 18% of the theological students believed in the resurrection of the body; 60% of the ministers but only 9% of the theological students believed in the devil as an actual person. Divorce and artificial contraception have finally been accepted by some Protestant denominations that rejected them a century ago. These changes in Protestant beliefs make differences between Protestantism and Catholicism even greater than they were and thus current tensions can be predicted upon an even wider religious basis than in the past. . . .

IX. Jewish-Gentile Relations

T HE Jewish population of the world is now estimated at 11.5 million, of whom 75 per cent live in three countries—the United States, the Soviet Union, and Israel. With approximately 5 million Jews, the United States is clearly the center of world Jewish population. Unlike Negroes, Roman Catholics, and most other American minorities, the Jews cannot be identified as either a racial, religious, or nationality group. The general assumption, of course, is that the Jews are a religious group. Yet "Gentile" (non-Jew), the term ordinarily used to identify their dominant group counterpart in intergroup relations, obviously has no specific religious connotation in the sense that Christian and Moslem have. Furthermore, there is evidence that tensions in Jewish-Gentile relations cannot be reduced to mere conflict in religio-cultural values; anti-Jewish feeling has seldom been exclusively or even largely a matter of prejudice and discrimination on religious grounds.

If the Jews are more than a religious group and if "anti-Semitism" is not based exclusively on religious differences, what is the identification involved in being a Jew? This is a complex question—one that has eluded a straightforward answer and has been a constant irritant to Jews and Gentiles alike. In the eyes of Gentiles it has created a mysterious Jewish figure; among the Jews it has compounded the uneasiness and difficulties of being Jewish.

Besides a hard core of religious identification, Jews also have some "racial" characteristics, not so much in the physical anthropological sense as in the social psychological meaning of the term. Jewish identification is also at times that of a nationality, a people with an idea of common tribal origin and destiny, with a distinctive language, a large common denominator of culture, and a nationalistic movement in Zionism.

There is even plausibility in the argument that American Jews warrant identification as a quasi-caste group. Like American Negroes in their relations with whites, Jewish-Gentile relations have been characterized by virtually all the criteria of caste, although not as stringently. The myth that Jews crucified and rejected Christ supplies a separating and degrading historical "experience"; status ascription is found in the belief that one is born a Jew or a Gentile. Intermarriage is tabooed by the mores if not by legislation; restriction in social interaction between Jews and Gentiles gives rise to a high degree of social separatism and parallelism. Jewish-Gentile interaction is also restricted formally in some public accommodations such as resort hotels, the quota system in higher education, and restrictive covenants in housing. Some personality traits—such as extroversion and upward mobility—that Gentiles consider virtues when manifest among themselves are looked upon as vices (loudness, aggressiveness, seeking control, etc.) when noticeable among Jews. Lastly, stereotypes of Jews and Gentiles are broadly etched, and occupational stratification remains a perennial source of tension.

In the last analysis, one may say that multiple identification applies to Jews in their relations with Gentiles. Practically speaking, however, Jews are those people who consider themselves to be Jews or are so regarded by others, no matter what the criteria of identification.

In the first reading of this section, Kurt Wolff presents a comprehensive outline of the sociology of the Jews. Here is a statistical picture through the 1940's of the Jews throughout the world, the evidence for considering Jews as a race, the essentials in Jewish culture, and attempts to explain modern anti-Semitism.

33. AN ELEMENTARY SYLLABUS IN THE SOCIOLOGY OF THE JEWS
BY *Kurt H. Wolff* *

PART I. SOME STATISTICS OF JEWS IN THE CONTEMPORARY WORLD

A. *World Distribution of Jews* (see Table 1).

B. *Nazism and World War II and Jewish Population.* Between 1933 and 1943, more than three million Jews emigrated or were deported

TABLE 1

JEWS IN THE WORLD

Continent and country	General population	Jewish population	Per cent Jewish to general population [a]
	(in thousands)		
Americas	274,200 [b]	5,500 [c]	2.0
North America and West Indies	153,600 [b]	5,000 [c]	3.3
Continental United States	133,200 [b]	4,800 [c,d]	3.6
South and Central America	120,600 [b]	500 [c]	.4
Argentina [e]	13,500 [b]	350 [c]	2.6
Brazil [e]	42,500 [b]	111 [c]	.3
Europe	530,000 [b]	9,500 [f]	1.8
Africa	150,000 [g]	600 [c]	.4
Asia	1,100,000 [g]	800 [c]	.1
Palestine	1,500 [b]	425 [c]	28.3
Australasia	10,000 [g]	25 [c]	.3
Total	2,171,000 [b]	16,700 [h]	.8

[a] Computed from preceding columns.

[b] "World Population in Transition," *Annals of the American Academy of Political and Social Science,* 237 (January, 1945).

[c] *American Jewish Year Book,* Vol. 46, 1944–1945 (Philadelphia: Jewish Publication Society, 1944).

[d] 1943 estimate: 5,199,200 (*American Jewish Year Book,* Vol. 46, *l. c.,* p. 491, note).

[e] South and Central American countries other than Argentina and Brazil have less than 50,000 Jews each.

[f] Arieh Tartakower and Kurt R. Grossman, *The Jewish Refugee* (New York: Institute of Jewish Affairs of the American Jewish Congress and World Jewish Congress, 1944), p. 337.

[g] Lester E. Klimm, Otis P. Starkey, and Norman F. Hall, *Introductory Economic Geography* (New York: Harcourt, Brace and Co., 1940), Statistical Appendix, Table I.

[h] Arieh Tartakower, "The Jewish Refugees," *Jewish Social Studies,* 4 (October, 1942), p. 313.

* Kurt H. Wolff, "An Elementary Syllabus in the Sociology of the Jews," *Social Forces,* XXIV (May 1946), 451–61. Reprinted by permission. Preface and most footnotes omitted.

from their respective countries of residence in Europe—almost one-third of all European Jews, or close to 18 per cent of all Jews in the world. If one adds the Jews who migrated within their respective countries of residence, the figure is estimated to amount to 5,261,000, or more than 55 per cent of all European Jews, and close to one-third of the total Jewish population of the world. Up to 1941 the emigrated or deported Jews included three-fourths of the Jews in Germany and Austria, and from ten to 40 per cent, respectively, of the Jews in Italy, Poland, Czechoslovakia, Rumania, France, and Belgium. Of this total number, approximately 800,000 Polish, Rumanian, and German Jews fled or were deported to Soviet Russia, and about 700,000 were admitted in other countries all over the world, including European countries, where many refugees stayed in expectation of their overseas visas and where many were caught after the outbreak of World War II. Between 1933 and 1943, among the various countries of immigration, the United States received the largest number, 190,000 or 23.5 per cent of the total. Next ranks Palestine with 120,000 or 14.8 per cent. The Western Hemisphere outside the United States received about 136,000 (17 per cent); Europe, about 283,000 (35 per cent); China, 25,000; Australia, 9,000; South Africa, 8,000. Almost 80,000, or half the Jewish refugees admitted to the United States between 1933 and 1941, came from Germany.

Most of these figures, and thus likewise some of those contained in Table 1, will be obsolete once we can more definitely ascertain how many millions of Jews have lost their lives in Nazi-dominated Europe through starvation, extermination, and the hazards of migration. As of late 1945,

TABLE 2

STATES HAVING THREE PER CENT OR MORE JEWISH POPULATION
(1937) [a]

	Jewish population	
State	*Number*	*Per cent of general population*
New York	2,206,328	16.70
New Jersey	267,970	6.50
Massachusetts	262,945	6.07
Connecticut	93,080	5.54
Illinois	387,330	4.96
Pennsylvania	434,616	4.43
Maryland	76,124	4.31
North Dakota	2,744	4.21
Rhode Island	27,813	4.02

[a] Source same as for Note c, Table 1. The percentages for the Jewish population are based on the total population for 1937 as estimated by the U.S. Bureau of the Census.

a well-documented estimate is 5,978,000—almost 72 per cent of all European, or 35 per cent of all Jews in the world.

C. *Some Figures Pertaining to the Distribution of Jews in the United States*. The total Jewish population of the nine States shown in Table 2 —3,758,950—represents 78.79 per cent of the Jewish population of the United States (4,770,647), while the total general population of these nine States—44,629,216 (1940)—represents only 33.90 per cent of the 1940 total general population of the United States (131,669,275).

The concentration of the Jewish population appears even more conspicuous if it is shown that the number of Jews residing in the five States with the largest Jewish communities (New York, Pennsylvania, Illinois, New Jersey, Massachusetts)—3,559,189—represents 74.61 per cent of all Jews in the United States, while the general (1940) population of these five States—39,753,449—makes up only 30.19 per cent of the total; hence the Jewish population is concentrated approximately two-and-a-half times as strongly as the general population.

Table 3 shows that the percentage of Jews in the general population

TABLE 3

PERCENTAGE OF JEWS IN URBAN PLACES AND
IN RURAL TERRITORY (1937) [a]

Type of community and area	Per cent Jewish to general population
Population 100,000 and over	10.94
25,000–100,000	2.77
10,000–25,000	1.22
5,000–10,000	.75
2,500–5,000	.63
Rural incorporated	.38
Rural unincorporated	.10

[a] Source same as for Note c, Table 1.

decreases with decreasing community size, being more than 100 times as high in the cities of 100,000 population and over as in rural unincorporated areas.

The Jewish population is even more highly concentrated in terms of its larger communities than in terms of its distribution by States. In 1937 there were 967 Jewish communities in the United States. Of these, 47 had 10,000 or more Jews each; the total population of these 47 communities—3,937,525—represented 82.54 per cent of all Jews in the United States. Four Jewish communities (New York, 2,035,000; Chicago, 363,-000; Philadelphia, 293,000; Boston 118,000) had 100,000 or more population each and totaled 2,809,000 or 58.88 per cent of all Jews in the United States, while the total general population of these four communities—13,533,913—represented only 10.29 per cent of the total general population of the United States.

D. *Jewish Immigration to the United States.* Three periods may be distinguished. From 1492 to 1815, approximately 15,000 mainly Sephardic (Spanish), Jews arrived. From 1815 to 1881, approximately 200,000, mainly German and Central European, Jews settled in this country— 13 times as many in these 65 years as in the preceding 325 years. From 1881 to 1940, approximately 3,500,000, mainly Russian and other Eastern European, Jews found their home here—16 times as many in these 60 years as in the preceding 390 years, or 233 times as many as in the first 325 years of American history. While the average number of immigrants per decade, for these last 60 years, thus amounted to almost 585,-000, it should be remembered that during the last decade (1933–1943), this number was less than one-third the average, namely, 190,000 (see IB above), in spite of the especially acute need for emigration from Europe. The paradox can be explained by the fact that since the Immigration Acts of 1921 and 1924 the United States has allotted only limited quotas of immigrants to each country of emigration.

PART II. THE QUESTION OF THE JEWISH "RACE"

The five (and other) subsubtypes of the Mediterranean subdivision (Figure 1, upper right corner) made up the population of ancient Palestine. As early as 50,000 B.C., according to recently found skeletons, individual differences made it untenable to speak of a Jewish subrace. Nevertheless, anthropometric measurements of contemporaneous Jews and surrounding populations in many parts of the world compel one to speak of a certain degree of ethnic identifiability of scattered Jewish groups, which seems to be irreconcilable with the above, but which can be explained by the relatively high degree of cultural separateness and endogamy of the Jews. In contrast to the Jews, other Mediterraneans who penetrated northward, e.g., the Etruscans, were wholly absorbed biologically *and* culturally; and yet it is probable that were one to make an intensive anthropometric study in Etruria (Tuscany) today, individuals with Etruscan features, if such could be defined, might be traceable.

Figure 2 gives a synopsis of the main Jewish migrations since 1000 B.C., thus providing a bird's-eye view of their present-day distribution as well as of their history.

The Yiddish-speaking ("Jewish," i.e., stationary medieval German plus elements of surrounding languages and some Hebrew) Ashkenazim (see Figure 2) are more differentiated among each other than are the Sephardim, but are less differentiated among each other than from the surrounding non-Jewish populations. The Sephardim are more similar to

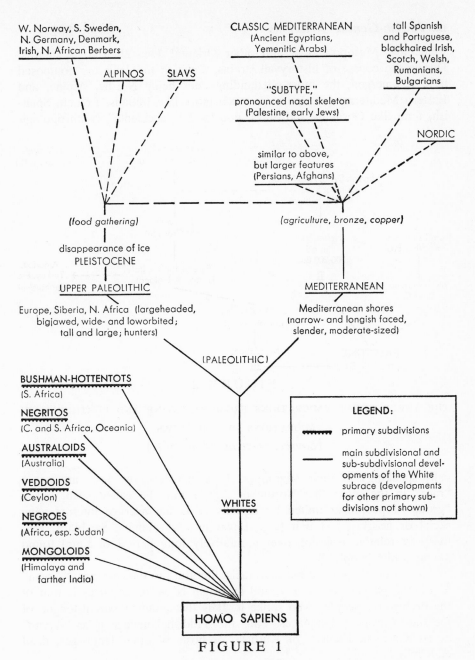

W. Norway, S. Sweden,
N. Germany, Denmark,
Irish, N. African Berbers

CLASSIC MEDITERRANEAN
(Ancient Egyptians,
Yemenitic Arabs)

tall Spanish
and Portuguese,
blackhaired Irish,
Scotch, Welsh,
Rumanians,
Bulgarians

ALPINOS   SLAVS

"SUBTYPE,"
pronounced nasal skeleton
(Palestine, early Jews)

NORDIC

similar to above,
but larger features
(Persians, Afghans)

(food gathering)

(agriculture, bronze, copper)

disappearance of ice
PLEISTOCENE

UPPER PALEOLITHIC

Europe, Siberia, N. Africa (largeheaded,
bigjawed, wide- and loworbited;
tall and large; hunters)

MEDITERRANEAN

Mediterranean shores
(narrow- and longish faced,
slender, moderate-sized)

(PALEOLITHIC)

BUSHMAN-HOTTENTOTS
(S. Africa)

NEGRITOS
(C. and S. Africa, Oceania)

AUSTRALOIDS
(Australia)

VEDDOIDS
(Ceylon)

NEGROES
(Africa, esp. Sudan)

MONGOLOIDS
(Himalaya and
farther India)

WHITES

LEGEND:

〰〰〰 primary subdivisions

──── main subdivisional and
sub-subdivisional devel-
opments of the White
subrace (developments
for other primary sub-
divisions not shown)

HOMO SAPIENS

FIGURE 1

PRIMARY SUBDIVISIONS OF MAN (HOMO SAPIENS) AND MAIN
SUBDIVISIONAL DEVELOPMENTS OF WHITES.

(*Adapted from Carleton Stevens Coon, "Have the Jews a Racial Identity?"*) *

* In Isacque Graeber & Steuart Henderson Britt, eds., *Jews in a Gentile World*,
(N.Y.: The Macmillan Co., 1942), pp. 20–37.

Yemenitic, Mesopotamian, and other Oriental Jews than to Spaniards. During the course of history all strains of which the Jews are composed have re-emerged, the most outstanding ones being Nordic, Alpine, and Eastern Mediterranean. Jews are much more like Italians, French, Spanish, than like Germans and Slavs, due to the "accidents" (anthropologi-

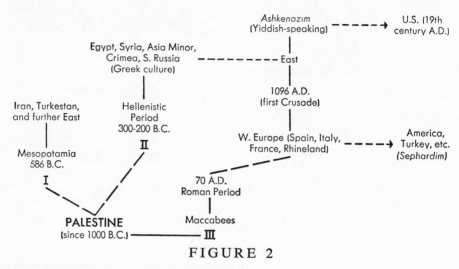

FIGURE 2

THE THREE GREAT EMIGRATIONS FROM PALESTINE AND FURTHER MAIN
MIGRATIONS OF THE JEWS.
(*Source: Same as for figure 1.*)

cally speaking) of their migrations. In conclusion: the Jews are not a "race" in the sense that Nordic or Alpine may be called such, but a "group of people as united biologically as is the average intermarrying social or geographical unit [e.g., Bavarians, Ukrainians, Swabians, etc., living in relative isolation over a relatively long period of time] found among white peoples." [1]

It should be pointed out that, racist literature to the contrary, "Aryan" is a language (not a "race"), and its origin is as unknown as is that of the prehistoric peoples who spoke it. It is the assumed parent-tongue of the Indo-European languages. Thus the Yiddish language is as "Aryan" as are German, English, or Kurdish, or hosts of other languages, dead and living.

[1] Carleton S. Coon, "Have the Jews a Racial Identity?" in Isacque Graeber and Steuart Henderson Britt, eds., *Jews in a Gentile World* (New York: The Macmillan Co., 1942), p. 35. For another physical anthropologist's concise and readable analysis of the racial position of the Jews see William Howells, *Mankind So Far* (Garden City, N.Y.: Doubleday, Doran, 1944), pp. 241–243.

PART III. ANTISEMITISM [2]

A. *Some Important Features of the Religio-Cultural Heritage of the Jews.*

1. God, originally probably local, early became the "Lord of Hosts," the commander of his soldiers, the Jews.

2. The interpreters of God's will were the priests, Levites, who developed the Torah, an elaborate body of laws which undifferentiatedly embody divine right (*fas*) and "everyday" right (jus).

3. The Prophets devaluated the sacrificial elements of the Jewish religion and further elevated the Torah. "Israel (the Jews) and the Law (the Torah) are one."

4. The universality of God, who avails himself of Assyria-Babylonia or of other peoples to punish the Jews for not having adhered strictly enough to the Torah, is a culture trait which prevented the Jews from becoming merely a religious sect and made them a nation or people— a people without territory and, subsequently, without a common language (Hebrew becoming, for the great majority, only a ritual language, if used at all).

B. *Characteristics of the Jews Explicable in the Light of Their Cultural Heritage* (See above) *and of Their Post-Biblical History.*[3]

1. Intellectualism, i.e., respect for learning due to high regard for the Torah and its study and to the necessity of reconciling conditions of the time with Torah teachings; hence legalistic and casuistic character of learning. (Legal heritage elaborated and incorporated in Talmud— literally, "study," "instruction," "doctrine"; nonlegal tradition, e.g., interpretations of scriptural passages, legends, historical notes, epigrams, theological discussions, integrated in the Midrashim—literally, "investigation," "interpretation.")

2. Business sense, developed because Jews were for long times and at many places prohibited from agriculture and, therefore, compelled to live in urban communities.[4] Trade and, particularly, peddling, pawnbrok-

---

[2] This part is largely based on Graeber and Britt, eds., *op. cit.* For reasons of space it is presented in outline form. Notes provide bibliographical references for classroom discussion, reports, term papers, and further study generally.

[3] History of the Ghetto and Jewish settlement patterns and personality types, especially in Chicago: Louis Wirth, *The Ghetto* (Chicago: University of Chicago Press, 1928).

[4] For more general information: relevant articles in *Universal Jewish Encyclopedia, The Jewish Encyclopedia, Encyclopaedia of the Social Sciences,* and other encyclopedias; Salo W. Baron, *Social and Religious History of the Jews* (New York: Columbia University Press, 1937), 3 vols., and *The Jewish Community* (Philadelphia: Jewish Publication Society, 1942), 3 vols., Cecil Roth, *The Jewish Contribution to Civilization* (Cincinnati: Union of American Hebrew Congregations, 1940); Uriah Z. Engelman, *The Rise of the Jew in the Western World* (New York: Behrman's, 1944) (largely demographic); *American Jewish Year Book, l.c.;* Arthur Ruppin, *The Jews in the Modern World* (London: Macmillan and Co., Ltd., 1934)—For the history of the

ing, and moneylending, were prohibited (only later stigmatized) to non-Jews.

3. Hypersensitivity, more intensive than among other "minorities," resulting from a long tradition of being torn between pride and humiliation—pride in the mission to represent monotheism (whose extreme for-

---

Jewish America: Levinger, *op. cit.;* Peter Wiernik, *History of the Jews in America* (New York: Bloch Publishing Co., 1930); *Americans, All: A Short History of American Jews* (Chicago: Anti-Defamation League, n. d.); Anita L. Lebeson, *Jewish Pioneers in America, 1492–1848* (New York: Brentano's, 1931).—For economic and occupational aspects of Jewish life in the United States: Editors of Fortune, *Jews in America* (New York: Random House, 1936); Jacob Lestchinsky, "The Position of the Jews in the Economic Life of America," in Graeber and Britt, eds., *op. cit.* pp. 402–416; Nathan Reich, "Economic Trends," in Oscar I. Janowsky, ed., *The American Jew, A Composite Portrait, l. c.,* pp. 161–182 (see also *ibid.,* pp. 294–295, for bibliography on the occupational distribution of Jews); several articles in *Jewish Social Studies,* Vol. 1, 1939 ff.; Gabriel Davidson, *Our Jewish Farmers and the Story of the Jewish Agricultural Society* (New York: L. B. Fischer, 1943) (Jewish farmers and the Jewish farm movement in the United States; a little-known aspect of Jewish life); Sophia M. Robison, *Jewish Population Studies, l. c.* (socio-economic and demographic studies of Jewish communities in Trenton, Passaic, Buffalo, New London, Norwich, Detroit, Pittsburgh, Chicago, Minneapolis, and San Francisco). The last-named book not only contains information on economics and occupations but also throws light on Jewish community life in the cities discussed.—More comprehensive Jewish community studies: Leonard Bloom, "The Jews of Buna," in Graeber and Britt, eds., *op. cit.,* pp. 180–199 (medium-sized metropolitan center of American industrial Midwest); Samuel Koenig, "The Socioeconomic Structure of an American Jewish Community," *ibid.,* pp. 200–242 (Stamford, Connecticut); Jessie Bernard, "Biculturality: A Study in Social Schizophrenia," *ibid.,* pp. 264–293 ("Milltown, Winnemac"; stimulating social-psychological theory); Uriah Z. Engelman, "Medurbia," *Contemporary Jewish Record,* 4: 339–348, 511–521, August and October, 1951 (statistical-average Jewish community in the United States); David G. Mandelbaum, "A Study of the Jews of Urbana," *Jewish Social Service Quarterly,* 12:223–232, December, 1935; Bessie Bloom Wessel, *An Ethnic Survey of Woonsocket, Rhode Island* (Chicago: University of Chicago Press, 1931); Hartford Communal Study Committee, *Hartford Jewish Communal Study 1937–1938,* Hartford, 1938; Joseph M. Papo, "The Jewish Community of Duluth," *Jewish Social Service Quarterly,* 18:219–231, December, 1941; Harold Orlansky, "The Jews of Yankee City," *Commentary,* 1:77–85, January, 1946; Kurt H. Wolff, "Traditionalists and Assimilationists: A Sample Study of the Jewish Population in Dallas, Texas," *Studies in Sociology* (Southern Methodist University), 4:20–25, Summer, 1940 (predominantly statistical); David G. Mandelbaum, "The Jewish Way of Life in Cochin," *Jewish Social Studies,* 1:423–460, October, 1939 (history and social life of contemporary Cochin in Southwestern British India, an old largely isolated Jewish community); M. J. Karpf, *Jewish Community Organization in the United States* (New York: Bloch Publishing Co., 1938); Abraham G. Duker, "Structure of the Jewish Community," in Janowsky, ed., *op. cit.,* pp. 134–160. The two last-named items deal largely with Jewish organizations.—Jewish organizations: *American Jewish Year Book, l. c.;* with special reference to refugees: Tartakower and Grossman, *op. cit., passim* and especially chaps. XIII and XIV; on Zionism: *American Jewish Year Book, l. c.;* Sulamith Schwartz, "Zionism in American Jewish Life," in Janowsky, ed., *op. cit.,* pp. 231–250; for classics in Zionist literature consult encyclopedias listed above.—Americanization of refugees from Nazism: Gerhart Saenger, *Today's Refugees, Tomorrow's Citizens* (New York: Harper & Brothers, 1941) (much concrete, but scarce statistical material).—Intermarriage: Milton L. Barron, "The Incidence of Jewish Intermarriage in Europe and America," *American Sociological Review,* 11:6–13, February, 1946 (contains many bibliographical references).

mulation is the idea of the "chosen people"), humiliation because prevented from instituting a national state of their own. These three characteristics appear to be more nearly objective than many others frequently attributed to the Jews, i.e., they are less created by a hostile attitude toward the Jews, are less biased, less mere stereotypes. For other "characteristics," see IIIE2e below.

C. *Some Important Characteristics of Contemporary Western Society, Especially the United States.*

1. Urbanization; industrialization; importance of occupation (job); breakdown of *Gemeinschaft,* i.e., importance of secondary contacts and complication of the social and economic order; nationalism; social disorganization and susceptibility to psychosis and faddism (e.g., Father Divine, Ku Klux Klan).

2. United States:

a. Mores of White, Protestant, Anglo-Saxon, rather than indiscriminate equality.

b. The broad base of low-economic, low-status jobs within the occupational pyramid is the seat of potential frustration; outlets for this frustration disappeared with the passing of the Frontier and with the decline of large-scale immigration (no new immigrants for earlier immigrants to look down upon—cf. Upton Sinclair, *The Jungle*).

D. *Jews in Contemporary United States.*

1. Fallacy that Jews control basic industries; true that Jews are over-represented in some parts of New York City and in some occupations— motion pictures, department stores, clothing, and less so in some others (theater, press, law, medicine).

2. Occupations in which Jews are overrepresented are themselves conspicuous, i.e., give social and economic prestige; also they are the ones that developed in the urbanized, non-*Gemeinschaft* sphere with its lesser discrimination against the Jews plus the Jews' greater skills in these occupations; possibly latent rural (and *Gemeinschaft*)-urban (secondary-contact society) tension channelled into, and exploited by, antisemitism.

E. *Sociology and Psychology of Modern Antisemitism.*[5]

[5] Graeber and Britt, eds., *op. cit.* (perhaps best single book on antisemitism and other problems of the Jews from the social-science, especially sociological, viewpoint); especially recommended: Talcott Parsons, "The Sociology of Modern Anti-Semitism," pp. 101–122; J. F. Brown, "The Origin of the Anti-Semitic Attitude," pp. 124–148; Miriam Beard, "Anti-Semitism—Product of Economic Myths," pp. 362–401; J. O. Hertzler, "The Sociology of Anti-Semitism through History," pp. 62–100 (rich in illustration but less important as theory); Anonymous, "An Analysis of Jewish Culture," pp. 243–263 (characteristics of Jewish and non-Jewish, especially American, cultures). The most useful all-around books on antisemitism are probably Hugo Valentin, *Antisemitism, Historically and Critically Examined* (New York: The Viking Press, 1936), and Lee J. Levinger, *Anti-Semitism, Yesterday and Tomorrow* (New York: The Macmillan Co., 1936) (good short bibliography). Best in its "historical and regional studies" is Koppel S. Pinson, ed., *Essays on Antisemitism* (New York:

Note: The term "anti-Semitism" was first used in 1879 by the German Wilhelm Marr.

1. Antisemitism as a social-psychological phenomenon can perhaps be best conceived of as passing through one or both of the following cycles:

Cycle 1: (a) Mos of antisemitism, (b) stereotype of Jew, (c) intensification of stereotyped Jewish traits, (d) intensification of hostility, (e) mos of antisemitism; cycle repeats.

Cycle 2: (a) Social disorganization, (b) insecurity, (c) frustration, (d) explosion of ingroup-outgroup tension, (e) hostile "racial" attitude, (f) stereotype of Jew, (g) intensification of stereotyped Jewish traits, (h) intensification of hostility, (i) social disorganization; cycle repeats.

2. Jews as scapegoats for frustration.

a. Jews are different from non-Jews: Jewish religion only non-Christian religion among Christians; no intermarriage; dietary habits; cir-

---

Conference on Jewish Relations, 1942). Of the various pertinent articles in the *Encyclopaedia of the Social Sciences,* those on "Antisemitism" by Benjamin Ginzburg and on "Race Conflict" by Hans Kohn are especially worthy of study. Valuable insights are found in Milton Steinberg, *A Partisan Guide to the Jewish Problem* (Indianapolis: Bobbs-Merrill Co., 1945), pp. 44–112; helpful data on specifics: Sigmund Livingston, *Must Men Hate?* (New York: Harper and Brothers, 1944); see also *Questions and Answers Concerning the Jew* (Chicago: Anti-Defamation League, 1942), and *Answers for Americans: "They Say the Jews. . . ."* (Los Angeles: University Religious Conference, n. d.). Of the many historical studies, in addition to Pinson *op. cit.,* may be mentioned: James Parkes, *The Conflict of the Church and the Synagogue: A Study in the Origin of Anti-Semitism* (London, 1934), and Joshua Trachtenberg, *The Devil and the Jews; The Medieval Conception of the Jew and Its Relation to Modern Antisemitism* (New Haven: Yale University Press, 1943). A useful brief introduction to the sociological view of antisemitism in M. Ginsberg, "Anti-Semitism," *Sociological Review* (British), 35:1–11, January–April, 1943. More factual, and with reference to the United States, are Alexander Lesser, "Anti-Semitism in the United States," *Journal of Negro Education,* 10:545–556, July, 1941 (especially contemporary antisemitism), and Max Meenes, "American Jews and Anti-Semitism," *ibid.,* 557–566 (especially valuable for its summary of numerous sociological and psychological surveys and tests). Antisemitism as an instrument of fascist power: David W. Petegorsky, "The Strategy of Hatred," *Antioch Review,* 1:376–388, September, 1941. Antisemitism, from the standpoint of social psychology, viewed as a psychosis: Read Bain, "Sociopathy of Anti-Semitism," *Sociometry,* 6:460–464, November, 1943. More specifically, but probably more debatably, antisemitism as unconscious hatred of Christ and Christianity: Sigmund Freud, *Moses and Monotheism* (New York: Alfred A. Knopf, 1939) (historically and hence fundamentally, unconvincing), and Maurice Samuel, *The Great Hatred* (New York: Alfred A. Knopf, 1941) (more plausible, be it only because without Freud's historical commitments). A study of American antisemitic organizations in the thirties: Donald S. Strong, *Organized Anti-Semitism in America* (Washington: American Council on Public Affairs, 1941). Literature on Nazi atrocities and Jewish life in Nazi-dominated Europe is numerous. On the latter topic, there are several valuably objective papers in *Jewish Social Studies;* as to the former, mention may be made of *The Black Book of Poland,* issued by the Polish Ministry of Information (New York: G. P. Putnam's Sons, 1942); of Leib Spiesman, "In the Warsaw Ghetto," *Contemporary Jewish Record,* 4:357–366, August, 1941; and of S. Moldawer, "The Road to Lublin," *ibid.,* 3:119–133, March–April, 1940.

cumcision (perhaps attenuated castration increasing Jew's inferiority feeling and at the same time increasing non-Jew's fear of Jew?); physiognomy.

b. Jews are like non-Jews: same God; same holy book (Old Testament); "family quarrel"; Jews are cultural and biological equals of non-Jews, hence conflict is more emotional than in case of White-Black-White-Yellow relations which on the whole can be better understood in terms of mere social distance.

c. Face-to-face ubiquity: Jews everywhere present; antisemitism everywhere readily understood (not a "domestic" affair).

d. Traditional scapegoat: ready availability of familiar channel of frustration (mos).

e. Characteristics of Jews transformed into hostile stereotypes:

Close attachment of Jews to Jewish culture becomes lack of attachment to "adopted" country (especially true in strongly nationalistic environments).

Bargaining ingenuity becomes "sharpness," "skinflintery," "smartness," "diabolical cleverness."

Jewish solidarity becomes "clannishness," "double morality," "Jewish world conspiracy" (*The Protocols of the Elders of Zion*).

Economic success makes all Jews money-bags.

Conspicuousness in certain occupations, especially in public entertainment, makes all Jews "show-offs," "loud," "egotistic."

Past migratory experience and adaptability of Jewish culture everywhere make Jews "cosmopolitan," "radical," but also "international plutocrats" and "capitalists."

f. Christ: killed by Jews, as many Christian children are taught in their religious-school textbooks; at the same time, Christ a Jew who must be loved; frustration resulting from this ambivalence readily diverted toward Jews (cf. Samuel, *op. cit.,* in Note 19).

g. Economic myths: "the guileless Gentile" (who had no part in the formation of "capitalism"); the "myth of Solomon" (whose wealth proves the existence of a Jewish business empire in Biblical times); the "myth of Shylock" (the Jew as the bloodsucker); the "international financier" (the Jew controls the finances of the world); mainly initiated by Werner Sombart and all untenable before even a slight knowledge of economics and history. These and other points are elements in vicious circles, i.e., they provoke the Jews to become, from self-defense and insecurity, more like the hated stereotypes, thus increasing hostility, etc. (see IIIE1 above). Psychologically, antisemitism works via the mechanisms of displacement (Jew, instead of true object of antagonism, is the target), of projection (Jew is accused of one's own motives), and of rationalization (Jews are inferior, anti-Christ, Bolsheviks, etc.).

h. Jews as scapegoats in outstanding crises of modern history: 1096 A.D., first Crusade (large-scale emigration of Jews to the East started;

see Figure 2); 1241, Mongolian invasion of Europe up to Silesia; 1348–50, Black Death; 1575, depression; 1618–48, Thirty Years' War; 1873, depression, followed by the formation of antisemitic parties, by antisemitic massacres and legislation in Russia, and by large-scale emigration of Russian Jews to the United States (cf. IE above).

F. *A Possible Policy Regarding Antisemitism.*

Long-range and widespread sociological and psychological understanding by Jews and non-Jews alike, of antisemitism and of all problems involved in it may eventually attenuate ingroup-outgroup tension.[6] But such understanding will be possible only if efforts toward it are linked up with the elimination of the more tangible causes of frustration (economic and technological) and of the moral causes of frustration (especially the obstructions to participation, or adequate participation, in democracy).

EDITORIAL COMMENT

A few generations ago, many responsible social observers predicted the inevitable crystallization of all the diverse population elements, including the Jews, into a new homogeneous "race" of Americans. The "melting-pot," as Israel Zangwill put it, would see the end of Jewish and minority group uniqueness, whether racial, religious, or ethnic in type. Yet, as analysts have made abundantly clear, there is an amazing tenacity to Jewish culture.

[6] Cf. *The Journal of Social Issues,* Vol. 1, Nos. 1 and 2, both dealing, in nontechnical language, with "Racial and Religious Prejudice in Everyday Living" and containing many valuable cases and policy suggestions regarding majority-minority relations, including the Jewish minority.—For forecasts regarding the fate of Jews: Jacob Lestchinsky, "The Post-War Outlook for Jewry in Europe," *Menorah Journal,* 30:13–37, Winter, 1942 (mainly economic); Salo W. Baron, "Reflections on the Future of the Jews in Europe," *Contemporary Jewish Record,* 3:355–369, July–August, 1940 (postwar plans); Morris R. Cohen, "Jewish Studies of Peace and Post-War Problems," *ibid.,* 4:110–125, April, 1941 (problems needing study and planning); *Jewish Post-War Problems, A Study Course,* prepared by the Research Institute on Peace and Post-War Planning of The American Jewish Committee (eight pamphlets, 1942–43: I, "Why Study Post-War Problems"; II, "The Two World Wars—A Comparison and Contrast"; III, "How the Jewish Communities Prepared for Peace During the First World War"; IV, "Europe between the Two World Wars"; V, "The Position of the Jews in the Post-War World"; VI, "Palestine in the New World"; VII, "Relief, Reconstruction and Migration"; VIII, "Jewish Survival in the Democracy of the Future").—Jewish life in a democracy: H. M. Kallen, "National Solidarity and the Jewish Minority," *Annals of the American Academy of Political and Social Science,* 223:17–28, September, 1942 (democracy seen as an orchestra, minorities being its integrating voices); contributions of numerous minorities, including the Jewish, to American culture; Francis J. Brown and Joseph Slabey Roucek, eds., *One America* (New York: Prentice-Hall, 1945) (Subtitle, "The History, Contributions, and Present Problems of Our Racial and National Minorities").—The instructor may want to call the attention of students who desire to follow Jewish current events to *Commentary* (formerly *Contemporary Jewish Record*) (monthly).

Often referred to as the eternal people, the Jews have somehow managed to retain their identity and their major cultural forms in American society and elsewhere. This has been true in spite of acculturation, assimilation, conversion, and other processes that have resulted in defection from the group.

What accounts for this persistence of the Jews and much of their traditional culture? How do Jews retain their identity as Jews in a Gentile world? Ira Eisenstein, in the following excerpt from one of his books, suggests that Jewish momentum socially and culturally can be explained by ten distinctive tendencies, institutions, and activities in Jewish life. These are the tendency to live together, the opposition to intermarriage, communal centers, religious activities, Jewish education, philanthropic activities, cultural activities, the upbuilding of Israel, secular nationalism, and fraternal organizations. Together they constitute the key to Jewish survival.

34. SOCIAL COHESION WITHIN JEWISH LIFE
BY *Ira Eisenstein* *

IF THE various tendencies that are breaking down Jewish life . . . met with no resistance, Jewish life would be ready to disappear. But certain signs of strength may be seen, as we look about us, which are helping to preserve Jewish life. . . .

The most important fact to be recognized is the momentum from the past which every Jew experiences. When an autoist shuts off the motor of his car, the car does not come to a stop at once; the momentum keeps the car moving for quite a time. Similarly, when the dynamo of belief in Jewish tradition was, so to speak, shut off after the Emancipation, Jewish life did not come to a stop at once; the momentum of many centuries carried Jewish life along for several generations. Thus, even if a Jew is indifferent to Jewish life, his contact with his father, or grandfather, keeps alive in him the consciousness that he is a Jew and that Jewish life persists. . . .

Momentum functions both as a cause and an effect. As a cause, it gives rise to a series of activities and institutions through which Jews express their Jewishness; the effect of such activities and institutions is to add to the momentum, operating thus to help to preserve Jewish life.

* From Ira Eisenstein, *Creative Judaism* (rev. ed.; New York: Jewish Reconstructionist Foundation, 1953), pp. 17–25. Reprinted by permission.

Following are some of these institutions and activities, together with some tendencies in Jewish life through which the momentum of Jewish life operates and helps to keep the Jewish consciousness alive.

1. *The tendency to live together.* The first important tendency that makes for Jewish survival is the habit of Jews to congregate in large numbers and to live close to one another. Consequently, large Jewish neighborhoods are formed. Jews come into frequent contact with one another. This is not due to any plan but to a desire to cling together. In some respects, it might not be such a good thing for Jews to settle, as they have settled, in the few large cities of the United States; but the effect for Jewish life has been that Jews have created institutions and organizations which reenforce Jewish life.

2. *The opposition to intermarriage.* One thing most Jews seem to agree on is that intermarriage with Gentiles is undesirable. No matter how far Jewish parents have drifted from Jewish life, the last thing in the world they would like to see is a marriage between their child and a non-Jew. And almost always the child will not marry a non-Jew out of consideration for his parents, because Jewish family life is close-knit. Strong family ties are characteristic of minority peoples generally; and the Jewish people is no exception.

3. *Jewish communal centers.* The opposition to intermarriage, alone, however, would not solve the problem of Jewish life; it might at best retard the process of breaking-down. For that reason, those Jews who have the future of Jewish life at heart have evolved a new type of institution, known as the Jewish community center, where Jewish young people can meet socially. Over three hundred centers have been erected since 1918. Before that time, the purpose of whatever Jewish social centers existed had been to Americanize the immigrant Jews. Soon, however, Americanization was seen to be inadequate as a program, and gradually, these institutions began to aim to develop "Jewish consciousness as a means to the highest type of spiritual life."

For this new purpose, however, a new program had to be worked out. Today, the Jewish community center constitutes one of the most important strongholds of Jewish life. It attempts to unite Jews of all opinions in the common task of providing cultural and recreational activities. The Jewish community center is one of the most effective bulwarks against intermarriage.

4. *Religious activities.* Despite the widespread tendency to be indifferent to Jewish religion, thousands of Jews continue to maintain religious institutions, and to observe religious rites. According to recent statistics, there are about 3,000 congregations in the United States with a combined membership of approximately 250,000 families. These congregations are organized into three large federations: the Union of American Hebrew Congregations, the United Synagogue of America, and the Union of Orthodox

Congregations of America. Each federation is, in turn, part of a large complex of institutions. For example, the Union of American Hebrew Congregations is served by rabbis trained at the Hebrew Union College— Jewish Institute of Religion. Each congregation within the Union conducts sisterhoods, brotherhoods, young peoples' groups and religious schools, all associated with their respective federations. Similarly, the United Synagogue of America obtains its spiritual leadership from the Jewish Theological Seminary, and the Orthodox congregations from the several large *yeshivot*. Each of the groups organizes new congregations and schools and publishes literature that interprets Jewish religion from its own point of view. . . .

At the turning points of life, Jews usually observe religious rites. Circumcision is very common. *Bar mitsvah* and confirmation are observed by large numbers of Jews. Almost every marriage between Jews is solemnized by a religious ceremony. Funerals are almost invariably conducted by rabbis, and religious rites are observed. The rites of mourning, *yahrzeit,* and memorial services are observed by many Jews who observe nothing else.

In general, it may be said that the tendency in the United States today among young people is toward a greater degree of observance. There is no longer the spirit of antagonism that prevailed a number of years ago.

5. *Jewish education.* Although the total number of children receiving a Jewish education is about thirty per cent, there has recently been an increase in the number attending schools. For the most part, the schools are connected with congregations, and instruct children from the age of seven to thirteen. There are also quite a number of Talmud Torahs supported by communal funds. There is an ever-growing number of Jewish parents who are concerned with bringing up their children as Jews and who are taking the trouble to give them some kind of Jewish education, whether it be the Sunday School type of training, ending in confirmation, or the more intensive training which gives greater prominence to the study of Hebrew. . . .

6. *Philanthropic activities.* Jewish philanthropy is one activity in which all who want to be identified as Jews participate. Through philanthropy a sense of Jewish responsibility is created, and once a Jew has taken some part in Jewish charitable work he is more inclined to concern himself with Jewish life in general.

The large number of charitable organizations has made it necessary, in each locality, to organize Federations or Welfare Funds. These now number 250 located in 236 cities in the United States, and they work together through the Council of Jewish Federations and Welfare Funds. They raise money for local charities, for agencies of social service, of recreation and education, as well as for national and overseas causes.

7. *Cultural activities.* a. *The Jewish press.* One of the most important factors in keeping alive the Jewish consciousness in the past has been the Yiddish press, which until recently served hundreds of thousands of readers. The newspapers printed in Yiddish contain, in addition to general news, very detailed accounts of what is going on in the Jewish world; in addition, they publish articles and stories on the various movements, institutions, and personalities in Jewish life.

The Anglo-Jewish press consists for the most part of weekly magazines, with some worthwhile monthlies and quarterlies. The scope of their contents is of course limited. But they contribute substantially toward keeping alive the Jewish consciousness of their readers.

More recently, radio and television have been employed to broadcast Jewish programs of drama, music, religious services and lectures.

b. *Literature and the arts.* In recent years, many fine books have been published in English on Jewish subjects. Indeed, most of the classics of Jewish literature are now available in translation, including the Talmud. Bible texts with commentaries, the traditional prayerbook with worthwhile notes, anthologies of Rabbinic literature, medieval philosophy, poetry, modern essays, history, fiction, the literature of modern Zionism— all these can now be read by those who do not understand Hebrew.

Juvenile literature, too, has developed during the past twenty years —along with juvenile books generally. Attractively illustrated and bound, charmingly written, they delight the young child.

The National Jewish Book Council has contributed greatly toward popularizing the Jewish book. Each year, it conducts Jewish Book Month, dedicated to bringing Jewish books to the attention of the public.

A similar organization, the National Jewish Music Council (both are sponsored by the National Jewish Welfare Board) encourages the use of Jewish records, the playing of Jewish compositions and the arrangement of concerts of Jewish music. Jewish Music Month is set aside each year to emphasize the important place that music should occupy in Jewish life. . . .

8. *The upbuilding of Israel.* The Zionist movement, begun in 1897, served, for almost two generations, as the most dynamic force in Jewish life. The enthusiasm, loyalty and sacrifice which this great enterprise aroused among tens of thousands of Jews throughout the world, was rewarded, in 1948, by the establishment of the State of Israel, and by the admission of Israel into the United Nations. In the course of the struggle to create the state, Jews in America organized many Zionist agencies. Hadassah, with its 300,000 members, is the largest organization of its kind in the world. The Zionist Organization of America, the Labor Zionist Organization, Mizrachi and many others, with their associated youth movements, created a network of active groups in every locality. . . .

9. *Secular nationalists.* Many outstanding Yiddish writers, artists and musicians are identified with this movement which originally stressed the

cause of socialism but which, more recently, has stimulated Jewish cultural activity.

The secular nationalist groups have established a fine educational system, several excellent libraries, museums, and research agencies, and have set up institutions where Jews may find a congenial atmosphere in which to carry on their social and cultural life.

10. *Fraternal organizations.* For those who, coming to the New World from the Old, felt the need for fellowship and mutual aid, fraternal orders were organized, to which any Jew might belong regardless of his religious views or affiliations. In addition, the fraternal orders developed philanthropic activities: orphan homes, infirmaries, hospitals, homes for the aged, etc., were supported by the fraternal organizations. Later, when the Federations took over these activities, the fraternal orders turned to educational work. The B'nai B'rith, for example, conducts Hillel Foundations in various universities. However, mutual aid, in the form of sick and insurance benefits, still figure most prominently in the *Landsmanschaften* (fraternities in which the members, or their parents, all come from the same locality in Europe).

Another type of fraternal order is that based on a common social philosophy, and devoted to spreading that social philosophy while at the same time carrying on many of the activities of a *Landsmanschaft.* An example of this type is the Workmen's Circle.

These are the various tendencies through which the momentum of Jewish life finds expression and which, therefore, help preserve that life.

EDITORIAL COMMENT

Centuries of experience in living as a minority group have given the Jews skills and versatility not often found among other American minorities. They are not fixed at a single status level with respect to all phases of their activities. Edward McDonagh, whose study of the status levels of Mexicans revealed considerable uniformity, has also compared the social, educational, legal, and economic statuses of American Jews. His conclusion is that, unlike the Mexicans, there is little uniformity between these various statuses in the case of the Jews.

The educational status of American Jews tends to be very high, a phenomenon that can be explained in considerable part by the emphasis on literacy and education in Jewish culture. At the other end of the spectrum is Jewish social status which tends to be very low as measured by tests of social distance. The other statuses examined by McDonagh—economic and legal—fall between the two extremes. In the article that follows, McDonagh describes the way in which he arrived at these conclusions.

35. STATUS LEVELS OF AMERICAN JEWS
BY *Edward C. McDonagh* *

To THE sociologist the attitudes of preference and prejudice toward the
Jews as a race are very real, though many of the bases for these attitudes
may be fallacious and meaningless in terms of scientific information. Few
social scientists would define the Jews as a distinct race, especially if the
term is to have any biological significance. Yet, despite the facts, the
Jews, in the minds of the prejudiced, constitute a different race from
"typical Americans."

Some scholars have vigorously refuted the assumption that the Jews
constitute a race. It is assumed that much of the "race" prejudice against
the Jews may be challenged and restricted with the proof that the Jews
should be defined as a cultural group united by a common religion and
welded together through the centuries by the combined forces of out-
group persecution and in-group preference. Hence, the Jews are, in terms
of sociological analysis, a cultural group, but often defined by typical
Americans as a race. If the Jews are considered to be a religious unit,
then many persons have reactions, not against the Jews as a race, but
against the Jews as a people with a distinct religion.

In the United States, as well as in most other countries, the prevailing method for tabulating the number of Jews is through a census of
religious bodies. At the present time there are about 5,000,000 persons in
the United States designated as Jews, or approximately 4 per cent of the
nation's population. Some of the Jews in the United States manifest the
operation of at least five major definitions, including religious, racial,
linguistic, ideological, and economic identifiers. For instance, comments
may be overheard concerning the importance of religious tolerance between Christians and Jews. Almost any discussion of minority groups will
evoke a reference to Negroes and Jews. The Jews are sometimes thought of
as a distinct linguistic group. In an ideological setting the impression may
be reflected that the Jews are communists, and, finally, they may be regarded in an economic sense as capitalists. No doubt these contradictory
facets are vital to an understanding of several status levels of these people.

The Jews are a race only in the sense that they may be defined so
by their critics. . . . A person is struck by the fact that even a moderate-
sized gathering of these people will indicate Teutonic, Mediterranean,
Mongoloid, and Negroid traits. While the Jews have a culture of Judaism
in common, they are best thought of as a people, many of whom aspire to

* Edward C. McDonagh, "Status Levels of American Jews," *Sociology and
Social Research,* XXXII (July–August 1948), pp. 944–53. Reprinted by permission.
Footnotes omitted.

be a nation. Hence, it becomes increasingly clear that the Jews have several statuses worth investigating that may throw some light on the role of these people in America.

I

Social status is a composite rating that designates the relative standing a person or group receives when compared with others. Each status . . . is a place or position in the scheme of social relations. One of the most objective measures of social status has been developed by Bogardus in his study of social distance. Social distance is the amount of sympathetic understanding existing between persons or groups. It is a measure of the amount of intimacy the evaluators would accord representative members of races, religions, etc. Slight distance is commensurate with high social status, and, conversely, marked distance refers to low social status.

In 1926 Dr. Bogardus asked 1,725 Americans on the Pacific coast to participate in a survey of attitudes of forty ethnic groups. He found that the German Jews ranked twenty-sixth from the top and that Russian Jews ranked twenty-eighth from the top. Less than 8 per cent of the persons indicated that they would marry into a Jewish family. American Jews placed German Jews first, Russian Jews second, and English Jews third. In 1946 Dr. Bogardus gave his social distance scale to 1,950 persons in six regions of the United States and found that the Jews were ranked in twenty-third place in a list of thirty-six ethnic groups.

In May, 1947 an exploratory social distance study was made by Dr. E. S. Richards and the writer to determine the relative social status of sixteen ethnic groups. The subjects in this study were two samples of university students, one a white group and the other Negro. Minor modifications were effected in the construction of the social distance scale for ease of scoring and groups selected. The results, however, were surprisingly similar to established ratings and suggest that white and Negro students accord the American Jew somewhat comparable status. White students from the University of Oklahoma ranked the Jewish group eighth from the top, and Negro students from Langston University ranked them thirteenth. White students accorded more status to the Jews than to the Chinese, Mexicans, Mulattoes, Filipinos, and Negroes. On the other hand, Negro students gave the Jewish group higher status than Japanese, Scotch, and German.

A second test of social distance was administered to the two groups. The subjects were asked to react to each of the sixteen ethnic groups, not in terms of average representatives, but in terms of outstanding representatives of each group. With this modification the white and Negro samples accorded the American Jew comparable rank status, namely, eleventh.

The similar status assigned to the Jews by white and Negro evaluators may suggest a biracial pattern of limited social status for the American Jew. A moderate social status to the Jews is perhaps objective evidence of the role of particularistic experience, hearsay, and the diffusion of anti-Semitism.

II

The legal status of the Jews is very difficult to comprehend with any degree of certainty. On paper, in this country, there is little evidence of discriminatory legislation against the Jews. However, there is a long history of low legal status for the Jews, which is still perpetuated through "private action" on the part of non-Jews in this nation.

. . . From the tenth century to the nineteenth the Jews had no share in the gradual evolution of political institutions, no rights of citizenship, no security of tenure, were forced to reside in segregated neighborhoods, and were compelled to serve as royal usurers as the price of residence. It was not until the middle of the nineteenth century that the Jews in Western Europe secured equal legal status with other citizens. In fact, the American Revolution offered Jews in this country complete legal equality before European nations were willing to do likewise.

The European example of differential legal status for Jews was revived with exactitude by the Nazis. Jews were removed from civil service positions, attendance in public schools was limited, all identification papers were stamped with a conspicuous "J." The lowered legal status of the Jew was symptomatic of coming pogroms and the systematic massacre of millions of these people in Germany and Poland.

Although there is little evidence in this country of differential legal status between Jews and non-Jews, yet there is a differentiation expressed through the informality of the mores. Without legal prohibitions the Jew may yet find it difficult to purchase certain residential property, to gain access to specific recreational areas and clubs, and to enter certain professions and businesses. A sign posted over the entrance to a recreational area reading "Gentiles Only" may test the very foundations of American freedom. When "private actions" were sanctioned by the courts, they had the power of legal expressions. Racial restrictive covenants have been written to exclude Jews as well as Negroes, Orientals, and American Indians. However, on May 10, 1948, the United States Supreme Court handed down the decision that restrictive real-estate covenants are lawful, as private agreements, but under the terms of the fourteenth amendment and the Civil Rights Act of 1866 they cannot be enforced by either state or federal courts. This important decision may stimulate the discrimination of Jews and other minority groups on a quasi-legal basis.

A hopeful and promising improvement of the legal status of American

Jews has been made in New York, Massachusetts, and New Jersey [as well as elsewhere]. These states have legislation ["fair practices acts"] which assures equal rights to all Americans. In many respects it is a significant trend that legislation is being enacted to invalidate some of the narrow and biased effectiveness of "race conscious" mores. America is attempting to guarantee to the Jews and other minority groups the human rights that the Germans under Hitler legally abolished. It may not be amiss, however, at this point to observe that Jewish refugees are often shocked by the degree of race consciousness existing in the United States. In fact, some of the refugees report about the same amount of ethnic prejudice against the Jews in this country now as was prevalent in Germany before the advent of Hitler. If this estimate is correct, it is all the more clear that legal action will have to come to terms with the mores that collectively deny human rights to Jews and others, not as individuals, but as groups of persons.

III

The academic success of the Jews depicts their high status as scholars and the prejudice against them as competitors. In the United States the Jews are predominantly an urban people with a strong tradition of scholarship. There are some bases for believing that they are the most academic-minded ethnic group in the United States. For instance, Terman found twice as many very bright boys and girls who were Jewish as the percentage of Jews in the general population of California at the time of the study. Historically, some of the great men have been Jews, and such names as Spinoza (philosophy), Mendelssohn (music), Freud (psychiatry), and Einstein (physics) immediately come to mind. The desire among the Jews for academic achievement has its historic roots and its great men, and is currently manifest in the disproportionate demand for professional training among Jewish students.

The tremendous desire of Jewish students to enter medical schools has met with the antagonism of the majority group. Inasmuch as the Jews have not developed their own professional schools in the United States, they find themselves at a marked disadvantage in securing admission to medical schools under the auspices of Christian denominations. Private and state universities in varying degrees have adopted the "quota system" as an arbitrary method of excluding a very large percentage of the applications by Jewish candidates. . . .

According to the . . . study by Frank Kingdon the percentage of Jewish graduates of City College of New York admitted to a medical school dropped from 58.4 per cent in 1925 to 15.0 per cent in 1943. The College of Physicians and Surgeons of Columbia University admitted 46.92 per cent of the class of 1920 as Jewish, but in the class of 1940 only 6.40 per cent of the class was Jewish. Of course, few professional schools admit the quota policy for screening Jewish candidates or other minority groups. On the other hand, the school of medicine at the University of Illinois a few years ago showed 41.80 per cent of the class as Jewish, while only 1.5 per cent of the class was composed of Negroes.

An examination of the 1946 application blanks from thirty-nine grade A medical schools disclosed that all wanted to know the applicant's religion, church preference, or church membership. In addition to church affiliation ten applications asked for the religion of the mother and father. Fifteen of the schools asked the race of the applicant and twenty-eight asked the race of the applicant's mother or father. Eleven applications called for information concerning change of name. Of course, such application questions in themselves may prove nothing, but they suggest much.

The demand for high educational status by Jewish persons has developed into a sharp issue. In fact, in a recent survey B'nai B'rith disclosed that the percentage of Jewish students in graduate and professional schools dropped from 14.2 in 1935 to 10.6 in 1946, and in dental colleges from 28.2 to 18.9. Both the demand and the percentage attending professional schools attest to the very high status Jews accord formal education. Discrimination against the Jews by the establishment of quotas may be an attempt to limit their status by this means. Would anti-Semites admit that to limit educational opportunities of the Jews is one way of limiting the economic status of these people?

[The trend more recently seems to be in reverse. According to the American Jewish Committee, "the admission policies of New York medical schools in 1952 show a marked decrease in discrimination compared to 1950. . . . Of seven medical schools in New York discriminating against Jews in 1950, one has ceased this practice altogether while the other six have reduced the incidence of discrimination. . . . What of the medical schools outside of New York? Most of those in the South, mid-West and West can easily avoid even the appearance of discrimination through acceptable geographic criteria which automatically exclude most Jews and Italians, who are Easterners. Certainly, it is far easier for a Texas Jew to get into a Texas medical school than it is for a New York Jew to get into any medical school. And the same is true for most of the other non-Eastern states. In the East, however, it is easy to document discriminatory practices in medical schools outside of New York. Nevertheless, schools in New York State remain the chief culprits. Yet great progress has been made in New York. . . . The tide of public opinion . . . has flowed swiftly against discrimination since the end of World War II. And an expanding national economy has attracted top students to other fruitful fields like engineering, physics and electronics. As a result, total applications for medical schools have declined from an annual high of 20,000 to 16,763 in 1952. Medical facilities now permit 7,600 to be admitted every year so that today, almost one out of two applicants are accepted, compared to one out of three several years ago. These widening opportunities have also opened the doors wider for Jews and Italians."] [1]

IV

No doubt one of the chief factors in the development of critical attitudes toward the Jew has been his alleged economic success, not his real economic status. For many Americans the Jews are stereotyped as great financiers who control much of the wealth in the United States. Ethnic relations have been limited between Jews and non-Jews because many of the latter have believed that the former decide the great economic issues of the day. *Fortune* magazine . . . asked the following question: "Do you think any of these groups are getting more economic power anywhere in the United States than is good for the country?" The following results were found: Protestant, 2 per cent; Catholic, 12 per cent; Jews, 36 per cent; Negroes, 8 per cent; none, 39 per cent; blank or confused statement, 11 per cent. This poll disclosed the interesting finding that most of the critical reactions against the Jews came from rural areas and in sections of the country where the Jews are not particularly numerous.

Perhaps the most reliable study of the economic status of the Jews in the United States was made by the editors of *Fortune* in 1936. This study revealed that at that time the Jews played little or no part in the great commercial houses of this nation. Of the 420 directors of the 19 members of the New York Clearing House in 1933 only 30 were Jews. They found no Jewish directors in the National City, Guaranty Trust, Hanover, First National, Chase, Bankers Trust, and the New York Trust. In the investment field the predominant Jewish houses consisted of Kuhn, Loeb & Company, Speyer & Company, J. & W. Seligman & Company, Ladenburg, Thalman & Company, and the Lehman Brothers. In foreign loans the highest Jewish house had not quite one-sixth of the amount of the highest non-Jewish house. There is no basis for purporting that the Jews command the banking field.

In heavy industries Jews do not occupy a prominent place; in the light industries, particularly in the sale of merchandise, they are more numerous. Eighty-five per cent of men's clothing manufacture and about 95 per cent of women's are said to be under the control of Jewish merchants. The fur industry is another virtual monopoly by Jewish businessmen. To a much less extent the motion picture industry has a number of prominent Jews. The essential observation concerning Jewish economic

[1] *The Committee Reporter,* November–December, 1953, pp. 5–6.

status may be found in the following conclusion: "Jews do not dominate the American scene. They do not even dominate major sectors of the American scene."

An interesting study is quoted by Karpf on the occupational status of Jewish and non-Jewish persons in New York City. It was found that about 17 per cent of the Jewish persons were engaged in retail and wholesale occupations, while for Gentiles the percentage was only 6; in broker and sales work the Jews amounted to 16.2 per cent and non-Jews 8.3 per cent; in skilled and unskilled jobs the Jews were 13.8 per cent and the non-Jews 22.4 per cent. In clerical, sales, and professional positions the percentages were about the same for both groups. In domestic occupations the percentages were 3.7 per cent Jewish and 13.5 per cent non-Jewish. . . .

In the United States the occupational distribution of Jews and non-Jews seems to have been more similar than it was in Germany. In 1933 a German census indicated that 61.3 per cent of all gainfully occupied Jews were engaged in trade and commerce in contrast to 18.4 per cent among the total population, but altogether they constituted only 2.5 per cent of all engaged in these fields in Germany. In law and medicine Jews made up comparatively large proportions, 16.3 per cent and 10.9 per cent, respectively.

In summary, with many qualifications in mind, it may be observed that the status levels of the American Jew vary with the particular status selected for analysis. In social status the American Jew appears to be rated within the Caucasian nationality groups, but nevertheless one of the lowest within this principal category; in educational status he appears to be very high, both in potentiality to achieve and desire to secure higher education; in legal status he appears on paper to be equal to other ethnic groups, but there are constant reminders of private agreements and selective mores against him; and, finally, in economic status he tends to be found in the business and merchandising callings which reflect a status approximating the "middle class."

EDITORIAL COMMENT

With the establishment of Israel as a Jewish state in 1948 came the inevitable charge—given the ambiguity in Jewish identification—that the new situation meant a divided or dual loyalty for the American Jews. Zionism, the nationalistic movement that made Israel possible, has always had strong support among millions of American Jews. By helping to establish a Jewish homeland, it is claimed that the American Jews have enhanced their own morale.

The movement has brought about self-knowledge, self-respect, and a sense of participation in the destiny of Jews in need elsewhere.

But a warm and affirmative feeling toward Israel, and kinship with Jews throughout the world have been confused by many Gentiles—and a segment of American Jews as well—with the question of loyalty to the United States. Survey research shows that the vast majority of American Jews want to maintain their identities as Jews and as Americans. Only a negligible number are interested in migrating to Israel, the majority feeling themselves an integral part of America and its way of life.

Johan Smertenko, in the article below, explains what Zionism and Israel have meant to the Jews of the United States and answers the charge of a divided loyalty that has been levelled against them.

36. HAVE JEWS A DIVIDED LOYALTY?
BY *Johan J. Smertenko* *

FOR more than fifty years, an increasing number of Jews in America have been engaged in a "foreign affair." With ever-growing interest and intensity they have participated in the effort to create a Jewish state in Palestine. Today, with the admission of Israel to the United Nations and the establishment of a minute . . . country of indefinite boundaries and uncertain future, this effort—known as Zionism—has achieved a measure of success. But this has served rather to increase than to diminish the sense of responsibility and involvement of Jewish Americans in the new state. And it has brought to the point of decision a question which has vexed and perplexed them through all these years but which they were under no compulsion to answer so long as the Jewish state was a prophetic ideal rather than a political reality.

The essential part of the question is whether American Jews are now liable to a dual allegiance. But around this nub are layers of social and political issues, some hoary with age and others of recent information, some affecting only the Jew and others touching basic American concepts of assimilation and nationality. Actually, the relationship of Jewish Americans to Israel will be determined neither by themselves nor by the new state, but by America. It is necessary, therefore, that all Americans un-

* Johan J. Smertenko, "Have Jews a Divided Loyalty?" *Harper's Magazine,* 199 (October 1949), 46–53. Reprinted by permission.

derstand the affiliation of Jews outside Palestine to Israel, the difference in position and attitude between Jewish Americans and Jews elsewhere, the effect of an independent Jewish state on the national status of the Jew in the United States and in other countries, and, most important, the role and responsibility of the American people in determining the final decision of the American Jew.

II

To many dispossessed and declassed Jews in Eastern Europe and in the Near East, to the Jews who lead an uncertain and uneasy existence in the antisemitic atmosphere of countries like South Africa where nationalist elements exploit prejudice against the Jew, Argentina where Nazi doctrines are still prevalent, or the Soviet Union where the Jew is persecuted as a "cosmopolitan," the land of Israel represents a hospitable haven for themselves and an inalienable home for their descendants. Their resolve to return to Palestine is motivated by a conscious and practical desire to escape the status of second-class citizenship and the stigma of alienness, to live unashamed and uninhibited by such characteristics of national peculiarity as accents, features, and gestures, to establish their own *mores* and determine their own destiny—in brief, to be equal, normal, and independent.

But it is also actuated by . . . nationalism. This is not at all a political phenomenon. It is, rather, the subconscious urge of any people with an intrinsic and sustained tradition to survive as a distinct entity, developing and demonstrating its particular genius in its own particular way. This national longing, as Mazzini put it, "to elaborate and express their idea, to contribute their brick also to the pyramid of history," is . . . associated by all expatriated peoples with a yearning for their homeland. . . . Though segregated in physical and psychological ghettoes, the Jews of the Eastern Hemisphere have been nationally sterile throughout the two thousand years of their exile. The urge to express themselves now operates with tremendous albeit subconscious power.

Moreover, the cataclysm of the second world war and the recent Arab conflict have added an emotional compulsion to the . . . motives that impel the persecuted Jews to Palestine. The survivors of Nazi extermination camps, the hounded Jews of Moslem countries, and all their oppressed kith and kin were forged into a nation both by Hitler's furnaces and by the ardent defense of the Israelis against the Arabs. The Jews experienced the profound difference between the roles of helpless victims and heroic patriots. A sense of patriotism as well as of security makes them feel that in Israel they can offer effective resistance to the threat of extermination. With a fervor that is born of emotional conviction rather than intellectual certainty, they believe that their future is inseparably linked with their ancient past and that their only hope for happiness lies in their ancient land.

III

Most of the Jews in the United States, however, do not share this conviction any more than they shared the martyrdom of European Jewry. They do not believe that life, liberty, and the pursuit of happiness are attainable only in Israel; nor do they feel the urge to seek expression for their Jewish personality. On the contrary, from Colonial days on, the majority of Jews who came to America bent every conscious effort to suppress their . . . nationalism and to conform to the *mores,* traditions, and attitudes of their adopted land.

This drive toward acculturation was given great impetus by the fact that in the middle of the nineteenth century Jewish immigration was welcomed. While Irish Catholics and, to a certain extent, German and Scandinavian immigrants were being attacked by the Know-Nothing party, Jewish immigrants found that the good-will and acceptance won by Colonial Jews had been extended to include them. Their appreciation of this welcome took the form of a phenomenally rapid adjustment to American life. They learned the language more readily and spoke it more fluently than other aliens. They adopted citizenship at the earliest opportunity. They discarded their traditional social customs and abandoned their cultural heritage as being out of tune with the young, materialistic civilization of which they so ardently desired to be a part. They even made fundamental changes in their religion to sanction the new mode of life.

If this process of acculturation had progressed unchecked to its natural consummation, there would be no question of Jewish allegiance today —nor even a "Jewish question." But two complementary factors arrested the process and created a situation that must be resolved before the question can be finally answered. The first is the growth of antisemitism in the United States; the second stems from it—the Jewish attitude toward America.

In this country, antisemitism is not a political movement like Nazism, but a prevalent attitude with wide social and economic ramifications. While the reasons for this phenomenon were many and various, the basic cause lay in the fact that the first world war brought an end to the American epoch of limitless resources and expanding frontiers. The postwar depression frightened old-stock Americans and centered their fears on the hordes of immigrants who had risen from their place as menials and laborers in undesirable fields to the rank of competitors in all of the many phases of American economic life.

Now the fear-engendered antagonism was directed chiefly against the Jews. They were the latest and most numerous immigrants; they were the immemorial scapegoat of Christian society for the discontents and hatreds provoked by our competitive culture. The average American was unconscious of these underlying causes and of the fact that his antagonism, rooted in the prejudice inherited from our medieval past, was being stimulated and exploited for mercenary gain and political advantage by antisemitic organizations. He declared that the Jew was a disagreeable and irritating fellow, objectionable as a competitor or a colleague or a neighbor. . . .

IV

Like all mass migrations, the Jewish exodus to America at the turn of the century was composed chiefly of the lowest social and economic class but, unlike others, these immigrants immediately sought to rise to a higher level. For they brought with them that consciousness of persecution which has for centuries stimulated Jews to a great achievement. Americans, though more aggressive and energetic than most peoples, could not feel that urge, compounded of physical necessity and psychic impulse. They quickened the tempo of their economic life to meet the competition, but they resented the additional effort and disliked the Jew for increasing the pace.

Similarly, Americans resented social intrusion on the part of the Jews. Sensitive to the point of an inferiority complex about their own social status, since with few exceptions they were of lower middle-class origin, they were provoked by the problem which the Jew presented. For the Jews rose . . . into the class of the socially eligible, as measured by standards of wealth, occupation, and education. Within one generation, the lowly peddler, tailor, junkman, or sweatshop worker wondrously won a place among the leading merchants, lawyers, physicians, and manufacturers of his community. But though he, or his children, had acquired the knowledge and means to admit him to the highest ranks of our commercial and professional life, this strenuous effort often left neither time nor energy for the acquisition of social graces. . . .

Obviously, the difference between Jewish parvenus and others who sought—and received—admission to our upper classes was due to the difference in speed with which the Jews emerged from the lower depths. The children of English tradesmen, Scandinavian peasants, German artisans, or Irish navvies climbed more slowly the rungs of the social ladder and acquired the polish time puts on things and men.

The "successful" Jews leaped the entire distance and arrived bristling with rough edges. To be sure, the Jews had the normal immigrant quota of people of "culture" and "good breeding." However, by and large these were neither financially successful nor socially ambitious, lacking the aggressive, competitive, and mercenary qualities that America demands from nine to five and deplores after office hours. But the arbiters of American "society" were not interested in the whys and the howevers. They decided that Jews were repugnant and undesirable, and their verdict was reflected in the popular attitude.

In the intellectual realm, too, there were grounds for antagonism. A temperamental difference irritated even those who are not normally susceptible to the prejudices of the masses. The American is liberal only in his traditions and principles; he is conservative in habits and attitudes. The immigrant Jew was orthodox in his traditions and beliefs; undisciplined in habits and attitudes. The American mind is the product of freedom, security, and contentment; the Jewish mind was the issue of persecution, insecurity, and unhappiness. The American is essentially pragmatic, interested solely in the specific issues that affect his well-being, and intolerant of general criticism; the Jew was a dialectician, concerned about everything that affects the social order, and neurotically critical. . . . These irritating differences . . . served to rationalize anti-Jewish prejudice in America and thus operated as a brake on the process of acculturation. Actually, due to the formative force of our environment, the second generation of white immigrants reaches the American norm in virtually every social characteristic. . . . So, at the same time that this antagonism was being implemented in the social and economic life of the country, the very reasons adduced for it were vanishing from the American scene. Both relatively, by comparison with other nationalities, or absolutely, by drawing a balance sheet of vices and virtues, it could be proved that most of the Jews in the United States conformed to the manners and traits of the average American. Such proof, poured forth in interminable protests, apologies, and rebuttals, had no effect whatsoever on the growth of antisemitism. As the American historian Bancroft observed long ago, "The prejudices of ignorance are more easily removed than the prejudices of interest. The first are blindly adopted, the second willfully preferred."

. . . At first manifestations of this prejudice "of interest" were so trivial that it seemed absurd to take them seriously, much less to combat them. That some exclusion was practiced against the Jew was deemed a ridiculous and un-American bit of snobbery more derogatory to the institutions which indulged in it than to the Jews. But gradually the blot of discrimination spread into an ever-widening stain of ostracism—from society to the school, from schools to offices, to shops and factories. And there followed, as a matter of course, exclusion from common privileges and communal enterprises. Today, it is no secret that Jews have great difficulty in gaining admission to the institutions of higher learning and that their opportunities for legal and medical training are limited to a minimum. It is equally well known that the professions of banking, engineering, and others are closed to all but a few and that the quasi-public-service corporations vigorously exclude them. In the mechanical trades the discrimination is almost as widespread as in the professions. . . .

Inevitably, these conditions influenced the Jewish attitude to America, and this reaction constitutes the second factor retarding acculturation.

V

The apparent paradox that the more Americanized a Jew became, the more conscious he grew of his lower-caste status is no paradox at all. Native in our country for two or more generations, conditioned by our environment, taught in our schools the fundamental equality of citizenship, he was more sensitive to the discrepancy between American ideals and practices, more resentful of race discrimination, more jealous of his rights and dignity than the ghetto-timid Jew of the Old World.

Automatically, and without realizing all the implications of their action, Jewish Americans took steps to meet the challenge of prejudice. Jewish clubs, fraternities, veterans' groups, etc., were the obvious answer to exclusion; so was voluntary segregation at vacation resorts or in sections of town and city. Increasing emphasis on Jewish education—a striking instance of which is the study of Hebrew in such uncompromising citadels of acculturation as Reform temples—was a conscious effort to intensify the Jewishness of the younger generation as a form of defiance to those who branded such Jewishness inferior. The renascence, through new members and fresh funds, of purely Jewish organizations, which had come into being to aid the immigrant and were dying as a result of his rapid Americanization, was a defense measure against the threat to Jewish civil rights.

But the most significant element in the Jewish reaction to antisemitism was the adherence of many Jewish native Americans to the Zionist movement. At the beginning of the century, Zionism in America was limited to the recent immigrants from Eastern Europe. It was at first ignored and later vituperously condemned and combated by the leaders of American Jewry who feared, even then, that an interest in Jewish nationalism would cast doubts on their loyalty and allegiance to the United States. Slowly and reluctantly, most of them were brought around to accept the philanthropic aspect of the movement, and this gave point to the sarcastic aphorism that the Zionist was a Jew who got money from another Jew to send a third Jew to Palestine.

However, the next generation of Jewish Americans, who returned from the first world war to see the Ku Klux Klan, the Dearborn *Independent,* and other antisemitic manifestations rampant in the land, found something besides a charitable institution in the Zionist movement. It became a compensatory substitute for the social activities from which they were excluded. Membership in Avukah (intercollegiate Zionist organization) offered some consolation to the youths who felt unwelcome in college societies; by joining Junior Hadassah, young Jewish matrons could engage in the same sort of ballroom charity as the members of the Junior League; and young and old found an outlet for communal enterprise in the annual drives for millions of dollars, with all the perquisites of organized philanthropy in the form of honors and offices, testimonial dinners, and pictures in the newspapers. Thus, although less than ten per cent of American Jewry was affiliated with the Zionist organization, it became the yeast-like nucleus of the Jewish community in almost every city and town.

Affiliation with Zionism, no matter how slight and superficial, established a pattern in Jewish-American life. By virtue of it, thousands found meaning and satisfaction in their daily experience. Its compensatory character strengthened its hold upon them. Almost imperceptibly, American Jews became involved in the problems and politics of the Zionist movement. Pride in the American contribution to the establishment of the Jewish state, both in funds and in political influence, added a sense of responsibility for the welfare of the persecuted Jew to what was once merely sympathy for his plight. Even without sharing the latter's nationalism, American Jews began to think of Palestine as the place where they had a particular interest and a personal stake. When Arab armies invaded Israel, thousands of Jewish Americans offered to enlist in the Israeli forces, and hundreds actually joined in the fighting.

VI

Taken in the aggregate, these actions constitute a definite departure from the American Jews' earlier ardent efforts at acculturation. They indicate a tendency toward separateness in individual interests and communal activities. The Zionists have exploited this tendency for their own laudable purposes. But the temptation to perpetuate it has given rise to the idea that American Jewry can be developed and crystallized as a cultural minority in this country.

"We American Zionists glory in our citizenship in the American nation and in our fellowship in the Jewish nationality," states a pamphlet issued by the Zionist Organization of America several years ago. "As we develop in this country an essentially Jewish life, with Jewish spiritual and cultural values, we shall to that extent also fulfill our obligation as citizens of America. American democracy confers the right, imposes the duty, upon every nationality to be loyal to its own heritage, to be true to its own best and noblest self." This idea is extended to its maximum in a report submitted at a national convention of the organization by a commission which devoted an entire year to a study of the question:

> "The Jews of Israel and the Jews out of Israel are bound together as one people with a common heritage of religion and culture. Jews everywhere have therefore a special concern for

the unimpeded flowering of Jewish civilization in Israel and for the tranquillity and happiness of the Jews in their ancient home. Moreover Jews everywhere anticipate the enrichment of their spiritual lives from the renaissance of Jewish culture in Israel.

Israel is a sovereign state. Only the citizens of Israel owe it allegiance. The establishment of Israel has in nowise affected the citizenship of Jews of other lands . . .

The existence and unity of the Jewish people have been and are basic postulates of the Zionist movement. An invariant aspect of the Jewish people, throughout its tri-millenial history, has been its attachment to the land of Israel. . . . The modern Zionist movement is an instrumentality fashioned by the Jewish people for the preservation of Jewish existence and the perpetuation of its unity by the re-creation of the Jewish state in Israel, the revival of Jewish culture, and the revivification of its creative forces. These aims are, in their very nature, as eternal as the Jewish people; and the responsibility for their pursuit and furtherance can never be finally discharged. . . .

(1) To safeguard the integrity and independence of the state of Israel as a free and democratic commonwealth by means consistent with the laws of the several countries whereof Zionists are nationals or inhabitants. . . .

(2) To assist in the organization of all Jewry for the above-stated purposes by means of local and general institutions in conformity with local law.

(3) To strengthen Jewish sentiment and consciousness as a people and promote its cultural creativity."

. . . The Zionist conclusion that the stimulus derived from Israel and the tendencies . . . discussed above would induce Jewish Americans to accept the . . . status of a cultural minority is entirely erroneous. Already we have seen that the creation of a Jewish state has tended to normalize the position of the Jew everywhere. It has given him a place of reference, a place in which his right to live is taken for granted. For the first time in two thousand years he is like other men in this respect. He "belongs." He is thus a free agent whose deliberate choice of a land is in itself a token of his desire to belong to it. . . . Like the Englishman, Frenchman, Italian, and others who leave their native soil to plant their roots elsewhere, he will know that this personal action has no bearing on the survival of his people and their culture. . . .

VII

It is only in the light of all these facts that the question of the Jewish American's loyalty to the United States can be seen clearly. The

issue of dual allegiance has been raised many times here in connection
with citizens of various nationalities. The Pilgrim Fathers protested against
the Scotch and Scotch-Irish on the grounds that their corporate affiliation
with institutions across the Atlantic constituted a menace to the new way
of life that "may well prove fatal in the end." Benjamin Franklin feared
that if the influx of Germans into pre-Revolutionary Pennsylvania were
not diverted to other colonies, the original settlers would "be not able to
preserve our language, and even our government will become precarious."
One hundred and sixty years later, Theodore Roosevelt called the Germans
"hyphenated Americans" and charged that their presence threatened the
security of our country. When Al Smith ran for the Presidency [in 1928],
there was serious as well as intemperate discussion on whether a Catholic's
allegiance to the Pope disqualified him for this high office.

More analogous to the present situation are the instances that followed the first world war, when Czechoslovakia and Poland were recon-
stituted and Ireland won her freedom. It is undeniable that the independence of these states was in a great measure due to the political,
financial, and even military support given to their mother countries by
Americans of Irish, Czech, Polish, and Slovak descent. The Irish, especially, opened a front here in their war against England, and behind this
front established their headquarters for propaganda and fund-raising, for
economic boycott and political pressure through candid and concerted activity in Congress. Dire conclusions were drawn from these exhibitions of
"divided loyalty." But the prophecies proved as untrue as the charges.
What actually happened when these states were reestablished was that a
substantial number of their people gave up American citizenship and went
back. The rest remained here and retained a normal interest and concern in the affairs of their countries of origin, no more and no less than
do Americans of English, Dutch, French, and every other stock.

. . . The first to raise the cry of "dual" allegiance against *all* Jewish
Americans were the very antisemites who have persistently denied the
Jew an equal place in our body politic. Zionist leaders promptly denied
the charge and again proclaimed the loyalty of *all* Jewish citizens. Their
denial was supplemented by the statement of Foreign Minister Sharett, on
taking Israel's seat at the UN Assembly, that "the state of Israel claims
no allegiance from Jews in other lands." On the other hand, the anti-
semitic accusation was echoed by a small though vociferous group of self-
styled "assimilated" Jews, who hastened to dissociate *all* such Jews from
"the fanatic Zionists." Haunted by the fear that the long-delayed establishment of a Jewish state would affect adversely their status as citizens,
they rushed into print to testify to their 110 per cent patriotism and
Americanism and to deny sharing the sentiments and efforts in support of
Israel.

. . . America will have the last word. She will determine whether this is the Jews' own, their native land. For assimilation is a dual and reciprocal process. Each individual is incorporated and digested by the surrounding mass much in the same way that a particle of food is absorbed by the amoeba. At the end, both the individual and the environment are mutually changed. When the United States is four per cent Jewish—not in population statistics only, but in the warp and woof of her character—then she will make her Jews 100 per cent American.

x. Minority Group Reactions and Adjustment

S EVERAL American minority groups and the problems they experience have been discussed in considerable detail in the previous sections. Many other minorities have been given only passing mention. None can be said to have possessed "typical" reactions to the prejudice and discrimination of which they have been targets. There is no typical response by minorities to their status. Historical, social, economic, and personality variables have evoked a variety or range of reactions, not only between different minority groups but within a given group itself.

At one extreme in the spectrum of possible minority group reactions is the psychological internalization of dominant group hostility, the process of self-hatred first recognized by Lessing and Lewin. At the other extreme there is militancy and belligerency in group identification expressed in race pride, ultra-orthodoxy, and nationalism.

Most American minorities have not reacted in these extreme forms. They have met the antipathy directed against them with other types of adjustment. In some cases they have accepted it, playing the inferior roles assigned to them. At other times they have sublimated by redirecting their thwarted drives into activities and organizations within their own group. Or they have retaliated—fighting back for equality by every means and technique available to them.

The best-known adjustments of all are assimilation and the related processes, amalgamation and acculturation. The second-generation, the native-born children of foreign-born parents, have been the most convenient frame of reference for studying these processes. It is estimated that as a nativity group, the second generation numbers nearly 24,000,000 Americans at the present time. Members of the second generation frequently undergo considerable cultural dualism and social marginality. At the same time that they are conditioned by their parents' old-world culture and minority group status, they are exposed to out-group cultural contacts and social values in school and elsewhere.

It is in the second and third generations, and among the newer, younger, and more dynamic personality types emerging among minority groups in general that the minority group reactions and adjustments of the future must be sought.

In the first reading of this section, Samuel Tenenbaum describes the anguished responses, at times, of minority groups to the statuses imposed on them. He stresses the fact that integration of personality is extremely difficult in the face of dominant group attitudes and actions.

37. WHAT HATE DOES TO THE VICTIMS
BY *Samuel Tenenbaum* *

MINORITY groups are reminded in countless ways, some subtle, some crude, that they are inferior. Booker T. Washington tells of a book popular in his youth which placed the shining, noble countenance of George Washington right next to a picture of an evil-looking, naked African, decorated with a ring in his nose and a dagger in his hand.

As a youth, Booker T. Washington looked at his black color and felt defiled and degraded. ". . . . Everything white was good and everything black was bad. . . . We always understood that God was white and the devil was black."

* From Samuel Tenenbaum, *Why Men Hate* (New York: The Beechhurst Press, 1947), pp. 169–76. Reprinted by permission. Most footnotes omitted.

A minority feels demeaned by any distinguishing characteristic. Livingstone relates how in Africa his white skin was a constant irritant and how his pallor, in contrast to the dark skin of the natives, made him feel tubercular.

In a dominant white civilization, Negroes spend fortunes, which they can ill afford, on beauty treatments to straighten out their wavy hair, while the whites spend greater fortunes to put waves into their straight hair. Even in their nationalistic magazines, colored readers find advertisements of skin bleaches and hair straighteners.

Negro mothers have been known to reject children who were very dark and shower affection on their lighter offspring. Among Negroes, there is a hierarchy, depending on color, and young men prefer for social and marital reasons light-colored Negro girls, and in the social scale they rank higher. In Negro colleges, light-colored Negroes feel superior to darker classmates.

Minorities are infected with the prejudices and discrimination of the dominant group. If the dominant group shows strong prejudices, then the "out-group" will. In a defense town, Negroes began to riot against Mexicans because the whites mixed the two up, and they refused to be confused with "greasers." In Denver, Colorado, a housing project intended for the most recent newcomers, who happened to be Mexicans and Negroes, ended in ignominious failure. The Negroes resented such close proximity to Mexicans. Likewise, Catholic Polish immigrants in Detroit, themselves an "out-group," resented inclusion in a Negro project. . . .

Because they had a longer time to live in a western environment, German Jews always regarded themselves as superior to Russian or Polish Jews. In fact, German Jews blamed all their troubles on recent immigrant Slavic Jews, especially Poles. If it were not for them, they said, Germany would not have embarked on its campaign of anti-Semitism. . . .

Spanish-Americans frown on Mexicans.

Old settled Negroes in the North regard their newly arrived racial brothers from the South with contempt.

The society pages of Negro newspapers are as snobbish, exclusive and as . . . devoted to the so-called social niceties as those of the whites. In fact, so punctilious is the behavior of the colored social aristocracy that they have been called "Black Puritans." . . .

Sixty per cent of the Jews and seventy per cent of the Negroes entertain unfavorable stereotypes, one against the other.[1] The Jews say Negroes are lazy, dirty, boisterous, stupid, etc. The Negroes say Jews are aggressive, sharp in their business practices, that they own everything. Many Jews discriminate against Negroes vocationally and socially. . . .

When the Negro attacks the Jew, he feels he thus becomes a 100

[1] Clark, Kenneth B., "Candor about Negro-Jewish Relations," *Commentary*, February, 1946.

per cent American, part of the dominant group. When the Southern Jew attacks the Negro, he feels he is aligning himself with the dominant whites. Minorities fall in with conventional discrimination patterns because they hope in this way to attain security and a sense of belonging which they crave. . . .

SOCIAL ADJUSTMENTS OF "OUT-GROUPS"

The hated can never be as wholesome or as normal in his attitude or in his living as the individual growing up free from discrimination and prejudice. He suffers from economic, social and educational handicaps. Because of these inequalities, he frequently has to live in slums, work at menial jobs, watch others get promotions and advancements which are denied him, and, even worse, he frequently has to adjust himself to frustrations resulting from undeveloped talents, skills, abilities.

Psychologically, also, he faces many difficulties that prevent normal development.

As one form of reaction, he may accept the slanderous charges of the dominant group. An individual who makes this kind of an adjustment tries to curry favor with the dominant group and he avoids his own. He is proud to be seen in the company of members of the dominant group and to claim them as friends. Feeling inferior, he humbles himself before this group, and he even may deny kinship with members of his own family. Accepting the prejudices of the dominant group, he frequently is quite willing to condone and even to join in the persecution of his own group. . . .

Another form of adjustment involves compliance with the position that the dominant group has established for the minority. This adjustment is best illustrated by the Negroes who act out the part of "Uncle Tom," meek, subservient, anxious to please, devoid of self-will. They do not rebel against discrimination, but accept it as their lot. They regard their more unruly compatriots as wild trouble-makers who can do nothing but harm.

Still another method of minority adjustment is to reject all the values of the community, to be passive and even to violate the established, conventional codes and traditions. Knowing its futility, such persons refuse to work hard to get ahead or to establish respectable homes and families. They are shiftless, irresponsible, generally described as "lazy ne'er-do-wells." More accurately, it might be said, they do not play according to the rules, for they realize how limited is their opportunity for gaining recognition for their talents and abilities and, as a result, they are sabotaging all the social values the community esteems, even to the point of violence and crime.

Opposed to this form of adjustment is that made by members of the minority groups who accept all the conventional values of their environment. They realize, however, that they cannot achieve them among the dominant group; hence, they seek respect, position and eminence among their own. They are ambitious and they work hard, as businessmen, scientists, teachers, ministers, journalists, statesmen and the like. In their entertainment and social life, they observe most punctiliously the decorum and the etiquette of the dominant group and they seek to attain a high degree of respectability—according to dominant group standards.

There are other individuals who are openly rebellious. Reflecting the strong solidarity and the jingoistic sentiment of the "in-group," they also are proud of their race and insist that it is their group who are superior to all others. They comprise the strong nationalistic element, who try to make a solidified "in-group" of their own minority group. Refusing to accept the lowly position which society forces upon them, they vigorously fight discrimination and prejudice. They generally are aggressive, proud of their origins, not only acknowledging kinship, but fearlessly taking a stand with their group for better or worse. Among the Negroes, it is this group which demands that their children should play with colored dolls, not white; that their people should pray to a colored God, not a white God. . . . Typical of this strong feeling are the words that Richard Wright puts into the mouth of Bigger Thomas in his book, *Native Son:*

> Every time I think about it, I feel like somebody's poking a red-hot iron down my throat. Look! We live here and they live there. We black and they white. They got things and we ain't. They do and we can't. It's just like living in jail. Half the time I feel like I'm on the outside of the world peeping in through a knothole in the fence.

Members of minority groups seldom possess the wholesomeness and the integration of personality that comes from growing up in a friendly, helpful, secure world. Many of them grow up with damaged personalities. At times, this sense of inferiority makes them aggressive, ambitious, shoving. At times, their sense of inferiority fills them with shyness, meekness and fear. At times, the consciousness of enveloping hostility makes them neurotic, so that they are robbed of peace and are denied a feeling of being adequate and worthwhile; at times, this makes them oversensitive, so that they are ready to fight any slight, those that exist and those that are only imaginary. . . .

EDITORIAL COMMENT

One of the first kinds of adjustment that American minorities have learned to make in reaction to their statuses and needs is to develop an organized, self-sufficient social life. Partly because of the barriers that separate them socially from the dominant group and partly because of a feeling of security derived from perpetuating what is culturally familiar to them, they have created for themselves a number of social, cultural, benevolent, nationalistic, and recreational institutions and organizations. The most important of these are mutual aid societies, the minority church, and the minority press.

The major purpose of mutual aid societies among minority groups is to provide benefits in time of sickness and death. However, they also function to facilitate social relations, preserve cultural values, and reenforce and perpetuate consciousness of kind. The minority church is often the nucleus for the formation of the group's organized life, and the minority press offers news and takes up issues that concern the group nationally or locally.

In organizing agencies, ethnic groups have been the most prolific of all. The following article is by two officers of the Common Council for American Unity who present their survey of this kind of adjustment to life in the United States and interpret its relationship to assimilation.

38. AGENCIES ORGANIZED BY NATIONALITY GROUPS IN THE UNITED STATES

BY *Yaroslav J. Chyz* AND *Read Lewis* *

EACH nationality group which has migrated to the United States has developed a wide variety of organizations to meet the fundamental human needs common to all mankind. His churches and religious organizations enable the newcomer to worship God according to his traditional faith and to enjoy the ritual and the hymns in which he has been reared. Newspapers and periodicals bring him news and needed information in his mother tongue. Fraternal benefit societies provide insurance in case of sickness or death. Singing and educational societies express his artistic and cultural interests. Clubs and lodges reflect his social needs. Political and relief organizations evidence his interest in and concern for his native land.

* Yaroslav J. Chyz and Read Lewis, "Agencies Organized by Nationality Groups in the United States," *The Annals of the American Academy of Political and Social Science,* 262 (March 1949), 148–58. Reprinted by permission.

AMERICAN CHARACTER OF ORGANIZATIONS

The nationality groups which came from English-speaking countries became the majority group in the United States and impressed their language and institutions on the new continent. The result has been a tendency to think of the agencies created by English-speaking groups as "American," and of similar developments on the part of other nationality groups as "foreign." Actually, all of them reflect the same basic human needs and are adaptations to American conditions. The fact that "foreign" languages are used in organizations developed by newer nationality groups tends to obscure the fact that the organizations themselves are essentially American and persist even when most of their members are unable to speak the ancestral language.

An Italian Catholic parish in the United States differs from a Catholic parish in Italy in very much the same way that a Protestant Episcopal congregation differs in its structure, scope, and mode of activities from a congregation of the Episcopal Church in England. An American newspaper in the Polish language is as American to a Pole in Warsaw as the New York *Times* is to a Londoner. Even such directly transplanted institutions as the German *Turnvereine* or the Czech *Sokols,* or such ritualistically strict bodies as the Orthodox Jewish congregations or the Russian Orthodox Churches, have developed characteristics and acquired peculiarities which single them out as "American" in the eyes of members of the original organizations.

There are, of course, exceptions to this rule, but they are rare and constantly decreasing. It could not be otherwise. The pattern of American life is so much an outgrowth of American conditions that any organization that wants to survive and develop must fit into it. On the other hand, that pattern offered and still offers so much freedom that it not only makes possible the survival of customs and cultural and social activities of various origins but also encourages the development of new organizational forms in which American and transplanted ways and usages are combined. Fraternal and benefit organizations, for example, which in America are the mainstay of many nationality group activities, have no counterpart in Hungary, Poland, or Slovakia. They are a purely American product.

The agencies organized by nationality groups in the United States may be grouped under three main heads: churches, secular organizations, and foreign-language press and radio. Of course, any rigid classification of agencies according to aims and activities is impossible. A fraternal benefit society may publish a foreign-language newspaper. A parish, or even a whole religious body, may devote a large part of its effort to educational and secular activities, especially those that aim to preserve the coherence of the group.

CHURCHES

Religious bodies are the oldest non-governmental forms of organization among all groups of Americans. Religion motivated the migration to these shores of the Pilgrims and the Quakers, the Scotch Presbyterians and the Belgian Protestants, the Moravian Brethren and the Swiss Mennonites, the French-Italian Waldensians and the Ukrainian Shtundists. Those who came here for other reasons were also for the most part religious people, and one of their first activities as a group was founding a congregation and building and maintaining a house of worship.

The oldest known white religious community in what is now the United States was the Catholic parish in St. Augustine, Florida, established in 1565. Because of their Spanish-Mexican membership and language, the Catholic missions and parishes in the American southwest and in California are the oldest non-English religious organizations in this country. The Dutch Reformed Church in New York, established in 1628, and the Swedish Lutheran congregations, founded among the Swedish settlers in Delaware by Reverend Reorus Torkillus about 1641, appear to be the first non-English Protestant religious communities. The first German Lutheran Church was established in New York in 1648. The first Jewish congregation was organized in Newport in 1658. The first Mennonites came to Pennsylvania in 1683. Moravian Brethren settled in the same colony in 1741. The first Russian Orthodox Church was established in Alaska in 1795. The Panna Maria, Polish Catholic parish in Texas, was founded in 1854. The Finns organized their first Lutheran synod in 1870. The first Greek Catholic Church serving Carpatho-Russians and Ukrainians was organized in 1885.

With the influx of larger numbers of their countrymen, the number of parishes and congregations grew and they began to organize themselves into dioceses, synods, provinces, conventions, and conferences. Numerous splits increased the number of religious bodies.

The oldest and largest single denomination among the non-English-speaking groups is the Catholic Church.

Catholic

According to the *Official Catholic Directory,* the Catholic population of the United States on January 1, 1947, was 25,268,173. It was organized in 14,742 parishes, 5,257 chapels, and 4,935 missions, and administered through 22 provinces and 99 dioceses.

The *Directory* lists some 2,000 parishes as being Armenian, French, German, Polish, Syrian, or of other nationalities and rites. Other sources indicate that at least 2,855 parishes are serving Catholics of Armenian, Assyrian, Belgian, Carpatho-Russian, Chinese, Croatian, Czech, Dutch, French, German, Hungarian, Italian, Lithuanian, Maltese, Polish, Portuguese, Rumanian, Russian, Slovak, Slovene, Spanish (Mexican and Puerto Rican), Syrian, and Ukrainian origin. Most of them are of Roman Catholic rite. A few hundred belong to the Armenian, Byzantine (Greek), Chaldean, Maronite, and Melchite rites. Among those of the Byzantine rite is the Ukrainian diocese having 138 Ukrainian parishes with 307,065 members. The so-called Pittsburgh diocese includes 165 Carpatho-Russian, 15 Hungarian, and 2 Croatian parishes with some 285,652 members. Assuming that these figures are typical, the total number of Catholics belonging to known non-English or nationality parishes exceeds five million. Another five million in all probability belong to nationality parishes although the latter are not identified as such.

Prominent among the characteristics that distinguish these nationality parishes are: (a) the use of the native language in all or some sermons and in some church songs; (b) certain additional rites and customs, such as the blessing of food before Easter, special Christmas customs, and distinctive marriage rites; (c) the celebration of holidays peculiar to the native country, such as St. Casimir's among the Lithuanians, St. Gennaro's and Our Lady of Mt. Carmel among the Italians, and St. Nicholas' among the Carpatho-Russians. In lay activities these nationality parishes differ from others by celebrations, both religious and secular, commemorating prominent personalities or events in the native country.

Protestant

The largest Protestant denomination among the nationality groups is the Lutheran Church. Most Americans of Danish, Estonian, Finnish, Icelandic, Latvian, Norwegian, and Swedish descent belong to it. Probably the majority of German-Americans are also Lutherans. There are Lutheran communities among the Hungarians and the Slovaks. The Lutheran Church is organized in some twenty national bodies which differ among themselves on dogmatic or organizational grounds: 2 Danish, 3 Finnish, 5 German, 1 Hungarian, 1 Icelandic, 1 Latvian, 5 Norwegian, 1 Slovak, and 1 Swedish. Altogether, according to 1945 statistics, they had 15,443 congregations and 5,119,153 members.

Next in numbers among the Protestant Churches are the Reformed religious bodies, with 3,986 churches and 981,875 members. Like the Lutherans, they are split into a number of central organizations: 3 Dutch, 1 German, 2 Hungarian, and 1 Slovak.

Baptist denominations have converts among many nationality groups. In some, special nationality Baptist bodies have been organized, such as the Czechoslovak Baptist Convention, the Hungarian Baptist Union, the Italian Baptist Churches, the Roumanian Baptist Association of North America, the Independent Baptist Church of America (Swedish), and others. Considerable Baptist missionary work is being conducted among the Spanish-speaking groups in the southwest. Various sects of

Baptists are represented among the 157 Protestant communities of Japanese-Americans.

The Church of the Brethren and other Brethren bodies, some of them known as Dunkers, chiefly of German and Swiss origin, have 4,300 congregations and 651,465 members. The Evangelical Church, of Methodist origin, has 1,194 churches and 255,881 members, almost exclusively of German descent. Sixteen Mennonite religious bodies have 1,116 churches and 110,725 members among the Pennsylvania Dutch and in other states. The Schwenkfelders and the Amana Church Society in the German group, the Huguenots among the French, the Waldensians with French-Italian membership, the Welsh Calvinistic Methodists who in 1920 joined the Presbyterian Church in the United States of America, and the Bohemian and Moravian Brethren of Iowa and the Evangelical Unity of Moravian and Bohemian Brethren in North America among the Czech-Americans, account for some hundred or more congregations and more than 10,000 members. Dissatisfaction with the Irish domination of the Catholic Church in America brought about the organization of the Polish National Catholic Church, which replaced Latin with Polish in its services and otherwise introduced several reforms. This church in 1944 had 146 parishes and 250,000 communicants. For similar reasons the Lithuanian National Reformed Church, with seven parishes and 3,225 communicants, was organized.

There are many smaller religious bodies in all the groups, in part the result of internal dissent and in part the result of proselytism by Protestant denominations. These bodies include: the Russian Dukhobors around Detroit and San Francisco; Russian Molokans in California; Old Believers around Pittsburgh; Ukrainian Shtundists in North Dakota; Polish Mariawites; the Armenian Evangelical Church; the Unorganized Italian Christian Churches of America; the Portuguese Evangelical Federation of Churches; the Italian Pentecostal Assemblies of God; the Hungarian and Ukrainian branches of the Assemblies of God; and many similar denominations. While they may not number more than 1,000 congregations, these smaller sects suggest the differentiation and dissent which find expression in a free country.

Eastern Orthodox

Most Christian immigrants from eastern and southeastern Europe and from the Near East, and their descendants, belong to a group of religious bodies with similar rites which use old Slavonic, Greek, Syriac, and Ukrainian languages in their liturgies and are either independent American religious bodies or are connected with the Eastern Patriarchs of Antioch, Constantinople, or Moscow or with church synods of their respective countries. The present unsettled religious conditions in a large part of eastern Europe have created dissension especially in the Russian

Orthodox Church, with one party favoring submission to the Moscow Patriarchate and the other advocating the creation of a supreme Russian Orthodox hierarchy outside the Soviet Union.

Other Orthodox Churches are the Albanian, Carpatho-Russian, Bulgarian, Greek (Hellenic), Rumanian, Serbian, Syrian, Ukrainian Orthodox, and Ukrainian Orthodox Autocephalous, with a total membership of 728,-860 in 880 churches.

Not connected with the above Orthodox Churches are religious groups of Armenians and Assyrians from Iraq and Iran. They have their own ancient churches: Church of Armenians in America (Gregorian) with 35 churches and 18,787 members; Assyrian Jacobite Apostolic Church with 4 churches and 3,100 members; and the Church of the East and of the Assyrians (Nestorian) with 10 churches and 3,000 members.

Non-Christian Religious Bodies

Jewish congregations are divided into three groups. The Orthodox group claims to have the largest numbers; in 1940, the Union of Orthodox Synagogues of America claimed 2,500 congregations as being affiliated with their group, numbering about 400,000 members and one million worshipers. The Conservative groups, organized in the United Synagogues, claimed the affiliation of 475 congregations with 250,000 members. The Reform group had 302 congregations affiliated with it, and about 150,000 members. In addition, there are 500 congregations without affiliation, and also a great number of "Holy Day" congregations which exist only for services on High Holy Days.

The members of the Jewish religious organizations, being of various national origins, participate in the activities of various groups, and even among themselves often form organizations according to the country of their origin. For example, the Sephardic Jews from Spain, Portugal, North Africa, and the Near East have synagogues of their own. In Brooklyn, New York there is an Arabic-speaking community mostly from Aleppo, Syria, and in Harlem a group of Abyssinian Jews.

Other non-Christian groups include Japanese Buddhists, who have 28 congregations in the United States, 19 of them in California; and Mohammedans, who have their mosques or places of worship in Washington, New York, Detroit, and probably also in San Francisco. The members of their congregations hail chiefly from Albania, Arabia, Egypt, Palestine, Iran, Iraq, Turkey, and Bengal and other parts of India.

One-third of Total Church Membership

The foregoing facts and figures are a convincing proof of the extent and vitality of religious life among nationality groups and of the importance and persistence of their churches. Those already referred to reach a total of some 15,000,000 members in more than 32,500 congregations: 5,092,-

000 members with 2,855 churches in the Catholic Church; 7,116,443 members with 24,998 churches in the Protestant denominations; 753,747 members in 929 churches in the Eastern Orthodox and other Eastern Churches; and some 2,000,000 members with 3,728 congregations in the different Jewish religious bodies.

These statistics are not always strictly comparable, because they are for different years; in some cases the latest figures available are [several] years old. Nor are the figures complete. The Baptist, Methodist, Pentecostal, Mohammedan, and Buddhist bodies have not been included in the foregoing totals, because not all the figures are available. Also, 5,000,000 or so Catholics who are members of nationality groups, although they belong to churches not specifically identified as nationality churches, as well as many of the 3,000,000 Jews living in communities with synagogues but not counted formally as members, would bring the total number of nationality membership in all denominations to some 23,000,000. This is more than 31 per cent of the 73,673,182 members of all denominations in the United States, as reported for the year 1947 by the *Yearbook of American Churches* and *The Christian Herald*.

While native languages are still used in most churches serving nationality groups, the use of English is becoming more widespread, especially in the Dutch, Danish, Norwegian, Swedish, and Jewish congregations. In the Catholic and even in the Eastern Orthodox churches, English sermons are heard more and more frequently. Social activities in the churches in which second and later generations participate are conducted almost exclusively in English in all groups with the exception of Spanish, French, and some German communities.

This trend toward English does not mean the loss of other nationality characteristics. Church traditions, rites, special holidays, social contacts, and intramarriage keep the church communities together even where the original language may have been changed. Many church activities are directed toward strengthening these internal ties. Parochial primary and secondary schools maintained by nationality churches often teach the native language and make the children acquainted with the culture and history of the group here and abroad. Immigrant clergymen rekindle the group spirit and strengthen the ties with the native country. Special colleges and seminaries in this country educate priests, ministers, and rabbis for service in their denominations. In these schools most subjects are taught in English, but with special attention to the language and culture of the group.

On the other hand, nationality group churches, as well as their central bodies, have developed traits and features which are typical of American church life but often entirely unknown in the "old country." Churches which in the "old country" were either state religions or state-supported have had to learn to exist on the material support of their members. The compulsory religious education has had to give way to voluntary Saturday or Sunday schools. The complete authority of the clergy in all church matters has been shared in varying degrees with lay members, who have freedom to disagree and even to carry their dissension to the point of seceding or forming a rival religious organization. Church activities extend to fields rarely entered by church organizations in other countries—large-scale welfare and charitable work, sports, summer camps, printing and publishing, participation in conferences, and consultations with representatives of other creeds.

Adaptation to new needs and conditions and survival among so many other and often rival denominations, along with maintenance of inherited beliefs and traditions, are proof of the vitality of the religious bodies of nationality groups. Many of them have already become and others are on the way to becoming an integral part of America, part and parcel of the diversity which is so characteristic of American religious life.

ORGANIZATIONS

Fraternal benefit organizations, in which members form local branches, lodges, or assemblies through which they pay monthly dues to a national body for some kind of insurance, are the oldest and most enduring of existing secular organizations in our nationality groups. Originally founded to assure the immigrant a decent burial, they have developed into a network of some 150 national organizations with more than three million members, insurance of about three billion dollars, over half a billion dollars in assets, and varied social activities in more than 31,000 lodges and branches, in all states of the Union. They support schools, museums, homes for the aged, orphanages, sport activities, publications, and adult education, and help their young members to pay for college education. Not all of them, of course, are engaged in all these activities or to equal degree in any of them. Smaller organizations are satisfied with fulfilling their benefit obligations to their members. Some of the largest support colleges or sponsor elaborate historical research relating to the group.

There are a large number of local fraternal organizations in which membership is limited to a particular city or a region. Like national organizations, most of them provide the usual sick benefits. Such local organizations are most numerous in the Jewish group, where they take the form of *Landsmannschaften* (societies of people from the same town or region in the native country), but also occur frequently among the German, Greek, and French groups, especially on the west coast, and also in the Scandinavian (Norwegian *bygdelag*) and some Slavonic groups.

Not a few national and some local fraternal organizations either publish or subsidize newspapers or publications. Eleven dailies, over fifty semiweeklies and weeklies, and about the same number of monthlies are supported in this way.

Several fraternal organizations do not carry insurance benefits, but are active chiefly in social, philanthropic, cultural, and educational fields. The largest Jewish organization—B'nai B'rith, established in 1843—has some 305,000 members in its 900 lodges and 580 chapters, helps Jews abroad, provides educational and social opportunities for its youth, and works for better understanding between Americans of Jewish and other faiths. The Order of the Sons of Italy in America unites some 125,000 members in 940 lodges for social purposes, for promotion of interest in Italian culture, and for organized participation in American life. The American Hellenic Educational Progressive Association (AHEPA) endeavors to integrate Greek and American cultures, while the Greek American Progessive Association (GAPA) is more interested in preserving Greek traditions and languages. The Federation of French Alliances in the United States and Canada maintains and propagates French culture and ideas in America.

Cultural and Occupational

Numerous singing societies cultivate and perpetuate native music among the German, Swiss, Swedish, Welsh, Norwegian, Russian, Ukrainian, and other groups. Almost every community with a large "foreign" population has local baseball, basketball, or soccer teams of "foreign" extraction. Jewish "Maccabees" compete with Slovak "St. Mary's," and Armenian "St. Gregory's" play against "Ukrainian Cossacks." The German *Turnvereine* and the Czech and Slovak *Sokols* unite physical culture with the maintenance of their group culture and ideals.

Japanese, Czech, Jewish, Finnish, and other farmers, Kosher butchers, German grocers, French cooks, Italian barbers, Russian lawyers and doctors, Swedish engineers, Norwegian seamen, Lithuanian organists, and other occupational and professional groups maintain local and regional associations of their own. There are associations to further folk dancing and to promote a study of a group's history in America. The American Scandinavian Foundation, the Carl Schurz Foundation, the Polish American Historical Commission of the Polish Institute of Arts and Sciences, the Menorah Society, the Swiss American Historical Society, the Finnish Suomi College, the Swedish American Biographical Society, and other similar institutions have made valuable contributions to the historical studies relating to their respective groups.

Political

Organized political activity on a national scale in the domestic field among nationality groups has always been and still is limited almost exclusively to the left-wing parties. This is partly due to the fact that many so-called "radical" ideas have been transplanted into America from abroad, and partly because the leftist parties look for recruits among American workers, so many of whom are of recent immigrant stock. In the past, the Socialist Party, the Industrial Workers of the World, the Socialist Labor Party had large nationality "federations" or "sections." Some of them survive. . . . Participation in other parties is organized through local "Polish" or "Italian" Republican or Democratic clubs, with an occasional state league or federation of such clubs.

In the foreign field, on the other hand, the activities of nationality groups are much more vigorous and diversified, especially among immigrants from central and eastern Europe. Unsettled conditions in some countries, sharp division of opinion regarding existing regimes, and efforts by political parties abroad have stimulated among the politically minded members of various groups interest and activities relating to the "old country," to an extent which some outside observers consider excessive. Actually, such interest and activities, in most cases, are limited to sharp articles in the foreign language press, a few conventions and resolutions, memoranda and delegations to administration and congressional leaders in Washington, and some financial help to the kindred groups and leaders abroad. Often these political interests and activities bring to the closer attention of our Government and the American public many urgent issues on which the United States must sooner or later take action. Information services issued by various nationality groups frequently contribute material which helps America to make up its collective mind on important international issues. . . .

Welfare

Charitable and welfare activities for the benefit of the needy members of one's group played a much more prominent part in the life of immigrants in the past than they do now. Fraternal benefit organizations resulted from such concern. At the present time several orphanages, more numerous homes for the aged, and a few hospitals and homes for the blind or crippled comprise the total of such activities. They are most numerous in the Jewish group. Otherwise, needy members of nationality groups must turn for help to general private and public agencies. On the other hand, activities for aid to kinsmen abroad have increased during and since World War II. Hundreds of millions of dollars are collected annually. All nationality groups have special committees for various forms of help to their kinsmen in other parts of the world. Many of them are members of the American Council of Voluntary Agencies for Foreign Service or have joined CARE—Cooperative for American Remittances to Europe, Inc.

The passage of the Displaced Persons Act of 1948 directed the activities of Croatian, Czech, Estonian, German, Hungarian, Jewish, Latvian,

Lithuanian, Polish, Russian, Serbian, Slovak, and Ukrainian relief organizations to the task of bringing their kinsmen to America and finding homes and employment for them. In the case of larger groups the task was not too difficult; but small American groups with large numbers of prospective immigrants, such as Estonians, Latvians, and to a degree Ukrainians, had to turn to religious organizations for help to carry on this work.

FOREIGN-LANGUAGE PRESS AND RADIO

Der Hoch-Deutsche Pennsylvanische Geschict-Schreiber, which made its appearance in Philadelphia in 1739, was the sixth American periodical and came into existence only 35 years after the first American newspaper, the Boston *News-Letter.* From that time on, the press in German and later in other languages grew until it reached its peak during the First World War with more than 1,350 publications in 36 languages. At the end of July 1948 there were 973 publications in 40 languages.

It is from Americans of foreign birth and their families that the non-English press draws the bulk of its readers. Not only do persons of foreign birth or parentage constitute almost one-quarter of the American population, but in the 1940 census as many as 21,996,240 persons in the United States reported some language other than English as their "mother tongue"—that is, the principal language spoken in their homes in their earliest childhood. These 21,996,240 persons, and consequently the foreign-language press, are concentrated in eastern and middle western states, on the west coast, and in the southwest. The states having the largest number of foreign-language publications are: New York 277; Illinois 127; Pennsylvania 83; California 60; Massachusetts 56; Ohio 50; Texas 49; Michigan 43; New Jersey 37; Wisconsin 24; Minnesota 23.

A quarter of the country's non-English publications, 249, are published in New York City. Chicago has 105. Other cities having 20 or more are Cleveland, Boston, Pittsburgh, Detroit, San Francisco, Los Angeles, and Philadelphia.

Almost all of the 95 non-English dailies and about 40 per cent of the 37 semiweeklies, 374 weeklies, and 467 periodicals are owned by individual publishers or by small corporations or partnerships. The rest are owned by religious, fraternal, or cultural organizations. They range all the way from small, struggling sheets printed and edited by a single individual to influential weeklies and large dailies, with circulation running into six figures, equipped with modern plants and capable of producing impressive Sunday editions.

All the dailies and 337 of the 411 weeklies and semiweeklies are newspapers in the strict sense of the word. In addition to carrying general news and editorials, some of them at the same time serve as organs of fraternal organizations. Depending chiefly on individual subscriptions or on organization support, foreign-language papers reflect the views of their readers much more closely than many of their English-language counterparts, which derive most of their income from advertising.

Almost 200 foreign-language publications are the organs of religious organizations, and some 300 are purely fraternal publications or are issued by political groups, cultural agencies, or trade interests. About 40 Spanish and Portuguese publications which, though published in the United States, circulate chiefly in Latin America fall in the last group. . . .

Contents and Character

As to content, foreign-language newspapers naturally devote most space to news about the "old country" or to events in their own group. At the same time, they carry a considerable amount of material on the American scene. Throughout its history, the foreign-language press has served as a sort of textbook and guide to American customs and institutions, American history, government, naturalization, and the thousand and one things a newcomer wants and needs to know in order to adjust himself to his American environment.

. . . In general, foreign-language newspapers encourage their groups to preserve their cultural heritage, religion, language, and social customs, and yet, at the same time, to find their place in the American community and participate in American life. . . .

Radio

Supplementing the foreign-language press, but of much less importance as a means of reaching the nationality groups in the country, are the more than 300 foreign-language radio programs which in 1948 were being broadcast each week in 26 different languages. These programs were broadcast from more than 125 different stations, located in some 26 states. Approximately 10 per cent of the programs are sponsored by religious groups, another 10 per cent by fraternal organizations, and the remaining 80 per cent are commercial undertakings aimed at the foreign-language market in a given locality.

In many cases the foreign-language broadcaster is connected with a local foreign-language newspaper. He usually buys a block of time from a local station and sells as much time as possible to local advertisers. The result is that most foreign-language programs are isolated units and, with notable exceptions, are disrupted by an overdose of commercials. While some stations have included features of outstanding cultural and educational value, most programs consist chiefly of music, news, entertainment features, and comment, which are supposed to appeal to different tastes and different sections of nationality groups.

As Affecting Assimilation

Do the agencies organized by American nationality groups—their churches, organizations, press—aid or hinder assimilation? The question, however interesting, is in a sense academic, for such agencies are an inevitable result of large-scale immigration. . . . Further, even as cursory a survey of nationality group agencies as has been possible here suggests they are here to stay, a permanent part of American life; that their apparent differences from the accepted "American pattern" are no greater than those shown once by the Quakers of Pennsylvania or the Mormons of Utah. Use of foreign languages will gradually in most cases give way to English, but most of the organizations, both religious and secular, will persist.

Do such agencies aid or hinder assimilation? The answer depends in part on what one means by "assimilation." If it spells loss of all group identity and unconditional acceptance of the language, customs, religious beliefs, and cultural patterns of New England, the "deep South," the West or Middle West—depending on where the newcomer happens to be settled—then these agencies must be counted an obstacle to assimilation. But if the essence of assimilation is, first of all, emotional identification with America and second, participation in general American life, if assimilation is considered not a one-way process but a mutual adjustment, then these agencies must be regarded as instruments of individual and group adjustment to America.

Agencies organized by a nationality or any other group naturally place a certain emphasis on the things—in this case, common heritage and language—which are the basis of the group's existence. To some extent, consequently, they tend to increase group consciousness as contrasted with emotional identification with America. It must be remembered, however, that most of these same agencies have been founded to meet the immigrant's needs in a new country. In a deeper sense, therefore, they are instruments of his adjustment and have a profound influence in furthering his assimilation. They facilitate, rather than prevent, his participation in such general American activities as trade unions and political parties and in local community affairs. . . .

EDITORIAL COMMENT

Assimilation, it is generally agreed, is a crucial process in the adjustment of American minority groups. Yet there is no consensus concerning its complete meaning and how it takes place.

Many Americans assume assimilation means the gradual absorption of a minority group by a dominant group. The end-product is alleged to be the loss of the minority's identity and the emergence of an enlarged and homogeneous society. This dubious oversimplification of what actually takes place in intergroup relations is based on an analogy, for assimilation was originally a concept that described a physiological process in which foreign or external substances are ingested by a living organism and transformed into body cells presumably in harmony with it. Even in physiological assimilation, however, it should be noted that the products are not identical body cells; rather, various types of cells are produced in adaptation to the different needs of the entire organism. Similarly, assimilation in the sociological sense of the term does not necessarily mean the complete, homogeneous merger of all the social units that are involved in the interaction.

Assimilation also does not refer to an exclusively one-way process in which the minority group passively accepts the social and cultural influences of the dominant group. It is, instead, a process of give and take, of mutual although unequal diffusion between the groups. Inasmuch as the dominant group by definition is more powerful in the interactive process, it is appropriate to speak primarily of *acculturation* or the adaptation of minority culture to the dominant group's culture. While acculturation is a cultural process within the framework of assimilation, *amalgamation* is the biological aspect of assimilation, referring to the mixture or blending of two or more groups through common offspring. In theory and, to a certain extent, in practice, acculturation and amalgamation can take place without each other, but one seldom occurs without some accompaniment by the other.

In the following selection, William Carlson Smith reviews the major theories about assimilation and examines some key variables in its operation in American society.

39. THE PROCESS OF ASSIMILATION
BY *William Carlson Smith* *

A. DEFINITION OF CONCEPT

The concept "assimilation" has been defined in a variety of ways.
The "melting-pot" theory. For many years, after 1909, Zangwill's dramatic parable of the *Melting Pot* symbolized the popular conception of

* From William Carlson Smith, *Americans in the Making* (New York: D. Appleton-Century Co., Inc., 1939), pp. 114–23. Reprinted by permission. Most footnotes omitted.

assimilation. In this great American cauldron we could "crystallize millions of aliens, of all nations, habits, and languages, flocking to us from every quarter of the globe, into a new homogeneous race, better and finer than the world had ever known." In eloquent words William Jennings Bryan pictured the outcome: "Great has been the Greek, the Latin, the Slav, the Celt, the Teuton, and the Saxon; but greater than any of these is the American, who combines the virtues of them all." This was a comforting theory and it was in full accord with the current *laissez faire* ideas.

The "Americanization" theory. When the United States entered World War I it became evident that thousands, if not millions, of immigrants living in our industrial cities had not been fused in the melting-pot. Then the "Americanization" theory came into vogue.

According to this position, all immigrants should divest themselves of their heritages immediately and take over a standardized American pattern for their lives. "The immigrant's . . . inheritance, no matter how much it may mean to him, becomes, upon his arrival in America, a 'foreign' impediment which must be forthwith cast away." In the words of Panunzio:

> Assimilation, as the word itself denotes, aims to make the foreign born similar to Americans in language, dress, customs, religion, and what not. It lays stress upon formal Americanization through naturalization. It insists that all immigrants must at all times use English and must put away their native customs, ideas, and ideals as soon as possible. In other words, assimilation tends to be a standardization.

According to this conception, assimilation was largely a negative process of denationalization. John Collier commented on this idea that it "rather indicates the taking over of the richly variegated cultural life of the many peoples coming to our shores and reducing them all to a deadly, dull Puritan drab."

The idea of conformity is basic in the popular programs of Americanization, or, more correctly, "spurious" Americanization. In the words of Arthur Evans Wood:

> It fosters on the part of the immigrant a barren conformity to dominant trends in religion, politics, leisure, business, consumption and other aspects of American life. Conform in many large and fundamental ways the immigrant must, if he is to survive. That is as a matter of course. But that he should become a Protestant, vote the majority ticket, 'root' for the home team, celebrate Mother's day, eat corn flakes, live beyond his income, divorce his wife, and speculate in city lots would not seem to exhaust the nobler opportunities that America holds for him.

In addition to *conformity,* the idea of *injection* is stressed by many. The immigrant is to be taught English and civics, he is to commit to memory certain portions of the Constitution, Lincoln's Gettysburg address, and literature filled with sonorous phrases. After he has learned to read he is supplied with patriotic literature, he is given full instructions relative to saluting the flag, and standing when the band plays the national anthem. Franklin K. Lane summarized this program thus: "One part ability to read, write, and speak English; one part the Declaration of Independence; one part the Constitution; one part love for apple pie; one part desire and willingness to wear American shoes; and another part pride in American plumbing will make an American of anyone."

The idea of rigid standardization is preposterous. In a complex society like ours there are religious sects, occupational, trade, or professional groups which have ideas, attitudes, and practices very diverse and they even have languages not wholly intelligible to outsiders. In Chicago the residents in the "Gold Coast" do not understand the dwellers in the adjoining slum, even though they be of old American stock.

It became evident that the Prussian method, or forcing process, was falling below expectations. The naive assumption that American clothes, practices, and customs were superior to all others and the spirit of condescension and coercion aroused a feeling of resentment among the foreign-born and the process of Americanization was actually retarded. . . .

The "ethnic federation" theory. Social workers in contact with immigrants thereupon formulated the theory of "ethnic federation," which, quite to the contrary, stressed the perpetuation of the cultural heritages of the different groups. According to this theory each group is to maintain its racial and cultural integrity and contribute of its own culture to American life. The resultant American culture then would be a symbiotic relationship of these several cultures existing side by side as distinct entities.

Culture units in such a situation, however, would not remain unchanged; assimilation would fuse them ultimately. This federation would make conditions favorable for assimilation and gradually the separate entities would tend to disappear.

A "sociological" theory. According to Kimball Young, "we may define assimilation as an interactional process by which persons and groups achieve the memories, sentiments, ideas, attitudes, and habits of other persons or groups and by sharing their experiences become incorporated with them in a common cultural life of the nation."

According to this conception the immigrant is not required to divest himself all at once of his heritages and be recharged completely with Americanism. While it is highly desirable for an immigrant to learn the English language, it is not absolutely necessary in order to act in concert with the native group. In fact, many useful citizens carry on much of their activity through the medium of a foreign tongue. It is a reciprocal process in which both native and alien participate and the result is a mutual enrichment. In this situation the several groups (like the fire and engineering departments of a city government), even though they engage in quite different activities, are cooperating, nevertheless, in a common enterprise. This idea implies that the various population elements are interacting, and that they are being blended into a common purpose. This gives opportunity for originality and individuality which have no place in popular conceptions of assimilation or Americanization. A dead-level like-mindedness is not the end product of this process.

Assimilation is not a static condition. It cannot be measured by any rigidly objective standard. There is no agreement as to what constitutes an assimilated immigrant. We may say in general that immigrants have become assimilated when they acquire the sentiments, attitudes, viewpoints, and behavior patterns of the Americans, and feel at home in the adopted country. Robert E. Park has expressed it thus: "In the United States an immigrant is ordinarily considered assimilated as soon as he has acquired the language and the social ritual of the native community and can participate, without encountering prejudice, in the common life, economic and political. The commonsense view of the matter is that an immigrant is assimilated as soon as he has shown that he can get on in the country. This implies among other things that in all the ordinary affairs of life he is able to find a place in the community on the basis of his individual merits without invidious and qualifying reference to his racial origin or to his cultural inheritance. Assimilation may in some senses and to a certain degree be described as a function of visibility. As soon as an immigrant no longer exhibits the marks which identify him as a member of an alien group, he acquires by that fact the actual if not legal status of a native." [1]

B. Nature of the Assimilative Process

Assimilation is inevitable. No matter what the situation may be, a change takes place in the immigrant who spends some time in America. Many try to steel themselves against any and all influences which may lead to a discarding of elements in the old cultural heritage and an adoption of anything from the new environment. Even then the inevitable happens. The Mennonites in Central Kansas settled in closed communities and tried to retain their national customs and habits through German schools, through religious instruction, and by restricting the association of their youth with Americans. Despite these precautions, however, changes came gradually; they could not stand against American influences. . . .

Assimilation a slow process. Assimilation is a slow process. Mere

[1] From R. E. Park, "Assimilation," *Encyclopedia of the Social Sciences,* New York, 1930, Vol. II, p. 281. By permission of The Macmillan Company.

externals, to be sure, can be changed readily, but assimilation goes far deeper and demands more time. "It is unwise to believe," according to Bercovici, "that a multitude of different peoples could have suddenly dropped all their culture, all their traditions, and all their customs, to adopt another culture and other traditions and other customs and habits. . . ."

Assimilation is not merely a process of acquiring the new but it also involves a discarding of the old. The immigrant slowly gives up his traditional ideas, standards, and practices and adopts those of the new country. Gradually the sentimental attachments to the old-world heritages relax and new loyalties are developed.

An unconscious process. In the main, the process of assimilation, as Samuel Gompers found, is an unconscious one and the person is incorporated into the life of the new group without being aware of it.

> Unwittingly I was reborn to become spiritually a child and a citizen of the United States. . . . Soon the currents of New York life crept over our Dutch-English threshold. One by one the members of our family group were swept into the life of our new home city. We learned its customs and found its opportunities.

Ernest Bruncken observed that the unconscious Americanization often became evident only when the immigrant returned to his homeland. A number of Germans planned to spend their last days in their ancestral abodes, but many of them soon retraced their steps to the adopted country. They found that the better part of a lifetime spent in the United States had left them more American and less German than they had imagined. Likewise G. E. Schiavo noted that probably the greatest disappointment in the life of the Italian immigrant has been his return to the scenes of his youth. Here, for the first time, he became aware of the great change that had come over him. Attuned, in some measure at least, to the whirlwind of American life, he could not adapt himself to the bucolic tranquility of his native village. And so he returned to the promised land with a new outlook upon life. His children should now grow up as Americans. He would provide for their education—the best they would be willing to accept. He might even send them to college. Such experiences are common to all groups.

Assimilation and amalgamation. Assimilation is often confused with amalgamation, since the two commonly go on together wherever different peoples come into contact. Amalgamation is a biological process; it is a mingling of blood and blending of . . . stocks through intermating and intermarriage. Assimilation, on the other hand, is a social, cultural, and psychological process; it involves the modification of attitudes, memories, ideals, and the fusion of cultural heritages. Either process may go on without the other: two . . . groups may become assimilated without biological intercrossing, or they may lose their . . . identities without any assimilation taking place. Usually, however, the presence of either one aids the other. Assimilation is conducive to intermarriage—that is, more frequent attachments develop between those who are closely akin in customs and language. On the other hand, intermarriage makes possible the primary contacts which are favorable to assimilation.

EDITORIAL COMMENT

In the course of American history minority groups have differed considerably in pace and extent of assimilation. If one compares several groups, he will readily note marked differences. Furthermore there is every reason to expect that differential patterns of assimilation will continue.

Such patterns are not fortuitous. Some demographic, cultural, and historical factors are conducive to assimilation whereas others are evidently hindrances. Insofar as these factors may combine to affect a given minority group in a manner quite different from other groups, one can expect differential assimilation to take place.

Sufficient thought and research on these variables of assimilation now are available to aid some sociologists in attempting to develop scales of prediction. In the following excerpt from their study of the social systems of American ethnic groups, Warner and Srole present one of the first of such attempts to produce a scale of assimilation and status. They come to the conclusion that, given the present rate of assimilation, the future of American ethnic groups appears to be a limited one.

40. DIFFERENTIAL ASSIMILATION OF AMERICAN ETHNIC GROUPS

BY *W. Lloyd Warner* AND *Leo Srole* *

1. ETHNIC GROUPS IN AMERICA

. . . American ethnic groups are sometimes classed with the minority groups of Europe, but while they show certain general characteristics in common the groups in America are quite different from those in Europe

* From W. Lloyd Warner and Leo Srole, *The Social Systems of American Ethnic Groups* (New Haven: Yale University Press, 1945), pp. 283–96. Reprinted by permission.

and more like the minority groups of Australia and South America. The roots of the minorities of Europe are buried deeply in the soil of the dominant country. Often the history of the subordinate group in a region is more ancient than that of the dominant one. In the United States the ethnic group's origins are known and felt to be "foreign." Yet these minorities arrived only a short time after the dominant culture had established itself.[1] Both the immigrant and host societies know that the so-called "old-American" culture is itself new and ultimately "immigrant." This feeling creates a certain toleration in the attitude of the host society.

The forces which are most potent both in forming and changing the ethnic groups emanate from the institutions of the dominant American social system. Our political organization permits all adults to be equal within its structure. Although at first this equality is largely theoretical, it gives the ethnic members an attainable goal as the political success of the Irish, Germans, Scandinavians, and Italians demonstrates. Our developing industrial and factory economy with its own hierarchy permits and demands that ethnic members move up and out of their ethnic subsystems into the common life of America. The public school teaches the people to adjust to the central core of our life, provides them with technical skills for their own advancement, and gives them some of the power necessary to become upward mobile in our class order. The school, in belief and partly in practice, expresses the basic principles of American democracy where all men are equal; when the school cannot make them equal it struggles to make them culturally alike.

The American family system breaks down and builds up ethnic subsystems. The ethnic parent tries to orient the child to an ethnic past, but the child often insists on being more American than Americans. Marriage also may maintain or disrupt the ethnic way of life. At marriage an individual may move out of his ethnic group into that of his spouse; or an individual who has become partly American may re-identify with his ethnic group and become more ethnic than in the past.

Cliques and associations also operate to increase or decrease ethnic identification. If the child in school becomes a part of an American clique he is likely to move rather rapidly into the American way of life. On the other hand, if he is rejected and forced to participate in ethnic cliques he may become closely identified with the cultural group of his parent. This is also true for adult cliques and for adult associations. On the whole, however, the evidence from Yankee City shows that cliques and associations increase the participation of ethnic people in the life of the larger community and accelerate assimilation.

Our class system functions for a large proportion of ethnics to destroy the ethnic subsystems and to increase assimilation. The mobile ethnic is

[1] The only exceptions are the American Indians and some of the Spanish-speaking minorities.

much more likely to be assimilated than the nonmobile one. The latter retains many of the social characteristics of his homeland. Most ethnics are in lower social levels. Some of them become self-sufficient, interact among themselves, and thereby reinforce their old ways of life. Some of the unsuccessfully mobile turn hostile to the host culture, develop increased feelings of loyalty to their ethnic traditions, become active in maintaining their ethnic subsystems, and prevent others from becoming assimilated. But, generally speaking, our class order disunites ethnic groups and accelerates their assimilation.

2. RACE, CULTURE, AND AMERICAN SUBORDINATE GROUPS

To understand the place of the ethnic group in the American social system it is necessary to see it in the larger framework of all the subordinate groups. A survey of the several types of subordinated groups in this country reveals that, excluding the subordination of lower-class old Americans, there are three basic types which are ranked as inferior. They are (1) the ethnic group, (2) the racial group, and (3) the ethno-racial group. The ethnic group carries a divergent set of cultural traits which are evaluated by the host society as inferior. . . . These cultural groups . . . form their own social world to nurse their members through a period of transition until these members "unlearn" what they have been taught and successfully learn the new way of life necessary for full acceptance in the host society.

The racial groups are divergent biologically rather than culturally. They possess physical traits inherited from their fathers and mothers which are divergent from those of the old-American white population. These traits have been evaluated as inferior. Such physical attributes as dark skin, the epicanthic fold, or kinky hair become symbols of status and automatically consign their possessors to inferior status. The Chinese, Japanese, and Filipinos of California, the Spanish Americans and Mexicans of the American Southwest, and American Negroes suffer from such evaluations of their racial differences. The cultural traits of the ethnic group, which have become symbols of inferior status, can be and are changed in time; but the physical traits which have become symbols of inferior status are permanent. Unless the host society changes its methods of evaluation these racial groups are doomed to a permanent inferior ranking.

From the researches done . . . on ethnic and racial groups, it now seems possible to present a conceptual scheme which places a subordinate group in its relative rank within our social hierarchy. It permits us to predict with some degree of success the probable degree of subordination each group will suffer, the strength of the subsystem likely to be developed by it, the kind of rank order it will be assigned, and the approximate period necessary for its assimilation into American life.

The conceptual scheme about to be described is based on the following propositions: First, the greater the difference between the host and the immigrant cultures, the greater will be the subordination, the greater the strength of the ethnic social systems, and the longer the period necessary for the assimilation of the ethnic group. On the other hand, those ethnic groups with small differences are quickly assimilated. Second, the greater the racial difference between the populations of the immigrant and the host societies the greater the subordination of the immigrant group, the greater the strength of the social subsystem, and the longer the period necessary for assimilation. Finally, when the combined cultural and biological traits are highly divergent from those of the host society the subordination of the group will be very great, their subsystem strong, the period of assimilation long, and the processes slow and usually painful. With these propositions in mind it is possible to construct a rough scale by which hypotheses may be developed about the relative ranking of each racial and cultural group in American life, the strength of its subsystem, and the period necessary for ultimate assimilation.

The people racially most like white "old Americans," the dominant people in America, are other Caucasians. Those least like them are the Mongoloid peoples, Negroes, and racially mixed, dark-skinned groups such as the peoples of India. The Caucasoid group lies at one extreme, and the Mongoloid and Negroid peoples at the other extreme of the range. To bring out the significant points about assimilation and to point up further questions on the subordination of subgroups, the Caucasoid immigrant population has been divided into those who are largely like the present old-American stock and those who are least like them. For convenience we can refer to the first as light Caucasoids and to the latter as dark Caucasoids. Those people with a mixture of Caucasoid and Mongoloid . . . , in particular mixtures from Latin America, occupy the next place in the range. The mixed . . . of Mongoloid and Caucasoid stock who resemble Mediterranean Caucasoids are followed by Mongoloids and Negroes. These considerations provide us with five categories: race type I, the light Caucasoids; race type II, the dark Caucasoids; race type III, Mongoloid and Caucasoid mixtures with a Mediterranean appearance; race type IV, Mongoloids and mixed peoples with a predominantly Mongoloid appearance; and finally race type V, Negroes and all Negroid mixtures.

A similar scale can be constructed for deviation from the dominant American culture. For purposes of the present analysis, the immigrant cultures may be divided into differences of language and religion. (Other customary behavior is associated with language and religion.)[2] . . . It is

[2] A finer cultural screening necessary for making sharper discriminations would divide the culture into more categories, but for general placement of the several groups, language and religion are significant; this is in part true because large bodies of customary behavior are associated with these two basic cultural phenomena.

clear that emphasis must be placed on religious differences. The dominant old-American religion is Protestant, and much of our customary behavior is closely integrated with a Protestant outlook on life. Our customary way of life is most like the English, and our language is but one of the several English dialects. The ethnic people most like us are English-speaking Protestants with a body of customary behavior no more deviant from our way of life than their language and religion. This cultural type is followed by Protestants who do not speak English and whose way of life is slightly more divergent from ours. The third type includes English-speaking Catholics and other non-Protestant groups. The fourth cultural type includes Catholics and other non-Protestants who do not speak English. The types least like us are the non-Christians, some of whom speak English and others who do not.

When these two scales, the cultural and the racial, are combined into a table, thirty possible categories logically result since there are six cultural types for each of five racial types. However, several of these categories do not exist in actual fact. For example, there are no English-speaking, Protestant, dark Caucasoids.

Table 1 succinctly presents the ethno-racial scale of differences between the dominant white American host society and the present ethnic and racial groups as well as the entering immigrant groups. In the left-hand column are the five racial types in the order of their similarity to the old-American white stock. Next to this column are the six cultural types serially arranged according to their similarity with old-American culture. The repetition of the six cultural categories for each racial type reveals that the racial evaluations made by the American host society are far more potent and lasting in the ranking of divergent peoples than those applied to cultural groups. For example, English-speaking Protestant Negroes possessing the same culture as the rest of the American group cannot be ranked as a subvariety of other English-speaking peoples; and it is obvious that they must be placed in a position inferior to all Caucasoid peoples, regardless of the cultural deviation of all the white-skinned peoples. The peoples most like white Americans, and therefore ranked highest, are the light Caucasoids who are Protestant and speak English. Those least like us are the non-Christian Negroes.

We will now turn to the second part of our analysis, presenting a way of ranking (1) the degree of subordination and social distance, (2) the strength of the racial and ethnic subsystems, and (3) the forms of American rank. A timetable predicts the approximate period necessary for the assimilation of each racial and ethnic group. For convenience a five-point scale has been set up for each. The degrees of subordination run from "very slight" through "slight," "moderate," "great," to "very great." The criteria for rating a particular group's degree of subordination are (1) freedom of residential choice, (2) freedom to marry out of one's own group, (3) amount of occupational restriction, (4) strength of attitudes in the host society which prevent social participation in such institutions as associations and cliques, and (5) the amount of vertical mobility permitted in the host society for members of the ethnic or racial group.[3]

TABLE 1

SCALE OF SUBORDINATION AND ASSIMILATION

Racial Type	*Cultural Type*

Racial Type I
Light Caucasoids
	Cultural Type 1
	English-speaking Protestants
	Cultural Type 2
	Protestants who do not speak English
	Cultural Type 3
	English-speaking Catholics and other
	    non-Protestants
	Cultural Type 4
	Catholics and other non-Protestants,
	    most of whom speak allied Indo-
	    European languages.
	Cultural Type 5
	English-speaking non-Christians
	Cultural Type 6
	Non-Christians who do not speak English

Racial Type II Dark Caucasoids	Cultural typing the same as for Racial Type I
Racial Type III Mongoloid and Caucasoid mixtures with Caucasoid appearance dominant (appearance of "dark" Mediterranean)	Cultural typing the same as for Racial Type I
Racial Type IV Mongoloid and Caucasoid mixtures that appear Mongoloid	Cultural typing the same as for Racial Type I
Racial Type V Negroes and all Negroid mixtures	Cultural typing the same as for Racial Type I

The presentation here is designed to give no more than a résumé of the operations and present only those necessary to understand the whole schema of ethnic and social subordination and assimilation. Any one group may be slightly out of place as, for example, the Catholic

[3] If each of these criteria is re-scaled from one to five and the results added and the sum divided by five, the quotient given provides a rough but fairly satisfactory index of the degree of subordination of each group. The light Caucasoids who are Protestant and speak English get an index of one, and the non-Christian Negroes an index of five, giving the first a rating of "very slight" and the latter "very great" subordination.

French or the Hungarians, but the relative place of most of the groups is accurate. The importance of this system of analysis is that each group's place is established in a total configuration of American society as the result of applying scientific propositions about subordination and assimilation which appear to be laws governing the relations of ethno-racial groups in the larger American society.

The criteria for the strength of the cultural or racial subsystem are (1) the power of the "church" over its members and degree of divergence of the "church" from the Protestant norms; (2) the presence of separate schools and the amount of control they exercise; (3) and (4) the political as well as the economic unity of the group; and (5) the number and power of ethnic or racial associations.[4] Our hypothesis is that the light Caucasoids who are English-speaking and Protestant develop the least powerful systems while the Negroes have the strongest.

Criteria for a timetable of assimilation are (1) the time taken for an entire group to disappear, (2) the proportionate number of people who drop out of a group in each generation, and (3) the amount and kind of participation permitted members of the group by the host society. The same procedure as described for the other categories produces a rough index for a group's assimilation: "very short" (see Table 2) means that the group is assimilated in a period of not more than one generation; "short" means more than one but less than six generations; "moderate," more than six; "slow," a very long time in the future which is not yet discernible; and "very slow" means that the group will not be totally assimilated until the present American social order changes gradually or by revolution.

To test these hypotheses about subordination and predicted assimilation, let us examine Table 2 in which many of the ethnic and social groups now in America are placed appropriately in the ethno-social scale. The people listed may also be regarded as referring to populations now outside America who in the future might be migrants should our present immigration law be modified.

Most of the peoples of the British Isles, including the North Irish but not the Catholic Irish, as well as the English-speaking Canadians and the other English-speaking peoples of the Dominions, belong to Cultural Type 1 of Racial Type I. According to our hypotheses, their subordination should be very slight, the subsystems they build very weak, and their period of assimilation usually less than a generation. Anyone familiar with the facts of such people's position in America knows that their actual place fits the one we propose for them. . . .

The Protestant Germans, Dutch, and Scandinavians of Cultural Type

---

[4] Each of the five characteristics of the strength of a subsystem can be redivided into a five-point scale and the same procedure can be used for determining the strength of the subsystem as that described for the degree of subordination.

TABLE 2

ETHNIC AND RACIAL ASSIMILATION

Cultural and Racial Type	Degree of subordination	Strength of ethnic and racial subsystems	Time for assimilation	Form of American rank
Racial Type I—Light Caucasoid				
Cultural Type 1. English-speaking Protestants. Tests: English, Scotch, North Irish, Australians, Canadians	Very slight	Very weak	Very short	Ethnic group to class
Cultural Type 2. Protestants not speaking English. Tests: Scandinavian, Germans, Dutch, French	Slight	Weak	Short	Ethnic group to class
Cultural Type 3. English-speaking Catholics, and other non-Protestants. Test: South Irish	Slight	Moderate	Short to moderate	Ethnic group to class
Cultural Type 4. Catholics and other non-Protestants who do not speak English. Tests: ("fair-skinned") French, French Canadians, Germans, Belgians	Slight	Moderate	Short to moderate	Ethnic group to class
Cultural Type 5. English-speaking non-Christians. Test: English Jews	Moderate	Moderate	Short to moderate	Ethnic group to class
Cultural Type 6. Non-Christians who do not speak English. Tests: ("fair-skinned") European Jews and Mohammedans from Middle East	Moderate	Moderate	Short to moderate	Ethnic group to class
Racial Type II—Dark Caucasoids				
Cultural Type 1	——	——	——	——
Cultural Type 2. Test: Protestant Americans (other "dark-skinned" Protestants)	Slight to moderate	Weak	Moderate	Ethnic group to class
Cultural Type 3	——	——	——	——
Cultural Type 4. Tests: "dark skins" of Racial Type I, Cultural Type 4; also Sicilians, Portuguese, Near Eastern Christians	Moderate	Moderate to strong	Moderate	Ethnic group to class

TABLE 2 (*continued*)

ETHNIC AND RACIAL ASSIMILATION

Cultural and Racial Type	Degree of sub-ordina-tion	Strength of eth-nic and racial subsys-tems	Time for assimi-lation	Form of Ameri-can rank
Cultural Type 5	—	—	—	—
Cultural Type 6. Tests: "dark-skinned" Jews and Moham-medans of Europe and the Near East	Moder-ate to great	Strong	Slow	Ethnic group to class

Racial Type III—Caucasoid Mixtures

Cultural Type 1	—	—	—	—
Cultural Type 2. Tests: Small groups of Spanish Americans in the Southeast	Great	Strong	Slow	Ethno-racial to class or color caste
Cultural Type 3	—	—	—	—
Cultural Type 4. Test: Most of the mixed peoples of Latin America	Great	Strong	Slow	Ethno-racial to class or color caste
Cultural Type 5	—	—	—	—
Cultural Type 6	—	—	—	—

Racial Type IV—Mongoloids

Cultural Type 1. Tests: Most American Chinese and Japa-nese	Great to very great	Very strong	Slow	Racial to semi-caste
Cultural Type 2	—	—	—	—
Cultural Type 3	—	—	—	—
Cultural Type 4. Test: Filipinos	Great to very great	Very strong	Very slow	Racial to semi-caste
Cultural Type 5	—	—	—	—
Cultural Type 6. Tests: East In-dians, Chinese, Japanese	Great to very great	Very strong	Very slow	Racial to semi-caste

Racial Type V—Negroids

Cultural Type 1. Test: Most American Negroes	Very great	Very strong	Very slow	Racial to color caste

TABLE 2 (*continued*)

ETHNIC AND RACIAL ASSIMILATION

Cultural and Racial Type	Degree of sub-ordina-tion	Strength of eth-nic and racial subsys-tems	Time for assimi-lation	Form of Ameri-can rank
Cultural Type 2				
Cultural Type 3. Test: Some American Negroes	Very great	Very strong	Very slow	Racial to color caste
Cultural Type 4. Tests: Negroid Puerto Ricans, etc.	Very great	Very strong	Very slow	Racial to color caste
Cultural Type 5				
Cultural Type 6. Tests: Bantu Negroes and West African Negroes	Very great	Very strong	Very slow	Racial to color caste

2 and Racial Type I, according to our hypothesis, are quickly assimilated into American life. The facts in general support this theory. Some of the Scandinavians and Germans, however, have formed sects that do not conform to the general rule we have laid down and present special problems which demand added dimensions to place them accurately in a timetable of assimilation.

The non-Protestant Christian groups who do not speak English are in Cultural Type 4. The great strength of the Catholic Church in organizing and maintaining separate ethnic groups is clearly illustrated here. The French, German, Belgian, and Dutch Protestants, it seems likely, assimilate very rapidly, develop less powerful subsystems, and are less subordinated than those of the same nationality and language who are Catholic. The Catholic Irish of Cultural Type 3 assimilate more slowly than the Protestant Irish despite the fact that in all other respects the two cannot be distinguished by most Americans. Whereas the Catholic Irish develop moderately strong subsystems and take many generations to assimilate, the Protestant Irish form very weak ones and almost immediately become assimilated.

Cultural Types 5 and 6 of Racial Type I include the light Caucasoid Jews, particularly those of Western Europe. We can best understand the place of the Jew and of the other peoples in this category if we glance down Table 2 to the same cultural types of Racial Type II (see "dark-skinned" Jews). A comparison of these categories of Jews tells us much about the place and problems of the Jew in American life. Jews and other non-Christians are likely to assimilate less easily than Christians, but the light-skinned Jew who is not physically different and thereby not burdened with negatively evaluated racial traits like his dark-skinned co-religionist assimilates more rapidly than those who belong to Racial Type II. In the first case five or six generations may see most of the group disappearing; in the latter the members of the group assimilate very slowly. . . .

The Catholics and non-Protestants of Cultural Type 4 and Racial Type II include a large number of nationalities such as Italians, Greeks, and French who are also found in Cultural Type 4 of Racial Type I. The subordination of the former group is likely to be greater and their period of assimilation much longer than those of the latter despite the fact that they are often co-religionists, speak the same language, and have the same body of customary behavior. The factor of race, or rather the strong negative evaluation of it by American society, is sufficient to explain most if not all the differences in ranking of the two groups.

The power of the evaluation of the racial factor becomes even clearer when Cultural Type 4, the Catholics and other non-Protestant Christians of Racial Type III (the Mongoloid and Caucasoid mixture), are compared with those of the dark Caucasoids. These Catholics, most of them dark-skinned Latin Americans, are heavily subordinated as compared with moderate and light subordination for the same type in the other two racial categories. The prediction for their assimilation is slow, which is to say there is no predictable time when they will disappear into the total population, whereas that of their co-religionists of lighter skin is predicted to be short and moderate. We see plainly that while the Catholic Church is a powerful instrument for the conservation of the ethnic tradition, it is much less powerful than the force of American organized "prejudice" against the dark-skinned people. The Negroid Puerto Ricans, Cubans, and West Indians who are of the same cultural type as the lighter-skinned peoples of these islands provide final and conclusive evidence that it is the degree of racial difference from the white American norms which counts most heavily in the placement of the group and in the determination of its assimilation.

The place of the English-speaking Protestant American Negro in our life yields the most eloquent testimony for this proposition. The Negro is culturally more like the white "old American" than the English and Scotch of Cultural Type 1, yet he occupies a very subordinate position where there is little likelihood of his ultimate assimilation unless our social order changes. Although the American Negro belongs to the same cultural type as the English and the Scotch, his racial ranking is near the bottom of the rank order.

These considerations of the relative rating of the cultural and social traits of American society bring us to consideration of the last column in Table 2. This has to do with the form of American ranking ultimately given each of these groups. All of the six cultural types in Racial Types I and II we predict will change from ethnic groups and become wholly a part of the American class order. The members of each group . . . are permitted to be upward mobile in the general class order. But all of the six cultural types in each of the Racial Types IV and V are likely to develop into castes or semi-castes like that of the American Negro. When the racial deviation reaches the Mongoloid and Negroid extremes the cultural factors are of little importance in the ranking of a particular group and race is all-important.

Racial Type III provides an interesting difference from the others. These ethno-racial groups are likely to divide into two parts: If and when the Spanish Americans and Mexicans lose their cultural identity, those of the more Caucasoid type will become a part of our class order and be capable of rising in our social hierarchy. The darker ones will probably become semi-caste. There is some evidence that it may be possible that this latter group will merge with the Mongoloid or Negroid groups. There is also fragmentary evidence which indicates that some of the Mongoloid groups may merge into the other dark-skinned castes.

The future of American ethnic groups seems to be limited; it is likely that they will be quickly absorbed. When this happens one of the great epochs of American history will have ended. . . .

Paradoxically, the force of American equalitarianism, which attempts to make all men American and alike, and the force of our class order, which creates differences among ethnic peoples, have combined to dissolve our ethnic groups. Until now these same forces have not been successful in solving the problem of race. The Negro and other dark-skinned groups are still ranked as color castes. . . .

EDITORIAL COMMENT

In the acculturation of American minority groups, no institution can be given more credit than the public school. For the Indians and Negroes, notable roles were once played by such agencies as the boarding school and the Freedman's Bureau respectively. During the period of "new" immigration beginning with the 1880's, vast numbers of adult immigrants from central, southern, and eastern Europe learned the rudiments of English and civics in "night schools" and "Americanization" programs.

Today in the case of all types of minority groups, schools provide the setting for the continuing acculturation of children. The question that public school educators have long asked and sought to answer is concerned with the identification of the variables associated with successful and unsuccessful acculturation. One of these basic variables discerned in relation to acculturation is social class, and it is this relationship that Allison Davis discusses in the reading that follows.

41. ACCULTURATION IN SCHOOLS
BY *Allison Davis* *

ACCULTURATION, which is the process of learning a culture different from that of one's parental family, is the chief problem of the ethnic, and of the lower-class white and Negro pupils in our schools both in learning and in personality development. An individual adolescent, born and socialized in Mexico, Italy, or China, undergoes acculturation when he learns American habits and values. Similarly, a native-born white or Negro child of inferior economic status undergoes acculturation when he begins to learn the culture of the school, for this culture is generally different from that of the lower-class child's own family. The culture of the school is [almost] everywhere middle class.

Acculturation includes both group and individual processes of cultural change. In the first sense, a Mexican or Sioux community undergoes acculturation when it changes its culture from a basically non-European to a basically European body of socially approved techniques, symbols, acts, and understandings of acts. In the second sense, an individual immigrant to California, born and socialized in Mexico or China, experiences acculturation when he learns [dominant] American cultural habits. . . .

BASIC VARIABLES IN ACCULTURATION IN SCHOOLS

In general, both the acculturation of the subordinate group and its participation with the dominant group in public schools are found to be most successful when:

the minority group of pupils is of approximately the same social-class level as the dominant group of pupils;

the minority is relatively small, constituting at the very most not more than 25 per cent of the school population;

the minority group came from the middle-class in its original home;

it has been in America a relatively long time;

it came from the same kind of community (*i.e.,* rural or urban) as that in which it now lives.

Social Classes and Cultural Behavior

To understand the pupils who come from the segregated ethnic communities, one must understand the cultures in which they have been

* From Hilda Taba and William Van Til (eds.), *Democratic Human Relations* (Washington, D.C.: The National Council for the Social Studies, 1945), pp. 266, 271–9. Reprinted by permission.

reared. Within each of these ethnic groups, however, there are several social strata. For the Anglo American, this fact should be the basic premise of all his evaluations of "Mexican," "Negro," or "Chinese" behavior. He must realize from the beginning of his work that there are several social classes of Mexican Americans, for example. Nothing discourages the average middle-class member of such groups so much as to be identified culturally with lower-class people of his group. In his culture, in his ambitions for his children, in his basic values and morals, he is cut to the same pattern as the middle-class Anglo American. He resents any effort to identify his behavior or goals with those of lower-class people.

The worst mistake, for example, which a teacher or administrator of the dominant group can make in his relationships with Mexican Americans is to assume that all Mexican Americans are similar in their educational goals and basic cultural pattern. Nor should he assume, as he often appears to do, that the Negro or Mexican pupil who leads his class or the student congress is a "sport" or "exception." The chances are overwhelmingly strong that he is the product of a middle-class home, where the parents exert powerful stimuli for school achievement. He is a middle-class child culturally. In most respects, he is the product of the same type of cultural environment which produced his teacher. This social-class motivation is the chief factor in the school behavior of the "good" and "ambitious" pupil. It is what the teachers constantly refer to obliquely, when they say that pupil "A" is a good student because he comes from "a good family."

Ethnic groups such as Mexican Americans or Italian Americans [often] undergo a marked social and psychological conflict in the process of acculturation in American habits. In . . . such cases, the ethnic culture and the American culture have unequal status or rank, in the eyes of both the American and the "foreigner." The Mexican culture, for example, gradually loses prestige with Mexican-American immigrants themselves. They come to prefer American culture, even when they cannot learn it. Their children not only prefer it, but are very likely to become ashamed of their parents' foreign culture. They learn to regard it with a certain feeling of social inferiority, especially when they reach high school, and become somewhat familiar with middle-class American standards.

"MEN OF TWO CULTURES"

It must be remembered always that the Italian, Polish, Mexican, or Chinese American, and to a lesser degree the lower-class white or Negro who is trying to become middle-class, are men of two cultures, having conflicting dogmas, values, and prestige. In this sense Robert E. Park described those who are undergoing acculturation as "marginal" men.[1] The basic conflict of the men of two cultures is that their two cultures have unequal prestige in the eyes of many.

[1] Robert E. Park, "Human Migration and the Marginal Man," *The American Journal of Sociology*, May, 1928, p. 893.

The Mexican, or Polish, or Italian American, as well as the lower-class white or Negro [often] comes to think of his original culture as inferior, and of the other culture as superior. This general characteristic of "second generation" groups is abundantly illustrated both in scientific studies and in autobiographical accounts.

ACCULTURATION OF LOWER-CLASS PUPILS

. . . Since the economic, occupational, and social goals of lower-class parents are quite different from those of middle-class people, the underprivileged child receives little stimulation or training for successful school work. The child sets his goal a little beyond that of his relatives and neighbors of the older generation. When he has bettered their mark, his prestige drive is extinguished. A great many white junior high school pupils in underprivileged areas in California answered the question on a written schedule, "Do you want to become an educated person?" with a negative. Their reasons were often realistic for a member of their communities and culture.

Because the parental and familial culture of the underprivileged group differs sharply from that of the middle class, the child finds his culture in conflict with that of the school which is . . . everywhere strongly middle class. The complaints of administrators and teachers in schools in lower-class areas in California, recently studied by the writer, were always the same, no matter whether white, Negro, or Mexican American was the low-status group in question. The first thing one was told invariably was that they were dirty and aggressive, in that order. . . . Children especially and some immature adults certainly make a persistent psychological association of dark color with dirt.

The list of group traits of the underprivileged pupil that the school constantly attacks in a headlong and generally uncomprehending manner, is as follows:

1. "Dirtiness"
2. Uncouth and aggressive language, cursing
3. Fighting
4. Ganging
5. Sexual precocity (from the middle-class age-norms)
6. Marring school property
7. Wearing "zoot suits," "severe drapes," earrings, high pompadours, heavy rouge or lipstick, and other types of clothing and make-up associated with groups of low status.

Thus the criticisms made by teachers of lower-class pupils are directed at violations of the basic middle-class controls against uncleanliness, verbal and manual aggressiveness, early sexual relations, lack of respect for property, and against certain lower-class symbols. . . .

With regard to psychological traits, lower-class pupils of all groups are thought by teachers to have, with very few exceptions, low intelligence—here the I.Q. is always immediately cited by the teachers as an ultimate measure of intelligence—and little "ambition."

One of the chief methods used by the public schools to freeze the social status of pupils is, as Warner, Havighurst, and Loeb have shown,[2] to assign them to curricula which lead to different levels of opportunity. The consequence of this sorting of pupils by the administrators is that many of these minority group members, especially those who are Negroes, remain unskilled, common laborers, although they have a high school education. For example, in the vocational curricula of the secondary schools, as administered in parts of California, there are serious handicaps to minority groups. To cite a specific case, one of the largest technical high schools has a policy of restricting pupils of certain minority groups to certain trades. The vice-principal of this school reported that Negro and Mexican American boys were steered away from the mechanical trades because they had "no ability" in these fields. He added that there was "no opportunity" for them in machine-shops, but admitted upon questioning that these restrictions were not entirely predictable in our society because war plants were then accepting workers from these groups. It was clear also that the pressure of labor unions upon the schools was involved in the vice-principal's decisions; he said, for example, that he discouraged Jews from studying printing because the local printing-trade unions would not accept Jewish members. . . .

The "maid's work" courses and the "remedial classes," both completely segregated usually, generate and maintain strong resentment to the public schools on the part of the Mexican American communities. . . . They [and other minority groups] wish training for their children that will give them a chance to compete with other American youngsters for industrial and white-collar jobs. Like all other groups in this country, they are unwilling to have their children educated solely for unskilled labor and domestic service. Certainly it is not the duty of the public schools to take the responsibility for freezing the occupational roles of ethnic and racial groups. The increasing complexity of the economic and social life of minority groups now demands a variety of types of education. . . .

EDITORIAL COMMENT

The final topic in this section on minority group reactions and adjustment is intermarriage, sometimes referred to as mixed marriage. Here is a phenomenon obviously dependent upon assimilation and directly related to other processes in intergroup relations as well. To many sociologists, intermarriage itself is the most significant process of all, for it presumably provides a precise index

[2] W. L. Warner, R. J. Havighurst, and M. B. Loeb, *Who Shall Be Educated?* (New York: Harper, 1944).

of trends in attitude, behavior, and possibility in dominant and minority group interaction.

Some Americans have even been willing to see intermarriage as the ultimate solution to problems in intergroup relations. If the process were to go far enough there would in fact no longer be any distinctive groups for intergroup relations. Ironically, however, others look upon intermarriage not as a solution but as a new social problem.

The following survey of research accomplishments and prospects includes a systematic consideration of these diverse significances and interpretations of intermarriage.

42. RESEARCH ON INTERMARRIAGE—
A SURVEY OF ACCOMPLISHMENTS
AND PROSPECTS BY *Milton L. Barron* *

PERIODICALLY since the end of World War I, American sociologists and their academic cousins, the demographers, have been exhorting each other to engage in research on a neglected aspect of human relations—intermarriage. In a multi-group society like the United States, they have maintained, the study of intermarriage may provide a precise, quantitative measurement of such vital and related sociological questions as the process of assimilation, the degree of internal cohesion in individual racial, religious and ethnic groups, and the extent of social distance between groups of these types.

But there have been other reasons for the attraction of social scientists to the analysis of intermarriage. Of interest to them is the considerable number of American people who have not adopted Israel Zangwill's romantic notion [1] that America is God's crucible, that the new society's complex ingredients should blend eventually by intermarriage into a race of supermen, combining the virtues of all races, creeds and nationalities. Indeed, many Americans today look upon the practice as a threat to their social values and way of life rather than as a panacea for their tensions in intergroup relations. For example, Gunnar Myrdal [2] found that most

---

* From Milton L. Barron, "Research on Intermarriage: A Survey of Accomplishments and Prospects," *American Journal of Sociology,* LVII (November 1951), 249–55. Reprinted from the *American Journal of Sociology* by permission of The University of Chicago Press.
[1] *The Melting-Pot* (New York: Macmillan, 1909).
[2] *An American Dilemma* (New York: Harper & Bros., 1944), 60–61.

Southern whites place the taboo on racial intermarriage in the highest rank among the various parts of their concern about the maintenance of the status quo between themselves and Negroes. Roman Catholic spokesmen in this country continually deplore "mixed marriage" with non-Catholics, and Protestant clerics are becoming increasingly vociferous not only in opposing such marriages but also in pointing to the Roman Catholic policy therein as an important issue in the struggle for power between the Catholic Church and other religious groups. Perhaps the best indication of Jewish anxiety about the "problem" is its popularity as a theme in plays and novels by and about Jews, especially and possibly significantly in terms of causation—in times of social disorganization like World Wars I and II. Ever since the astonishing response to Anne Nichols's comedy about Abraham Levy's marriage to Rose Mary Murphy during the armistice of the first war [3] there has been a steady procession of other works, some of them more prominent than others.[4]

Sociologists may well ask themselves why so many Americans consider intermarriage to be a social problem. A tentative answer is that the practice is a grave threat to the people's values of identity, homogeneity and survival. As one writer sees the menace in operation with reference to Jews: "The one great factor, making for group survival, is the ability to keep offspring within the group. As between two or more groups, intermarriage is forever a source of danger to the less favorably situated group, since the younger generation is usually anxious to escape the inherited hardship. The severance of relations favorable to exogamous marriage thus becomes the desideratum of every minority. . . ." [5] Not infrequently the problem-mentality of those resistant to the practice, especially clergymen, is expressed in terms of "culture conflict," a concept borrowed from the social scientists. Intermarriage, it is maintained, should be avoided because conflict almost invariably results between culturally disparate mates and harmfully affects their children. The validity of this claim will be weighed in a subsequent section of this article. At this point it is appropriate to suggest that there are two flaws in such a rationalization for resistance. First, there are occasionally only nominal differences at the most between intermarrying mates. Secondly, important cultural differences often stratify husbands and wives, let us say, of the

---

[3] *Abie's Irish Rose* (New York: Samuel French, 1924) was the stage play. In 1927 it was published as a novel by Harper. Subsequently it became a movie film, and more recently it has been a radio serial presented weekly by one of the major broadcasting networks.

[4] Some of the better known novels dealing with Jewish-Gentile intermarriage have been Gwethalyn Graham, *Earth and High Heaven,* (Philadelphia: Lippincott, 1944); Sholem Asch, *East River* (New York: Putnam, 1946); Norman Katkov, *Eagle At My Eyes* (New York: Doubleday, 1948); and Myron Brinig, *Footsteps on the Stair* (New York: Rinehart, 1950).

[5] Julius A. Leibert, "Somatic Jews," *Liberal Judaism,* XIII (December 1945), 56–60.

very same religious affiliation. Yet few priests, ministers and rabbis preach caution or refuse to officiate at such technically non-mixed marriages.

What have American sociologists and demographers learned about intermarriage? Their research findings may be organized and summarized as follows:

1. *Causal factors.* What are the social and psychological forces which induce intermarriage? Studies in New York City, Los Angeles, Burlington, Woonsocket, New Haven and Derby [6] have shown that an unbalanced sex ratio and numerically small representation lead some groups into considerable incidence of intermarriage. But even more important, in contrast to the theme of "America divided" expressed by most writers on intergroup relations, is that in this immigrant-receiving society our heterogeneous groups have developed cultural similarities and social proximity to a surprising extent. For example, residential propinquity, a well-known factor in courtship, not only because of the premarital contacts facilitated but also because of the economic and cultural similarities implied, is found to be an important correlate of intermarriages as well as inmarriages. Our communities' ecological areas are not homogeneous with regard to race, religion and nationality.

Premarital studies also indicate that young people of diverse groups are led into marital ties through economic propinquity and similarity, both occupational and spatial; by close association and common experiences in the amount, type and locale of education, and by recreational contacts. Indeed, the high degree of similarity in economic and educational status of those who intermarry lends support to the prediction of the ultimate emergence of clearly defined ingroups and "consciousness of kind" along these lines.

Religious and racial intermarriages also occur today because of the inefficacy of institutional control by church and state. Historical as well as contemporary evidence demonstrate that churches and synagogues cannot effectively curb religious intermarriage in societies where church and state are separate and civil marriage, accordingly, is an alternative to a clerical ceremony. As far as racial intermarriage is concerned, the point is perhaps best made by way of illustration. There were cases of such marriage in California long before October 1, 1948, the date when that state's law prohibiting the practice was ruled unconstitutional by a decision of the State Supreme Court. In short, easy social contact and a cultural common denominator negate much of the prohibitive impact of institutional control.

But that is not all. Sociologists also have several hypotheses to explain why intermarriage occurs which need to be tested in future empirical studies. It is proposed that post-adolescence and the premarital years con-

[6] Comparison of the findings may be found in Milton L. Barron, *People Who Intermarry* (Syracuse: Syracuse University Press, 1946), pp. 251–323.

stitute an age of rebellion against the more conservative values of parents, which, coupled with the conflict between generations and the emancipation from family control brought on by extramural and secular experiences in education and the economy, are conducive to intermarriage. For many young Americans the cultural relativity with which they are indoctrinated in public school systems and the psychological association which they develop between the intermarriage taboo and "backwardness" are also conceivably significant in this context. A likely explanation is to be had too in the individualistic choice of a marriage partner embedded in the "romantic complex" of American culture. And lastly, one must consider the roles of self-hatred among many members of minority groups and the drive toward upward social mobility, both of which may find expression in marriage outside the group.

2. *Patterns.* A second type of research activity has centered upon patterns of incidence and selection. Which groups tend to intermarry more than others? Which groups are selected most frequently by other groups? And what are the dynamics or trends of incidence and selection in intermarriage over the years? Sociologists who pose these questions in their community studies generally find that intermarriage occurs most often between ethnic groups, less often between religious groups and least between racially defined groups. This, of course, is not only useful in terms of evaluating the relative cohesive strength of group types, but it is suggestive of possible realignments in the structure of American society.

Unquestionably the most valuable sociological study in this connection was made by Ruby Jo Reeves Kennedy in New Haven.[7] Marriage records in that community for 1870, 1900, 1930 and 1940 were analyzed, and over each time interval there was found to be an increase in the percentage of those intermarrying from most—*but not all*—groups. The proportion of Protestants intermarrying with non-Protestants and Roman Catholics with non-Catholics for example, declined slightly over the last measured decade. This is more important than it may seem to the casual observer, largely because it disrupts the armchair, speculative idea that intermarriage relentlessly increases in the dimension of time in a smooth, unbroken pattern. It supports the contention that no mystical force pushes any aspect of intergroup relations in a single direction.

The most interesting pattern discovered by Dr. Kennedy is rhetorically mentioned in the title of her article. Negro-white intermarriages in New Haven have been practically nonexistent on the one hand. Ethnic groups, on the other hand, have intermarried at a very high rate, but not indiscriminately. Rather they have tended to intermarry within the confines of the apparently hardening lines of religion. Catholic nationalities have intermarried with other Catholics; Protestants have chosen other

---

[7] "Single or Triple Melting Pot? Intermarriage Trends in New Haven," *American Journal of Sociology,* XLIX (January 1944), 331–39.

Protestants; and Jews, probably in large part because their religious and ethnic characteristics coincide, have married Jews. Thus we have had the pattern of the "triple melting-pot."

The need for further research on this aspect of intermarriage is obvious. The communities studied so far have been few in number, mostly concentrated on the Eastern Seaboard. It is important that we get a more adequate regional coverage. Secondly, many more studies are needed on the dynamics of intermarriage. Are second and third generation Americans intermarrying more than their first generation parents and grandparents elsewhere than New Haven? Thirdly, studies of intermarriage incidence and selection must keep within reasonable distance of the ever-changing calendar. It is absurd in terms of time as well as place to assert that "Americans intermarry" according to a pattern of a triple melting-pot when all we really know is that residents of one community, New Haven, were demonstrating such a pattern ten years ago.

3. *Consequences.* The third and last major kind of research on intermarriage has dealt with the consequences of the practice in family life. How do intermarried mates and their children fare in numerical size, personality development and interpersonal relations, religious affiliation and participation, and success or failure as measured by the criteria of divorce, desertion and separation?

The fragmentary research of this sort so far has been concerned mainly with religious intermarriage and will be summarized below. First, one should be reminded that such research has been challenged by the vested interest, social myopia and wishful thinking of many laymen. To be sure, few but racists and fundamentalist zealots now argue against intermarriage on the grounds of detrimental biological consequences. But there are numerous people who insist on a consequence of overwhelming doom for those who intermarry in social and cultural matters. For example, at the annual conference of the Rabbinical Council of America in January, 1950, Rabbi Israel Tabak of Baltimore, then president of the Council, contended that such marriages are 90 per cent unsuccessful and that they "undermine the stability of the home, increase the number of unhappy marriages and bring children into the world with a rift in their souls which can never be healed." [8]

Very unusual and seemingly more objective and realistic is a recent statement by another rabbi: "There are many Jews who . . . deprecate mixed marriage on simple practical grounds. Marriage, they argue, involves at best many problems and difficulties. Why complicate it still more? Why enter on a union with a reduced chance of success? This would be an impressive argument if we should show that a majority, or even a dangerously high percentage, of intermarriages are failures. We do not, in fact, have reliable statistics; nor do we have a satisfactory way of measuring success in marriage. . . . Everyone knows of successful inter-

[8] *New York Times,* January 31, 1950.

marriages, and they are not so rare as to be labeled startling exceptions." [9]

Another preliminary to the results of empirical studies concerning intermarriage consequences is in order. It is the review of relevant theory formulated by specialists in the field of marriage and the family. For the most part they have assumed that extreme differences in background should foster marital discord rather than rapport. They have suggested, for instance, that the element of mixture is a focal point for conflict in some cases of intermarriage in that it becomes the scapegoat for tensions which originate elsewhere in the marital relationship; it is an easy substitute explanation for a couple's poor adjustment in, let us say, financial affairs. At the same time, however, the theorists have maintained that the consequences of any marriage depend upon the total situation, and not merely upon the fact of mixture. That is, a marriage's inner solidarity is affected not only by its various parts but also by the influences of those with whom the couple has had and continues to have social ties. Theoretically, no type of marriage contains within itself the germs of its own inevitable failure. Success or failure depends upon total adjustment rather than upon the mere elements of difference.

Accompanying this theory pertinent to the husband-wife relationship in intermarriage there is the theory regarding the children of such marriage. Most prevalent is the notion that lack of adequate identification and the status of marginality and outcaste are the burdens they must bear. At least one sociologist has speculated that in order to avoid the situation, one adjustment probably at work in society is the greater exercise of birth control so that the number of children born of such marriages is less than the number born of "pure marriages." [10] For those religiously intermarried couples who do have children there are known to be several alternative adjustments. An early European practice sanctioned by law in some countries and transplanted informally to the United States is for the boys to follow the religion of the father and the girls that of the mother. Another practice is for all members of the family—parents as well as children—to assume the religious affiliation of one of the parents. Still another is for one parent and all the children to join one denomination while the other parent remains in his own. Next is the "compromise" alternative—that is, the parents become members of a neutral religious body like the Universalists or Unitarians and raise their children accordingly. Idealists try one of two other alternatives: either the children are exposed to both of the parents' divergent faiths, or they plan to allow their children to make up their own minds when they reach the age of discretion.

Occasionally the problem of religious identification of children of

---

[9] Bernard J. Bamberger, "Plain Talk About Intermarriage," *The Reconstructionist,* XV (December 1949), 10–14.

[10] M. C. Elmer, *The Sociology of the Family* (Boston: Ginn and Co. 1945), 195.

intermarriages comes before the courts, and in two of such cases recently important precedents may have been established. A test case in Texas was concerned with the legal validity of that part of the Roman Catholic Ante-Nuptial Contract and Promises signed by the non-Catholic in a "mixed marriage" which states "that all children, both boys and girls, that may be born of this union shall be baptized and educated solely in the faith of the Roman Catholic Church, even in the event of the death of my Catholic consort. In case of dispute, I furthermore, hereby fully agree that the custody of the children shall be given to such guardians as to assure the faithful execution of this covenant and promise.". . . The decision in court was that the promises signed are not valid in law; they are only binding in "good faith."

The second case was in New Jersey and dealt with the question of the religious affiliation of children of "mixed marriages" in the event of a divorce. The mother, a Jewess, had married and divorced a Roman Catholic. There were two children of the marriage, a ten year old son and a 5½ year old daughter, the mother insisting on raising them as Jews, the father insisting on his religion. The Court of Errors and Appeals decided in the mother's favor after the father had contended that the right to control religious training is vested exclusively in the father. The court rejecting this, cited the state law that each parent has an equal right in the matter, and noted that in the divorce case the custody of the children had been awarded to the mother. Therefore she had the right to raise the children in the religion she saw fit.

What systematic and empirical data has sociological research uncovered about the consequences of intermarriage? The most fruitful study was conducted a short time ago by Judson T. Landis at Michigan State College.[11] For three years Dr. Landis had collected information on their parents' marriages from the students in marriage lecture sections, such as age when married, occupation, education, religion, present marital status, whether either parent changed his or her religious faith at or after marriage, which parent took the responsibility for providing religious training, how much conflict over religion had been evident to the children, and the eventual faith taken by the children, the students themselves.[12]

Of the 4,108 families whose histories were thus analyzed, it was discovered that almost two-thirds of the parents had inmarried as Protestants, 573 families had parents inmarried as Catholics, and in 346 cases there had been intermarriage between Catholics on the one hand and 305 Protestants and 41 persons of no religious faith on the other. In 192 of these

[11] "Marriages of Mixed and Non-mixed Religious Faith," *American Sociological Review,* XIV (June 1949), 401–7.

[12] The study's significance has two restrictions. It does not reflect a cross section of the American population, but rather it represents the background of young people in college in the Midwest. Secondly, because of the method used in collecting the data, the results shed light only upon intermarriages in which there are children. A study of childless intermarriages would probably show different results.

346 intermarriages, each spouse retained his or her own religious affiliation after the marriage; in 113 of the cases either the Catholic or the Protestant changed to the faith of the other.

What about the comparable divorce rates of the inmarrying and inter-marrying parents? [13] The rates were lowest in non-mixed Catholic marriages; next came non-mixed Protestant marriages; higher were the rates in Catholic-Protestant intermarriages, and highest of all was the percentage of divorce in marriages involving a partner with no religious faith. Analysis showed that the Catholic-Protestant intermarriages had a better chance to avoid divorce when one mate—particularly the Protestant wife or the Catholic husband—changed to the faith of the other mate. Further analysis showed that it made a difference to the divorce rate whether the mother was Catholic or Protestant in the intermarriage. There were three times as many divorces in intermarriages between a Catholic man and a Protestant woman as there were in cases in which the husband was Protestant and the wife Catholic.

Landis's explanation for this significant differential is that fewer factors make for tension in intermarriages in which the mother is Catholic. This is because the mother-role and Roman Catholicism are more likely to be "constants" or inflexible; the father-role and Protestantism, on the other hand, are more likely to be "variables" or flexible. Consider, for example, the serious question about the religious training of the children. "In the American home," Landis observes, "the mother is more likely to be a church member and is more apt to take the responsibility for the religious instruction of the children. When a man who has no faith or is a Protestant marries a Catholic woman, he signs the ante-nuptial agreement and does not find it difficult to abide by the agreement when his children are born. He expects his wife to be responsible for their religious training. There is then no great cause for conflict in this type of a mixed marriage. If the mother is Protestant the marriage seems to have many more serious problems. The Protestant mother has agreed that the children will be baptized Catholic, and yet she can hardly bring up her children in a faith which she herself does not accept. Since the major responsibility for religious training falls upon her, she will probably bring the children up in the only faith she knows and believes in. This means that the agreement made before marriage must be scrapped. The Catholic husband is more apt to be a church member than the Protestant husband who marries a Catholic. It may be quite a blow to him to find that his wife will not have the children baptized into his faith. Conflict results since many Catholic fathers cannot give up without a struggle. The Catholic father not only has

---

[13] Professor Landis acknowledges that the divorce rate is not an accurate index of marital success or failure. This may be illustrated by low divorce rates in cases where the wife is Roman Catholic and yet the situation is unhappy for her. Inasmuch as three out of four divorces are granted to women in the United States, a devout but unhappy Roman Catholic wife cannot take the initiative toward divorce, whereas most unhappy Protestant wives are free from any dogmatic restrictions to do so.

his own conscience to live with but he is also constantly aware of the attitude of his church and of his family when they see his children being brought up in the Protestant faith."

How were the children of Landis's study actually brought up? First, the data showed that Elmer's previously mentioned theory of intermarriage adjustment by limitation of offspring is substantiated. The students whose parents had intermarried had fewer brothers and sisters than those whose parents were non-mixed. Catholic women married to Protestants had had 2.2 children; Protestant women married to Catholics, 1.9; both Catholics, 3.6; and both Protestants, 2.7. The most common tendency was for the children, especially daughters, to follow the faith of the mother, this being the case for approximately 75% of the girls as compared with 65% of the boys. This is consistent with the students' description of the parental responsibility for religious training in their homes. The most frequent policy was that "mother took all responsibility for the religious training"; the second in frequency was that "our parents told us about both faiths but let us decide for ourselves when we were old enough."

Conspicuous by their absence in Landis's study as well as in other studies are data about the consequences of Jewish-Gentile intermarriages. However, before we can rest assured about the adequacy of our knowledge about the consequences of the intermarriage process, sociologists must also meet the challenge to do more research on a larger sampling of socio-economic groups in our society than that implied in the college level. They must pursue studies of intermarriage among those people who are childless; they need to interview cases of intermarriage in order to check on their statistical analyses. More needs to be known, too, of the degree or lack of acceptability of intermarried couples by the individual's family of orientation. Other studies should be made of inmarriages and intermarriages which have not ended in divorce or separation in order that we may determine success or failure in terms of other meaningful standards. And there is a call for research on intermarriages between members of different Protestant denominations and sects, in which cases the problems of adjustment may often be as great as those between the major religious affiliations of Catholic, Protestant and Jew.

One final task confronts American sociologists. It is to bring to the attention of laymen the inconsistency of their conservative attitudes toward intermarriage on the one hand with their activities on the other hand in creating social and cultural conditions favoring intermarriage. Sending children to public schools and to centres of higher education away from home; the struggle against restrictive covenants, job discrimination and quota systems; participation in interfaith activity are but a few practices which lead inevitably to intergroup contacts that sometimes become love and intermarriage. The recognition of this dilemma is a fundamental beginning to any intelligent approach to the problem.

XI. Toward Intergroup Harmony and Equality

FINDING the solutions to problems in intergroup relations is no longer regarded as the prerogative of the minority groups themselves. Along with the conviction that prejudice and discrimination are costly to everyone, not only to minorities, the formulation of goals and techniques and the implementation of action programs gradually have come to be responsibilities shared by all.

What are the ultimate goals or aims of action programs in intergroup relations? What should be the goal? In fact, what is intergroup "harmony"? On these questions there is no agreement, for at least five different goals are discernible: homogeneity, tolerance, cultural pluralism, peace, and equality.

Similarly, there are differences of opinion about what techniques and programs are most effective in reaching these goals. Until evaluations and action research give us better answers, we shall go on employing a variety of techniques. According to Goodwin Watson, one classification for these techniques is the following seven-fold scheme.

First there is *exhortation,* including such activities as the commemorations of Good Will Week, Brotherhood Week, posting placards and slogans based on such themes, and using the mass media of communication for conveying one's message. The second type of action, intercultural *education,* includes both the dissemination of knowledge and the reorientation of unfavorable emotional and attitudinal tendencies. Third, there is *participation,* covering the "get acquainted" programs wherein members of different ethnic groups exchange visits and participate in intergroup contact of a more permanent nature in residential and work propinquity. *Revelation,* the fourth type of action program, is the disclosure of such things as the sources and backers of hate movements, the findings of surveys on community relations, publications available, etc. Fifth is *negotiation,* the type of action in which middle-of-the-road personnel serve as mediators in the conflict between dominant and minority groups. In *contention,* the sixth type of program, militancy is the keynote; through their leadership, minorities demand, insist, and struggle. *Prevention,* the seventh, is action that meets the problems of intergroup tension before the symptoms become more acute. It includes such programs as predicting areas of potential conflict through "race-tension" barometers, periodic polls on intergroup problems, training public officials such as the police to minimize their own prejudices, and removing general sources of frustration through the provision of better employment, housing, recreational, and educational facilities. The latter suggests another type of action, *legislation* and its corollary results—executive orders and litigation—all of which are operative toward equality of treatment and opportunity.

In the selection that follows Robin Williams considers the five different goals of action programs, the causal assumptions upon which they stand, and the two major avenues through which the techniques for improving intergroup relations can operate.

43. BASIC ASSUMPTIONS AND PRINCIPAL TECHNIQUES IN INTERGROUP ACTION PROGRAMS BY *Robin M. Williams, Jr.**

RECENT years have brought a striking increase in the number and activity of organizations working in the field of intergroup relations. . . . When to all these are added the many other groups and agencies which deal with or affect intergroup relations without having this as their central or explicit purpose, the multiplicity of efforts to "do something about" the problems sensed is a most impressive aspect of the current scene. Millions of dollars are being expended annually in direct attempts to influence intergroup relations, while thousands of people give their energy and talent to the work of organizations in this field. The amount of activity is eloquent testimony to both the recognized urgency of the problems and the amount of good will and civic concern which can be mobilized for action.

Existing organizations exhibit a wide variety of philosophies, aims, strategies, and technics. Johnson's classification of national agencies in race relations gives a good indication of the range:

> A classification of the 75 organizations on the basis of strategies and techniques gives the following result: 15 agencies engage to some extent in programs of action and community organization; 13 are concerned with education in the schools; 37 carry on some form of adult education program; 10 promote cultural and recreational activities; 5 act through the courts to secure legal redress; 11 engage in serious research; and 7 are active primarily in promoting legislation. These are by no means mutually exclusive functions; actually, an organization may have several functions. . . .[1]

BASIC ASSUMPTIONS UNDERLYING ACTION PROGRAMS

Research on the control of intergroup tensions requires as a first step an analysis of the underlying *goals* and *causal assumptions* upon which action is predicated. Inspection of existing programs shows that such assumptions are very frequently implicit and taken for granted, and

* From Robin M. Williams, Jr., *The Reduction of Intergroup Tensions* (New York: Social Science Research Council, 1947), Bulletin No. 57, pp. 7–19. Reprinted by permission.

[1] Charles S. Johnson, "National Organizations in the Field of Race Relations," *The Annals*, 244:118 (1946).

that it is sometimes problematic how much awareness exists as to the implications of the actions which are in fact undertaken. Often, perhaps even typically, a single agency is aiming toward several goals at the same time: It may be engaged in carrying on lawsuits, organizing intergroup conferences, preparing and disseminating propaganda, bringing pressure to bear on legislative bodies, and carrying on research. There are instances in which some of the assumptions which may be inferred from the programs in operation appear to be incompatible with the nominal objectives of the organization. Thus it may happen that an organization which states its goals in terms of increasing mutual understanding and amity is carrying out a program against discrimination sufficiently militant to increase conflict in the immediate situation, whatever its long-term results.

Every action program must assume, above all else, that through organized purposive efforts it is possible to exert an appreciable degree of control over intergroup behavior. Control is meaningful in terms of specific groups in particular circumstances, but to speak of the possibilities of "society controlling its minority problems," for example, is meaningless. What we can directly observe is the concrete behavior of particular individuals, groups, or organizations. When we ask what "we" can do about any social problem it is clear that "we" cannot refer to an abstract total society but simply to particular parts of the society. There are definite possibilities and limitations as to the control which can be achieved by any given agency or group with a certain position in the social structure, with certain funds and personnel at its disposal, with particular authority or power, with defined channels of communication, and so on. Choices of alternative methods and techniques are likely to be profoundly affected by the kind of judgments made as to the degree of control possible.

Beyond this, existing programs differ in the goals which they assume are worth while or feasible. At one extreme are those activities which seem to be guided by the assumption that the final goal is complete acculturation of different ethnic or, more rarely, racial and religious groups to one relatively homogeneous set of beliefs and behavior patterns. This orientation is historically derived from the melting-pot theory with its emphasis on "Americanization" or assimilation. Although this extreme version is much less common now than in the past, it is still manifest in some current intercultural programs. The opposite assumption visualizes a mosaic type of society in which many separate groups retain their traditional cultural characteristics and in which there is a minimum of contact among different groups; for the integration of the whole society reliance is placed on philosophies of tolerance, supported by common and interlocking economic and political interests, or on various kinds of suppression and authoritative controls. The "equal but separate" *modus vivendi* which so often has been invoked in Negro-white relations derives in part from this basic postulate. Somewhere between these contrasting points of view, so far as cultural groups are concerned, is the orientation known as cultural pluralism or "cultural democracy." Although often a vague and somewhat inconsistent position, cultural pluralism as usually represented envisions an end-situation in which (1) a considerable portion of the cultural distinctiveness of various groups will be retained, but (2) there will be extensive interaction among all groups, and (3) at least a minimal body of *shared* values and traditions will be emphasized.

Recently there has been more and more serious questioning of both the possibility of actually eradicating differences in any near future and the value of such a goal, even if it could be achieved. To many, the melting pot has begun to represent flat uniformity imposed by a dominant group. The persistence of existing cultural differences has been increasingly recognized as bound up in many ways with fundamental sources of individual and group integrity. At the same time workers in the field of intergroup relations have seen the impressive growth of extensive intergroup contacts in an industrial, urban, secular, mobile society. Intergroup problems have become less sharply localized. Physical separation of groups has become more difficult to maintain. Aside from other factors, including that resistance to any form of "segregation" which the nominally dominant American value-system encourages, these facts in themselves have cast serious doubt upon even the feasibility of a mosaic-type society. Thus, in effect, doctrines of cultural pluralism have represented a compromise solution, conscious or unconscious, of the dilemmas just sketched.

Another important axis of decision involves questions as to the relative weight to be given to the achievement of gains in group status, rights, and privileges as against the avoidance of conflict and the preservation of harmonious intergroup relations. These questions entail complex considerations of pace and timing under varied circumstances. Existing agencies have made contrasting decisions, so that we have such comparisons as that between the Congress of Racial Equality and the National Association for the Advancement of Colored People, on the one hand, and the Southern Regional Council or the Urban League, on the other. The labels of "militancy" or "gradualism" often more nearly reflect contrasting choices of pace than differences in ultimate purposes. . . .

Action requires not only a choice of goals but also a selection of means—a selection which is affected by the ends chosen but not completely determined by them. The selection of means also rests upon cause-and-effect assumptions: if *this* is done, then *that* will follow. Analysis of the specific causal assumptions which are implied in current action programs amounts to a formulation of a great many particular hypotheses. . . . Here it is necessary only to outline a few of the broadest premises which appear to operate in the selection of methods and techniques in actual programs.

1. One of the most obvious of these premises guiding strategy is, in its least sophisticated formulation, "Give people the facts and prejudice will disappear." In this crude form the assumption is rarely made explicit, yet much intercultural activity is carried on as if the proposition were accepted. A recent critique of educational programs maintains: "Perhaps the most glaring defect of intercultural education as it functions at present is that is it geared for the most part only to intellectual values. It assumes—an assumption yet to be empirically confirmed—that ignorance is the real barrier, that the truth will set men free, that the objective facts about race and race prejudice are sufficient automatically to eliminate bias and suspicion and hatred." [2] Under repeated criticisms of this sort, the claims made for the imparting of information are growing more modest, frequently taking the form of asserting no more than that "the facts will have *some* influence." Even this is sometimes qualified by indicating the need for a relatively long period and many cumulative and mutually supporting educational influences.

Insofar as it is assumed that presentation of facts will reduce intergroup prejudice, a further premise is necessary: that prejudice is unrealistic, a function of ignorance or of "distorted stereotypes," of "false pictures in the mind," of "warped social perception." For unless prejudices represent erroneous information or ignorance, the presentation of correct facts can not be expected to change the hostile attitudes.[3] An implicit belief in the efficacy of information is extremely common [4] and is often expelled in one context only to reappear in another.

In one sense the opposite of the viewpoint just mentioned is the doctrine that group prejudices are subject to reduction or elimination *only* by changing "underlying interests" or "needs." This assumption most commonly takes the form of stressing, and acting on the basis of, a belief in the dominant importance of economic competition and economic deprivation. This often underlies the efforts of those who attack intergroup problems by working for measures intended to provide greater economic security for all, to increase job opportunities for "underprivileged" elements, and so on. An extreme development of the postulate that economic interests are determinants of prejudice leads to diagnosis in terms of alleged inevitable consequences of a competitive, capital-

[2] Charles I. Glicksberg, "Intercultural Education: Utopia or Reality," *Common Ground,* 6(4):64 (1946).

[3] It does not necessarily follow, of course, that presentation of facts would be the only way to change even a prejudice which was a function of inadequate or false information.

[4] Even where there is a careful recognition of the multiple origins of prejudice, isolated statements may imply that the central element is a false stereotype which may be brought into line with the facts, which are assumed to differ from the stereotype. Thus: "The practical goal of studying prejudices is to provide a foundation for changing prejudices so as to square the stereotypes with the facts." (Ronald Lippitt and Marian Radke, "New Trends in the Investigation of Prejudice," *The Annals,* 244:176.)

istic system; the corollary program of action is then sometimes visualized as a fundamental transformation of at least some aspects of the economic and political structure. Thus it is said that prejudice is not a "moral problem" but represents an ideology maintained because of its usefulness in perpetuating a system of differential privileges. In this view prejudice can be eradicated only by altering the social structure which gives rise to "interests" that are served by intergroup hostility along the lines of religious groupings.[5]

On the other hand, among those who stress certain psychological needs as the central element in prejudice, there is sometimes a tendency to assume that direct change in the individual's emotional organization is the major effective strategy which can be employed. This psychiatric emphasis, however, has met with weighty objections when presented as an exclusive approach, e.g., limitations of time and trained personnel, the pervasive influence of group situational factors, and the consequent frequency of "relapses." At present it is not a common assumption among agencies working in the area of intergroup relations. The question of how much emphasis should be placed upon treatment of individuals' emotional needs, however, does suggest the more general question to be outlined next.

2. A second basic assumption underlying a great variety of specific techniques may be presented in two opposing formulations: that action should be directed toward (a) a direct change in values or attitudes, *or* (b) a change in those aspects of the situation which are regarded as productive of existing attitudes and behavior. Very few concrete programs are based exclusively on one or the other. With the rather elaborate specialization of agencies which has come about, part of the varying emphasis toward one pole or the other represents a kind of division of labor and not necessarily an unconditional espousal of one as the only approach. Furthermore, many groups which confine their activity largely to education and publicity are well aware of the importance of situational factors. But they often find these factors inaccessible to control under existing circumstances and so concentrate upon direct influencing of attitudes.[6] Although the choice of approaches is thus not a clear index of cause-and-effect assumptions, it is true that such opposing assumptions are made, corresponding activities are carried out in many specific situations, and definite opinions are held as to the feasibility, effects, and costs of the alternative programs. But again, the systematic evidence which would be required to reach a scientific judgment on the

[5] An almost pure example of this approach is found in Herbert Aptheker's *The Negro People in America* (New York: International Publishers, 1946).

[6] In some cases the demands of the more militant groups for "action" rather than "words" reflect a feeling on their part that many information-education-propaganda efforts are largely "ritualistic" in the sense of having little effect and of serving as a substitute for efforts to change the real situation.

merits and demerits of these alternatives for meeting a range of social situations does not yet exist.

3. "Contact brings friendliness." This is the extreme and unqualified phrasing of a general assumption manifest in a great many current activities. . . .[7] At this point we need only note that there is evidence that some kinds of contact sometimes are followed by increased mutual understanding and friendliness, and that the reverse is also true. There is a growing awareness that future action and research must define the whole context of intergroup contacts more carefully in order to arrive at practically useful specifications.

4. To what extent is it wise to focus public attention upon intergroup relations, upon the problems they represent, and upon changes or attempts to bring about changes in group relations? What are the effects of publicizing intergroup tensions and instances of hostile behavior? Should the *intergroup* character of contacts be stressed or minimized? How should hostile rumors be handled? On questions of this kind the opinions of educators and administrators range from the belief that "the best way to handle intergroup relations is to say as little as possible about them" to the policy of singling out minorities and intergroup tensions for explicit attention.[8] In its most general form the issue is that of the differential consequences of direct and publicly labeled approaches as against indirect, nonmanifest methods of influencing group relations. In actual practice the policies range from continual emphasis on intergroup labels to minimizing intergroup differences, avoiding the posing of direct issues-in-principle, relying on fait accompli techniques, and in general keeping intergroup problems from the center of attention.

Probably no other question of approach in this field has been more extensively—and heatedly—discussed than this. For all its vigor, the discussion has failed to produce definite conclusions or even an appreciable consensus of opinion. The only reasonably certain point is that no clear answer of "good" or "bad" can be expected when the question is raised in general terms; casual observation indicates that the results of alternative policies vary with the specific types of situations in which they are followed. What is needed first of all is a series of repetitive studies to determine the concomitants of particular actions, based upon assumptions at one pole or the other. Only when these studies are complete can we hope to arrive at verified general conclusions.[9]

[7] The related but not completely homologous proposition is that segregation increases the likelihood of intergroup tension and hostility.

[8] Cf. Theodore Brameld, *Minority Problems in the Public Schools* (New York: Harper & Brothers, 1946), pp. 11, 14, 30, 161.

[9] It should go without saying that these statements do *not* imply (1) that action must wait until this terminal goal has been reached; nor that (2) even the most complete conceivable program of scientific study will settle all the practical problems of policy decision in concrete cases. In the first place, circumstances are indefinitely

5. The great amount of effort currently devoted to arranging special occasions for intergroup association would hardly be expended except for the assumptions that (a) the experience changes behavior, and (b) there is a transfer of the changed behavior to other, more usual, types of situations. Thus, an interracial summer camp is presumably not an end in itself, nor is such a project likely to be undertaken exclusively for the possible symbolic values for the public at large. Inferentially, it must be believed that the participating individuals will behave in appreciably more desirable ways in future situations. Analogies from transfer-of-learning studies concerned with skills and academic subjects are not very helpful in evaluating such a belief, for the social and emotional contexts are radically different. However, as far as can be discovered, there is now no scientifically acceptable evidence on behavior transfers from various types of special intergroup contacts to other situations.

The assumptions examined thus far do not include nearly all the orientations, nor even those of widest generality, implied by current activities. Enough have been described, however, to provide the background for a brief review of specific techniques which are employed in control programs. . . .

TECHNIQUES FOR CONTROLLING INTERGROUP RELATIONS

Fundamentally, there are only two avenues through which human behavior may be controlled.[10]

First, one may operate on *the situation within which people must act,* or upon their perception of the situation, without attempting directly to alter their attitudes, sentiments, or values. The pressure for a given type of behavior then comes either from (a) revealing information which affects the way in which individuals visualize the situation," [11] or from (b) actual or potential alteration of the situation itself. In the area of intergroup relations an example of the first type of pressure would be the effective imparting of facts convincing white workers that inclusion of Negro workers in an industrial union would increase the organization's bargaining power. A hitherto unrecognized aspect of the situation might thus become a factor in changed group relations. Random examples

---

varied, and there is always need for seasoned judgment. Scientific analysis, however, can provide the data necessary for economy in decision making. Action, based on ordinary experience and reasoning, will continue; but it should have a progressively more dependable basis as research proceeds along these lines.

[10] See Talcott Parsons, "Propaganda and Social Control," *Psychiatry,* 5:551–572 (1942). A somewhat different but compatible classification is given by Charles Strother, "Methods of Modifying Behavior," *Journal of Social Issues,* 1(3):46–52 (1945).

[11] Cf. the aphorism of W. I. Thomas: "If men define . . . situations as real, they are real in their consequences." ("The Relation of Research to the Social Process," in *Essays on Research in the Social Sciences,* Washington: The Brookings Institution, 1931, p. 189)

of the second type of alteration would include penalties for intergroup aggression, or rewards for cooperation; removal of legal disabilities; economic changes resulting in greater security and lessened competition in the occupational field.

Among organizations which are primarily and explicitly working on intergroup relations, the most common type of effort to change the actual situation is probably that of arranging for social contact between members of different groups. Such arrangements are of many different kinds, ranging from special, temporary and limited contacts to continuing and intensive association. Another approach designed to change a given situation is the establishment and maintenance of special-purpose organizations within a given group. This is exemplified by attempts to divert potentially disruptive activities of adolescents into constructive channels through boys' clubs and the like. It is illustrated also by more significant organizations for defense, protest, and pressure within minority groups. A third approach directed toward actual change in situational factors is through the law and law-enforcement; in the cases of Negroes, Japanese Americans, and certain immigrant groups, legal factors are the focus of much organized effort.

The second main avenue of control is through *direct appeal to the values or attitudes of individuals,* without necessarily changing the actual or potential situation of action in other respects.[12] Here belongs much of the whole panoply of propaganda: use of shared symbols, prestige appeals, redefinition of values, affirmation of moral norms, manipulation of anxiety and guilt, etc. Direct efforts to change attitudes on intergroup relations generally fall into a few fairly distinct types:

(1) The attempt is made by various specific techniques to show that differences in the characteristics of various groups are not inevitable or biologically fixed. This has been of first-rank importance in the case of the Negro.

(2) There is the approach which minimizes the differences in values and behavior, and stresses the elements common to both parties in the conflict. Thus, for example, important common elements in the religious beliefs and practices of Protestant, Catholic, and Jewish groups may be emphasized; or rational membership and common socio-political beliefs may become the focus of attention.

(3) The range of intragroup variation is highlighted as a way of attacking categorical definitions of the situation. In this approach one assumption (explicit or implicit) is that the recognition of individual and

---

[12] "There are two methods available for meeting this problem [ethnic conflict]: first by altering the actual or potential situations in which people act; second, by appealing to the sentiments of individuals without necessarily altering the situations but by manipulating symbols, changing attitudes or influencing their 'definition of the situation.'" (Simon Marcson, "The Control of Ethnic Conflict," *Social Forces,* 24: 162.)

subgroup differences will weaken stereotypes and introduce a realistic flexibility in intergroup attitudes.

(4) Appeal is made to larger social codes, religious values, or legal precepts. Approaches in this category are almost infinitely varied, including dramatization of Constitutional rights, and affirmation of codes of fair play and other ethical precepts. To be at all effective, efforts along these lines must be based upon an adequate consensus with regard to the relevant codes among the persons to whom the "propaganda" is directed. What constitutes an adequate consensus in any particular case is often a difficult problem of fact finding.

(5) Emphasis is placed upon those achievements and qualities of members of a specific group which are rather universally esteemed and especially upon those which do not fit the group stereotype. In the case of Negroes, for example, this may involve publicity concerning achievements in literature, science, medicine, military activity, business, and other fields apart from traditional "Negro arts." Qualities of dependability, integrity, serious industry and the like may be highlighted as an antidote to stereotyped pictures of contrary qualities.

(6) The desired behavior (tolerance, cooperation, etc.) is linked with persons who are prestige symbols and the objects of mass identifications on other grounds. This approach may use any of the preceding types of appeal, but implements them by association with particular, valued personalities. So, for example, motion picture actors with whom large proportions of the population are assumed to have made identification are shown appealing for or demonstrating the behaviors which are the goal of the propaganda effort. Under some conditions this technique may result in the important by-products of weakening the presumption of group support for hostile intergroup actions. This becomes highly significant when prestige symbols are used to redefine permissive behaviors, as when persons who symbolize authority publicly act to reinforce desired attitudes or to discourage undesired behavior. Persons who represent the dicta of conscience, especially religious leaders and political officers, frequently serve this function: Pope Pius XI issues an encyclical condemning antisemitism; a minister speaks out against group hostility; the President establishes a Committee on Fair Employment Practice.

The more specific techniques which have been used by agencies concerned with promoting intergroup cooperation or with improving the status of a particular group include almost every conceivable mode of influencing human behavior. Goodwin Watson has classified these activities into seven patterns: exhortation, education, participation, revelation, negotiation, contention and prevention.[13] Three of these are primarily in

[13] In a survey for the Commission on Community Interrelations, published as *Action for Unity* (New York: Harper & Brothers, 1946). A summary may be found in the Commission's *Facts on Friction*, No. 9 (February, 1946).

the area of direct attempts to change attitudes or values—exhorting to ideal patterns, educating, and revealing new facts. Social contact across group lines (participation) represents a situational alteration which is assumed to affect subsequent behavior. The remaining patterns include both situational alterations and direct approaches to attitudinal change. . . .

EDITORIAL COMMENT

Intercultural education, one of the most popular techniques in the promotion of intergroup harmony, is built upon three assumptions. First, the divisive factors in human relations are taught and learned; therefore, intergroup rapport can also be taught and learned. Second, the development of such rapport serves an important ideal of democracy—the fullest development of all human beings. Third, the processes of developing this rapport must be designed in terms of the nature of both the individual and the social group.

One of the best-known programs in intercultural education is the Springfield Plan, named for the community in Massachusetts where it was first developed. During the 1930's, some of the school authorities in this New England industrial community of 160,000 people began to recognize that their conception of Springfield was more fiction than social fact. It was no longer predominantly Yankee and Protestant; most of the residents were now Roman Catholic Irish, French Canadians, Poles, and Italians. Others were Negroes, Greeks, Chinese, Mexicans, Filipinos, and Jews. Prejudice and most forms of discrimination prevailed in the community.

Deciding that Springfield's educational system should be more realistic and that it was false to assume that democracy had been realized, the superintendent of schools proposed action at several levels, especially in the hiring of teachers and the revision of the academic curriculum. Clyde R. Miller, long known for his interest in and contributions to intercultural education, describes briefly in the following reading some features of the Springfield Plan.

44. EDUCATION FOR FAIR PLAY—
THE SPRINGFIELD PLAN
BY *Clyde R. Miller* *

. . . IN a sense, the so-called Springfield Plan of education began as an attempt to strengthen in children and adults in one community the democratic rights and obligations—political, economic, social, and religious—threatened by the increasing prestige of Fascist successes.

The educational approach . . . represented by the Springfield Plan goes much further than the mere preaching of sweetness and light.

This approach holds that the disparity between moral preachments, so often part of a school program, and what actually takes place in the world out of the school can be lessened first by avoiding the moral clichés and secondly by practicing fair play in school and out.

Such a program involves the enlistment of the schools and of many adult community groups in a positive, continuous program under responsible leadership.

In Springfield the leadership has been in the superintendent of schools and the Board of Education. The first thing that the superintendent of schools in Springfield (Mass.), Dr. John Granrud, did, when this program started in the fall of 1939, was to appoint a committee to see what the problem was.

This committee found that biases and attitudes associated with bitterness and actual and potential violence among different groups represented forces outside the school. True, some of the teachers and other school people represented those biases and attitudes, but essentially the school mirrored an outside world.

In an imperfect world the teaching of democracy in the schools has been idealized; the world outside too often was reflected as perfect. There were Negro children and Jewish children and Catholics and Protestants and young folks with "foreign" names who knew that they were unlikely to get a fair chance when they left school. The Negro boy, so the committee reported, was well aware that in the competition for jobs he would not stand a chance with a white boy. The youngster of a foreign-sounding name often was well aware that he would not stand a fair chance for a job in competition with a youngster of Anglo-Saxon name. It was apparent that if democracy was to work better inside of a school system, it must be working better outside at the same time. This meant that the

* From Lyman Bryson, Louis Finkelstein, and Robert M. MacIver (eds.), *Approaches to National Unity* (New York: Harper & Brothers, 1945), pp. 314–20. Used by permission of Harper & Brothers.

problem of changing attitudes must be a community problem linking press, radio, church, business group, labor union, and social agencies with the schools.

In the . . . years that have elapsed since 1939, precisely this type of organization has grown in Springfield. The Council of Social Agencies and the Adult Education Council and various industrial and welfare groups worked with the schools in making realistic an approach to today's problems in neighborhoods of the city of Springfield, in the community as a whole, in the state, in the nation, and in the world.

This seems a big order. It is. It has meant during the past . . . years that, in addition to teaching as well as usual the traditional tool subjects, the schools have had to make great changes in their own teaching methods and curriculum to deal realistically with today's world outside the school.

There has been frank recognition that students must be filled with a zeal for fair play and for a rational approach to the issues which divide individuals and groups. Building this zeal has been characterized by indoctrination which begins in the nursery school. This pervades all grades through junior college and, thanks to enlightened groups, it pervades neighborhoods and the community. It has been an indoctrination for fair play; it has been continuous and community wide. After several years that community believes it is beginning to see results.

Perhaps the most interesting of the methods used at the high-school level are those involved in the study of the technique of propaganda, persuasion, and public opinion, which has been advocated by Dr. Huxley, H. G. Wells, and so many others. . . . It is the intention that before any youngster leaves high school he will know how to recognize propaganda and persuasion, how to distinguish that which is good from that which is false, how to protect himself against irrelevant facts and opinions diverting him from relevant facts and opinions in his consideration of any issue. The cliché that there are two sides to every argument is seen for what it is in these units. There may be a dozen sides.

Even in the lower grades, children are prepared for this rational approach to life's problems by a type of teaching which helps them distinguish between fact and opinion. Two plus two equals four is a fact. Helen has the prettiest dress of any girl in our third grade is an opinion. Some may think that Ethel has the prettiest dress. Seven plus six equals thirteen is a fact. Thirteen is unlucky is an opinion, and yet it is an opinion to which great newspapers, hotels, and business institutions defer.

At the teacher-training level, Springfield College has offered and will continue to offer for teachers and citizens an extension course which relates contemporary problems to the processes of persuasion with the idea of making demagogues less effective.

This course, for example, has emphasized the importance of the conditioned reflex as related to actions based on group bias. Teachers and community leaders learn that as a stimulus a red light can cause not only people but horses to stop automatically. So can a stimulus like the words Jew or Catholic or Wall Street or labor union cause people of conditioned minds to reject and condemn automatically those who are called by such names.

With the common propaganda devices, the course considers the mental processes that are involved in biases and attitudes. 1. The process of custom or tradition by which, as William James and William Graham Sumner pointed out, most of our actions, thoughts, and feelings are regulated. 2. The process of anxiety or fear which, if stimulated, can bring mental and emotional states that are not only contagious but epidemic; and the very efficacy of modern communication by press and radio has made millions of people the victims of mental diseases associated with fear. . . .

And the other processes, leadership, missionary, frustration, and rationalization—all are studied and related to today's conflicts and persuasions. Finally, emphasis is given to the importance of creative thinking or analysis or scientific approach—call it what you will—which, when coupled with good will, offers the most hope for a better world.

Springfield, of course, has borrowed liberally wherever it could. It has used its own initiative in adapting ideas and methods to conditions peculiar to the Springfield community. Other cities which have been moving in this same direction have been helped by Springfield, but they, too, have helped Springfield. Pittsburgh, Columbus, Detroit, Cincinnati, Santa Barbara, Los Angeles, Newark, Hartford—these and many other communities—[have been] working along lines briefly indicated in this report. . . .

To change attitudes quickly among large numbers and throughout the nation, it is necessary to increase the number of communities working actively for education for fair play. This is not so difficult. If even one citizen in a community sees what needs to be done and has the zeal to make a start, he can interest others. He can bring together other business men, labor leaders, school-board members, educators, ministers, civic leaders. All that is essential is that somebody does need to make a start. . . .

EDITORIAL COMMENT

While most people concede that the schools can play an important role in the reduction of intergroup tensions, few are sensitive to the crucial position of the police in intergroup relations. Ever since 1943, when so many race riots broke out throughout the country, the feeling has grown that municipal authorities and officials have a clearcut responsibility to prevent such outbreaks and to help improve relations between the groups that are found in most cities. A particular responsibility is to protect the legally prescribed civil rights of all the residents of the community, regardless of their specific group identification.

This places a burden upon police departments in an area in which they have traditionally been unprepared. Training in the tasks of prevention seems to be their chief hope for a successful role in handling problems of intergroup relations.

The professionalization of police work and its newly realized role in intergroup relations began, for the most part, on the West Coast. The authors of the following article about the role of the police are well-equipped for their task, both having specialized in police training and problems of minorities in the state of California.

45. THE ROLE OF POLICE
BY *Davis McEntire* AND *Joseph E. Weckler* *

THE RESPONSIBILITY of police in controlling group prejudice has been nowhere more positively stated than in the Report of the Peace Officers Committee on Civil Disturbances, a body appointed by the Governor of California following the "zoot suit" riots in Los Angeles in 1943. Under the chairmanship of Attorney General Robert W. Kenny of California, this Committee of eight high-ranking peace officers stated:

> The police play a vitally important role in race relations. No agency of government can be more effective in furthering good race relations and in preventing race riots than the police. *Police can prevent race riots.* Not only can they prevent such riots from occurring, but should they occur, intelligent police methods can minimize their consequences. At the same time, lax police policies contribute to race riots and antiquated methods of coping with riots can greatly aggravate their consequences.

The series of race riots in 1943 startled police departments all over the country into awareness of the dangers of racial tensions. The Di-

* Davis McEntire and Joseph E. Weckler, "The Role of Police," *The Annals of the American Academy of Political and Social Science,* 244 (March 1946), pp. 82–9. Reprinted by permission.

rector of the Federal Bureau of Investigation warned the International Association of Chiefs of Police in that year of "civil violence, race riots, and insidious campaigns against minority groups.". . . Many police departments, resolved not to be caught unprepared have formulated plans for control of "civil disturbances" or "unusual disorders" as race riots are euphemistically termed. With few exceptions, such plans relate chiefly to tactics and the efficient mobilization and utilization of police forces. The realization that "police can prevent race riots" has been of slower growth.

Prevention requires a more fundamental but less spectacular approach than the techniques of suppressing a riot. A first requisite is a professional attitude on the part of police officers toward their job and toward human relations. There are recognized police techniques for implementing a preventive policy, but they will avail little unless at least the commanding officers understand the problem and take a professional attitude toward its treatment.

ATTITUDE OF POLICE

The accepted standard of police attitude toward human relations is impartiality. Outside the Southern states, most police officers are not only committed to the principle of impartiality, but they firmly believe that they are in fact fair and impartial in their dealings with persons of different racial, ethnic, or religious groups. Recruit and in-service training schools for police emphasize justice, equality, and impartiality. Yet, as the Law Enforcement Coordinator of California has observed, police officers "often fail to realize that their prejudices make impartiality impossible. Believing, as many do, that 'Negroes have criminal tendencies' leads to unconscious discrimination." [1]

It is only natural that police recruits should share the prejudices of the population from which they come. Myrdal describes the average Southern policeman as "a promoted poor white with a legal sanction to use a weapon. His social heritage has taught him to despise the Negroes and he has little education which could have changed him. . . . Probably no group of whites in America have a lower opinion of the Negro people and are more fixed in their views than Southern policemen." [2]

Although in the North and West, professional standards of police are far higher than in the South, they are still considerably below those usually required of other public servants concerned with human relations, such as teachers and social workers. The educational requirements for

[1] Robert B. Powers, Law Enforcement Coordinator, California Department of Justice, unpublished report.
[2] Gunnar Myrdal, *An American Dilemma* (New York: Harper & Bros., 1944), pp. 540–41.

police work in most cities are not high, and in the training of police officers little attention is given, as a rule, to the human relations aspects of police work.

The police are an outstanding example of a public agency deeply involved in social problems which has made almost no use of the contributions of social science. In fact, most policemen have a lively, if uninformed, contempt for anything which smacks of "social work." The result is that the police recruit rarely receives any viewpoints or factual information which might take the place of his prejudices. Hence, the average policeman, in his dealings with members of minority groups, is likely to be guided less by knowledge than by the sterotyped conceptions prevalent among the less informed sections of the white population, from which he, himself, comes. His experiences are chiefly with the hoodlum and criminal members of minority groups and serve only to deepen and confirm his prejudices. He comes to regard Negroes, for example, as generally lazy, lustful, thieving, and bellicose; and he is likely to view the misconduct of a particular Negro as "typical Negro behavior," since he has had neither training nor experience which would teach him otherwise.

An outstanding example of stereotyped thinking by police officers is a report submitted a few years ago by a high ranking Sheriff's officer in a large western county to a Grand Jury on the extent and causes of crime among the local population of Mexican extraction. This group lived and continues to live under conditions of poverty, bad housing, segregation, and discrimination. These conditions the officer dismissed as relatively unimportant as causes of crime. The main factor, he maintained, was "biological." Mexicans, he thought, had an inherent lust for blood, an inborn desire to kill or at least let blood, which "has come down through the ages" from the times when the ancient Aztecs practiced human sacrifice. Negroes and Filipinos, the report went on to state, were governed by the same biological tendencies.

Such ideas will impress most social scientists as too fantastic even to merit rebuttal. Nevertheless, the report in question was submitted as an official report of a large Sheriff's department, with the approval of the department head. It was considered a reliable and authoritative analysis of the problem. Obviously, in so far as police officers are persuaded that the members of any group, recognizable by skin color, are biologically criminal, there is no possibility of an impartial, professional approach to the problems of intergroup relations. The standard of impartiality becomes merely a cover for prejudice when policemen are guided by ideas of racial group criminality such as those expressed in the above-mentioned report. If an officer is convinced that Negroes as a group are criminally inclined, he will see no breach of impartiality in arresting a Negro on very slight suspicion. If he believes that any Mexican or Negro suspect will try to put a knife in his back at the first opportunity, there will be nothing unfair from his point of view in a ready use of gun or club against such individuals.

MINORITY ATTITUDE TOWARDS POLICE

It is axiomatic among police officers that they must have the confidence of the public in order to do an effective job of law enforcement. They do not have, in most cities, the confidence of the minority group populations. Many Negroes look on the police as an enemy and expect to be discriminated against and mistreated if arrested. The same is, to a large extent, true of Mexicans, especially of the youth. These attitudes are rooted in the whole status of minority groups in America. Because they are subordinated and discriminated against in many ways, the police officer, as a representative of society, often appears to them as the symbol of repression.

The policeman in the South has definitely the dual responsibility of preserving the peace and preserving the caste order or keeping the Negro "in his place." The southern Negro learns through experience to appreciate the policeman for what he is, namely, the symbol and guardian of "white supremacy." When the southern Negro migrates to the North or West, he carries his acquired traditional attitude with him and sometimes it is perpetuated by his contacts with police in the new locale. The above mentioned Sheriff's report, for example, must have convinced every Negro, Mexican, and Filipino who read or heard of it that he didn't have a chance in the Sheriff's office.

The average police officer does not know that many minority group persons are deeply suspicious and afraid of him. Not knowing this, the policeman is likely to interpret the behavior of such persons in his presence as prima facie evidence of wrongdoing of some sort. If an officer is inclined to stereotyped thinking, his low opinion of minority peoples will be confirmed by behavior which he observes but fails to understand. At the same time, his prejudices, expressed in word or deed, will increase the mistrust of minority groups toward the police.

PROFESSIONALIZATION OF POLICE WORK

Basic improvement in the ability of police to work effectively in interracial situations may be expected as the professional standards of police work are raised. During the past quarter-century, as E. W. Lester, former Deputy Chief of Police in Los Angeles, has said, police work has developed "from the category of unskilled labor to a semi-profession." [3] The development of civil service systems, career service, and

[3] E. W. Lester, "Tolerance in Police Work," training lecture, Los Angeles Police Department, mimeographed.

specialized training all testify to the increasing professionalization of police work. . . . It is well known that the higher a person's educational level, the less likely he is to be blindly prejudiced toward minority groups. Hence, to raise the educational standards for police recruits would have a very salutary effect. The police officer needs not only specialized training in the technicalities of law enforcement; he needs also a broad education to enlighten his prejudices and equip him to understand human relations and the social problems in which he will be inescapably involved.

The benefits of better trained police personnel will, of course, not be limited to the prevention of racial disorders. Minority group relations are only an unusually exacting phase of a police department's public relations. If minority groups are mistrustful of police, it is also true that police generally do not enjoy the degree of public respect and confidence which they should have in order to do the best job of law enforcement. Where police departments handle the general public with professional competence, they are usually able to take minority group problems in stride. It has been the history of race riots that they have nearly always occurred in a setting of official incompetence and neglect, accompanied by widespread loss of public confidence in the police. An eminent foreign observer, noting that college training for teachers and social workers is taken for granted, suggests that "a college education should be even more urgently required for fulfilling the duties of a police officer." [4] While this recommendation may seem visionary in view of present standards, most police officers probably will agree that their responsibilities are not less important than those of teachers or social workers whose professional standards are much higher.

Raising the educational standards for police recruits is a long-term goal. The problem of preserving interracial peace is immediate and urgent. To meet the immediate problems, special in-service training for police officers has been widely advocated and in some instances adopted. Ideally, as the best that can be done in the immediate situation, such training should be extended to all police officers in any city where racial disturbances are potential. At the minimum, training should be given the commanding officers, and, in any event, it should start with them. If the commanding officers in a police department will study the problem confronting them and learn to understand it, they will be enabled to establish sound policies and to issue specific instructions for the action of policemen in specific circumstances.

THE RICHMOND PLAN

As an illustration of a practical type of in-service training in race relations for police officers, the plan adopted by the Richmond, California,

[4] Gunnar Myrdal, *op. cit.*, p. 544.

Police Department deserves special notice. Richmond is typical of the smaller West Coast communities which have been greatly expanded by an influx of war workers. Located on the east shore of the San Francisco Bay, this city became the site of major shipbuilding activity. . . . Many of the newcomers were Negroes. Racial tensions were noticeable throughout World War II, and there has been fear that they might grow more severe with postwar reduction in employment.

The Richmond police have been alert to the dangers inherent in the changed racial make-up of their city. To strengthen its preventive program against the threatening situation at the end of the war, this Department . . . carried through an intensive short course of training for a selected group of officers and is proceeding with training of its entire personnel. Comments of officers participating in the program indicate that the training has been well received and is considered valuable by the men receiving it.

The Richmond plan was developed in cooperation with the Office of the California Attorney General and the American Council on Race Relations. It provides for a combination of reading, group discussion, and expert consultation. There have been no formal lectures. Instead, the basic idea has been to center the training on concrete problems of police work as expressed by the policemen themselves, and to bring out practical solutions through round-table discussion. In accordance with this plan, the initial group of fourteen Richmond officers held five daily conferences of two hours each. Discussions were led by a social scientist from the staff of the American Council on Race Relations. Various readings on prejudice, anthropology, race riots, and police practice were assigned to be read by the officers individually and discussed in the group. Discussions were enriched by the presence at each meeting of one or more outside consultants. The latter included several high-ranking officers from the State Department of Justice and the Parole Board, themselves former police officers, and representatives of the National Association for the Advancement of Colored People and the Japanese American Citizens League, brought in to express the point of view of these minority groups.

Neither the discussion leader nor consultants attempted to dominate the conferences or force acceptance of any predetermined conclusions. Every person at the conference table stood on equal basis with the others and everyone was there to contribute and to learn. The discussion leader raised problems for discussion, encouraged the individual policemen to analyze their own experiences, and tried to help the group arrive at common judgments on the various problems discussed. The consultants were actually the "life" of the conferences. The state law enforcement and parole officials spoke with experience and authority. The minority group representatives were able to speak with equal experience and authority of the point of view of their respective groups. Few, if any, of the police officers present had ever heard the viewpoint of a minority group directly expressed by an authorized and eloquent spokesman, and it was a revelation to them. Several officers remarked that the conferences would have been more than worth while if only for the contribution of the minority group representatives.

The whole emphasis of the Richmond discussions fell on prevention. Discussion of a policeman's selfish interest in reducing racial tensions, gaining the confidence of minority groups, handling the normal incidents of police work in such a manner that they would not take on the aspect of racial incidents, and preventing racial clashes, was participated in by all present. It was generally agreed that when a race riot occurs, the prestige of the police is almost certain to suffer and the job of law enforcement is rendered much more difficult for a long time. The discussions touched on the underlying causes of racial tensions—prejudice, discrimination, the slave tradition, residential segregation, the frustration and aggressive reactions of many minority group members, and related matters. Most of the time, however, was devoted to discussing the actual problems of policemen and practical solutions. The discussion of prejudice brought the significant conclusion that prejudice is the result of ignorance and fear and a policeman cannot do his job properly if he is ignorant or frightened or both. With respect to race riots, the officers agreed that they frequently had to deal, in the normal course of their duties, with situations which contained the makings of a riot; and their handling of routine incidents had much to do with whether the riot potential declined or grew.

RESULT OF CONFERENCES

The conferences produced two significant results in addition to whatever help the participating officers may have gained directly. One was a unanimous recommendation of the officers to their chief of police for the establishment of a Human Relations Detail in the police department. On the basis that "everybody's business is nobody's business," this group of officers felt that one or two men should be specifically assigned to the investigation of racial incidents, rumors, and related duties. Another important product was a training bulletin containing the conclusions of the conferences in brief, outline form, for the study and guidance of all officers in the department.

Following the conferences, a two-hour panel discussion was presented before the entire personnel of the police department. The discussion was presented twice at different hours in order that all officers might have opportunity to attend. The panel included several of the expert consultants who had joined in the earlier conferences, together with several officers from the conference group. In this way an attempt was made to acquaint the entire force with the main conclusions of the conferences. The next step, in accordance with the training plan, was the setting up of additional small discussion groups within the department.

What Richmond did is practicable, feasible, and can be done by any police department which wants to equip its men to deal more intelligently with the law enforcement problems of race relations. Careful consideration of the type of training program developed in Richmond should go far toward overcoming some of the common objections of police officers to training in race or any other phase of human relations.

Undoubtedly, the two greatest barriers to more widespread training of this type are the aversion of the average officer to anything suggesting "social work" to his mind, and his defensive animus against "outsiders coming in to tell us how to do police work." These resistances stem partly from the general anti-intellectual bias of police at their present professional level and partly from the group-defensiveness of police, for they, too, are a minority group with many characteristics of minority group behavior. Nevertheless, it is becoming increasingly recognized that the successful police officer has to be something of a practical psychologist —he has to understand human behavior. In the Richmond program, "outsiders" and police worked together. Most of the "outsiders" were, in fact, former policemen. In group discussions, the policemen did the talking; they talked about their own problems, and they arrived at their own conclusions. An intangible but perhaps the greatest benefit of the training conferences was the increased confidence, remarked on by several observers, with which these officers approached racial problems. They felt, for the first time, that they understood the problem; it was no longer an ominous mystery, and they felt sure of their ability to deal with it.

RECOMMENDED TECHNIQUES

When once a foundation of knowledge has been laid, there are recognized techniques which any police department can adopt to implement a preventive program. The Report of the California Peace Officers Committee on Civil Disturbances contains a list of thirty-nine suggestions.[5] Among the more important of these techniques are the establishment of working liaison with organizations in the community concerned with interracial or intercultural relations, including minority group organizations; investigation and counteraction of inflammatory rumors; inclusion of members of different racial and religious groups on the police force; cooperative programs with school authorities to eliminate racial animosity

[5] See also: J. E. Weckler and Theo Hall, *The Police and Minority Groups*, Chicago: International City Managers Association, 1944; Davis McEntire in collaboration with Robert B. Powers, *Police Training Bulletin: A Guide to Race Relations for Police Officers*, Sacramento: State Department of Justice, 1946.

among school children; systematic observance of trouble symptoms; and a public relations program through the press, radio, and talks of peace officers before organized groups.

A strategic task in executing a preventive program is to win the confidence of the minority peoples. It is of no avail to condemn the minority groups for lack of cooperation with police or to attempt to fix blame on them for real or imagined shortcomings. Police must accept the fact that they are generally feared and distrusted by Negroes and other minority groups. Exceptional efforts will be necessary to develop a friendly and cooperative attitude among these groups. The absence of formal discrimination is not enough—a police department must scrutinize its practices and the attitudes of its personnel for discriminations of which they may not be aware, and then proceed with a vigorous public relations program to convince the minority groups of the department's determination to afford equal justice. Police departments will not see the necessity for this unless they have made prior study of the problem, which goes back to the basic need for training. Also, as previously noted, unless the individual policeman is made aware of his prejudices, he will be unable to act in a genuinely impartial manner. In any case, as one officer remarked during the Richmond conferences: "Good public relations are dependent not on what we are but on what the people think we are. It is a matter of reputation rather than character with which we are concerned." To help establish a desirable reputation with minority groups, police departments should make special efforts to inform the minority press of constructive police action. Special pains should be taken to give public credit when it is due to police officers who are members of minority groups. And such officers should have full opportunity for advancement within the department strictly according to their merits as policemen.

PRACTICES TO BE AVOIDED

One pitfall to be avoided is the failure, often well intentioned, of police to recognize and stay within the proper field of law enforcement. The idea is prevalent among policemen, as among white people generally, that minority groups are "all right in their place" and that it is the policeman's job to help keep them there. This is standard practice in the South. In the North and West, police often consider it their duty to keep the races apart and so they try to keep Negroes out of white areas and vice versa, sometimes refuse to issue permits for cabarets except on the assurance that there will be no mixed patronage, and look with suspicion upon any racially mixed couples or groups. Such police activities are, of course, entirely outside the proper field of law enforcement but they are usually excused as means of keeping the peace. Experience indicates, however, that arbitrary racial separation devices probably aggravate rather than ease tensions. In any case, such measures are inevitably regarded by minority groups as enforced segregation and the policeman is made to appear as the symbol of repression.

Special efforts, too, must be made to avoid what may be termed "paternalistic discrimination." Policemen frequently take the attitude that minority groups cannot be expected to observe the standards of conduct as are expected of the rest of the community. Hence, gambling, prostitution, and other vicious activities are allowed to flourish in Negro neighborhoods although they would be sternly suppressed anywhere else. This not only exposes the children and other people in such neighborhoods to an excessive risk of vicious associations, but it supports the belief among the Negro population that the police don't care about crime as long as it affects only Negroes.

CONCLUSION

The touchstone to successful police relations with minority groups lies in professionalizing police work. A really effective police officer will approach all situations with a detached point of view and an understanding of the social forces that create police problems. Such a policeman will give equal consideration to all individuals as a matter of course regardless of their racial, cultural, or religious affiliations.

EDITORIAL COMMENT

Anti-discrimination legislation, a heavily used technique in the situational control of intergroup problems, is subdivided into three types. The oldest are civil rights laws, the various state enactments forbidding any place of public resort, amusement, or accommodation to discriminate against a customer because of race, religion, or nationality. Civil rights laws began to be enacted by the states following the decision of the United States Supreme Court in 1883 that the federal government had no power to outlaw such discrimination. These laws, according to Will Maslow, have not proved very effective for five reasons: public prosecutors regard offenses in this area to be trifling and they are unwilling to prosecute unless furnished with airtight cases; the party discriminated against often prefers not to assume the burden of a profitless lawsuit; jail sentences are almost never imposed and fines are small, encouraging those subject to the laws to treat the fine as an ongoing business expense; the one powerful sanction—the suspension or cancellation of license—is generally missing from these laws; only a few states have recognized the crucial importance of enforcing a civil rights law by setting up a specialized state agency to administer it.

Group defamation laws comprise a second kind of anti-discrimination legislation, but very little is done either by the states or the federal government because the constitutional guarantees of free speech have outweighed any "clear and present" danger to society. In 1935, for example, New Jersey made it a criminal offense to circulate, publish, or utter in public any statement which "incites, counsels, promotes, or advocates hatred, violence or hostility against any group of persons . . . by reasons of race, color, religion or manner of worship." But in 1941 the Supreme Court of New Jersey declared the law unconstitutional.

The third and probably most effective kind of anti-discrimination legislation is on behalf of fair employment and educational practices. Before President Roosevelt's executive order 8802 on June 25, 1941, creating a temporary, federal Fair Employment Practice Committee, there had been very few attempts to prevent by law any discrimination in employment. This was due largely to the prevailing constitutional doctrine that the state government could only regulate those industries concerned with the "public" interest. Thus, the few state laws in existence had been directed only against discrimination in the cases of work-relief applicants and teachers or other public employees, or against discrimination practiced by public contractors and labor unions. Violation of these laws had generally been a misdemeanor. Furthermore, there was no special administrative machinery to translate the law on the books into the law in action. As a result the laws were not enforced.

The temporary, federal Fair Employment Practice Committee established in 1941 by executive order forbade discrimination in government service, defense industries, and trade unions. It required all government contracts to contain provisions obligating contractors not to discriminate. The Committee was headed by the late Bishop Francis J. Haas and it was given the power to investigate complaints, conduct hearings, make findings of fact, make recommendations, use persuasion and conciliation, and issue "directives" without sanctions. It lacked the power to proceed except on receipt of complaint; it had no power to compel witnesses to attend hearings or to produce documentary evidence. The peak appropriation it ever received was $500,000, and at no time did it employ a staff much larger than a hundred people. After World War II the Committee died for lack of congressional appropriation.

On July 1, 1945, the first state fair employment practice law was passed in New York State, establishing a state commission against discrimination. By 1955, there were eleven such state laws, differing from the executive order of 1941 in several respects. To

begin with, they were laws, not executive orders; they were meant to
be permanent, not temporary; they provided for a special agency
with sanctions for enforcement; and they were not limited to public
employment.

In 1948 New York State took the initiative once more in
enacting a fair education practice law. This law makes it an unfair
practice for a post-secondary school to discriminate against anyone
seeking admission as a student because of race, religion, or nationality. The only schools exempt by the law are religious denominational institutions, which may admit students of their own religious
affiliation and exclude others as long as they do not discriminate
on the basis of race and nationality.

In the following article, the late Bishop Haas and G. James
Fleming, both veterans of the President's Committee on Fair Employment Practice as chairman and regional director respectively,
recount some of the lessons learned by experience during the war
years.

46. STEPS TO FAIR EMPLOYMENT
BY *Francis J. Haas* AND *G. James Fleming* *

EXPERIENCE during the war years points to several steps necessary to
facilitate the full and nondiscriminatory employment of the so-called
"minority groups" into American industry, with the maximum harmony
and the least disruption of production. The numerous experiments, to be
followed by more general practice, indicate that it is possible to maintain
employment patterns without paying unfair regard to race, religion, . . .
or nationality background. These steps are:

1. *Self-education and self-conviction on the part of management and
policy-making and policy-enforcing officials.* Unless management has examined the pros and cons and convinced itself of the soundness of the
position it has taken, its next steps will be half-hearted, unsure, stupid, or
trouble instigating. The employer, it is assumed, has put himself through
something like a course of reading, conferences, round-table discussions,
and inspection trips, and of course, has not forgotten that he needs workers.
Then he reaches a favorable decision, and the policy is no longer a matter
for discussion but one to be put into effect.

2. *The taking of a firm position by management once it has decided
to adopt the new policy.* This step is very important and becomes in-

* Francis J. Haas and G. James Fleming, "Personnel Practices and Wartime
Changes," *The Annals of the American Academy of Political and Social Science,* 244
(March 1946), pp. 48–56. Reprinted by permission. Footnotes omitted.

creasingly so, as management proceeds to win support for the new program. Experience has shown, for instance, that nearly every strike by white workers against the introduction of Negroes may be traced to the lack of a firm stand by the employer or, even worse, hints by responsible management representatives that management itself was not "solid" behind the new program. Such was the case, for example, in the Packard Company strike of 1943, when 25,000 white workers staged a 7-day walkout against the use of Negroes on the production line; so, also, most certainly, in the 1944 street car tie-up by operators of the Philadelphia Transportation Company. And there are many other examples.

3. *Informing, and seeking the cooperation of the labor organization with which the company has an agreement.* By not taking the union by surprise, management is able to count on the support of the union officers and those to whom rank and file workers will turn to ascertain whether the new program is "on the up and up" or whether it is antiunion. If a union is friendly to fair employment, this step will be most fruitful; if it is not, early counseling with it will at least save management from being accused of "springing" something on the union. In many places the first suggestion to employ without discrimination has come from the unions.

4. *A program of education for workers, especially for supervisory staff, and of assurance for all workers.* All workers want to know, first of all, whether or not any new policy or practice will affect their pay, their working hours, their status, and their security. They are suspicious of whatever may look like "speed up" or "union-busting," and are likely to distrust whatever is new or altruistic when introduced by management. Accordingly the plan should not be overdone, and it should flow through the usual channels of worker education, appealing to the best motives, stressing the positive. It cannot take the place of all the other steps. It is only one of them.

5. *Careful selection first of minority group workers and careful selection then of the departments to which they are sent and the foremen or supervisors to whom they are assigned.* Acceptability is a matter of joint acquiescence, both on the part of those who are to accept and those to be accepted. The education of workers is not enough without the proper orientation of the new workers, both to their occupational responsibility and to the tradition, habits, and personality factors which must be met and overcome—and overcome in such a way as to help the general objective of fair employment.

6. *Careful follow-up and fullest integration.* Modern industry involves more than going to a workbench and going home at the end of the day. It includes everything from lavatories to rest rooms, from music at lunch time to an all-round schedule of athletics and games. The new worker should be made to feel that he "belongs" to the full activities of the firm, and the old workers should be led to see, as part of the education program,

that all privileges and opportunities are open to all. Attempts to block or cause confusion in the new policy of the company should be watched for and dealt with firmly and without compromise. Such straightforward action prevents many later headaches. . . .

RESULTS DISPROVE MYTHS AND FEARS

"Employers need only to approach the matter [of employing Negroes] practically and objectively, using the proved rules of good management practice as a guide," observes the American Management Association in its special research on *The Negro Worker*. Those who have made this kind of approach and who have been both earnest and honest have been able to overcome the worst of their fears, the record shows. They have been able to control those group prejudices which first caused employers to say, "Our workers won't stand for this."

At first, personnel men—accustomed to past traditions which excluded Negroes from certain occupations—were confused, even where they were not bitterly opposed. One investigator observed: "In the absence of any well-defined techniques for overcoming some of the objections to the use of Negro workers, personnel directors frequently found themselves confused when confronted with new and complicated situations. Likewise the selection of competent workers for training and placement often presented a difficult task for interviewers and personnel representatives."

Some personnel directors were afraid of their shadows and, instead of providing their companies with personnel leadership and direction, tried to do no more or go no further than they thought their employers would approve at first presentation. Increasingly, however, personnel men—not all by any means—have come to see that there is economic soundness in nondiscriminatory employment practices because, instead of a part of each personnel dollar being spent in finding ways *not* to employ or utilize some otherwise acceptable workers, under a regime of fair employment all of each personnel dollar is used for the exclusive purpose of employing needed workers.

Wartime experience has shown them that there are good and bad, efficient and inefficient workers among all groups, regardless of race, religion, or national origin. They have also discovered that Negroes *can* be trained and have been trained for occupations requiring all levels of skill, and covering every occupation listed in the *Dictionary of Occupational Titles*.

PERSONNEL MEN LEARN ANSWERS

Personnel officials have learned the answers to the arguments raised against employment of Negroes, along these lines:

Anti-Negro Argument 1:

Negroes have no mechanical aptitudes.

Personnel Department Rebuttal:

Thousands of Negroes completed defense courses in mechanical skills; over 100 plants reported . . . the employment of Negroes in every technical, professional, and supervisory job listed in the *Dictionary of Occupational Titles*. Negroes in the Army Air Forces were flying fighter planes in combat.

Argument 2:

Negroes and whites cannot work together (mix together).

Rebuttal:

Negroes and whites do work together as school teachers and policemen in many cities; as construction workers in others; as welders, carpenters, power drillers on street transportation systems. . . .

Argument 3:

The Negro is more susceptible to disease, has more disease.

Rebuttal:

All workers in company, regardless of race, are required to submit to medical examination; those diseased are not employed, thus all workers are equal from point of view of disease. (If no medical examinations are given, the responsible management should provide for same.)

Argument 4:

Why force Negroes on us in the factories?

Rebuttal:

The smart personnel man will always start his nondiscrimination program with employment of a Negro or Negroes in his own department or on the top management level. (Davis suggests a "neat," attractive, well-qualified Negro girl in the employment office itself.) Some personnel directors add Negro interviewers or "assistant personnel directors" to their staffs.

Sometimes an employer faced an individual employee who said: "If you employ Negroes I will have to quit this company, though I'll hate to." And the employer had to reply: "We'll be very sorry to lose you after all these years, but this is a free country and there is no way I can stop you from leaving." Usually, after that answer the white worker would return to his job and settle down to learning how to work in the same plant with Negroes.

After studying 300 plants in all parts of the country, in which he found over 100,000 Negro workers (18,435 skilled; 30,500 semi-skilled; and 49,389 unskilled), Julius A. Thomas, industrial secretary of the National Urban League, described the change in the employment practices towards Negroes as the explosion of many myths. He wrote:

"The war has exploded many myths about racial differentials in industrial adaptability and not the least significant are those that affect the Negro worker. The first of these myths to vanish in thin air concerns the Negro's assumed inherent limitations in acquiring certain skills. . . . In the early days of the war the writer talked with dozens of personnel men who glibly argued that Negroes were emotionally incapable of mastering certain mechanical operations. The record gives conclusive proof that skills and capacities have no relation to the race of a worker.

"The second myth to disappear concerns the introduction and integration of Negro workers. It is worth noting that only three out of 300 plants included in the survey segregated Negro and white workers, and in these cases, the segregation applied only to Negro skilled workers and machine operators. Unless the caste relationship of Negro and white workers was disturbed, there was no demand for segregation. Only six plants reported separate eating and comfort facilities, and all of them were located in the South. . . ." [1]

WHAT THE FUTURE HOLDS

For the future . . . there are too many unknowns. If there is economic order, if there is political stability, if jobs are plentiful, many of the changes . . . in personnel practice will continue, employers will continue finding ways to control those prejudices which lead to job discrimination, and Negroes and other minority group workers will hold a substantial part of their wartime gains. At worst, as long as the United States is the United States, there must be some residue of benefit because of the jolt that personnel practice and policy—and the thinking of personnel men— have received. . . .

EDITORIAL COMMENT

For generations one school of thought has held that enacted law, judicial decision, and executive order could not eliminate prejudice and discrimination. The "mores," so it was argued, are not amenable to directed change, but must evolve gradually in conformity with their own principles. Sumner and other sociologists have

[1] Julius A. Thomas, "Wartime Changes in the Occupational Status of Negro Workers," *Occupations, the Vocational Guidance Magazine* (April 1945), p. 404.

been quoted in support of the point of view that "you cannot legislate prejudice out of existence."

In reply, many argue that while enacted law and court decisions are unable to control an attitude—prejudice—they can certainly exercise some control over overt behavior—discrimination. The law does not have to be passive, a reflection of the folkways and mores. It can be a dynamic agent altering traditions and cultural patterns. If discriminatory laws are effective, there is no reason why anti-discrimination legislation should be any less effective.

In the next reading, two social scientists, one a political scientist and the other a sociologist, examine the question with reference not only to legislative action but also to related processes, such as court decisions.

47. CAN MORALITY BE LEGISLATED?
BY *John P. Roche* AND *Milton M. Gordon* *

IT is . . . timely to examine the relationship between law and mores, between the decrees of courts and Legislatures and the vast body of community beliefs which shape private action.

While it is not perhaps customary to think of the Supreme Court as a legislative body, the cold fact is that in the desegregation cases, the nine justices have undertaken to rewrite public policy in at least seventeen states and innumerable communities. Indeed, it would be difficult to find a recent Congressional enactment that equals in impact and scope this judicial holding. Whether one approves or disapproves of such judicial acts, it is clear that the court has undertaken a monumental project in the field of social engineering, and one obviously based on the assumption that morality *can* be legislated.

Opponents of the desegregation decision have, with the exception of a fringe of overt white supremacists, largely founded their dissent on the principle that law can not move faster than public opinion, that legal norms which do not reflect community sentiment are unenforceable. They cite the dismal failure of Prohibition as a case in point, urging that basic social change—however desirable—must come from the bottom, from a shift in "grassroots" convictions.

On the other hand, the court's supporters maintain that virtually

* John P. Roche and Milton M. Gordon, "Can Morality Be Legislated?" *The New York Times Magazine,* May 22, 1955, pp. 10, 42, 44, 47, 49. Reprinted by permission.

every statute and judicial decree is, to some extent, a regulation of morality. Indeed, they suggest, if the moral standards of individuals were not susceptible to state definition and regulation, we would never have emerged from primitive barbarism.

In this article, we shall examine from the viewpoint of the social scientist the evidence on both sides of the question, and see if it is possible to extract any meaningful conclusions.

First of all, we must delve into the relationship that exists in a democratic society between law and community attitudes. While this is a treacherous area, full of pitfalls for the unwary generalizer, it seems clear that, as distinguished from a totalitarian society, law in a democracy is founded on consensus. That is to say that the basic sanctions are applied not by the police, but by the community. The jury system institutionalizes this responsibility in such cases as "mercy killings" or those involving "the unwritten law" by finding citizens who have unquestionably killed "not guilty."

Conversely, juries applying other sections of the criminal code— notably those penalizing subversion—will often bring in verdicts of "guilty" based not so much on technical guilt as upon the proposition that the defendant should be taken out of circulation. In another area of the law, insurance companies, faced with damage suits, have learned to shun juries like the plague. Indeed, they will frequently make unjustified out-of-court settlements in preference to facing a jury that begins its labors with the seeming assumption that no insurance company of any standing would miss $100,000.

From this it should be clear that in the United States law is a great deal more, and simultaneously a great deal less, than a command of the sovereign. Thus one can safely say that no piece of legislation, or judicial decision, which does not have its roots in community beliefs, has a chance of being effectively carried out.

To this extent, it is undeniable that morality cannot be legislated; it would be impossible, for example, to make canasta playing a capital offense *in fact,* even if the bridge-players' lobby were successful in getting such a law on the books. This is a fanciful example, but in our view the Volstead Act and the Eighteenth Amendment were no less unrealistic in objective: like H. L. Mencken's friend, Americans seem willing to vote for Prohibition as long as they can stagger to the polls.

Excluding these extreme efforts to legislate morality, which are obviously unsound, we now come to the heart of the problem: Under what circumstances will an individual accept distasteful regulation of his actions? To put it another way: What are the criteria which lead an individual to adjust his acts to the demands of the state?

Specifically, why do people pay taxes when they disagree strongly with the uses to which the money will be put? A large-scale tax revolt, as the French have recently discovered, is almost impossible to check without recourse to martial law and police state methods, but the average taxpayer grouses and pays. While Americans are not, by and large, as law-abiding as their British cousins, it is probably fair to say that most of us obey most laws without even reflecting on their merits.

This problem of the basis of legal norms has proved a fascinating one to sociologists. In the past fifteen years some significant new thinking on the subject has grown out of empirical research, more incisive analysis, and general observation of large-scale experiences with legal desegregation in important areas of American life such as employment, public housing and the Armed Forces.

The older categorical view stated in classic fashion by the sociologist William Graham Sumner, was that law could never move ahead of the customs or mores of the people—that legislation which was not firmly rooted in popular folkways was doomed to failure. The implication was that social change must always be glacier-like in its movement and that mass change in attitudes must precede legislative action.

The newer viewpoint is based on a more sophisticated and realistic analysis of social processes. In the first place, it questions the older way of stating the problem in terms of all or nothing. Any large, complex society, with its multiplicity of social backgrounds and individual experiences, contains varying mores and attitudes within itself. On any given piece of legislation there will not just be supporters and enemies; rather there will be many points of view, ranging from unconditional support, through indifference, to unmitigated opposition.

Thus, the degree of success that will attend such an enactment is the result of a highly complex series of interactions and adjustments among people with diverse attitudes toward the measure itself and toward the imposition of legal authority. Furthermore, it is predictable that a large segment of the population will be basically neutral, if not totally indifferent.

To put the matter in an even broader framework, the prediction of behavior must take into consideration not only the attitudes of the individual but also the *total social situation* in which his behavior is to be formulated and expressed. For instance, people with ethnic prejudice are likely to express themselves in a social clique where, say, anti-Semitic jokes are *au fait,* but will restrain themselves in a group where such remarks are greeted with hostility. Once the bigot realizes that he must pay a social price for his anti-Semitism, he is likely to think twice before exposing himself to the penalty.

In this connection, Robert K. Merton, Columbia sociologist, has set up an incisive classification, suggesting that four major groups can be delineated:

(1) The all-weather liberal, who can be expected to oppose prejudice and race discrimination under any set of social conditions; (2) the

fair-weather liberal, who is not himself prejudiced, but who will stand silent or passively support discrimination if it is easier and more profitable to do so; (3) the fair-weather illiberal, who has prejudices, but is not prepared to pay a significant price for expressing them in behavior, preferring rather to take the easier course of conformity; and (4) the all-weather illiberal, who is prepared to fight to the last ditch for his prejudices at whatever cost in social disapproval.

If we apply this classification to such a problem as desegregation, it immediately becomes apparent that the critical strata, so far as success or failure is concerned, are groups two and three. Group one will support the proposal with vigor and group four will oppose it bitterly, but groups two and three will carry the day.

But because groups two and three are not crusaders, are not strongly motivated, they are particularly susceptible to the symbolism of law. Thus the fact that fair employment practices have been incorporated into law, or that the Supreme Court has held school segregation unconstitutional, will itself tend to direct their thinking toward compliance.

The symbols of state power are to the undedicated nonrevolutionary mighty and awesome things, and he will think long and hard before he commits himself to subversive action. Consequently the law tends to become, in another of Merton's phrases, a "self-fulfilling prophecy"; that is, a statute tends to create a climate of opinion favorable to its own enforcement. As John Locke long ago pointed out, the great roadblock to revolution is not the police but the habits of obedience which lead the law-abiding majority to refrain from even legitimate and justified resistance.

American experience over the past decade and a half seems to confirm this hypothesis. By legislative action, executive order and judicial decision, the race prejudices of Americans have been denied public sanction. Fair employment practices commissions, of national scope during the war and subsequently operative in a number of states and municipalities, integration of the Armed Forces, integration of many segregated schools, elimination of "white primaries" and removal of racial restrictions in many professional associations—all these have provided a living laboratory for the study of the impact of law on the mores.

At virtually every stage in the development, strong voices were raised to plead that morality could not be legislated, that an end to discrimination must await an unprejudiced public. Yet, the results indicate a high degree of compliance, some covert evasion, and only a few instances of violent resistance.

Moreover, it should be kept in mind that the success of desegregation laws or orders need not be measured against a hypothetical standard of 100 per cent but against the usual standards of law enforcement. Even laws against homicide and rape, which have overwhelming community support, are occasionally violated.

But, while laws may restrain behavior, is there any evidence to indicate that attitudes are affected? Here the evidence seems clear: the law itself plays an important part in the educational process. Again the key to analysis is the social situation.

Legislation and administrative orders which have prohibited discrimination in such areas as employment, the Armed Forces, public housing, and professional associations have brought people of various races together—often with initial reluctance—in normal day-to-day contact on an "equal-status" basis where the emphasis is on doing a job together. Contact of this kind gives people a chance to know one another as individual human beings with similar interests, problems and capabilities. In this type of interaction racial stereotypes are likely to be weakened and dispelled.

Such a favorable change of attitude as a result of personal contact has been reported in a number of studies. In one carefully designed research project, Morton Deutsch and Mary Evans Collins found that white housewives who had been assigned to public housing projects which were racially integrated tended to develop favorable attitudes toward Negroes, while the vast majority of those who occupied segregated housing tended to remain the same in their racial views. A study of integration in the Army reached a similar conclusion.

Findings such as these support a considerably broader and more complex conception of the relations between legal norms and human acts and attitudes than did the older, simpler Sumner thesis. In this more comprehensive analysis, law itself is seen as a force which, in its impact, does more than prohibit or compel specific behavior. Indeed, in its operation, law actually provides the setting for types of social relationships—relationships which may have a profound effect on the very attitudes which are necessary to adequate enforcement of the statute in question.

We thus come down to the final and crucial problem. It is plain that under some circumstances morality can be legislated, while under other conditions, the laws prove impotent. But what are the specific factors which must be evaluated? What criteria can be offered as a guide to intelligent and effective action in these touchy areas of belief, superstition and vested prejudice? The following four considerations are suggested as a beginning:

First, the amount of opposition and its geographical spread. If a random of 15 per cent of the population, roughly gauged, oppose some regulation, there will probably be little difficulty in gaining public acceptance and enforcement. However, and this is particularly relevant to the desegregation problem, if the 15 per cent all live in one compact geographical area where they constitute a majority, control local government and supply juries, the magnitude of the problem is much greater.

Second, the intensity of opposition. This is a qualitative matter, for, to paraphrase George Orwell, while all Americans are created equal, some are more equal than others. A proposal which is militantly opposed by "opinion-formers" in the American community—for example, ministers, lawyers, newspaper editors—will have much harder sledding than a nose-count of the opponents would seem to justify, and, conversely, a measure which receives the support of this key group, or significant segments of it, can overcome a numerically large resistance.

Much of the success of the Negro in overcoming his legal, social and economic disabilities has been an outgrowth of the strong stand on his behalf taken by church leaders, journalists, trade unionists, business men and politicians who have created a climate of opinion favorable to Negro claims and who have based their assertions on the values which constitute the American Creed: Equality of treatment under law and human brotherhood under God. With this quality of support, much can be accomplished even against great numbers.

Third, the degree to which sanctions can be administered. Here we turn to the practical problems of enforcement, and it is at this point that Prohibition really should have run aground long before it was in-corporated into public policy. Home manufacture of alcoholic beverages has, according to well informed sources, even survived in the Soviet Union, and if the M.V.D. is incapable of banning private brew, there is little reason to suspect that a democratic society could handle the job.

It can not be emphasized too often that general principles of morality are no stronger than the instruments by which they are implemented; it would thus be legislative folly to try to prohibit people from disliking Jews, Negroes, Catholics, or Protestants. However, making gin in the bath-tub, or disliking minorities, is not action equivalent to segregating school children on the basis of their pigmentation.

Because it is nearly impossible to regulate what goes on in millions of private homes, it does not follow that enforcement of desegregation in public institutions will be equally difficult. In sum, false and misleading analogies must be avoided, and each proposal must be examined on its merits to determine whether or not it is enforceable.

Fourth, the diligence of enforcement. It is extremely important that enforceable regulations be diligently enforced. This is particularly true in the initial period when public attitudes (specifically, the attitudes of Merton's groups two and three) are in the process of formation. Flagrant refusal to obey usually is designed as a symbolic act to rally the undecided, and strong action at such a time will convince many wavering minds that the best course is compliance.

The Milford, Delaware episode—where parents, stirred up by agita-tors, refused to send their children to a desegregated school—is a good case-study of what should not happen; there vigorous action by the state authorities, such as occurred under similar circumstances in Baltimore, would have dampened the ardor of the fanatics and decimated their fellow-travelers. The danger is that successful symbolic defiance plants the dragon seed and brings into the resistance movement those who would otherwise remain interested and sympathetic spectators—at a distance.

In short, to ask, "Can morality be legislated?" is actually to pose the wrong question. What types of morality, under what conditions, and with what techniques for enforcement are qualitative considerations which fragment the question into more answerable units. Our analysis suggests that, although large-scale local considerations may call for special circumstances of implementation, the majesty of the law, when supported by the collective conscience of a people and the healing power of the social situation, in the long run will not only enforce morality but create it.

EDITORIAL COMMENT

Basic to all the other techniques examined so far is one of self-evident merit in the reduction of intergroup tensions and the eventual achievement of intergroup harmony—research. This is especially needed in unraveling the subtleties of prejudice that are still not fully understood. But when independent research findings about prejudice are fed into traditional types of educational programs, they are likely to be ineffective in changing the prejudices of the audience.

One possibility for overcoming this problem is the action-research project. Its major assumption is that people can be guided to participate in research and to discover thereby the facts concerning their own prejudices. This experience in turn can lead to the acceptance of the facts and induce changes in attitude and behavior.

New trends in the investigation of prejudice and action-research procedure are the topics discussed in the following article by Ronald Lippitt and Marian Radke.

48. NEW TRENDS IN THE INVESTIGATION OF PREJUDICE

BY *Ronald Lippitt* AND *Marian Radke* *

THE NEED for an understanding of the dynamics of prejudice has no equivalent in importance in the social sciences. In no other aspects of in-

* Ronald Lippitt and Marian Radke, "New Trends in the Investigation of Prejudice," *The Annals of the American Academy of Political and Social Science*, 244 (March 1946), pp. 167–76. Reprinted by permission. Most footnotes omitted.

terpersonal and intergroup relationships is there a more urgent need for social sciences to "get out and do something."

Prejudice is not a new subject. Yet, we are ill adapted to cope with the problems of prejudice which have grown increasingly acute in the social evolutions of recent years.

The customary context of prejudice is in the fields of racial, religious, and class tensions. Its implications, however, extend to all aspects of group living and of personal-social relationships. In methods of bringing up children, in manners of dress, in food habits, in differential standards for men and women, in preferred forms of leadership, in the way in which a factory or organization is run—in these and innumerable other areas, distorted social perceptions, or prejudices, play a significant role. The close interdependence of perception and conduct points to the very practical and consequential role of prejudice in social living.

OBSTACLES TO STUDY OF PREJUDICE

Scientifically, more than the usual number of difficulties are involved in the study of prejudice. The literature in this field, until very recently, shows a narrow emphasis on the surface aspects of the problem; an immaturity of approach is reflected in the nature of the questions asked in the research, and in the nature of the data obtained. Descriptive data of a static variety constitute the major proportions: How many persons, what kind of persons, have prejudices against what kinds of objects or people? What is the content of the prejudices? What is the direction and the degree of discrepancy between prejudice and reality? To what sociological data (socioeconomic level, age, sex, and so forth) can these prejudices be related? For these questions, techniques of measurement are at hand which can readily produce quantitative results. It is quite another matter to obtain by these means an understanding of the dynamics of prejudice. Sensitivity to the interplay of crucial factors in the development and maintenance of prejudice and in changes of stereotypes is woefully slight.

Advance in theory and treatment of a problem follows closely in the wake of the correct formulation of the problem. Herein lies one of the greatest needs. We cannot afford to continue the study of prejudice on a purely descriptive level. Productive investigation requires theories, concepts, and inquiry into all aspects of the problem, including (1) the nature and genesis of prejudice, (2) interactions among prejudices within the individual and between individuals, (3) the maintenance of prejudice, and (4) the changing of prejudices.

A second difficulty encountered by the student of prejudice arises from the fact that the data necessary for understanding combine the disciplines of psychology, sociology, anthropology, economics—indeed the whole gamut of the social sciences.

Third, prejudices have social consequences; findings have social implications. Not all of society, not every group or individual, is eager to accept or act upon the research implications. Resistance to putting to scientific test old convictions and comfortable philosophies discourages free research. This liability operates not only on the level of problem formulation; it is ever present in the analysis and interpretation of data in the field of prejudice. Research on prejudice has special significance from still another point of view, as a method of changing prejudiced attitudes and behavior. The development of a procedure whereby the results of research are more readily carried over into action and application is an inestimable need. The action-research procedure as such a method is given special attention in this article.

NATURE OF PREJUDICE

Prejudice we have defined as a type of stereotype which does **not** coincide with the facts. The data which shed most light on the real nature of prejudice are to be found in analysis of the conditions under which these distorted stereotypes arise, persist, or are changed. It is important to take a comparative approach, using data from a variety of contexts, to gain a deeper understanding of the dynamics involved, freed somewhat from the peculiarities of any one context in which prejudice has been investigated.

Demonstrated repeatedly in a variety of kinds of research is the independence of many stereotypes from the actual experiences of the individual. Horowitz' studies of the attitudes of southern and northern white children toward Negroes showed that contact or lack of contact with Negroes did not materially influence the attitudes of the white children. In another study, children who had had no personal experience with members of either of two minority groups were found with strong and definite prejudices toward these minorities. . . .

Knowledge and vicarious experiences have been equally disappointingly ineffective in many instances in changing prejudices. Studies of the influence of education on attitudes and beliefs regarding Negroes give evidence on this point.[1] Numerous illustrations are found in the field of diet therapy, of the persistence of old superstitions and taboos against certain foods after instruction and demonstration proved their falsity.

---

[1] B. Samelson, "Does Education Diminish Prejudice?" *Journal of Social Issues,* Vol. 1 (1945), pp. 11–13; D. Droba, "Education and Negro Attitudes," *Sociology and Social Research,* Vol. 17 (1932), pp. 137–41; D. Young, "Some Effects of a Course in American Race Problems on the Race Prejudice of 450 Undergraduates at the University of Pennsylvania," *Journal of Abnormal and Social Psychology,* Vol. 22 (1947), pp. 235–42.

On the other hand, there are studies in which changes in attitudes, beliefs, or behavior have been effected.[2]

The findings of studies such as these have advanced our knowledge one step closer to a more precise formulation of the problem. We have learned not to ask whether or not knowledge or experience affects prejudice, but to ask *what kinds* of knowledge or interaction, in *what kinds* of situations, give rise to or change prejudices. The specific variables involved in the change must be isolated. In this connection such factors as power relations, dependency, leadership, . . . and the ties with other value systems in the individual, need careful study. . . .

GENESIS OF PREJUDICE

Perhaps a prior question to those relating to the conditions under which prejudices are found concerns the genesis of prejudice. In a study by Marian Radke in which children nine to eighteen years of age were questioned about their attitudes toward Jews and Negroes, data on the genesis of these attitudes were obtained. The responses of the younger children showed general attitudes of dislike and rejection, but were more or less without specific stereotypes. The older children's responses, in addition to general negative attitudes toward these groups, included specific characterizations and stereotypes. The children had had none or a minimum of personal or day-to-day experience with either of the minority groups studied.

From these results the following hypothesis may be formulated: Prejudices are frequently part of the general acculturation process. The child growing into the culture of his group learns first to accept the reaction of an authority (parent, teacher, friend) to an object, idea, or group as something "good" or "bad" without understanding the reasons for this reaction of the authority. Only later does he learn the meaning of the response, or does he acquire rationalizations for his negative or positive attitude. Just as the young child learns to avoid the hot stove because of his mother's warning "no" at each approach toward the stove, in similar fashion he learns, without benefit of personal experience, but through the derogatory references of the adults, to feel only dislike or disgust for the "dirty Japs," the "Red menace," the not-to-be trusted Catholics or capitalists or labor unions or foreigners. Long before the groups thus labeled

[2] F. Smith, "An Experiment in Modifying Attitudes Toward the Negro," Ph.D. Thesis in the Library of Teachers College, Columbia University, New York City, 1933; A. Marrow and J. French, "Changing a Stereotype in Industry," *Journal of Social Issues,* Vol. 1 (1945), pp. 33–37; K. Lewin, "Forces Behind Food Habits and Methods of Change," in *The Problem of Changing Food Habits:* Report of the Committee on Food Habits (C. Guthe, chairman), Bulletin of the National Research Council, 108, 1943.

have any reality for the child, they represent for him an undesirable. Then to support his sentiments he obtains specific negative qualities which he can apply to the groups—rationalizations for his prior sentiments.

The acquisition of prejudices, seen like other acculturation processes, has important implications for research and practice: prejudices cannot be conceived of or treated without careful consideration of the medium in which they arise and persist.

INTERACTIONS AMONG PREJUDICES

The interdependence of prejudices within the individual has been given relatively little attention experimentally, except for correlational studies in which the presence of a given attitude is related to the presence or absence of a second. In a number of studies, certain attitudes such as antisemitism and Jim Crowism . . . frequently occurred in clusters. These clusters might well be studied from the standpoint of the dynamic interrelationships among prejudices; the ease of holding one kind of prejudice if another is held; the ease of changing the perception of a given event if certain other prejudices exist around it in the individual or group.

In a study of ideologies of Mennonite and non-Mennonite children, Kalhorn discussed the way in which the same standards of behavior, such as obedience to parents and doing household duties, were related to very different religious and secular value systems in different children and in the two subcultures. The same is undoubtedly true of prejudices.

Thus the antisemitism of the individual who perceives the social world as one in which world economic-political competition is the dominant theme is of a very different nature from the antisemitism of the "valley-minded" individual whose horizons do not extend beyond the rival and conflicting religious dogmas of his local community.

A prejudice against drinking milk is one thing for the high school girl who sees it as a "fattening" food and is trying to stay thin; it is a prejudice of quite a different nature for an adult in certain parts of Asia where milk is never used in any form for human adult consumption.

Understanding of a prejudice, like understanding of a value or standard of behavior, is, therefore, understanding the background . . . in which it is embedded, as well as knowing the particular psychological region in which it is located.

Just as the behavior of the person in the immediate situation in influenced by the larger background situation, so the specific prejudices of the individual are reinforced or diminished by the existence or absence of other prejudices. Accepting one belief may make it easy or impossible to accept another attitude or prejudice of a given sort. . . .

A leader of a club of Negro and white children who believed that there are certain racial differences in temperament and personality repeatedly attributed the quarrelsome and fighting behavior in his group to the Negro club members.

A prejudice against employing women workers prevents the employer from seeing objectively the comparable work records of men and women, and allows him to think only in terms of the added liabilities of employing women.

Depending upon the pattern or system of prejudices to which a given prejudice is linked, it will be reinforced or weakened in different kinds of situations and at different times.

DYNAMICS OF MAINTENANCE OF PREJUDICE

Theoretically, we may conceive of prejudices in the same way as any other aspect of interpersonal and group living. The concept of a quasi-stationary equilibrium, developed by Kurt Lewin in regard to group processes, is applicable here. A culture is maintained at a given level of functioning, and is, under most circumstances, remarkably "watertight," or resistant to change. . . .

Prejudice should be seen as part of the cultural equilibrium in which the individual or group lives. It, like any other aspect of the culture, is maintained by many forces and counterforces; many factors must be considered, such as status maintenance, suppression or fear of suppression of one group by another, values, and power relations between groups. A given prejudice cannot be isolated from this total group process. A change in prejudice is, therefore, equivalent to a change in the level of the equilibrium. The futility of attempts to change a prejudice by a direct single-item attack is fully comprehensible in this light. A prejudice does not exist in a vacuum; a "change" attempt which treats it as if it did is doomed to failure, or at best, only temporary success.

CHANGING OF PREJUDICES: ACTION-RESEARCH

The questions raised concerning the conditions under which knowledge or experience is effective in changing stereotypes may now bear re-examination in light of the concept of quasi-stationary equilibria in relation to the dynamics of the maintenances of prejudice. Only if the knowledge or experience has the effect of permanently disturbing the balance of forces maintaining the prejudice is a lasting change accomplished. This can be accomplished, theoretically, in several ways: Either the change attempt is made on so broad a front that all or nearly all the forces preventing or creating change are affected at one and the same time (in which case there is a total restructuring of the . . . field), or the change is brought about by affecting a key area which in turn affects a related area and so on, thus building up a beneficial spiral which eventuates in the restructuring of the . . . field.

One procedure for the changing of prejudices in line with the preceding discussion is a step-by-step method that involves fact finding. This procedure is discussed in greater detail below.

One of the facts most frequently found in studies of prejudice is that an inconsistency exists between the thinking and the action of an individual or a group. Prejudiced behavior occurs in spite of objective knowledge of facts upon which unprejudiced behavior could be based. Values are expressed verbally which contradict the behaviors and attitudes which are manifested.

Data on attempts to re-educate prejudiced behavior reveal that when the usual re-educational procedure points out this inconsistency, even without directly attacking it, two reactions frequently occur: (1) the challenging facts presented by the "educator" are rejected as not valid by using one or another of the ego defense mechanisms, e.g. the data are inadequate, the fact collector was biased and so forth; (2) the awareness of the inconsistency brings feelings of guilt which lead to tension and anxiety but very seldom to changed behavior with regard to the prejudice. As Lewin and Grabbe [3] have pointed out, a basic problem in the process of re-education is spontaneous, voluntary acceptance of the new values and behavior patterns, and the most effective stimulus to, and reinforcement of, change is belonging to a group of persons who feel and act in the desired way.

A number of recent research projects have tried to take these factors into account in experimenting with a fact-finding procedure which will serve not only to discover prejudiced attitudes and behavior, but also to encourage changes in the conduct of the prejudiced individual or group. This research method has been called "action-research" in . . . recent statements by research organizations focusing on the study of conflict and misunderstanding between ethnic groups.

The major assumption in action-research is that individuals and groups can be guided to participate in a research role in discovering the facts about their own prejudices. There is evidence that this type of research experience makes possible, psychologically, the acceptance of facts and their implications for changes in attitude and behavior which under other circumstances would be rejected or "not seen." Because of the almost uniform failure of re-education programs in combating prejudice, and because the authors believe the action-research project offers an opportunity for social scientists to fulfill an important unique function as scientists in a democracy, the remainder of this article is an analysis of the action-research procedure.

[3] K. Lewin and P. Grabbe, "Conduct, Knowledge, and Acceptance of New Values," *Journal of Social Issues,* Vol. 1 (1945), pp. 53–64.

ACTION-RESEARCH PROCEDURE

Analysis of eight . . . studies using the action-research approach reveals the following major points of procedure:

1. Initially *a group-need to discover some facts exists or is created.*

This may be the aroused curiosity of a community to know how it compares in certain aspects with other communities, or it may be the desire of the group to discover how well it is achieving its objectives, why it is having the problem it is, or what the facts of its present operation would suggest for improvements. Not only must the group be able and willing to recognize that a problem or "need to know" exists, but it must take the attitude that "there are ways of finding out" and "finding out will be worth while. . . ."

Usually the action-research worker discovers that the group is well aware of certain problems but unable to accept the need for a further factual diagnosis as a step toward solution. As a spokesman of one group said . . . "We know what our gripes are, so I guess we ought to know what to do about them." Research on prejudice often finds this close linkage between strong feelings and the assumption that these feelings automatically reveal the direction of "what to do about it." For this reason the next two steps of the action-research approach to prejudice are very important.

2. In the second place, *the group, or representatives of it, share in the deciding of "what do we need to know?"*

At this stage the research technician, who has been accepted in a consultant or guiding role, takes the attitude that, to answer the questions posed by the problem which has been agreed on, people on the inside of the group probably have excellent hunches as to what kind of facts are needed and where they may be found. . . .

. . . The final list of hypotheses, and facts needed to test them, are a combination of ideas from research workers and group members. As Marrow and French point out, this early involvement in research procedure is essential if the facts which are discovered are to be accepted as valid and conclusive enough to combat prejudice in the group of fact finders.

3. *Scientific research instruments are constructed.*

At this stage, in each project, the research worker was willingly delegated the role of specialized technician. Now decisions had to be made as to the wording, the form, and the sequence of the questionnaire or interview schedule or observation check sheet or rating scale. Two major questions confronted the research personnel in each case: (1) What would be the best instrument, or set of instruments, from the methodological point of view? (2) What types of research instruments would laymen be able to use with satisfactory reliability and validity? . . .

4. Further achieving of the "objectivity role" occurs in *making decisions about sampling* and *learning to use the research tools reliably.*

In each of the studies some of the most interesting discussions took place around the problems of sampling. In several cases a hesitant research technician was much surprised to discover how eagerly the lay research committee grappled with the problem of getting enough facts from the right places to "have proof." Numerous insights about inadequate bases for research conclusions were grasped and verbalized during this stage of the projects, and helpful suggestions made from inside knowledge of the population as to refined sampling breakdowns.

The motivation to learn to use the instruments correctly also proved to be high. Interviewers were ready to be observed and to discuss the problems of personal bias. In two cases regular reliability checks were instituted and the results were reviewed with great interest. Where the training procedure was well represented, it was found that becoming an objective human instrument was tackled as a challenging and absorbing problem. In another case the refined mechanics of data collection were never perceived as necessary, and a sloppy job was done by a number of the workers.

It is our conclusion that laymen are very receptive to "learning how to be objective" or "to be scientific," and can do a very creditable job of it when limited training is conducted in an interesting fashion, and if, as noted in the next paragraph, there is proper supervision to ensure quick success.

5. *Supervision of data collection must help to ensure success and deal sympathetically with discouragement problems.*

In one project, a major drop of morale occurred when the mechanics of making appointments with interviewees proved difficult. The layman researchers must be relieved of as much drudgery of this sort as possible. In another study, the observers felt very discouraged about "how little they were getting" until the research worker did a rough tabulation of several observations with them to show how the cumulative data began to build up a picture. Little group sessions on difficulties and interesting anecdotes proved one of the most successful techniques of correcting mistakes and ensuring a feeling of progress, and thus securing consistent motivation in the early stages before internalized criteria of achievement made feelings of success more possible.

6. *Evidences of attitude change often appear during this phase of participation in fact gathering.*

One administrator who was participating in making observations of staff operation remarked, "You certainly see things differently when you are looking for facts." An interviewer who had just finished her interviews with several adolescents said reflectively, "You really see things through different eyes when you are trained to listen and not be on the defensive." These laymen were discovering that when taking an "objectivity role" and playing the game according to the research rules there was little room or need for the distortions of ego defensiveness and attitude bias that belonged to their "regular citizen role."

7. *Collaboration in putting the facts together and interpreting the facts requires special skill of the research technician.*

Two temptations beset the research personnel in this phase of an action-research project: (1) to take the data off to a room with a calculating machine and come back with the results, or (2) to assign a lot of tabulation drudgery to the lay research workers. In the most successful projects, the work of setting up the first tables of data was done by the research technicians, who then shared this first stage of results with groups of laymen with the question, "What do you begin to make out of these? What lines do you see for further analysis?" The excitement of making sense out of the fragmentary elements of data was thus shared, and, because of this, much "tougher facts" could be faced without psychological rejection. . . .

8. *Sometimes more is needed than a change in the values and social perception of the individual or group.*

In most cases the changed outlook, which comes with the new ability to see and accept the facts, results in changed action, particularly if it has been a group acceptance. But sometimes understanding the facts does not automatically ensure skill in behaving differently. A group of head nurses recently discovered why they were having so much trouble with aggressive behavior of medical students on their wards. The understanding carried with it the implication that they needed to change their behavior toward the students quite radically. But they discovered that new behaviors, like new tools, are often awkward to handle on first usage, and result in a sense of failure. To overcome this difficulty, the nurses set up practice situations where one nurse could keep her role as head nurse and others would become medical students. In this secure situation of "not playing for keeps," the new behavior pattern was tried out, co-operatively evaluated, and perfected to the point of ensuring success.

9. *Spreading the facts to other groups by oral and written reports can be a final step—and a new first step.*

In four of the studies reported here, representatives of the lay group participated in the writing up of research reports, and in two cases they presented these reports orally at meetings of other groups. There is no research evidence, positive or negative, that changes in prejudiced attitudes or behavior occurred in the other groups because of the reading or hearing of the reports, but there is evidence that one important result was achieved. Several requests originated from other groups to have similar projects of their own. It is doubtful that material written or reported by unknown "experts" would have met with this type of acceptance and stimulated the readiness to enter into "the experience of measurement."

SUMMARY

The practical goal of studying prejudices is to provide a foundation for changing prejudices so as to square the stereotypes with the facts. Experiments in change are, likewise, the most valuable scientific means to understand the nature of prejudice.

Research in this field must examine the genesis of prejudice in the group and in the individual, the interrelation between various prejudices, the factors which maintain them, and the conditions for changing them.

From the research emerges a concept which links the prejudices of the individual with the standards or culture of the group, and which views the culture of the group or subgroup as a quasi-stationary equilibrium. In the same way that the individual grows into other aspects of the culture, he grows into prejudices. Any discrepancy between the individual and the group results in action of forces on him to make him want to return to the group level. Group prejudices themselves are due to many factors, economic, political, traditional, and organizational. Any attempt to change must take into account this totality instead of any one aspect.

A basic factor in instituting and maintaining a change in the individual is the creation of psychological forces in him to want to leave his present level, and the removal of restraining forces which otherwise hold him at that level. After the situation has been made fluid enough to permit a change, and after a change has been effected, it is important that the new cultural equilibrium be permanently stabilized.

A procedure is discussed here which uses fact finding as a means of bringing about change through a step-by-step method on a group level. It obtains from the members of the group a degree of involvement first on an intellectual level, separate from action or fears of what action or change entails. This takes the person out of many aspects of his real situation in which forces prevent change. On the intellectual level a change . . . is achieved. The individual accepts the new insights as facts, since the group approves. The group as a whole moves along because the individual members at no time have to depart too far from the group standards. This anchoring of the individual's behavior in group standards at the same time stabilizes his attitudes and behavior at the new level.

EDITORIAL COMMENT

In research and scholarship on intergroup relations, it is quite likely that the general tendency to ignore other cultures and to concentrate on the "American style" of prejudice and discrimination limits one's understanding of problems and hampers the development of effective action programs. This, of course, is not only characteristic of American intergroup relations; it is a parochialism that has hampered American sociology in general.

No social scientists are better equipped for a cross-cultural perspective of a given social problem than the anthropologists. Many of them have been vitally interested in the problems of intergroup relations, not only in their own society, but, as one might expect, in other societies as well, particularly peripheral ones. Gene Weltfish, who attempts to outline the needed perspective in the article that follows, for several years conducted field research among a number of American Indian tribes in Oklahoma, New Mexico, Arizona, Louisiana, and North Dakota.

49. NEEDED FACTS AND IMPLICATIONS FOR ACTION BY *Gene Weltfish* *

. . . IT is clear that all efforts must be directed toward a realistic program for *changing the conduct,* or the potential conduct, of individuals or groups of persons in situations where conflict exists, overtly, or latently, along lines of racial [nationality] and religious cleavage. Experience and educational experimentation have proved that many educational attempts which seem to make a contribution in this direction will have no effect when measured against these criteria. Certain types of emotional appeal fade quickly in their effect; logical intellectual approaches frequently fail to have any influence on behavior or attitudes; programs which provoke constructive action in one case of conflict completely fail in another. We are just as vitally in need of facts about how action, rather than just the addition of knowledge, can be stimulated by intercultural educational experiences, as we are in need of more facts about the roots and mechanisms of . . . prejudice as they operate in daily living. Both types of problems are considered below:

* Gene Weltfish, "Some Problems on Which We Need More Facts—and Some Implications for Action," *Journal of Social Issues,* I (February 1945), 47–54. Reprinted by permission.

PERSPECTIVE ON THE "AMERICAN STYLE" IN PREJUDICE AND DISCRIMINATION

We need more facts about the pattern of prejudice and discrimination in different cultures to aid us in getting perspective on educational possibilities in working with "human nature" in our own culture. Ruth Benedict points out that, "In Europe there is general agreement that the policy of dominant ethnic groups which roused most group antagonism was the common one of forbidding the use of the other's mother tongue, closing out schools conducted in that language, etc. . . . But in the United States the social situation and the psychological attitudes differ qualitatively. All immigrant groups have wished to learn English and by the second generation have prided themselves on their fluency. No one has ever proposed that a better intercultural policy would include public schools in the language of each immigrant group. The truth is that all minority groups want a share in the general American life—if not in the first generation, at least by the second or third. What they object to is being shut out. Our American Negroes demand that they give their blood to the bloodbank, or that they get assigned to combat service. They do not, like so many European minorities, resist recruiting if possible, boycott schools, and demand to be let alone.

"This contrast in the dynamic of group cleavages in Europe and the United States can be generalized: in Europe resentments have been aroused by interference with local customs, initiative or status quo; they want to ward off this interference. . . . The theme in minority accusations in the United States is resentment of obstacles placed in the way of social, economic, or political opportunities by the dominant groups—and equally, the dominant groups complain that labor or the Negro is putting obstacles in the way of their 'freedoms' of private enterprise or of white supremacy. They both want a green light ahead, not, as in Europe, to wall themselves in.

"In the United States, therefore, the dynamics of better minority relations is quite simply not putting obstacles in the way of minority groups' social opportunities. It means the actual practice of civil liberties, and defining these for the dominant groups, so that liberties shall not be cutthroat. In Europe it means, far more often, insisting on certain areas of life where laissez-faire will be the rule—allowing use of mother tongue, local practices, customary law, etc. . . ."

Looking in another direction for comparative perspective Benedict points out that the expression of prejudice by means of aggression against a scapegoat individual or group is almost if not entirely missing in the character structure and group dynamics of the Japanese. She says: "The Japanese react powerfully to anything they construe as insult, but the scapegoat psychology is certainly hard to find."

Margaret Mead contrasts the British and American attitudes toward minority-majority group conflict relationships. The British place a positive valuation on compromise while for the American compromise usually means "giving in," "giving up," "losing the main point." The British see the majority position as equivalent to the position of secure strength and right, and see compromise as the act of the wise, strong, secure, bending down, generously and *prudently* (Because "the heresy of today is the orthodoxy of tomorrow.") including some of what the minority wants in the whole final decision. If the American group loses a point in negotiation it sees itself as "being pushed around," "having the wool pulled over our eyes," being "outwitted and outmanoeuvred." Thus in the British position, taking up majority-minority positions is a prelude to agreement among all; but in the American position it is a prelude to ignoring the minority, and if possible eliminating them. The American version of what to do with a cleavage is to absorb the other side, to assimilate it completely.

These observations, and the implications for action which they suggest, point clearly to the need for more comparative analysis to help us become aware of the "American style" in group hostilities, and to discover what the most strategic methods are for constructively channeling these hostilities and tensions in our culture and in our American personality makeup.

PREJUDICE AND GROUP IDENTIFICATION

Amazing as it may seem social psychology does not know very much yet about what it means for an individual's behavior and thinking that he belongs to various groups. It is one of the most perplexing facts about anti-Semitism, for example, that the same individual will be friendly with Jewish persons in some situations but violently antisemitic in others. Antisemitic action and expression seem often to be linked with situations in which the individual feels as a member of a specific group—political, church, professional, etc. It is of great importance to find out in what social roles individuals conduct themselves as anti-Semites. Individuals who belong to few groups, or have strong feelings of personal insecurity, seem to need to take on the total "coloration" of each new group membership more completely and to lose any inclination to "show" any "backbone" in opposition to the group codes existing in the situation of the moment. The question comes up frequently in working with delinquent gangs whether the group as a whole must be broken up because of the strong reinforcement which the members provide each other in living up to their particular group style of behavior and thinking in resistance to all efforts at reeducation. Where racial or religious prejudice is the basis of organized group action, and therefore of satisfaction to the members, we need to raise this same question.

These considerations emphasize the importance of the leaders in setting the style of group life, and of groups with high status in our social structure setting the example for other groups. Edward L. Bernays makes some specific suggestions about the possible role of one of the dominant groups in our society. He says, "American business is one of the most powerful forces in this country and can affect social change more quickly than even government because its controls are centered in the hands of fewer people.

"Since business has an enlightened self-interest in maintaining equilibrium and peace at home in its relations with purveyors, customers, workers, the whole society, business has a major stake in eliminating group tensions, in bringing about accommodation and equilibrium among all groups. Business has also mastered the techniques of adult education, persuasion, and suggestion better than any other single force. The . . . millions of dollars spent . . . in advertising is an index of the emphasis business places on this phase of its work. Business, up to the present, has been wary, afraid of taking social leadership in this field.

"It is said that it will act when public opinion makes demands of it for social action. Business has not led public opinion in this field. Business usually acts as a leader. In this crisis situation business is acting like a canny politician, with ear to the ground. The tradition of American business is pioneering. It is ironic that it should step back and wait for someone else to lead in this field. Business simply cannot wait because the country cannot wait.

"What field of business will undertake this important step? Big business, as it is called, must undertake the responsibility. Big business has most at stake. It can exert social control most quickly because millions of men are working with it. The right to work on an equal basis with other citizens, and the economic status of the Negro, is certainly basic to the problem of group tensions. Economic insecurity for the Negro means psychological insecurity, frustration and aggression.

"The keynoting effort of those working in the field of better group relations should be directed at getting key business men and the important financial interests, which work with the broad economic structure of the United States, to recognize that it is in their enlightened self-interest to deal with the problem realistically within their field. An effort should be made to get them to adopt the techniques of integration of Negroes that have already been so successfully adopted by many of America's defense industries in many parts of the country. This, in turn, will give an impetus to other phases of business which looks to the leadership of "big business" in all its doings. This leadership, based upon enlightened self-interest, will cut through the folkways and the habitual points of view and actions, because it is given social sanction by the groups to whom these people look for leadership.

"Labor unions, in turn, through the impetus already given to their own attitudes by the leadership of some of the unions will modify their attitudes predicated on the same basic philosophy of leadership. A tremendous leverage will be given to the whole situation. The other groups that are working with the problem will have impetus, flow, given to their own efforts and a situation which now appears to be so stalemated can get that momentum in terms of social goals which is so elemental to accelerating evolutionary progress in our democracy."

The sociometrists have consistently stressed the need for social actionists to study the role of "key people in the community" more carefully as one of the most strategic approaches to the problem of social change. Much more study of this problem should be made by applied scientists who have the job of changing the prejudice pattern of the community.

THE SATISFACTION-VALUE OF BEING PREJUDICED, OR DISCRIMINATED-AGAINST

It is often possible to show the prejudiced group that on no rational grounds—economic, social, political, etc.—does it stand to gain by aggressive obstruction of the minority group. And almost as often the prejudice continues unabated or even intensified by the increased consciousness of the contradiction between their "official belief in democracy" and their prejudiced behavior or attitudes. It is also possible frequently to point out to members of the minority group that a change in their tactics would "draw less fire" and make for more rapid progress, and to find from subsequent observation that many of the discriminated-against persons seem to want to draw fire by continuing or even intensifying the irritating behavior. The ego-satisfactions derived from interpersonal aggression or martyrdom are often a far more important factor than economic, political, or ideological differences which might appear to be the basis of the cleavage. Fact-finding on this problem is of greatest importance for a diagnosis of the possibilities and most appropriate methods of re-education. It seems probable from the evidence to date that many individuals and groups must go through what amounts to a therapeutic experience rather than the more typical conception of an educational procedure before ego-anchored prejudices can be yielded up for new constructive sources of satisfaction. . . .

LEGISLATION AND EDUCATION

Often this problem is argued as an "either-or" proposition. Should slower educational processes be depended upon to solve the group friction or should legal pressures be brought to bear to see that "rights are guaranteed"? Usually it is foolish to ask such a question rather than to consider the proper balance of the two approaches and their timing in the total campaign to reduce discrimination and prejudice. One of the problems is that often the perception of minority group members by the majority group is so distorted by "living at a distance" because of segregation policies, biased reporting, etc., that some kind of legal force is necessary to bring members of the two groups into a close enough relationship for the discriminators to learn from experience how inadequate their stereotypes have really been. . . .

"But you can't legislate prejudice" is often the reply. This is quite true, but what we need is a lot of experimentation to answer such questions as: What kind of preparational education will make it possible for a community to profit by the increased contact of group members that follows legal anti-discrimination measures? How can legal force be used to get the community over the first hump of resistance without deepening the lines of psychological cleavage? Perhaps even after school days are over most of us can profit by a bit more compulsory education when we insist on playing truant from some of the most basic courses in the curriculum of daily living in a democracy.

EDITORIAL COMMENT

Throughout this volume there have been frequent references to "the American Creed," the set of norms that calls for equality, justice, and dignity in intergroup relations as well as in other forms of human relations. Frequent mention has also been made of another tradition, unofficial and less explicit but powerful in its motivation and approval of inequality and its justification of prejudice and discrimination against minority groups.

In a sense, then, all relations between races, religious groups, and nationalities in American society have been subject to two diametrically opposed philosophies. The first may be called social inclusivism; the other is social exclusivism. One posits intergroup harmony and equality whereas the other evokes just the opposite. Both are American philosophies, whether we approve of them or not.

The concluding essay, by Harry Overstreet, a philosopher, compares the two philosophies or creeds in broad terms and then considers the contributions that the social and psychological sciences have made in support of one of them—social inclusivism.

50. SOME CONTRIBUTIONS OF SCIENCE TO THE EASING OF GROUP TENSIONS
BY *Harry A. Overstreet* *

Two conflicting philosophies about human relations contend for mastery in America. They might be called *exclusivism* and *inclusivism*. According to its own inner logic, each prescribes a method for relating groups within a society. The one calls for segregation and the denial of full rights to certain individuals; the other for the removal of segregation and the granting of full rights to all.

Obviously one of these philosophies must eventually prevail, for no people can happily remain half exclusivist and half inclusivist. . . .

Today, among the most powerful influences for lessening group exclusivism are the sciences. This may seem surprising, for it is said over and over again that the sciences have no ethical import. Yet thanks to them we have been passing through a revolution of the mind which has been putting the highly questionable philosophy of exclusivism increasingly on the defensive.

Through the social and psychological sciences the influence has been direct. By creating a clearer understanding of man and his world, anthropology, sociology, and psychology have helped to discredit old folk tales about groups and peoples; old prejudices about color and race; old superstitions about ethnic and national superiority. Through the physical sciences, the influence has been less direct, but powerful nevertheless. By their discoveries, and the inventions that have followed, these sciences have brought about an unprecedented new mingling of men, so that the lines of difference between people have become less sharp. The physical sciences have also performed a service to our minds that is difficult to measure by domesticating the concept of "the personal equation." They have made us aware of the danger of importing wish-thinking and our own unchecked impressions into the judgments we make about people. This has done more than can easily be measured to discredit subjective thinking about groups and races and to rouse active suspicion against theories unverified by objective research.

In the following, I shall confine myself to the social and psychological sciences. I should like to call attention to four major contributions they have made that are now decisive aids against exclusivism.

In the first place, thanks to these sciences, we now know that there

* From Lyman Bryson, Louis Finkelstein, and Robert M. MacIver (eds.), *Approaches to National Unity* (New York: Harper & Brothers, 1945), pp. 61–70. Used by permission of Harper & Brothers.

are greater differences between individuals within any racial or culture group than there are between the groups themselves. This serves to discredit those who maintain that there are pure, self-contained groups, readily distinguishable from others; and that the differences between these groups are unbridgeable. Again, these sciences have demonstrated that group prejudices—preferences for our own and antagonism to other groups—are not something born in people but are created by the peculiar man-made conditions of their culture. Being man-made, they can be unmade by man. Again, they have shown how individuals inevitably become conditioned by their cultural environments and how changes in these environments can make them into different individuals. Finally, they have shown how cultural environments can be changed so as to bring about more desirable relations between individuals and groups.

Thanks to conclusions such as these, we are now learning to think of individuals as being what they are chiefly because of the conditions under which they live. We do not any longer think of them as having immutable "racial" qualities or cultural "essences." When we are told, for example—this has been a stock in trade of American segregationists—that Negroes are "by nature" shiftless, and/or immoral, and/or without ambition, we need no longer bow as to superior judgment. We can ask, first, for the statistical justification of such assertions . . . ; and second, we can ask that there be an objective description and critical evaluation of the environment in which Negroes live.

The more a scientific attitude toward group problems prevails, the more such swift generalizations as the above are placed on the defensive. Increasingly, they are compelled to justify themselves by rigorous, objective evidence. Group prejudice is always strongest where there is no enlightened facing of the facts. The most decisive aid, therefore, which the psychological and social sciences are now rendering, is to make enlightened fact-finding not only fashionable but obligatory. When people get the habit of challenging every statement unsupported by critically assembled facts, group prejudice is on the way out.

A second important contribution which these sciences have made has been to give concreteness and specificity to the hitherto vague concept of the "good life." As long as the "good life" was a metaphysical concept, it could be argued about endlessly without bringing people to a clear idea of what it concretely meant. It was always easy to say of the individuals of a suppressed group—this used to be said of Negro slaves—that they really were "happier" in their simple ways and did not seem to need what people in other groups needed. Such a statement rested heavily upon the metaphysical vagueness of the term "happy life." The social and psychological sciences have put an end to this. They have made clear the conditions that are prerequisite if individuals of any race or group or status whatsoever are to fulfill their life. They have worked out for us (through empirical research) an irreducible minimum of psychological needs. These they have found to be at least six: (1) work, of the kind that is individually satisfying and socially approved; (2) decent living conditions; (3) adequate education; (4) the respect of one's fellows; (5) equality before the law; (6) participation in the government of one's life.

When several of these are lacking, we can now say without more ado that those particular conditions for the realization of the "good life" are absent and need to be supplied. We can do more: we can say sharply and with the complete support of these sciences, that unless these specific conditions are fulfilled, results will follow that are bad not only for the individuals who are denied the indispensables of life, but also for those who deny them. This is a vast help toward overcoming the unwillingness of a dominant group to improve the conditions of a suppressed group. People of a dominant group might not easily respond to pleas for "justice" to Negroes; for to them, full justice might imply all kinds of undesirable possibilities, like social equality and intermarriage. Members of a dominant group might, however, find it hard convincingly to disagree with the proposition that absence of self-respecting work leads to deplorable results: the demoralization of the individual and his potential danger to society. They might be willing, therefore, to make provision for such work. In similar manner, they might be brought to see that substandard housing and substandard education are bad for those subjected to these conditions and dangerous for those who subject them; and they might be persuaded to do something about these evils. To ask the dominant group to show respect to the Negro—even to the slight extent of ceasing to treat him with discourtesy—might not win such ready response; but in our new psychological atmosphere, it becomes increasingly obvious that humiliating people is dangerous business and that courtesy is wiser. Likewise, individuals of the dominant group might be brought to see that equal treatment before the law must be granted for the very safety of themselves as well as in elementary decency to members of the subdominant group.

In short, people need not be race idealists to work for better housing or for better vocational and educational opportunities. Members of a dominant group are far more likely to work for the "good life" of "inferiors" if they know the hazards to themselves that the absence of certain necessary conditions entails. This, to be sure, is not a very high order of motivation. But if it brings about better treatment of the members of the suppressed group, it may even in the end serve to make the dominant group *prefer* to treat them thus. In any event, thanks to the sharp, aseptic analyses of the social and psychological sciences, it becomes harder for members of a dominant group to ease their conscience with a hazy metaphysics of the "happiness" or "carefreeness" of the "childlike" people they intend to keep suppressed.

A third contribution which these sciences have made has been to place a new emphasis upon the "individuality" of all individuals. This is important; for the gravest danger to clear and just thinking about people of a subdominant group has been the habit of regarding them not as individuals but as group members. This person, for example, is not Simon Cohen, a gifted student of philosophy, but a "Jew." This other person is not Richard Horton, an honest civil service worker, but a "Negro." By getting us accustomed to a certain new concept—that of "personality adjustment"—the psychological sciences have done much to overcome this mischievous tendency toward "label thinking."

Personality adjustment is no longer an esoteric concept. It belongs increasingly to the common consciousness. Because of its practice in schools, clinics, Y.M.C.A.'s, churches, and elsewhere, the knowledge is now widespread among us that many individuals are maladjusted and that troubles result from this both to the individuals and to the society to which they belong.

The stress laid upon personality adjustment tends to focus attention upon the individual himself quite apart from his membership in a group . . . , except as such membership affects his personality integration. This is of no small importance to our problem of group tensions. Most of the angers against individuals of despised groups are really angers against the groups. Indeed, the only safeguard of the group-hater is to steer clear of recognizing admirable qualities in individuals of the group. If a Jew-baiter, for example, were once to admit that some Jews are far better than many Gentiles, the whole question of the relation between Jews and Gentiles would become too complicated for him to handle. Thus the more strongly the habit is formed among people of regarding individuals as individuals, the more they are likely to change undiscriminating condemnation into some measure of understanding.

While personality adjustment began with the effort to straighten out obviously maladjusted individuals, it has now become a preventative, and not merely a remedial, technique. The interest of those who undertake such adjustment has broadened from that of extracting square pegs from round holes to that of preventing the square pegs from ever getting into round holes. Thus it has become a way of discovering the abilities and disabilities of all individuals insofar as these bear upon the chances for wholesome success in life.

A fourth contribution of the social and psychological sciences needs mention. People have hitherto been proud of their group exclusiveness. It has seemed to give them distinction and prestige. Thus the member of the Ku Klux Klan has seemed to enlarge his sense of personal significance by associating himself with others in what he believed to be the heroic defense of white supremacy. In a similar manner a member of an antisemitic group has grown big with importance.

Studies in the pathology of hate have begun to make us see that a

life devoted to an unremitting hatred is one that is psychologically and often physically ill. The normal restraints of critical judgment are removed;
mental and emotional reactions become hysterical; angers and fears possess the individual; the constant sense of foes that threaten is combined
with a sense of unquestionable superiority. The paranoiac pattern, in
short, becomes apparent.

In the past twenty-odd years of psychological and physiological research, it has been discovered that continuous, excessive anger tends to
bring about physical illness. Man does not hate his fellow man with impunity. Hate engenders poisons that invade the system, fog the mind. It
is no longer fashionable to boast that one cannot control his angers. The
scientific climate of opinion is now such that a person who is forever ful-
minating hatred against people is regarded as a somewhat absurd figure,
and psychologically stupid to boot.

It becomes increasingly clear that generosity and good will are
health-giving attitudes. More and more, therefore, we are inclined to be
wary of the hater; for we begin to realize that hate cannot be long continued without impairing physical well-being and mental balance.

A similar psychological wariness is being bred in us toward all claims
to superiority, whether of class, race, nation, or religion. The person who
claims superiority for his group—and for himself as a member of his group
—is inevitably on the defensive. Inevitably he lives in a state of suppressed or overt rage against those who question his claims. Inevitably,
then, he builds rationalizations to justify himself and his group. As he
creates these rationalizations, he is increasingly less able to judge human
situations with objectivity. He becomes, in short, a person with a mind
slanted in his own and his group's favor and furious at those who deny
his estimate of himself and his elite companions. The upshot of it all is
that indulgence in superiority feelings is carried on at one's mental and
spiritual peril.

The foregoing contributions of the social and psychological sciences
have created among us a new climate of opinion. Living in this new scientific climate, we are beginning to feel as far removed from traditional
views about racial and group superiority as, in the theatre, we are removed
from our former naive acceptance of villain and hero in melodrama. We
have grown wiser about the subtleties of life. The confident slogans of
"white supremacy," "Nordic supremacy," "Protestant-white supremacy,"
"Gentile supremacy," seem pathetically uninformed and out of date. It is
as if we were suddenly viewing life in a new perspective. The achievement of generous relations among human beings no longer seems like a
utopian dream but just plain, good sense. Human beings are human beings. As old Shylock once said: "Hath not a Jew eyes? hath not a Jew
hands, organs, dimensions, senses, affections, passions? fed with the same
food, hurt with the same weapons, subject to the same diseases, heal'd by

the same means, warmed and cooled by the same winter and summer, as a Christian is?" The sciences have removed—or are rapidly removing— the artificial barriers between us and are enabling us to see one another as human beings.

Up to the present time, support for the ideal of the "brotherhood of man" has had to depend solely upon men of good will. The "realists" of the world scoffed at the idea of brotherhood, pointing out to these "soft idealists" the brutal facts of man's "natural" antagonisms. These antagonisms of group and race have been so persistent among us that for centuries the "realists" have had it all their own way. Now, however, the situation changes. Thanks to the social and psychological sciences, it is the "realists" who are now on the defensive. All their confident, wishful assertions about natural superiority and inferiority are compelled to run the gauntlet of scientific scrutiny. When they come out at the other end, they look like sorry specimens of their former selves.

For the first time in history, in short, the ideal of the brotherhood of man, or, expressed in more accurate terms, the ideal of human association on a basis of moral equality, has become underpinned by four powerful sciences: biology, anthropology, sociology, and psychology. All these together completely contradict the notion of rigid lines between superior and inferior groups, and emphasize instead the variability, flexibility, and wide adaptability of human nature. Science, in short, is now on the side of the men of good will. . . .

Index

A NOTE ON THE TYPE

The text of this book was set on the Linotype in a face called
TIMES ROMAN, designed by STANLEY MORISON for *The Times*
(London), and first introduced by that newspaper in 1932.

Among typographers and designers of the twentieth century, Stanley Morison has been a strong forming influence,
as typographical adviser to the English Monotype Corporation,
as a director of two distinguished English publishing houses, and
as a writer of sensibility, erudition, and keen practical sense.

In 1930 Morison wrote: "Type design moves at the pace
of the most conservative reader. The good type-designer therefore realises that, for a new fount to be successful, it has to be
so good that only very few recognize its novelty. If readers do
not notice the consummate reticence and rare discipline of a new
type, it is probably a good letter." It is now generally recognized
that in the creation of *Times Roman* Morison successfully met
the qualifications of this theoretical doctrine.

Composed, printed, and bound by KINGSPORT PRESS, INC.,
Kingsport, Tennessee. Paper manufactured by P. H. GLATFELTER
COMPANY, Spring Grove, Pennsylvania. Designed by HARRY
FORD.

Date Due

MAR 11 66	NOV 2 1 84		
APR 20 '66	AUG 02 '88		
MAY 12 '66			
APR 9 '69			
APR 7 '70			
MAY 6 '70			
DEC 9 '70			
DEC 8 '7			
AP 26 '78			
SE 2 8 '81			
OC 12 '81			
OC 23 '81			
FE 1 6'83			
MR 1 '83			
APR 2 5 84			
NOV 7 84			
GB	PRINTED	IN U. S. A.	